Studies in Neuroscience, Consciousness and Spirituality

Volume 7

Series Editors
Harald Walach, Poznan University of the Medical Sciences, Poznan, Poland and Witten/Herdecke University, Dept. Psychology, Witten, Germany
Stefan Schmidt, University Medical Center, Freiburg, Germany

Editorial Board
Jonathon Schooler
University of California, Santa Barbara, CA, USA
Mario Beauregard
University of Arizone, Tucson, USA
Robert Forman
The Forge Institute, USA
B. Alan Wallace
Santa Barbara Institute for Consciousness Studies, CA, USA

More information about this series at http://www.springer.com/series/10195

Mohamed Safiullah Munsoor

Wellbeing and the Worshipper

Insights Into an Islamic Spiritual Order

 Springer

Mohamed Safiullah Munsoor
Dehiwela, Sri Lanka

ISSN 2211-8918   ISSN 2211-8926 (electronic)
Studies in Neuroscience, Consciousness and Spirituality
ISBN 978-3-030-66133-5   ISBN 978-3-030-66131-1 (eBook)
https://doi.org/10.1007/978-3-030-66131-1

© The Editor(s) (if applicable) and The Author(s), under exclusive license to Springer Nature Switzerland AG 2021
This work is subject to copyright. All rights are solely and exclusively licensed by the Publisher, whether the whole or part of the material is concerned, specifically the rights of translation, reprinting, reuse of illustrations, recitation, broadcasting, reproduction on microfilms or in any other physical way, and transmission or information storage and retrieval, electronic adaptation, computer software, or by similar or dissimilar methodology now known or hereafter developed.
The use of general descriptive names, registered names, trademarks, service marks, etc. in this publication does not imply, even in the absence of a specific statement, that such names are exempt from the relevant protective laws and regulations and therefore free for general use.
The publisher, the authors, and the editors are safe to assume that the advice and information in this book are believed to be true and accurate at the date of publication. Neither the publisher nor the authors or the editors give a warranty, expressed or implied, with respect to the material contained herein or for any errors or omissions that may have been made. The publisher remains neutral with regard to jurisdictional claims in published maps and institutional affiliations.

This Springer imprint is published by the registered company Springer Nature Switzerland AG
The registered company address is: Gewerbestrasse 11, 6330 Cham, Switzerland

Acknowledgements

Life's journey is a process, where intermittently one gets an opening to carry out a substantive piece of work, which bears some fruits for the one involved, as well as for others who can derive benefits from it. This research is one such fruit, which I hope you will be able to benefit from—getting a spiritual taste of it, as well as enable to see the bigger picture that emerges from the synthesis of the data.

With my whole being my heartfelt gratitude to the Divine, the 'Light upon Light'[1] that pervades all—the total community of life and the Universe that is manifested as mysteries and realities of life[2]—for providing me with this life and what is entails. For my beloved parents, Mr. Munsoor Zainudeen and Mrs. Sithy Rafeeka, who nurtured me with love, while encouraging me to don this path and who have since passed on. To my dearest wife and spiritual partner, Husna, and my loving children, Hannah, Wardah, Leena and Inaam, as well as my son-in-laws, Umair and Mousa, and my grand-daughter, Liyana Maariyah, for their continued love and immeasurable support. My heartfelt appreciation to our extended families for their sustained help during our life's journey, which has eased our burden. A special tribute to our Sri Lankan-Austrian friends who have made a positive difference to me and my family during our 4-year stay in Vienna. Likewise, my sincere gratitude to our family friends and our in-laws for their support during our long stay in Saudi Arabia, where this research was initiated in 2013.

My special thanks to Sheikh Dr. Jahid Sidek the Head of the spiritual Order Naqshabandiyyah Khaliddiyah, Malaysia, for giving me the permission for the study, without which this research would not have been possible. My appreciation to the Manager of the Residential Centre Mr. Idris Hussein for providing access to the seekers in the Order and guiding me as and when required. Interacting with

---

[1]This is derived from the Qur'anic verse, [Surah Al-Nur 24:35–36], where this is elucidated in terms of gaining an insight of the parable of the Divine presence "Allah is the Light of the heavens and the earth".

[2]This citation is from Dr. Thomas Berry, a cultural historian and scholar of the world's religions, especially Asian traditions from his book The Great Works: Our Way into the Future (1999).

the seekers was a special experience from which I gained very valuable insights on their transformation and how the Order functions. My great appreciation to them for their unreserved sharing of their first-hand experiences and to whom I am deeply indebted. Mr. Abdul Raheem, a Sri Lankan based in Malaysia has helped me selflessly through out my frequent visits during my study and research, which had greatly facilitated my life. Professor Dr. Hassanuddeen Bin Abdul Aziz Raheem (IIUM, Malaysia) guided me in finding the appropriate institution to carry out my research Dr. Ahmad Najaa' Bin Mokhtar and Dr. Muhammad Khairi Mahyuddin from the USIM, Malaysia gave me their valuable time and guidance. I am grateful to all of them.

A special word of appreciation to my thesis supervisor Dr. Che Zarrina Saa'ri and staff of the University of Malaya (Academy of Islam), Malaysia, as well as to my IDB and KAICIID colleagues who helped me by providing valuable feedback and guidance on my research. My profound thanks to the Sheikhs of the Naqshabanddiyya Awaisia tariqa Hazarath Muhammad Ahsan Baig and Syed Bunyad Hussain Shah for providing with the needed guidance and sharing the excellent methodology for deepening my contemplative practices, which has spurred my own transformation. I was initially guided to this system of meditation-behaviour and offered advice by the following to whom I am indebted—As-Seyyed Quraish Moulana, Amir Abdul Wahid Pallie and Mr. Jamaldeen Ashraf Ali Abdulla. Special thanks to all the seekers (*murids/sathis*) who have offered their knowledge to me as well as sharing their finer points of experiential learning.

My appreciations to all teachers, classmates, friends and colleagues from whom I have benefitted through out my life and continue to do so. Finally, my appreciation to the Springer Publishers (Harald Walach, Stefan Schmidt, Cristina dos Santos, Christopher Coughlin, Anita Rachmat and Nagajaran Paramasivam) for their efforts and for accepting to publish this piece of empirical research. My thanks to the two blind peer reviewers whose comments were very useful in shaping the manuscript.

Contents

1 Introduction 1
2 Conceptual Framework for Worship (Ibadah) 17
3 Conceptual Framework for Morality (*Akhlāq*) 93
4 Research Approach and Methodology 127
5 Case Study of a Spiritual Order, Malaysia 141
6 Spiritual Leadership and Self-Development Model 241
7 Summary and Conclusion 323
Appendices 337

About the Author

Dr. Mohamed Safiullah Munsoor is currently an international development consultant. He previously worked as a Director, Programmes, KAICIID (www.kaiciid.org) from 2017 to 2020. He was responsible for setting the programmtic direction and operationalization of the multi-faceted work of KAICIID in the area of interreligious dialogue and peace building.

Safiullah studied in Sri Lanka, Australia, United Kingdom and Malaysia. He obtained his first PhD from the University of Reading, UK, in International and Rural Development with a focus on Local Organisations. His second PhD focused on developing a Model of Spiritual Leadership and Self-Development (University of Malaya, Malaysia) by exploring the landscape of an Islamic Spiritual Order. He is a Master Practitioner in Neuro-Linguistic Programming and Neuro-Semantics and is a member of the International Society of Neuro-Semantics, USA.

Safiullah worked as the Manager for the Islamic Solidarity Fund for Development (Global Poverty Fund of US$2.5 billion) of the Islamic Development Bank (Multilateral Development Bank), Jeddah, Saudi Arabia from 2008 to 2017. He was responsible for the programme management and out-reach division, while being the overall strategy and programme coordinator for the Fund.

Safiullah's international career in development spans over three decades. He has worked with Save the Children (Norway) and the Canadian International Development Agency and spent nearly 20 years of his career with several United Nations organisations. He has worked in Asia, the Pacific, Africa, the Middle-East and Europe covering more than 20 countries. His professional work primarily focuses on poverty reduction, capacity building, strategic planning, program development and management. He has a high level of international expertise in community-driven development (CDD) and championed this within the IDB, as well as implemented several programmes in Asia and Africa. More recently, his attention has turned to social co-existence and peace building, while exploring the inter-section between peace and development. He is currently pursuing psychodynamic counselling moving from organisational and community development to focus on individuation and self-transformation.

He has a long-standing interest in religion and spirituality and has studied Yoga, Buddhist meditation and Islamic Sufi contemplative practices. He is a meditative practitioner within the Islamic tradition and has pursued it seriously for over two decades. He teaches mindfulness meditation to families, friends and colleagues who are interested in it. He has an increasing number of publications in the field of spirituality, self-development and well-being (https://www.linkedin.com/in/dr-m-safiullah-munsoor-ab715940/edit/birthday/). His personal interests include walking, meditation, music and reading. He is married and has 4 children.

Safiullah is seeking for a research institution that will accommodate him to further his research and teaching in integrated spirituality and well-being as well as share his knowledge and skills in terms of community-driven development having had global experience and expertise in this field. He can be contacted by email at safimunsoor@gmail.com or mohamed.safiullah@gmail.com.

Chapter 1
Introduction

1.1 Overview

Life has never been more comfortable for a sizeable part of the global population, with technological advances infiltrating every facet of our lives. Notwithstanding this, poverty remains a chronic issue, as do greater levels of anxiety, depression, and substance abuse (including drugs and alcohol), with accompanying negative impacts on people's general sense of wellbeing. This trend seems to transcend geographic, cultural and religious boundaries, affecting mankind irrespective of faith or orientation.

The state of affairs outlined above begs several questions: what ails society? Why are people not content with their lives? Why are they not striving to achieve a sense of wellbeing? Why are individuals turning to external dependencies to sustain their lives, with obvious related costs and side effects? Is this connected to their way of life and their psychology it terms of their attitude or is it to do with the way they understand their faiths through their belief systems or else not having any religious or spiritual orientation and meaning to life?

Within the contemporary context, there seems to be a resurgence of spirituality and its related practices, with a decline in association with formal religions, at least in Europe. For example, there has been an increased number of research into 'spirituality and the workplace', as well as spiritually related practices being adapted into health and fitness schemes. In this light, there has been investigations into faith-based traditions particularly Buddhism (meditation) and Hinduism (yoga) but less so in terms of Islam and its contemplative practices. I use religion and spirituality synonymously within the text even though within the current context, this has become bifurcated due to extraneous factors.

This study attempts to understand some of these questions through exploring the workings of an Islamic spiritual Order, Naqshabaanddiyah Khaliddiyyah, Malaysia and by laying bare the essential elements that are required to transform the lives of this particular group of seekers. It explains the need for the development of the outer self (form), including rituals, prayers and other acts of worship, while focusing on the inner (spirit) state, with an aim to awaken (*yaqza*) oneself in a spiritual sense. This is accomplished by drawing upon the Islamic tradition and its Prophetic model, and with reference to other faith traditions and contemporary sciences, where relevant. It is to be noted that this research has been done within the framework of the Sunni tradition and therefore draws upon it to a large extent. The Shia tradition,[1] which is a rich domain of spirituality, is referred to only when and where relevant since it is not a comparative study and thus outside the remit of this study. However, it was found in our exploration that there are more similarities than differences between the two mystical traditions, that is, Irfan (Shia) and Sufism (Sunni)[2] and this is highlighted where relevant.

Health, as defined by the WHO (2014) is, "a state of complete physical, mental and social wellbeing and not merely the absence of disease or infirmity." This definition is challenged by Sulmasy (2002), who proposes a biopsychosocial-spiritual model, where spirituality is subsumed within health since it has an impact on well-being (see Chap. 6)[3]. The attainment of a wholesome lifestyle has been thrust upon us as a solution to achieving a balanced way of living. Wellbeing can

---

[1] The spiritual Order under study is of Sunni orientation and also one of the few Orders which traces its lineage-silsila to Khalip Abu Baker since most orders link up to Khalip Ali (may God honour His countenance on both) through the Prophet (our peace and salutations). While the debate ensues between the Sunni-Shia traditions, given that both believe in the Oneness of God, accept the Qur'an in totality and the finality of the Prophet, this study makes some reference to Shia spirituality where and when required since it falls with the overall Islamic framework. There are some fatwas issued in this regard which includes from the Grand Muftis of Al-Azhar–Mahmoud Shaltoot in 2021 and Ahmed el-Tayeb (2016). This is reinforced by the Amman Message (https://ammanmessage.com), a statement calling for tolerance and unity in the Muslim world issued on 9th November 2004, by 500 Islamic Scholars from over 50 countries. This related to such matters as defining who is a Muslim, excommunication from Islam (*takfir*) and principles related to delivering religious opinion (*fatwa*). The scholars who supported the Amman message included Grand Imam Shaykh Al-Azhar, the Grand Ayatollah Al-Sayyid Ali Al-Sistani, the Mufti of Egypt, the leading Shi'i clerics (both Ja'fari and Zaydi), the Grand Mufti of the Sultanate of Oman, the Islamic Fiqh Academy in the Kingdom of Saudi Arabia, the Grand Council for Religious Affairs of Turkey, the Grand Mufti of the Hashemite Kingdom of Jordan and the Respectable Members of its National Fatwa Committee, and the Shaykh Dr. Yusuf Al-Qaradawi.

[2] The Amman Message 2004 above cited had this as a part of their statement: In accordance with the Shaykh Al-Azhar's *fatwa*, it is neither possible nor permissible to declare whosoever subscribes to the *Ash'ari* creed or whoever practices real *Tasawwuf* (Sufism) an apostate. Likewise, it is neither possible nor permissible to declare whosoever subscribes to true Salafi thought an apostate. Equally, it is neither possible nor permissible to declare as apostates any group of Muslims who believes in God, Glorified and Exalted be He, and His Messenger (may peace and blessings be upon him) and the pillars of faith, and acknowledges the five pillars of Islam, and does not deny any necessarily self-evident tenet of religion. There was a recognition of eight schools of sharia/fiqh (madhahib) and varying schools of Islamic theology: (1) Sunni Hanafi, (2) Sunni Maliki, (3) Sunni Shafi'i, (4) Sunni Hanbali, (5) Shia Ja'fari, (6) Shia Zaydi, (7) Zahiri, and (8) Ibadi. It also forbade declaring an apostate anyone who is a follower of: (1) the Ash'ari/Maturidi creed, (2) real *Tasawwuf* (Sufism), and (3) true Salafi thought.

[3] Dr. Daniel Sulmasy is a palliative care physician and a Catholic Franciscan monk (Sulmasy 2002).

1.1 Overview

be enhanced by creating a space to cultivate peace, by adopting a life style with an appropriate approach and an attitude of tolerance, which provides the basis for abating negative emotions and behaviour. Does religion in general and Islam in particular outline a pathway to a state of wellbeing? This is one of the questions that is addressed in this exploration of the spiritual Order in the light of emerging neuroscientific evidence, as well as in reference to humanistic psychology and spiritual leadership.

In a contemporary context, the concern with the quality of life is becoming more pressing due to what has been termed 'the social acceleration of our culture', as well as a greater degree of 'individualisation and functionalisation' of our lives which seems to be resulting in 'continuing discontentment and stress' (Rosa in Schmidt and Walach 2014). 'Stress' here is defined as "physiologic or psychologic perturbations that throw us out of balance" (van Wijk et al., in Schmidt and Walach 2014), while 'stress-related responses' mean, for example, contemplation-meditation translating into "the set of neural and endocrine adaptation that help us to re-establish homeostasis" (Sapolsky in Schmidt and Walach 2014), thus becoming a therapy.

This empirical investigation[4] aims to understand the nature of the spiritual Order and its accompanying system—including its leadership, that is, the role of the exemplar (Sheikh), its approach, methods and tools—and the effects that it has on the wellbeing of the seekers (*murids*) who follow it. One of my key arguments is that Islam has a spiritual architecture, with its role models, that can be utilised for modelling and developing oneself. Development of the self refers to spiritual growth, improving one's state of wellbeing and behaviour, with a greater level of awareness and consciousness. Here, 'spiritual' is defined as "the search for the sacred" (Pargement and Mahoney 2002), and sacred is defined as "concepts of God, and transcendent reality, as well as other aspects of life that take on divine character and significance by virtue of their association with, or representation of, divinity". Within this context, a 'spiritual order' refers to "a group of people who join together for religious or similar reasons and live according to particular rules" (Cambridge University Press 2021).

A counter claim and argument that is presented—especially within the current phase of extremism and violence—is that Islam does not have a spiritual architecture for self-development and is ritualistic in its outlook. These claims are dealt with in great detail in Chap. 5—case study and Chap. 6—the integrated discussion and analysis.

In light of the above, the objectives of this study are:
Primary Objectives:

---

[4]This research results from primary and secondary data collected, analysed and interpreted for a Ph.D. thesis which has been presented and successfully defended in 2017 and successfully completed in 2018.

(1) Based on an in-depth assessment of the spiritual Order, to develop a model exploring the associations between spiritual leadership and self-development of its seekers.
(2) To understand the nature of the spiritual Order, its leadership, and the impact has on its seekers.

Specific Objectives:

(1) To identify, through a non-intrusive process of inquiry, the spiritual landscape of the Order including its concepts, metaphors, and the guiding principles that enhance and contribute to self–development.
(2) To identify the essential features and traits of the relevant spiritual role models or exemplar-Sheikh.
(3) To develop a model of the state of excellence of the role model, namely, the Sheikh and the workings of his Order.
(4) To identify spiritual practices that go towards positively contributing to the spiritual and emotional wellbeing of practitioners.

Given the complexity of the subject, I used qualitative research adopting the interpretative phenomenological approach (IPA),[5] which provided an avenue to understand the social, spiritual and experiential landscape of the Order. As a means of developing an effective dialogue, 'clean language'[6] was used, which is a method of posing very few questions and building on the authentic narrative of the seekers themselves through key informant interviews and focus group discussions. This ensured that I did not impose my own narrative and thoughts into the process of the seeker's understanding.

The research was augmented by using methods such as neuro-linguistic programming (NLP),[7] to build the profile of the exemplar. This was combined with the

---

[5] In Smith and Osborne's exposition of the Interpretative phenomenological approach (IPA) they point out that IPA uses hermeneutics (understanding how language is used) and symbolic interactionism (making sense of the personal and social world of others and how meanings are constructed). They, however, caution to not accept all of what the individual says but to be critical in understanding things as they transpire (Smith and Osborne 2003).

[6] James Lawley and Penny Tompkins (2016) say that the therapist David Grove who developed the system for 'Clean Language' reflected and "wondered what it would be like to fully preserve and honour a client's experience with minimal interference by the therapist." He achieved this by identifying a number of very simple questions with a particular syntax and a unique delivery method. These questions contained a minimum of presupposition and were therefore called 'Clean Language.' What he discovered was the more he used Clean Language, the more clients naturally used metaphor to describe their symptoms. When Clean Language questions were then directed to the metaphors and symbols, unexpected information became available to the client, often with profound results. He found that the less he attempted to change the client's model of the world, the more they experienced their own core patterns, and organic, lasting changes naturally emerged from "the system".

[7] The NLP is a contested methodology and has been subjected to scrutiny and not found to be robust and scientific. Notwithstanding this, its modelling methods and the meta-programme is seen to be well grounded and a useful avenue for understanding people and how their model themselves. This

results of a questionnaire, which provided responses from the seekers to validate the qualitative research approach. Using thematic analysis, the resulting data was interwoven with Islamic scriptural citations and examples of the Prophetic[8] way of life, as well as relevant theoretical references. Relevant data from neuro-science[9] and humanistic psychology was used to corroborate the findings of the study and produce a rich tapestry of the spiritual world of this Order.

The data generated by this study is primarily an emic viewpoint which "results from studying behaviour as from inside the system",[10] hence the seekers presented their own narratives and spiritual landscapes including their experiences, concepts and beliefs, within their framework of Islam. The emic perspective is especially important in creating insight and understanding of cultural nuances. Given this situation, I strived to incorporate the etic dimension—that is, studies of behaviour from outside a particular system—by providing my own reflections as an outsider augmented by views and data from external studies and perspectives. In this light, I am attempting to position this work within a balanced perspective in relation to the tension that often arises from the emic-etic dimension, even though it will be objectively difficult to lay aside totally my own subconscious biases.

1.2 Context

Within the framework of Islam, one subject that has received unbalanced attention as well as a mixed reaction within the contemporary context is self or spiritual-development, as compared with Hinduism (yoga), Buddhism (mindfulness meditation), or Judeo-Christianity, with its monastic and kabbalah traditions. The latter faiths being underlined by the Judeo-Christian[11] ethos-values have to a large

---

comes from my own experience of becoming a Master Practitioner of NPL-NS (Neuro Linguistic Programming-Neuro-Semantics).

[8] The salutation of Prophet Mohammad with Peace and Blessings be Upon him should be evoked when ever one comes across it, as it should be with all other Prophets. Given that there will be general readers of this manuscript it is not mentioned when ever the Prophet's name is referred to but it is implicitly intended.

[9] Neuroscience was used to bring together the emerging findings from various acts of worship from Hinduism (yoga) and Buddhism (meditation), while building a case of Islam derived from its own spiritual practices. Humanistic psychology was utilised in order to make reference to leadership and self-development in the light of various works including that of Abraham Maslow and Carl Rogers.

[10] The terms emic-etic was first coined by a linguistic theoretician Kenneth Pike (1964) in his cultural anthropological studies and thereafter expanded by others.

[11]
(1) Yoga (Sanskrit) is a group of ancient spiritual practices originating in India. As a general term in Hinduism, it has been defined as referring to "technologies or disciplines of asceticism and meditation which are thought to lead to spiritual experience and profound understanding or insight into the nature of existence." Yoga is also intimately connected to the religious beliefs and practices of the other. Raja Yoga, known as simply as yoga in the context of Hindu

extent laid down the foundation for Western society. Both within Buddhism and Hinduism, there have been numerous scientific experimentations that have been carried out, which have recorded benefits of their respective contemplative practices on the health and wellbeing of its practitioners (see Sect. 2.4).

In a contemporary sense within Islam, there has been a general neglect of these traditional Islamic practices of self-development (*tasawwuf*) unless one is a part of what is commonly known as a '*ṭarīqa*'[12] or other relevant Islamic orders, which literally means 'a way or a path', essentially a spiritual order.[13] Notwithstanding this, presently one sees these types of practices, largely drawn from the Buddhist and Yogic tradition, being incorporated into a professional work or in a clinical setting often by a clinician who has found value in it.

Nizamie et al. (2013), Isgandarova 2018, and Rothman (2020) points out that Islamic and Sufi oriented practices have been incorporated in order to augment cognitive behaviour therapy or has formed the core in some transpersonal psychotherapy interventions. In this light, the therapist works with the client's belief system and practices like prayer and meditation (*dhikr*). They essentially highlight that the value framework of patience (*sabr*), trust in God (*tawwakul*), contentment (*riḍa*), thankfulness (*shukr*) and belief in the mercy of God, may provide a basis for changing the negative cognitive schema of the clients. This study deals with these above mentioned aspects both from a theoretical (Chaps. 2 and 3) as well as empirical point of view (Chaps. 5 and 6).

There has been a re-emergence for the usefulness and adaption of spiritually related practices (mindfulness meditation, yoga), which are being secularised for all intensive purposes. Otherwise, one generally spends insignificant amounts of time on these practices, and this space is inadvertently being replaced by various

---

philosophy, is one of the six orthodox (*astika*) schools of thought, established by the Yoga sutras of Patanjali (Indian religions).

(2) Buddhist meditation encompasses a variety of meditation techniques that develop mindfulness, concentration, tranquility and insight. Core meditation techniques are preserved in ancient Buddhist texts and have proliferated and diversified through the millennia of teacher –student transmission.

(3) Merton (2004) expounds on Eastern Christians having a shared tradition, arguing that they became divided during the early centuries of Christianity in disputes about Christology and fundamental theology. In general terms, Eastern Christianity can be described as comprising four families of churches: the Assyrian church of the East, the Eastern Orthodox churches, Oriental Orthodoxy, and the Eastern Catholic churches.

[12]*Ṭarīqa* or 'ṭuruq' (singular), which is "associated with the mystical teaching and the set of spiritual practices and rituals that are performed within this order, with the ultimate aim of seeking *haqiqah* or ultimate truth" (Marzouqi 2013).

[13]This study focuses on what is commonly termed a Sufi order. There are other orders, with an inward focus and orientations within Islam that need to be studied in order to gain a comprehensive understanding of their nature and impact on their followers. In this sense, I do not discount those orders, which do not fall under the rubric of Sufi related orders and my due respect to all orders whatever their orientation, which strives in the cause of the divine without harming and being tolerant of others. I believe in the principle of 'do no harm' to oneself and others, which is a Prophetic code.

1.2 Context

types of entertainment for the senses, that occupies almost all of one's free time as well as the mind, such that one is no longer able to harmonise oneself with silence. Yet, in times of crises, either to oneself or those close to us, we are forced to seek help from the world of psychological practitioners and/or spiritual role-models and their related practices, in order to find a sense of peace and solitude. On a general note, one can say that a large focus of contemporary life is on physical and aesthetic development with little attention paid to inward self-development from which fundamental issues such as drug based dependencies or forms of addiction can arise. This is the case not only with the general population but could also be true of various religious communities, where the focus has narrowed down to solely the outer (formalistic) rather than the inner state of one's development, which from time-to-time is manifested as conflict and violence both within oneself, one's faith and between faiths.

In a contemporary context, the psychologist and psycho-therapist have taken on at least parts of the functions of a traditional spiritual role model. But even though this could be effective, therapists are confined by certain boundaries like cost, time, flexibility, professional work ethics etc., The therapist does not necessarily serve as someone you can role-model on, as is the practice within spiritual orders or ṭariqas and thus can only play a limited role in shaping their client's lifestyle or context.

A note of caution needs to be underlined here about spiritual orders, although in general they tend to have sound role-models, an observation is that, there is a tendency for some of them to become sectarian in nature and to veer at times from the traditional Islamic framework. Thus, finding a sound spiritual order and an exemplar or Sheikh is generally not an easy task, however, there are criteria against which one needs to validate their conduct in order to find a sound guide (see Sect. 2.5).

While on the one hand, the modern life-style has made living more comfortable in terms of material wellbeing; conversely, however, life has become more stressful due to the competitive nature of work and living. This has led to a challenge that Walsh (2016) outlines as follows:

"In modern affluent societies, the diseases exacting the greatest mortality and morbidity such as cardiovascular disorders, obesity, diabetes, and cancer are now strongly determined by lifestyle...smoking, physical activity, alcohol intake, and diet exert a major impact on mortality, and even small differences in lifestyle can make a major difference in health status... The importance of healthy lifestyles for treating multiple psychopathologies, for fostering psychological and social well-being, and for preserving and optimising cognitive capacities and neural functions."

In this light, Walsh (2016) succinctly articulates that:

"Therapeutic lifestyle changes (TLCs) are under-utilised despite considerable evidence of their effectiveness in both clinical and normal populations. TLCs are sometimes as effective as either psychotherapy or pharmacotherapy and can offer significant therapeutic advantages...[They can] include exercise, nutrition and diet, time in nature, relationships, recreation, relaxation and stress management, religious or spiritual involvement, and service to others."

In a contemporary sense, it is relevant to examine the role of religion, which subsumes spirituality,[14] within the context of the scientific and technological advancement that has culminated in our modern age.[15] There are two perspectives: One is that religion, its dogmas and rituals have become irrelevant in the modern or post-modern world since religion is not able to provide a basis for people to reconcile themselves with the contemporary world view. The second view, which is a critique of the first, is that religion with its embedded spirituality, including its rituals, is still alive since it is not intrinsically antagonistic to the modern world (Cladis 2006).[16]

I argue that there is a renewed interest in learning from religious and spiritual role models in order to deal with the vagaries of life. These religious or faith-based practices associated with the development of one's self are now being utilised for a variety of functions, including dealing with anxiety and depression, maintaining a healthy life style, developing dialogue and discourses, and finding meaning in life. Many of these practices have been taken out of their religious context and secularised, by being given a purely 'scientific perspective'. This includes Mindfulness Based Stress Reduction (MBSR)[17] and Mindfulness Based Cognitive Therapy (MBCT).[18] Both of these methods, derived from Buddhist practice, have been adapted within psychology and are used to treat a range of conditions, from pain management to anxiety and depression. This highlights the immense need for contemplative practices as well as the development of one's character and behaviour,

---

[14] Within the contemporary context, religion is often separated from spirituality due to a loss of confidence in religious institutions, resulting from poor leadership, policies and corruption. In essence most, if not all, of the stress-reduction, some psychotherapeutic practices as well as societal values and education systems have been derived from different faiths. To push this point further, a large body of scientific works including medicine, mathematics, chemistry, physics, biology etc. have been closely linked with the evolutions of various religions, including Islam, which played a paramount role during this period.

[15] Ernest Gellner (2006) definition of the modern age as being industrialised, urbanised, egalitarian at least in name, with compulsory education for all, and vastly more populous than before.

[16] Cladis cites the eminent sociologist Emile Durkheim who, in his earlier work, predicted the demise of religion. This position was changed in his later works where he argued that it would prevail and influence modernity. His conception of religion changed to include a variety of human beliefs and practices.

[17] MBSR was developed by Kabbat-Zinn, a Scientist, after having studied Buddhism and utilising its meditative methods, which is a moment-to-moment awareness of oneself, either one's breath or body without evaluating the emerging thoughts. This training of the self-perception of one's breath, bodily sensations, posture etc. and linking it with the alienated parts of the body, is seen to be therapeutic. It has been shown to have numerous benefits on well-being.

[18] MBCT was developed by Zindel Segal, Mark Williams and John Teasdale, based on Jon Kabat-Zinn's Mindfulness-Based Stress Reduction program. MBCT is designed to help people who suffer repeated bouts of depression and chronic unhappiness. It combines the ideas of cognitive therapy with meditative practices and attitudes based on the cultivation of mindfulness. The heart of this work lies in becoming acquainted with the modes of mind that often characterise mood disorders while simultaneously learning to develop a new relationship to them.

these are key ingredients to shape one's life positively. The Contemplative Tree in Sect. 2.3 provides a range of these contemplative or devotional practices and methods within the Islamic framework.

1.3 Value Addition

In recent years, there have been some emerging scientific based studies relating to Islamic practices (Ibrahim et al. 2008; Doufesh et al. 2012; Aldahadha 2013; Roky et al. 2003; Afifi 1997; Roky et al. 2000), which are yielding interesting results that point to the positive mind-body impact relating to contemplative and devotional practices. However, there is a need for more research, especially in investigating meditative and contemplative practices given the variability of practices and orientations.

There seems to be a general neglect of the spiritual self within a context or what can be termed as spiritual development (*tasawwuf*) within Islam, perhaps due to a number of reasons:

(1) either a lack of comprehensive understanding of the concepts, methods, and tools used within Islam;
(2) the minimalistic approach taken by people due to pressures of time;
(3) a lack of understanding of the merits of these practices including their purpose and value;
(4) an understanding that some of these practices are not following the Prophetic tradition and are therefore an innovation (bid'a);
(5) current scholars mainly focusing on the outer rituals and losing focus on inward development.

Notwithstanding this, Islam has had a long history of communities of practices, or spiritual orders, dating back to the sixth century. These orders are generally low key meaning not competitive, pursue a variety of contemplative practices, and are still active across the globe (see Chap. 5).

There has been a general tendency by a segment of the Muslim populace to be preoccupied with the Sharī'a,[19] especially in terms of the rules and regulations governing one's life and the outward acts and rituals, which are no doubt altogether important in Islam. This, however, has to an extent overshadowed the inner dimension of Islam (*tasawwuf*), with its core emphasis on self and spiritual development, which includes *akhlāq* (behaviour, attitude, code of conduct) and *'ibādah* (worship). *Dhikr* (remembrance of God) and several other contemplative practices fit well

---

[19]Sharī'a (Arabic) is the body of Islamic religious law. The term means "way" or "path to the water source"; it is the legal framework within which the public and some private aspects of life are regulated for those living in a legal system based on Muslim principles of jurisprudence and for Muslims living outside the domain. Sharī'a deals with many aspects of day-to-day life, including politics, economics, banking, business, contracts, family, sexuality, hygiene, and social issues.

within the Sharī'a and sunnah (action and words) of the Prophet. Some of the key concepts aforementioned are discussed in detail in Sect. 2.3 and 2.5.

The Arabic language has a wide array of texts that deal with the issue of the development of self in an in-depth manner. They are, however, not generally accessible to the public due to language restrictions, their contents, style of presentation, as well as a general ignorance of substantive works of some eminent Islamic traditional scholars. There have been an increasing number of materials available in English, but this has largely been for specialist readers who are interested in spirituality and which are not freely accessible to the common reader. In recent times, there have been attempts by some Islamic scholars to elucidate these areas to the general English-language reader, as we shall see in the discussion encapsulated in the literature review (Sects. 2.1–2.6). However, first hand empirical studies of these spiritual orders are not common and even rarer are those that effectively combine both theory and practice, let alone integration of different disciplines within it.

1.4 Knowledge Gaps

There are several emerging research studies, especially in the field of neuroscience, that point out the positive impacts of 'mindfulness meditation' (University of California, Berkeley 2016), which in-effect are a fundamental aspect of many religious traditions including Islam. Mindfulness is a form of awareness and intuitive knowing, from moment to moment, of what is going on inside oneself and that of the outside world, which is cultivated through meditation without judgement. This forms a way of training one's attention over time so that one is able to concentrate, for example, on prayers without the mind wandering. In Islam, this is called 'khushu', a type of absorption in worship. This state of concentration is conducive towards a state of deeper contemplation where one feels that God's is witnessing you (murāqaba).

This field of inner development, which is facilitated by spiritual orders and their leadership, using traditional practices, and which appears to have an impact on its seekers, has been one area that has not been well researched. This is especially so in the light of the emerging data relating to neuroscience of numerous benefits in terms of well-being and the process of self-development.[20]

Given the above, there is a need to articulate and present succinctly to the reader the process of role-modelling, and the specific approaches, and methods that can be

---

[20]There are increasing observations of changes in the characteristics of individuals resulting from long and deep meditative practices as cited in several articles (Schmidt and Walach 2014). Purely from an empirical point of view, this does not come as a surprise for those who have observed over time that those who are truly spiritually oriented are calm in their disposition and of good character, which can be seen across the faiths.

1.4 Knowledge Gaps

used for self-development within the Islamic framework. This needs to be examined on two levels, one is the theoretical and the other operational:

(1) The former includes the broader Islamic framework –including much of the body of belief (*'aqidah*), theology (*kalām*), the legality (*fiqh*), and the philosophy (*falsafah*)—that lays down the fundamentals and the variances within Islam. This is very much the rational or the cognitive dimension, connected with brain functions.

(2) There are within Islam the non-rational or a more operational level, those areas that are more related to the heart, which include the Prophetic revelation (*waḥy*), divine inspiration (*ḥadith qudsi*), the states of mind in worship including contemplative practices (prayer, fasting, supplication, repentance), a meditative state of being (*khushu* or absorption in worship), intuition (*badīha*), illumination (*tanwīr*), a kind of knowing related to telepathy (*firāsah*), with states of the heart relating to compassion, empathy, love, and charity. These are more related to spiritual and emotional states of the heart, not necessarily related to cognitive actualisation.

What this study attempts to build is a model of factors associated with spiritual leadership and self-development, factoring in both the rational (brain—cognition, intellect) and the non-rational (heart—revelation, intuition, inspiration, emotion) aspects that are required for the development of the self within the spiritual Order under study. In doing so, it will elaborate the organisational workings of the Order with its various variables that that go into making it work.

Without the development of both aspects mentioned above, there can be an unbalanced state of self-development. Perhaps this can be best summed up in the saying of Imam Malik (Khan 1976, p27): "Whosoever, without adequate knowledge of *fiqh* (law) acquired *tasawwuf* (inward science) becomes...a sinner. He who acquired both both becomes an accomplished believer". This, then, refers to a more holistic perspective of Islam, which should focus on both the outer/external and the inner/internal. Based on the research data set from the case study, the discussion (Chap. 6) puts this into context by presenting and discussing a model of spiritual leadership and self-development and the brain-heart inter-link.

While research linking spiritual practices with mental and physical wellbeing can be justified in its own right, there is an additional element to this particular study. This is related to the question often asked by those who are not Muslims, as to whether Islam has these types of resources in terms of virtues and self-development, which other major religions have more ostensibly available within their domain. When Muslims start to look at other traditions and practices to find solace and peace of mind, they have essentially missed out on the inner dimensions of Islam. This, then, needs to be effectively articulated, which reflects the knowledge gaps as outlined below:

- To develop a model of spiritual leadership and self-development after mapping out the metaphoric, symbolic, and conceptual landscape of a spiritual leader within the order;

- To develops the nexus between worship and morality, as well as the rational (brain) versus the non-rational (heart), which needs to be better articulated within English-language Islamic literature;
- To provide empirical data and first-hand insight into contemplative practices within Islam, including a framework relating to meditation-contemplation and neuro-science.

One of the limitations of the scope of this study is that no scientific experiments were conducted relating to collecting neuro-science data, which is well beyond this initiative. In essence what has been recorded, analysed and synthesised is the subjective experience of seekers, where interviews were triangulated with a survey questionnaire. This was then corroborated by both re-checking it internally with the seekers for internal validity, as well as supporting it with other similar studies that have been done externally, for establishing a form of external validity.

It is to be noted that in order for spiritual practices—especially contemplative practices including meditation—to gain objectivity and credibility within the scientific domain, one needs to correlate the deep stages of meditative experiences with "traditional-independent psychological markers of the different levels and/or sub-levels identified by standard scientific protocols" (Shear, in Schmidt and Walach 2014). This detecting of the changes in the levels of consciousness and the resulting neuro-scientific changes could then lead to the development of a 'theory of the mind'[21] and meditation being considered as a 'methodology for exploring consciousness'. Having stated this, for those who are spiritually inclined, it is the experience and the transformation that matters whether it conforms with the scientific framework is a different question.

When one discusses spirituality, the United Nations Sustainable Development Goals (SDGs) do not generally come to mind, and this important nexus and narrative between spirituality and the SDGs does not feature in the development or the humanitarian discourses. However, a closer examination of the process and impact of spirituality and well-being (Chap. 3, Fig. 3.4) on the mind, body and behavior is significant, as seen in the data set in Chap. 5. This relates to SDG goal number 3 (good health and well-being – afiya or holistic health). Further to this, SDG goal number 4 (quality education – tarbiyah) has application within the Order consists of religious-spiritual contents, methods and processes of learning and a set of tools, which serves as a vehicle during the educational process of the seekers. This process of raising awareness accompanied by mutual respect and tolerance for the other, which embodies adab or code of ethics towards male and female, impacts both

---

[21] Maps relating to the levels of the mind or consciousness have been developed from various traditions and on a phenomenological basis have similarities even though they may be different on a metaphysical framework of their respective faiths. This has been recorded for yoga, Vedanta, and other orthodox Indian systems (*darsana*). There are levels of consciousness of the mind, which have been articulated within Islamic literature and these are elaborated in Fig. 2.1 and Chap. 6 of this study, which deals with the nature of the soul and its attributes as well as compares the stages of consciousness of Islam and the Vedanta one of the oldest faith traditions, which believes in one God, (Chap. 6).

genders (SDG goal number 5 on gender equality and empowerment). Even though the data relating to gender is insufficient to make a robust statement, a brief sketch of women's participation is outlined based on my observations. Finally, SDG goal 16 on promoting peace, justice and inclusive society is examined before drawing relevant conclusions. The implications of the data on these spiritual practices on the mind, body and behaviour has been presented in Chap. 5 and discussed in the light of the SDG[22] goals and indicators in chapter 6 with relevant conclusions outlined in Chap. 7.

1.5 An Overview of the Structure

This work is categorised into seven main chapters. The introduction (Chap. 1) provides an overview of the research exploration, with the objectives, context including its justification, key claim and counter claim and the context. Based on the two core dimensions within Islam, that is, worship (*'ibādah*) and morality (*akhlāq*). The second section (Chaps. 2 and 3) is divided into two conceptual frameworks, the first dealing with worship and the second dealing with morality.

The above essentially constitutes the required background literature and research which underpins this study. The first framework deals with the soul and its attributes with reference to western psychology, the diseases of the soul and its treatment, contemplative practices and wellbeing and neuro-science (Chap. 2). The second framework deals with the right way to God (with a focus on ethics) and the way of the Prophet and his leadership (Chap. 3).

The third section (Chap. 4) outlines in some detail the methodology of the study and the philosophical basis driving it. The results together with the interpretation and analysis are presented through building a detailed case study of the spiritual Order in Malaysia (Chap. 5). This integrates both interview and survey data and is subjected to interpretation by the researcher. Then, in Chap. 6, the integration of the full data set with related theories and concepts is discussed and an integrated analysis and synthesis is presented. Finally, conclusions (Chap. 7) are drawn from the whole study with regards to its summary and significance and the scope for future research.

---

[22] The 2030 Agenda for Sustainable Development, adopted by all United Nations Member States in 2015, provides a shared blueprint for peace and prosperity for people and the planet, now and into the future. At its heart are the 17 Sustainable Development Goals (SDGs), which are an urgent call for action by all countries - developed and developing - in a global partnership. They recognize that ending poverty and other deprivations must go hand-in-hand with strategies that improve health and education, reduce inequality, and spur economic growth – all while tackling climate change and working to preserve our oceans and forests; The 17 Goals Sustainable Development https://sdgs.un.org/goals.

References

Afifi, Z. E. M. (1997). Daily practices, study performance and health during the Ramadan fast. *The Journal of the Royal Society for the Promotion of Health, 117*(4), 231–235.

Al-Bukhari (Arabic–English), with compilation by Al-Imam Zain-ud-Din Ahmaf bin Abdul-Lateef Az-Zubaidi. Chapter 7 No: 433 & Chapter 8 No: 436. Saudi Arabia: Islamic University, Al-Medina Al-Munawwara.

Aldahadha, B. (2013). The Effects of Muslim Praying Meditation and Transcendental Meditation Programs on Mindfulness among the University of Nizwa Students. *College Student Journal, 47*(4), 668–676.

Cambridge University Press. (2021). *Order, Cambridge Dictionary*, United Kingdom. https://dictionary.cambridge.org/dictionary/english/order

Cladis, M. S. (2006). Modernity in Religion: A Response to Constantin Fasolts "History and Religion in the Modern Age". *History and Theory, 45*(4), 93–103.

Doufesh, T., Faisal, K., Lim, S. & Ibrahim, F. (2012). EEG spectral analysis on Muslim prayers. *Applied Psychophysiology and Biofeedback 37*(1), 11–18.

Esch, T. (2014). The Neurobiology of Meditation and Mindfulness. In S. Schmidt & H. Walach (Eds.), *Neuroscientific Approaches and Philosophical Implications* (Vol. 155). Switzerland: Springer.

Gellner, E. (2006). *Nations and Nationalism* (2nd edn.). New York: Cornell University Press.

Ibrahim, F., Abas, A. B. W., & Cheok, N. S. (2008). Salat: Benefit from science perspective. In *Department of Biomedical Engineering, Faculty of Engineering*. Kuala Lumpur: University of Malaya.

Isgandarova, N. (2018). Muraqaba as a mindfulness based therapy in Islamic psychotherapy. *Journal of Religion and Health, 58*, 1146–1160. https://doi.org/10.1007/s10943-018-0695-y.

Khan, A. Y. (1976). *Dalail-Us-Sulook: The Objective Appraisal of the Sublime Sufi Path*, Idarah Naqshbandiah Owaisiah, Murshad Abad Mianwali, Pakistan.

Lawley, J. & Tompkins, P (2016). *The Art of Clean Language, The Clean Language Collection*. http://www.cleanlanguage.co.uk/articles/articles/109/1/Less-Is-More-The-Art-of-Clean-Language/Page1.html.

Marzouqi, H. (2013). *Ṭarīqa Islam: Layers of Authentication*. Qatar: Arab Center for Research and Policy Studies.

Merton, T. (2004). *The Wisdom of the Desert: Sayings from the Desert Fathers of the Fourth Century*. USA: Fonsvitae Publishing.

Nizamie, S. H., Katshu, M. Z. U. H., & Uvais, N. A (2013), Sufism and mental health, *Indian Journal of Psychiatry, 55*(Indian Mental Concepts 1—Supplement January 2013), pp. S215–S223.

Pike, K. (1964). *Tagememics: The Study of Units Beyond The Sentence*, National Council of Teachers of English, USA.

Pargament, K. I., & Mahoney, A. (2002). Spirituality: Discovering and conserving the sacred. In C. R. Snyder & S. J. Lopez (Eds.), *Handbook of Positive Psychology* (pp. 646–659). Oxford: Oxford University Press. https://psycnet.apa.org/record/2002-02382-047.

Roky, R., Iraki, L., Haj Khlifa, R., Ghazal, N. L., & Hakkou, F. (2000). Daytime alertness, mood, psychomotor performances, and oral temperature during Ramadan intermittent fasting. *Annals of Nutrition and Metabolism, 44*(3), 101–107.

Roky, R., Chapotot. F., Benchekroun, M. T., Benaji, B., Hakkou, F., Elkhalifi, H. & Buguet, A. (2003). Daytime sleepiness during Ramadan intermittent fasting: polysomnographic and quantitative waking EEG study. *Journal of Sleep Research, 12*(2), 95–101.

Rothman, Abdallah (2020). *Midnight Moments, Session 20, Continuing the Journey*. UK: Cambridge Muslim College. https://www.youtube.com/watch?v=I3DE5MpfiPk&list=PLBUQOvJ_NYrAawK3603c13NXfHhxPia0f.

Saligman, M. (2007). Hard Talk. In *BBC Asia Services*.

References

Segal, Z., Williams, M., Teasdale, J., & Kabat-Zinn, J. (2006). Mindfulness-Based Stress Reduction program. In: *Your Mindfulness Guide to Cognitive Therapy, Mindfulness-Based Cognitive Therapy (MBCT)*. http://mbct.com.

Shaltoot, M. (2021). Shaeikh Mahmud Shaltut's Fatwa about Shia Madhab, 1959. https://www.icit-digital.org/articles/shaykh-mahmud-shaltut-s-fatwa-about-shia-madhab-1959.

Smith, J. A., & Osborn, M. (2003). Interpretative phenomenological analysis. In Smith, J. A. (Ed.). *Qualitative Psychology: A Practical Guide to Methods* (pp. 53–80). London: Sage.

Sulmasy, D. P. (2002). A biopsychosocial-spiritual model for the care of patients at the end of life. Gerontologist, Oct; 42 Spec No 3:24–33. https://doi.org/10.1093/geront/42.suppl_3.24.

Tayeb, A. (2016). *Grand Mufti calls for greater tolerance between Sunni and Shi'a*, Albawada News, 24th February, 2016, https://www.albawaba.com/news/grand-imam-al-azhar-calls-more-tolerance-between-shias-and-sunnis-809470.

The 17 Goals | Sustainable Development https://sdgs.un.org/goals. (2018). The 2030 Agenda for Sustainable Development. https://sdgs.un.org/goals.

University of California, Berkeley. (2016). Mindfulness, What is Mindfulness? In *Greater Good: The Science of Meaningful Living*. http://greatergood.berkeley.edu/topic/mindfulness/definition.

Walach, H. (2014). Meditation—Neuroscientific Approaches and Philosophical Implication. New York: Springer.

Walsh, R. (2016). Life Style and Mental Health. In *American Psychologist* (Vol. 66, 7, pp. 579–592, 2011). California: University of California, Irvine College of Medicine. https://www.apa.org/pubs/journals/releases/amp-66-7-579.pdf.

WHO. (2014). *Mental Health: A State of Well-Being*. http://www.who.int/features/factfiles/mental_health/en/.

Chapter 2
Conceptual Framework for Worship (Ibadah)

A comprehensive literature review is carried out in Chaps. 2 and 3, where Chap. 2 provides a conceptual framework for worship (*'ibādah*), including an exposition into the soul (2.1), the diseases of the soul and its treatment (2.2), contemplative practices (2.3), and well-being and the worshipper (2.4). Chapter 3 covers the conceptual framework for morality and includes the right way to God (3.1) and the spiritual path of the Prophet (3.2).

2.1 Conceptual Framework for Worship: An Islamic Perspective with Reference to Self in Western Psychology[1]

2.1.1 The Soul (Heart) and Its Attributes

The subject of the soul is a perennial one and this research attempts to decipher and understand the soul, the spiritual self, and its differentiation from the corporal self. This largely uses the body of knowledge as articulated by Abu Ḥāmid Muḥammad ibn Muḥammad al-Ṭūsi al-Ghazāli (1058–1111) in his seminal work-the Revival of Religious Sciences (*Iḥyā Ulūm al-Dīn*) (1995), Shahāb al-Din 'Umar ibn Muḥammad Suhrawardi (1144–1234) in his—the Knowledge of the Spiritually Learned (*'Awārif al-Ma'ārif*) (1991), Taqi al-Dīn Aḥmad ibn Taymiyyah (1263–1328) in his *Diseases of the Heart and their Cures* (*Amrāḍ al Qulub wa Shifa uha*) (2010), and Ibn Qayyim al-Jawziyya (1292–1350) in *Spiritual Disease and*

---

[1] An earlier version of this particular article under the same title was published in an academic journal Afkar No: 16 (January 2015), pages 93–118, Academy of Islamic Studies, University of Malaya.

its Cure (Al-Dāi wa al-Dawa) (2006). One eminent and early scholarly work on this subject is by Imam Harith ibn 'Asad al-Muḥāsibi (781–857), who was one of the forerunners in Islamic *tasawwuf* (inward science) and a notable theologian said to have influenced Imam Ghazāli (Smith 1980; Sa'ari 2007). Related references, including those from Western psychology on the self, with special reference made to Abraham Maslow (2011) and Carl Rogers (1991), are interwoven within the text.

2.1.2 Key Concepts

Some of the key terms that are defined here are *nafs*, *rūḥ*, *qalb* and *'aql*. Imam Ghazāli defines the soul, also termed the heart or qalb, as "that perfect, simple jewel-like substance whose only business is recollection, memorisation, contemplation, discrimination and careful consideration, and it accepts all branches of knowledge and does not grow weary of receiving abstract images free of matter. This jewel-like substance or the rational soul (nafs al-nāṭiqah) is the leader of the spirits and the commander of the faculties and all serve it and comply with its command" (Al-Ghazali 1995).

Imam Ghazāli refers to the soul, or an immaterial thing cited, as *'laṭifah'*, with its attributes. There are scholars who hold the view that there is only one *'lata'if* and that is the heart (*qalb*), while others say that there are five *'laṭa'if* (Khan 1976), which have been mapped out, with the *qalb* (heart) being the key, followed by the *rūḥ*(spirit), *sirri* (innermost conscience), *khāfi* (hidden depth), and *ahkfā* (most hidden depth). These then become the different facets of the soul. They become points of focus for the remembrance (*dhikr*) of certain Islamic Sufi orders, referred to as subtle spiritual organs, which is not necessarily a practice amongst the general body of Muslims. Some even call such practices innovation (*bid'a*) since it was not exactly practiced during the time of the Prophet. As far as one can discern even though the Prophet himself meditated for thirteen years on top of a mountain in a cave on top of mount Hira, Makkah, there seems to be no documentation on the type of meditation that he performed except to say that it may have been a process of emptying one'is mind.

I argue that whatever it takes to deepen consciousness of God without the use of external means is worthy even though the exact methodological evidence is not contained with the Prophetic narration (*ḥadīth*) there are numerous references to *dhikr* (remembrance) in the divine scripture as cited in the discussion that follows.

Imam al-Muḥāsibi (Smith 1980), in discussing the heart, bases his evidence on the Qur'ān:

$$\text{لَّا مَنْ أَتَى اللَّهَ بِقَلْبٍ سَلِيمٍ}$$

...(and when) only he (will be happy) who comes before God with a heart free of evil. (Qur'ān, al Shura, 26:89)

2.1 Conceptual Framework for Worship: An Islamic Perspective with...

$$\text{إِلَّكَذَلِكَ نَسْلُكُهُ فِي قُلُوبِ الْمُجْرِمِينَ}$$

Even so do we (now) cause this (scorn of Our message) to pervade the hearts of those who are lost in sin. (Qur'ān, al Hijr, 15:12)

He sees the *qalb* as the essence of the self, which is immaterial, controlling the conscious nature of man, as well as an instrument that enables reality to be perceived and interpreted. There is a repeated emphasis in the divine scriptures on the heart, which is a facet of the soul, and the seeking of its development:

$$\text{اِأَفَلَمْ يَسِيرُوا فِي الْأَرْضِ فَتَكُونَ لَهُمْ قُلُوبٌ يَعْقِلُونَ بِهَا أَوْ آذَانٌ يَسْمَعُونَ بِهَا فَإِنَّهَا لَا تَعْمَى الْأَبْصَارُ وَلَكِن تَعْمَى الْقُلُوبُ الَّتِي فِي الصُّدُورِ}$$

Have they then never journeyed about the earth, letting their hearts gain wisdom, and causing their ears to hear? Yet, verily, it is not their eyes that have become blind – but blind have become the hearts that are in their breasts! (Qur'ān, al-Ḥajj, 22:46)

$$\text{اِوَلَقَدْ ذَرَأْنَا لِجَهَنَّمَ كَثِيرًا مِّنَ الْجِنِّ وَالْإِنسِ لَهُمْ قُلُوبٌ لَا يَفْقَهُونَ بِهَا وَلَهُمْ أَعْيُنٌ لَا يُبْصِرُونَ بِهَا وَلَهُمْ آذَانٌ لَا يَسْمَعُونَ بِهَا أُولَئِكَ كَالْأَنْعَامِ بَلْ هُمْ أَضَلُّ أُولَئِكَ هُمُ الْغَافِلُونَ}$$

...and men who have hearts with which they fail to grasp the truth, and eyes with which they fail to see and ears with which they fail to hear. (Qur'ān, al-A'rāf, 7:179).

Skellie (2007), in commenting on the various works of Imam Ghazāli, states that is it not clear whether he held the view that the soul was material or immaterial in its nature. He says that some hints that allude to its material nature are found in the Alchemy of Happiness (*Kimiya al-Sa'ādah*); *nafs* is seen as the vehicle (markab) of the heart; similarly, in *al-Risalah al-Laduniyya*, the nafs is termed the animal spirit (*al-rūḥ al-ḥaywāni*). Skellie points out that the clearest hint to its material nature is in *Mizan al-Amal*, when Imam Ghazāli refers to the two meanings of the soul as the animal soul (*rūḥ al-ḥaywāni*) and the human soul (*nafs al-insāniyyah*). I argue that this above-mentioned reference of Imam Ghazāli applies solely to the immaterial nature of the soul, where analogies and imageries such as 'the vehicle of the heart' are used to capture one's imagination rather than alluding to its material nature.

In discussing the '*rūḥ*' there are two meanings that are alluded to. The first meaning applies to a material thing within the heart, called the 'life force, which gives the impetus to hear and which vibrates the whole body, akin to an electric current. The second meaning is an immaterial and subtle thing, also referred to as the soul, which distinguishes life from the lifeless. It is something about which not much is known. When the Prophet was asked about the soul, he referred to the Qur'ān, where God says: 'And They will ask about (the nature of) divine inspiration (*rūḥ*). Say: "This inspiration (comes) at my Sustainer's behest; and (you cannot understand its nature, O men since) you have been granted very little of (real) knowledge" ' (Qur'ān, Al-Isra, 17:85).

Like *rūḥ*, *nafs* has two meanings; firstly, it refers to passion or the base, lower self, which embodies greed, anger and other evil attributes. A prophetic saying captures this: "Truly in the body there is a morsel of flesh which, if it be whole, all the body is whole, and which, if it be diseased, all of it is diseased. Truly it is the heart" (An-Nawawi 1977). Secondly, it refers to the situation when the passion has been removed and it assumes different forms as it goes through stages of purification and refinement. This is where the self becomes aligned with the soul or the heart. This discussed in detail in Sect. 2.1.4 below.

To bring some clarity to the over-lapping terms of *nafs* and *rūḥ*, a differentiation is cited that states the distinction lies in their respective attributes; when a soul is infused into a child, it is the *rūḥ*. As life proceeds, as both good and bad traits are acquired, and life becomes associated with the physical body, it is termed the *nafs* (Khan 1976). Imam Suhrawardi (1991) states that *nafs* has two meanings: (i) *nafs-i-shay* (the *nafs* of a thing), which effectively forms the *dhāt* (essence) and the *ḥaqīqah*(truth) of a thing; and (ii) *nafs-al-nāṭiqah-al-insāni* (the human rational *nafs*), which is also called the human natural soul.

'Aql likewise has two meanings (Al-Ghazali 1995). Firstly, it refers to the intellect or the medium through which the 'true nature of the material things are known and its seat is in the soul'. Secondly, it alludes to the 'power to understand the secrets of different learnings', a subtle essence manifested as knowledge, which is contained within the intellect. These two aspects, one with a material base and the other immaterial, are interdependent. This is reinforced by the *hadiths* that state that the first thing that God created was the intellect (Al-Ghazali 1995). A particular point of view is that revelation (*waḥy*) comes from the universal intellect, while inspiration comes from the universal soul by a process of emanation. Islam affords a prime place to the intellect, which also includes reason, the ability to discern between right and wrong, good and evil, the real and the illusory, all of which enable man to get nearer to God (Schuon 2006). The Qur'ān aptly articulates this in 39:9 and 19:20, the latter being a metaphor for those who are ignorant or whose hearts are blind:

أَمَّنْ هُوَ قَانِتٌ آنَاءَ اللَّيْلِ سَاجِدًا وَقَائِمًا يَحْذَرُ الْآخِرَةَ وَيَرْجُو رَحْمَةَ رَبِّهِ قُلْ هَلْ يَسْتَوِي الَّذِينَ يَعْلَمُونَ وَالَّذِينَ لَا يَعْلَمُونَ إِنَّمَا يَتَذَكَّرُ أُولُو الْأَلْبَابِ

Say; are those who know and those who do not know equal? (Qur'ān, Zumar, 39:9)

2.1 Conceptual Framework for Worship: An Islamic Perspective with...

وَمَا يَسْتَوِي الْأَعْمَىٰ وَالْبَصِيرُ
وَلَا الظُّلُمَاتُ وَلَا النُّورُ

The blind and the seeing are not alike, nor are the depth of darkness and the light. (Qur'ān, Fāṭir 35:19–20)

This is followed by his citing of Ibn Juryj, who said, 'The *rūḥ* and *nafs* are in the body of a person, being separated by something resembling a ray of light' (Picken 2011). Here Imam Muḥāsibi points out the differentiation between the *rūḥ* and the *nafs* and at the same time their intrinsic link with each other (Smith 1980). Ibn Qayyim alluding to the *nafs* and the *rūḥ* brings about some clarity into the discussion when he states, 'The difference is in the way of the attributes and not in terms of entity' (in *Kitāb-ar-Rūḥ* by Ibn Qayyim, cited in Khan 1976). Thus they are both of the same body yet their distinction can be found by way of their characteristics.

Al-Attās sums up the meaning of the four key terms related to the human soul as 'an indivisible, identical entity, a spiritual substance, which is the reality or very essence of man' (Al-Attas 2001). He adds that this alludes to *kamāl*, or perfection of being, which is a unifying principle. As Imam Ghazāli states (Sa'ari 2007), it has the power to transform something potential to something actual and forms a spiritual entity, called *al-rūḥāniyyah*, which is created but is in effect immortal, confined neither by space or time. *Al-rūḥāniyyah* can be known through the intellect and by means of observing what originates in it (Al-Attas 2001). Given that it has varied states, it is called by different names: for example, when it is involved in intellectuality and learning it is termed 'intellect'; when it governs the body, it is called the soul. In a similar vein, when it receives intuitive illumination, it is called the 'heart' and when receiving its own world of abstract entities, it is described as the 'spirit' (Al-Attas 2001). In this sense, it is manifesting itself in all these different states.

2.1.3 The Structure of the Soul (Nafs) and the Stages of Its Development

Within Islam, the understanding of the self is linked with its spiritual dimensions. The concept of *nafs* in the Qur'ān is translated as self or soul, and as described in its verses, the *nafs* traverses three distinct stages in its life:

(i) Before birth all souls are with God and they all bear witness that Allāh is their Lord (Qur'ān, Surah al-A'rāf, 7:172)
(ii) Life on earth, where our purpose is to worship Allah (Qur'ān, Surah al-Dhāriyat, 51:56)
(iii) The Hereafter, where we will be held accountable for all our actions and be either rewarded or punished. (Qur'ān, Surah al-Qāri'ah 101:5–8)

The structure of human individuality within the domain of Islamic psychology can be comprehended through the three primary elements: *nafs* or ego-self; *qalb* or heart; and *rūḥ* or spirit (Helminski 1999). The *nafs* or self consists of the ego-self, the natural-self, and the carnal-self, and it is seen as a complex manifestation linked to the body and inter-twined with its pleasure and survival. It has no limit to its desires, be they concerning its body or personality, and it needs the spiritual self (*rūḥ*) to guide and liberate it. The connection between the spiritual self (*rūḥ*) and the natural self (*nafs*) is that the former needs the latter, in order to 'aspire towards completion, or perfection' (Helminski 1999). The heart or *qalb* is captured as the core of our being, the soul, where our deepest and most comprehensive knowing takes place, including its psychic function. A schema of the development of the *nafs* or self, as derived from Imam Ghazāli's *Iḥyā* and Imam Suhrawardi's *Awārif al-Maārif* with backing from the Qu'rān, is outlined in Fig. 2.1.

It is to be noted that the knowledge of the soul or psyche is sometimes referred to as 'Islamic psychology' even though this field goes beyond this into the metaphysical realm. Thus, in-effect, one may not find the answers that one is seeking since the approach, tools and methods for this purpose may be different from the material sciences. Moving from the above state of *nafs al-ammārah bi-su* (animal self) to that of the self that is reproachful (*nafs al-lawwāmah*), Imam Muḥāsibi (Smith 1980) draws an analogy of a beast of burden, which is wild and must be tamed with constant discipline so that it becomes useful to the master, by which he moves towards the Lord.

This movement is a process, where at the early stages the struggle is still going on, with the higher soul gradually beginning to gain the upper hand. This struggle and tribulation continues, until with time, effort, and the mercy of the Lord, Satan (*Iblīs*) and his hosts have been routed and the lusts of the flesh no longer make any appeal; the soul has become a captive, in complete submission to the Will of its Lord (Smith 1980). The self is now at rest and is called *nafs al-mutma'inna* (see Fig. 2.1), the self at peace with itself and in unison with the soul and all its facets. A more stratified and ascending gradation of the evolution of the self is presented in Fig. 2.2 (Chisthi 2007).

2.1.4 Illustrations of the Characteristics of the Soul

In order to understand the complexity of the soul, Imam Ghazāli sketches its attributes by drawing an analogy of a secret army. This is best illustrated in Fig. 2.3, where the soul at the centre is seen as the king, with the embedded intellect acting as conscience and one's actions acting as ministers which govern. From this, we see that greed and anger both have a role in so far as they maintain their functions well within the limits of feeding the body and fending off threats. Beyond this, both of these traits take over the mind-body function and become detrimental. Thus this needs to be viewed within a context of a spectrum rather than being bipolar.

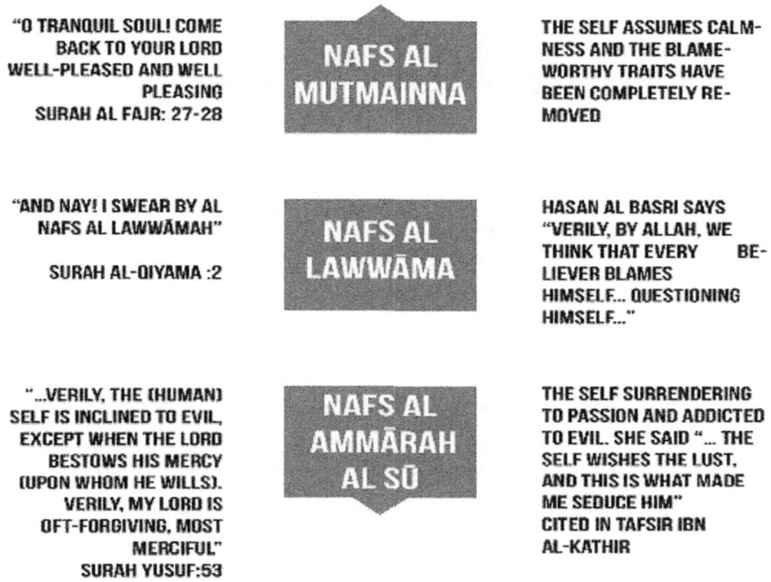

2.1 Conceptual Framework for Worship: An Islamic Perspective with... 23

Qur'anic Verse	Stage	Description
"O TRANQUIL SOUL! COME BACK TO YOUR LORD WELL-PLEASED AND WELL PLEASING SURAH AL FAJR: 27-28	**NAFS AL MUTMAINNA**	THE SELF ASSUMES CALMNESS AND THE BLAMEWORTHY TRAITS HAVE BEEN COMPLETELY REMOVED
"AND NAY! I SWEAR BY AL NAFS AL LAWWĀMAH" SURAH AL-QIYAMA :2	**NAFS AL LAWWĀMA**	HASAN AL BASRI SAYS "VERILY, BY ALLAH, WE THINK THAT EVERY BELIEVER BLAMES HIMSELF... QUESTIONING HIMSELF..."
"...VERILY, THE (HUMAN) SELF IS INCLINED TO EVIL, EXCEPT WHEN THE LORD BESTOWS HIS MERCY (UPON WHOM HE WILLS). VERILY, MY LORD IS OFT-FORGIVING, MOST MERCIFUL" SURAH YUSUF:53	**NAFS AL AMMĀRAH AL SŪ**	THE SELF SURRENDERING TO PASSION AND ADDICTED TO EVIL. SHE SAID "... THE SELF WISHES THE LUST, AND THIS IS WHAT MADE ME SEDUCE HIM" CITED IN TAFSIR IBN AL-KATHIR

Fig. 2.1 Stages of development of the *Nafs* (self) based on Qur'ānic verses

The weakness of the soul and its progressive ascension in the first three main stages, what Margret Smith (1980) calls Muḥāsibi's psychological theory, are:

(i) '*Nafs al-ammārah bi-su*': The lower soul (*nafs*) represents the seat of appetites and of passion, the 'flesh' with its sinful lusts. This leads one to sinful states while striving for one's own self-interest. As the Qur'ān says, 'Verily, man's inner self does incite (him) to evil, and saved are only they upon whom my Sustainer bestows His grace!'(Qur'ān, Yusuf 12:53). Imam Muḥāsibi (Smith 1980) warns us of the nature of the *nafs*, if you give in to it, it will lead you in a downward spiral to the death of your spiritual self, while leaving it alone will take you to its own dictates and you come under its control. He says, 'Place it where God Almighty placed it and describe it as He described it and withstand it according to His command, for it is a greater enemy to you than Satan (*Iblīs*) himself, and *Iblīs* gains power over you only by means of it and your consent to it.'

(ii) '*Nafs-al-Lawāmma*': Imam Muḥāsibi (Smith 1980) says that the lower soul is akin to the beast of burden, which needs to be tamed, and therefore needs a variety of disciplines, so that it can serve the immediate master, which will then enable the person to serve the Ultimate Master. At this stage, the soul struggles with its desires and there is critical self-inquiry; with discipline over time, the soul starts to take the upper hand and becomes a reproachful soul (*nafs-al-lawāmma*). In this light, the Lord says, 'But nay I call to witness the accusing voice of man's conscience!' (Qur'ān, al-Qiyamah, 75:2). Asad,

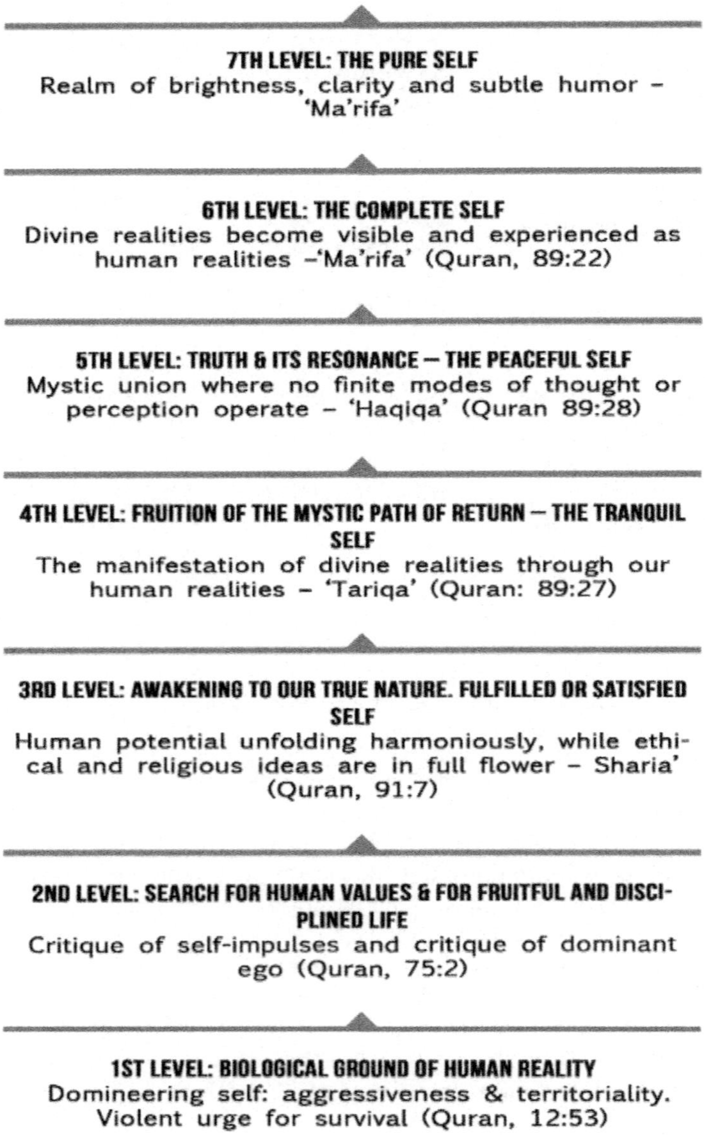

7TH LEVEL: THE PURE SELF
Realm of brightness, clarity and subtle humor – 'Ma'rifa'

6TH LEVEL: THE COMPLETE SELF
Divine realities become visible and experienced as human realities –'Ma'rifa' (Quran, 89:22)

5TH LEVEL: TRUTH & ITS RESONANCE – THE PEACEFUL SELF
Mystic union where no finite modes of thought or perception operate – 'Haqiqa' (Quran 89:28)

4TH LEVEL: FRUITION OF THE MYSTIC PATH OF RETURN – THE TRANQUIL SELF
The manifestation of divine realities through our human realities – 'Tariqa' (Quran: 89:27)

3RD LEVEL: AWAKENING TO OUR TRUE NATURE. FULFILLED OR SATISFIED SELF
Human potential unfolding harmoniously, while ethical and religious ideas are in full flower – Sharia' (Quran, 91:7)

2ND LEVEL: SEARCH FOR HUMAN VALUES & FOR FRUITFUL AND DISCIPLINED LIFE
Critique of self-impulses and critique of dominant ego (Quran, 75:2)

1ST LEVEL: BIOLOGICAL GROUND OF HUMAN REALITY
Domineering self: aggressiveness & territoriality. Violent urge for survival (Quran, 12:53)

Fig. 2.2 The stages of meditative progression & consciousness (Chisthi 2007)

2.1 Conceptual Framework for Worship: An Islamic Perspective with...

Fig. 2.3 Illustration of some functionalities of the soul based on articulation by Imam Ghazāli

in his commentary on this verse, (al-Qiyamah, 75:2, 109) adds that man's reproaching soul is the subconscious awareness of his own shortcomings and failings.

(iii) '*Nafs-al-Mutma'inna*': Once the soul becomes reproachful, the higher nature has taken over and it is in a better position to wage war successfully against the lower soul. This is where human nature is seen at its best, 'the soul at rest' (*nafs al-mutma'inna*). At this juncture, the 'lust of the flesh' is no longer an issue and 'the soul has become a captive, in complete submission to the Will of its Lord', while becoming the 'soul at rest'. In this context, the Lord says, '(But unto the righteous God will say,) O thou human being that has attained to inner peace! Return thou unto thy Sustainer, well-pleased (and) pleasing (Him): enter, then, together with My (other true) servants—yea, enter thou My paradise!' (Qur'ān, al-Fajr, 89:27–30)

The Lord says:

$$\text{فَأَمَّا مَن طَغَى}$$

$$\text{وَآثَرَ الْحَيَاةَ الدُّنْيَا}$$

$$\text{فَإِنَّ الْجَحِيمَ هِيَ الْمَأْوَى}$$

'For, unto him who shall have transgressed the bounds of what is right (to the good of his soul), that blazing fire will truly be the goal.' (Qur'ān, al Nāzi'āt, 79:37–39)

Imam Ghazzali (1995) draws an analogy of the soul as an army with an external and an internal eye; the hands, feet, eyes, ears and tongue are the former, and greed for food and drinks is the latter. He then organises these into four divisions: the first, the division of greed, which benefits the soul by providing the desire for food and drinks which is necessary for the functioning of the body. The second, the open division, uses anger to move the bodily organs to produce the object of greed, namely power and strength. The third division, the senses, with their powers of sight, hearing, smell, taste and touch, are manifested through the five organs to help the human being function properly. The fourth division lies secretly in the brain, generating the power of ideas, thoughts, memories, retention and consolidation. The analogy that is drawn here defines the importance of both the internal organs and the senses to maintain the equilibrium of the mind-body.

2.1.5 The Soul as a Special Vehicle

The high stature of the soul is best portrayed in the divine communication, which said:

$$\text{إِنَّا عَرَضْنَا الْأَمَانَةَ عَلَى السَّمَاوَاتِ وَالْأَرْضِ وَالْجِبَالِ فَأَبَيْنَ أَن يَحْمِلْنَهَا وَأَشْفَقْنَ مِنْهَا وَحَمَلَهَا الْإِنسَانُ إِنَّهُ كَانَ ظَلُومًا جَهُولًا}$$

'Verily, We did offer the trust (of reasons and volition) to the heavens, and the earth, and the mountains; but they refused to bear it because they were afraid of it. Ye man took it up...' (Qur'ān, Al-Ahzāb, 33:72)

The souls were in pre-existence, when God said to them:

$$\text{وَإِذْ أَخَذَ رَبُّكَ مِن بَنِي آدَمَ مِن ظُهُورِهِمْ ذُرِّيَّتَهُمْ وَأَشْهَدَهُمْ عَلَى أَنفُسِهِمْ أَلَسْتُ بِرَبِّكُمْ قَالُوا بَلَى شَهِدْنَا أَن تَقُولُوا يَوْمَ الْقِيَامَةِ إِنَّا كُنَّا عَنْ هَذَا غَافِلِينَ}$$

'Am I not your Sustainer?' and they answered, 'Yes indeed!' (Qur'ān, al A'rāf, 7:172)

Imam Ghazāli says that by virtue of the trust placed in humans, all else has been made subservient to them. This trust he says is *ma'rifa*, or divine knowledge, and *tawhīd* (Oneness). The objective of purifying the soul is to rekindle the light of divine knowledge, as God tells us:

$$\text{أَفَمَن شَرَحَ اللَّهُ صَدْرَهُ لِلْإِسْلَامِ فَهُوَ عَلَى نُورٍ مِّن رَّبِّهِ فَوَيْلٌ لِّلْقَاسِيَةِ قُلُوبُهُم مِّن ذِكْرِ اللَّهِ أُولَٰئِكَ فِي ضَلَالٍ مُّبِينٍ}$$

'Could then, one whose bosom God has opened wide with willingness towards self-surrender unto Him, so that he is illuminated by a light (that flows) from his Sustainer...' (Qur'ān, al Zumar, 39:22)

Imam Haddād (Al-Haddad 1990) best captures the spiritual journey of the soul when he describes its pre-existence, it then being infused into an infant, where it grows through the life stages until it passes away from this world and goes into the next, with the soul in the *barzakh* (Isthmus or intermediate stage), until the day of reckoning. When the screen of sins and obstructions are lifted from the soul, it sees the pictures of the unseen things, where the world of signs and the unseen world unite into *rububiyyah* or the presence of God's being, which encompasses everything. There is no existence of anything except of God, His action, His sovereignty (Al-Ghazali 1995).

2.1.6 Disciplining of the Soul and Actions to Get Near to God

In terms of disciplining the soul or inner self, the Lord then speaks about a reward for those in control thus:

$$\text{وَأَمَّا مَنْ خَافَ مَقَامَ رَبِّهِ وَنَهَى النَّفْسَ عَنِ الْهَوَىٰ}$$
$$\text{فَإِنَّ الْجَنَّةَ هِيَ الْمَأْوَىٰ}$$

'But unto him who shall have stood in fear of his Sustainer's Presence, and held back his inner self from base desires, paradise will truly be the goal!' (Qur'ān, al-Nāziāt, 79: 40–41)

The bodily organs, such as hands, the feet and the internal organs all have their respective functions which keep the body in a state of equilibrium. The soul, with its embedded intellect, acts as ministers controlling and overseeing all related functions, both external and internal, that impacts on the mind-body complex (see Fig. 2.2).

It is the servant's duty to purify the soul and make efforts with true and sincere intentions. As Imam Muḥāsibi says, one of the key gateways in the path of man to God, which propels him to divine knowledge, is the 'gate of the intention and its purification, which leads to the will to do good in secret and openly, in things great and small' (Smith 1980). The Jibrīl *hadīth*—related on the authority of Umar ibn al-Khattab and recorded both in Sahih Bukhari and Muslim (An-Nawawi 1977), lays down a comprehensive framework in Islam, whereby, the Angel Jibrīl both asks the questions and confirms the response from the Prophet Muhammad on the fundamental concepts of Islam, *iman* and *iḥsān*. Regarding *iḥsān*, the Prophet said, 'It is to worship Allah as though you are seeing Him, and while you see Him not to know truly He sees you'. *Iḥsān* has been interpreted in several ways, including sincerity of purpose, right action, goodness, charity, and also as excellence in whatever one does, especially in worship. This is further reinforced by the Prophetic saying, 'Actions are but by intentions and every man shall have but that which he intended'[2] (An-Nawawi 1977). This in effect forms the doorway to the purification of the soul, through directing due attention to God.

The trigger to action is intention thus Islam emphasises that every action should be preceded by a proper intention and sincerity in purpose. As Imam Muḥāsibi says with regards to experiential learning and self-realisation of God that, 'Many a man lives his life and dies when his hour comes, without having realised the importance of this' (Smith 1980). The most pertinent Prophetic *hadīth* is that, 'Indeed there is in the body a piece of flesh which if it is sound then the whole body is sound, and if it is corrupt then the whole body is corrupt. Indeed it is the heart', referring to the soul, which is also called the spiritual heart.[3] This is teamed up with the Qur'ānic injunction where God says:

$$\text{إِنَّ اللَّهَ لَا يُغَيِّرُ مَا بِقَوْمٍ حَتَّىٰ يُغَيِّرُوا مَا بِأَنْفُسِهِمْ وَإِذَا أَرَادَ اللَّهُ بِقَوْمٍ سُوءًا فَلَا مَرَدَّ لَهُ وَمَا لَهُم مِّن دُونِهِ مِن وَالٍ}$$

'Verily, God does not change men's condition unless they change their inner selves' (Qur'ān, al-Ra'ad, 13:11)

This calls for ways and means to educate oneself and purify one's heart. Asad (2011) refers to this verse as 'an illustration of the divine law of cause and effect (*sunnat Allah*) which dominates the lives of both individuals and communities.'

Within this framework and in terms of disciplining one's self, there are numerous writings, notably those of Imam 'Abdullah Anṣāri (2011), Imam Ghazāli (1995), Sheikh Ibn 'Arabi. (2008), Imam ibn Qayyim al-Jawziyya (in ed. Zakariya 2006), Sheikh 'Abd al-Qāder al-Jīlāni (1977), Ibn Hazm al-Andalusi (1998), and Imam Sidi ibn Zarrūk (2001), whose writings can be broadly articulated as follows:

(i) Guiding Principles: Concept and principles that guide and orient one towards God;
(ii) Morality (*akhlāq*): A code of conduct or behaviour that maximises benefits and leads to good, including virtuous characteristics, while excluding blameworthy ones;
(iii) A Guide-Teacher: Getting guidance from one who has traversed the path on how to develop oneself to a higher state and check one's ego is vitally beneficial to purifying the soul; Methods-Tools: Ways and means of dealing with one's *nafs* or self at different stages of its development;
(iv) Repentance (*tauba*)—Supplication (*dua*): Repentance and supplications that evoke one to turn towards the Lord and the proper ways of doing this.

---

[2] This *hadīth* was related on the authority of Umar ibn al-Khattab and recorded both in Sahih Bukhari and Muslim.

[3] This *hadīth* is reported in Bukhari n.d. and Muslim n.d.

2.1 Conceptual Framework for Worship: An Islamic Perspective with...

(v) Remembrance of God (*dhikr*): Practices and rituals, including prayers, recitation of the divine scriptures, and remembrance, which deepen understanding of oneself and others.

The soul is like a fortress; frequent attacks are made on it by the devil and therefore it is necessary to safeguard it through its doors, which are made up of the character and conduct of the human being in which it lives. In this context, there are twelve doors of which one must be aware and take care of, Imam Ghazāli (1995) tells us:

(i) Anger and sexual passion, when the intellect becomes weak;
(ii) Hatred and greed: the Prophet said, 'Your love for anything makes you deaf and blind' (Abu Dawud, al-Adab, 14/38; Ahmad, al-Musnad, 5/194);
(iii) Eating to satisfaction: eating to your heart's content or excessive consumption intoxicates the mind and prevents you from prayers, increases your passion, decreases compassion and increases the chance of disease;
(iv) Love for fine things: the love for material things leads to greed, selfishness and attachment to the world;
(v) Dependency on people: undue dependency on people leads to losing trust in God and losing sincerity when one works to solely gain the praise and favor of people;
(vi) Hastiness and absence of steadiness: haste in action leads to faults, blunders and regret which is why the Prophet told us, 'Hastiness comes from the devil and delay comes from God', God says:

خُلِقَ الْإِنْسَانُ مِنْ عَجَلٍ سَأُرِيكُمْ آيَاتِي فَلَا تَسْتَعْجِلُونِ

'Man is a creature of haste.' (Qur'ān, al-Anbiyā, 21:37)

(vii) To possess wealth beyond necessity: fuels insatiable desires and greed. This becomes the focus of one's existence causing one to lose focus on life's true purpose;
(viii) Miserliness and fear of poverty: this leads to another door, whereby people are prevented from being charitable, which encourages hoarding and generates greed for wealth;
(ix) Staying in bazaars: this is where people while away their time, consuming themselves with things that are worldly and becoming heedless of God;
(x) Love for sects and hatred for opponents: there is a tendency to hold on to one's sect and develop a hatred for others outside of this. This leads to discord and fracture in society as well as damaging one's own heart;
(xi) When ordinary men are the leaders of religion: when those who do not have the necessary learning, wisdom and education take the position of religious leadership they pose a potentially great danger to society and are capable of misguiding people;

(xii) **Bad opinion about Muslims**: This is seen as an issue which has ramifications, whereby people spin their opinions about others causing malice. The Lord says:

$$\text{يَا أَيُّهَا الَّذِينَ آمَنُوا اجْتَنِبُوا كَثِيرًا مِّنَ الظَّنِّ إِنَّ بَعْضَ الظَّنِّ إِثْمٌ ۖ وَلَا تَجَسَّسُوا وَلَا يَغْتَب بَّعْضُكُم بَعْضًا ۚ أَيُحِبُّ أَحَدُكُمْ أَن يَأْكُلَ لَحْمَ أَخِيهِ مَيْتًا فَكَرِهْتُمُوهُ ۚ وَاتَّقُوا اللَّهَ ۚ إِنَّ اللَّهَ تَوَّابٌ رَّحِيمٌ}$$

'O you have attained faith! Avoid most guesswork (about one another) – for behold, some of (such) guesswork is (in itself) a sin...' (Qur'ān, al-Hujarāt, 49:12)

The eminent physician and scholar, Abu Zayed Ahmed Ibn Sahl Al-Balkhi (1006–1056), practiced psycho-social healing because he understood that one's emotional and spiritual state affects one's physiological and physical health (Abdullah 2011). Thus, he combined a code of conduct ('*adab*') with philosophy (*falāsifah*), to impart ethical training for managing oneself and thereby developing one's soul. There are an increasing number of neuro-science studies that have identified and discussed the positive impact of these spiritual practices on wellbeing or on the mind-body, which is something to think about seriously in the current context of work-life balance and mental health (Abdullah 2011). This is elaborated in Chap. 6 with regards to Islamic Psychotherapy.

2.1.7 The Human Mind and Thoughts

The Prophet (cited in Ghazāli 1995) encapsulates the mind and its nature in three examples that he cites. Firstly, the mind is like a sparrow, which changes every moment. Secondly, the mind is like water in a pot, which changes state when it is heated. Thirdly, it is like a feather in an open field, which is turned over again and again. In the light of virtues, vices and doubtful things, the heart-soul and mind (intellect) takes three forms, as outlined here by both Imam Ghazāli (1995) and Sheikh Ibn Taymiyyah (2010):

A **Sound Heart**: God-fearing, nurtured by divine service and free from bad conduct. This type of mind is where good thoughts and knowledge are reflected and the Lord bestows his blessings on it, saying:

$$\text{لَيْسَ عَلَى الَّذِينَ آمَنُوا وَعَمِلُوا الصَّالِحَاتِ جُنَاحٌ فِيمَا طَعِمُوا إِذَا مَا اتَّقَوا وَآمَنُوا وَعَمِلُوا الصَّالِحَاتِ ثُمَّ اتَّقَوا وَآمَنُوا ثُمَّ اتَّقَوا وَأَحْسَنُوا ۚ وَاللَّهُ يُحِبُّ الْمُحْسِنِينَ}$$

'Those who have attained faith and do righteous deeds incur no sin by partaking of whatever they may ...and continue to be conscious of God and to believe, and grow ever more.' (Qur'ān, al-Mā'idah, 5:93)

The above type devoid of blameworthy traits, where the carnal self has been subjugated to the control of the soul. In this state, it is blessed with nine virtues: gratitude, patience, God-fearing, poverty, asceticism, love, commitment, reliance on God, good thoughts and other good qualities, and it becomes free from vices and evils. This type of self is termed *nafs al-mutma'inna*, where the Lord says, in 89:27–28:

$$\text{يَا أَيَّتُهَا النَّفْسُ الْمُطْمَئِنَّةُ}$$
$$\text{ارْجِعِي إِلَىٰ رَبِّكِ رَاضِيَةً مَّرْضِيَّةً}$$

'O thou human being that hast attained to inner peace! Return thou onto thy Sustainer, well-pleased (and) pleasing (Him) ...' (Qur'ān, Sura al-Fajr, 89:27–28)

A **Corrupt Heart**: This is a heart-soul and mind full of passions, low desires and other evils. This leads to the door to Satan to be opened and for the doors to the angels to be closed. The reference is to a state as stated by the Lord in 25:43:

$$\text{أَرَأَيْتَ مَنِ اتَّخَذَ إِلَٰهَهُ هَوَاهُ أَفَأَنتَ تَكُونُ عَلَيْهِ وَكِيلًا}$$

'Hast thou ever considered (the kind of man) who makes his own passion his deity?' (Qur'ān, al-Furqān, 25:43)

This refers to *nafs al-ammārah bi-su* (beastly self), where the self predominates the soul with its darkness. This is a strong statement admonishing humans for their greed, which itself is triggered by desires that make them forget God. It refers to erecting inner statues within one's mind built on emerging desires. A subtler type of shirk, or associating partners with God.

A **Mixed Heart**: A mind that is a mixture of good and evil, which vacillates depending on the side towards which it is tilted. It swings between good (or good guidance) and evil deeds (or misguidance). The two forces fight until one of them is triumphant. This can be referred to as *nafs al-lawwāma* or the self-critical self, where there is intense competition between the self and the soul.

2.1.8 Islamic and Western Psychological Perspectives

There is often confusion in terms of understanding what the soul, the spirit, the heart, and the intellect are, given that they are often used inter-changeably. Essentially the term *nafs* is the concept of self in Islam, which is synonymous with what is called the self in the Western context. Research in Western psychology, interestingly, resonates with the stages of development of the *nafs*, where 'possible selves' (Markus and Nurius 1986) are defined as 'ideal selves that we very much like to become, and the selves we are afraid to become' and they can be manifested as evil self, alcoholic self, depressed self, critical self, loving self etc.

Even though there are no spiritual gradations in Western psychology as there are in Islam, as described above, this stratification is important from two viewpoints. Firstly, this stratification provides the potential for individuals to change and develop themselves. Secondly, the strata can 'provide the essential link between the self-concept and motivation', to bring about change. Maslow's theory of self-actualisation of the human being is also indicative of the development of the self from a lower state to a more evolved state of being and maturity (Maslow 2011), what Carl Rogers calls those who have 'become' or attained 'full-humanness' (Rogers 1991). The concept of self-actualisation is discussed in relation to spiritual actualisation in some detail in Chap. 6.

The notion of self in Western psychology is different from that of Islam, as is evident in the discussion that follows. From a behaviourist viewpoint, 'the self-concept has an aura of mysticisms not far removed from the concept of the soul' (Epstein 1973). As can be deduced from the definitions cited in Table 2.1, with the exception of Carl Jung's definition below and his related theories, the concept of self and its development seems to be largely rooted within the worldly realm, in that it is fashioned by how one feels about oneself, as well as what others perceive about you as an individual. There seem to be no concepts or direction connecting one to a spiritual dimension or to the next life, which Islam embodies.

Al-Attās (2001) sums up the Islamic world view when he states that the focus on worldly ends does not pose an issue in Islam and does not necessarily exclude spiritual aspects; rather, both this world (*dunya*) and the next (*ākhirah*) are inter-linked and cannot be separated. In this sense, worldly works, service to people, and looking after one's family are seen as spiritual, part of the act of worship. According to Al-Attās, the *qalb* (heart) is seen as the mid-point of the psyche, halfway between the *nafs* (self) and *rūh* (spirit) and includes the subconscious and superconscious faculties of perception, memories and complexes. What is alluded to here by Al-Attās is the intellect (*'aql*), with its related faculties of consciousness, which are embedded within the heart or the soul. The *rūh* or spirit, referring to the spiritual self or essence, is outlined as an impulse or command of God. It can be a transmitter sending signals to the heart, having some key servants including reason, reflection and conscience. The development of individuality or the totality of a person results from the inter-relationship between the three above-mentioned dimensions, the heart (*qalb*), spirit (*rūh*), and the self (*nafs*) (Helminski 1999).

2.1 Conceptual Framework for Worship: An Islamic Perspective with...

Table 2.1 Multiple definitions of the self in western psychology (Epstein 1973)

Definition	Source
Self as designated in speech in the first person singular: I, me, my, mine and myself. It is through the subjective feeling that the self can be identified. Linked to the concept of a 'looking glass', where an individual perceives himself/herself in a way that others perceive him/her	Cooley (1992)
Expanded on Cooley's definition stating that there are as many selves as there are social roles, with some being significant while the others are specific to particular situations and of minimal significance	George Mead (1934)
Similar to Cooley and Mead, where the self arises out of social interaction, where he identified the self-system as: an organisation of educated experience called into being by the necessity to avoid or minimise incidents of anxiety. This dynamism is an explanatory conception and is not a thing or not such as superegos, egos, ids, and so on	Sullivan (1953)
Two fundamental approaches, firstly, self as a knower, secondly, self as an object of what is known. The first proposition was totally rejected, while the second was referred to as whatever the individual views as belonging to himself including the material self (own body, his family and possessions), the social self (views others hold of the individual), and spiritual self (emotions and desires). Self-viewed as having unity and differentiation and being intimately associated with emotions as mediated through self-esteem	William James (1950)
Self-concept seen as the nucleus of personality, where personality is defined as the organisation of values that are consistent with one another. It involved the constant assimilation of new ideas and rejection or modification of old ideas, where the concepts are organised into a unified system, which is preserved	Lecky (1945)
Self-concept defined as those parts of the phenomenal field, which the individual has differentiated as definite and fairly stable characteristics of himself	Snygg & Combs (1949)
View common with Lecky, Snygg and Combs. Self is defined as an organised, fluid, but consistent conceptual pattern of perceptions of characteristics and relationships of the 'I' or the 'me' together with values attached to these concepts. Self-concept includes those characteristics of the individual that he is aware of and over which he exercises control. A threat to it produces anxiety	Rogers (1951)
Behaviour is organised around cognitive structures, with the self being one such structurehierarchically organised and subject to change, generally from the lower to higher order constructs. There are different types of selves including somatic self, social self etc.; depending on the moment in time	Sarbin (1995)
Proprium: All regions of our life that we regard as peculiarly ours. Those aspects are considered as of central importance to the individual and they contribute to the inward sense of unity	Allport (1995)

(continued)

Table 2.1 (continued)

Definition	Source
Self-concept as a self-theory, where an individual as unwittingly constructed about himself as an experiencing, functioning individual, and it is part of a broader theory that he holds in relation to his entire range of significant experiences. The fundamental aspects of the self-theory are to optimise the pleasure-pain balance of the individual over the course of a life-time; to facilitate the maintenance of self-esteem, and to organise the data of experience in a manner which allows coping with it	Epstein (1971)
Self is defined as '... compromising of the totality of the person, both conscious and unconscious and is distinct from both the ego and the persona – conscious aspects of personality'	Carl Jung (in Glassman and Hadad 2004)

Imam Muḥāsibii (Smith 1980) describes ongoing internal dynamics, where the higher nature of man constantly struggles with the lower self (*nafs*), which urges it to pass through the gateway of the senses, "the seat of the appetites and of passion, the 'flesh' with its sinful lusts". In a similar vein, Ibn 'Arabi in his Divine Governance of the Human Kingdom (Helminski 1999), encapsulates the inner struggle when he states:

> The conflict between reason and the evil-commanding self is caused by their very nature, which induces each of them to try to dominate the whole of the human being and to be the ruler of it. Even when one of them is able to conquer the whole realm, the other still strives to regain what it has lost and to repair what has been destroyed. This swing between the two opposing states forms the consciousness of humans, whereby transcending the evil-commanding self forms the very essence of the spiritual journey.

The Prophet characterised the best man as the one whose soul is God-fearing, a concept called '*taqwa*' (piety), where there is no deceit, no deception, no treachery, no contrivance and no hatred. For God says, 'Consider the human self, and how it is formed in accordance with what is meant to be and how it is imbued with moral failings, as well as with consciousness of God' Qur'ān, ash-Shams, 91:7:

$$\text{قَدْ أَفْلَحَ مَن زَكَّاهَا}$$

$$\text{وَقَدْ خَابَ مَن دَسَّاهَا}$$

'To a happy state shall indeed attain he who causes this (self) to grow in purity, and truly lost is he who buries it (darkness).' Qur'ān, ash-Shams, 91:9–10

The soul is the medium which absorbs both light and darkness according to one's intentions and actions. In this regard Imam Ghazāli (1995) points out that the vision of the soul is through the subtle essence or *laṭīfah* by which spiritual things are seen, 'it is an immaterial thing or formless *laṭīfah* or basic subtle element which has got connections with the material heart ... it catches the knowledge of God and spiritual world. It is punished and rewarded.' This can take the form of dreams or it can be in a wakeful state. In referring to the blindness of the soul, God says:

$$\text{وَمَن كَانَ فِي هَذِهِ أَعْمَىٰ فَهُوَ فِي الْآخِرَةِ أَعْمَىٰ وَأَضَلُّ سَبِيلًا.}$$

... for whoever is blind (of heart) in this (world) will be blind in the life to come (as well). (Qur'ān, al-Isrā, 17:72)

The Lord refers to the sight of the soul when He says:

$$\text{مَا كَذَبَ الْفُؤَادُ مَا رَأَىٰ}$$

This is reinforced by what God said:

We gave Abraham (his first) insight into (God's) mighty dominion over the heavens and the earth (Qur'ān, al-An'ām, 6:75)

There are different streams of knowledge, namely that concerning the intellect and that concerning religion. For the salvation of the soul, the intellect, despite being necessary to discern things, is insufficient on its own and, in this regard, anyone applying blind faith (*taqlīd*) without the intellect is a fool, while anyone relying only on the intellect without divine guidance is a proud person (Al-Ghazali 1995). Thus, the two strands should be woven together. Imam Ghazāli likens the intellect to food and religious education to medicine, where both are necessary for a healthy body. In a similar vein, for a diseased soul, the medicine is the *Sharī'a* in terms of the duties as prescribed by the Prophet, which if followed acts as a necessary medicine for its sickness.

The transmission of knowledge of the soul takes three forms, namely, the prophecies of the Prophets (*wahy*); inspiration (*ilhām-kashf*); and the whisperings of the devil (*waswās*). An important distinction is presented, whereby thoughts are divided here into good and bad. The state of the soul is thus captured: 'the soul changes from one condition to another. This effect on the soul is called *khawātir* and out of it there grows will and then intention' (Al Ghazāli 1995). Knowledge in the above light can be seen as being bi-polar along a continuum, where, for example, things can be good-bad in varying degrees. As a general axiom, there are always two aspects to things in nature, the exception being God, who is One.

Having presented an exhaustive list through which one can be misled, Imam Al Ghazāli (1995) advises what can drive away the devil: 'when the devil which is like a hungry dog comes to your door, fill yourself with constant *dhikr* or remembrance of God; when the soul is heedless of remembrance, the machination of the devil comes in.' This means that whatever thoughts and actions one may have or do, it is necessary to stay focused on the Lord, so that the devil cannot seep into your soul. Focusing on the here and now, or a state of mindfulness, has now become a form of meditative practice that has an impact on the brain and well-being of individuals (Williams 2015).

The difference between Buddhism and Islam within the context of meditation, is that in Islam it is not mindfulness for mindfulness' sake but the focus on the Divine. It is recommended that one recites a verse from the Qur'ān titled *āyat al Kursi* or The Verse of the Throne (Qur'ān, al-Baqara, 2:255), which drives away the devil and the preoccupation of the mind with negative thoughts.

Imam Ghazāli points out: 'Clear your soul first from passion and greed and then take the medicine of *dhikr*. When *dhikr* enters such a heart which is free of thoughts other than God, the devil flees away from it, as disease goes away ...' The other aspect is supplication to God, where He says:

> And if My servant ask thee about Me behold, I am near; I respond to the call of him who calls ... (Qur'ān, al Baqara, 2:186).

2.1.9 Discussion

The subject of the soul and its attributes is a vast subject that cannot be comprehended within one study and therefore what is dealt with here is only an insight into it. It is, however, found that the inner science of the development of the self is deeply embedded within the Qur'ān, as well as in the sayings of the Prophet; it is a guide to mankind on how to develop oneself. The most striking feature of the soul, is its propensity to good and evil depending on which side you nurture, and thus lies man's potential to become a saint or a sinner. The soul is a complex entity and, as the Qur'ān has articulated, only a little knowledge has been vouchsafed to us.

From the little that we understand, it seems that the soul has multiple functions in the way it governs itself and it appears that the intellect (*'aql*), which is embedded within it, guides it in terms of decisions made, while the heart (*qalb*), which is intrinsically linked to the soul, has its active cognition and ability for empathy, and is seen as an intermediary between the soul and the spirit, all encompassed within one spiritual entity. The *rūḥ*, or the spirit, is seen as a radiant light that animates the body and is akin to the electricity that keeps things alive: that is, the life force. There is a clear distinction between the notion of soul in Islam and the Western psychological perspective; in the former the soul or the heart (which is used interchangeably) is from God and serves one both in this world and the next life, while according to the Western secular perspective the self, as it is called, is confined to this, material, life, which withers away after death.

Within the Islamic framework, as outlined in the Divine's words, there are stages in the development of the self, from an animal or beastly self (*nafs al-ammāra bi-su*), to a self that is blameworthy or has developed a level of awareness (*nafs al-lawāmma*), to a more stable state of being at peace with oneself and the Lord (*nafs al-mutma'inna*). As the self becomes more purified and virtuous, then it integrates with the soul-heart and establishes a more intimate connection with God, from whose domain it originated.

In order to travel through the various stages, there are methods and tools embedded within the acts of worship, as well as in having good morality (*ahklāq*), which is manifested in a courteous code of conduct (*adab*). There is thus an 'inward science' within Islam, which enables the development of the self in preparation for life in this world and, more importantly, for the next world. Thus, the soul's purpose is to produce not only an altered state of consciousness but also a deeper comprehension of God as the Creator and Sustainer of the universe (Badri 2000).

The Prophet portrayed Islam as a 'middle-way' (*ummatan wasatan*) and in this light Imam Khwāja Kamāl Ud-Dīn says, 'It is not the killing of human passion which makes high morality, but the balancing of them to certain measures, which creates healthy morals and produces spirituality' (Kamal-Ud-Din 1923). Islam recognises that there is a role that passion does play in sustaining the human life especially in terms of its nutrition and reproductive roles. The focus in Islam is overcoming the beastly self, the focus on which pre-disposes one to connect with God.

On the other hand, within the context of Western psychology, there is the self and its development, what Maslow called the progression towards self-actualisation or, as Carl Rogers calls it, full-humanness. There appears to be no concept of the soul in Western psychology, as in Islam and in the Judeo-Christian tradition; rather, the self seems to be anchored very much in this material world, and the preparation is only in the light of this world and not the next life. There are tools and methods within Western psychology, which range widely from cognition and behavioural therapies to people-centred therapy. Most recently, spiritually oriented practices have been incorporated into these therapies, including mindfulness and meditation, thus reinforcing some of the traditional and spiritual methods used within religion.

The Islamic framework outlined above illustrates a rich tradition for self-development. Given that the focus within Islam goes beyond this life and into the afterlife, the methods of self-development appear to be an integral fabric of the faith, which is rigorous and time-tested by the sages. Thus, these methods are thought to be highly beneficial within the context of current society in shifting attention from the extrinsic to the intrinsic self, for real change can come only from within.

2.2 Disease of the Soul and Treatment

2.2.1 Context

The soul, which is from the domain of the Lord (Qur'ān, al-Isra 17:85) with all its complexity, is the vehicle that animates our lives and that which subsists on when we pass away (Al-Ghazali 1995). Thus, giving it the utmost attention is important especially in relation to the diseases that affects it. When Imam

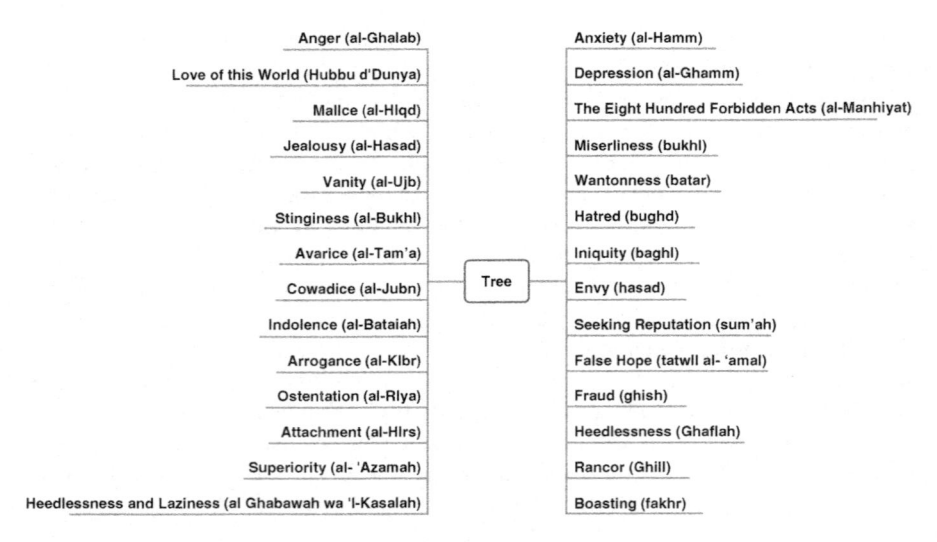

```
                Anger (al-Ghalab)              │  │  Anxiety (al-Hamm)
     Love of this World (Hubbu d'Dunya)        │  │  Depression (al-Ghamm)
                Malice (al-Hlqd)               │  │  The Eight Hundred Forbidden Acts (al-Manhiyat)
                Jealousy (al-Hasad)            │  │  Miserliness (bukhl)
                Vanity (al-Ujb)                │  │  Wantonness (batar)
                Stinginess (al-Bukhl)          │  │  Hatred (bughd)
                Avarice (al-Tam'a)             │  │  Iniquity (baghl)
                Cowadice (al-Jubn)          ──[Tree]── Envy (hasad)
                Indolence (al-Bataiah)         │  │  Seeking Reputation (sum'ah)
                Arrogance (al-Klbr)            │  │  False Hope (tatwll al-'amal)
                Ostentation (al-Rlya)          │  │  Fraud (ghish)
                Attachment (al-Hlrs)           │  │  Heedlessness (Ghaflah)
                Superiority (al-'Azamah)       │  │  Rancor (Ghill)
  Heedlessness and Laziness (al Ghabawah wa 'l-Kasalah) │  Boasting (fakhr)
```

Fig. 2.4 The tree of bad manners (al-Akhlāq al-Dhamimah—The Ruinous Traits)

Muhammad al-Busayri inquired from Shaykh Abu'-Hasan al-Kharqani concerning negative psychological states, he pointed to seventeen states (Kabbani in ed. Hussain et al. 2008) affecting our souls, while other notable scholars have identified similar as well as those that are different.

2.2.2 The Ruinous Traits-Emotions of the Heart

For the sake of comprehensiveness, these ruinous traits are firstly, captured as a tree diagram—developed using the ruinous traits as derived from four eminent scholars Sheikh Abul Hasan al Karkarni, Imam Mawlud al-Yaqubi, Imam Abu Hamid al-Ghazāli and Imam Ibn Hazm al-Andalaus—with the each of the branches manifesting one particular negative psychological state as illustrated in Fig. 2.4.

Table 2.2 captures many common ruinous traits as identified by the four scholars and these include: (i) anger, (ii) love of this world-attachment, (iii) hatred-malice, (iv) pride-vanity, (v) envy, (vi) stinginess-miserliness, (vii) greed-excessive sexual passion, (viii) harm of the tongue-backbiting, (ix) arrogance, (x) heedlessness, (xi) ostentation and (xii) wantonness-extravagance, (xiii) superiority-love of power and show. In Table 2.2, similar traits have been linked together given that their meanings or inherent qualities are similar. These ruinous traits according to the above mentioned scholars, have significant negative psychological states and emotions that cause the diseases of the heart or soul. These are outlined in the Table 2.3.

In this study, an informed decision is made to analysis only the traits that are commonly identified by the selected eminent scholars, while elaborating on the

2.2 Disease of the Soul and Treatment

Table 2.2 List of ruinous traits-emotions as identified by selected eminent scholars

	Shakyh Muhammad Mawlud al-Yaqub	Shakyh Abul Hasan Kharqani	Imam Abu Hamid al-Ghaz_li	Shakyh Ibn Hazm al-Andalus
1	Anger	Anger	Anger	Arrogance
2	Love of this world	Love of this world	Attachment to this world	Greed
3	Hatred	Malice	Hatred	Ruthlessness
4	Envy	Jealousy	Envy	Envy
5	Vanity	Vanity	Love for wealth	Ostentation
6	Miserliness	Stinginess	Miserliness	Miserliness
7	Iniquity	Cowardice	Greed	Covetousness
8	Rancor	Indolence	Sexual Passion	Hypocrisy
9	Wantonness	Indolence	Love of power and Show	Lying
10	Arrogance	Arrogance	Harm of the Tongue	Backbiting
11	Ostentation	Ostentation	Pride and self-praise	Extravagance
12	Relying on other than God	Attachment		
13	Blameworthy modesty	Superiority		
14	Heedlessness	Heedlessness/Laziness		
15	Fear of poverty	Anxiety		
16	Displeasure with divine decree	Depression		
17	Fantasizing	The 800 forbidden acts		
18	Fraud			
19	Derision			
20	Displeasure with blame			
21	Antipathy towards death			
22	Oblivious to blessing			

types, implications, and factors to treat them, as well as backing these up with evidence from the scriptures and where relevant with supporting scientific evidence. These traits were one of the components used to develop the questionnaire which was given to the seekers (see Chap. 5 and Appendix 2).

Table 2.3 Diseases of the heart (soul) & its treatment (Qur'ānic citations from Asad 2011)

Characteristics—Vice	Implications	Treatment	Supporting evidence—scriptural
Greed: Excessive or rapacious desire, especially for food, wealth or possessions	Laziness.	Hunger and Thirst	Qur'ān: Remain, then, conscious of God as best as you can, and listen (to Him), and pay heed. And spend in charity for the good of your own selves: for, such as from their own covetousness are saved – it is they, they that shall attain to a happy state! (al-Taghabun 64:15-16)
	Lack of clarity of thought	Eating only when one is really hungry	
	Diseases (diabetes, cholesterol, high blood pressure, gout etc.)	Finishing eating before one's hunger is fully satisfied	Qur'ān: But as for him who is niggardly and thinks that he is self-sufficient, and calls the ultimate good a lie, for him We shall make easy the path towards hardship and what will his wealth avail him when he goes down (to his grave)? (al-Layl 92:8-11)
	Inability to perform divine duties in a timely manner.	Becoming aware of false hunger	
	Difficulty of performing professional duties		Ibn 'Abbas and Anas bin Malik reported: Messenger of Allah said, "If a son of Adam were to own a valley full of gold, he would desire to have two. Nothing can fill his mouth except the earth (of the grave). Allah turns with mercy to him who turns to Him in repentance" (Bukhari n.d. and Muslim n.d.)
			Qur'ān: Alluring unto man is the enjoyment of worldly desires through women, and children and heaped up treasures of gold and silver, and horses of high mark, and cattle and lands. All of this may be enjoyed in the life of this world – but the most beauteous of all goals is with God. (āl Imran 3:14)

2.2 Disease of the Soul and Treatment

Excessive sexual passion: One is preoccupied with thoughts and deeds, that lead to venturing beyond legitimized relationships.	Psychologically affects the individual with its dependency and impacts the family	Not being alone with the opposite gender
	Negatively impacts society and can contribute to family break-up	Abiding by God's Laws
		Observing Fasts
	Increases chances of contracting STDs	Early marriage
		Hunger
	Encourages human trafficking and prostitution	Restricting one's sight on the opposite gender and on thoughts associated them
	Loss of sense of right and wrong/morality	Involvement in some work

Qurʾān: Tell the believing men to lower their gaze and be mindful of their chastity: this will be most conducive to their purity; indeed, God is aware of all what they do. (al-Noor 24:30)

Qurʾān: And who are mindful of their chastity, (not giving way to desires) with any but their spouses – that is, those who they rightfully possess (through wedlock): for, then, behold, they are free of all blame, whereas such as seek to go beyond that (limit) are truly transgressors. (al-Muʾminun 23:5–7)

(continued)

Table 2.3 (continued)

Characteristics—Vice	Implications	Treatment	Supporting evidence—scriptural
Excessive Anger: Feeling or showing strong resentment, displeasure and wrath, occurs frequently and is difficult to control:	Hidden pride of the oppressor and disobedient person	Taking a path of moderation between not being angry at all and being excessively angry	Qur'ān: Who spend (in His way), in time of plenty and in time of hardship, and hold in check their anger, and pardon their fellow-men because God loves the doers of good. (āl Imran 3:134)
	Damages relationships	Controlling it through practice	Abu Huraira reported Allah's Messenger (may peace be upon him) as saying: "The strong man is not one who wrestles well but the strong man is one who controls himself when he is in a fit of rage." (Sahih Muslim Book 032, 6313)
	Loss of self-control and rational faculty, resulting in atypical behaviour	Engaging the mind in more necessary matters	
	Becomes revengeful and greedy	Knowing that God does not love anger and following this path	Narrated by Abu Huraira: "A man said, 'Advise me!' The Prophet said, 'Do not become angry and furious.' The man asked (the same) again and again, and the Prophet said in each case, 'Do not become angry and furious.'" (Sahih Bukhari, Book 073, Hadith 137)
	Loss of sense of right and wrong	Becoming detached and getting rid of the love of this world	
	Oblivious to advice and council	Being silent	Bahz ibn Hakeem reported: "The Messenger of Allah said, 'Verily, anger corrupts the matter just as vinegar spoils honey.'" (Al-Mu'jam Al-Kabeer 16385, Shu'b al-Iman 7805, Grade: Hasan (fair) according to Al-A'jluni)
	Use of abusive language	Changing posture	
	Can result in assault and murder	Prostration and supplication to God	
		Taking ablution	
		Remembering God	
		Being mindful of retribution	

2.2 Disease of the Soul and Treatment

Hatred: The feeling of one who hates; intense dislike or extreme aversion or hostility	Revenge Envy Happiness at the sorrow of others Non-Cooperation Backbiting Ridicule Assault	To forgive someone who has done wrong to you To remember that if you forgive you will be forgiven Reflect on the result of your intended action before you do a thing	On the authority of Abu Huraira who said: The Messenger of Allah said: "Do not hate one another" (Muslim) "You will never enter Paradise until you believe. And you will not believe until you love one another. Certainly, I shall guide you to something that, if you do it, you will love one another: Spread the greetings (of peace) among yourselves." (Recorded in Muslim) "Creeping upon you is the disease of the peoples before you: envy and hatred. And hatred is the thing that shaves. I do not say it shaves hair, but it shaves the religion. By the One in whose hand is my soul, you will not enter Paradise until you believe. And you do not believe until you love one another. Certainly, let me inform you of that which will establish such for you: spreading the greetings (of peace) among yourselves." (Ahmad, Tirmidhi)

(continued)

Table 2.3 (continued)

Characteristics—Vice	Implications	Treatment	Supporting evidence—scriptural
Envy: Feelings of discontent or covetousness with regard to another's advantages, success, possessions etc.	The envious person loves that the person envied should be deprived of their blessings. This is enmity and it is unlawful	Accepting that whatever others get are gifts from God	Qur'ān: Have they perchance, a share in (God's) dominion? But (if they had), lo, they would not give to other people as much as (would fill) the groove of a date-stone! (al-Nisa 4:54)
	The envious person wishes to have the gifts of the envied persons, such as his power, material and non-material things. This is lawful but not commended	Curing it with knowledge and action, noting that envy is injurious both in this world and the next	Qur'ān: He [Satan] said, "Tell me, is this (foolish being) the one whom Thou hast exalted above me? Indeed, if Thou wilt but allow me a respite till the Day of Resurrection. I shall most certainly cause his descendent – all but a few – to obey me blindly!'" (al-Isra 17:62)
	The envious person does not wish to have identical things but similar things. This is commendable in some cases and not in others	Knowing that no harm reaches the envied person, rather the result is that your own mind becomes filled with sorrow and difficulties	Anas ibn Malik reported: The Messenger of Allah said, "Envy consumes good deeds just as fire burns wood." (Source: Sunan Ibn Mājah 4208)
	Envy becomes expressed as backbiting and falsehood	Knowing that the envied person will get the virtues of the envious person	Abdullah ibn Mas'ud reported: The Prophet said, "There is no envy except in two cases: a man whom Allah has given wealth and he spends it according to its right, and a man whom Allah has given wisdom and he judges and teaches with it"
		Doing the opposite action intended to the envied person, turning guilt into praise, pride into humility and hurt into helpfulness	

2.2 Disease of the Soul and Treatment

Wantonness: Given to self-indulgence, complete recklessness and unrestrained sexual behaviour.	Being excessive and wasteful Not sharing one's wealth with others Descent into debt through the pursuit of an exuberant lifestyle	Using hunger intentionally as a tool to restrain oneself leading to greater understanding Internalizing that too much of anything is not healthy, especially food, and leads not only to physiological issues but impacts negatively on the spiritual heart Remembering the hereafter and that God does not love those who are extravagant Reflecting on previous generations and civilisations, which exulted in their wealth, who are now not even positively remembered, while their soul awaits final judgment	Qurʾān: And pay heed unto God and His Apostle and do not (allow yourself) be at variance with one another, lest your heart and moral strength deserts you. And be patient in adversity. And be not life those (unbelievers) who went forth from their homelands full of self-conceit and a desire to be seen and praised by men; for they were trying to turn others away from the path of God – the while God encompassed all their doings (with His might). (al-Anfal 8:46-47) Qurʾān: (Now) Behold, Qarun was one of the people of Moses; but he arrogantly exalted himself above them – simply because We had granted him such riches that his treasure-chest alone would have been too heavy a burden for a troop of ten or even more. (al-Qasas 28:76) Qurʾān: Hast Thou ever considered (the kind of man) who makes his own desires his deity, and whom God has (thereupon) let go astray knowing (that his mind is closed to all guidance), and whose hearing and heart He has sealed, and upon whose sight He has placed a veil? Who then can guide hi, after God (has abandoned)? Will you not, then bethink yourself? (al-Jathiyah 45:23) Qurʾān: And since they cannot respond to this they challenge, know that they are following their own likes and dislikes and who could be more astray than he who follows (but) his own likes and dislikes without any guidance from God? (al-Qasas 28:50)

(continued)

Table 2.3 (continued)

Characteristics—Vice	Implications	Treatment	Supporting evidence—scriptural
Ostentation: Pretentious or conspicuous show, of wealth or importance; display intended to impress others.	Performing acts of worship for others to see, thereby nullifying its intention and benefits	Sincerely seeking purification from God from four things:	The Messenger of Allah said, "Verily, what I fear most for you is the lesser idolatry." And he elaborated, "It is showing off. Allah the Exalted will say to them (who show off), on the Day of Resurrection when the people are being rewarded for their deeds: Go to those whom you wished to show off in the world and look for your reward with them." (Musnad Ahmad Hadith 23119)
	Laziness and non-motivation to do things when people are not around	i) love of praise	
	The tendency to increase or decrease one's ritualistic actions due to praise and non-praise.	ii) fear of blame	
		iii) desire for worldly benefits from people	Abu Sa'id al-Khudri reported: The Messenger of Allah entered upon us while we were discussing the False Messiah. He said, "Shall I not tell you about what I fear for you more than the presence of the False Messiah?" We said, "Of course!" He said, "Hidden idolatry; that a man stands for prayer and beautifies his prayer because he sees another man looking at him." (Ibn Majah Hadith 4202)
	Doing things for other than the Lord	iv) fear of harm from people	
		This is developed from the belief that only God can cause benefit or harm	
	Being disappointed when things do not turn out well		
	Adopting behaviour that is not entirely yours seeking to please someone else, which can lead to hypocrisy		Allah's Messenger said: "If anyone wants to have his deeds widely publicised, Allah will publicise (his humiliation). And if anyone makes a hypocritical display (of his deeds) Allah will make a display of him." (Sahih Muslim Book 42, Hadith 7115)

2.2.3 The Implications of the Ruinous Traits and Their Treatment

This section will list the 13 traits that have been flagged repeatedly by some selected eminent scholars. These traits have been presented below in a standardised format for ease of understanding. The implications are outlined and then treatment elaborated, which is backed by the scriptures and ḥadīths where this type of evidence is available.

2.2.4 The Origins of Ruinous Traits

While it is crucial to identify ruinous traits and treat them based on the pointers from the Qur'iān and the ḥadīths, it is important to gain a more in-depth understanding of their root causes. In this vein, Sheikh Ibn Hazm, Imam Abu Zakariya al Razi (313AH/925AD), and Imam Ghazāli provide their perspective on the genesis of some key ruinous traits in Figs. 2.5, 2.6, and 2.7.

According to Sheikh Ibn Hazm (Al-Andalusi 1990) the root cause of traits that destroy humans are injustice, greed and ignorance, for example, ruthlessness arises from covetousness, which is derived from envy, which in turn comes from desire and greed. This formulation differs from Imam al-Razi (Fig. 2.5), who sees miserliness and covetousness as the source from which envy arises, which then leads to evil. Even though three of the traits mentioned by Imam al-Razi are the same as with Ibn Hazm (Fig. 2.6), their analysis and interpretation of the origin is different. One firm agreement between them however is that envy is a ruinous trait that leads to evil or improper behaviour. Imam Ghazāli (1995) points out that hatred arises from anger in one's mind and outlines eight evils that comes out of the anger-hatred inter-link

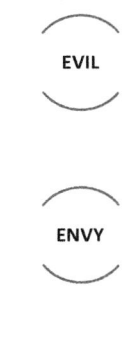

Fig. 2.5 Imam Razi's perspective on the genesis of ruinous traits)

EVIL

ENVY

MISERLINESS & COVERTOUSNESS

Fig. 2.6 Imam Ibn Hazm's perspective on the genesis of ruinous traits

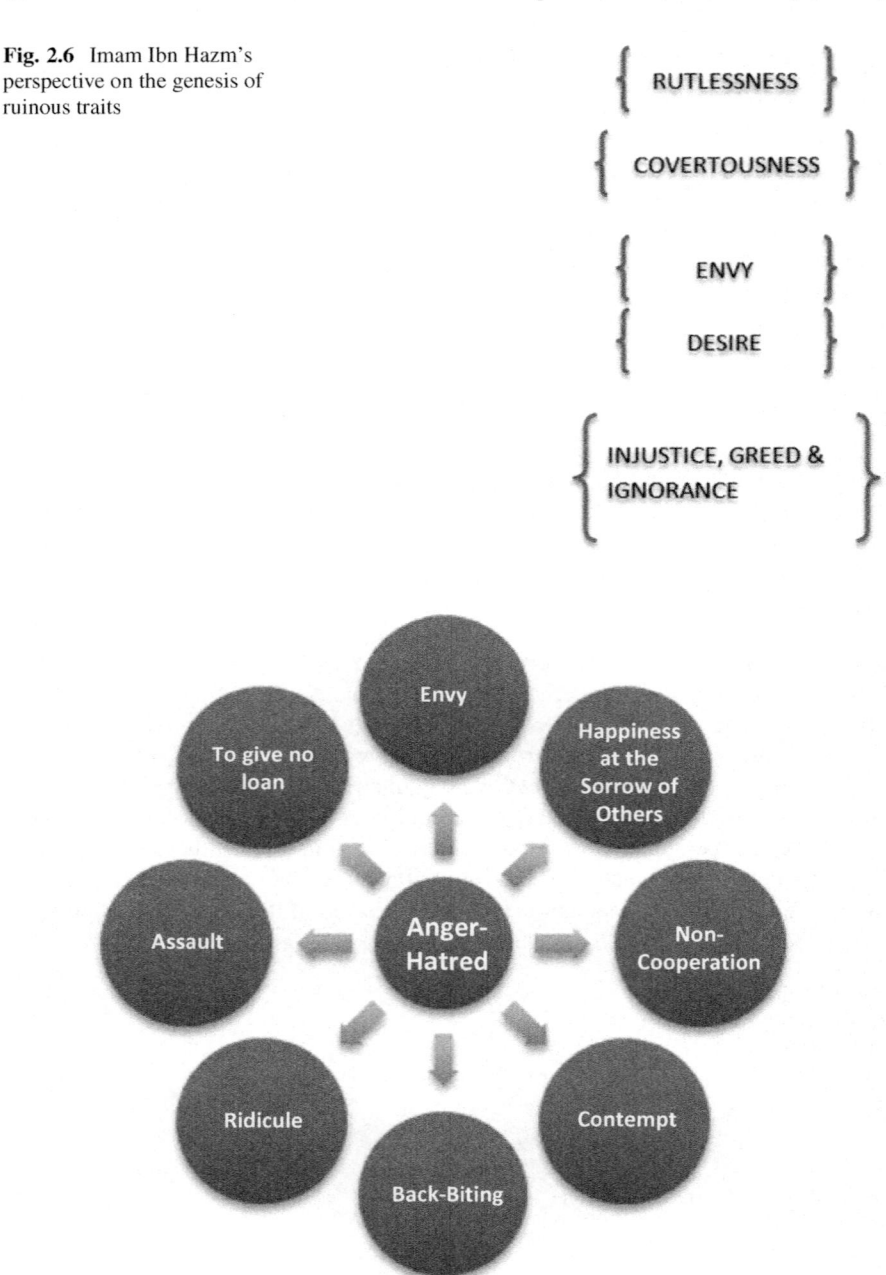

$$\{ \text{RUTLESSNESS} \}$$
$$\{ \text{COVERTOUSNESS} \}$$
$$\{ \text{ENVY} \}$$
$$\{ \text{DESIRE} \}$$
$$\{ \text{INJUSTICE, GREED \& IGNORANCE} \}$$

Fig. 2.7 Imam Ghazāli's perspective on the genesis of ruinous traits

2.2 Disease of the Soul and Treatment 49

Table 2.4 Diseases of the heart (soul) & its treatment (Qur'ānic citations from Asad 2011)

Characteristics—vice	Implications	Treatment	Supporting evidence—scriptural	Supporting evidence
Harm of the tongue (backbiting): To attack the character or reputation of (a person who is not present) and/or to speak unfavourably or slanderously of a person who is not present. (Al-Ghazali 1995)	Useless talk	Silence	Prophet: He who keeps silent gets salvation.	Qur'an: O you who have attained to faith! Avoid much guess work (about one another), for behold, some of (such) guesswork is (in itself) a sin; and do not spy upon one another, and neither allow yourself to speak ill of one another behind your backs. Would any of you like to eat the flesh of your dead brother? Nay you would loath it! And be conscious of God. Verily God is the Acceptor of repentance, Dispenser of grace. (al-Hujarat 49:12)
	Quarrels	Good conduct	Prophet: Silence is a rule and few observe it.	
	Disputes	Speaking well	Prophet: He who is safe from the harm of his belly, sexual organs and tongue is safe from all troubles.	
	Rebukes	Refraining from back-biting		
	Scolding	Reducing speech to only what is necessary		
	Harsh words	Concise statements	Prophet Jesus was asked, tell us a thing by virtue of which we can enter paradise. He said, don't talk. They said, we shall not be able to do that. He said, then don't talk except good.	Qur'an: Not even a word can be uttered but there is a watcher with him, ever present. (Qaf 50:18)
	Cursing	Using sweet words		
	False speaking	Increasing knowledge of the effects of bad deeds		
	Self-Praise	Not arguing and excessive questioning	God: Don't back-bite one another. Do you like to eat the flesh of your dead brother? Rather you abhor it (Qur'an, 44:12)	
	Disputes			
	Ornamental talk			
	Excessive talk			
	Obscene talk			
	Hypocrisy			

(continued)

Table 2.4 (continued)

Characteristics—vice	Implications	Treatment	Supporting evidence—scriptural	Supporting evidence
Attachment (to the world): An act of attaching or the state of being attached. A feeling that binds one to a person, thing, cause, ideal, or the like; devotion	It severs the way of divine service.	Using prayer and fasting as tools to save oneself from passion	Prophet: The world is a prison to believers and a paradise to unbelievers.	Qur'an: 'All who buy the life of this world at the price of the life to come – their suffering shall not be lightened, nor shall they be succoured!' (al-Baqara 2:86)
	Entraps people with its attraction and causes dependency.	Utilizing only what is essential and leaving the rest.	Prophet: He who loves the world injures his hereafter and he who love his hereafter injures his world.	Qur'an: 'Would you content yourselves with (comforts) this worldly life in preference to (the good of) the life to come? But the enjoyment of life in this world is but paltry thing when compared with the life to come!' (al-Tauba 9:38)
	The hearts are affected negatively by its separation.	Reminding ourselves frequently that everything in the world will pass away	Prophet: Love of the world is the root of all sins	
		Being reminded of the signs of God, death and the final destination	Prophet Jesus: Don't take the world as your Lord. If you do so, it will make you a slave.	
	Greed for materials things becomes the causes of man's calamities.		Prophet Jesus: Know that the root of all evil is the attachment to the world.	Qur'an : 'And nothing is the life of this world but a play and a passing delight; and the life in the hereafter is by far better for all who are conscious of God. Will you not, then, use your reason?' (al-An'aam 6:32)
	Causes quarrels amongst people due to increasing wealth		Prophet Jesus: Love of both this world and the next cannot remain united in the heart of a believer, just as water and fire cannot remain united.	
	Addiction to materials things leads to the sickness of the body and mind		Prophet: Don't keep your mind engaged in the thoughts of the world.	Qur'an: 'O Men! Be conscious of your Sustainer and stand in awe of the Day. God's promise (of resurrection) is true indeed: let not, then, the life of this world delude you, and let not (your own) deceptive thoughts about God delude you!' (Luqman 31:33)
	The greater the urge to seek happiness the greater the sorrow		Prophet Jesus: Who is there who constructs a house in the currents of sea? Don't take it as your permanent abode.	

2.2 Disease of the Soul and Treatment

Boasting & arrogance: Offensive display of superiority, pride or self-importance by virtue of wealth, knowledge, lineage, beauty etc. Arrogance: Kibr is the force behind the act of Boasting (Mawlid 2011)	Arrogance signifies the glorification and aggrandizement of the self Manifested as contempt and scorn towards others Making others feel less than yourself. Loss of humility and compassion Difficulty of performing professional duties	Realizing that one's blessings are from God and He can take them away at any moment Remembering and reflecting on our origins and from what we were made Reflecting on the limitations of our bodies and our dependency on things Realizing that life by its nature is in constant flux; riches are temporary and beauty fades To become aware that blessings are coupled with responsibilities To know that the highest honour in the sight of God is by the servitude to the Lord and with this comes the benefits and this is not based on beauty, power, wealth, lineage and authority.	God: "God does not love the arrogant and the boasting ones" (Qur'ān, 31:18, 57:23). God said: "I will divert My signs from those who show arrogance without right" (Qur'ān, 7:146). Prophet: Verily, Allah does not look at your appearance or your wealth but rather He looks at your heart and your actions. (Muslim) God: "He does not love those who wax arrogant" (Qur'ān, 16:23). God: "Indeed, the most honourable of you in the sight of God is the most God-fearing of you. Surely, God is all knowing and all-aware" (Qur'ān, 49:13). God: 'Perished is man! How ungrateful he is! From what stuff did He create him? From a sperm drop He created Him and proportioned him' (Qur'ān, 80:16–19).	Qur'an : Has there (not) been endless span of time before man (appeared) –a time (when he was not yet a thing to be thought of)? Verily, it is We who have created man out of a drop of sperm intermingled, so that We might try him (in his later life): and therefore, We made him a being endowed with hearing and sight. (al-Insan 76:1–2) Qur'an: He who has created death as well as life, so that He might but you to a test (and thus show) which of you in best in conduct, and (make you realize that) He alone is almighty, truly forgiving. (al-Mulk 67:2) Qur'an: Have We not given him two eyes, and a tongue, and a pair of lips, and shown him the two highways (of good and evil)? But he would not try to ascend the steep uphill road. (al-Balad 90:8–11)

(continued)

Table 2.4 (continued)

Heedlessness: Careless; thoughtless; unmindful; lack of attention or a state of forgetfulness to what is more important in one's life.	Being heedless of divine purpose, remembrance of God and acts that one is obligated to accomplish	Keeping good and sincere company.	Imam al-Junayd: A pathogen which is the cause of all other diseases of the heart.	Qur'ān: [the time of] their Reckoning draws near to mankind, while they turn away in heedlessness. (al-Anbiyā 21:1)
		Seeking repentance and forgiveness (istighfar).	God: "You were heedless of this. Now We have removed your veil from you, so your sight this day is sharp!" (Qur'ān, 50:22).	Qur'ān: O Mankind! There has now come unto you an admonition from your Sustainer, and a cure for all (the ill) that may be in men's hearts? And guidance and grace onto all who believe (in Him). (Yunus 10:57)
	Forgetting things that are important	Reflecting at the day's end and recounting the good and the bad that one does and repenting for it.		
	Loss of sense of purpose and meaning of life	Visiting the righteous people in the path of God – the prophets (al-Nabbiyin), the Truthful one (al-Saddiqin); martyrs (al-Shuhada) and the righteous (al-Salihin).	God speaks of those who do not profess faith and not accepting the message of the Prophets as having a cover (ghishawah) over their eyes (Qur'ān, 2:7).	
	Given the closure of one's door to the mind, not seeing reality as it should be seen and experiencing the grace of God		Prophet: Show me the truth as truth and give me the ability to follow it; and show me falsehood as falsehood and give me the ability to avoid it.	
	Does not develop the inward state or character of oneself	Visiting ones who have passed away as a reminder of reality.	God: "O you who believe invoke benediction upon (the Prophet) and salutations of peace" (Qur'ān 33:56).	
		The frequent benediction on the Prophet.		
		Reciting the Qur'ān with reflection (tadabbur) awakens the heart.		

2.2 Disease of the Soul and Treatment

Love of wealth & power & show: The possession of control or command over others; authority; ascendancy: power over men's minds.	Power gives the means to earn wealth by ethical and unethical means Wealth may earn power but this may not necessarily be the case Both wealth and power can be used and abused to control the minds of people Wealth can be taken away but generally power cannot since it is an influence over one's mind Wealth and power can change a person and make him/her arrogant and haughty Inherent fear of losing one's wealth and power leading to anxiousness	Realizing that one is accountable for one's deeds and actions in the next world. Reflecting that one cannot use wealth and power all the time to accomplish things and there is liability, which catches up with you, where you are taken into account. . Realizing that wealth and power vanish and that spiritual knowledge and freedom will be carried with the soul. Realizing that seeking name and fame is unlawful within the perspective of Islam, unless it comes to you by itself. Realising the greater the power the greater the chances of one's downfall or becoming the target of death.	Prophet: It is sufficient for the evil of a man if he is pointed to regarding his temporal and spiritual work. Prophet: God does not look at your figure but He looks into your hearts and actions. . Imam Ali: Spend but don't disclose it. Don't raise your personality to attract the attention of the people, rather keep it secret and remain silent, you will then be safe. . Hazrath Ibrahim ibn Adham: He who loves name and fame does not know God to be true.	Qur'an, Al-Qasas 28:83: As for that (happy) life in the hereafter, We grant it (only) to those who do not seek to exalt themselves on earth, nor yet to spread corruption for the future belongs to the God conscious. Hazrath Abu Tayyab: He who loses time in earning wealth for the fear of poverty creates wants. Abu Musa reported: Two of my cousins and I entered the house of the Prophet. One of them said, "O Messenger of Allah, appoint us as leaders over some lands that Allah the Exalted has entrusted to your care." The other said something similar. The Prophet, said, "Verily, by Allah, we do not appoint anyone to this position who asks for it or is anxious for it." Source: Sahih Muslim 1733

(Fig. 2.7): Envy, happiness at the sorrow of another, non-cooperation, contempt, backbiting, ridicule, assault, and not to give loans to the one whom one does not like.

The term '*hasad*' is used for envy, which Ibn Hazm (Al-Ghazali 1995) also equates with a sense of laziness, while it is also used in the context of the 'evil eye'. This has a very negative impact on the mind, bringing about anxiety, insomnia, resentment and anger. Ibn Hazm says that the evil eye is primeval and universal, while Francis Bacon is cited as saying that the concept of the evil eye, which represents the glance on an object with evil intent, is common across all cultures and society. Thus, envy is seen as one of the most ruinous traits and in this light Imam Ibn Hazm recommends a number of treatments for overcoming it, as follows:

(i) Do not spend extravagantly
(ii) Lead a moderate lifestyle
(iii) Do not be arrogant with people
(iv) Try to soften hearts
(v) Be charitable to the needy
(vi) Invoke God's name, seek His blessing and protection
(vii) Do not be boastful of one's strength
(viii) Cultivate goodwill

Imam Ghazāli (1995) stresses the need to apply the opposite of the evil intended as a medicine to combat envy: for example, if it causes pride then treat with humility; if the intention is to mention guilt then praise the person, and if the intention is to destroy then help the person.

2.2.5 Discussion

There are a many significant aspects that emerge from the review and analysis, notably that there are myriad ruinous traits of what contemporary psychologists call negative emotions. The tree diagram (Fig. 2.4) represents 22 of them, each symbolising a branch of the tree. This is a metaphor to signify that each branch carries with it a body of its own content, which gives it its inherent characteristics. What is most fitting is that this is not a purely academic analysis but one that has implications and profound negative impacts on one's heart or mind and that results in causing pain, confusion and disease. This starts with a thought in one's mind, which is envious or hateful and this builds up negative emotions, which then impact the spiritual heart. This can subsequently precipitate as psychological and medical conditions as it is empirically observed within the contemporary context of anxiety, depression and unhappiness. Such is the profundity of the spiritual heart being affected by these ruinous traits and the need for human beings to take careful care of it before it becomes diseased.

It will be noticed that not all of the 22 emotions have the same negative impacts, some are more pernicious than others and the 13 emotions that were repeatedly

2.2 Disease of the Soul and Treatment

flagged by eminent scholars were analysed in Table 2.2, where their implications, as well as treatment were elaborated. The pattern that emerges from the implications is the destructive impact on the individual. This, however, does not seem to stop at the individual level but impacts those on whom the negative emotions are directed, for example, envy results in a state of anxiety and hatred on the envier and has negative energy or evil eye on the envied person, this concept is prevalent in many societies and cultures as pointed out by Francis Bacon.

What is most significant from the analysis is to bring attention to the fact that the extremes of what could be termed as good emotions—charity, humbleness, kindness, compassion—if taken to the extreme could become a weakness leading to extravagance, abasement, being abused etc. In a similar vein, bad emotions like anger, greed, pride, attachment to the world, wantonness etc. become very destructive forces that affect both the individual, as well as the family around them and society at large.

In light of the above, Ibn Hazm's analysis of the mid-point of the vices being the best position, for example, the position of modesty being between arrogance and extreme humbleness or abasement of oneself; and courage being a medium course between fear and rashness. Thus, Ibn Hazm (1990) says, "Virtue is a medium course between two vices." In this sense, Ibn Hazm's definition of virtue is aligned with Aristotle's golden middle way but this does not apply to evil deeds such as theft, murder, envy, treason etc., given that they are inherently evil and should be rejected outright. This leads us to the position as articulated by the Prophet that Islam is the middle-way or the middle-path (*ummatan wasatan*).

A connection is seen here with these points of view, where people want more than their needs (greed) while concurrently being not willing to part with what they have for the fear of losing it. This in-effect portrays a sense of injustice or perpetuating inequality by not sharing, while not factoring that all provisions (*rizq*) is from the Lord and this has been determined for a person before the individual came into existence (Mas'ud 2006). Given that there are both good and evil within humans, there is a need to follow contemplative spiritual practices (prayers, *dhikr*, *fasting*, *zakah* etc.), combined with good morals, which enable one to tide over these ruinous traits.

It can be stated that the external purifications and rituals, prescribed in the *Sharī'a*, are to give structure to one's life combined with the social and legal controls that keep one on track and give life order. However, the tradition of *tasawwuf* or the purification of the inner self—also called *tazkiyatun nafs*—is a central core of Islam and this addresses the diseases of the heart and the treatment of ruinous character. The treatment, as seen from Table 2.2, covers a wide range of approaches, methods and techniques pertaining to the body and mind:

(i) Body: Observing fasts including abstaining from food, water; regulating one's eating and sexual acts.
(ii) Mind: This can be categorised into contemplative practices and other practices that include remembering God consistently, recitation and reflection of the divine scriptures; asking for forgiveness; forgiving those who do wrong to you,

cultivating silence, reflecting on death; reflecting on one's life, supplicating to God; reflecting on the impermanence of life etc.;
(iii) Behavioral and other practices: Doing the opposite of bad habits (reversing the process), being in the company of the pious people (*ṣohba*); giving charity (*zakah* and *sadaqa*); sharing from things that you love; being compassionate.

This is what I would call attaining equilibrium in terms of both the body and mind, by feeding one's body when hungry and sharing one's wealth and/or efforts with others, while deepening one's sense of worship, which is all encompassing. Worship is used as a state of mindfulness of God, oneself and others, a relationship that keeps one in a state of contentment and in check.

The importance of emotional wellbeing for health is being backed by an increasing body of evidence from diverse fields of epidemiology, social sciences as well as experimental research, which points to the failure of the health system for not taking into consideration mental and social health. Here social health refers to overcoming social diseases such as dependency and misuse of alcohol and drugs, domestic violence, and child abuse, which fall within the gambit of the ruinous traits within an Islamic perspective. Concurrently, emotional wellbeing is critical given that emotional distress forms one of the preconditions to physical illness.

In the light of the above, treatment of the diseases of the heart in effect predisposes one to a healthier life. Looking at wellbeing from a psycho-spiritual perspective whereby identifying the ruinous or negative traits and treating them as exemplified in Tables 2.2, inter-links with the concept of social and mental wellbeing and is thus key to social and emotional wellbeing. Here, we see science fitting into the spiritual realm, which is evidence based and has been developed over millennium. This indicates that religion should subsume Spiritual Psychology (Husain 2005), defined as 'an applied field which focuses on the knowledge that a person has or possess in terms of beliefs, resources, experience, and behaviours; and the importance giving to spiritual practices and rituals in order to increase wellbeing'.

Islam, thus, has within its framework and tradition both aspects that are articulated above to bring about a balance of life both for the body and the mind. This can be best encapsulated in the statement where Imam Malik stated, 'Islam without *ḥaqīqa* (inward) is lame and Islam without *Sharī'a* (outward) is heresy' (Kabbani 1995).

2.3 Contemplative Framework and Practices: An Islamic Perspective

2.3.1 Introduction

Contemplative practices form the cornerstone of Islam and infiltrates every facet of life, as the ensuing discussion demonstrates. These can be categorised into seven main types of practices, ranging from stillness through to generative, ritual, and activist, relational, creative and movement practices. The 'tree of contemplative practices' was used within the Islamic context to map out seven main categories of practice derived from the divine scripture, as well as from the words and practices of the Prophet and the Sages.

2.3.2 Context

Contemplative practice is a key to building one's mind and body and overcoming the negative emotions or ruinous traits that plague human beings. Before delving into the practice itself, it is imperative to examine its main categorisations and understand the framework within which it is embedded. The contemplative framework is presented as the tree of contemplative practices based on the framework of the Centre of Contemplative Mind in Society (2007) (Fig. 2.8). This is presented as seven major branches, which can be condensed into three dimensions:

(i) The practices where the mind and more specifically the heart predominate, namely, stillness and creative practices;
(ii) Where the collective behaviour predominates, including generative and relational practices;
(iii) Where the body predominates, including activist, movement and ritualistic practice. The above practices represent a wide spectrum, embracing the mind-heart-body-relationships

2.3.3 The Fundamentals of Contemplative Practice

The Jibril ḥadīth, signified by the visitation of the Angel Jibril to Prophet Muhammad, lays down the framework for the faith (Ibn Daqiq 2014). During this visit, the Prophet was questioned on three fundamental aspects of Islam, and the questions and Prophetic responses are outlined here:

i. What is Islam? Islam comprises of five pillars:

   (a) The testimony of faith that there is no other God but God, which denotes a negation and an affirmation (*Shahada*).
   (b) Prayer five times a day (*Salah*).
   (c) Obligatory charity (*Zakah*).
   (d) Fasting (*Saum*).
   (e) Pilgrimage (*Hajj*)

ii. What is *Iman*? *Iman* comprises six articles of faith:

(a) Belief in the Oneness of God.
(b) Belief in the Angels.
(c) Belief in all the Prophets.
(d) Belief in the divine Scriptures.
(e) Belief in the Day of Judgment.
(f) Belief in pre-destination (*qada qadr*).

iii. What is *Ihsan*? *Ihsan* is interpreted as virtue and excellence in one's intention and actions. The word Islam derives from the root word 'salam', which means 'peace'; it also contains the meaning of being in total submission or surrender to God. *Iman* means to have faith in one's heart, while *Ihsan* is excellence in worship and in dealing with oneself and others.

The pivotal aspect of Islam is the shahada or the testimony of faith, which states that there is no other God but God and that Prophet Muhammad is His prophet. The most critical belief is in the Oneness of God, which is called *tawhid*. This forms the bedrock from which all else is derived, including all contemplative practices. Sheikh Hamza Yusuf, commenting on the work 'Vision of Islam' (Chitick and Murata 2002), describes the *shahada* as having a vertical dimension through its connection with God; this is quintessential to Islam, where one is to fully surrender to God. The horizontal dimension, or *iman*, with its inherent beliefs as described above, is the link to the chain of all prophets going back in time. The dimension of depth, *ihsan*, is 'worshipping God as if you see Him, while you don't see Him, He sees you.' (Ibn Daqiq 2014) As will be noted, the other five pillars of Islam also form part of the contemplative practices under the ritualistic-cyclic, as well as the silent practices (see Fig. 2.8).

2.3.4 Contemplative Practices in Islam

As seen in the Tree of Contemplative Practices (Fig. 2.8), there are seven major branches, defined as stillness, generative, creative process, relational, activist, ritualistic-cyclic, and movement practices. This categorisation has been undertaken based on the nature of the practices, each of which is expounded below:

(1) **Stillness** focuses on quietening the mind and body, in order to bring about a state enabling one to turn to God. Within the Islamic framework, there are several elements that can be categorised under stillness: contemplation, meditation, repentance, supplication, centering, reflection, thinking about death, and silent ritual prayer. In discussion, there is often confusion between contemplation and meditation. In Islam, contemplation appears repeatedly in the Qur'ān, "And He has made the night and the day and the sun and the moon subservient (to His laws, so that they be of use) to you, and all the stars are subservient to His command: in this, behold, there are messages indeed for people who use

2.3 Contemplative Framework and Practices: An Islamic Perspective

MOVEMENT PRACTICE
Mindfulness while sitting eating drinking and journeying

GENERATIVE PRACTICES:
Loud prayer, congregational prayer, loud dhikr and Durood on the Prophet

RELATIONAL PRACTICES:
Dialogue, mentoring, spiritual guidance, narrating stories, listening

CREATIVE PROCESS PRACTICES:
Poetry, prose, calligraphy, art and journal writing

ACTIVIST PRACTICES:
Voluntary umra (pilgrimage), voluntary services & supporting others in need, protests

STILLNESS PRACTICES:
Contemplation & meditation, silent ritual prayer, repentance, centering reflection, silence and seclusions, hunger and vigilance

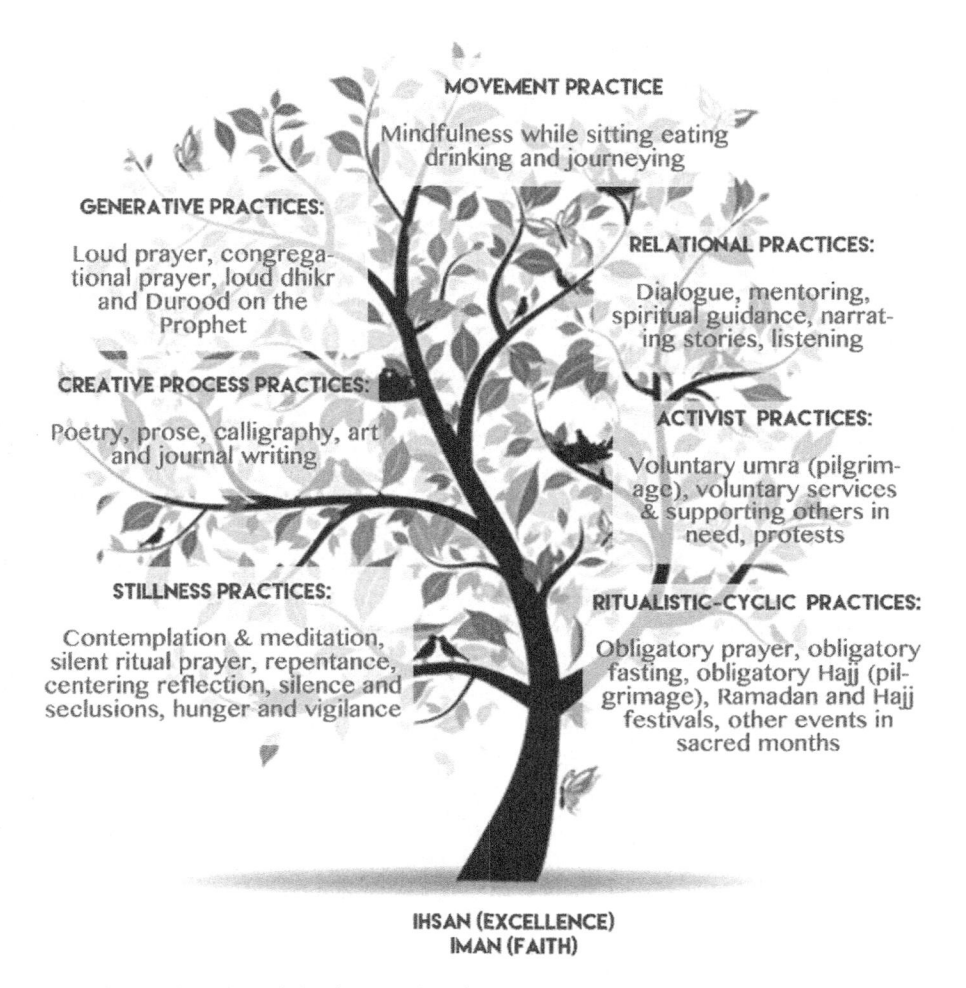

RITUALISTIC-CYCLIC PRACTICES:
Obligatory prayer, obligatory fasting, obligatory Hajj (pilgrimage), Ramadan and Hajj festivals, other events in sacred months

IHSAN (EXCELLENCE)
IMAN (FAITH)

Fig. 2.8 Islamic contemplative framework and practices

their reason" (al-Nahl, 16:12). This means taking cognizance of things within you and without, which involves observation, reflection, and internalization of human beings and their total environment including the celestial systems.

Schuon (2006) equates intellectualism with contemplation; he does this by framing it within the context of the unity of God and in relation to Islamic metaphysics, where he says that psychologically this is manifested in certitude (*yaqīn*) in God and the serenity that arises therefrom. Schuon cites Sheikh al-Alawi, who sums up that 'the profound meaning of religious practices and the reason they exist is for the remembrance of Allah, which means that all the Sharī'a, all the dogmas, all the practices reside in the *dhikr* (remembrance of God).' Schuon describes the essence of meditation thus: 'To close the eyes is in fact to exclude the world, and to pronounce the Name is to affirm God.' This, he states, is excluding *Maya* (artifice, illusion), while affirming *Atma* (the real or true self) and closing the eyes is the nafy (negation) of the *shahadah (la Ilaha)*; pronouncing the Name is the *ithbat (illa Allah*—affirmation). This refers to creating a state of non-existence of oneself or of one's ego on one hand and the appearance of a sense of a Higher Being on the other.

Ibn 'Arabi discusses meditation in the context of spiritual unravelling saying:

> We empty our hearts of reflective thinking, and we sit together with al-Ḥaqq (The Real) on the carpet of adab (pious conduct) and murāqaba (spiritual attentiveness) and presence and readiness to receive whatever comes to us from Him – so that it is God who takes care of teaching us by means of unveiling and spiritual realization (Morris 2005). The seeker focuses on 'perfect collectedness in contemplation (murāqaba) and if God's grace persists then he may attain vision (mushāhada)' (Schimmel 1975).

From another perspective, the Ignatian (Catholic) tradition defines meditation as an attempt made to understand God, while contemplation is the focus on a single symbol or word (Annunciation Trust 2008). Imam Ghazāli (1995) describes meditation as, 'To keep one's thought towards God, the One who keeps watch over you and to keep all thoughts involved in Him.' He adds that meditation results in the generation of knowledge about God (ma'rifa), which impacts both the body and the mind. Thus, Imam Ghazāli points out that meditation is both a state of presence of mind of oneself and knowledge about God and as such he defines six stages of spiritual effort:

i. *Mushārata* (taking account of passion): Making conditions to better oneself by purification of the soul *(tazkiyatun nafs)*, which forms the bedrock of the road to salvation. God says, 'Indeed he succeeds who purifies it. And indeed, he fails who corrupts it.' (Qur'ān, al-Shams, 91:9–10) When this verse was recited, the Prophet used to say, 'O Allah! Give my soul what is good and You are its Guardian and Master, and the best to purify it.' Imam Ghazāli says you have to be careful to not become careless for even a moment especially with guarding one's eyes, ears, tongue, stomach, sexual organs, hands and feet. Thus, he says, you need to instruct them 'to save the soul from these sins' (Al-Ghazali 1995).

ii. *Murāqaba* (deep meditation): The essence here is to 'worship God as if you see him and while you see him not He sees you' (Ibn Daqiq 2014). Imam Ghazāli uses the term 'meditation' in connection with three introspective types of action: (a) sincerity *(ikhlas)* in relation to virtuous action and purity of intention; (b) examination of one's sinful actions and repentance; (c) observance of rules and laws in relation to lawful action.

iii. *Muhasaba* (taking account of oneself) (Al-Ghazali 1995): Taqwa or piety refers to obeying Allah's orders and refraining from what He has forbidden, being accountable for one's deeds before being recompensed, while being mindful of the good deeds for the next life (Qur'ān, al-Hashr, 59:18). Kaliph Omar said, 'Take account of your actions before accounts are taken from you and weigh actions before they are weighed upon', while the sage Hasan al Basri says, 'A believer takes guard over oneself' (Al-Ghazali 1995).

iv. *Muʿaqabah* (punishment of oneself): Punishing oneself as a result of bad conduct or intention. This involves doing the opposite of the bad act or reprimanding oneself for the act performed. It also offers opportunities to gift things that one possesses or offers self-sacrifice by fasting or performing other acts of worship (Al-Ghazali 1995).
v. *Mujahada* (exerting efforts): Exerting effort and conducting oneself against one's dictates, that is where sins move far away from you. The female sage Shaonah says there are two safeguards at the time of your final exit from this world, namely, 'to keep sorrow attached to your heart and place the love of God above any temptation.' This entails the striving of the soul in the way of God, constantly fighting against one's lower desires to attain the pleasure of The Almighty (Al-Ghazali 1995).
vi. *Muataba* (self-rebuke): Imam Ghazāli stresses that there is no greater enemy than one's own baser self (*nafs*), which, if left unrestrained, will lead you to evil and ultimately the destruction of your soul. The *nafs* is like a wild animal, which without harsh discipline cannot be tamed. It must be rebuked frequently and brought into submission before the will of God, thus transforming it into the self-accusing soul (Al-Ghazali 1995).

As seen from the six categories above, meditation within Islam is a fluid concept, which Imam Ghazāli (1995) articulates as having two key factors. Firstly, there is the act before the action, which refers to the intention of the seeker, verifying if one is doing it for the sake of God, for human dictates or at the prompting of the devil. Thus, 'Verily works are according to one's intentions, and each person is (gets) what he intends', as the Prophet Muhammad stated (Ibn Daqiq 2014). In a similar vein, Prophet Jesus outlined: an action, which is especially good, follow it; an action, which is especially bad, avoid it; an action, which is difficult to ascertain, as to its goodness or badness, entrust it to one who knows it (Ibn Daqiq 2014). The second key factor is one's state of mind during the action, in relation to which the Prophet Muhammad asked three questions: 'How have you done it?, Why have you done it?', and 'For whom have you done it?' (Al-Ghazali 1995). This, then, ascertains if it was done according to permissible means and if the act was performed not to show off but sincerely for God'.

The term 'meditation' within Islam refers to the final query by Angel Jibril to the Prophet, 'That is worshipping God as if you see Him (mushāhada), while you see Him not, he sees you (murāqaba)'. In this case, the aspirant is in a state of focusing on God, with the intention of the Lord turning towards him. This takes two forms, the silent remembrance (*dhikr al-khafi*) and the loud remembrance (*dhikr al-lisān*), where the focus is on one single attribute of God. There is sound evidence in the Qurʾān to support the need for a meditative mind, as indicated here: (i) 'God (Allah) watches you.' (Qurʾān, al-Nisa 4:1); (ii) 'Does he not know that God sees him and hears his word?' (Qurʾān, al-ʿAlaq 96:14); (iii) 'And remember your Lord within yourself, humbly and with fear and without loudness in words in the mornings and in the afternoons' (Qurʾān, al-Aʿrāf 7:205).

The sage Ibn al-Mubarak commenting on 'Allah watches over you' (Al-Ghazali 1995) says that this refers to keeping the thought in mind as if you are seeing God, while the sage Ibnul Ata says, 'Constant meditation over truth is good divine service' (Al-Ghazali 1995). Meditation is not done for its own sake but to develop the state of one's heart or soul, to transcend from one state to another and to enable one to get closer to God. In this light, seven progressive stages are mapped out by the seeker in the spiritual path, as shown in Fig. 2.3.

Reflection (*tafakkur*) is another type of meditation which is more cognitive, God particularly calls on mankind to reflect on the creation and created things. This is one of the central themes in both the divine scripture and the Prophetic tradition. Ibn 'Arabi's writing on Islam unfolds this spiritual intelligence (Morris 2005), which comprises experience, reflection and right action, which together form a framework for comprehending the Divine. Several Qur'ānic verses urge one to reflect:

(i) 'And among His wonders is this: He creates for you mates out of your own kind. So that you might incline towards them, and He engenders love and tenderness between you: in this, behold, there are signs indeed for people who reflect!' (Qur'ān, al-Rum, 30:21);
(ii) 'Do they not contemplate within themselves? Allah has not created the heavens and the earth and all that is between them except in truth and for a term appointed. But truly many of mankind are disbelievers in the meeting of their Lord.' (Qur'ān, Rum, 30:8)
(iii) 'And He has made the night and the day and the sun and the moon subservient (to His laws, so that they be of use) to you; and all the stars are subservient to His command: in this, behold, there are messages indeed for people who use their reason!' (Qur'ān, al-Ankabut, 29:20).

In the above light, we can point out that meditation within Islam includes two key dimensions, where it is discursive, with reflection and focus on words and deeds, and non-discursive in terms of its silent prayers and silent remembrance (*dhikr*), where the focus is on observing God, who is formless and being mindful of His overarching presence. This discussion is taken up again in our next chapter on wellbeing and the worshipper.

Ibn 'Arabi discusses four transformative pillars (see Table 2.5) (Ibn 'Arabi 2008): silence, seclusion, hunger, and vigilance, which in effect are all stillness practices. These four transformative pillars are comprehended by the aspirant and by the one who is more advanced in knowledge, called the verifier, according to their own states (ḥāl) and stations (maqām) of consciousness, and also in reference to a particular domain of divine knowledge (*ma'rifa*).

Regarding silence (*samt*) and seclusion (*uzla*), Abu Hurayrah narrates that the Prophet said, 'Whoever believes in God and the Last Day, let him say what is good, or let him be silent' (Abu-l-Qasim 2002). Similarly, Imam Qushayri says silence is security but points out that it is, concurrently, important to command what is good and forbid evil although one needs to be silent in the presence of God (Abu-l-Qasim 2002). Shakyh Ibn 'Arabi (Ibn 'Arabi 2008) and Imam Qushayri (Abu-l-Qasim 2002) articulate two types of silence, namely, the outer and the inner. The

2.3 Contemplative Framework and Practices: An Islamic Perspective

first is the silence of the tongue, where one does not speak except about God, while the silence of the heart is where one refrains from any thoughts about created things. In the first case, the burden of the person is lightened, while the latter is a speaker of wisdom. When both the tongue and the heart are silent then one's innermost consciousness (*sirr*) becomes apparent and the Lord gets closer to the person (Ibn 'Arabi 2008).

Seclusion is linked with silence, given that when one withdraws from human company then silence sets in. Seclusion can be categorised firstly, as physical seclusion from others and this belongs to the aspirant (*murid*). The second type is having no attachment to created things in one's heart and this is of the verifier (*muhaqqiq*), which comes from deep contemplation. This is called witnessing or '*mushāhada*', 'what the heart retains of the form of the One contemplated'. Ibn 'Arabi states that if this is done on a sustained basis, it can lead to grasping the mysteries of Divine Unity (*wahdaniyya*), where it brings the quality of Uniqueness (*ahadiyya*), as outlined in the Table 2.5. As he says, seclusion bequeaths knowledge of this world (Ibn 'Arabi 2008).

Imam Qushayri outlines a distinguishing factor between seclusion (*uzla*) and retreat (*khalwa*), where *uzla* refers to detaching from humankind, while khalwa is gaining intimacy with God (Abu-l-Qasim 2002). Imam Qushayri points out that seclusion is not mere physical isolation but separating blameworthy qualities and replacing them with thoughts of the Divine, whilst still being amongst people. This type of seclusion, which is a Prophetic practice has been adopted by various Islamic orders, with different types of focus, some on teaching and learning, while others more on the remembrance of God (*dhikr*), while observing acts of prayers and fasting.

Based on my experience there are only a handful of Orders that practice the silent remembrance and deep type of meditation (*murāqaba*) and these are largely within the Sufi Orders. These streams of practice, which cultivate silence and meditative practices have been somewhat diffused over time, with undue emphasis on the outer than inner practices. These types of inner practices have the potential to change human behaviour and bring about peace and contentment as some neuro-scientific data seems to indicate, while empirically inner insights have been experienced and known by the seekers of the spiritual paths.

Regarding hunger (*ju'*) and vigilance (*sahar*), these two are linked, since hunger leads to vigilance (Ibn 'Arabi 2008). Ibn 'Arabi distinguishes hunger not necessarily as an empty belly but a longing for something, while vigilance means being awake or refraining from something, but on a deeper level having perpetuity. Imam Qushayri (Abu-l-Qasim 2002) uses the term '*murāqaba*' instead of '*sahar*' to mean a state of witnessing or watchfulness of God's presence, but they essentially have the same meaning. Imam Qushayri adds that preservation of this knowledge of the consummate awareness of God is essential in cultivating it and forms the foundation of good action. This, he says, cannot be accomplished unless one empties oneself through a process of self-observation and inner accounting (*muhasaba*). One sees that this has resonance to what is now called mindfulness and concentration meditation.

Table 2.5 Four pillars of knowledge

The four pillars (*arkan*)	Spiritual states		Spiritual stations and secrets (*at / asrar*)	Domains of knowledge (*ma'ārifa*)
	For the aspirant (*murid / salik*)	For the verifier (*muhaqqiq / muqarrab*)		
Silence (*Samt*)	Safety from harm	Intimate conversation	Inspiration (*wahy*)	God (Allah)
Seclusion (*Uzla*)	Transcendent of all attributes		Divine unity (*wahdaniyya*) & Uniqueness (quality) (*ahadiyya*)	This world (*dunya*)
Hunger (*Ju'*)	Humility, submission, servility, lack of self-importance, calm, indigence, absence of base thoughts	Delicacy of feeling, serenity, intimacy, non-worldliness, transcendence of ordinary humanness	Eternal self-subsistence (*samadaniyya*)	Satan (*shaytan*)
Vigilance (*Sahar*)	Cultivating the moment	Cultivating the moment, assuming lordly attributes	Everlasting self-existence (*qayyamiyya*)	The self (*nafs*)

Ibn 'Arabi (2008) says that there are two forms of hunger: firstly, voluntary hunger, which is that of the seekers and secondly, obligatory (involuntary) hunger, which is that of the verifiers or more advanced students of knowledge. Hunger has spiritual states and stations; for the seeker it includes humility, submission, indigence, discretion, tranquil emotions and an absence of base thoughts, and for the verifiers it is characterised by delicacy of feelings, serenity, intimacy (with God), disappearance of worldliness and transcendence of ordinary human characteristics through the Lord. The last, says Ibn 'Arabi, represents the station of eternal self-subsistence (*al-samadani*), where the Lord provides openings for the verifiers. He says, 'Hunger bequeaths the knowledge of Satan, may God preserve us and you from him'.

Ibn 'Arabi (2008) says, 'Vigilance is the fruit of hunger, for an empty stomach drives away sleep'. As in the case of hunger, vigilance also has two types. The first is the eye's vigil, which aims to maintain the spiritual intention in the heart aimed at pursuing the quest. Secondly, the vigil of the heart is the state of awakening from the state of forgetfulness and seeking contemplation. 'Vigilance bequeaths knowledge of the self', says Ibn 'Arabi.

(2) With regard to **Generative Practices**, the intent here is to forge a platform for evoking common thoughts and feelings through acts of devotion and prayers. The congregational prayers (which are highly valued and firmly encouraged)

are where the loud recitation from the Qur'ān forms a point of focus for three out of the five ritual obligatory prayers. The weekly Friday sermon forms an established generative practice largely focusing on the current social and cultural issues of society that need to be addressed. The collective recitation of peace on the Prophet and loud *dhikr* (remembrance of God) offers a devotional platform for generating energy and forging solidarity.

(3) **Creative Process Practices**: As with other traditions, the art and architecture of Islam has been heavily influenced by the religion: however, they differ from most others in that traditionally, figurative art has been excluded. Rather, the creative process focuses on the beauty of God's creation through geometry and floral forms inspired by nature. The repetitive geometric shapes and symmetry that have become a hallmark of Islamic art and architecture, with their aesthetic sense and tranquillity, provide the ambience for the mind to be oriented towards the infinite. In this sense, it manifests beauty with its three essential elements, namely, symmetry, proportion and harmony. Poetry and prose have formed a rich tradition within Islam within both the Arab and Persian regions; more specifically the mystical tradition, expressed through the likes of Jalaluddin Rumi, Omar Khayyam, Ghalib, Firdows, Hafiz, Ibn 'Arabi and others who have used the medium to create awareness of and orient people's minds towards God. They speak of the connection between man and God and create a longing in the hearts of man to draw closer to their Creator.

(4) **Relational Practices**: these Islamic traditional practices include the relationship between a sheikh or spiritual teacher (*murshid*) and a seeker (*murid*) and this takes the forms of dialogue, mentoring, and spiritual guidance. This is generally linked to conduct within the confines of the *Sharī'a* and more specifically the development of the inward state or the self. This practice of *tasawwuf*, is a science of self-development within Islam, that although it has been preserved within some societies, it unfortunately has been lost in others.

(5) **Activist Practices**: This largely covers those actions done outwardly that benefit oneself and others, including service to others and protests for justice. Service to others forms a core part of Islam, both in the context of helping those in need and benefiting them (*sadaqa* or voluntary giving and *zakah* or obligatory giving); this enables one to overcome one's selfishness and rise above one's ego, a goal which is central to Islam.

(6) **Ritualistic or Cyclic Practices**: This essentially comprises the five pillars of Islam, including declaration of faith (shahada); performing the obligatory prayers (*salah*); giving obligatory charity (*zakah*); fasting and performing pilgrimage (*hajj*) if one can afford it. Given that the shahada has already been discussed, the other four pillars will be outlined here.

Prayer (*salah*): The ritual prayer, which is performed five times a day, was a command given to the Prophet in his meeting with God in the seventh heaven, highlighting its importance as a pivotal aspect of faith. When one examines it in the light of the Tree of Contemplative Practices, one can identify the following characteristics. It is a stillness practice since the majority of the prayer is undertaken in silent contemplation. The Prophet used to be silent during the first part of the ritual prayer. When asked about his silence, he replied that he used it for supplication as follows: 'O Allah, remove my sins from me as far as You have removed the East from the West. O Allah, purify me from sins as a white garment is purified from filth. O Allah, wash away my sins with water, snow and hail' (Maqsood 1998). One of the most recommended voluntary acts is the '*tahajjud*' prayer, as God says, 'And rise from thy sleep during part of the night (as well) as a free offering from thee' (Qur'ān, al-Isra ,17:79). The above prayer is performed during the last third of the night, the most still period of the day. As Rabia Al-Adawiyya said, 'Oh Lord: The Stars are shining, and the eyes of man are closed and kings have shut their doors and every lover is alone with his beloved and here am I alone with Thee'. (Knysh 2010).

General vigilance needs to be observed throughout the prayer's rhythmic movement for excessive movement nullifies the prayer. This realises the principle of 'the still body instils a still mind'. The ritual prayer, in effect, represents movement meditation with set patterns and contemplative focus:

(i) Generative practice: Congregational prayers are a platform for people to get together, this is strongly encouraged as a basis for solidarity as well as spiritual cohesion. A narration of the Prophet supports this, 'A faithful believer to another faithful believer are like bricks in a wall, supporting each other. While (saying this) he clasped his hand and interlaced his fingers'. (Bukhari quoted in Maqsood 1998).

(ii) Activist practice: There are many voluntary or supererogatory prayers which are done as additional spiritual activities. These are important in their own sense since the five daily prayers are done out of a sense of obligation, with the understanding that they are a duty which must be performed, while voluntary prayers are done out of love for God.

Schuon (1998) captures the canonical prayer as a centrepiece when he says, 'The prayer integrates man into the rhythm of universe adoration and—through the ritual orientation of the prayer towards the *Ka'ba*—into its centripetal order'. This movement of prayer then gives it a unified global force of worship of God both in space and time, connecting people from all walks of life and forms a repetitive cycle across the variations in time between countries.

While ritual prayers can be called movement meditation, which includes the synchronisation of both physical and mental coordinates, one observes that it can become mechanistic, when it is performed perfunctorily. If this is done, then it loses its meaning and effects since the consciousness is absent from the individual. This is one of the issues that does not allow a deeper level of meditation and connection to one's inner self and the divine. Perhaps this may also be a reason why prayers do not necessarily have an impact on the person who is performing them.

'*Zakah*': This is an important facet of Islam, which not only entails obligatory sharing a defined portion of your wealth, but more crucially parting with your desire to retain it. Schuon points out that 'the alms (*zakah* or obligatory and *sadaqa* or voluntary act) vanquish egoism and avarice and actualise the solidarity of all creatures, for alms are a fasting of the soul, even as the obligatory fast (Ramadan) is an almsgiving of the body' (Schuon 2006). He further adds that 'almsgiving is detachment with regards to the world'. Imam Ghazāli (1995) as stated below says that *zakah* is the 'purification of properties' and it has three main causes for being a pillar of Islam: (i) Appreciating the Oneness of God and abiding with His decree and that 'Promise reaches perfection when a Unitarian has got no object of love except the One'.; (ii) Miserliness is the trigger to destruction, as the Prophet says, "There are three destructive guilts - to obey miserliness, to follow lower desires and self-conceit. The Lord says 'those who are saved from miserliness have attained salvation' given that it purifies the self and one's material possessions"; (iii) Expressing gratitude for the gifts of God, which are innumerable and range from one's body and mind to all of the material and non-material things.

Fasting: This consists of fasts both during Ramadan as well as voluntary fasts. Imam Ghazāli (1995) states, 'Fasting is half of patience and patience is half of faith'. Fasting is one of the unique acts of worship which is hidden from people, where one does not necessarily see the other doing it. Therefore, there is no inherent *'riya'* or ostentation in it, as the Lord says, 'Every good action will be rewarded from ten to seven hundred-fold but the fast is for My sake and it is I who will reward him for it'. The Prophet said, 'Everything has got a gateway and the gateway of worship is fasting' and 'the devil runs through the human body like the circulation of blood; curb it with hunger'. Schuon (2006) asserts that 'Fasting is detachment with regards to desire, hence with regards to ego' and 'Fasting cuts man off the continual and devouring flux of carnal life, introducing into the flesh a kind of death and purification'. Similarly, Ibn 'Arabi (2008) emphasises that eating to satisfaction tends to provide more energy to the limbs, which causes it to commit a string of actions, taking one away from the main aim and intention of worshipping God.

Hajj: This is an obligatory act, if one can afford it. Schuon (2006) says, 'The pilgrimage is the return to the Centre, the Heart, the Self', while adding, "The Pilgrimage is a prefiguration of the inward journey towards the '*Ka'ba*' of the heart and purifies the community, just as the circulation of the blood, passing through the heart, purifies the body" (Schuon 1998).

(7) **Movement Practices**: In Buddhism, movement meditation is part of the various forms of meditation and it is taught to monks and laypersons alike, one example of which is the walking meditation. In Islam, there is little conscious teaching of it in the present day, even though meditation forms the very core of Islam. Being mindful of what one is doing, as well as saying prayers or uttering God's remembrance at all times are fundamental to the Islamic way of life. One of the best examples in Islam of movement meditation is the ritual prayer, where one is intended to be fully observant of oneself and the presence of the Lord. The Lord says, 'Worship me sitting, standing and sleeping' (Qur'ān, al-Nisa, 4:103). Presence of mind in prayers and daily living infiltrates every aspect of the life of a Muslim and this awareness of God is the cornerstone of worship. Thus, consciousness of God is the central theme and it should be a part of bodily movements, which then brings about focus and tends to reduce the chatter of the mind.

2.3.5 The Direction and Impact of Contemplative Practices

There are two distinct benefits derived from contemplative practices. The first is the emerging data from neuro-science on the positive effects of spiritual practices (Goleman 1991), ranging from ritual prayers to remembering God or meditation (*dhikr*) to fasting. From a scientific perspective, whose scientific data sets are from various religions and more recently from practices within Islam (Afifi 1997, Ibrahim et al. 2008, Ibrahim and Ahmad 2013, Doufesh et al. 2012); all point to physiological and psychological changes that lead to a sense of wellbeing. Secondly, the experiential data generated from individuals' experiences of these spiritual practices and their sense of well-being and meaning generated by these practices. Here, we touch only upon the former, while focusing on the spiritual impact of these practices and their frame of reference. Suffice to say that there is a whole framework within Islam called '*tasawwuf*', or 'inward science', which has a wealth of theory and perhaps limited groups of practitioners in regard to the global Muslim population.

Here only some essential aspects are drawn upon to give a snapshot of its framework for developing the self. Contemplative practices are generated through obligatory acts of worship, voluntary acts of love and seeking closeness to Him. God essentially does not benefit from our worship, but it is our prescription for developing ourselves and overcoming our inherent and acquired weaknesses. In the light of this, seven stages have been conceptualised by the Sages, with references from the Qur'ān, as represented in Fig. 2.2. These practices are generally done under a Sheikh or Master, who not only teaches how it is to be done but also observes the students (*murids*) and guides them through a combination of demonstration, lectures, one-to-one counselling, spiritual guidance and techniques of reflection and non-formal education. This type of learning is what can be termed as experiential learning, which is validated through a series of dialogues and observations both by the Sheikh and his/her peers. As the case study in Chap. 5 documents and elaborate, these practices are transformational in nature and can lead to a contended life for the seekers.

2.3.6 Discussion

The terms 'contemplation' and 'meditation' have generally been used interchangeably to mean the same thing. The dictionary defines contemplation as the act of contemplating; thoughtful observation or full or deep consideration; reflection; religious contemplation. Meditation means the act of meditating, continued or extended thought; reflection; contemplation; transcendental meditation, devout religious contemplation or spiritual introspection. As defined above, there is hardly a difference between these two terms.

2.3 Contemplative Framework and Practices: An Islamic Perspective

Within Islamic thought, the Qur'ān frequently refers to contemplation of the signs of God both within oneself and externally. While in Islamic literature itself the words 'contemplation' and 'meditation' have been used interchangeably, a distinction can be drawn. Contemplation refers to being mindful and reflecting (*tafakkur*) on the signs and attributes of God, as well as recollection (*thakur*) of them. Meditation (*murāqaba*), meanwhile, has a deeper sense, meaning movement from the stage of contemplation to absorption, where one tries to witness God (*mushāhada*) or, failing that, that God sees him (*murāqaba*). There are numerous groups within Islam with their own methods of remembrance of God; this can take many forms, depending on the group, from loud pronouncements to one where silence is used either by itself or by using one's breath as a point of attention as in the spiritual order, the Naqshbandiyyah *ṭarīqa* (path) method. This process is accompanied by emptying the mind of everything other than God leading to a state of absorption in Him, as done by the Prophet during his retreats at Mount Hira for 13 years, prior to receiving Prophethood. Imam Shadhili, the first Sheikh of the Shadhili spiritual order (*ṭarīqa*) best captures the essence of this when he says:

> You who wander in deserts away from your own consciousness, come back to yourself to find all existence summed up in you. You are the way and reality of perfection. One in whom the great consciousness of God dwells (Jurji 1938).

Every act is an act of worship done in a state of witnessing the Presence of God, and this is the most recommended of states, in line with the Qur'ānic injunction, 'Worship me sitting, standing and sleeping' (Qur'ān, al Imran, 3:191). In order to deepen one's consciousness of God, several methods have been outlined including rigorous training and meditative practices with their inherent disciplines of hunger, vigilance, silence, and seclusion.

In this light, there is a difference between the Islamic and Ignatian (Catholic) traditions of the word 'meditation'. The Ignatian understanding of contemplation is rooted in the imagination of God and in this sense is more cognitive. In the Islamic context, meditation is a state of absorption (*khushu*), while contemplation is focusing on an attribute of God, which ideally should not conjure images since He is formless and shapeless; the emphasis in both cases is more on the heart than on a cognitive process. This can be best explained by the categorisation of meditation into non-discursive - silent remembrance and prayers versus the discursive, where one focuses on the repetition of the names of God and loud prayers, which can involve a series of images (see Sect. 2.4). The similarity between the two traditions is the focus on God, even though the point of divergence is the concept of the Trinity within the former context.

In the Buddhist tradition, meditation essentially refers to quietening the mind through following the flow of the breath (*anabaena sati*) with deep reflection on oneself or a process of introspection (*vippasana*), that is, observing oneself without being judgmental or evaluating one's thoughts. Both aspects are a part of Islam in terms of quietening one's mind. However, Buddhism gives an orientation that is completely different. In Buddhism there is no concept of God the Creator as such and the focus is not on a Supreme Being but on the self (Goleman 1990), whereas in

Islam one must be mindful of God witnessing, reflecting on the signs of God, being introspective, where if one was to receive Divine Grace, experience an opening of divine manifestations (*tajalliyat illahiyyah*). In our normal realm of life, the latter is generally confined to the Prophets and the special category of people who are deemed close to God.

Why contemplate or meditate? The fundamental reason for contemplative practice is that it helps one to become fully aware of oneself and one's behaviour towards others and God. Thus, there are clear profits to be derived from contemplation and meditation. This is well articulated in the Qur'ān where the Lord says, 'Consider the human self, and how it is formed in accordance with what it is meant to be, and how it is imbued with moral failings as well as with consciousness of God. To a happy state shall indeed attain he who causes this (self) to grow in purity, and truly lost is he who buries it (in darkness)' (Qur'ān, al-Shams, 91:7-10). Asad commenting on these verses points out that, firstly, the concept of self means not only the physical aspect but also the whole being with its essence of life. Secondly, he points out the concept of moral free will, whereby man can choose to rise to great heights of consciousness (*taqwa*) or to debase himself and become lowly (*fujur*).

Likewise, Ibn 'Arabi articulates four pillars of spiritual transformation paired together: hunger-vigilance and silence-seclusion. These are aimed at overcoming the lower, base desires and transforming the self into spiritual actualisation. Hunger allows one to curb the desire (*nafs*). The desire for food frequently leads one to overeat, with negative implications in the long term. Fasting is seen to bring about a state of heightened awareness, which aids spiritual activities and brings about a state of vigilance apart from being a route to detox one's body. Vigilance is congruent with meditation and with the modern-day use of the term mindfulness. Silence refers to both that of the tongue and, more importantly, to the silence of the heart, when the focus of thought is none other than God. Seclusion is the silence of the heart, this includes not only physical seclusion from people but also the higher state which means being amidst the crowd but at the same time being fully mindful of the Lord, in other words, being present while being absent or attached to the world.

These above four are enablers as articulated by Ibn 'Arabi; they empower the seeker to 'tame the beast' or lower base desires, as Imam Muḥāsibi articulates, and move upwards into the seven levels of consciousness (Fig. 2.2). Within an Islamic perspective, the effort is very important but taken alone it is insufficient to make spiritual progress. In this sense, the Prophet refers to two concepts, namely, trust in God (*tawakkul*), where one exerts effort and then puts trust in God, and God's mercy (*raḥma*), the light that shines on the heart to liberate it.

The Tree of Contemplative Practices indicates the wide repertoire available within Islam of practices that fit into the seven categories shown in Fig. 2.8 The five pillars are subsumed within ritualistic practices, while the voluntary practices, born out of love and/or fear, constitute the other categories. As is evident, there are a plethora of practices ranging from activist, relation and generative rituals, to stillness and creative practices. Although the ritualistic practices are obligatory, acceleration of spiritual progression generally occurs in those who involve themselves in voluntary practices. There is special reference and attention given to stillness practices within Islam and this is supported both by the divine scriptures and the words and actions of the Prophet.

The Qur'ān tells us, 'Worship me in silence and in awe in the morn and in the night' (Qur'ān, āl Imran 3:41). In this light, the essence of Islam is having the consciousness of God in whatever one does, hence being in a state of meditative awareness and living. As already noted when habituation sets in or prayers become mechanistic, one tends to lose the focus on oneself and have difficulty connection with God since it requires a presence of one's mind and heart.

The most critical factor is the role of the teacher or the spiritual master, who has attained a certain level of self-actualisation and who is able to both teach and guide the seekers (*murids*). There are still traditional organisations where types of experimental learning take place, but most of which do not necessarily promote themselves. There has been critiques of sheikhs or exemplars of the spiritual orders because of the veneration given to them by the seekers who follow their path which in some cases falls to excess. While this is a valid point, I would point out three key aspects. Firstly, there still exists sheikhs who are sincere and genuine in their deliberation and are able to guide seekers. In this case, one can use the benchmarks that has been developed to find a sheikh who is sound (see Chap. 5). Secondly, it is a tested pathway, where one can derive several benefits as the case study in Chap. 5 has demonstrated. Thirdly, before one critiques and is blinded by labels, it is appropriate to join an order and then experience it oneself, so long as one is able to find a sheikh who possess the right characteristics.

Given the context of modern society, where people have high levels of anxiety, stress, violence, and diseases associated with disorders, these types of spiritual practices could be integrated into their daily lives in order to mitigate them. There is a need to adopt the format, tools and methods of learning that have beneficial neurological effects, which impact the well-being of individuals and groups undergoing such learning. These practices not only have an impact on their wellbeing but also enhance their character under the tutelage of a sheikh or master. This, then, forms the inward sciences of Islam, which aim to develop the whole individual similar to other esoteric traditions in other faiths.

2.4 Wellbeing and the Worshiper: A Neuroscience and Islamic Perspective[4]

A growing body of scientific data indicates that meditation in the long-term results in changes to the brain structure, a concept termed neuroplasticity. This has led to

---

[4] An earlier version of this article was published under the title Wellbeing and the Worshipper: A Scientific Perspective of Selected Contemplative Practices in Islam in the academic Journal Humanomics, Vol. 33, Issue 2, 2017, pages 163–188, Emerald Publishing Limited. This was co-authored by Dr. Hannah Safiullah Munsoor.

contemplative practices like meditation, prayers and fasting being studied within the context of 'human physiology, and a kind of pan-human technology of human spiritual development' (Andresen 2002). Within the Islamic framework, *salah*, *dhikr* (meditation) and fasting were found to be beneficial for both the body and mind. However, as compared to the Buddhist and Hindu tradition, there has been comparatively little research into Islamic contemplative practices. Hence, there is a dire need to carry out further research where the focus tends to be on the inner than necessarily on the outward aspects of Islam.

2.4.1 Introduction to Neuropsychology, Religious and Spiritual Experiences

This section deals with some key terms and definitions relating to this research. It further outlines brain structures and functions which is related to understanding the nature of contemplative practices and spiritual experiences.

Contemplative Practices There are many categories of contemplative practices within Islam, as depicted by the Tree of Contemplative Practices from the Society of Contemplative Mind (Fig. 2.8); for the sake of this discussion, however, only meditation (from stillness practice) and prayer (from ritualistic practice) will be defined. Andresen (2000) points out that carving out a working definition of meditation poses the danger of limiting this complex phenomenon and overlooking the subtleties involved in the process. Similarly, prayer eludes a precise definition, given that it is a subjective experience. Taking this into consideration, Andresen and Smith provide a framework to distinguish these practices, presented in the Table 2.6.

Mindfulness and Spirituality Mindfulness meditation can be categorised as a non-discursive meditative practice where the focus is on the breath while thoughts are observed without evaluating them. In its broadest sense, the purpose of meditation from a spiritual perspective, be it Eastern or Western, should be to rise above one's limited self. Wilber (2011) presents a comprehensive definition of spirituality; having four dimensions, each with its own truth, that when taken together form a whole: (i) involves peak experiences or altered states with varying time spans and is not dependent on age or stage; (ii) represents the highest levels; (iii) is a separate development pathway; (iv) is an attitude signifying the states of openness, trust and love. Wilber sums up by stating that true spirituality is a change in the levels of consciousness, which can be either temporary or permanent. From an Islamic viewpoint, spirituality involves the changing levels of consciousness, which are states of spiritual development that are articulated by some scholars and directly referenced in the Qur'ān. From the perspective of spiritual orders, this change occurring within one's self and in one's behaviour towards the self and others is experientially known, and this forms the basis of sustaining these practices. This thesis demonstrates this transformation through the investigation which has resulted

2.4 Wellbeing and the Worshiper: A Neuroscience and Islamic Perspective

Table 2.6 Definition of meditation and prayer

Method	Characteristics	Type of meditation
Discursive Meditation	Recitative: e.g., invocations and homage to deities Gestural: as in ritual gesture and movement in groups Mental: guided contemplation and confession of sins	Prayer: mental states that entertain thoughts/objects serially. The mind focuses on a series of thoughts and images
Non-Discursive Meditation	Recitative: mantra practice, Jesus prayer and Muslim prayer (*salah*); recitation of the Scriptures (Qur'ān, Bible, Torah) and remembrance of God (*dhikr*) Gestural: Mudra practice or religious dance Mental: Single pointed meditation	Meditation: mental states that entertain a single thought/object serially. Characterised by the mind being focused upon a single object without voluntary discussion or involuntary distraction towards the objects

in the case study presented in Chap. 5 of the Naqshabandiyyah Khalidiyyah spiritual Order (*ṭarīqa*).

Basic Brain Neurobiology and Structures in Relation to Contemplative Practices The most important brain region linked to spiritual experience is the limbic system, which is composed of the hypothalamus, amygdala, hippocampus, and the frontal lobe. Some of the limbic system's key functions vis-à-vis contemplative practices are outlined below: (i) The limbic system is reported to play a crucial role in spiritual and religious experiences (d'Aquili and Newberg 2000; Saver & Rabin 1997) (ii) The amygdala controls and modulates higher order emotion and motivational functions, specifically relating to arousal and fear (Morris et al. 1996; d'Aquili and Newberg 2000), while also being involved in attention, learning and memory; (iii) The hippocampus plays a major role in information processing, including new memory, new learning, cognitive mapping of new environments and focusing attention. The hippocampus inhibits the transfer of information between the brain regions (d'Aquili and Newberg 2000); (iv) The inter-connection between the amygdala, the hypothalamus and the hippocampus, with their various roles of controlling emotions and inhibiting the transfer of information, is deemed to be important in generating religious and spiritual experiences (d'Aquili and Newberg 2000).

Spiritual Psychology and Islamic Psychology Given that spirituality has a clear impact on our physiological and psychological wellbeing, how does it relate to our mental state? Hussain (2000) defines spiritual psychology as a unified field with the following aspects: (i) it links body, mind, heart and spirit; and (ii) it establishes the relationship between theory and practice. In order to elucidate this definition, Hussain draws a contrast with cognitive psychology, which deals with empirical research on human mental life or processes and spiritual psychology, which emphasises the self and its development. Spiritual psychology forms a significant part of the Islamic framework; some key areas are discussed below.

Originating from the time of the Prophet Muhammad, there was formulated within Islam the inner science of *tasawwuf*. This is supported by numerous Qur'ānic citations and prophetic narrations that discuss the self; a hallmark divine writ being, '... to a happy state shall indeed attain he who causes this (self) to grow in purity, and truly lost is he who buries it (in darkness)' (Qur'ān, 91:9-10). It is important to note the inference of this verse, denoting the intention and effort required for the seekers to grow. Unfortunately, this emphasis on this inner development aspects in Islam has withered over time and needs to be rekindled.

There are also numerous works by traditional Islamic scholars that deal with Islamic psychology in some depth, notably the writings of Imam 'Abdullah Anṣāri (2010), Imam Ghazāli (1995), Ibn 'Arabi (2008), Imam ibn Qayyim al-Jawziyya (2006), Sheikh 'Abd al Qāder al-Jīlāni (1977), Ibn Hazm al-Andalusi (1998) and Imam Sidi ibn Zarrūk (2001), to name a few.

Experiential and Experimental Research Goleman (1990), a psychologist who also spent time as a monk, in discussing the Tibetan and Western models of mental health, points out that he 'was astounded to find that cradled within every great religious tradition there is a psychological system, the esoteric part of the religion'. As Goleman highlights, to overcome these negative traits is to retrain both the attention (through prayers, meditation) and the perceptual habits (through seeking repentance, supplication, forgiving others and oneself, mirroring of one's habits, sitting in the company of those who have changed) aimed at transforming oneself. To this day, this inner science forms the foundations of certain Islamic movements and organizations and manifest in various parts of the world.

Experimental Research Evidence: Hindu and Buddhist Perspectives, Including the Relaxation Response Outlined below is experimental evidence resulting from well-documented Eastern contemplative traditions that can be summarized as follows:

(i) There are many different types of meditation, from Yoga and Transcendental Meditation (Hinduism) to Mindfulness, Tantric Meditation (Buddhism and Yoga) and the relaxation response, which has also been derived from these traditional spiritual practices.
(ii) All of these meditative practices have been observed to produce benefits for the body and mind, even though the effects on physiology and psychology differ from one to another.
(iii) The spectrum of physiological benefits ranges from lower cholesterol, hypertension and heart rate (both systolic and diastolic) to the activation of the autonomous system, with increased alpha and theta brain waves.

(iv) There is, however, a need for longitudinal studies of specific types of meditation in order to confirm their respective specific effects on the mind and body.

There have been numerous benefits as evident from a systematic review of current evidence on Buddhist Vipassana meditation (also called *mindfulness meditation), wherein Alberto Chiesa included controlled and cross-sectional studies (Austin, J.A 1997 in J. Andresen (2000) (see Table 2.7). There were neuroplasticity or structural changes found in the brains of people who meditate as follows:

(i) Strong activation in the rostral anterior cingulate cortex (plays a role in regulating blood pressure and heart rate and certain higher level functions such as attention allocation, reward anticipation, decision-making etc.), as well as in the prefrontal cortex (plays a role in executive functions—focusing attention, planning, predicting, coordinating and adjusting complex behaviours etc.) of the brain.
(ii) The following areas were thicker in the meditators compared to the controls: regions associated with attention, interception and sensory processing, including the prefrontal cortex and the right anterior insula (maintains attention and focus, sustains task performance, detects salient events and coordinates with other parts of the brain etc.)
(iii) Greater levels of grey matter concentration were found in the right anterior insula, as well as in the left inferior temporal gyrus (involved in processing visual stimuli relating to form and colour, memory and its recall, perceptual and spatial awareness etc.) and right hippocampus (helps to process and retrieve memories, conversion of short-term to long-term memories, etc.).

In light of the above, the psychological changes observed were as follows: a decrease in alcohol-related problems and psychiatric symptoms as well as positive psychosocial outcomes, a significant decrease in the avoidance of negative thoughts as compared to controls, more mature defense mechanisms and coping strategies accompanied by greater levels of maturity and better tolerance of common stressors.

The Impact of Islamic Contemplative Practices on Mind and Body At present, research on Islamic contemplative practices has just skimmed the surface. The sections below outline key experimental research into Islamic contemplative practices of ritual prayer, meditation and fasting in the context of well-being and health implications, with special focus on neuroscientific findings.

Ritual Prayer (Salah) The Islamic ritual prayer (see Fig. 2.9) has been shown to have beneficial effects on the physical and mental aspects of human physiology, such as that by Ibrahim et al. (2008). The most comprehensive investigation on Islamic ritual prayer or Salah from a physiological and neuroscientific standpoint was carried out at the University of Malaya by Ibrahim et al. (2008). Here, the implications of ritual prayer on the body and brain were examined.

Table 2.7 Experimental evidence from various forms of contemplative practices

Method	Types	Experimental results	Relevant references
Buddhist meditation	Mindfulness-based meditation	(i) Reduces stress	(i), (ii) and (iii) Astin, J.A 1997 in J. Andresen (2000)
		(i) Helps prevent relapse in the case of affective (mood) disorders (depression, bipolar disorder and anxiety disorder).	(iv) Kabat-Zinn, J, Lipworth 1982 in J. Andresen (2000)
		(iii) Reduces overall symptomology, increases domain-specific sense of control in practitioners' lives & scores highly in terms of spiritual exposure	
		(iv) Controls chronic pain	
The relaxation response	Bio-feedback & Self-regulation	(i) Alleviates negative states associated with heart disease, hypertension, stress, behavioural coping and substance abuse	(i) Bradley & McCanne 1981; Engel 1997.
		(ii) Reduces blood pressure levels significantly.	(ii) Benson et al., 1971 in J. Andresen (2000)
		(iii) Treats hypertension and cardiovascular diseases	(iii) Benson & Alexander & Feldman, 1975; in J. Andresen (2000)
Yoga	meditation & bio-feedback	(i) Reduces heart rate and blood pressure.	(i) Benson, Rosner & Marzetta, 1973 in J. Andresen (2000)

2.4 Wellbeing and the Worshiper: A Neuroscience and Islamic Perspective

Transcendental meditation	Progressive muscular relaxation	(i) Lowers systolic & diastolic blood pressure. (ii) Significantly improves exercise tolerance. (iii) Reduces exercise-induced myocardial ischemia in patients with known coronary artery diseases.	(i) Kinsman, R.A & Staudenmayer, H. 1978 in J. Andresen (2000) (ii) Zamarra et al, 1996 in J. Andresen (2000) (iii) J.W. Schneiden, R.H. Besseghini, T. Robinson, D.K & Saferno, J.W (1996)
Yoga	Hindu Tantric Meditation	(i) Increases autonomic activation. (ii) Increases alpha and theta power. (iii) Shows minimal evidence of EEG-defined sleep (iv) Decreases autonomic orientation to external stimuli.	(i), (ii), (iii), (iv) Corby, J.C 1978 in J. Andresen (2000)

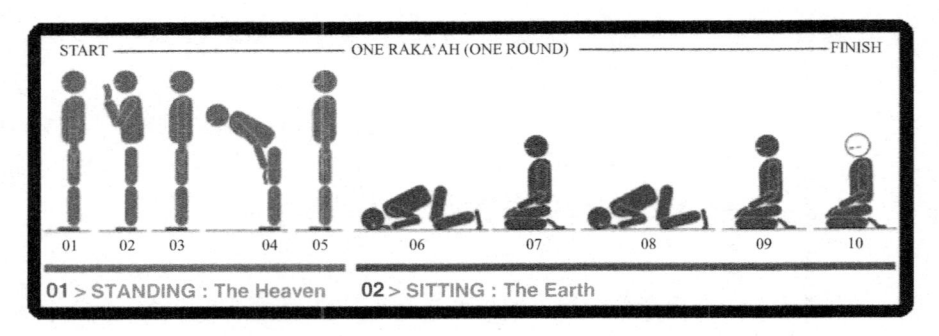

Fig. 2.9 The order of sequence during Salah (Piet 2011)

Salah and Body Composition In investigating the impact of one prayer on body composition, bio-impedance analysis—BIA[5] (Khalil et al. 2014) readings were used as a health indicator and taken before and after prayer of 47 Muslim students. Individuals satisfying all pre-stipulated essential conditions of prayer compared to their counterparts demonstrated: (1) higher phase angles, signifying larger quantities of intact body cells and membranes, (2) higher body capacitance, signifying the ability of cells to store energy, and (3) a lower body resistance value, an indicator of good blood vessel elasticity (Biodynamics Corporation 2014). Thus, individuals who satisfied all conditions of prayer had better body compositions compared to their counterparts.

Ibrahim et al. also examined the impact of the ritual praying five times a day on body composition. Findings indicated that participants, who performed all five prayers, compared to counterparts who did not, demonstrated higher phase angles, body capacitance values, basal metabolic rates and body cell mass. This indicates that individuals observing prayers regularly had a healthier body composition overall. Furthermore, being able to fully comprehend the meaning of recitation during prayer was shown to provide an added advantage to body composition compared to those with little to moderate understanding. Specifically, individuals able to fully comprehend the meaning of recitations showed a higher phase angle, body capacitance and total intracellular reading (an indicator of blood flow efficiency).

This above study noted that praying in congregation as opposed to individually was also demonstrated to produce a healthier body composition, with higher phase angles, body capacitance and lower body resistance levels. The act of bodily contact during congregational worship is thought to be responsible for the improved composition, since it allows for electrical signals to flow from one individual to the next.

---

[5]BIA is a noninvasive, low cost and a commonly used approach for body composition measurements and assessment of clinical conditions. It includes a variety of methods: the frequency based, the allocation based, bioimpedence vector analysis and the real time bioimpedance analysis system.

Ibrahim et al. further investigated the impact of *taraweeh* prayer (a voluntary prayer performed during Ramadan, consisting of 20 *rak'ahs* or rounds) and fasting during Ramadan on body composition. Findings indicated that after 20 days there was an increase in phase angle, basal metabolic rate, lean body mass and ratio of intracellular water compared to body weight. Further observed was a decrease in resistance value, glucose and fat mass compared to initial values. These results demonstrate that *taraweeh* prayer and fasting are comparable to the effect of moderate aerobic exercise and a calorie-restricted diet. Furthermore, the study provided support for the beneficial nature of fasting, in line with Islamic perspectives. While these findings seem promising, there is a need for further research, where these studies are repeated using similar methodologies and tools in order to establish the reliability of these studies.

Salah and the Heart The heart plays a major role within the Islamic framework as the spiritual centre of man. As such, many of the tenets and rituals within Islam are concerned with the purification of this organ. Indeed, the Prophet is reported as saying:

> Truly in the body there is a morsel of flesh which, if it be sound, all the body is sound and which, if it be diseased, all of it is diseased. Truly it is the heart (Al-Bukhari 1994)

This connection between the heart and brain has been supported by research in neuroscience. According to the neuro-visceral integration model, there are direct and indirect neural pathways linking the heart and brain, which are involved in cognitive, autonomic and affective responses (Thayer and Lane 2009). For instance, modified or reduced Heart Rate Variability (HRV) is associated with conditions like congestive heart failure, diabetic neuropathy, increased levels of anxiety and post-traumatic stress disorder (PTSD), as has been recorded by Bildstrom et al. 2003, Brosschot et al. 2007, and Cohen et al. (1998). Thus, the HRV is said to serve as an indicator for the health of the brain more than of the heart (Thayer et al. 2012).

A recent meta-analysis of research linking cerebral blood flow to HRV demonstrated the importance of the heart in regulating cognitive, affective and autonomic response in the brain (Thayer et al. 2012). Significantly, studies show that brain regions involved in the perception of danger and safety, such as the amygdala and medial PCF, are also connected with HRV. These findings provide support for the notion that HRV is a vital indicator of health, adaptability and stress. Thus, this also illustrates the vital role the heart plays in the control of overall health. Moreover, it provides a scientific understanding of the heart's role, which lies at the very center of the Islamic perspective. The question then arises if this refers to the physical or to the spiritual heart and this is explored further in Chap. 6 in the discussion of findings.

The Impact of Salah on the Brain The impact of Salah (ritual prayer) on brain activity has been investigated in a study measuring alpha waves using EEG (Doufesh et al. 2012). Nine Muslim participants performed four rounds of the afternoon (dhuhr) prayer and EEG measurements were taken in three conditions: before prayer, during prayer with recitation of Qur'ānic verses, and during prayer without any recitation. No significant difference was found in alpha waves between the conditions of prayer with recitation and without recitation. In line with previous studies, significantly higher alpha waves were found in the occipital (located at the back portion of the brain and associated with interpreting visual stimuli and information) and parietal brain (located in the middle section of the brain and associated with processing tactile sensory information such as pressure, touch and pain) regions during prostration in both conditions compared to any other prayer positions and the resting state.

In examining different positions during the *salah* on the brain, Ibrahim, Abas and Ng (in Ibrahim et al. 2008) investigated the pauses of movement prevalent throughout *salah*, using EEG measurements in two separate studies. The first study measured the alteration of brain signals at the point of pauses during *salah*. Specifically examined were the points of *tuma'ninah*, when there is a brief pause before moving onto the next posture. Also measured was the pause during *i'tidal*, where the individual rises from the bowing posture and pauses briefly before going into the prostrate position. Pausing allows individuals to gather their thoughts, thereby creating a state of composure. The second study examined the effects of the complete act of *salah* on the brain, with EEG measurements taken before and after the prayer. Results from the first study showed an increase in alpha frequency signals when participants assumed the pause positions, indicating a state of relaxation. Results from the second study indicated a higher frequency reading from gamma signals (activated when processing activity is present) compared to the state before *salah*. Further studies are required to aggregate the data, as well as test their reliability, so that more conclusive inferences and results can be obtained.

Meditation In a rare study of meditation among Muslims, Aldahadha (2013) examined the impact of *salah* as a form of both Muslim Praying Meditation (MPM) and Transcendental Meditation (TM) on the mindfulness skills of university students. TM, a straightforward meditation practiced for 20 minutes twice a day, involves an individual seated in a relaxed position with eyes closed. This form of meditation is said to provide not only a restful state but one of awareness too. The experience of an increased state of awareness, lacking in the mental load that typically accompanies one's train of thought, has been termed 'transcendental consciousness' (Tanner et al. 2009).

The above-mentioned study was carried out over a period of three months on 354 students, who were given the MPM questionnaire (Al Kushooa) and the Kentucky Inventory of Mindfulness Skills (KIMS) prior to training. Following the three-month training, the KIMS was re-administered. Findings indicated that MPM not only showed an increase but also predicted the impact of the KIMS. Furthermore, the additional practice of TM training produced a significant increase in self-reported mindfulness on the KIMS, compared to the group practicing MPM alone. These findings indicate that Muslim ritual prayer is not only predictive of mindfulness but also demonstrates enhanced effects when culminating with additional meditative practices like TM, which is akin to the Islamic practice of *dhikr* or remembrance of God. On a practical level, as per my discussions with members of some spiritual orders practicing both ritual prayers and *dhikr*, their quality of attention is seen to be much better than those purely doing ritual prayers. This is confirmed by my own experiences having done both seriously and consistently for almost two decades. This needs to be further tested scientifically to confirm its reliability and validity.

Fasting Fasting, whereby one refrains from food and drink from dawn till dusk, is the fourth pillar of Islam. It is obligatory during the month of Ramadan. There are, however, voluntary acts of fasting that are recommended throughout the year; for instance, the Prophet used to fast on Mondays and Thursdays and fasting during the first 10 days of the month of *Hajj* is highly valued. Research into the impact of Islamic fasting on health has focused on physiological aspects, such as energy intake, lipid profile and body weight. A recent review of literature on the impact of Ramadan on health and wellbeing concludes that while findings varied due to individual differences between subjects (for instance, health conditions, eating, lifestyle and cultural habits etc.), it remains safe for all healthy individuals (Alkandari, Maughan, Roky, Aziz & Karli, 2012). Overall, studies seem to indicate that fasting can be beneficial for health, provided it is carried out with individual health in mind and in line with medical advice.

There have been very few studies investigating the impact of Islamic fasting on the brain. One study, a polysomnographic and quantitative waking EEG study, examined daytime sleepiness during Ramadan (Roky et al. 2003). An increase in daytime sleepiness was found both through subjective and objective measures, and this was correlated with metabolic changes, specifically a decrease in body temperature. These findings may provide an explanation for the decrease in psychomotor, learning and motor functioning during Ramadan (Afifi 1997; Bigard et al. 1998; Boussif et al. 1996; Roky et al. 2000).

Clinical Implications of Fasting Studies on fasting, both on rodents and humans, have demonstrated that it may postpone the aging process, help the prevention and treatment of certain diseases and reduce the side-effects of chronic dietary intervention (Longo and Mattson 2014). A recent review on the implications of fasting on cellular metabolism and clinical applications showed that chronic fasting improved longevity, partly by reconditioning metabolic and stress resistance pathways (Longo and Mattson 2014). In rodents, intermittent or periodic fasting was shown to prevent heart disease, cancer, diabetes and neurodegeneration. Fasting in humans decreases rates of hypertension, obesity, asthma and rheumatoid arthritis (Longo and Mattson 2014).

The Effect of Fasting on the Brain Evolutionarily speaking, a preservation technique of mammals is to be active when hungry and inactive when satiated (Weindruch and Sohal 1997). This is demonstrated in studies of mammals during food deprivation, where decreased organ size (except the brain) have been reported. This demonstrates the need for greater cognitive functioning in circumstances where food is sparse. Among rodents, intermittent fasting is shown to enhance cognitive function, learning and memory, as determined by behavioral enhancements in sensory and motor function tests (Singh et al. 2012; Fontàn-Lozano et al. 2007).

Fasting, Aging and Disease Studies on humans have consistently supported animal data on the impact of fasting in delaying aging and its related diseases. The most important factors in aging, accelerated by a gluttonous lifestyle, are: (1) oxidative damage to proteins, DNA and lipids; (2) inflammation; (3) accumulation of dysfunctional proteins and organelles; and (4) elevated glucose and insulin (Bishop et al. 2010; Fontana and Klein 2007). Fasting two days a week for overweight women at risk of breast cancer demonstrated reduced oxidative stress and inflammation (Harvie et al. 2010), while in elderly men there was a reduction of body weight and fat and elevation of mood (Teng et al. 2011).

Other age-related effects of fasting observed in humans are the inhibition of the TOR motor pathways (a central regulator of cell metabolism, growth, proliferation and survival, Laplante and Sabatini 2012), the stimulation of autophagy (a physiological process involving the degeneration and recycling of cellular matter), and ketogenesis (the formation of ketone bodies, compounds resulting from fat metabolism) (Harvie et al. 2010; Sengupta et al. 2010). Thus, fasting is shown to conserve against aging and to help prevent related diseases.

Fasting and Neuro-Generation Much of the understanding of the effects of fasting on nervous and cognitive functions comes from animal data. Studies on calorie restrictions in humans have shown improvements of cognitive function in overweight women (Kretsch et al. 1997) and elderly participants (Witte et al. 2009). Likewise, participants with mild cognitive impairments who underwent a low glycemic diet for a month demonstrated improved visual memory via cerebrospinal fluid biomarkers of metabolism and brain bioenergetics (Bayer-Carter et al. 2011).

The evidence from animal and human data suggests that fasting can be beneficial in optimizing health and reducing the risk of disease. Animal studies have demonstrated robust and replicable benefits on the health indices from fasting, such as greater insulin sensitivity and reduced levels of blood pressure, body fat, insulin, glucose, atherogenic lipids and inflammation. Furthermore, fasting is shown to have positive functional outcome in animal and some human models of disease like cancer, myocardial infarction, diabetes, stroke, Alzheimer's, dementia and Parkinson's disease.

Mind-Body Interactive and Global Well Being The Contemplative Tree (Fig. 2.8) shows a wide spectrum of practices relating to worship, where contemplative or meditative practices are but one significant component. What is paramount within the religio-spiritual framework as outlined above, including ritual prayers, meditation, fasting and other related practices, is that they have been shown to have an effect on the mind and body. These practices provide meaning, direction, a sense of solace and, as neuroscience is now indicating, a sense of both physical and mental wellbeing. Table 2.8 shows the effect of worship on well=being at different levels of society. Wellbeing refers to the 'absence of negative conditions or feelings, the result of adjustment and adaptation to a hazardous world' (Corey and Keyes 1998). Thus, it subsumes and goes beyond the physiological and psychological realm and from an individual to a communal and societal level culminating at a global plane.

2.4 Wellbeing and the Worshiper: A Neuroscience and Islamic Perspective

Table 2.8 Worship, wellbeing and its implications

Domain	Type of worship	Impact	Implications
Individual	Prayer	Decrease in heart and brain activities	Having direction
	Meditation		Sense of being
	Fasting	Lowering of metabolism and better cellular functioning	Generally being in a peaceful state
		Alert mind with a greater level of consciousness	Able to interact better
Community	Worship on festive events	Greater level of cellular and electrical activity	A sense of collective at a community level
		Societal cohesion	Sharing of material goods
		Inculcates greater community discipline	
Societal	Congregational prayer	Higher level of energy	Sharing of spiritual events with wider society
	Collective fasting	Collective sense of belonging	
		Greater level of giving/charity	Forging solidarity at societal level
	Group Meditation		
Global	The collective togetherness termed "*ummah*"	Social Cohesion	A greater sense of global solidarity
		Social Solidarity	Collective sharing and giving, which is transnational
	Collective rites and rituals (Hajj and 'Umrah). Inter-generational practices (calligraphy, poems-prose, song)	Social Networking	Sharing of common symbols and icons
			Societal inter-relations

The deliberations in this study within the context of well-being and relating to Islamic rites and rituals can be categorised into four main domains, namely, individual, community, societal and global as outlined in Table 2.8.

At an individual level, worship in all its manifestation has a physiological, psychological and physical impact as several of the studies flagged in this paper have indicated. But, in a sense, it goes beyond the individual and enables one to relate to others better. When these types of individuals who profess faith with a tolerant attitude, devoted to contemplative practices and interacting with others, they are able to forge groups that foster a sense of direction and meaning to life. This sense of togetherness at a community level can result in a platform for sharing and caring as seen in communities across the world.

At societal level, what Islam calls for is not only for prayers and fasting together with the other rituals but a focus on a holistic way of life. In this light, worship only forms one segment, while the other is the interaction with other beings and one's conduct in any transaction (mu'amalat), which also constitutes worship. In this light, religion and its traditions in its various forms have been instrumental in developing various contemplative practices ranging from prayers, meditation, contemplation, repentance, supplication, voluntary support to others in need, to name a few. These, by and large, are seen to provide meaning to life, its direction, optimism (having faith), infusing a sense of stillness and calmness through its contemplative practices and affording methods for socialisation based on faith and social justice, which is the bedrock of Islam. In this way, Islam provides a societal framework which forms a basis of how human beings should live their lives.

Overall, empirical evidence seems to resonate with the beneficial nature of age-old religious practices on the body and mind. While physical wellbeing is key to maintaining the mind-body balance, spiritual and emotional wellbeing seem to have a pervasive impact, not only on one's physical and mental states but on interpersonal connections too. The existing body of literature on contemplative practices within Hindu and Buddhist traditions has highlighted their valuable impact on health. Specifically, practices such as yoga and meditation are associated with effects such as lowered heart rate and blood pressure, increased activation of the autonomic nervous system, reduced stress and chronic pain, as well as neuroplasticity especially for the longer-term meditators.

Salah Research on Islamic contemplative practices, despite its diversity, has been limited. Ibrahim et al's (2008) study demonstrated the beneficial impact of *salah* on body composition. This can perhaps be used as a tool to gain a healthier body composition in the short-term but more importantly, it is the mental connection with the divine, and the ensuing physiological and psychological responses that have made it stand the test of time. Within Islam, Jabir ibn Abdullah reported that the Messenger of Allah said with regards to the five times prayer, "If there was a river at the door of anyone of you and he took a bath in it five times a day, would you notice any dirt on him? They said, "Not a trace of dirt would be left" (Bukhari 2015).

Thus, these findings provide a deeper insight into the nature of purification that is to be gained through the process of the Islamic ritual prayer. In examining the impact of ritual prayer or *salah* on the heart, Ibrahim and Ahmad (2008) found that the prostrate position was particularly beneficial since there was a significant increase in blood flow to the brain compared to other positions. Indeed, the act of prostration is greatly revered within Islam; the Prophet is reported as saying, "The closest that a servant is to his Lord is when he is in prostration" (Muslim 2019).

Furthermore, neuro-scientific research has demonstrated the heart-brain connections, emphasizing the vital role the heart plays in overall physiological and psychological health (Thayer et al. 2012). In this vein, the Prophet is reported as saying:

Truly in the body there is a morsel of flesh which, if it be sound, all the body is sound and which, if it be diseased, all of it is diseased. Truly it is the heart (Bukhari 1994)

Thus, such findings provide a scientific dimension to the act of worship and the nature of vital spiritual organs. Given this, an interesting area of investigation would be the heart-brain connection during Islamic worship, for instance, the effect of prostration during Islamic prayer on the brain using neuro-imaging technology.

Studies on the brain during *salah* found significantly higher alpha waves in the occipital and parietal regions when the body was in the prostrate position (Doufesh et al. 2012). No significant difference was found in alpha waves between the conditions of prayer, that is with or without recitation. Additionally, Ibrahim et al. (2008) found alpha waves during the pause position throughout *salah* and gamma waves after *salah*, compared to before *salah*. Alpha frequency activation is correlated with spiritual activities like yoga (Vialatte et al. 2009; Arambula et al. 2001), tai chi (Field et al. 2010) and zen meditation (Yu et al. 2011). These results demonstrate that the mere movement of *salah* creates a state of relaxation similar to that of meditation. Given that alpha waves are associated with a state of relaxation and gamma waves with processing activity, these findings are congruent with the Islamic concept of *salah*. Here, prayer is seen as a space for contemplation, as well as one that offers a sense of calm thus providing a form of sustained meditation over time. One important aspect of Ibrahim et al.'s (2008) research is that the prayer is only as effective as the concentration with which it is carried out, relating to the concept of *khushu* or the state of absorption in God.

Meditation Aldahadha's (2013) study on Muslim prayer and transcendental meditation highlights the likeness between *salah* and meditative states. It demonstrates the enhanced effects on an individual's state of mind of combining prayer and meditation. Much like meditation, *salah* involves a shift in one's focus from the external materialistic world to the inward, spiritual realm. While the predominant focal point within Islam in the modern day seems to be on ritual prayer, meditation holds a special place within the Islamic tradition. This is epitomised in the narrative by Aisha, which captures the moment of Qurʾānic revelation, which occurred while the Prophet was on one of his meditative retreats:

The first revelation that was granted to the Messenger of Allāh, was the true dream in a state of sleep, so that he never dreamed a dream but the truth of it shone forth like the dawn of the morning. Then solitude became dear to him and he used to seclude himself in the cave of Hirāʿ, and therein he devoted himself to Divine worship for several nights before he came back to his family and took provisions for this (retirement); then he would return to Khadījah and take (more) provisions for a similar (period), until the Truth came to him while he was in the cave of Hirā (Al-Bukhari n.d.).

Thus, themes of seclusion, contemplation and meditation were very much a part of the Prophet's life, even before the birth of Islam as it is known today.

Fasting The data from animal and human studies have elucidated the neurophysiological underpinnings of fasting, its general benefits and certain cautionary measures (Longo and Mattson 2014). These indicate that fasting can delay aging and the onset of related diseases and is shown to improve cognitive function. Within Islam, fasting forms an important tenet. On the surface, it involves restraint from food, drink and sexual pleasures. At a deeper level, restraint encompasses the restriction of the senses such as sight, hearing, speech, feeling and smelling from an unnecessary information overload. At the highest level, fasting involves the mind, thinking of God and the life after death. The Prophet Muhammad is reported as saying, "Fasting is a shield" (Bukhari 2015) against much of the physical and psychological behaviour that can harm a person. Through the above findings a much clearer picture can be gained of the mechanisms through which fasting purifies and protects the body.

Certain studies have found that fasting can increase daytime sleepiness and decrease psychomotor, learning and motor functioning during Ramadan (Roky et al. 2003, Afifi 1997; Bigard et al. 1998; Boussif et al. 1996; Roky, Iraki, Haj Khlifa, Ghazal, & Hakkou 2000). While these findings can be viewed as providing support for the negative impact of fasting, it provides an important learning opportunity for Muslims from a religious standpoint. It highlights the finite nature of man when in a vulnerable position, such as a state of hunger, consequently producing a state of remembrance of God.

The neuro-physiological research presented generally highlights the beneficial nature to the overall health of Islamic contemplative practices of the ritual prayer or *salah*, meditation and fasting. Findings demonstrate that caution needs to be exercised when fasting if it pertains to individual health. These studies do have certain limitations; for instance, the studies on *salah* and meditation had small sample sizes and consisted of participants from the same region. Nevertheless, these have provided a foundation that future research can build upon with the use of larger and more diverse samples. Furthermore, these studies are pioneers in a virtually unexplored territory, that is, the impact of Islamic contemplative practices on neurophysiology. Thus, this presents scope for future research within the field.

While Islamic contemplative practices have demonstrated a valuable tool for self and spiritual development, the ruinous-blameworthy-virtuous-praiseworthy model of positive and negatives traits provides a viable framework for understanding key areas of development. In line with Goleman's insights gained from Tibetan meditative practices and psychology, Islam offers a rich tapestry of tools and methods, those that focus one's attention, like prayers and meditation, and those, including fasting, charity, supplication, sharing and caring for others, that if practiced can offer self-improvement.

In light of the above, a reversion to a more traditional form of Islam may be what is required in answer to the fast-paced lives that most of us lead. Following in the footsteps of the Prophet Muhammad and more traditional societies, adapting meditative/contemplative practices in addition to the prescribed prayers may help to improve one's overall mindfulness, which in turn has numerous physiological and psychological benefits. The research above has highlighted the beneficial nature of Eastern, including Islamic, contemplative practices. While the empirical study of Islamic contemplative practices is relatively new, these findings provide another dimension to the understanding behind these practices from a scientific perspective. It demonstrates that Islam, for its followers, offers systematic methods and tools for self-development at a physiological, psychological and spiritual level.

At a clinical level, such findings offer the possibility of integrating Islamic contemplative practices into forms of psychotherapy, for instance, an Islamic form of Mindfulness CBT (Cognitive Behavioural Therapy). Aligning therapy with religious beliefs may make it more acceptable for Muslims to seek and undertake therapy. This approach is of crucial importance in light of the turmoil within the Muslim world, which has resulted not only in a surge of refugees and displaced persons but also individuals channelling their frustrations in unconstructive ways. Thus, this highlights the importance for greater research into and understanding of Islamic contemplative practices and its impact on individual and collective levels.

References

Abdullah, F. (2011). Therapeutic ethics: Managing anger, negative thoughts and depression according to Al-Balkhi. AKFAR, *Journal of 'Aqidah and Islamic Thought*, BIL12: Rabi' al-Awwal (1432H/Feb, 2011), 79.

Abd al-Qāder al-Jīlāni. (1977). *The removal of cares (Jala Al-Khawatir): A collection of forty-five discourses*. Kuala Lumpur: S. Abdul Majeed & Co.

Abu-l-Qasim' Abd'al-Karim bin Hawazin al-Qushayri. (2002). *The Risalah: Principle of Sufism*, (trans. by Rabia Harris, eds. Laleh Bakhtiar, Seyyed Hossein Nasr.). Chicago: Great Books of the Islamic World Inc.

Afifi, Z. E. M. (1997). Daily practices, study performance and health during the Ramadan fast. *The Journal of the Royal Society for the Promotion of Health, 117*(4), 231–235.

Al-Attas, S. M. N. (2001). *Prolegomena to the metaphysics: An exposition of the fundamental element of the worldview of Islam* (2nd edn.). Kuala Lumpur, Malaysia: International Institute of Islamic Thought & Civilization (ISTAC).

Allport, G. W. (1955). *Becoming: Basic considerations for a psychology of personality*. New Haven & London: Yale University Press.

Al-Ghazali. (1995). *Ihya Ulum Id-Din* (vol. III) (trans.: Karim, M.F.). New Delhi: Islamic Book Services.

Alkandari, J. R., Maughan, R. J., Roky, R., Aziz, A. R., & Karli, U. (2012). The implications of Ramadan fasting for human health and well-being. *Journal of Sports Science, 30*, 2012, Issue, Supplementary Issue – Ramadhan and Football, https://doi.org/10.1080/02640414.2012.698298.

Asad, M. (2011), *Al-Qur'an*, "Translated by Muhammad Asad", The Message of the Qur'an, Kuala Lumpur: Islamic Book Trust.

Al-Ghazāli. (1995). *Ihyā Ulum-Id-Din: The book of religious learning* (vol. iv). New Delhi: Islamic Book Services.

Al-Ghazālī, Abū Ḥāmid Muhammad b. Muhammad al-Ṭūsī. (2007). *Wonders of the heart* (trans.: Skellie, W.J.). Kuala Lumpur: Islamic Book Trust.

Al-Haddad, I. A. A. (1990). *The lives of man* (trans.: Badawi, M.). Aligarh, India: Premier Publishing Company.

Al-Jawziyyah, I.-Q. (2006). *Spiritual disease and its cure*. In Sheikh Zakariya (Ed.). London: Amiraat Al-Firdous Ltd.

Aldahadha, B. (2013). The effects of muslim praying meditation and transcendental meditation programs on mindfulness among the University of Nizwa Students. *College Student Journal, 47*(4), 668–676.

Andresen, J. (2000). Meditation meets behavioural medicine. The story of experimental research on meditation. *Journal of Consciousness Studies, 7*(11–12), 17–74.

Andresen, J. (2002). *Meditation meets behavioural medicine.* In Andresen, J. & Forman, R. (Eds.). *Cognitive models and spiritual maps* (pp. 17–73). Exeter: Imprint Academic.

An-Nawawi. (1977). *Forty Hadith, 3rd Edition, Hadith no: 6* (trans.: Ezzedin, I. & Johnson-Davies, D.). Damascus: The Holy Quran Publishing House. Retrieved from https://www.faithinallah.org/an-nawawi-on-the-excellence-of-prescribed-prayers/.

Annunciation Trust. (2008). "Meditation and contemplation", last accessed October 2008. Retrieved from: https://www.annunciationtrust.org.uk/approaches/meditation_contemplation.shtml.

Ansari, A. (2011). *Stations of the Sufi path: The 'One Hundred Fields' (Sad Maydan) of Abdullah Ansari of Herat.* Trans: Nahid Angha. London: Archetype Publishers.

Arambula, P., Peper, E., Kawakami, M., & Gibney, K. H. (2001). The physiological correlates of Kundalini Yoga meditation: a study of a yoga master. *Applied Psychophysiology Biofeedback, 26*(2), 147–153.

Badri, M. (2000). *Contemplation: An islamic psychospiritual study* (trans.: Abdul-Wahid Lu'Lu'a). Herndon, Virginia: International Institute of Islamic Thought.

Bayer-Carter, J. L., Green, P. S., Montine, T. J., VanFossen, B., Baker, L. D., Watson, G. S. & Craft, S. (2011). Diet intervention and cerebrospinal fluid biomarkers in amnestic mild cognitive impairment. *Archives of Neurology, 68*(6), 743–752.

Bigard, A. X., Boussif, M., Chalabi, H., & Guezennec, C. Y. (1998). Alterations in muscular performance and orthostatic tolerance during Ramadan. *Aviation, Space, and Environmental Medicine, 69*(4), 341–346. https://europepmc.org/article/med/9561280.

Bildstrom, S. Z., Jensen, B. T., & Agner, E. (2003). Heart rate versus heart rate variability in risk prediction after myocardial infarction. *Journal of Cardiovascular Electrophysiology, 14*(2), 168–173.
Retrieved November 2, 2014 from https://www.biodyncorp.com/tools/450/understanding_printout.html
Retrieved November 2, 2014 from https://www.biodyncorp.com/product/450/body_capacitance_450.html
Retrieved November 2, 2014 from https://www.biodyncorp.com/product/450/phase_angle_450.html
Retrieved November 2, 2014 from https://www.biodyncorp.com/product/450/resistance_450.html

Bishop, N. A., Lu, T., & Yankner, B. A. (2010). Neural mechanisms of ageing and cognitive decline. *Nature, 464*(7288), 529–535.

Brosschot, J. F., Van Dijk, E. & Thayer, J. F. (2007). Daily worry is related to low heart rate variability during waking and the subsequent nocturnal sleep period. *International Journal of Psychophysiology, 63*(1), 39–47.
Retrieved from https://www.ncbi.nlm.nih.gov/pmc/articles/PMC1114432.

Bukhari, Al. (1994). *Book of belief* (vol I) (trans.: Khan, M. M.). Riyadh: Dar-Us-Salam.

Bukhari, Al. (2015). A prophetic saying narrated by a companion Abu Huraira, recorded in Sahih Bukhari. Al-Tanazil. Accessed 6th May, 2015. Retrieved from https://al-tanzil.com/Excellence_of_Prayers.html; Edited from: https://www.faithinallah.org/an-nawawi-on-the-excellence-of-prescribed-prayers/.
Retrieved from: https://www.firstpeople.us/FP-Html-Legends/TwoWolves-Cherokee.html.

Chisthi. (2007). *The stages of the development of the soul*, last modified 2nd October 2007. Retrieved from: https://www.chisthi.ru/soul_development.html.

Chitick, W., & Murata, S. (2002). *The vision of Islam, Hamza Yusuf commentary* [CD No. 2]. California: Alhambra Productions, Inc.

References

Cohen, H., Kotler, M., Matar, M. A., Kaplan, Z., Loewenthal, U., Miodownik, H., & Cassuto, Y. (1998). Analysis of heart rate variability in posttraumatic stress disorder patients in response to a trauma-related reminder. *Biological Psychiatry, 44*(10), 1054–1059.

Cooley, C. H. (1902). The looking-glass self. In C. Lemert (Ed.). *Social theory: The multicultural readings* (2010) (p. 189). Philadelphia: Westview Press

d'Aquili, E. G & Newberg, A. B. (2000). The neuropsychology of religious and spiritual experience. *Journal of Consciousness Studies, 7*(11–12), 251–266.

Doufesh, H., Faisal, T., Lim, K. S., & Ibrahim, F. (2012). EEG spectral analysis on Muslim prayers. *Applied Psychophysiology and Biofeedback, 37*(1), 11–18.

Epstein, R., & Komorita, S. S. (1971). Self-esteem, success-failure, and locus of control in Negro children. *Developmental Psychology, 4*(1, Pt.1), 2–8. https://doi.org/10.1037/h0030371.

Epstein, S. (1973). The self-concept revisited: Or a theory of a theory. *American Psychologist, 28*(5), 404–416. https://doi.org/10.1037/h0034679.

Field, T., Diego, M. & Hernandez-Reif, M. (2010). Tai chi/yoga effects on anxiety, heart rate, EEG and math computations. *Complementary Therapies in Clinical Practice, 16*(4), 235–238.

Fontàn-Lozano, Á., Sáez-Cassanelli, J. L., Inda, M. C., de los Santos-Arteaga, M., Sierra-Domínguez, S. A., López-Lluch, G. & Carrión, Á. M. (2007). Caloric restriction increases learning consolidation and facilitates synaptic plasticity through mechanisms dependent on NR2B subunits of the NMDA receptor. *The Journal of Neuroscience, 27*(38), 10185–10195.

Fontana, L. & Klein, S. (2007). Aging, adiposity, and calorie restriction. *Jama, 297*(9), 986–994.

Goleman, D. (1990). *Tibetan & western models of mental health*. In Goleman, D., & Thurman, R.A.F (Eds.). *Mindscience: An east-west dialogue*. Boston: Wisdom.

Goleman, D. (1991). *Tibetan and western models of mental health*. In Goleman D. and Thurman R (Eds.). *Mindscience: An east-west dialogue* (pp. 89–102). Massachusetts, Boston: Wisdom Publications.

Glassman, W. E. & Hadad, M. (2004). *Approaches to psychology*. United Kingdom: Open University Press.

Harvie, M. N., Pegington, M., Mattson, M. P., Frystyk, J., Dillon, B., Evans, G. & Howell, A. (2010). The effects of intermittent or continuous energy restriction on weight loss and metabolic disease risk markers: a randomized trial in young overweight women. *International Journal of Obesity, 35*(5), 714–727.

Helminski, K. (1999). *The knowing heart: A Sufi path of transformation*. Boston & London: Shambala.

Husain, A. (2005). *Spiritual psychology*. New Delhi: Global Vision Publishing House.

Ibn 'Arabi, M. (2008). *The four pillars of spiritual transformation* (trans.: Hirtenstein, S.). Oxford: Anqa Publication in Association with Ibn Arabi Society.

Ibn Daqiq al-'Id. (2014). *A treasury of Hadith, Hadith No; II, A Commentary on Nawawi's selection of forty prophetic traditions* (trans. by Mokrane Guezzo). UK: Kube Publishing.

Ibn Hazm al-Andalusi. (1998). *In pursuit of virtue: The moral theology and psychology of Ibn Hazm a-Andalusi*. London: Ta-Ha Publishers.

Ibn Qayyim al-Jawziyyah. (2006). *Spiritual disease and its cure*. London: Al-Firdous Ltd.

Ibn Taymiyyah Taqî ad-Dîn Ahmad. (2010). *Disease of the heart and their cures* (trans.: Abu Rumaysah). Birmingham: Daar Us-Sunnah Publishers.

Ibrahim, F. & Ahmad, W. W. (2008). Study of heart rate changes in different salat's positions. In *Presented at 4th Kuala Lumpur International Conference on Biomedical Engineering*.

Ibrahim, F., Abas, A. B. W. & Ng, S. C. (2008). *Salat: benefit from science perspective*. Kuala Lumpur: Department of Biomedical Engineering, University of Malaya.

Imam, G. (1995). *Ihya Ulum-Din* (vol. III) (trans.: Karim, M.F.). New Delhi: Islamic Book Services.

James, W. (1950). *The principles of psychology* (2 volumes in 1). New York: Dover Publications.

Jurji, E. J. (1938), *Illumination in Islamic Mysticism. A translation, with an introduction and notes, based upon a critical edition of Abu-al-Mawāhib al-Shādhilī's treatise entitled Qawānīn ?ikam al-ishrāq*. Princeton Oriental Texts, Iv. 9 × 6, (pp. x + 130). Princeton: Princeton University Press.

Kabbani, M. H. (1995). *The Naqshabandi Sufi Way: History and Guidebook of the Saints of the Golden Chain* (pp. 1–469). Chicago: Kazi Publications.

Kabbani, S. M. H. (2008). *Sufism and the perennial conflicts of good and evil*. Kuala Lumpur, KL: Globe Vision Publishing House, University of Malaya.

Kamal-Ud-Din, K. (1923). *The threshold of truth, higher studies in Islam series 1*. London: The Basheer Muslim Library, The Islamic Review Office, The Mosque, Working.

Keyes, C. L. M. (1998). Social well-being. *Social Psychology Quarterly, 61(2)*, 121–140 (20 pages); American Sociological Association. https://doi.org/10.2307/2787065.

Khalil, F. S., Mohktar, S. M., & Ibrahim, F. (2014). The theory and fundamentals of bioimpedance analysis in clinical status monitoring and diagnosis of diseases, MDPI (Multidisciplinary Digital Publishing Institute), Basel, Switzerland, 4th June 2014, last retrieved 2nd March 2020, https://creativecommons.org/licenses/by/3.0/, https://www.ncbi.nlm.nih.gov/pmc/articles.

Khan, M. A. (1976). *Dalael-E-Sulook: An objective appraisal of the sublime Sufi path*. Pakistan: Idarah-E-Naqshbandiah Owaisiah.

Knysh, A. (2010). *Islamic mysticism: A short history*. Leiden, Boston: Brill.

Kretsch, M. J., Green, M. W., Fong, A. K. H., Elliman, N. A. & Johnson, H. L. (1997) Cognitive effects of a long-term weight reducing diet. *International Journal of Obesity, 21*(1), 14–21.

Laplante, M. & Sabatini, D. M. (2012). mTOR signaling in growth control and disease. *Cell, 149*(2), 274–293.

Lecky, P. (1945). *Self-consistency; a theory of personality*. New York: Island Press.

Longo, V. D. & Mattson, M. P. (2014). Fasting: molecular mechanisms and clinical applications. *Cell Metabolism, 19*(2), 181–192.

Morris, J., Frith, C., Perrett, D. et al. (1996). A differential neural response in the human amygdala to fearful and happy facial expressions. *Nature, 383*, 812–815. https://doi.org/10.1038/383812a0.

Maqsood, R. W. (1998). *The muslim prayer encyclopaedia: A complete guide to prayers as taught by the Prophet Muhammad*. New Delhi: Goodword Books

Markus, H. & Nurius, P. (1986). Possible selves. *American Psychologist*, 954.

Maslow, A. (2011). *Towards a psychology of being*. New Jersey: Martino Publishing.

Mas'ud, Ibn. (2006) cited in Saihi Muslim, Islamic Revival. Retrieved from https://islamicsystem.blogspot.com/2006/07/seeking-your-provisions-rizq.html.

Mead, G. (1934). *Mind, Self, and Society: From the Standpoint of a Social Behaviorist*, edited, with an Introduction, by Charles W. Morris, Chicago: University of Chicago Press.

Morris, J. W. (2005). The reflective heart: discovering spiritual intelligence in Ibn Arabi's Meccan illumination. Louisville: Fons Vitae.

Muslim, Al. (2019). *Muslim book of prayer*, 979 Retrieved from https://www.sahihmuslim.com/sps/smm/sahihmuslim.cfm?scn=dspchaptersfull&BookID=4&ChapterID=187.

Picken, G. (2011). *Spiritual purification in Islam: The life and works of al-Muhasibi*. UK: Routledge.

Piet, M. (2011). The most basic prayer. Retrieved from https://markpiet.wordpress.com/2011/01/20/the-most-basic-prayer-02/ Religious Facts. (n.d.) Hadith 1. Retrieved from https://www.religionfacts.com/library/hadith/1.

Rogers, C. (1991). *On becoming a person: A therapist's view of psychotherapy*. USA: Mariner Books/Houghton Mifflin Company.

Rogers, C. R. (1951). *Client-centered therapy*. Boston: Houghton Mifflin.

Roky, R., Iraki, L., HajKhlifa, R., Ghazal, N. L. & Hakkou, F. (2000). Daytime alertness, mood, psychomotor performances, and oral temperature during ramadan intermittent fasting. *Annals of Nutrition and Metabolism, 44*(3). https://doi.org/10.1159/000012830.

Roky, R., Chapotot, F., Benchekroun, M. T., Benaji, B., Hakkou, F., Elkhalifi, H. & Buguet, (2003). A daytime sleepiness during Ramadan intermittent fasting: polysomnographic and quantitative waking EEG study. *Journal of Sleep Research, 12*(2), 95–101.

Sa'ari, C. Z. (2007). *Al-Ghazālī and Intuition: An analysis* (trans.: al-Risalah al-Ladunniyyah). Kuala Lumpur: University of Malaya.

References

Sarbin, T. R., & Jones, D. S. (1955). An experimental analysis of role behavior. *The Journal of Abnormal and Social Psychology, 51*(2), 236–241. https://doi.org/10.1037/h0046648.

Saver, J. L., & Rabin, J. M. D. (1997), The neural substrates of religious experiences. In S. Salloway, P. Malloy, J. L. Cummings (Eds.), *The neuropsychiatry of limbic and subcortical disorders* (p. 196). Washington: American Psychiatric Press.

Schuon, F. (1998). *Understanding Islam* (pp. 1–195). Indiana: World Wisdom Inc.

Schimmel, A. (1975). *Mystical dimensions of Islam*. North Carolina: The University of North Carolina Press.

Schuon, F. (2006). *Sufism: Veil and Quintessence, A new translation with selected letters*. In Cutsinger, J. (Ed.). Bloomington, Indiana: World Wisdom Publication.

Sengupta, S., Peterson, T. R., Laplante, M., Oh, S. & Sabatini, D. M. (2010). mTORC1 controls fasting-induced ketogenesis and its modulation by ageing. *Nature, 468*(7327), 1100–1104.

Sheikh Muḥyiddin Ibn 'Arabi. (2008). *The four pillars of spiritual transformation*. Oxford: Anqa Publication in Association with Ibn Arabi Society.

Sidi, Z. (2001). *The poor man's book of assistance* [16 CDs]. California: Al-Hamra Production.

Singh, R., Lakhanpal, D., Kumar, S., Sharma, S., Kataria, H., Kaur, M., & Kaur, G. (2012). Late-onset intermittent fasting dietary restriction as a potential intervention to retard age-associated brain function impairments in male rats. *Age (Dordr), 34*(4), 917–933.

Smith, M. (1980). *Al-Muhasibi: An early Mystic of Baghdad, Islamic book foundation, publication no: 52*. Pakistan: Lahore.

Suhrawardi, Shahab–u'd-Din 'Umar b. Muhammad. (1991). *The Awarif-ul-Maarif* (trans.: Wilberforce Clarke, H.). Lahore: Sh. Muhammad Ashraf.

Snygg, D., & Combs, A. W. (1949). *Individual behavior: A new frame of reference for psychology*. New York: Harper & Brothers.

Sullivan, H. S. (1953). *The interpersonal theory of psychiatry*. New York: W W Norton & Co.

Tanner, M., Travis, F., Gaylord-King, C. & Haaga, D. (2009). The effects of the transcendental meditation program on mindfulness. *Journal of Clinical Psychology, 65*(6), 574–589.

Teng, N. I. M. F., Shahar, S., Manaf, Z. A., Das, S. K., Taha, C. S. C. & Ngah, W.Z. (2011). Efficacy of fasting calorie restriction on quality of life among aging men. *Physiology & Behavior, 104*(5), 1059–1064.

Thayer, J. F., & Lane, R. D. (2009). Claude Bernard and the heart–brain connection: further elaboration of a model of neuro-visceral integration. *Neuroscience and Biobehavioral Reviews, 33*, 81–88.

Thayer, J. F., Fredrikson, F. M., Sollers III, J. J. & Wager, T. D. (2012). A meta-analysis of heart rate variability and neuro-imaging studies: implications for heart rate variability as a marker of stress and health. *Neuroscience & Biobehavioral Reviews, 36*(2), 747–756.

Vialatte, F. B., Bakardjian, H., Prasad, R., & Cichocki, A. (2009). EEG paroxysmal gamma waves during Bhramari Pranayama: a yoga breathing technique. *Consciousness and Cognition, 18*(4), 977–988.

Weindruch, R. & Sohal, R. S. (1997). Caloric intake and aging. *The New England Journal of Medicine, 337*(14), 986.

Wilber, K. (2011). Waves streams, states and self: Further considerations for an integral theory of consciousness. *Journal of Consciousness Studies, 7*(11–12), 145–176.

Williams, M. (2015). Oxford Centre for Mindfulness. Retrieved from: https://oxfordmindfulness.org.

Witte, A.V., Fobker, M., Gellner, R., Knecht, S. & Fiöel, A. (2009). Caloric restriction improves memory in elderly humans. *Proceedings of the National Academy of Science USA, 106*, 1255–1260.

Yu, X., Fumoto, M., Nakatani, Y., Sekiyama, T., Kikuchi, H., Seki, Y. & Arita, H. (2011). Activation of the anterior prefrontal cortex and serotonergic system is associated with improvements in mood and EEG changes induced by Zen meditation practice in novices. *International Journal of Psychophysiology, 80*(2), 103–111.

Chapter 3
Conceptual Framework for Morality (*Akhlāq*)

This chapter deals with the right way to God (Sect. 3.1), which sets the pathway to appropriate behaviour and acts as a moral compass. The most appropriate in this light is the role–model of the Prophet and his spiritual leadership and life are duly portrayed (Sect. 3.2).

3.1 *Riazat* or Efforts for Good Conduct in the Way of God

3.1.1 Introduction

Morality, which is generally associated with religion, spirituality and ethics, is deeply rooted within every religion and culture, no matter if it is different in its theology and orientation. The concept of morality contains within itself prescriptions and narratives with its interlinked code on conduct. It has a wide scope being within many different traditions including the aboriginal cultures to the scriptural based religions including Hinduism, Jainism, Buddhism, Judaism, Christianity, Islam and other faiths.

This chapter analyses the topic of *riazat* or efforts of good conduct in the way of God, attempting to understand its types and nature. This is done while drawing answers from the body of Islamic literature, and concurrently connecting, where relevant, interpretations of morality within other religions and cultures. The central focus of this study is that efforts towards good conduct are not only important for their own sake but is the bedrock for developing oneself both in this world and in the next life. In this light, it lends support to the thesis that both worship (*'ibādah*) and *riazat* (good conduct) are both inter–woven into the fabric of developing excellence (*iḥsan*), which is fundamental to Islam.

From a point of review, the focus is on Imam Ghazāli's (1058–1111) articulation of *Riazat* or efforts in the ways of God (Al-Ghazāli 1995), while being complimented by the Moral Theology and Psychology of Ibn Hazm al–Andalusia (994–1064) (Al-Andalusi 1998). There were several other texts that were used in order to enrich the review and discussion including the work of Muhuyiddin Ibn 'Arabi (1165–1240) (Ibn 'Arabi 1998) on spiritual transformation.

As a prelude to this chapter, the key definitions and the dimensions of morality are explained. This is followed by the inherent qualities of human character, while trying to understand the formation of the character of the child. The question of whether human nature can be changed is then addressed, with the identification of vices and virtues and their accompanying traits. This is underpinned by the functions of prophethood and its values and, finally, the types of religious training and exercises that are required to shape one's character are expounded. It ends with a detailed discussion followed by a conclusion.

3.1.2 Key Definitions and Dimensions of Morality

By understanding the key terms and from references in the light of the Qur'ān and *hadīth*, one is able to build a picture of what Islamic morality means and its link to good conduct in the way of God. It is key to understand that there is an intrinsic link between good conduct and the state of the soul and its inclinations. Good conduct is half of faith, while bad conduct is the disease of the soul that affects not only this life but that which is beyond (Al-Ghazāli 1995).

Ibn Hazm (1998), while explaining what good conduct is points out that the Arabic word *khuluq*, with its plural *akhlāq*, refers to "character, natural disposition or innate temper, and has been also used to signify "customs or habits" or that which "becomes second nature" as a result of things becoming internalised. He says that *khuluq* means "morality" and derived from the same root as khalaqa, referring to "created or fashioned".

When the Messenger was asked about good conduct, he stated: "Make due allowance for man's nature, and enjoin the doing of what is right; and leave alone all those who choose to remain ignorant" (Qur'ān, al–Araf, 7:199). The Prophet further elaborates that good conduct is to re–establish severed relationships and to pardon the one who oppressed you. This is tied in with the statement where he says, "I have been sent to complete the best of conducts" and that the "best in faith of the believers is the best amongst you in good conduct" (Al-Ghazāli 1995).

Ibn Hazm (1998) points out that there are two explicit references to the term *khuluq* or moral behaviour in the Qur'ān. In the first case God makes reference to the people of Prophet Hud[1] who said, "This (religion of our) is none other than

---

[1] Prophet Hud, who was after Prophet Noah and before Prophet Salih is mentioned a few times in the Qur'ān (26:123–140; 46:21–26). He was the Prophet of the 'ād people who occupied a large tract of the Southern Arabia. The 'ād according to the Qur'an forsook God and oppressed their own people and exhibited arrogant and immoral behavior. The tomb of Prophet Hud is said to be

that to which our forebears clung" (Qur'ān, al–Shuara, 26:137), where Muhammad Asad (2011) explains this as "the innate habit of the earlier people". The second case underlines the character of Prophet Muhammad when the Lord says, "For, behold, thou keepest indeed to a sublime way of life" (Qur'ān, al–Qalam, 68:4), here *khuluq* refers to "a way of life" which Aisha captures the character of the Prophet when she said, "his way of life (*khuluq*) was the Qur'ān" (Asad 2011), which has been reported by many of the Prophets companions.

3.1.3 Inherent Qualities of Human Character and the Formation of a Child's Character

There seems to be an intrinsic link between good conduct and the state of the soul, with its inclination towards good or bad. This is framed within the context of creation, when the Lord created the Prophet Adam with earthly material and then infused His spirit onto him. In this context, Imam Ghazāli (1995) alludes that there is a connection of the body with the earth and the soul with the Creator. This can be further supported by the Qur'ān, where God says, "And they will ask about (the nature of) divine inspiration *(rūh).*" Say "This inspiration (comes) at my Sustainer's behest" (Qur'ān, al–Isra, 17:85). There appears to be an intrinsic correlation between conduct and the state of the soul, as Imam Ghazāli explains, the human nature is anchored in the soul and actions flow out of it. In order to understand the above statement, Imam Ghazāli provides the following categorisation, where he says that the nature of the soul is divided into four kinds: (1) power of discerning knowledge; (2) power of administration or anger; (3) power of greed; and (4) power of adjustment to the above three natures. Within this framework, when knowledge is able to develop and mature then it is able to discern truth from falsehood and good from bad, and thus knowledge is the anchor for good conduct. This is supported by the statement "granting wisdom unto whom He wills; and whoever is granted wisdom has indeed been granted wealth abundant" (Qur'ān, al–Baqara, 2:269).

Ibn Hazm (1998) says that when God created the soul there were several capabilities that were embedded in it, including a sense of justice, which acted as a rudder to seek for fairness and truth. He supports this by the statement from the Qur'ān where God states, "Behold, God enjoins justice, and the doing of good and the generosity towards (one's) fellow–man; and He forbids all that is shameful and all that runs counter to reason as well as envy; (and) exhorts you (repeatedly) so that you might bear (all this) in mind" (al–Nahl, 16:90). This is further augmented by a stronger statement: "O You, who have attained to faith! Be ever steadfast in upholding equity, bearing witness to the truth for the sake of God, even though it be against your own selves or your parents and kinsfolk. Whether the person concerned

---

in Hadhramaut, Yemen cited in Note 1040, The Holy Qur'an, Trans. and commentary—Abdullah Yusuf Ali.

be rich or poor, God's claim takes precedence over (the claims of) either of them. Do not, then, follow your own desires, lest you swerve from justice ..." (Qur'ān, al–Nisa, 4:135).

Inherent in the soul is understanding and reason, which help us navigate the path to virtue, enlightening the way of darkness and enabling us to discern what is right (Ibn Hazm 1998). Perhaps one of the main dimensions of the Qur'ān that non–Muslims, as well as some Muslims, may not readily notice is the emphasis on the use of one's reason and mind and, in this sense, it becomes a religion of inquiry and investigation rather than blind faith. This is illustrated by several verses of the Qur'ān, where God says, "Or (dost thou deem thyself equal to) one who devoutly worships (God) throughout the night, prostrating himself or standing (in prayer), ever mindful of the life to come, and hoping for his Sustainer's grace?" Say 'Can they who know and they who do not know be deemed equal' (Qur'ān, al–Zumar, 39:9).

The above statement is reinforced by two other verses: firstly, "Give then, this glad tiding to (those of) My servants who listen (closely) to all this is said, and follow the best of it; (for) it is they whom God has graced with His guidance, and it is they who are (truly) endowed with insight!" (Qur'ān, al–Zumar, 39:17–18) Secondly, "In this behold, there is indeed a reminder for everyone whose heart is wide–awake—that is (everyone who) lends ear with a conscious mind" (Qur'ān, Qaf, 50:37). Truth and thereby faith, is arrived at through the knowing and conscious mind, which in turn leads the individual to right conduct.

Ibn Hazm (1998) points out that the term *qalb* or heart refers to the mind and not the material heart or the organ which pumps the blood throughout the system. He states that the light of the mind enables the soul to discern between right and wrong, for example, through the avoidance of foolishness and bad desires, including anger, which trigger fanaticism and tribal values. He further points out that obedience to God is the key to all virtue and disobedience to all vices and this forms the essential criterion to discern right from wrong.

3.1.4 Can Nature be Changed?

Imam Ghazāli (1995) poses the question, 'Can nature be changed?' He goes on to state that it is a mistaken belief to think that it cannot and this he says arises from two main reasons. Firstly, if indeed nature cannot be changed, then education and learning would be of no use, the objective of education being not merely the acquisition of knowledge but the development of the human mind and nature. where the Prophet said "make your conduct good." He argues that even the lower animals can be changed by training and in the same light humans can be changed by training, education and habits. In cases of the some of the strong elements, like passion, anger, and pride, which sway us from living aright, these aspects can be managed by applying rules, regulations and control and these can take you to the highest degree of development.

3.1 *Riazat* or Efforts for Good Conduct in the Way of God

The second reason is the mistaken belief that greed, passion, anger, and pride can be completely uprooted. These are needed for humans to live, where, for example, if there was no greed for food, this would affect one's well–being. Khwaja Kalam–ud–Din (1924) lends support to this statement highlighting that the natural impulses in humans are fundamental to human nature and crushing this instinct, as in some religions, does not produce the balance that is required for life.

3.1.5 Vices and Virtues and its Traits

A powerful statement is made by Khwaja Kalam–ud–Din (1924), where he states, "Nothing, in itself, is good or evil in the moral world." This also resonates with Immanuel Kant who begins his treatise, The Fundamental Principles of the Metaphysics of Morals (1785), with the famous statement that "Nothing can possibly be conceived in the world, or even out of it, which can be called good without qualification, except a good will."

Before we proceed any further, it is necessary to define vice and virtue and its normative definitions. Vice is defined by the Oxford English Dictionary as: (1) immoral or wicked behaviour; (2) an open sewer of vice and crime; (3) criminal activities involving prostitution, pornography, or drugs; (4) an immoral or wicked personal characteristic; (5) a weakness of character or behaviour. Virtue on the contrary is defined as: (1) behaviour showing high moral standards; (2) a quality considered morally good or desirable in a person; (3) a good or useful quality of a thing: (4) (archaic) virginity or chastity. The Islamic perspective and definitions of vice and virtue as derived from the Qur'ān and the *sunnah*, which are articulated by Ghazāli (1995) and Ibn Hazm (1998), are outlined in Table 3.1. What is noteworthy is that some of the vices can be seen from the perspective of a continuum (see Table 3.2), where either extreme is considered a vice, while the virtue is found in the middle position.

Apart from the vices, (Ibn Hazm 1998), points out seven cardinal sins that are:

(1) Polytheism or associating others with God
(2) Magic
(3) Murder
(4) Devouring the possessions of orphans

Table 3.1 List of Virtue and Vices

Vices	Virtues
Oppression	Justice
Greed	Patience
Lustful	Loving
Covetousness	Modesty
Deceitfulness	Truthfulness
Pride	Humility

Table 3.2 The continuum of Virtue and Vice

Vices	Virtue	Vices
Hate	Love	Envy
Extravagance	Benevolence (Generosity)	Miserliness
Haughtiness	Bravery	Cowardice
Deception	Wisdom	Genius

(5) Practicing usury
(6) Fleeing from the dangers of war, when it is necessary to defend oneself
(7) Spreading malicious gossip about an innocent, devout women.

He further adds others to this list, namely:

(8) The utterance of falsehood or false witness
(9) Unkindness to one's parents
(10) Telling lies about the Prophet
(11) Exposing one's parents to other's insults
(12) Ingratitude towards God and others
(13) Backbiting
(14) To torture or kill animals except as necessary for food
(15) To deprive a thirsty person of water
(16) To steal.

Concerning virtue, Imam Junaid al-Baghdadi as cited in Imam Ghazāli (1995) says that there are four acts that will raise a person to the highest ranks and these are patience, modesty, generosity, and good conduct. Al Ghazāli also cites Ibn Abbas, who when asked what honour is, quoted the verse in the Qurʻān: "Verily, the noblest of you in the sight of God is the one who is most deeply conscious of Him" (Qurʻān, al-Hujurat, 49:13).

Ibn Hazm (1998) saw virtue as multi-faceted and able to be categorised into three major domains, namely the religious, the intellectual, and the moral. The religious virtue includes religious duties and obedience to God, whereas intellectual virtue encompasses wisdom and good judgment, and moral virtue incorporates courage, prudence, justice, chastity and faithfulness. Having given virtue this broad and multiple scope, Ibn Hazm, however, points out that it stems from one main virtue, the disciplining of one's soul to be obedient to God.

There is a clear distinction between vices and virtues and the two extremes result in a disease or a kind of addiction. Thus, it is the middle course that brings about equilibrium in the personality. As Ibn Hazm (1998), points out, "Virtue is a medium course between two vices" (See Table 3.2). He then provides an example where courage is a medium between fear and rashness. Courage in this sense, enables the fighter to stand up and have the courage to fight but not to throw himself into the line of fire, which is rash. Perhaps, this is the reason for the Prophet to state that

3.1 *Riazat* or Efforts for Good Conduct in the Way of God

Islam is a middle path, where the Qur'ān points out, "And thus have We willed you to be a community of the middle-way" (Qur'ān, al-Baqara, 2:143). Muhammad Asad (2011) elaborating on this refers to a community that maintains an equitable balance between extremes, while being appreciative of the nature of humans and their possibilities.

Imam Ghazāli (1995) points out that the majority of people are inclined one way or another, for the middle-way he says is a straight path "narrower than a hair and more sharped edged than a sword." In light of this, Khawja Kamal-ud-Din's statement puts things into perspective: "It is not the killing of human passion which makes morality, but the balancing of them to certain measures, which creates healthy morals and produces spirituality" (Khwaja Kalam–ud–Din 1924).

3.1.6 The Functions of Prophethood and its Values

Ibn Hazm (1998) discusses the three crucial roles of the prophets, which he says are required to maintain ethics and the morality of the soul:

(i) The teaching extended in terms of teaching the rectification of the morals of the soul, including the practicing of justice, generosity, chastity, truthfulness, courage, patience, meekness and mercy, while avoiding the opposites of these virtues
(ii) Providing protection against oppressors and transgressors, who would otherwise impact negatively on their lives and property
(iii) Guiding people in having a good life in this world and the next and facilitating them to achieve salvation

His conclusion in this regard is that God is the source of all knowledge and morality, and he has, through sending the prophets at various junctures in human history, guided man on how best to communicate and behave with others.

3.1.7 Types of Religious Exercises and Training

There are many obstacles in the path of humans especially in terms of aligning with the guidance that God has provided us so that we can gain nearness to Him. For the Lord himself says, "I have placed a screen in their front and a screen in their back and then I covered them and they do not see" (Qur'ān, Ya Sin, 36:9). Imam Ghazāli (1995) points out that for religious person there are four walls before them:

(1) The wall of wealth—one needs to be satisfied with the bare necessities of life.
(2) The wall of honor—moving away from name and fame and all that it brings.

(3) The wall of Madhahab[2]—differences of opinions in religious matters need to be tolerated and the blind following of a particular sect needs to be avoided.
(4) The wall of sins—repentance of past sins, restraint from acts of oppression, and compensation to the oppressed should be adhered to, in order to remove one's sins.

Once the above have been accomplished, then the concerned person needs to be secure within a type of a fort, which will protect him/her from evil or harmful things since the straight path in one and the other paths with their temptations are many. The fort of this path has walls says Imam Ghazāli, namely, solitude or silence, which can increase the power of intellect and encourage fearfulness of God; hunger, which melts the fat of the heart resulting in softness and humility creeping in; and sleeplessness, which makes the heart bright, pure and radiant, while too much sleep makes it dead and hard.

In a similar vein as Imam Ghazāli (1995), Ibn 'Arabi (2008) explains that there are four dimensions of knowledge, which in-effect encompass the path to God, as well as their impact on the soul, that is, silence (*samt*), seclusion (*uzla*), hunger (*ju*) and viligence (*sahar*), which have been already dealt with in some detail in Sect. 2.3.4:

Imam Ghazāli (1995) makes an intriguing statement when he asserts that first one has to close the knowledge that is gained through the five senses, so that clean and pure knowledge can arise to the surface from the bottom of the heart. He goes on to say that except when it is really necessary, there is no need to necessarily gain knowledge through the five senses. In this sense, perceptional reality as we know may or may not be correct, which we call human error. He concludes by citing the preciousness of the traveller in the path of religion, whose journey requires him to overcome such obstacles as the love of wealth, fame, attachment to the world and the inclinations towards the realm of sin. All of these have to be given up from the heart, requiring a long, hard and sustained effort in order to achieve a state of nearness to God. Another way, he says, is the silent *dhikr* or remembrance of God, where the focus is on the utterance and the tongue, after much repetition, becomes closed and his heart opened. As the Lord says, "Verily, in the remembrance of Allah do hearts find their rest" (Qur'ān, al-Ra'ad 13:28).

3.1.8 Discussion

Can humans find moral values, or do we need divine providence to find it for us? Modern forms of humans have existed for around 200,000 years, and there is evidence from various scriptures that there have been prophets and guides sent to

---

[2] It should be noted that Madahab here does not refer to the four Schools of Thought or Law within Islam (Hanafi, Maliki, Shafi and Hanbali) but refers to the sects and cults that have grown within Islam that proclaim sole ownership of the truth.

3.1 *Riazat* or Efforts for Good Conduct in the Way of God

humanity to steer their conduct towards God, thereby providing a moral compass. Even though there is much variation in cultures, some pre-dating the Abrahamic faiths including Islam, some key values of life seem to be universal and forms the social fabrics of human society. This includes such things as not to kill, not to steal, not to take others property, respecting people, their rights and dignity etc. In this sense, there is an innate sense of justice and conduct that has been programmed into us as humans and throughout history there have been divinely guided people known as prophets and sages, who have steered us in the right direction.

Riazat, meaning good conduct in the way of God, is subsumed with the rubric of *akhlāq* or morality, which is a broader concept. This is deeply rooted within the Qur'ān and the way of the Prophet, who was sent as a 'mercy to mankind' in order to perfect morals. *Akhlāq* is so crucial that even if you immerse yourself in worship but do not have good conduct, your position becomes weak in the eyes of God. A Prophetic supplication that highlights this is, "O Allah, You have fashioned my body well; please fashion my morality well" (Kolkailah 2012).

From these above statements it is evident that both virtues and vices are underlined by the Islamic tradition; we are urged to unburden ourselves from our egoist states, while giving due consideration to others, where justice is spelt out as a key principle of equity and caring for the less fortunate, which forms the bedrock of Islam.

Nothing is inherently good or bad but rather it is the intention behind it that makes it so, except good will as articulated by Kant (Folse 2003). Here, the reference is to the intention of an individual being the prime mover in determining if an action is good or bad, and goodwill referring to universally accepted things, such as intelligence, wit, judgment, courage, resolution, perseverance, power, riches, honour, health etc. Even though the above statement is true within the context of varying environments, evil does exist in this world, which history informs us results from the ways that people decide to act on the free will that God has given them and for which they are then responsible.

This, then, has implications for how one behaves. It poses the fundamental question: is good or bad conduct a result of one's character, which is derived from nature, or can it be nurtured and developed? Even though everyone has their own base/original character, Imam Ghazāli says that through education and training one can change oneself, as well as through the company that one keeps, as stated by the Prophet.

Within the context of the human realm, what do other theistic and non-theistic religions say about right and wrong conduct? It is important to examine this aspect since we live in a multi-cultural and multi-religious world and need to be mindful of varying perspectives that have a bearing on society at large. If Buddhism, which is a non-theistic way of life, is examined, it lays down ten vices or what are called negative emotions, where there are three vices of the body, four vices of speech, and three of the mind. The ones of the body are: killing, stealing and sexual misconduct. The vices of speech are: divisive speech, false speech, harsh speech, and senseless gossip; while the three mental vices are: covetousness, harmful thoughts and intentions, and wrong views (Dalai Lama 1998). This shows that in

Fig. 3.1 Johari window
(Source: De Victoria 2008)

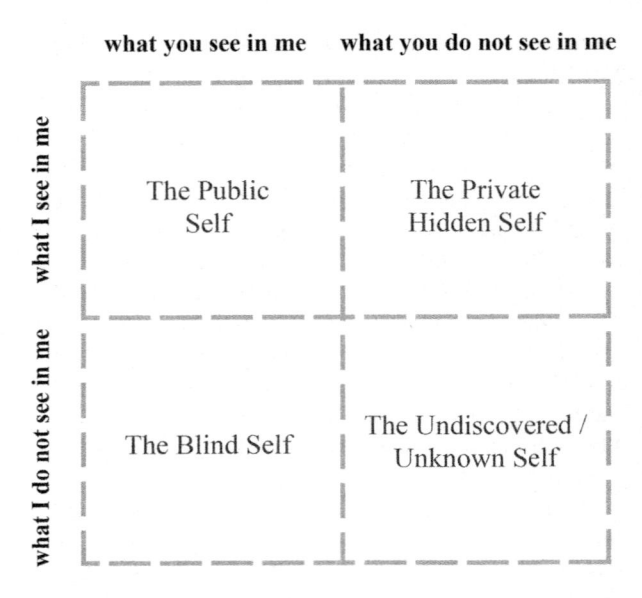

	what you see in me	what you do not see in me
what I see in me	The Public Self	The Private Hidden Self
what I do not see in me	The Blind Self	The Undiscovered / Unknown Self

terms of conduct, theistic and non-theistic religions outline more or less similar deeds, acts, or thoughts and, in this sense, there is a universal nature that points to divine guidance and providence.

Within the context of spiritual development, which is concomitant with self-development, perhaps one can assert that a greater level of awareness is brought about by the development of the soul through its various processes of ascension, namely, from its beastly self, to that of the blaming self and finally to the soul at peace, as cited in the Qur'ān and as articulated by Imam Muḥāsibi (Smith 1980) and Imam Ghazāli (1995). Why this is so paramount is that good conduct and striving towards God are necessarily interconnected not only with good behaviour, but also with the evolution of the soul to better states in achieving nearness to the Lord, where one finds peace.

Developed by Joseph Luft and Harry Ingham, in psychology the "Johari Window" (Fig. 3.1) offers a way of looking at how personality is expressed (De Victoria 2008). Outlined below is an inter-psychic and interpersonal communication grid, which provides a basis in creating a greater sense of awareness about oneself as did the Prophet and his Companions.

This above tool draws out the conscious and the sub-conscious areas of one's life, what you do and do not see about yourself, or that of which one is not aware, which is also called the blind self. The latter can be known by asking others about yourself and determining what they observe and which you may not know. This is exactly what Hazrat Omar bin Khatabb, the second Kaliph and the sage Hazrat Daud Tai have recommended their companions to do. This shows that there was a high level of awareness of the self and its methods of development during the time of the Prophet, which is lacking today.

3.1 *Riazat* or Efforts for Good Conduct in the Way of God

There is a whole system of good intentions, behaviour, and acts of worship, which have been well articulated by several Islamic scholars of repute based on the Qur'ān and *sunnah*, including Imam Muḥāsibi (Smith 1980), Imam Ghazāli (1995), Imam 'Abdullah Ansari (2010), Imam al-Mawlud (2012), 'Abd al-Qader Al-Jilani (1997), Ibn Ataullah Iskandari (2006) and several others. Their work deals with combating the vices of greed, miserliness, wantonness, hatred, envy, ostentation, vanity, anger, fraud, rancour, heedlessness etc, as well as developing the virtues of repentance, magnanimity, chivalry, devotion, patience, intention, striving, discipline, refinement, self-examination etc. The Prophet, the companions, and the sages who followed them have set a up a solid framework, which when combined with proper guidance, good company and an effort leading one to inner peace has positive implications both for this life and the next.

Bad conduct is not only impedes spiritual development but has wider implications as witnessed in the recent global financial crisis that had a significant negative impact in many parts of the world (Rahn 2010). This, for example, was attributed to greed on the part of the lending institutions and rating agencies, who did not follow the rules and encouraged or tolerated fraud on the part of the borrowers, falsifying documentation, in addition to government and management failure.

What is most intriguing when one examines virtues and vices from a perspective of a continuum, the middle position is seen as the most suitable one, where, for example, extravagance and miserliness are both vices and benevolence including generosity is considered a virtue. This was also found to be the case with other concepts, which are reflected in the Table 2.5. This in a sense, reinforces the view of taking a balanced approach and lays credence to the Prophet's statement of Islam being a middle-way (*ummathan wasathan*). This position is also echoed by the Buddha, where he experimented with the extremes and then came to a conclusion of the middle-ground (*majjihima padipada*)—even though the orientations of the religions are different. One needs to look beyond *riazat* or efforts of good conduct in the way of God and see the bigger picture within the framework of *akhlāq* (morality), which subsumes *riazat*. Thus, the moral compass derived from the Qur'ān and the *sunnah* including *riazat* are instruments to get near to God, and this should form a holistic path within the Islamic perspective. It needs to be understood that it is not confined to the normative definition of worship alone, but also combines virtuous conduct towards other human beings and God, which elevate the soul. It is striking the balance or the middle way (*ummatan wassatan*) that affords one the ability to sail through this life and the next, rather than taking the path of extremes.

There are specific practices within the tradition, which provide a solid psychological basis for examining oneself and re-asserting the state of our morality, such as mirroring or emulating the good qualities one sees in others, checking one's faults, the constant remembrance of Allah, seeking forgiveness and forgiving others etc. Yet one needs to be cognisant that good attitude and behaviour is not the raison d'etre but a vehicle for one's development. Since good conduct combined with worship provides a basis for developing one's spiritual states (*ḥāl*) and stations (*maqām*) in moving on to a higher state of consciousness or nearness to God, which is the reason of our existence.

3.2 The Spiritual Journey and the Leadership of Prophet Muhammad: Integrating Morality with Worship

3.2.1 Introduction

This section demonstrates through the use of traditional sources that the Prophet was a human being of the highest calibre and a role-model who changed the face of humanity. Within the contemporary context Martin Lings aptly portrays the evolving situation, which captures our modern state of life: "One of the functions of the Word-made book, with a view to the primordial religion that Islam claimed to be, was to reawaken in man his primeval sense of wonderment, which with the passage of time, had become dimmed or misdirected" (Lings 2005). In order to explicate the above mentioned statement, there is a need to examine the life of the Prophet to map out how he lived, which has its basis in the Qur'ān. The Qur'ān says "Indeed you have in the Messenger of Allah an excellent example for any one whose hope is in Allah and the Final Day, and remembers Allah much" (al-Ahzab 33:21). Let us now turn our attention to understanding the Prophetic model of living.

A review of most biographies of the Prophet, portrays the pre-Islamic period, his early life, and role as head of the family, a statesmen, a religious and political leader, where the historical focus is on the several battles that he had to wage to protect the nascent and emerging group of new Muslims. From the earliest biographies by Ibn Ishaq (Guillaume 1995), Ibn Waqidi (Faizer 2011) and Ibn Hisham (2002) to the more recent ones including Haykal (1993), Mubarakpuri, 2002a and 2002b, Ghazali (1995), Salahi (1995), Bashier (1990), Ali Nadwi (2014), Abu Khali (2003); provides an overall sketch of the life and character of the Prophet, profile of his wives, events, campaigns, expeditions, treaties, engagement with other nations, where there seems to be undue focus on the battles that he had to wage. While it is necessary from an historical perspective, this is to miss the main point of his mission, which the Qur'an says as:

> "...We have sent unto you a Messenger from among yourselves, who recites unto you Our revelations and purifies you, and teaches you the scripture and wisdom, and teaches you that which you did not know." (Quran 2:151).

> "You have indeed in the Messenger of Allah a beautiful pattern (of conduct) for any one whose hope is in Allah and the Final Day, and who engages much in the Praise of Allah." [Quran 33:21].

This is backed by the *ḥadith* or narrative to 'perfect human character'. This signifies spiritual guidance which is offered by the Prophet to purify oneself, have cordial relationship with others and cultivate consciousness of God, which essentially calls for an integration of both worship (*ibadah*) and morality (*akhlaq*). Apart from the biographical works that are mentioned here, who are largely Muslims, with a few exceptions as noted below, there have been some notable figures who were non-Muslims, who outlined the intention and the character of the Prophet as par excellence, which rebuts some of the slanders which have been unfairly advocated.

I have found a few works (Schimmel 1985, al-Yahusbi 1991, al Tirimidhi 2002, Lings 2006, Khalidi 2009, Chopra 2010), which deals with certain aspects of the Prophet's spiritual journey and states, which to me is the quintessential aspect of his universal mission. In this light, the section presented below is an attempt to gain greater insight into his spiritual pathway of the Prophet, in order to fill this essential gap in literature, while making reference to the theories of the notable humanistic psychologists, Abraham Maslow (2014) and Rogers (1991) to see the Prophet's life into a contemporary perspective.

3.2.2 The Prophetic Model

The Prophet Muhammad was born in the sixth century into one of the notable clans of Makkah (Mecca), an epicentre from time immemorial, the home of the Ka'ba. The religion of Prophet Abraham with its monotheistic creed had been lost and the people had turned to many gods and idols to whom they made sacrifices and prayed to. Figure 3.2 provides a spiritual timeline as well as some key events in the life of the Prophet.

The love of the Prophet Muhammad reigns high amongst the Muslims due to his position in Islam as the best of creation and the beloved of Allah, he is seen as the role model to be emulated. The question that begs to be asked is, do Muslims emulate both the Prophet's inner and outer states? The answer to this would lie in the attitude and behaviour of the Muslims and how closely they actually follow the role model of the Prophet, as will be seen in the ensuing discussion. The shahada or declaration of the Islamic faith itself requires one to testify in the Oneness of God and that the Prophet Muhammad is His Prophet. Thus, the Prophet is tied into the very fabric of the faith, for he has authenticated the divine message and is thus the Messenger (*rasul*) who carried the message, as well as a Prophet (*nabi*) who delivered a new one superseding the older scriptural messages and/or confirming it.

3.2.3 The Prophet's Code of Conduct and Sense of Morality

The approach in this section, will be to identify the traits of the Prophet, which essentially falls within the framework of *akhlāq* (morality), including his code of conduct, outlining its definition and providing supporting evidence to back it up. As the tables below show (Tables 3.3 and 3.4), the Prophet's character was infused with virtuous qualities that manifested in his code of conduct and is a part of his spiritual legacy. The Islamic ethos is to follow the Prophetic model by emulating these virtues. One of the better ways to capture the behaviour of people is in their

Fig. 3.2 Timeline of the prophet

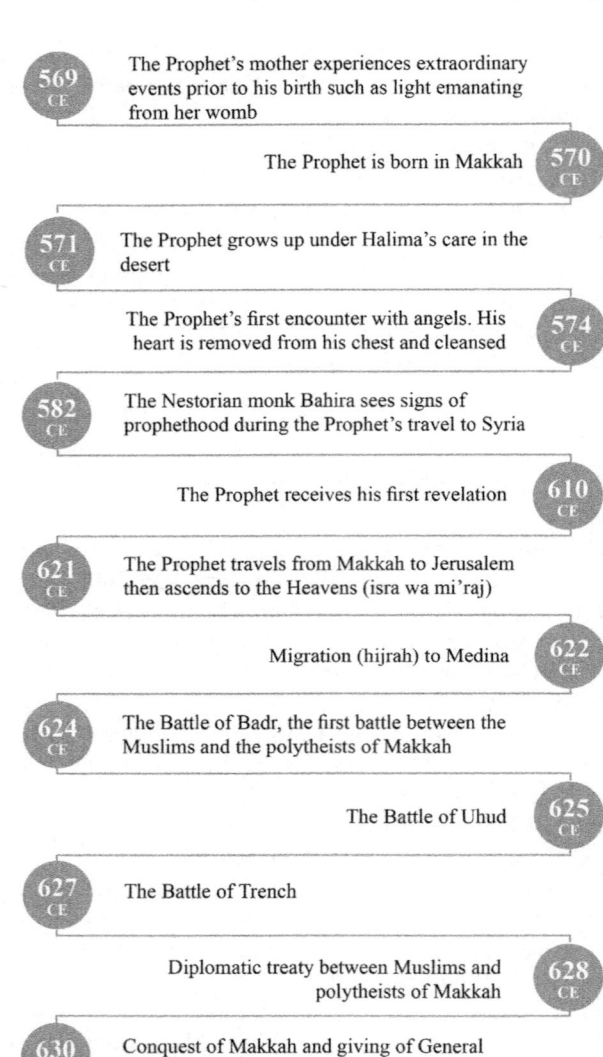

- **569 CE** — The Prophet's mother experiences extraordinary events prior to his birth such as light emanating from her womb
- **570 CE** — The Prophet is born in Makkah
- **571 CE** — The Prophet grows up under Halima's care in the desert
- **574 CE** — The Prophet's first encounter with angels. His heart is removed from his chest and cleansed
- **582 CE** — The Nestorian monk Bahira sees signs of prophethood during the Prophet's travel to Syria
- **610 CE** — The Prophet receives his first revelation
- **621 CE** — The Prophet travels from Makkah to Jerusalem then ascends to the Heavens (isra wa mi'raj)
- **622 CE** — Migration (hijrah) to Medina
- **624 CE** — The Battle of Badr, the first battle between the Muslims and the polytheists of Makkah
- **625 CE** — The Battle of Uhud
- **627 CE** — The Battle of Trench
- **628 CE** — Diplomatic treaty between Muslims and polytheists of Makkah
- **630 CE** — Conquest of Makkah and giving of General Amnesty by the Prophet
- **632 CE** — Farewell speech. The Prophet passes away

3.2 The Spiritual Journey and the Leadership of Prophet Muhammad:...

Table 3.3 Identifying some key traits of the prophet

Type of Adab	Definition	Supporting evidence
Compassion	A strong feeling of sympathy for peoples who are suffering and a desire to help them.	Anas bin Maalik says, "I remained in the service of the Prophet for 10 years. He never once told, "Be off". When I did something, he never asked me "Why did you do that?" When I did not do certain task, he never asked me why I did not do it. He had the best of character amongst all people" (al Tirimidhi 2002).
Loving	A feeling or showing love and affection for somebody/ something.	The Prophet's loving nature is manifest in his interaction towards children, as well as his wives: it is reported about his granddaughter Umama that, "Once or twice he brought her with him to the Mosque perched on his shoulder kept her their while he recited the Qu'rān, putting her down before the inclination and prostrations and restoring her to his shoulder when he resumed his upright position" (Ibn Ishaq 1967).
Gratitude	The feeling of being grateful and wanting to express your thanks.	The companion of the Prophet Mughira bin Shu'bah and Abu Huraira said that the Prophet performed such lengthy optional prayers (nafl) that his leg became swollen and Mughira said, "You undergo such great difficulties, whereas Allah has forgiven your past and future sins." The Prophet responded, "Should I not be a grateful servant?" (Tirimidhi 2002, (248) Hadith Number 1, 269; (249), Hadith Number 2, 270; (250), Hadith Number 3, 271).
Equity	A situation in which everyone is treated equally.	One of the Prophet's helpers had an issue with a Jew regarding the status of the Prophet vis-à-vis Prophet Moses, where the Prophet cited the Qur'ān, "We make no distinction between any of them" (Al-Qur'ān, Al-Baraqa 2:136).
Generosity	The fact of being generous (willing to give somebody money, gifts, time or kindness freely).	The Prophet on one of his expeditions becoming aware of the situation of poverty of Jabir son of Abdallah, asked to buy his camel and then paid him an ounce of gold and then also returned his camel to his surprise. (Lings 2005)
Steadfast	Not changing in your attitudes or aims.	"Even if you do a little worship be steadfast in it".
Modesty	The regard for decency of behaviour, speech, dress etc…	Abu Sa'eed Khudri says that the Prophet was more bashful than a virgin in her veil. When the Prophet did not like something, it could be seen on his face (but because of the excessive modesty he did not mention it). (Tirimidhi 2002, (341) Hadith Number 1, 377)

(continued)

Table 3.3 (continued)

Type of Adab	Definition	Supporting evidence
Brave	Willing to do things, which are difficult, dangerous or painful; not afraid.	When the Quraysh were preparing a large army to confront the growing but yet small band of Muslims, most opinions were not to leave Medina but the Prophet articulated thus: "It is not for a Prophet, when he hath put on his armour, to take it off until God hath judged between him and his enemies. The victory is yours, if ye be steadfast" (Lings 2005).
Freedom	The right to do or say what you want without anyone stopping you.	When the Prophet's uncle Abbas sent his slave Aby Rafi as a gift to the Prophet and he set him free instead of making him work for him (Lings 2005).
Justice	Amongst others, the fair treatment of people.	A pact was established to do away with injustice, when the Prophet was young, where he said "I was present at the house of Abd' Allah bin Judan and so excellent was the pact that I will not exchange my part in it for a herd of red camels, and if now, in Islam, if I was summoned unto it, I will gladly respond" (Lings 2005).
		When the Prophet first entered Medina and his camel alighted at a particular place, he bought the piece of land from the two orphans Sahl and Suhail even though they wanted to give it to him free (Lings 2005).
		After the first battle called Badr, the Prophet gave orders to treat well all captives even though they had to be bound (Lings 2005).

interactions with others and the table below presents the character of the Prophet and his code of conduct at assemblies. What is apparent from his conduct is that he was a person who was very considerate and civil, contrary to many rulers and leaders who are authoritarian and arrogant to their subjects.

3.2.4 The Prophet's Worship and his Spiritual Nature

Knowledge is the central tenant that the Prophet emphasised in his discourse and actions. The divine revelations form the fountainhead of knowledge, this is captured in the message: "And if all the trees on the earth were pens and the sea, with seven seas behind it to add to it, yet the Words of Allah would not be exhausted. Verily Allah is All-Mighty, All-Wise" (Qur'ān, Luqman 31:27). Table 3.4 encapsulates its importance. Within Islamic cosmology, knowledge is divided into three main domains, namely, the divine directly from God; the rational and the intuitive.

3.2 The Spiritual Journey and the Leadership of Prophet Muhammad:... 109

Table 3.4 Behaviour of the prophet at assemblies

Snapshot	Situation	Supporting evidence
Profile of the Prophet	Prophet's behaviour in assemblies and his mode of interaction.	Imam Hassan stated stated that his younger brother Imam Hussain asked about the conduct of the Prophet in his assemblies from his father Imam Ali, who thus described it: (1) He was always happy and easy mannered. (2) There was always a smile and sign of happiness on his blessed face. (3) He was soft natured and when people wanted his approval, he easily gave consent. (4) He did not scream while speaking, nor was he rude or spoke indecently. (5) He never over-praised anything nor exceeded in joking, nor was he a miser. (6) He kept away from undesirable language and did not make as if he did not hear something. (7) He completely kept away from three things: from argument, pride and senseless utterance. (8) He did not disagree or insult anyone, nor look for faults of others, he only spoke from that which merits and rewards was attained. (9) When he spoke those present bowed their heads in such a manner, as if there was a bird sitting on their heads. (10) Whenever one spoke to him, the other would keep quiet and listen till he would finish. (11) He exercised patience at the harshness and the indecent questions of a traveller. (12) If someone by way of thanks praised him, he would remain silent. (13) He did not interrupt when someone was talking and did not begin speaking when someone was busy speaking." (Tirimidhi 2002, Hadith number 9, 369–370).

Knowledge ('ilm) and the intellect ('aql) form core elements within Islamic epistemology or the theory of knowledge and have a much wider scope and connotation than in the Western context as it has given the "Muslim civilisation its distinctive shape and complexion" (Rosenthal 2007). Rosenthal asserts that there is no other term which has been more pervasive within Islam as 'ilm, in terms of its "depth of meaning and wide incidence of use."

Within the Islamic context, the Qur'ānic narrative was a precursor to the development of knowledge, which was orally learnt and then transformed into a written form. The frequency with which the term 'ilm occurs in the Qur'ān, as well as the emphasis given to it by the Prophet himself, are without doubt are evidence its prime importance. In this context, Rosenthal (2007) states that the Prophetic concept of knowledge "set intellectual life of Islam on its basically unchangeable course".

The *sunnah* of the Prophet which has been operationalised from the Qur'ān lays the platform for the development of the Islamic civilisation. The height of Islamic civilisation took place in what can be termed historically as the medieval period, albeit that this is a misnomer that this period is perceived as backward given the significant contribution Islam made to science, society and the intellectual tradition.

This Islamic ethos with its body of knowledge, accompanying rules, regulations and mission expanded not only in terms of territory but in increasing the knowledge base of society resulting in a height of intellectual civilisation. This trend influenced both Eastern and Western societies and left its mark in history having influenced many fields of learning including mathematics, architecture, medicine, astronomy etc; (BBC 2020) even though it is not readily acknowledged in a contemporary context (Table 3.5).

Table 3.5 Knowledge as a Central Tenant of Islam

Type of knowledge	Supporting evidence	Reference
Rational	Reason is arrived at by giving attention to things, by developing a surmise or an experience or based on a premise and in some cases reasons is supported by sense perceptions.	Imam Sadr-ad-din al-Qonawi (Rosenthal 2007)
Revelatory	The Qur'ān is "the form of knowledge that comprises the variety of possible conditions affecting existing things", which is also implied as a 'form of divine attribute of knowledge' directly from God.	Imam Sadr-ad-din al-Qonawi (Rosenthal 2007)
Illumination (*tanwīr*)	Illumination (*tanwīr*), which is defined "...as the casting of an idea into the intellect (*al-aql*) by means of overflowing (*al-fayd*)"	Imam Sadr-ad-din al-Qonawi (Rosenthal 2007)
Intuition (*badīha*)	The light that God casts into the breast of humans, which is not derived from rational arguments or rational proofs.	Imam Abu Hamid al Ghazali (Ghazāli 2007)
Action Based (Prophetic Sunnah)	The sunnah's formed the operationalisation of Qur'ānic knowledge to everyday life by the Prophet. The former was recorded immediately and transmitted through time, while the latter was orally sustained and later on recorded as text.	These are encapsulated in the six major traditional works including: Bukhari, Muslim, Tirimidhi, Ibn Majah, An Nasai, Dawood.
Dreams	This refers to the Prophetic dreams that he had, which were visions, which unfolded over time.	Imam Ahmed recorded that Ai'sha stated, "The first thing that began happening with the Messenger of Allah from the revelation was dreams that he would see in his sleep that would come true. He would not see any dream except that is would come true just like the (clearness of) the daybreak in the morning" (Ibn Kathir's Tafsir 2003:532).

Knowledge, which took varied forms in the life of the Prophet, is evident in every sphere of his life from the mundane to the scared. However, the Prophetic knowledge was pitched at different levels and articulated depending on the level of understanding and trust of the person concerned. This is evident as outlined below:

(i) Only a part of the spiritual journey was shared with the community, the Prophet shared the first part (al-Isra), which was from Makkah to Jerusalem, while his ascension to the celestial zone (al-Miraj), the seven heavens and the meeting with the Lord was only shared with his very close companions. Thereafter articulated as a question and answer dialogue

(ii) Narrated (by Abu Huraira): "I have memorized two kinds of knowledge from Allah's Messenger ( ).. I have propagated one of them to you and if I propagate the second, then my pharynx (throat) will be cut off" (i.e. killed) (Bukhari 1994).

(iii) "Allah will exalt in degrees those of you who believe, and those who have been granted knowledge. And Allah is well-acquainted with what you do" (Qur'ān, al-Mujadilah 58:11).

(iv) Say: "Are those who know equal to those who know not? It is only men of understanding who will remember" (Qur'ān, al-Zumar 39:9).

Having shown some of the human nature of the Prophet, there are many dimensions that underscore his spiritual nature and that bring out his uniqueness and sanctify his mission and journey.

3.2.5 *'Ibādah (Acts of Worship)*

This section deals with some of the key tenants of Islam, which the Prophet practiced and became part of his way of life. It also highlights some of the mental states that embodied his life and that are key to sustaining one's state of worship and enhancing spiritual progress. The contents of Tables 3.6 and 3.7 highlight the five pillars or principles in Islam—The Oneness of God; the ritualistic prayer, the obligatory payment (zakah), fasting and the performance of the journey to Makkah (*hajj*).

The Prophet performed these obligatory rites but went much beyond them in the performance of optional acts, which he intensified in most cases beyond the normal call of duty.

3.2.6 *States of the Prophet*

One of the most crucial aspects of the Prophet's life which is not often discussed and practiced is his reflective inner, as well as the outer states that he maintained (see Table 3.7). These are explained below. Imam Ali Ibn Abi Talib states when asked

Table 3.6 Identifying key acts of *'Ibādah* (Worship) of the Prophet

Type of 'Ibādah	Description	Supporting evidence
Salah (ritual prayer)	A ritual set of words and actions taught to the Prophet by Angel Jibril and sanctioned by God during the Prophet's ascent to Heaven. A type of movement and still meditation, with word chanting and silence laced into one	The Angel Jibril showed the Prophet how to purify for worship, as well as the various movements in prayer including standing, the inclining, the prostrating and the sitting, with its repeated magnification (Lings 2005). In addition to evening and dawn payers, there were voluntary prayers performed following the same pattern. The Prophet mentioned that one third of the night was blessed "Each night, when a third of it has yet to come, our Lord—the blessed and exalted be He!—descendeth unto the nethermost heaven," and He saith; "Who calleth onto Me, that I may answer him? Who prayeth unto Me a prayer, that I may grant him it? Who asketh my forgiveness, that I may forgive him?" (Bukhari 1994). Abu Hurayrah asked the Prophet, what do you say during the silence between takbir (the start) and the recitation? He said: "I say—O Allah, remove my sins from me as far as You have the East from the West. O Allah, purify me from sins as a white garment is purified from filth. O Allah, wash away my sins with water, snow and hail" (Al Muslim as cited in Maqsood (2001).
Recitation of Qur'ān	The divine scriptures sent to the Prophet are to be recited and reflected upon. The celestial sound itself serves as a form of meditation.	God says, "or add to it (at will); and (during that time) recite the Qur'ān calmly and distinctly, with thy mind attuned to its meaning. Verily, the hours of night impress the mind most strongly and speak with the clearest voice" (Qur'ān, al-Muzzammil 73:4,6). The Qur'ān enjoined long recitation of its own verses, while the Prophet recommended various litanies of repentance and praise (Lings 2005).
Fasting	Abstaining from food and drink but also includes the restraining of the five senses. A detox for the mind and body.	God says, "O you who believe! Fasting is prescribed to you as it was prescribed to those before you, that you may acquire *taqwa* (piety)" (Qur'ān, Al-Baqara 2:183).

(continued)

3.2 The Spiritual Journey and the Leadership of Prophet Muhammad:... 113

Table 3.6 (continued)

Type of 'Ibādah	Description	Supporting evidence
Zakah	An obligatory charity for those who can afford it from their annual savings.	"Islam is erected on five cardinals; bearing witness that there is no deity except Allah and that Muhammad is God's Messenger; establishing prayers; paying the poor-due (*zakah*); making the pilgrimage, and fasting the days of the month of Ramadan" (Ibn Daqiq al-'Id 2014).
Hajj-'Umrah	A ritualistic pilgrimage of Abrahamic tradition, which was made obligatory upon those who can afford it.	The Prophet only performed two Hajj (one when he was in Makkah and one from Medina), which was combined with his last sermon in Arafah, a historical speech that laid down the rights of different races, women and children. There was only 4 'Umrahs that he had performed.
Sadaqa	A voluntary act of charity not only referring giving money but also other acts to help people in need	Abu Huraira narrates that the Prophet said "My heirs must not distribute Dinars and Dirhams. From my assets, after deducting the expenditure of my women (family), and the *aamils* (workers), whatever is left over must be given as *sadaqa*" (Tirimidhi 2002, Hadith number 5, 441). Rubayyi bint Mu'awwidh bin Afraa said, "I bought to the Prophet a tray full of dates, and some small cucumbers. The Prophet gave me a handful of jewellery" (Tirimidhi 2002, Hadith number 14, 374).

about the silence of the Messenger of God said, "He was silent for four reasons: forbearance, caution, appraisal and reflection. His appraisal lay in constantly observing and listening to the people. His reflection was upon what would endure and what would vanish. He had forbearance in his patience. Nothing provocative angered him." Then he added, "He was cautious about four things: in adopting something good which would be followed, in abandoning something bad which would be abandoned, in striving to determine what would be beneficial for his community and in establishing for them what would combine the business of this world and the next" (Qadi 'Iyad 1991).

Some key aspects are outlined in the Table 3.7, namely, state of poverty; keeping vigil especially night vigil; maintaining silence unless required; non-attachment to things or being non-materialistic; being in a state of mindfulness or heightened sense of awareness; being contended or satisfied with states and situations; maintaining a state of cleanliness and being physically fit and working, as well as practicing martial arts. What is apparent is that apart from the obligatory and ritualistic acts of worship, the Prophet maintained certain states especially of the mind and a healthy physical constitution, which were a part of his inner and outer states.

Table 3.7 Identifying the State of the Prophet

Type of *'Ibādah*	Description	Supporting evidence
State of Poverty	Simplicity of living and contentment with the bare minimum. Involuntary as well as voluntary state of poverty	The People of the Bench (Ahl-al-Suffah), were the poor and the refugees, who had lived on a bench at the end of the mosque, the Prophet and his household took responsibility for their welfare (Lings 2005). Aisha, the wife of the Prophet reports, "We, the family of Muhammad, did not light a fire for months in our homes. We sustained ourselves on dates and water" (Tirimidhi 2002, Hadith number 4, 394). Abu Talha says, "We complained to the Prophet about the severe pangs of hunger and showed him the stones fastened to our stomachs. A stone was fastened on the stomach of every one of us due to severe hunger. The Prophet showed us two stones fastened onto his stomach" (Tirimidhi 2002, Hadith number 5, 395). Anas reported that "The Prophet did not store anything for the next day."
Dhikr	A deeper immersion into meditation, which is both through sound as well as silence, with focus on the names and attributes of God. The focus is on the words, the presence of yourself and on your breath.	Abu Ma'bad, the freed slave of Ibn Abbas said, "In the lifetime of the Prophet, it was the custom to remember Allah by glorifying, praising and magnifying Allah aloud after the compulsory congregational prayers (salah)." Ibn Abbas further said, "When I heard the Dhikr, I would learn that the compulsory congregational prayer had ended" (Bukhari 1994). God says, "And remember the Name of your Lord and totally devote yourself to Him with complete devotion. Lord of the East and the West; there is no God but he, so take Him as a trustee" (Qur'ān, al-Muzammil 73:8-9). God says, "So when you have accomplished your rituals remember Allah as you remember your forefathers or with far more remembrance" (Qur'ān, al-Baqara 2:200). God says, "So bear with patience all that they say, and glorify the praises of your Lord, before the rising of the sun and before (its) setting. And during a part of the night (also) glorify His praises also (so likewise) after the prostration" (Qur'ān, Qaf 50:39-40).

(continued)

3.2 The Spiritual Journey and the Leadership of Prophet Muhammad:... 115

Table 3.7 (continued)

Type of *'Ibādah*	Description	Supporting evidence
		Abu Huraira narrates that the Prophet stated, "The example of the one who remembers (glorifies the Praises of) his Lord in comparison to the one who does not remember (glorify the Praises of) his Lord, is that of a living creature compared to a dead one" (Bukhari 1994).
Silence	Remaining without speaking: does not confine itself to only words but also the silence of the heart, without all its clutter.	God says, "Their sides forsake their beds, to invoke their Lord. In fear and hope, and they spend out of that We have bestowed on them" (Qur'ān, As-Sajdah 32:26).
Non-Attachment/ detachment to Material Things	Not craving for material things and only confining oneself to essential needs, while accepting "At the time of great need, a woman presented him with a sheet and he wore it as he was in need of it. A person came and asked him for it, he presented the sheet to the person" (Tirimidhi 2002). Ibn Abbas reports on the Prophet, "Taking of loans and fulfilling the needs of others when the creditors came, and if some resources had come from somewhere, he would pay the debts, and did not go home till everything was given to the needy" (Tirimidhi 2002). On the authority of Abu'l Abbas Sahl Ibn Sa'd al-Sa'idi narrates that a person came to the Prophet and said, "O Messenger of Allah, tell me about an act that if I were to perform it, God will love me and also people will love me." The Prophet said, "Be unattached to this world, and God will love you; and be unattached to what people possess and they will love you" (Ibn Daqiq al-'Id 2014). On the authority of the son of Umar, the Prophet took him by his shoulder and said, "Be in this world as a stranger or a traveller passing through" (Ibn Daqiq al-'Id 2014).	

(continued)

Table 3.7 (continued)

Type of 'Ibādah	Description	Supporting evidence
	'Ali Ibn Abi Talib sums up the Prophet's guidance, "Do for this world as if to live forever and for the next world as if to die upon the morrow", and "To be always ready to depart is to be detached" (Lings 2005).	
Keeping Vigil	A period of time when people stay awake, esp. at night, in order to watch a sick person, say prayers, protest, etc..	God says, "O you wrapped up! Stand (to pray) all night, except a little. Half of it or less than that, a little..." (Qur'ān, al-Muzzammil 200:1-3). Asad (2011) points out that the term wrapped can be understood as in a literal sense as wrapped up in a cloak or in a metaphorical sense as being wrapped up in sleep or even wrapped up in oneself. He goes on to state that whatever may be the linguistic sense "it implies a call to heightened consciousness and deeper spiritual awareness on the part of the Prophet."
		The companions of the Prophet took the above commandment as applying to themselves and they would keep long vigils (Lings 2005).
		The Prophet stated an ideal to be followed: a third of the 24 h daily cycle should be for worship, a third for work and family, with the last third including time spent in sleep and at meals (Lings 2005).
State of Mindfulness	Being in a state of awareness of the things that one does without being judgmental. Within the Islamic context this means concerted focus on God, without any other forms of thought.	The Prophet stated, "Verily this day ye are at a station which is rich in reward and rich in treasure, for him who is mindful of what he is about and who is devoteth to this soul thereunto in patience and certainty and earnestness and effort" (Lings 2005).
Physicality	The quality of being physical rather than emotional or spiritual.	Fit and well set with a flat stomach. The Prophet commented to one of the companions, "the bulge would look better on someone else."

(continued)

Table 3.7 (continued)

Cleanliness	The state of being clean or the habit of keeping things clean.	God says, "O you enveloped in garments! Arise and warn! And magnify your Lord! And purify your garments! And keep away from al-Rujz (idols)!" (Qur'ān, al-Muddaththir 74:1-5). The companions did not only perform the ablution but also ensured that their garments were free of defilement
Contentment	A feeling of happiness or satisfaction	The Prophet insisted that, "All is well with the faithful whatever the circumstances" (Lings 2005).

3.2.7 Spiritual Leadership and the Prophet

One key reason for examining spiritually-oriented leadership is that these leaders have been found to be more effective and transformational in nature than leadership in other settings (Revees 2005). Motivation, which is spiritually-oriented and faith-based is identified as a 'distinguished variable', which is the cause of much of the transformational leadership (Revees 2005). The sense of commitment that these types of leaders have are said to be derived from their 'own conscience and internalised values' derived from a spiritual sense of connectivity with a higher power (Revees 2005). As seen in the discussions above, the best illustration has been the life of Prophet Muhammad, who was able to transform the people from their state of ignorance to a more enlightened state.

In Ibn Khaldun's articulation, work or craft is seen as a metaphor, whereby one personally grows both his/her social roles and technical skills (Kriger and Seng 2005). Within the Islamic context, worship and services are intrinsically linked, where as we have seen in the example of the Prophet, that good works and right conduct (see Sects. 3.1 and 3.2) shape the soul or the inner self towards good and leads to better connectivity with God. The rapidly expanding societies of the world, with its global outreach have called for a re-examination of organisational structures and their roles and responsibilities. In this sense, a more holistic leadership is called for, that "integrates the four fundamental arenas that define the essence of human existence—the body (physical), mind (logical/rational), heart (emotions, feelings), and spirit" (Moxley cited in Fry 2003).

It is argued that spiritual leadership is necessary for the transformation, as well as the success of learning organisations, and in this light, "spiritual leadership taps into the fundamental needs to both the leader and follower for spiritual survival so they become more organisationally committed and productive" (Fry 2003). In this context, spiritual leadership is defined as "comprising the values, attitudes, and behaviours that are necessary to intrinsically motivate one's self and others so that they have a sense of spiritual survival through calling and membership" (Fry 2003).

Table 3.8 Qualities of spiritual leadership

Vision	Altruistic love	Hope/Faith
Broad appeal to key stakeholders	Forgiveness	Endurance
Defines the destination and journey	Kindness	Perseverance
Reflects high ideals	Integrity	Do what it takes
Encourages hope/faith	Empathy/Compassion	Stretch goals
Establishes a standard of excellence	Honesty	Expectation of reward/victory
	Patience	
	Courage	
	Trust/Loyalty	
	Humility	

The qualities that are often associated with spiritual leadership that are outlined in the Table 3.8, which subsumes the characteristics of the Prophet.

3.2.8 Discussion

The Prophet by virtue of his 'triad relationships' (see Fig. 3.3), was able to transform himself and others as well as society at large, through reverberating his message as an 'art of living' globally. Some have taken this message and fully transformed themselves and others, while some have taken the minimum or else have misunderstood it. In this light, the Prophet who the Qur'ān says "We have not sent you but as a mercy to all the worlds" (Qur'ān, al-Anbiyā, 21:107), forged within Islam the outer and the inner tradition of self-development, with its varying tools and methods. This led to the transformation of the pagan society into a unified whole, with its emphasis on building moral character and developing one's inner consciousness.

This is best understood in merging together of three essential components as outlined in Fig. 3.3, namely the intra-relationship with oneself, the inter-relationship with one's community, and the supra-relationship with one's God. This can be called the triad relationships.

This triad is most crucial for the self-development: if you do not develop yourself how can you develop others? This is a challenge, a struggle (jihad), which goes on and that needs to be well managed for otherwise the inner self could lead one to destruction. In a similar vein, there is the challenge of the relationship with others including communities, enabling one to go beyond one's selfish self and help those

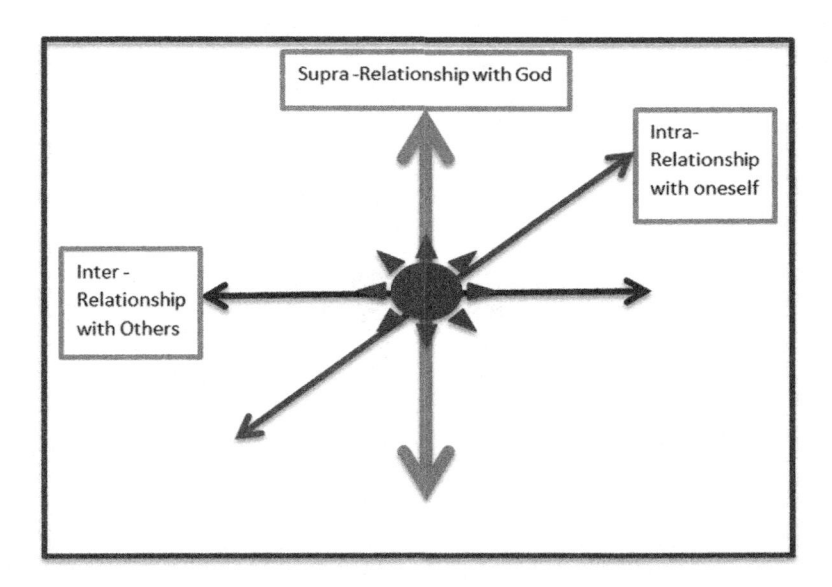

3.2 The Spiritual Journey and the Leadership of Prophet Muhammad:...

Fig. 3.3 The triad relationship with God, Man and Community

in need, preventing social conflict and the disruption of society. For example, the 'Arab Spring' as a case in point, where greed and bad governance including a lack of care for others stretched the people's patience and led to revolts. Then the finale is one's relationship and sustained dialogue with God, which enables one to connect and strengthen oneself. In my view, the integrated concept of the triad that the Prophet taught led to a shift in the paradigm of human development, which transformed individuals and societies.

Tariq Ramadan (2009) encapsulates the essence of the above: "a teaching method relying on gentleness, on the common sense of individuals, and on their understanding of commands, the Prophet also strove to teach how to put their instincts to sleep, so to seek, and how to resort to diversion to escape evil temptations... that a moral sense should be developed not through interdiction and sanction but gradually, gently, exactingly, understandingly and at a deep level."

The Prophetic journey is a spiritual one, where one's intention, orientation, thoughts and practices resulted in a pristine state, enlightening his soul and demonstrating how one prepares for traversing into the next domain or life. The life processes, its manifestations and the impact the Prophet had on life and society points to an extraordinary personality, who was highly spiritual, who reached the highest stage with the rare occurrence of his meeting with the Lord (al-isra wal mi'raj). The Prophet was above normal human standards. This is testified by the divine scriptures itself, where God states that, "And verily you on an exalted standard of character" (Qur'ān, al-Qalam, 68:4) and as evidenced in his extraordinary life.

Fig. 3.4 Key dimensions of human well being

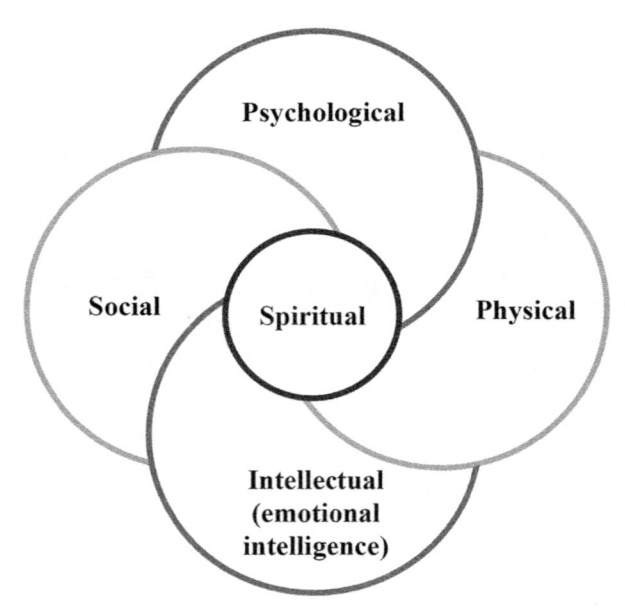

The Prophet stated, "Beware! There is a piece of flesh in the body, if it becomes good (i.e., reformed), the whole body becomes good, but if it gets spoilt, the whole body gets spoilt, and that is the heart" (Bukhari 1994). The heart is inter-changeably used with the soul in the Qur'ān. This forms the essence of the inter-link of all of these traditions, that is, to mould and shape the outer and specifically the inner states of our being, which has a vital carrier—the Soul—and which is prone to both good and bad, tilting towards one's orientation and action. Thus, dealing with one's ego states and inner conflicts needs a combination of appropriate methods and tools together with a guide who can provide the required guidance in relation to dealing with the spiritual and psychological-emotional issue that facilitates one to move towards a more balanced life.

Each of the below mentioned (see Fig. 3.4) are what can be called a tradition, given that each one has a range of tools and its own narrative. This is drawn from the life of the Prophet and is expounded below.

Intellectual Tradition Knowledge was a basis of action: as Rosenthal (2007) points out in his thesis 'Knowledge Triumphant', the emphasis on knowledge in Islam changed the whole course of history and resulted in a civilization that contributed to many facets of endeavour, both human and scientific. What is apparent in the life of the Prophet is the transmission of knowledge in its myriad forms including: revelation (*wahy*—Qur'ān); illumination (tanwir e.g. *hadīth qudsi*—inspired), intuition (badiha), sunnah (Prophetic words and actions), dreams (visions) and rational (ma'qool and ijtihad is by way of reasoning). These dense layers of knowledge embedded themselves within the fabric of Islam and laid the foundation and the pathway for its development. Thus, the faith does not ask one to follow it blindly but with understanding of its purpose and content.

Spiritual Tradition Righteousness (*birr*) and piety (taqwa) are both traits that were central to the life of the Prophet be it in the light of worship (*'ibādah*) (see Table 3.6) or code of conduct (adab) (see Table 3.7) and are key to understanding what it enshrines. Sheikh Al-Qayyim (2007) defines them as '*birr*' representing integrity and excellence of a human being, where one cannot achieve any virtue without it, while piety (taqwa) is a means and a way leading to *birr*, that is, obeying Allah with *iman* and *ihtisab* (counting on Allah's promised reward for a given deed). He points out that deeds or actions should emanate "from pure *iman* and not from customs, desires or pursuit of (worldly) praise or status in order to be counted being acts of obedience that brings one close to God."

Contemplation and Mindfulness The obligatory prayer being one such spiritual act, which the Prophet prayed with complete absorption or 'khushu', which is a state of mindfulness. According to context of iḥsan as revealed in the Jibril ḥadīth: "Worship God as if you see Him (mushāhada), while you see him not, He sees you (murāqaba)" (Ibn Daqiq al-'Id 2014). This is a state of witnessing within the movement meditative practice, namely, the prayer. This is then done with concentration and stillness in its various states and graceful movements, while contemplative on sounds of prayer and focusing on the spot of prostration. Section 2.4 outlined the tangible health benefits of worship including on the body composition, the heart and the brain. In this light, a whole new science has emerged called Neuro-Theology (Newberg and D'Aquili 2000).

The Prophet, in a ḥadīth recorded by Ahmed and Nasa'i, referred to prayers as "the coolness of my eyes." His combination of the obligatory prayers with the optional prayers, which he did intensively devoting a third of the night for this purpose, so much so that his leg used to swell from it and when his wife asked why he prayed so much when he had been promised Paradise by God already he responded, "Should I not be a grateful slave?" (Jawsiya 1997) It is stated that, "When anything distressed the Prophet he prayed" (Abu Dawood cited in Maqsood 2001) both to seek comfort and guidance from his Lord.

The Prophet used the term mindfulness, which is now frequently used in relation to meditation and neuro-science, when he articulated according to his companion Al-Agharr al-Muzani, when he said, "My heart is invaded by unmindfulness, and I ask Allah's pardon a hundred times in the day" (Abu Dawood cited in Maqsood 2001). This effectively implies the focus that we need to have on being mindful, that is, God consciousness, which forms the quintessential of worship and one's state of being.

Fasting or Abstinence as a Method of Restraint Fasting by the Prophet was not only confined to the obligatory fast but to optional fasts that were undertaken twice weekly combined with other fasts that occurred during the special months of the Islamic journey. Food as a general rule was only eaten when hungry and as required by the body and there was a general level of conscientiousness not to over-eat. Is this not a contemporary recipe for staying healthy?

Ritual Practices as a Point of Raising God Consciousness The Hajj, which is an obligatory pilgrimage, with the proviso that one is able to afford it, and 'Umrah, the lesser pilgrimage being optional. All pilgrims are required to wear the most basic attire, two pieces of white unstitched cloth, that are almost shroud like. This pilgrimage itself is where one effectively leaves all material possessions behind and gathers to seek Oneness, while purifying oneself of all of the sins and psychological baggage that one carries during a lifetime. All of the du'ās or supplications of the Prophet during the Hajj, as well as 'Umrah signify this, for example, the unitary focus to the exclusion of all else: "Here I am, O Allah! Here I am! There is no one who is Your partner, here I am! Surely all praise and blessings are Yours, and dominion. You are without companion" (*Talbiya*, which is an often-recited phrase during both Hajj (bigger pilgrimage) and 'Umrah (smaller pilgrimage)). This then is a state of mindful contemplation of the Lord of the East and West, the Universal; the God of all.

Inter-Relationship Tradition—Being Chivalrous The Prophet's profound generosity of both obligatory and voluntary giving was to such an extent that all that he received was exhausted by nightfall. This characterizes him as being non-materialistic and someone who did not live for this world but the next. Chivalry, which forms a quintessential part of Islam, was embodied by the Prophet by his generosity, the courage to do things selflessly and without fear of poverty, one of the conditions he put forth for proper faith or *iman* was, "what you love for yourself you should love for your brother" (Ibn Daqiq al-'Id 2014). This is the golden mean or golden middle way, which is part of the Aristotelian philosophy and of all religious traditions including Hinduism (Vedas), Judaism, Christianity, Islam, as well as in the non-theistic religions Jainism, Hinduism and Buddhism. In this light, it denotes love for humanity, parting with your wealth, debasing your ego and greed, so that you do not hoard or become miserly, which is one of the ruinous traits that affects negatively one's soul.

Combining Worship and Morality Good Code of Conduct: All of the above-mentioned acts, which form the pillars of the Islamic faith, are done routinely but yet in the life of the Prophet we see the depth as well as the breath of his worship. His life is laced with acts of worship and devotion. However, one sees that this is not confined to strictly acts of worship, and even the 'muashaaka' or human interaction, as well as daily actions of life including transactions (mu'amalat) should be accompanied by virtuous acts. Thus, it is not only appropriate to worship but also that one's conduct and behaviour should be aligned or in harmony, and not harming or hurting people.

As evidenced in Tables 3.3, 3.4, and 3.5, there were a spectrum of virtuous traits. In this light, the nexus between '*ibādah*-worship and *akhlāq*-morality, which subsumes one's code of conduct is the key, as seen in the model of the Prophet. What has been outlined is a combination of an extensive range of devotional acts to be done with intensity and commitment.

Psychological Tradition The Mental States of the Prophet: While recognising the value of proper worship and its inter-link with one's virtuous code of conduct, one of the most crucial aspects of human existence, which is increasingly backed up by hard scientific and empirical data, is how one responds to oneself and his/her environment. In this light, the life of the Prophet lays down the mental and the conscious states that underpinned his life, which are most crucial if one is to emulate him and prepare for the next life:

(i) Being God Conscious (*taqwa*): This is the crucial thread that is woven throughout all aspects of the Prophet's life, being and thoughts, be it in prayer, meditation, human transaction, life with his family, and in the battles that he had to overcome. This is maintaining a state of mindfulness.

(ii) Being in a State of Poverty (*zuhud*): This was a conscious state that he chose in order to create a balance between both spiritual and material life. It enabled him to not be attached to material things and find contentment with little. This balanced approached he took is evident in his formula for eating, "One third food, one third water and one third empty."

(iii) Being Contented (*rida*): Though the Prophet was tested with numerous hardships throughout his life, he was always seen with a smile on his face, he participated in conversations and joined in laughter but not excessively. He was satisfied with what he had and constantly thanked God in all situations without complaining.

(iv) Being Mindful (*mubaalin mutanabbih*): Whatever the Prophet did, be it worship or in his daily routine, he did it with a sense of mindfulness and presence. This is manifest in all his daily actions, be they partaking of food or looking in the mirror, he had a prayer for each, and his ritual prayers were always conducted in a state of absorption.

(v) Being Grateful (*shukr-imtinan*): Although he was granted salvation he would pray long into the night out of gratitude to God and whenever something significant happened he went down in prostration to Him. This gratitude extended to everyone around him, as he said, "If one is not grateful to a human being one cannot be grateful to God."

(vi) Having Fortitude (*wujud althabat*): His patience knew no bounds and is called '*sabrun jameelun*' or beautiful patience, which characterised the Prophet Jacob who trustingly waited for his lost son the Prophet Joseph. This is manifest in the agreements that he forged with his enemies, minority groups, and in his general dealing with people from all walks of life.

(vii) Cultivating Silence (*ziraeat alsamt*): It is known that the Prophet would speak only when necessary and otherwise maintained and cultivated silence. The highly recommend night vigil and early morning prayers and remembrance of God (*dhikr*) is characteristic of this, as well as not talking until '*fajr*' or morning prayers was a sunnah or practice of the Prophet

(viii) Being Non-Materialistic and Non-Attached (*kawnuha ghyr almadiya/murtabita*): One aspect that is repeatedly seen in the life of the Prophet is his sharing of material wealth and his spiritual rites and blessings. When he received money or goods, he would distribute it all before he returned home, while never accepting charity. His non-attachment is evident in his orientation of 'being a traveler or a stranger in this world', underlining the transient nature of life and things. This is backed by the rendition of his Companion Anas, where he said that the Prophet drew a line on the sand and said, "This is man, this is his hope, and this is his moment of death. As he is in the process of hoping that the closest line gets to him, which is his moment of death surrounding him" (Ibn Daqiq al-'Id 2014). The Prophet said, "The love of this world is the beginning of every sin" (Ibn Daqiq al-'Id 2014), which is backed by a recipe for a contended life, "The person who is unattached to this world puts his heart at rest in this world and in the next, while the one who desires this world tires his heart in this world and the next" (Ibn Daqiq al-'Id 2014).

Physical Tradition: Being Physically Fit Part of the holistic tradition that the Prophet brought was the focus on physical well-being and fitness, that was evident in his life as well as his companions. This was characterised by him having a flat stomach and his participation in martial arts including archery, swordsmanship, wrestling and horse riding. Additionally the Prophetic diet was largely plant based with meat being consumed infrequently. This aligns with the dictum 'a healthy body is a health mind' and vice versa, which needs careful reflection in this day and age of excessive consumption and lack of exercise.

References

Abdullah Ansari. (2010). *The Sufi Path—Stations of the Heart: Sad Maydan: The One Hundred Field* (Angha, N., Trans.). Cambridge, UK: Archetype.
Al-Ghazāli, Abu Hamid (1995). Ihya Ulum-Din (Vol. III). (Karim, M. F., Trans.). New Delhi: Islamic Book Services.
Al-Jilani, Abd Al-Qadir (1997). *Al Ghunya li-Talibin: Tariq al-Haqq Sufficient Provision for Seekers of the Path of Truth* (pp. 1–170). (Holland, M., Trans.). Florida, USA: Al-Baz Publishing, Inc.
Ali Nadwi, A. H. (2014). *Prophet of Mercy (Nabiyy-i Rahmat)*, Trans. Dr. Mohiuddin Ahmad, London: Turath Publishers.
Asad, M. (2011). *The Meaning and Explanation of the Qur'ān*. Kuala Lumpur: Islamic Book Trust.
Bashier, Z. (1990). *Sunshine at Madinah: Studies in the Life of Muhammad*, Markfield: The Islamic Foundation.
BBC. (2020). *The Islamic World in the Middle Ages (12th–15th Century)*. https://www.bbc.co.uk/bitesize/guides/zx9xsbk/revision/8
Bukhari. (1994). Chapter 32, 100:103 in Al-Imam Zia-ud-Din Ahmad bin Ahmad in Abdul-Lateef Az-Zuaidi Summarized Sahih Al-Bukhari: Book of Knowledge (Khan, M.K., Trans.). (Original work published in ninth Century-810-870 CE). Riyad: Maktaba Dar-us-Salam.
Chopra, D. (2010). *Muhammad: A Story of the Last Prophet*. New York: Harper Collings.
Dalai Lama. (1998). *The Four Noble Truths: Fundamentals of Buddhist Teachings* (2nd edn.). In Side, D. (Eds.) (Jinpa, G. T., Trans.). New Delhi, India: Harper Collins Publishers.
Daqiq al-'Id, Ibn. (2014). A Treasury of Hadith: A Commentary on Nawawi's Forty Hadith, Hadith XIII, The Perfection of Faith. (Guezzou, M., Trans.). In *Original Work of Abu*

References

Zakaria Mohiuddin Yahya Ibn Sharaf al-Nawawi, published in 13th Century (1234-1277 CE). Markfield, England: Kube Publishing.
De Victoria, S. L. (2008). *The Johari Window*. http://psychcentral.com/blog/archives/2008/07/08/the-johari-window.
Faizer, R. (2011). *The life of Muhammad: Al-Waqidi's Kitab al-Maghazi*, Ed. Rizwi Faizer and Trans. Rizwi Faizer, Amal Ismail and AbdulKader Tayob. New York/London: Routledge.
Folse, H. (2003). *Comments on Kant's Ethical Theory*. http://www.loyno.edu/~folse/Kant.html.
Fry, L. W. (2003). Towards a theory of spiritual leadership. *The Leadership Quarterly, 14*(6), 693–727.
Ghazāli, Abu Hamid Muhammad. (2007) Al-Ghazāli and Intuition: An Analysis, Translation and Text of al-Risalah Al-Ladunniyyah (Che Zarrina Sa'ari, Trans.). In *Original text published in 11th Century (1058-1111 CE)*. Malaysia: Department of Aqida and Islamic Thought, Academy of Islamic Studies, University of Malaya.
Ghazali, A. H. (1995). *Ihya Ulumu-Din - The Revival of Religious Sciences*, Trans. Fazlul Karim, 5 Volumes. New Delhi: Islamic Book Services.
Guillaume, A. (1955). *The life of Muhammad: A Translation of Ishāq's Sīrat Rasūl Allāh*. Introduction and Notes by A. Guillaume, Professor of Arabic in the University of London (pp. xlvii, 813). New York: Oxford University Press.
Hisham, I. (2002). *Sirat Ibn Hisham: Biography of the Prophet*, Trans. Abus Salam. H. Harun. India: Al-Falah Foundation.
Ibn Kathir, I. (2003). *Tafsir Ibn Kathir (Abridged) Volume 1–10* (Surat At -Taghabun to the end of the Qur'an) Abridged by Mubarakpuri S.R. (2nd edn.). Riyadh: Darussalam.
Ibn 'Arabi, Muhyiddin, Hilyat al-Abdal. (2008). *The Four Pillars of Spiritual Transformation: The Adornment of the Spiritually* (Hirtenstein, S., Trans.). London: Anqa Publishing.
Ibn Ataullah Iskandari (2006). Ikhmaalush Shiyam Perfection of Morals. (Mujilisul Ulama of South Africa, Trans.). South Africa: YMMA.
Ibn Hazm al-Andalusi. (1998). Al-Akhlāq wa'l-Siyar, In Pursuit of Virtue: The Moral Theology and Psychology of Ibn Hazm al-Andalusi (Laylah, M.A., Trans.). London: Ta Ha Publishers Ltd.
Imam al-Mawlud's Matharat al-Qulub. (2012). *Purification of the Heart: Signs, Symptoms and Cures of the Spiritual Diseases of the Heart* (Yusuf, H., Trans.). USA: Sandala Inc.
Ishaq, Ibn. (1967). *The Life of Muhammad, A Translation of Ishaq's Sirat Rasul Allah*. Reissued (Original work published in 8th Century (704-770 CE). Pakistan: Oxford University.
Jawsiya, Ibn-ul-Qayyim. (1997). Patience and Gratitude, An abridge translation of 'Uddat assabirin WA dhakhirat sah-shakirin; Nasiruddin al-Khattab. In *Original Publication in 13th Century*. London: Ta-Ha Publication.
Khawaja, K. U. D. (1924). *The Threshold of Truth: Higher Studies in Islam Series 1*. The Mosque, Working, UK: The Islamic Review Office.
Khalidi, T. (2009). *Images of Muhammad: Narratives of the Prophet in Islam Across the Centuries*. New York: Doubleday publishers.
Kolkailah, N. (2012). Beauty and Body Image: Part III. In *Virtual Mosque*. http://www.virtualmosque.com/personaldvlpt/character/beauty-body-image/.
Kriger, M., & Seng, Y. (2005). Leadership with Inner Meaning: A Contingency Theory of Leadership Based on the Worldviews of Five Religions. *The Leadership Quarterly, 16*, 779.
Lings, M. (2005). Reflection of the Al-Qur'ān, Surah Al-Rum, XXX, 30, Muhammad his life based on earliest sources. Pakistan: Suhail Academy Lahore.
Lings, M. (2006). *Muhammad: His Life Based on the Earliest Sources by Martin Lings* (final edn.). United Kingdom: Inner Traditions.
Maslow, A. H. (2014). *Toward a Psychology of Being*. Floyd: Sublime Books.
Maqsood, R. W. (2001). *The Muslim Prayer Encyclopaedia: A Complete Guide to Prayers As Taught by the Prophet Muhammad*. UK: Goodword Books.
Mubarakpuri, S. R. (2002a). The Sealed Nectar: Biography of the Noble Prophet (sws). Riyadh: Darussalam Publishers & Distributors.

Mubarakpuri, S. R. (2002b). *When the Moon Split: A Biography of Prophet Muhammad*. Riyadh: Darussalam Publishers & Distributors

Newberg, A. B. & D'Aquili, E. G. (2000). Neuropsychology of Religious and Spiritual Experience. In Andersen, J. & Forman, R. K. C. (Eds.) *Cognitive Models and Spiritual Maps*. United Kingdom: Imprint Academic.

Ramadan, T. (2009). *In the Footsteps of the Prophet; Lessons from the Life of Muhammad*. Oxford: Oxford University Press.

Reave, L. (2005). Spiritual values and practices related to leadership effectiveness. *The Leadership Quarterly, 16*(5), 655–687. https://www.researchgate.net/publication/222725013_Spiritual_values_and_practices_related_to_leadership_effectiveness.

Salahi, A. (1995). *Muhammad: The Man and Prophet: A Compete Study of the Life of the Prophet if Islam*. Dorset: Element Books Limited.

Schimmel, A. (1985). And Muhammad Is His Messenger: The Veneration of the Prophet in Islamic Piety (studies in religion). Chapel Hill and London: The University of North Carolina Press.

Smith, M. (1980). *Al-Muhasibi: An early Mystic of Baghdad, Islamic book foundation, publication no: 52*. Pakistan: Lahore.

Revees, A. (2005, April). Emotional intelligence recognizing and regulating emotions. *AAOHN journal, 53*(4), 172–178.

Rogers, C. (1991). *On Becoming a Person: A Therapist View of Psychotherapy*. New York: Houghton Mifflin Company.

Rosenthal, F. (2007). *Knowledge Triumphant: The Concept of Knowledge in Medieval Islam*. USA: Brill, Leiden.

Tirimidhi, Abi Eesaa Muhammad bin 'Eesaa bin Sorah. (2002). In *Shamaa-il Tirmidhi, Original Work Published in the 9th Century–824–892 CE* (Muhammad bin Abdurrahman Ebrahim, Trans.). New Delhi, India: Islamic Book Services.

Qadi 'Iyad, Ibn Musa al-Yahusbi. (1991). *Muhammad: Messenger of Allah; Ash-Shifa of Qadi 'Iyad. Original work published in 12th Century*. Granada, Spain: Aisha Abdrrahman Bewely. Medina Press in association with Islamic Book Trust Malaysia.

Chapter 4
Research Approach and Methodology

4.1 Research Objectives and Context

The type and nature of research requires building a sensitive approach and methodology that is able to effectively capture data and analyse and interpret it within the different theoretical domains. To accomplish this, a general approach to this research is firstly outlined in order to set the framework within which this research will be carried out. This is followed by presenting the various methodologies that this research will utilise, while elaborating on the methods, tools and types of sample. Next, the sampling framework and the criteria for selecting relevant organisations are outlined. The section that follows deals with how the data is analysed. Finally, the ethics pertaining to this research are articulated.

4.2 General Approach and Methodology: Within the Religious-Scientific Nexus

4.2.1 Qualitative Research Approach

Qualitative research "can preserve chronological flow, see precisely which events led to which consequences, and derive fruitful explanations" (Miles and Huberman 1994) before the theory is built based on field research. It enables one to investigate and generate a phenomenon grounded within a theoretical reality. Factoring in the nature and the complexity of the research on spiritual oriented organisations, such approaches are "used to uncover and understand what lies behind any phenomenon about which little is yet known" (Corbin and Strauss 1990).

4.2.2 The Interpretative Phenomenological Approach

The predominant approach for the purposes of this research will be the interpretative phenomenological analysis (IPA), which calls for mapping out subjective experiences and thinking patterns of people within the spiritual order. Smith and Osborne (2003) capture the essence of IPA thus:

> The aim of interpretative phenomenological analysis is to explore in detail how participants are making sense of their personal and social world, and the main currency for an IPA study is the meanings, particular experiences, events, states hold for participants. The approach is phenomenological in that it involves detailed examination of the participant's life-world; it attempts to explore personal experience and is concerned with an individual's personal perception or account of an object or event, as opposed to an attempt to produce an objective statement of the object or event itself. At the same time, IPA also emphasises that the research exercise is a dynamic process with an active role for the researcher in that process.

There is no social world beyond people's perceptions and interpretations. It is subjectivist, that is, subjectively understanding the actions based on which social reality is defined. A critique that should be borne in mind in this type of research is that there is an inclination to use a loosely-structured emergent, inductively-grounded approach to data gathering (Miles and Huberman 1994) and thus a tighter design is called for that enables one to delineate constructs with clarity and to focus on that which is able to be verified and validated.

It is expected that the combination of research methods will involve IPA, which subsumes 'Clean Language and Symbolic Modelling' and NS-NLP (Neuro-Semantics–Neuro Linguistic Programming), in addition to the use of a survey methodology, which is more positivist in its approach. This will enable the research to yield data that has multiple viewpoints and is therefore well grounded within its reality and constitutes a form of methodological triangulation. This, however, is cast within the Islamic tradition, whereby it is compared and contrasted against the framework of the divine scriptures and the sayings of the Prophet, which largely covers universalities, albeit some specificities.

4.2.3 Research Design and Strategy

The research strategy for this study was to combine both the survey method as well as in-depth interviews, thus using both quantitative and qualitative methods. The focus was on measuring frequencies and cross-tabulation, while qualitative analysis and qualitative coding used included priority ranking and Venn diagramming.

4.2.4 Methodologies

The four methodologies used, which are "discreet but inter-related aspects for a thorough going methodology on religion" (Andersen and Forman 2000) are: doctrinal analysis (based on divine writ from the Prophets-Messengers); social expression (tradition, rituals, faith based, and cultural norms and behaviour); subjective experience (religious and spiritual experiences) and scientific (objective) research.

This research adopts a combined approach, namely relevant doctrinal analysis of the Qur'ān and sunnah, social expressions of the Sheikh and the seekers, subjective experiences of the seekers, and in a limited way scientific (objective) survey research on the seekers. This research uses the thematic analysis approach, which subsumes the interpretivist-phenomenological (also called the constructivist), thus covering the social expression and the subjective experience on one hand, and the scientific (objective) research that has a positivistic approach (subsumes empiricism and realism), with its limited use, built on the qualitative data generated by the former.

The four-fold methodology with its predominant IPA approach includes related models and methods as outlined in Table 4.1. The first is the Prophetic Model based on the divine writ and the way of life of the Prophet, which has been fully covered in Sect. 2.6. The second two methods reflected in the Table 4.1, namely Symbolic Modelling (SM) & Clean Language (CL) and Meta Programme Modelling originate from cognitive sciences, systems theory and NS-NLP.

Except for the first and the last models and methodologies outlined in the table below, all of the others can be categorised under the general rubric of the 'grounded theory approach' since they rely on data being generated from the subjects or clients, based on which theories, concepts, and principles are built. Only the survey method

Table 4.1 The models used for this research

Meta-models	Approach/psychologies	Purpose
The divine writ & the prophetic model	Religious-spiritual psychology	Comparing and contrasting against the divine writ (the Qur'ān) and the sayings and actions of the Prophet
Symbolic Modelling (SM) & Clean Language (CL)	Interpretative-phenomenological—constructivist	Modelling the Leader-Sheikh and the seekers-followers in the respective organizations
Meta-profiling-NS NLP	Interpretative-phenomenological—constructivist	Modeling some key aspects of the Leader-Sheikh
Quantitative—survey	Positivistic (empiricism & realism)	The survey is constructed based on the key concepts and themes derived from the comprehensive literature review to elicit independent views of the seekers

can be classed as being positivist and a different method from the other three, with this providing a varying perspective on the same research. Each of these approaches and methods are briefly outlined.

4.3 Islamically Guided Methodology

The divine scripture (Qur'ān), the actions and saying of the Prophet (*ḥadīth*), and eminent Islamic scholarship on spirituality and development of the self will be used to guide this research (see chapter 2 and 3). Apart from the divine transmission of knowledge (revelatory—*waḥy*), which were confined to the Prophets, from an Islamic viewpoint there are two fundamental domains of knowledge transmission. These are the senses through which we receive and then translate knowledge into action, which includes the cognitive faculties, and secondly, the heart (*qalb*) and the soul (*nafs*) through which is unravelled the inspiration, intuition and illumination. These are cited in the scriptures and sayings of the Prophet, "And God has brought you forth from your mothers, womb knowing nothing—but He has endowed you with hearing (sam,a), and sight (*basar*), and minds (*fuād*), so that you have cause to be grateful" (Qur'ān, Al-Nahl (16), Verse 78). The objective of purifying the heart-soul is the rekindling of divine knowledge, "Could then, one whose bosom God has opened wide with willingness towards self-surrender unto Him, so that he is illuminated by a light (that flows) from his Sustainer ..." (Qur'ān, al-Zumr (39:22).

4.4 Approach to Modelling

Some key pointers from the clean language approach on modelling Lawley and Tompkins (2011) were used as outlined below.

Modelling human excellence: The question that is prompted is what is modelling? It is a process that happens over a period of time and involves two key aspects: observing someone who is achieving something and establishing a map or sequence (a model) of what they are doing. There are three fundamental types of modelling of human experience, namely, metaphoric, conceptual and symbolic (Table 4.2 see second column)

Table 4.2 Relationship between levels, modelling and models

Logical levels	Types of modelling	Models
Spiritual & identity	Metaphoric modelling	Metaphoric model
Beliefs & capabilities	Conceptual modelling	Strategies of genius
Behaviour & environment	Symbolic modelling	Meta-models

i. Metaphoric (sensory): In every day experiences, the senses scan both the internal and external environment and record their different states. This is done through the visual (seeing), auditory (hearing), tactile (touch), olfactory (smell), and gustatory (taste), as well as through kinaesthetic and internal bodily movements.
ii. Conceptual: Concept, categories, and classes are ways of understanding abstract and complex ideas. It is a method of making sense of the world and the environment around us and this is done through constructing concepts in our minds. They are perceived as a higher order state than the sensory and the material world that surrounds us.
iii. Symbolic: This is a way that the mind is able to draw from the material-sensory realm to represent the conceptual and abstract forms, which is shared with others in order to make them understand a state of mind. In this light, it uses symbols however does not only relate to symbols as such but to links with a pattern that has a personal relevance for the individual.

Deriving from the work of Robert Dilts, modelling is categorised into six levels, with similarities being paired together as follows:

i. Environment and behaviour, given that they are observable through the five senses—seeing, hearing, smelling and tasting follows, which pertains to sensory modelling;
ii. Beliefs and capabilities are mental processes perceivable through inference and therefore required conceptual descriptions, thus this related to conceptual modelling;
iii. Spirituality and identity form a pair, given that the most common way of realising this is through metaphors and symbols and thus symbolic modelling.

This research will attempt to use all three-paired categorisation above, where the sensory and the conceptual is derived from the use of NS-NLP, while symbolic modelling is generated through the use of SM and CL processes. Each of these is elaborated below in Appendix 1A–1C.

4.5 The Process of Modelling

4.5.1 Sampling Methods and Tools

As Fig. 4.1 indicates, the three essential components of the Symbolic Modelling (SM) are: Metaphors, Modelling and Clean Language (CL) itself. Each of these are outlined below:

Metaphor (The Medium) Metaphors are a medium of expression, that are easy to understand but are complex in themselves. "The essence of metaphor is understanding and experiencing one kind of thing in terms of another" (Lakoff and Johnson

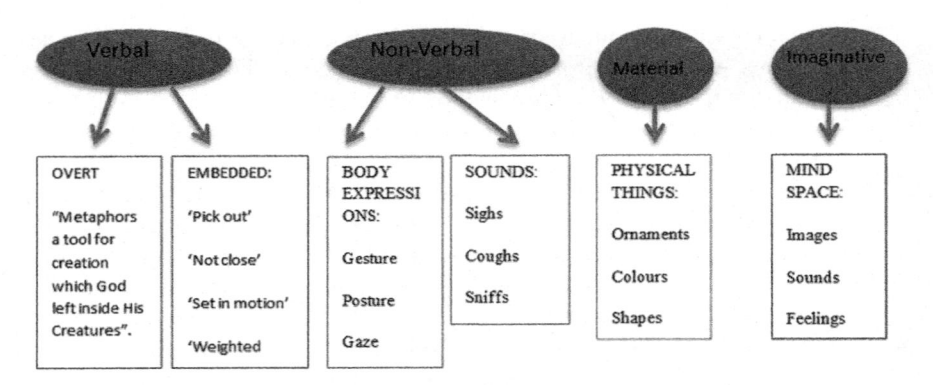

Verbal		Non-Verbal		Material	Imaginative
OVERT	EMBEDDED:	BODY EXPRESSIONS:	SOUNDS:	PHYSICAL THINGS:	MIND SPACE:
"Metaphors a tool for creation which God left inside His Creatures".	'Pick out' 'Not close' 'Set in motion' 'Weighted'	Gesture Posture Gaze	Sighs Coughs Sniffs	Ornaments Colours Shapes	Images Sounds Feelings

Fig. 4.1 Ways to express symbolic domains (from Lawley and Tompkins 2000)

2000). It is a deep mode of explaining things but presented in a simplistic form: for example, reaching for the stars means that one is aiming very high, while stating that we feel like a fish out of water implies that we are out of place. It is a way of "carrying across our experience of the physical into the abstract mental realm" (Lawley and Tompkins 2011). Metaphors are composed of a number of inter-related components, which combine to form it and where they can be a whole or a part of it—words, objects, mental images, and so on—and can be classified into four domains as shown in Fig. 4.1.

These four domains and six varying categories represent a spectrum of the way humans communicate and the faculties that we are endowed with. The symbolic expressions together with the subject-clients metaphors converge to form the 'Metaphor Landscape', as termed by Lawley and Tompkins, and in the light of SM the interest is "in the personal nature of symbols and metaphors (where) this idiosyncratic symbolism connects a person to their history, their spiritual nature, their sense of destiny and to the 'unknown or hidden' aspects of their life" (2000). Metaphor "makes the intangible tangible, it embodies relationships and patterns, and captures the essential nature of experience" (2011), giving the mind a way of dealing with complex experiences (Fig. 4.2). Here clean language is used to map out the metaphors and this is used for modelling, which provides the outcome of this process.

The criticality of metaphors to life is best expressed in that, "We define our reality in terms of metaphors and then proceed to act on the basis of the metaphors. We draw inferences, set goals, make commitments, and execute plans, all on the basis of how we in part structure our experience, consciously and unconsciously by means of metaphors" (Lakoff and Johnson 2000). Metaphors could be one of the many ways that we organise and structure our thought processes.

Modelling (The Method) Research in general tries to draw out generalities and this forms a deductive process of starting from the big picture and then generating

Fig. 4.2 A symbolic modelling outline

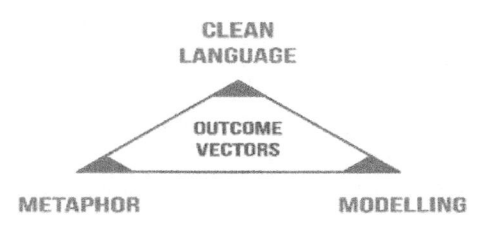

CLEAN LANGUAGE

OUTCOME VECTORS

METAPHOR   *MODELLING*

data in order to arrive at a conclusion about it. On the other hand, SM within the grounded theory perspective "seeks out the distinctive and idiosyncratic organisation of each individual's map of the world" (Lawley and Tompkins 2011) and from this perspective, it is a process of inductive research, where data is derived from the individual or organisation aimed at building the bigger picture or generalising to the sample or the subject in question. The key focus of SM is the exploration of the client's metaphoric world as seen from their perspective, within the context of their sense of time and space, which is manifested using their own words and non-verbal aspects.

This is best represented in David Grove's articulation of the process, where he called it "a trialogue between facilitator, client, and their metaphor landscape" (Lawley and Tompkins 2011). In this process of understanding the world of others, it is essential to set aside one's own perceptual space, in order to be able to empathies with that of the client, and not to mix it with one's own.

There are four fundamental modelling processes that have been identified and that are used in the modelling process. These are outlined below:

- Identifying: To begin mapping out aspects that are important from a client's perspective, which can be an attribute, a symbol, a relationship, a pattern or a context. It is appropriate to give an identity to it so that it becomes distinguishable.
- Develop Form: To explore and deepen one's understanding of what has been identified, which makes it more amenable, so as to gain a more comprehensive insight. This will mean elaborating on its attributes, so that it emerges more fully.
- Relate over Time: To put it into context, whereby one is able to discern the sequence of events—before-during-after—as well as examine the temporal relationships, namely, cause, effect, contingency, pre-condition, provenance (place of origin) and expectancy.
- Relate across Space: To come to an understanding of the relationships or intra-relationships vis-à-vis separate things, places, frames, contexts etc.

The illustration of this process and how elements inter-relate is given in Fig. 4.3.

Clean Language (The Means) Three functions of CL have been identified, namely, to acknowledge, orient, and send the client on a quest, with its four components—the syntax, vocal qualities, gestures, and clean questions.

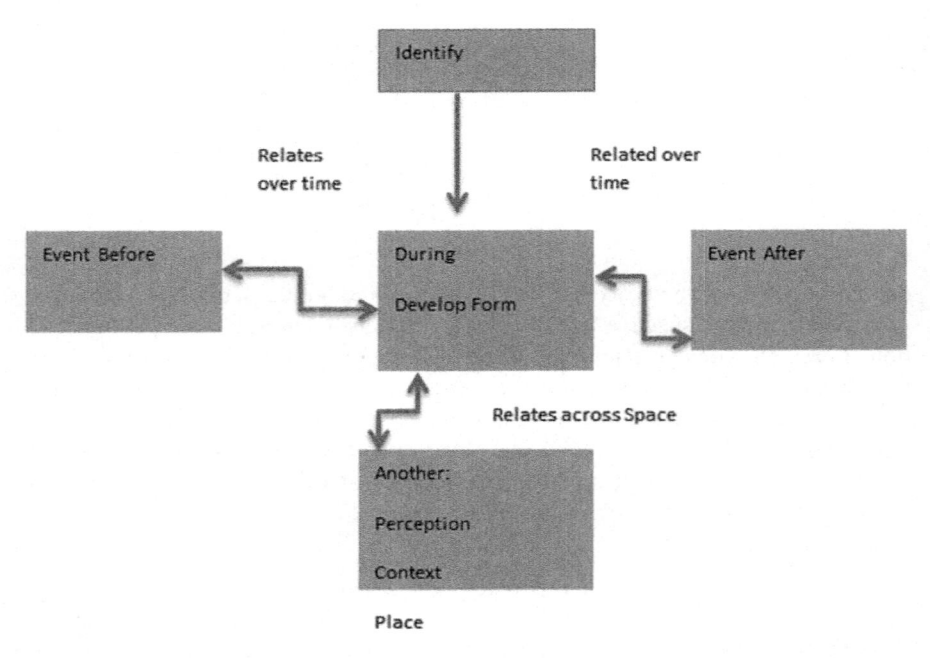

Fig. 4.3 Basic process of modelling

CL affects and directs attention, and importantly it is termed 'clean' since "it is sourced in the client's exact vocabulary, it is consistent with the logic of their metaphors" (Lawley and Tompkins 2011). CL has been found to enhance the rigour and authenticity of interview-based qualitative research, which can provide greater confidence for the researcher in the validity of the findings of qualitative research.

CL can also assist in the promotion of ethical research practice by reducing the risk of misrepresenting participants. It has further been "demonstrated (that) the potential of Clean Language as a specific, systematic method for eliciting naturally occurring metaphors in order to provide in-depth understanding of a person's inner symbolic world" is considerable (Lawley and Tompkins 2011).

4.5.2 Symbolic Modelling (SM) and Clean Language (CL) Questionnaire Model

The CL questionnaire is a non-intrusive technique of questioning, which facilitates the interviewee in reflecting on their responses and building on it iteratively. In this sense, it is does not interject the thinking of the interviewer and bring related biases into the process of information flow (see Appendix 1A and 1B).

There are four basic questions, which are the key questions around which the interviews, the focus group discussions, and the key informant interviews have taken place. SM and CL were used as a means through which communication was carried out with the Leader-Sheikh, as well as with the members of the organisation, in order to map out their perceptions, as well as the impact that these practices are having on their wellbeing. The danger of imposing the researcher's own perspective into the research needs to be mindfully observed and this is called outcome vectors.

4.6 Neuro-Semantic and Neuro-Linguistic Programming

NLP is the "study of the structure of subjective experience" underlined by Neuro-Semantics (NS) (Hall and Bedenhamer 2009), which deals with the underpinning values, belief systems, and the meaning of life. The use of NS-NLP has a repertoire of meta-programs especially for modelling individuals (see Appendix 1C). The spectrum of categories has been developed through original research by Richard Bandler and John Grinder, who identified an approach to examine 'the deeper structure of human behaviour, and a set of explicit models, applications, and tools derived from this approach' (Hall and Charvet 2011). This was further elaborated by Michael Hall to include NS. These four meta-programs domain enables a higher-level categorisation from the primary state of thinking, emotion, choice or meanings to another state called the meta-state, which effectively becomes the perceptual filters through which one views the world (see Appendix 1C).

Sampling Methods and Tools One of the programs within NS-NLP is called Meta-Profiling. This is a process of understanding the thinking patterns of individuals. It is categorised into four main areas, namely the cognitive (thinking), emotional (feeling), conative (choices) and semantics (meanings).

The aim in the case of this research model was the excellence of the Leader-Sheikh and then on the members utilising NS-NLP. The eliciting of data for the meta-programming outlined was only confined to the Sheikh-Exemplar suggesting that NLP-NS was used in a limited sense as compared to the complexity involved in the whole modelling process.

Sampling Models and Templates The purpose of this framework of meta-programs is to understand the repertoire of perceptual filters and patterns that one utilises when one communicates, encodes and decodes information. These will be used as benchmarks for the purpose of understanding and categorising the dialogue with the Leaders-Sheikhs of the Order.

There could be cross-cultural issues given that both the meta-program and CL were developed within a Western context and are in this case being applied to the Malaysian-Muslim context. This research is therefore one of the few, if not the first research,[1] which uses both of the above methods to elicit data, at least in the Malaysian context.

Overall Format for Modelling Template for the Leader-Sheikh Through the dialogue developed with the interviewees their relevant perceptual filters or metaprograms were identified, in addition to mapping their motivation patterns including values, beliefs and assumptions, as well as their strategies of communication. This was translated into a workable format that enabled the provision of a summation and sequencing of the process of modelling (see chapter 5). This was the basis for developing the meta modelling for the Leaders-Sheikhs based on their metaprograms and the different processes involved.

4.7 Survey Approach

In the positivist approach, the core assumption is that facts can be collected on the social world independent of how people would interpret them and can be assessed using a positivistic instrumentation or methodology (Open University Press 1996). In this sense, the researcher is detached from the topic under investigation, thereby presuming an objective position, whereby data is collected aimed at drawing out generalisations and explaining human behaviour through the use of theories.

The survey methodology derived from the positivistic approach will be used once the data collected from those under the IPA approach has been conceptualised. This will enable the researcher to have greater clarity of the concepts, categories and traits. The survey methodology will be built using the responses from the subjects-clients, being more relevant having been generated inductively which will strengthen the data generated. See Appendix 2 for sample questionnaire.

The interviewees only had a few introductory questions, and then the interviewee's narrative was used to build the data, thus maintaining the originality and minimising the biases of the researcher. The questionnaire formulated for the survey was constructed based on the comprehensive literature review. The questionnaire was initially constructed by the researcher and pre-tested with a few colleagues and thereafter finalised. The initial questionnaire was undertaken in the English language and then translated into Bahasa Malayu. This was then re-checked with a senior member of the Order, revised, and then finalised before being distributed.

---

[1] This is accordingly to James Lawley, one of the co-founders of Clean Language together with Penny Tompkins as per our email exchanges subsequent to their guidance that they offered me on its methodology.

4.8 Sampling Method, Frame and Criteria of Selection of Organizations

The focus will be on selected seekers of the Spiritual Order as per the criteria given below and their Leaders-Sheikhs.

Method The method used in this case is 'selective sampling' from qualitative research, whereby a sample due to its inherent nature is selected for study. On a general note these orders operate in a low-key manner and are not commercially oriented. Selection criteria have been developed in order to ensure that these Orders have a history and are a functional entity, having the characteristics as shown below.

Selection Criteria for the Order The Order was selected based on the following criteria, in that it:

 i. should be an Order of the Islamic faith, which should be both preaching as well as practicing its message—a Community of Practice (Lave and Wenger 1991);
 ii. should not be confined to one area, be from different geographic areas, thus having a spatial dimension;
 iii. should be a functional organisation, which has been in existence for at least one generation, thus representing a stable organisation;
 iv. should have an outreach based on its ability to function and attract members, thus being a functional and an effective organisation.

The researcher took part in selected acts of ritual worship with the resident seekers, taking part in two of their general dhikr (remembrance of God) ceremonies, and attending one lecture, while having intense discussions with the seekers who were members. Apart from this, three of the books written by the Sheikh were obtained and relevant sections marked out. These were translated from Bahasa Malayu to English and then used for referencing where relevant.

Sampling Frame—Level of the Order The approach to identifying and gaining access to the selected spiritual order for the study was through a key informant who presented two spiritual orders having different lineages and orientations. Initially the researcher approached two orders in Malaysia, but it was only possible to gain access to one, namely, Naqshbandi Khalidiyyah, given that there was no response from the other. In this sense, it was a qualitative sample but it was not purposeful, as the researcher himself had no preference in the selection of the order.

Sampling Frame—Level of the Self-Individual There are two groups of seekers, namely, the general seekers who belong to the Naqshbandiyyah Khalidiyyah Order and the residents of the rehabilitation centre, which has become a part of the Order, and which has a group of resident seekers within it. The resident seekers are drug addicts/ex-drug addicts and HIV patients: a couple of the members were transgender. The interviews and the survey were administered to both groups within the Order, with particular attention paid to the resident seekers. In terms of the interaction and the interview process, the IPA was essentially adapted to explore the personal and spiritual world of the seekers and the Sheikh. The survey data constructed from the literature review augmented the data generated from the interviews.

Sample Size and Geographical Distribution There was one very detailed case study carried out in geographical locations in one country, Malaysia. A relevant case study format was developed for this purpose, in order to represent the conceptual themes generated from the data set. This case study is presented in chapter 5.

Sampling and Data Collecting A total of 60 questionnaires were handed out, with 32 being completed and returned, which represents a response rate of over 50%. The original questionnaire was in English and this was translated into Bahasa Malayu, and then on its completion re-translated into English. Excel was used to input the survey data and then relevant charts and figures were developed.

In-depth interviews were held with the Sheikh and 10 other respondents, of whom five were centre residents and five were general seekers or *murids*. (see Appendix 3A & 3B) A total of 18 hours of interview recordings were made, all of which were in English and in one or two cases from Bahasa Malayu to English. All of these were carefully transcribed and re-checked by the researcher.[2] The INVIVO qualitative data analytic package (see Appendix 1D) was used to qualitatively code the interviews, develop queries, and draw relevant models, with cross tabulation being done for some data and concepts.

Qualitative Data Analysis Methods and Techniques In order to facilitate the analysis of the qualitative data, the INVIVO software package was used to identify concepts, themes and codes. This then was used to build the thematic analysis. Interviews, survey data, as well as other observations that are generated from the field were inputted into it and then used to identify commonalities and differences, as well as particularities. It enabled the drawing of maps, figures, tables etc. which could then be used for textual analysis, as well as building relevant narratives.

Approach to Analysis The following approach was followed in collectivising, processing and analysing the data developing as outlined below (guided by Braun and Clarke 2006):

  i. Identification of Respondents: The respondents were identified by asking the key informant in the Order who to interview in terms of their knowledge, while for the survey the questionnaires were given without any pre-selection.
  ii. CL approach: Given that the approach to eliciting information was following the CL approach, the questions were kept to a minimum, while trying to build the conversation based on their own narratives

---

[2]There were 10 persons interviewed, that is, the Sheikh and 8 seekers (murids), of whom 5 where general seekers and 5 being resident seekers of the Centre. There is a total 26 interview transcripts in total. In Appendix 3A & 3B, these transcripts have been consolidated, where in each document set, the relevant transcripts of each person has been inserted into.

4.8 Sampling Method, Frame and Criteria of Selection of Organizations

iii. Documentation: While the audio recording was on going, the researcher took detailed notes of the conversations and maintained a memo for theoretical notes.
iv. Comprehension of data: The audiotapes were transcribed and doubled checked by re-listening to the audiotapes. Audio tracks that were inaudible were left out.
v. Generating codes: The transcripts were read in detail and then relevant codes were identified in the light of the respondent's narratives, while also benefitting from the discourses in the literature review.
vi. Building data & codes: Relevant data extracts from the interview data set were segmented into each of the codes.
vii. Identifying & naming themes: The codes were then collated into higher-level categories or themes.
viii. Thematic analysis & voices of the respondents: Analysis was carried out where relevant after most data extracts, which was largely paraphrased so as not to lose the originality and the accuracy, where relevant concepts and theories were woven into the analysis.
ix. Factoring in literature review: While undertaking the analysis, including coding and building thematic categories, the concepts and data from the literature review was used to support the data, where required.
x. Synthesis of data, codes and themes: After these processes were completed, a separate chapter was developed synthesising the data and developing thematic illustrations, as well as drawing out a model for the spiritual leadership and self-development. The synthesis is presented in chapter 6.
xi. Reflexivity: Given that I am myself interested in *tasawwuf* and a member of a ṭarīqa (albeit outside Malaysia), there is a need to look at the data set critically, as well as be aware of my own inherent personal bias that exists in the collection and analysis of data.

Survey Data Analysis Once the questionnaire had been dispensed and relevant data collected, Excel was used to landscape the data. Thereafter, the data was segmented according to the different concepts and categories, and relevant charts and graphs developed based on frequencies. This was then selectively ranked to derive priorities.

Ethics and Triangulation The use of all of the above approaches and methods enabled a form of triangulation, where the data generated are seen from different angles with the aim to strengthen its reliability. The data collected from the organisation was cross-checked with the seekers to establish internal validity, while external validity was derived from cross-comparison. This strategy also ensured that the ethics of the whole process are maintained since the clients-subjects have verified the accuracy of their responses. Written consent was obtained on behalf of the Shiekh of the Order who agreed for the research to be carried out, as well as for it to be published.

References

Andersen, J. & Forman, R. K. C. (2000). Methodological pluralism in the study of religion: how the study of consciousness and mapping spiritual experiences can reshape religious methodology. *Journal of Consciousness Studies, 7*, 11–12, 7–14.

Braun, V., & Clarke, V. (2006). Using thematic analysis in psychology. *Qualitative Research in Psychology, 3*, 77–101. https://doi.org.10.1191/1478088706qp063oa.

Corbin, J. & Strauss, A. (1990). *Basic qualitative research: grounded theory, procedures and techniques*. USA: Sage Publication International.

Hall, M. L. & Charvet, S. R. (2011). *Innovations in NLP: For challenging times*. UK: Crown House Publishing Limited.

Lakoff, G. & Johnson, M. (2000). Metaphors we live by. In J. Lawley & P. Tompkins (Ed.), *Metaphors in mind: Transformation through symbolic modelling*. London: The Developing Company Press.

Lave, J. & Wenger, E. (1991). *Situated learning*. UK: Cambridge University Press.

Lawley, J. & Tompkins, P. (2000). *Metaphors in mind: Transformation through symbolic modelling*. UK: The Developing Company Press.

Lawley, J. & Tompkins, P. (2011). Symbolic modelling: emergent change through metaphors and clean language in hall. In L. M. Hall & S.R. Charvet (Eds.). *Innovations in NLP for challenging times*. UK: Crown House Publishing.

Miles, M., Huberman, M. A. (1994). *A expanded source book: Qualitative data analysis* (2nd edn.). London: Sage Publications.

Open University. (1996). Engaging in Educational Research, Open Learn Course, www.open.edu/openlearn/education-development/education/engaging-educational-research/contentsection-0.

Smith, J. A., & Osborn, M. (2003). Interpretative phenomenological analysis. In J. A. Smith (Ed.), *Qualitative psychology: A practical guide to research methods* (pp. 51–80). London: Sage Publications, Inc.

Chapter 5
Case Study of a Spiritual Order, Malaysia

5.1 Introduction

The aim here is to capture the data in its original form, interpret it and integrate it where and when necessary with Qur'ānic and *ḥadīth* literature citation. This chapter is divided into the following main sections:

(1) General overview: The evolution of spiritual orders in general is outlined. The development of the Naqshabandiyyah *ṭarīqa* is sketched out, followed by outlining the Naqshabandiyyah Khālidiyyah, the Order under study.
(2) Organisational overview: This includes outlining the *ṭarīqa*'s objective, management, and inherent characteristics of the seekers, as well as their motivation and expectations.
(3) Spiritual dimensions: This includes its creed (*aqidah*), the process of self-realisation of the seeker, and the nature of the role of the Sheikh, as well as the process of spiritual Modelling of the Sheikh.
(4) Key approaches, methods, and tools: This is elaborated under *tarqiyah* (spiritual grooming), *tarbiyah* (education) and *tazkiyah* (spiritual purification).
(5) Well-being and the worshipper: This includes elucidating on a key concept identified by this research, namely, the heart-brain connection. This is followed by ascertaining the impact of worship on its seekers and finally touching upon their related spiritual experiences.

The detailed discussion and its theoretical and practical implications, which flows out from this chapter are presented in Chap. 6. This is where the data set is synthesised and the model for spiritual leadership and self-development is crafted, to encapsulate the workings of the Order and its key variables, as well as the impact it creates on the seekers.

5.2 General Overview of the Spiritual Orders and the Naqshabandiyyah ṭarīqa (Order)

5.2.1 The Evolution of Spiritual Orders

Movements, orders and organisations form the fulcrum around which human life is organised and evolves for the better or worse. This study is about one such Order, commonly called 'ṭarīqa', meaning a spiritual path. The name of the selected Order is Naqshabandiyyah Khālidiyyah, located in Malaysia. These types of spiritual Orders focus on the inward science of Islam known as 'tasawwuf' or inward contemplative practices, while observing the 'Sharī'a' or the body of knowledge governing largely the outward aspects of Islam.

Deriving from a general critique within certain quarters of Islam, the question can be posed as to whether 'tasawwuf'—or what is commonly called Sufism—is a concept alien to Islam or not? This is best responded to by gaining a historical perspective. Imam Malik said, "Whoever studied *tasawwuf* (inner development) without *fiqh* (law) is a heretic, and whoever studied *fiqh* without *tasawwuf* is corrupted, and whoever studied *tasawwuf* and *fiqh* will find the truth and reality of Islam." Perhaps the current situation is summed up best by a saying a millennia ago, during the time of the Prophet 'tasawwuf' was a reality without a name and now it is a name without a reality. Hujwiri supports this position that during the time of the Prophet and his immediate predecessors, the name 'tasawwuf' did not exist but its essence or reality was a part of everyone. In the same vein, Ibn Khaldun says that in the first three generations, *tasawwuf* was too general to have a specific name: however, when the dislocation occurred between people becoming worldlier and less spiritual, those devoting themselves to worship become known as Sufis.

The second century hijra (800 CE) witnessed a paradoxical movement, where Islam expanded exponentially during the Umayyad period while witnessing the formation of state institutions and internal rifts within the community. This trend underlined the emerging bifurcation, which formed one of the causes for trying to circumvent the fear of the loss of the spirit of Islam. This spurred the formation of these types of spiritual orders focusing both on the exoteric and the esoteric aspects of Islam, which became later known as *ṭarīqas*, meaning the path.

Imam Qushayri encapsulates this changing trend: "People began to differ and levels of development became distinguishable" (2002), this led to a shift in perception, where those totally devoted to God became known as ascetics and devotees, as opposed to simply being Muslims. The first such circle was of the eminent scholar and ascetic Imam Hasan al-Basri and his followers, who passionately emulated the Prophet. They translated the way of the Prophet into the traditionalist movement called '*ahl al-ḥadīth*'. He had a unitary conception of both the inward and outward aspects of Islam anchored within the ideal community, as was during the time of the Prophet.

There were several orthodox and traditional Sufi orders that originated in various regions. A list of some selected orders includes:

1. Qādiriyya led by Abd al-Qādir (d. 1166—Iraq, Iran and Middle-East),
2. Shādhiliyyah led by Abu-Hasan Shādhili (d. 1258—Morocco and expanded to Africa),
3. Chishtiyyah led by Mu'in ad-Din Chishti (d.1273—Iraq),
4. Mevlavi led by Jalal ad- Din Rumi (d.1273—Turkey),
5. Ahmad al-Rifā 'i led the Rifā 'iyya (d. 1320 –Iraq and Middle-East, Turkey, Eastern Europe and Spain),
6. Naqshabandiyyah led by Baha' al-Din Naqshaband (d. 1389—Central Asia and Europe),
7. Khalwati led by Umar Al-Khalwati (d. 1397—Iran, Iraq, Syria, Turkey), and
8. Ni'matullahiya led by Nur al-Din Ni'matallah Vali (d. 1431—Iran).

5.2.2 An Overview of Naqshabandiyyah ṭarīqa and Naqshabandiyyah Khālidiyyah

The Naqshabandiyyah order was founded by Sheikh Baha al-Din Naqshaband (800AH/1400CE), who came from Bukhara, Uzbekistan, which then was a part of the Persian speaking world. The order rapidly spread into Asia and Europe; it was very influential both as an esoterically oriented movement, as well as being sociopolitically active and a part of some of the resistance movements in Asia (Mogul India), Ming and Ch'ing areas (China, Central Asia, Afghanistan and Turkey) and Europe (the Balkans and during the Czarist period in what was then the Russian Empire).

Currently, the Naqshabandiyyah is a worldwide movement with a number of orientations and branches, including Naqshabandiyyah Haqqāni, Mojjadijiya, al-Sufia, Khālidiyyah, Awaisiyya etc. The Naqshabandiyyah order is unique in terms of its methodology of *dhikr* and it is said that, "it is a way (that is) closest and easiest for students to get to some degree of unity with God, even though the pupils lack the properties and have not fully prepared to receive a rank this high in esteem" (Kabbani 1995). Its main focus is on silent *dhikr* (*sirr* or *dhikr qalb*—remembrance in the heart), even though some *ṭarīqas* also include the louder forms of *dhikr* (*jahir* or *dhikr lisan*—remembrance of the tongue).

Naqshabandiyyah Khālidiyyah,[1] *Tasawwuf* and Self Development: The Naqshabandiyyah Khālidiyyah has similar roots to most Naqshabandiyyah *ṭarīqas*, starting with the Prophet at the helm, with its silsila (chain of lineage) coming through Abu Bakr al-Siddique, Salman al-Fārisi and several generations to Sheikh Khālid al-Baghdadi. This Order is similar to the Naqshabandiyyah Haqqāni in its silsila, before then branching off to four other splinters of *ṭarīqas*. This chain then converges again, culminating in Sheikh Sulaiman al-Zuhdi through to Sheikh Abdul

---
[1] The Facebook page of the Naqqshabandiyyah Khaliddiyyah can be viewed through https://www.facebook.com/drjahidsidek/.

Wahab Rokan (Indonesia) with two other Sheikhs before the current Sheikh Jahid Sidek.[2] Appendix 3A & 3B presents the personal interview document numbers and anonymised initials of the names of the seekers.

In the context of Naqshabandiyyah Khālidiyyah and *tasawwuf*, the key is its position within the Islamic orthodoxy, its core practice and methodology of remembrance of God (*dhikr*). A recent inquiry into this order by Omar and Zarrina (2011) sums up some essential features within which the order Naqshabandiyyah Khālidiyyah is grounded:

1. The practice of *wuquf qalbi* (witnessing the presence of God) is one of the eleven pillars of the Naqshabandiyyah Order, which is the main guideline to achieve *ma'rifa* of Allah (divine knowledge of God).
2. Eight of the eleven pillars have been developed by Shaykh 'Abd al-Khāliq al-Ghujdawani (d.575/1179), while the other three pillars were perfected by Shaykh Baha' al-Din Naqshaband (d.791/1388) (Abu al-Zahra' 2002). The former is the Sheikh of the latter
3. The *Wuquf qalbi* practice (a state of witnessing or that God is witnessing you) is a pillar introduced by Shaykh Baha' al-Din Naqshaband, where he described it as mandatory as it is the essence of every *dhikr* practice (Abu al-Zahra' 2002).
4. *Wuquf qalbi* must be maintained throughout the *dhikr* process, as well as in those activities outside the *dhikr* hours (Nizar in Omarand and Zarrina, 2011, p 92)).
5. *Wuquf al qalbi* is a practice that is closely related to other pillars introduced by Shaykh 'Abd al-Khāaliq al-Ghujdawani prior to Shaykh Baha'al-Din ('Abd al-Majid 1997).
6. The pillars previously mentioned were: disciples must remember Allah (*hudur*) in each exhalation of breath (hush dardam); the mind and thoughts are not influenced by other than Allah (*nazar bar qadam*); migration from condemned behaviour to commendable behaviour (*safar dar watan*); the heart must always have *dhikr* with Allah even when being with the community (*khalwa dar anjuman*); perpetual *dhikr* using prescribed *dhikr* (*yad kard*); constant supplication to Allah using a special prayer i.e. *Ilāhi anta maqsūdi wa riḍāka maṭlūbi* (My God, You are my destination and Your pleasure is what I seek); protecting the heart from any intruding thoughts other than Allah (*nakah dashat*); to be in constant remembrance (*dhikr*) with Allah without being forced (*yad dashat*).
7. The other two pillars introduced by Shaykh Baha' al-Din Naqshaband other than *wuquf qalbi* are *wuquf zamani* and *wuquf 'adadi*. The meaning of *wuquf zamani* is that a disciple must constantly check his being every 1 or 2 h, whether he is in the state of remembering Allah or otherwise. *Wuquf 'adadi* is when any disciple performing the *dhikr al-nafy wa al-'ithbat* (negation and affirmation of God), the *dhikr* must always be in odd numbers Abd al Majid (in Omarand and Zarrina, 2011 (p93)).

---

[2]The biography of the Sheikh including the books that he has written is given in the website in bahasi Malayu -https://drjahidsidek.wordpress.com/biografi/.

8. *Wuquf qalbi* represents the meaning of perpetual remembering of Allah (*dawam al-dhikr ma'a Allah*). Therefore, it is not surprising it is deemed as a pillar of the Naqshabandiyyah Order.

Omar and Zarrina (2011) conclude their research inquiry by stating that the Naqshabandiyyah Khālidiyyah's *tasawwuf*-based practices, especially the *wuquf qalbi*, is not divergent from the point of view of the Order's past. Thus, the practices are within the pillars and principles of the Naqshabandiyyah *ṭarīqa* in general and that any technical variations or interpretations are grounded within this and the framework of fitting the Malaysian context.

5.3 Results and Analysis

This section largely uses primary data, backed up with secondary data where necessary. It thus forms the main data set for the research in building the case study.

5.3.1 Case Study on the Naqshbandiyyah Khālidiyyah Ṭarīqa (Order)

The Naqshabandiyyah Khālidiyyah was 'selectively sampled' based on specific criteria within the methodology of the study, namely that it should be an indigenous organisation, which is both functional and has been operational for over a generation (the criterias are outlined in Chap. 4).[3]

5.4 General Organisational Framework

5.4.1 Organisational History

The organisation's leader is a Malaysian academic and Sheikh, Dr. Jahid Sidek. This *ṭarīqa* is headquartered in Kuang, Selangor, South of Kuala Lumpur. I spent several weeks collecting interview data from the Sheikh, the management of the Centre, its residents, as well as with its general *murids* (seekers), while reading some of the literature written by the Sheikh.

---

[3] In order to capture the authenticity of the interviews, the exact words of the interviewees have been retained to the extent possible so as not to change the meanings of their articulation. Therefore, the flow of the English language may seem different to the body of the main text.

The *ṭarīqa* has several sub-centres of the organisation spread across the various regions including in the north, south and centre of Malaysia. The number of *murīds* runs into several hundreds, with some estimates of around 500 core seekers, largely based in Malaysia. As a part of the *ṭarīqa*, an NGO has been established called 'Istana Budi' (a rehabilitation centre) so that it can take care of some of the social and legal functions of catering for a group of special people, including drug addicts, HIV-AIDS patients and trans-gender persons. These residents, who at any one-time number around 30, have either been abandoned by their families or are seekers of a spiritual path. This NGO acts as a welfare and shelter home. As the Manager explains:

> "It is a welfare home of course but mainly we cater for people with HIV because this is a *farḍ kifāya* (communal obligation). We started in 2009, before then, there was no Muslim organisation who had this sort of setup. So most of these people who have HIV are taken up by the Christians missionaries and the Buddhist associations, Hindu temples but there was no Muslim organisation ... we are pioneers actually." (Interview document No:3 – Appendix 3).

It is to be understood that the predominant organisation is the *ṭarīqa*, that is the spiritual Order, while the NGO itself caters for the special needs of the residents and gives it the legal status. On a general note Islamic spiritual orders have been in existence for more than a millennium, while the concept of NGOs is a relatively new phenomenon.

5.4.2 *Ṭarīqa's Objectives*

The objectives of the *ṭarīqa*, which is the core organisation, are summed up by a very senior seeker, who manages the residential centre:

1. The first objective is *da'wah* (propagation), focusing mainly on *'aqīdah* (creed), which is trying to bring back people to believe in only one God. People still believe in black magic, in talisman, in a lot of other things, which they think give them a lot of benefits but in actual fact are shirk or blasphemy.
2. The second is the treatment of diseases; spiritual, mental and physical. These are done under the Manara Treatment Centre (within the Istana Budi), where the Islamic reflexology technique is practiced.[4] Treatment is for both ordinary

---

[4] Islamic reflexology has been developed by the Sheikh of the Order. It is a type of acu-pressure technique, whereby a slender cutting from the branch of a particular tree is used at the different locations of the body depending on the type of illness, where it is lightly and repeatedly beaten on the specific location or around about it, with the dispensation of prayers from the Qur'ān. The duration varies from 5 to 10 min or more and once this is completed a very cold water bath is administered with prayers once again. I took part in the Islamic reflexology treatment as well as in their sessions of *dhikr*—remembrance of God. Interestingly, a similar technique was used by one of the Sheikhs of Masjid al-Aqsa in Jerusalem, Sidi Shaykh Muhammad al-Rifā'i. Drug addicts were taken into the desert, wrapped in white cloth and this technique of light beating was

or conventional diseases, for people with heart failure and hypertension through to migraines and all sorts of diseases. It is said that they treat common diseases successfully.
3. The development of the self through multiple methods as cited here represents the road to 'self-actualisation' where the human traverses through progressive levels.[5]

5.4.3 Organisational Perspective

The management of the *ṭarīqa* itself has been decentralised by the Sheikh, so that each of the peripheral centres of the *ṭarīqa* take care of their own sub-organisation and collection of funds. They mobilise funds from their respective geographic regions and membership, which enables them to take care of the functioning of the organisation. This forms part of the efficiency of the centre, while the effectiveness is maintained by the Sheikh himself, who visits these centres on a regular basis to impart knowledge, as well as perform the *dhikr* or meditation. This enables the main goal of the *ṭarīqa* to be sustained.

The funding for the NGO, where many of the residents themselves are an active part of the *ṭarīqa*, is explained by the Manager: "Funding is mainly ... with our own funds but then we get support from the Selangor Religious Council, Malaysia. This council channel their *zakah* or obligatory contribution through us."

One of the many challenges is the health conditions of the residents and there is a concerted effort to find solutions:

> "The death rate is very high, about 5–6 per year out of the 30 (around 20 per cent) of the residence. So our mortality is very high; treatment and rehabilitation services is given to deserving residents, to provide residents with counselling, motivation, guidance services and a sustain(able) way of life, to fostering good relationship with the general public and acceptance by family members because we encourage the family members to come and visit them. Self-actualisation of one's potential to explore one's talent and abilities, seeking for employment, they do get well and go outside again. They do get well and once they get ill again they come back here." (Interview document 1 - Appendix 3).

---

administered together with prayers and *dhikr*. This was related to me by Dr. Rosina Fawzia al-Rawi al-Rifā'i, who was a student of the Shaykh above mentioned who had heard about it. She is now a leader of a spiritual group in Vienna, Austria (www.fawzia-al-rawi.com). She teaches the practice of meditation, breathing techniques, working with divine names and healing. I, together with my wife, had an opportunity to be a part of this circle for several months in Vienna.

[5] What Maslow calls 'self-actualisation' or a higher level of understanding and realisation from an Islamic perspective is to reach gnosis of God or '*ma'rifa*', where the philosophical and theological basis of the latter is well articulated in greater depth as evident in numerous traditional Islamic sources. This is elaborated in detail in Chap. 6, where self-actualisation is compared to and differentiated from spiritual actualisation.

It is thus a centre that essentially provides a space for this type of resident to continue their medical treatment while enhancing learning and putting into practice spiritual methods and tools in order for them to work towards self-actualisation.

Number and Types of Seekers There were two main groups of seekers or respondents: those who were resident in the main centre and the general membership of the Order. In terms of the survey there were 32 respondents, out of which 18 (56%) were residents, while 14 (44%) were general members of the order. In terms of the interviews, there were ten seekers interviewed out of which five were centre residents, while five were general seekers including one female.

The residents were mainly drug addicts, HIV patients and a couple who were transgender. They are seekers who want to transform their lives or who were referred by the hospital. The majority of residents were also active members of the Order and involve themselves in the various acts of worship and remembrance of God. The data analysis generated by the questionnaire was analysed collectively, that is, both for the residents and the general seekers, given the relatively small sample size, so that a consolidated perspective could be elicited.

The Age of the Seekers As seen in Fig. 5.1, the largest group of seekers were between the ages of 40–50 years (28%), followed by the age group 50–60 (25%), then 30–40 years (16%), 60–70 years (13%), with smaller numbers belonging either the younger category (20–30 years) or the much older (70–80 years). In sum, the majority of the respondents were middle-aged to elderly.

Educational Levels of Seekers Fig. 5.2 shows that the largest group of the seekers, nearly 43%, had either high school-level education, or university degrees or were diplomas holders (28%), followed by a minority who had completed primary school (12%) or had a vocational certificate (3%).

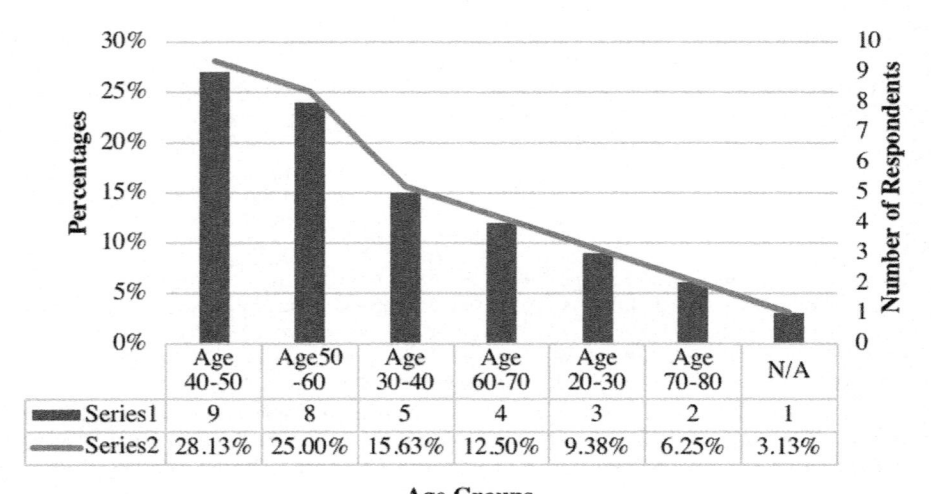

	Age 40-50	Age 50-60	Age 30-40	Age 60-70	Age 20-30	Age 70-80	N/A
Series1	9	8	5	4	3	2	1
Series2	28.13%	25.00%	15.63%	12.50%	9.38%	6.25%	3.13%

Age Groups

Fig. 5.1 Age of respondent

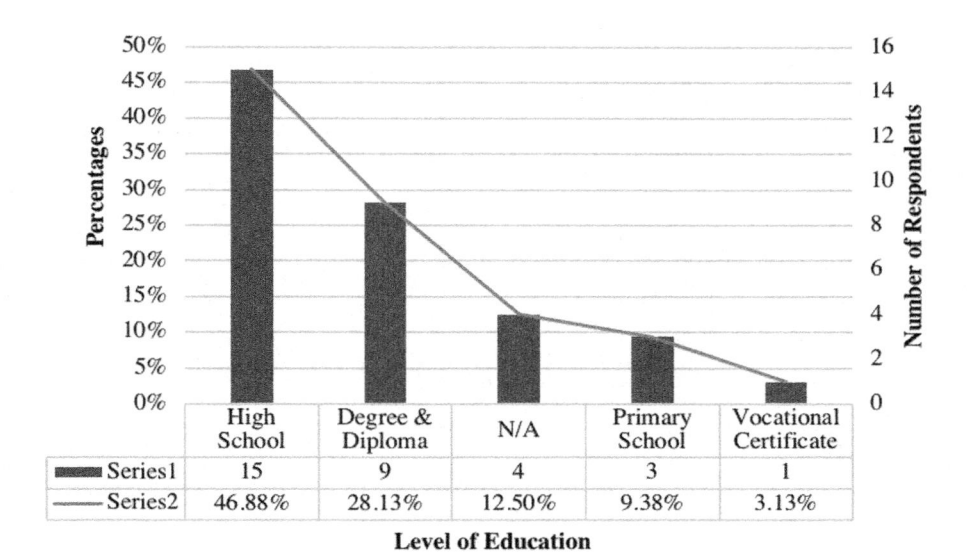

5.4 General Organisational Framework

Fig. 5.2 Educational levels of the respondent

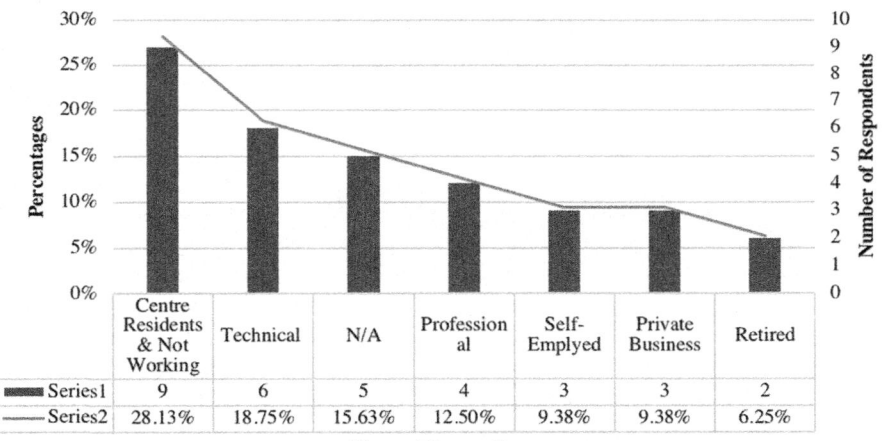

	High School	Degree & Diploma	N/A	Primary School	Vocational Certificate
Series1	15	9	4	3	1
Series2	46.88%	28.13%	12.50%	9.38%	3.13%

Level of Education

Fig. 5.3 Status of occupation of respondents

	Centre Residents & Not Working	Technical	N/A	Professional	Self-Emplyed	Private Business	Retired
Series1	9	6	5	4	3	3	2
Series2	28.13%	18.75%	15.63%	12.50%	9.38%	9.38%	6.25%

Type of Occupation

Occupational Status of the Seekers The residents of the centre formed the largest group (28%), who on account of their drug addiction or being HIV patients had given up their respective careers, even though the majority of them had been to high school. This is followed by those who were in the technical field (19%) and professionals (13%), while a minority were either self-employed (9%), had a private business (9%), and were retired (6%) (see Fig. 5.3).

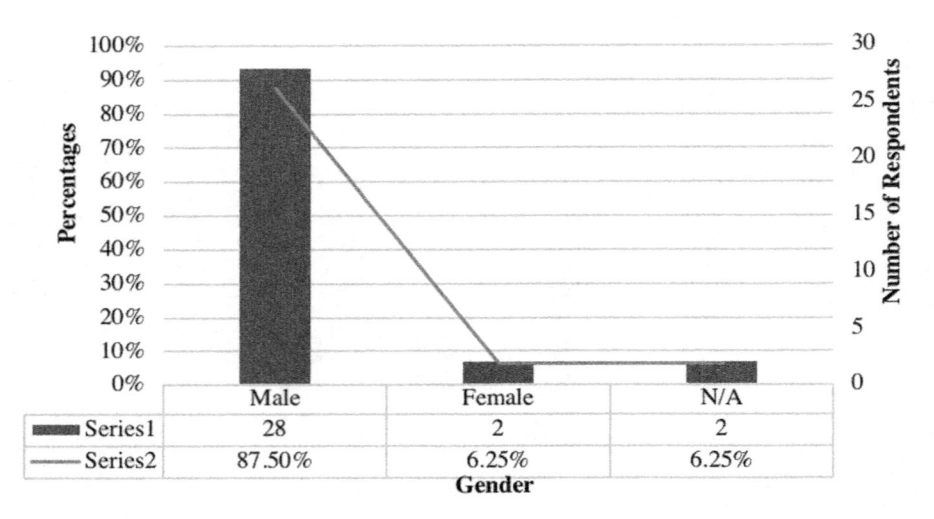

Gender	Male	Female	N/A
Series1	28	2	2
Series2	87.50%	6.25%	6.25%

Fig. 5.4 Gender of respondents

Gender of Seekers The seekers were predominantly male (87.5%), with a minority being female (6%), while some of seekers had not stated their gender (6%) as reflected in Fig. 5.4. There was some difficulty getting to the female seekers given the religio-cultural situation, as perhaps the time was not sufficient to gain trust and access.

Duration with the Organisation As indicated in Fig. 5.5, the largest group (41%) did not state the duration that they had spent with this organisation, followed by those who had been up to 6 months (38%). Some 16% had been there for 1–4 years, with a minority, that is, two of them having been with it for 15 years and 18 years (3% respectively). Regarding the group that did not respond and on a general note relating to the residents, they are normally at the Centre for a couple of years and then leave, while for general seekers there is a tendency to stay on, especially for those who like the Sheikh or the benefits that they derive from the Order. There could be some that leave the Order if they are not able to sustain their efforts.

Motivation and Expectation Motivation for Joining The motivation of seekers to join this organisation, as well as their expected outcomes are captured in Fig. 5.6. The most significant motivations were found to be: to prepare for the next life (65%) and to learn better behaviours (50%). This is followed by service to others (31%) and being in the company of like-minded people (28%), to learn spiritual practices (16%), and having wide access to others (13%) and 'others', that is to get closer to God, while trying to gain '*ma'rifa*' or knowledge of the divine (13%).

Expectations for Joining the Organisation As indicated in Fig. 5.7, the most significant factor was 'to change myself for the better' (30%), followed by the same

5.4 General Organisational Framework

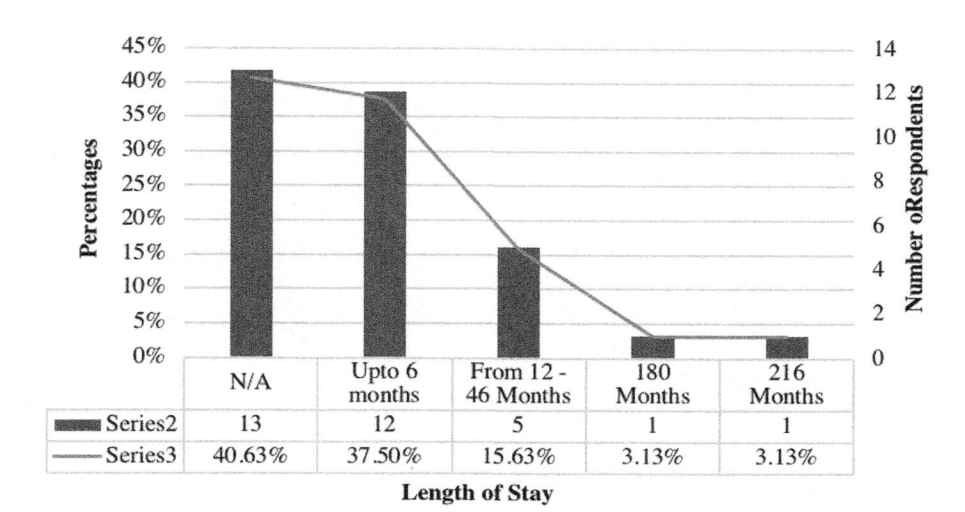

	N/A	Upto 6 months	From 12 - 46 Months	180 Months	216 Months
Series2	13	12	5	1	1
Series3	40.63%	37.50%	15.63%	3.13%	3.13%

Length of Stay

Fig. 5.5 Length of duration with the organisation

	To prepare the next life	Learn better behaviours	Do good to Others	Have company of like minded	Learn spiritual practices	Have access to wider newtwork	Others
Series1	21	16	10	9	5	4	4
Series2	65.63%	50.00%	31.25%	28.13%	15.63%	12.50%	12.50%

Motivations for Joining

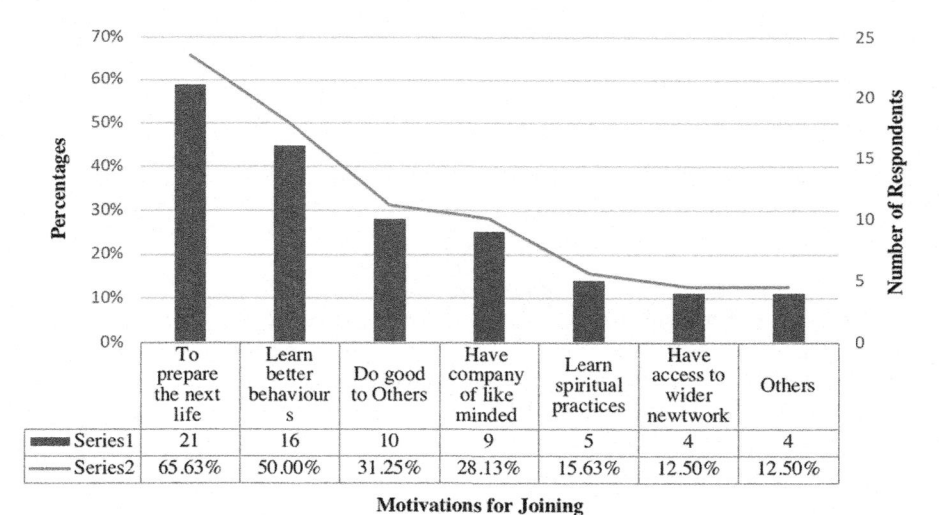

Fig. 5.6 Motivation for joining organisation

score of 17% each for 'becoming calmer', 'gaining blessing' and to 'learn more spiritual practices' respectively. This was followed by 'to learn more about faith' (15%), with other expectations being 6%.

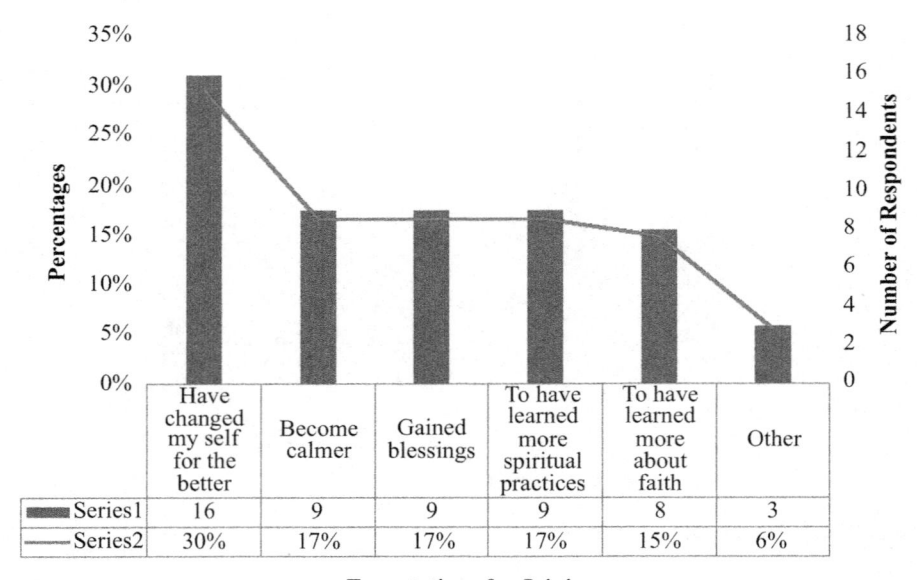

	Have changed my self for the better	Become calmer	Gained blessings	To have learned more spiritual practices	To have learned more about faith	Other
Series1	16	9	9	9	8	3
Series2	30%	17%	17%	17%	15%	6%

Expectations for Joining

Fig. 5.7 Expectations for joining organisation

5.5 The Spiritual Dimension of the Order

5.5.1 Spiritual Dimensions

This section begins with the foundational aspect of the faith, which is required for ascertaining if the Order is within the Sharī'a given the challenge from certain quarters that Sufi Orders have a corrupted 'aqīda or creed of Islam. This is followed by underlining the concept of self-realisation, which was found to be a key trigger element for the seekers, combined with the role modelling of the Sheikh, which then follows.

5.5.2 The Foundational Aspects of Faith (Tawheed)

The most fundamental aspect in Islam is *tawheed*, the Unity of God, and all else rests on this concept. In this regard, it is important to see the perspective of the seekers, as well as the Sheikh and some of these are given below. The resident imam (see Appendix 3 document no: 2) says relating to the power of God in the Qur'ān:

> "The parable of those who seek protectors from other than Allah is that of a spider who builds a house; but indeed, the weakest of houses is the spider's house – if they but knew." (Ankabut, 29:41)

5.5 The Spiritual Dimension of the Order

He adds, "Allah's power is like that. Nobody hurts Allah. Allah can agonize this entire world alone ...powerful". When asked about the change in his life he explained: "It has changed because I hope that when Allah loved me very much, whatever I do is because of Allah." He goes on to cite the Qur'ān,

> "And whoever does a wrong or wrongs himself but then seeks forgiveness of Allah will find Allah Forgiving and Merciful." (al-Nisa 4:110)

The above seeker continues: "In your heart you must do what you can to get it." He says that his change was triggered through *tauba* (repentance) or through *dhikr* (remembrance of God).

> "To do *dosa* or sins? For me it's very simple, to let people know why you perform *salah* (ritual prayer)? I perform *salah* because of Allah, that's why I appreciate my Rasulullah - the Prophet. If Rasulullah did not get this love, nobody can know Allah ..." (Interview Document 1 - Appendix 3)

As referred to above, there are many factors that have come together for the resident imam through the process of repentance and *dhikr*, including permanent trust (*tawakkul*) in God. The resident imam (Interview Document 2—Appendix 3) and his friend outlined their concept of *tawheed* of God and by his reference to the Prophet:

> "That's why in the Qur'ān Allah said, are you listening, are you hearing? ...Allah teaches you how good you are; your eyes, ears and your mouth, which all has its rhythm. This process is faster and better than light ..."

The citation to the divine writ here is for humans to become aware of themselves, their surroundings and the cause behind it all being God. The Head of Reflexology discusses *tawheed* (Interview Document 3—Appendix 3):

> "...about doing more *dhikr* and putting ourselves down so that Allah can fill the empty glass. We remember ...the words in the Qur'ān. How to say, we are together ...That's the first thing, how do you honour the *tawheed*? It's a very interesting question. It is by mentioning Allah, Allah, Allah. The *tawheed* is a kind of a belief. How to improve, glorify ...only practically."

The above reference is to the methodology of getting to know God by becoming humble (putting one's self down), emptying one's mind and filling it with the name of God, which in effect is the essence of *tawheed*. The Centre Manager (Interview Document No: 1 -Appendix 3) articulates his understanding of *tawheed* thus:

> "Praise of God, the attributes of God, Allah, Allah *Qayyum* (Everlasting and Eternal) – He is everything and all those things. At least if you sing or lie down, you sing about the ninety-nine attributes of God. That is better than just dreaming away nothing or at least you want to *salawat* (praise of the Prophet). That is even better because God says (citing the Qur'ān, al-Azhab 33:56): 'Allah and His Angels send blessings on the Prophet: O ye that believe! Send ye blessings on him, and salute him with all respect'."

The above seeker continues:

> "That is a command on you; 'Send ye blessings on him, and salute him with all respect '. Yes, so, I say God has commanded you to say it and you just do not care a damn. At least if you prayed 17 *rak'a* (one complete daily prayer cycle), you would be saying the *salawat* – praise on the Prophet"

The point of reference here is the replacing of unwanted rumination of thoughts not by 'dreaming away' but by a state of worship that brings about a focus on God, on Oneness (*tawheed*). Here we observe the attempt to inculcate a sense of mindfulness, focusing the mind and avoiding unnecessary thoughts. From these above renderings of the seekers, one can conclude that their comprehension of the Oneness is in line with the traditional Islamic orthodoxy, where nothing is partnered with God and reliance is solely on Him.

5.5.3 The Seekers, their Self-Realisation and Reflections

One of the fundamental elements that emerges from the data set is that most of the residents who were drug addicts and HIV patients wanted to change their lives. This trigger of wanting to change was the same for the general seekers, it prompted their search for an exemplar and a place for this purpose. A professional banker, a general seeker, shares his process of self-realisation:

"You know sometimes, this thing is all from God, Allah is giving me something that makes me stop. ... you know Allah teaches us a lot of things that humans don't know, and we do not how Allah actually teaches us. Because when you are on the road and people overtake you and you get angry, so actually Allah is teaching you how to be patient. But you do not see it. When you remember God, sooner or later ... it's not that today you take *bay'a* (oath of loyalty), ... you know today or tomorrow you will get something from Allah. No, sometimes it takes a longer time ... So we have to think more about *ākhira* (the next world). Last time I was a hot-tempered person and *Alhamdulillah* (praise the Lord) this has now stopped." (Interview Document No: 7 - Appendix 3).

Here, he is outlining his process of change and the gradual resolving of the ruinous trait—in this case anger—that takes time to change. As already noted, anger was the worst ranked of the ruinous traits by the seekers. The orientation of the afterlife and its frequent reminder seems to anchor oneself regarding the existing reality and makes a way to prepare for the next life.

The above seeker then shifts his discussion to the obstacles that the seeker faces in his path of spirituality:

"And get away from all the distractions. We humans are attracted to money, attracted to properties ... or the other obstacle that distracts you from the remembrance of God. When you see money, you are thinking about money and you have already forgotten about Allah. The focus is that you don't think too much of the things that will stop you from the remembrance of God." (Interview Document No: 7 -Appendix 3).

Then he moves his discussion to an historical perspective:

"You know I was with my Sheikh in 1990, and you know there was some improvement on my side. I realised that it takes a long time. It's not immediate, say 1 year or 2 years ... You know from 1990 until now, I keep on following the first one (Sheikh). My Sheikh was Imam Issak somewhere in 1990–1992 after my Sheikh passed away, I followed Dr. Jahid Sidek (the current Sheikh) from then onwards till today. It's a long period." (Interview Document No: 7 - Appendix 3).

5.5 The Spiritual Dimension of the Order

There are two aspects that can be deciphered here, first, in relation to the Prophetic saying of 'We have completed the smaller *jihad* (struggle) and now have a bigger *jihad* (struggle)'. When asked by his companions what is the bigger, he said it was the struggle with *nafs* or self. Secondly, that it takes time to unlearn and re-learn habits and behaviours and empty oneself of all of the unwanted chattering that goes on in one's mind. The above seeker turns his discussion to highlighting the heart-mind link and the spiritual oath of allegiance:

> "Turning towards Allah actually you know to make ourselves, to make our hearts and minds always to be thinking of Allah (*dhikrullah*). If you don't *dhikrullah* then you do not know how to make your whole being. You know staying alive to remember Allah.... Before 1990, before I joined this *ṭarīqa* and I was praying but you know during prayer, I was thinking who am I praying to? Who is Allah? All kinds of questions arose. For three times, I wanted to see him (the Sheikh), but I couldn't but sometimes I can't see him because sometimes he is so far... During that time, we don't have highway route but now there is highway route and its very fast ... So, there is a difference between before *bay'a* (oath of allegiance) and after *bay'a*." He adds about the ruinous traits, "You know sometimes when you see outside there is still pride" (Interview Document No: 7 - Appendix 3).

The reference here is to being able to find a guide who can fast-track one's self-development and the positive difference it makes to take the oath of allegiance with the Sheikh. The focus of attention on remembering God (*dhikr*) is flagged as a method of getting nearer to God, of knowing oneself, and then being able to know God. This seems to resonate with many of the spiritual orders that I have come across, where there is emphasis on prayers, *dhikr* and the guidance of the Sheikh.

The Sheikh himself talks about having hope (*amal*) by citing the Qur'ān (Interview Document No: 5—Appendix 3):

> "And He will provide... from where he never could imagine. And whosoever puts his trust in Allah, then He will suffice him. Verily, Allah will accomplish His purpose. Indeed, He has set a measure for all things." (al-Talaq 65:3)

The Sheikh is pointing out that it is the level of trust or *iman*—the faith that one's has in God and for those who fully turn to Him, for God alone is sufficient. Ibn Kathir (2003) comments on the word '*taqwa*' or piety where he states: '*taqwa*' of Allah is obeying what He has commanded and avoiding what He has forbidden. Then Allah will make a way out for him from every difficulty and will provide for him from resources he never anticipated. My conception of piety in this context goes well beyond permissible and avoidance, where one believes in God's existence no matter what, where even if he/she sins, that God's mercy and love transcends beyond the rights and wrongs. I believe this was one of the elements that provided the motivation for the seekers especially those at the centre, that is, the drug addicts and the HIV patients, to form the basis for their transformation. This provides a spiritual space for healing.

The Centre Manger outlines the obstacles of the evolving self and some aspects for its development (Interview Document No: 1—Appendix 3):

> "Your stations (*maqām*) to states (*ḥāl*), if you don't perform it, you feel you have the feeling of guilt that you have not performed. It is the feeling that you have lost something, and then like it is gone forever, it is not like prayers, where you miss the prayer you can delay it. But once it is gone it is no longer there..."

The reference to the states ($ḥāl$) is a certain state of mind or consciousness, which the seeker experiences from time to time, and this is a temporary state (Suhrawardi 1991). The states over time and with the mercy of God become stations (*maqām*), which have more of a permanent nature, like reaching a state of contentment. It is one of the hallmarks of a person who is positively changing in a spiritual sense, that he/she is attracted to prayers and feels a loss if one misses it. Thus, this then is a nourishment to the soul. The above seeker adds:

> "... So anyway coming back to that it is like a business. There is no loss, no gain and if you perform well – because even in prayer you make a lot of mistakes, and a lot of things coming in between ... and you instead of getting back your capital, you actually have a loss... and so for the one who is in loss, you have to perform a lot of things ... So if you only do the part, you don't get your capital and you lose, because during the performance (of prayers).. there are a lot of loop holes.. and this is where you lose. This is the reason you cannot depend only on the compulsory obligation." (Interview Document No: 1 - Appendix 3).

What the seeker is stating above is the necessity of doing the optional prayers as a supplementary reinforcement for any gaps or deficiencies in the ritual or obligatory prayers. The seeker elaborates:

> "I feel that my life is better arranged. I mean before that—this is in realm of faith, the inner faith, where things are happening to you...I mean money comes and goes and at those times we did not realise or see it ... this is given by God or it is reward ... But now we know this is God's 'qaḍa qadr' (fate), that things happened and a lot of things happened like this morning." (Interview Document No: 1 - Appendix 3).

The resident imam discusses his current state of mind and heart, where he told his "parents ... sister, if you want me to live with you, take me here (to the Centre), I don't want to go back to my old life." It was asked whether he maybe wanted to build up his strength so that he could 1 day go out without anybody, to which he replied: "Yes ... you need time." Stating that he had been here for almost 2 years, he was asked about his reason for joining. He responded: "I was not close to religion. Bad friends and empty mind." He explained this further: "When you take drugs, you think you are better than other people." (Interview Document No: 2—Appendix). This is something that has been stated earlier by the ex-sailor, that one needs to build up sufficient strength to go outside into the wider world once again amidst all of the attractions and dependencies, which would be a true test of faith and change in one's behaviour. As far as the residents are concerned this factor of actually going out into the real world posed one of the challenges to test if their transformation was able to sustain itself.

The above seeker was asked, "So what else would you like to happen for the future? Are you strong enough to go out? Or you still trying to cope?", to which he replied, "Not yet." The resident imam, was asked, "How about you, is it different or same?" To which he said, "The same", and that he also has HIV. When asked why he started taking drugs, he answered, "The reasons are friends and an empty mind ..." and now he "wanted to change my life, just step by step." He said, "I was 15 years old and was involved on and off with drugs ..." and when asked what made him stop, said, "I feel sick. Thinking hard about dying..." (Interview Document No: 4—Appendix 3).

5.5 The Spiritual Dimension of the Order

Both the resident imam and his friend underline this symbolic concept of 'empty minds', where there is no sense of belief or direction or constructive engagement, combined with the influence of bad friends, which had previously led them to drugs and other dependencies. The crux of the matter is getting out of these dependencies through spiritual methods, with related guidance and support. When asked how the above seeker had heard about this Centre, he says it was from his sister. When asked about his experience of engaging in spiritual acts compared to heroin, he said, "It is better ... even here I say to you, if I get a lot of money I never think to go out to buy something" (Interview Document No: 2—Appendix 3). This indicates some level of change, where the urge for drugs has subsided.

The supervisor of the Centre, who is a seeker, says (Interview Document No: 8—Appendix 3):

> "Everybody in life has an experience, my life was ... not a very true and good life before. A lot of sins committed, a lot of wrong doings, and I don't know but suddenly 1 day, I felt I must go and refer to Tuan Guru (Sheikh), because I've been to other places, other Sheikhs and *ṭarīqas*..."

This charts the course of a seeker gaining self-realisation and trying to find the right Sheikh as well as methods to trigger the change. An earlier reference was made to joining other *ṭarīqas*, however, coming here to the Centre triggered the change based on the calm mind-set of the Sheikh, the immediate supportive and disciplined environment, the method of *dhikr* as well as the peer support.

The Centre supervisor outlines his contact with the Sheikh and his experience within the organisation (Interview Document No: 8—Appendix 3):

> "But I think the change is gradual – you begin to tolerate, you gain more patience, because I used to lose my temper – young men are gregarious and ..aggressive, but I'm very disciplined. So, if I see things not to my taste, I let it out. But later on, I realised that I cannot do it that way all the time, because some people can take it, some people don't. So gradually I'm able to adjust to the needs of the person rather than my need, it is the other way around."

The above seeker adds that:

> "In the past, I use to say like this thing is going to be black, and no other colour, but when it comes back to me green or yellow, red, I don't accept it. But now I will accept, but I will ask the guy to explain, why is it red? Or green? Or grey? And not black? ... even though I was a teacher, but you know in the class we do practice a sought of communication. But as a leader within certain groups, especially managing people from different levels of educations and different background of life, you have to adjust to things to this situation." (Interview Document No: 8 - Appendix 3)

This refers to a breach of old thought patterns and adapting to new ones, which could have been caused by many factors both intrinsic—age, reflection, realisation, depth of *dhikr*, evolving patience, as well as extrinsic including the Sheikh's guidance, the environment and the peer group support.

The friend of the resident imam discusses the process of his self-realisation and his joining the organisation (Interview Document No: 4—Appendix 3):

> "I came here after my late father passed ... after ... four months, I had a dream where he came to me and said 'Son, how long do you want to be like this? Please change your ways,

please find something that you can do. Please, don't waste your life' ... Yes he came in my dream. So, I got up and I prayed. Yes, I prayed, Allah why must I do this? Why did you send me in like this? Please I need to change, I need to at least open my heart to become someone, only for my Server ... I have to stop to do bad things. After prayers, after *dhikr*, I went to sleep before there's something that happened there, myself and my brother, that is my younger brother, said, find something to do, don't waste yourself, don't rush yourself here. You have got a lot of things to do, so please make peace, so I fell asleep. I was thinking, what shall I do? I will go to my brother's house with my mum, leaving everyone, and then I got hooked back on drugs."

This is the seeker's is first flash of dreams, where it seems that his subconscious is being prodded by his late father. Even though he had some form of realisation that what he was doing was negatively affecting him, there was no systematic channel available for him to be guided, thus highlighting the need to have systems in place such as this *ṭarīqa*. The above seeker captures some of the obstacles in his way:

"Yes, let's say for one month plus I was trying to steal, trying to cheat people then after a year, I stopped ... so I went to a centre (a different one) ... something like rehab but its better, there's no drugs and it is drugs free. There I start methadone, it is just like drugs also to stop people on being drugs, but it's still the same, it's being on drugs also that's how it is. I cannot see that I am normal and I say I want to kill myself. I went to hospital. So, I say is there any place I can (go) ... and they say, yes you have to go to (a) place, Sungai Buloh hospital, but I have a what do you call it? HIV virus. Yes, but I don't want to be with my family. I want to be in one place that I can peacefully see that there's no drugs. So, someone gave me the number of Haji, this Centre Manager, and then I called him. When I called, he was in the hospital somewhere in the canteen. I spoke to him and I said I take drugs and I have HIV, can I come stay at your place? He said where are you, I say I am in the hospital, can you come and see me downstairs? And then I saw him he brought me here." (Interview Document No: 4 - Appendix 3).

The struggle that we see here is one where the seeker wants to wean himself off all drug dependencies, even methadone, which is used as an interim drug, an opioid for drug addicts. This moment of self-realisation and desire for change has been found as a central factor in most residents, as a basis for change. The seeker continues on his ongoing struggle: "I will have to fight that one fight. Fight, fight ... But I think I will stay here until I die and *dhikr* until I die. *Inshā'Allāh" (if God wills). Yes, that's what I think. So, I think maybe I found the right road that I want to be in this dhikr group.*

When asked how often dreams come, he says: "Quite often. Each time I get dreams I get down and I pray, I wake up and pray my *tahajjud* (night vigil) ... grateful to Allah." Additionally, when asked about the types of dreams, he says they are: " ... getting closer to Allah to change my ways and to remind me who I am so there's ... Allah and Rasulullah (Prophet) but to become like Prophet Mohammed ... It is in my heart (and) in my mind because I think is this true and true to me. And I say this is the last chance that Allah is giving to you use it in the right way." When asked to expand about who said this, he highlights that: "I say to myself. Use it as good as possible because there's no getting this type of treatment, pull you closer to Allah ... remind me of Allah ... and it is a nice group where we can talk we can share about our Islamic things." (Interview Document No: 4—Appendix 3).

The resident here is alluding to both his consciousness and subconsciousness being involved in his evolving state of transformation, which are manifested through his dream states. He expresses his determination when he says 'fight, fight' and his getting into a deeper state of contemplation by his night vigil and ritual prayers that he performs. His goal is the emulation of the Prophet, which is done through modelling the Sheikh, as well as reading about the life of the Prophet by using the library at the Centre.

The nurse, who is a seeker, says:

> "I follow Tuan Guru (the Sheikh) and then when I started I took the *Bay'a* (oath of allegiance), I had to pray. I pray *salah tauba* (prayer of forgiveness) and then ask Allah for guidance with the past. It was great; you know everybody will be so scared after taking *Bay'a* thinking that it is something really wrong. But after taking *Bay'a*, I find that more truth is being revealed. The closeness, how we wish for perfection of *akhlāq* (morality) back to famous *ḥadīth* urges ... Allah will make you realise ..." (Interview Document No: 6 - Appendix 3).

Here there is a combination of methods ranging from close guidance of the Sheikh, taking the oath of allegiance, prayers of repentance and reflection on the divine scriptures. She is alluding to a change in orientation of working towards getting close to God after taking the oath of allegiance. She outlines the state of her mind and heart:

> "I find that I fight (mentally) a lot. I am quick tempered, hot tempered but you know, (the Prophet's companions) knew that coming back from a (physical) war was not easy but yet (sic) the war on the *nafs* (self) is the greatest. Now it is the greatest war and you have to do it daily, and I will do this until I die. So I stayed (at home) and then the goodness of Allah was making me to look after my mother. It becomes my duty to look after her, then I was offered to come here (the Centre) because of all the Beauty and Majesty of Allah. But so, when I came here after four years of divorce, I did not realise that Allah still wants me to be married. So I married him (the Centre supervisor) and that is why am here and we find we seem to have compatibility, we asked Tuan Guru for his blessing." (Interview Document No: 6 -Appendix 3).

5.6 Spiritual Modelling

5.6.1 Modelling the Sheikh and the Change Process

In pursuing the conversation with the female seeker, she makes reference to the discussion with her husband, who is also a part of this organisation, highlighting that one of the things that was mentioned was the development of the soul by being with the Sheikh. When asked how she believes this was undertaken, she responds: "Observing his character." When asked to elaborate she says:

> "You feel that he is very patient. We learn because... to be like him. You try to copy (him) as much as possible. So when you come here as husband and wife then this is the good part. Because when we are under one guru.. then you remind each other. If you feel.. in a (state

of) loss, then I keep remembering why not, this is how our guru does it and then we absorb that behaviour so you solve the problem." (Interview Document No: 6 - Appendix 3).

Here she is outlining the process of modelling the Sheikh by observations, as well as inculcating the values that are being taught by the Sheikh. It is to be noted here this includes both the verbal and the non-verbal aspects, where the latter being the Sheikh's demeanour, behaviours and value system, which are captured in the NLP Modelling exercise in Chap. 6. When asked to give an example about her change of behaviour, she explains:

> "This is small. If you look at the big thing as small, then the small thing is nothing. So if you solve things with Sharī'a (Islamic knowledge and *fiqh*) it is difficult, but with *haqīqa* (reality) then it becomes easy. Because when you solve problem you look at Allah and Allah's *taqdīr* (destiny) and easily you want to follow the step by step in Sharī'a, so it can be difficult. That is true but when you try to participate you find the truth there." (Interview Document No: 6 - Appendix 3).

An essential point is made here that it is not sufficient to merely follow rules, rather one needs to apply and adapt to situations and this she points out is through utilising '*haqīqa*' or 'reality on the ground'. This refers to using one's intuition rather than following set ways which may not be applicable to the context. Within *tasawwuf* itself there is a graduation framework which is outlined by In Brown's Dervishes (in Suhrawardi (1991, p 283) he cites the Qadiri order and the graduation framework as follows:

1. Sharī'a: observes the stipulated rites of Islam;
2. *Ṭarīqa*: attains a stage of closeness to God with great piety, virtue and fortitude.
3. Ma'rifa: has attained a type of divine knowledge.
4. *Ḥaqīqa*: becomes joined to the truth, where God is in all things that he sees.[6]

Imam Suharawardi says many reach the first and second stage but only a few reach the fourth stage.

When asked if she herself sees any changes within herself and whether her family have seen any changes in her, she responds:

> "I don't know because I don't question them but I can feel that they sort of place the value of being married to him, they sort of think that maybe there was a gap (age), after sometimes they observe that there was a difference, they seem to be attached to him and they like him." (Document no: 6, Appendix 3)

The query was then posed about when she undertook '*ibādah* (worship), and whether it impacted on her *akhlāq* (morality), she answered by outlining the two contrasting qualities of God:

> "So, it is a relationship between '*abdi* (slave) and Khāliq (Creator)...realising the Beauty and Majesty of Allah...you are always moving at the will of Allah...it is easier said, so long as you keep the *dhikr* and the *murāqaba* (meditation) that Allah is always watching you." (Interview Document No: 6 - Appendix 3).

---

[6] This order of the graduation framework here is shari'a, tariqa, ma'rifa and haqiqa and is different to its general formulation, which is shari'a, tariqa, haqiqa and ma'rifa.

5.6 Spiritual Modelling

The change process within herself, here, is seen through the reflection on her husband, a type of 'mirroring'. There are two key concepts that are underlined here, one is the slave (human)—Creator (God) relationship, a relationship of submission which forms the core of Islam and emanating from it, knowing one's place in the world. The second is that in terms of change, she is outlining what the Sheikh had mentioned about the continuum of *Jamal* (Beauty) and *Jalal* (Majestic) and what is in-between, which are attributes of God.

In explaining the relationship between the two variables, that is, worship and *akhlāq* (morality), she outlines what kind of relationship it is:

> "It the relationship between the servant and the Lord...the Khāliq (the creator) and the '*abdi* (slave)... Yes '*ibādah* also has an impact and the guru also impacts your *akhlāq*. This is because when you also keep getting close to God almost every day. We always follow (Sheikh), so there in the lessons that he imparts to us, there is also knowledge there for people who remember *akhlāq* (morality). It's not that just we stay at home and do our '*ibādah* at home, it is not only on the '*ibādah*, even when you are treating other people or looking after the sick, it's all '*ibādah* isn't it? So whatever you do, the servitude to the Lord, then it is the '*ibādah*..." (Interview Document No: 6 - Appendix 3).

The worship that she is highlighting is a holistic concept not just confined to prayers, which is the essence of an Islamic lifestyle even though many do not have this perspective or put this into practice. The point that is underlined here is that worship, as well as the lectures combined with the rules laid out by the Sheikh including the code of conduct, impacts morality or *akhlāq*.

The resident Imam now turns to outlining his state of mind and emotions:

> "...Allah will give you a better state (spiritual) where you will stay. You do around three months directly. ...one night I cried, I don't know why. Automatically. Nobody forces me to cry, that is, something is touching me inside, there is something about it...I am very strong, and God gives you (a chance) to change your life. Why do you never see that? Why do you never think about that? My heart says like that. Yes, through Allah. Before I forget to say thank you to Allah, before I forget to say *Inshā'Allah* (if God wills). Before I never say *salaam waleikum* (peace be upon you too), I never respect anybody, now it has changed a lot." (Interview Document No: 2 - Appendix 3).

The process of reflection (*tafakkur*) and change is emphasised in the above narrative, with emotions being manifested in combination with mental space afforded by divine forgiveness and hope. Here one sees a process, whereby the seeker is re-directing himself to fall in track with the code of conduct within Islam. When asked about the reasons for the change, the resident Imam pointed out that:

> "It has changed because I hope when Allah loved me very much; whatever I do is because of Allah. He said in the Qur'ān 'if you do whatever I say truly and hope for Me to forgive you and you will do properly, then you will get it'. Now seriously I follow and I just get it into my heart, I do not know how to discuss about my heart. If you do not ever do it (turning towards God) you will not get it." (Interview Document No: 2 - Appendix 3).

This rendition stated above represents a point of convergence of love, hope, belief, intention and action, where striving (*jihad*) is being emphasised to get this feeling of closeness to God. Perhaps it is in this type of convergence that change occurs, where he is referring to 'get it into my heart', and 'do what you can to get it'.

The professional artist outlines his state of mind and the ensuing change after he discovered he had contracted HIV:

> "Yes! I couldn't accept it actually the first time...but after my mom, my sister (spoke to me), they are very positive towards me...my school friends with whom we have grown up together they are so positive. They said, it's okay, so I was like, okay, give it a try and when I was in the hospital... you know when I look at myself, I am in the film and music industry so am like a modern person, involved in filming shows and wearing boots. So, I was thinking like, do you want to be a good Muslim and if so, I have to change not only the inner side but even the way of my appearance in society... So, I tried to change whatever things, you know. And Alhamdulillah I am quite happy now. Like the doctor was so amazed, within less than three weeks I came off from the hospital. So, they said, 'Oh your progress is quite good'. And I think it is because I do pray and pray and pray; the *tahajjud* (night vigil) and prayers - really helps." (Interview Document No: 9 - Appendix 3).

One sees here the professional artist highlighting the difficulty he faced, while arriving at a state of self-realisation, with a change of his worldview, and thus a change of outlook both internally and externally. The facilitating factors here seems to be the support of friends and family and his emphasis on prayers and night vigil, which provide comfort. The above seeker outlines some aspects of this change:

> "Very difficult, but my mom always tells me just make sure you are close to Allah and things will be easy, which I tried, and Alhamdulillah (praise the Lord). You know I never miss my *salah* (ritual prayer). I try to be a good person, so I am more relaxed you know. Even like you, the people who surround me are totally different kind of people. So, I can go through that, you know. I have learnt to accept things and I learnt to be more patient (sabr). It looks very funny; it looks so weird, sometimes I was thinking like my mom doesn't love me that's why she sent me here but after (my) experience and everything... I look at the positive side (and) have learned a lot." (Interview Document No: 9 - Appendix 3).

This above seeker is consistent with his prayers, conforming to rituals and learning to accept the difficulties in being patient, which helps him be at ease. His initial integration to this group was difficult due to his foreign exposure but he has within a short time learnt to accept and adopt his ways to suit the situation. When asked how long he has been at the Centre and what was the turning point, he says:

> "Two weeks really. I think the turning point was when I got the news (of my HIV) in the UK. I was not sick. That's why when I think that I started crying, I was like Allah is so great and that's like why He didn't get me sick over there." (He says he went through a process of questioning, where he says,) "Why He didn't get me sick when I was working? When I was at home (Malaysia) only then He gives me this sickness. So, it is a lot of wonderful things I guess." (Interview Document No: 9 - Appendix 3).

When the above seeker was queried, "So when did you know?", he says:

> "I got to know (about my HIV) here in the hospital ... I think two months ago. The TB was very bad because the fungal infection had already gone to my brain...but the doctor said forget about the HIV because you can take something for the HIV but the TB is already gone to your brain and also my kidney, so we have to clean that first. So that's what the doctors have been doing, and so far so good, every week when I go to see them there is a progress... then I always listen to what they want, like they say my heart is not normal. So, I will change my diet, no more acidic food, and no more these things so things can be better." (Interview Document No: 9 - Appendix 3).

5.6 Spiritual Modelling

It is to be noted that in the Centre even though the focus is on spiritual activities, the relevant medical treatment is on-going, with the Centre's nurse's intervention and referral to the hospital. An Islamic scholar[7] calls this active repentance when one gets treatment and help from others and passive repentance when you appeal to God and he says both are required. These are vulnerable times for the professional artist, who has recovered from the current illness and is coming to terms with his current predicament with a sense of the realisation of God being good to him. This is a very positive outlook rather than questioning one's life and beliefs and having a negative attitude. This is the acceptance of one's situation and in a greater sense, God's will, a fundamental premise in Islam. The above seeker continues sharing his experiences:

> "It was like (an) awakening because I am not a good person ..in the industry. I am in the glamorous world. I have done a lot of things, a lot of naughty things, and when Allah gives me a chance like this for me it is like a miracle, you know how much He loves me so much. So, that is why I can take it, you know, slowly I realised things can heal me and can accept... At first my Mom said that I ... should come.. here, I could not accept that. Then I told her that the *dhikrullah* (remembrance of God) kind of things; my impression towards that was not so good ... and then if you don't have guru, I can see that some of these people have mentors. ... but when I think back my mom was telling me, we have to cleanse your body, in order for you to... because you will take a long time... so, I said okay. That is how I can accept things..." (Interview Document No: 9 - Appendix 3).

When asked whether cleansing the body also cleanses the mind, he points out that:

> "Yes, because the *dhikrullah* (process and method of remembering God) is something about, if you tell me yoga yes, because I was exposed to this kind of thing. So basically *dhikrullah* is something new to me and I am quite happy that Allah loves me and brings me to this kind of thing." (Interview Document No: 9 - Appendix 3).

He is addressing here a misperception by some Muslims about having a Sheikh and doing *dhikr*, which is a hallmark of those practicing *tasawwuf* (inward science). His perception changed when he came to the Centre and had a chance to observe things first-hand. His mother's role in creating the required awareness and referring to him to this Centre has been a significant move towards his acceptance and his eventual learning to accept and try to integrate with the group. When asked about his status within the Centre, he outlines:

> "Because I am still under my injection, the strong injection, so once I finish that I will start the *Bay'a* (oath of allegiance)... (and) my *salah* (ritual prayer)... it so funny that I was asking my mom... that before this when I pray, you know like I am catching up with time that's it. But now, when I pray, it takes a period of time because for me I can do the *tauba* (repentance), my *salah tauba* (forgiveness prayer). I can feel that I am near to Allah, before

---

[7] Said Nursi was an eminent Islamic Turkish-Kurdish Scholar (1876–1960) whose thoughts are expressed in many of his books. He founded a nondenominational movement, the Nur Movement, which advocated for a reinterpretation of Islamic according to the needs of modern society. He believed that change can come only within the changed mindset not through transformation of institutions by themselves (Yucel 2010).

it was like some reaction ... but now I feel like I have done so many bad things and how Allah can accept me for what I am." (He continues to highlight his observations): "He gave me a very good chance so I just have to make good use of it. Because I think He has already given me three chances. Yes, the first time I ignored, the second time I ignored, and this is the third time and I feel like this is going to be my last time..." (Interview Document No: 9 - Appendix 3).

The shift is apparent by his approach to prayers currently and previously, where he is now able to be in a state of absorption and concentration, which is combined with the ritual repentance prayers and being aware that this could be his last chance. This is a process of transformation that he is underlining here, coupled with a sense of healing. When the above seeker was asked about his past history, he expounded:

"That was when I got sick like five years ago... not very serious sickness, just a normal sickness and I always tell myself like I take vitamins and I am not going to get sickness. So, I feel like if God says you have to get the sickness, you have to. I learnt my lesson because when I think back, then I felt like oh my God, I am so arrogant to God. I think like I am so good but actually no, you know... I used to be stubborn... so I have learnt my lesson but forever now my family comes first, my children..." (Interview Document No: 9 - Appendix 3).

What is witnessed here is an acute sense of awareness of oneself, one's arrogance and travelling along the path being given an opportunity to relive life and improve one's spiritual states. The above seeker talks about his state of awareness:

"Before I was like, yes because I was so busy working until my mom said, like you go for the money you go nowhere... What you should do is that pray to Allah and get the right *rizk* (provision) from Him. I can see the money, where I got sixty-thousand but I don't know where the money went, I repaired my car and still the car cannot be moved. I spent a lot when I renovated my house, then (the) contractor ran away. So, these kinds of things make me think like what my mom said is true. And now even though I am not working, the *rizk* is always there and am quite relaxed. I just hope this will last for long. You know some people when they see... death they go back to normal. So, this really helps, because just to remind me like, you know you cannot do so many things because you are a Muslim. So, you can do certain things and you cannot do others and I am very comfortable with it." (Interview Document No: 9 - Appendix 3).

Three elements can be discerned in the above narrative. First, what is pointed out is the lack of work-life balance and that when an unexpected situation or emergency transpires, one is thrown off balance. Second, the concept of *rizk* or that one's life provisions are already measured according to the Islamic tradition and realising this affords one comfort to navigate one's course of life, irrespective of the difficulties that one experiences. Third, the daily remembrance of death is a Prophetic sunnah (tradition) and it does have a sobering effect. As the above seeker says, 'they go back to normal'.

The Head of Islamic Reflexology was asked about what it is to stop one depending on external things and depend on Allah only, to which he says (Appendix 3 document no:3): "When everything else happens, we refer to Allah, so we don't have to argue much. He was then queried as to how he thought the breakthrough occurred, and he explained, "The reason is what the Qur'ān said your body will shake and you will get sweat when you mention Allah's name. You are not using

5.6 Spiritual Modelling

your eyes, you close your eyes then you are using your heart's eyes. When you close your eyes, your heart's eyes will open then when you open your eyes your heart's eyes is closed, understand that? You see?" This referenced example is like the Prophet Musa in the Qur'an, where God tells us:

وَلَمَّا جَاءَ مُوسَىٰ لِمِيقَاتِنَا وَكَلَّمَهُ رَبُّهُ قَالَ رَبِّ أَرِنِي أَنظُرْ إِلَيْكَ قَالَ لَن تَرَانِي وَلَٰكِنِ انظُرْ إِلَى الْجَبَلِ فَإِنِ اسْتَقَرَّ مَكَانَهُ فَسَوْفَ تَرَانِي فَلَمَّا تَجَلَّىٰ رَبُّهُ لِلْجَبَلِ جَعَلَهُ دَكًّا وَخَرَّ مُوسَىٰ صَعِقًا فَلَمَّا أَفَاقَ قَالَ سُبْحَانَكَ تُبْتُ إِلَيْكَ وَأَنَا أَوَّلُ الْمُؤْمِنِينَ

"And when Musa came at the time and place appointed by Us, and the Lord (Allah) spoke to him; he said: O my Lord! Show me (Yourself), that I may look upon the mountain; if it stands still in its place then you shall see Me. So when his Lord appeared to the mountain. He made it collapse to dust, and Musa fell down unconscious. Then when he recovered his sense he said. Glory be to You, I turn to You in repentance and I am the first of the believers." (al-A'rāf 7:143)

The above seeker continues:

"Before he fainted, he said to close his eyes and using his heart's eyes to open, then when it opened, he mentioned the Tusina (name of a mountain) not inside his eyes but inside his heart. When Prophet Musa saw the Tusina in his eyes then only Allah's spiritual manifestation affected his *rūḥ* (spirit) and then his *rūḥ* separated from him for 40 days. So, whatever knowledge that Allah put in Prophet Musa is *sirr*(secret). Everything you say is inside the *sirr*(silent *dhikr* or remembrance), so every knowledge you want you have to *dhikr* with your eyes close. Then the knowledge comes to you, *Inshā'Allah*." (Interview Document No: 3 - Appendix 3).

The citation here of the Qur'ān, as well as his own experience, is to point out that God can only be experienced in the heart, that is, in one's mind's eye and not by the physical senses. Here he is using the incident of Prophet Musa to illustrate his point. On a general note, it could be said that the depth of the Prophetic experience and its divine interventions are different from that of other human beings. The above seeker further illustrates:

"For example, I tell you, when you put Allah's name with one touch, what is called touching... you pull (out) one Allah's name and you pull the whole world. Allah's name must be very heavier. You don't understand what is clue (meant) by that. But when you glow (spiritual light), automatically those things flow inside your heart, you can explain those things, how this thing went... and how the world is very light." (Interview Document No: 3 - Appendix 3).

The expression here is the total absorption in Allah's name, which touches the heart and when the heart is free from anyone but Allah, then the light of God flows into to it. The 'glow' here is a kind of manifestation of the light (*nūr*) that God gives those in His path, when matters are entrusted to God it makes the burden of humanity/human existence light. This is the experiential learning that can only be known through the process of deep meditation. The above seeker further expounds:

"Other times, yes that I am nobody. You feel *tawaddu* (a state of humbleness and that one is nothing in the presence of God) ... although there is Prophet Mohammed who is at the highest level but he is as a slave to Allah. Then in person, there are a few on this level, for example, those having patience. First, we start with repentance, patience and gratitude... so at this level we will feel serious... So when you are lucky enough to flourish, all these things, if you have to be patient and the patience is of very high potential. Some people, they learn..." (Interview Document No: 3 - Appendix 3).

Once again, the concept of the slave-Master relationship is highlighted, and this is also true for the Prophet, who saw himself in this way. This leads to one to assume a position of humility that deflates one's ego and opens one up to better deal with people and be closer to God. The virtue of patience is highlighted as a path finder, which together with seeking forgiveness and being grateful (*shukr*) would lead to being more calm and collected manner. These are some of the traits that can lead to a process of self-actualisation using Maslow's terminology. His use of the word flourish refers to a state of spiritual growth and human flourishing.

The sailor, when asked so how long he planned to stay, responded: "If I find myself ready to go out I will but I just want to really change myself. But now I am not ready to go out yet." When prodded further on how he felt he could really change himself, he said: "Change yourself, get nearer to God, stay in the jungle, really just be nearer to God." He has been able to start changing his state of mind though the various methods as outlined above, combined with the environment in which he is now living, which enables him to sustain his spiritual practices. (Interview Document No: 10—Appendix 3).

The resident who is a friend of the resident Imam discusses dreams, a subject of importance within Islam, saying, "Quite often I get.. each time I get dreams I get down and I pray. I pray well. Each time I get a dream I wake up and pray my *tahajjud* (night prayer or vigil), how grateful I am to Allah." He was asked about the type of dreams, and points out that it is, "About getting closer to God, getting closer to Allah to change my ways and to remind me who I am so there's .... Allah and Rasulullah (messenger of Allah)... but to become like Prophet Mohammed." When asked further about where he feels dreams when he has them, he stated:

"In my heart" (and when prodded where) "In my mind because I think is this true and true to me? And I say this is the last chance that Allah is giving to you use it in the right way... I say to myself, use it as good as possible because there's no getting give you this type of treatment, pull you closer to Allah... reminds me of Allah ... nice group where we can talk we can share about our Islamic things." (Interview Document No: 4 - Appendix 3).

This above narrative alludes to both consciousness of God and immersing oneself in acts of worship, as well as an indication of the process of internalisation as manifested in dreams in the above data extract. The situation is more pronounced in these types of cases since they are HIV sufferers and the residents see this as their final attempt to change themselves.

The nurse who is also a seeker in this *tarīqa*, highlights her reflections about the Sheikh and her learning:

"It is a lot to do with *sohba* (companionship) with the Guru (Sheikh). It is very important because that is how I learn about the Prophet. All the *sahabas* (companions) were always

5.6 Spiritual Modelling

around him, observing him and questioning him. So actually all my life, I was looking for what is life all about, it just comes from Allah. I seem to get the question: what is life really about? Then when you say the *shahada* (testimony of faith), there is no God but God... what is the secret there. There is one Abdul Abidin and another person were talking about the *sira salikeen* (the seeker on a straight path). I was listening to them. It sought of touched my heart, then awareness comes in and then you want to practice sincerely. Meantime as I read books on *tasawwuf* (inner aspects of Islam) to go on the Sufi path. It is said that you have to look for a teacher, in order to go through path; you cannot be without a teacher. If the teacher is not within the territory, you have to go out of the country. Because it is so important, I said where am I going, and as I was *tafakkur* (reflecting), on all those words, it so happened that Tuan Guru (Sheikh) was coming over to my *surahu* (smaller mosque). So, every time when he comes, if I am off duty, I will make sure that I will go for the after *maghrib* session. So, he was touching on all the key topics using the one *kitab* (book)." (Interview Document No: 6 - Appendix 3).

The process of learning is emphasised here, which captures both the verbal and non-verbal aspects of listening to the Sheikh, practicing and reflecting, and in the process one's heart is touched or the words and its subsequent action become internalised and a part of you. This is akin to Albert Bandura's (2011) social learning theory that encapsulate this process of modelling by observing others, the four necessary conditions are outlined: (1) attention, (2) retention, (3) reproduction and (4) motivation. This will be elaborated on in the discussion session in Chap. 6.

The process of self-discovery is outlined by her, where she draws a continuum in terms of knowledge, which encompasses both the external-Sharī'a (body of knowledge including *fiqh* or law) and the internal-*haqīqa* (reality), with the latter being based both on experience and intuition. The concept that she uses, namely, *tawajjuh*(spiritual attention), which Schimmel (1975) explains as the bonding between the Sheikh and the *murid* (seeker) and thus, "Concentration upon the sheikh, which later orders, mainly the Naqshbandiyya, considered necessary for the successful performance of *dhikr*... the sheikh, too, would practice *tawajjuh* and thus 'enter the disciple's heart' to watch him and to guard him.' When queried about the effect of *dhikr*, she details:

> "Yes *dhikr* has of course affected me a lot, it's the basis of our existence. The more you practice *dhikr* and the more you get. The guru (Sheikh) always tells us that everything the whole universe is in *dhikrullah* (state of remembrance of God), so how come we are not in *dhikr* so that is a lot to do with *tafakkur* (reflection), we have to do that a lot ... because you have to let Allah nourish you with that, it is a gift. Because when you find difficulty you have to let Allah help you with that. Because its Allah's gift you cannot just say that you can do it or you can't. If Allah feels like you're ready to be gifted then Allah gifts you at that time so you cannot be impatient knowing that you put yourself in that station, which is not meant for you... this is when all the *nafs* (ego) and the *shaytan* (devil) will all comes in. So you always have to be aware about the practice of *dhikr*, it is so important and you always have to be aware of the *shaytan* that is always trying to destroy the relationship with the *Khāliq* (Creator). Realise the position of *'abdi* (servant)... the more you feel that you are *'abdi*... keep polishing as the Tuan Guru (Sheikh) says until you die..." (Interview Document No: 6 - Appendix 3).

Here, she is outlining the importance of consistency in doing the *dhikr*, that is remembering God, while at the same time reflecting within oneself. This can also be understood as the synchronisation of the heart through the process of *dhikr* and reflection, which is the concept of alignment with the heart and the brain (elaborated in Chap. 6). She says that if you keep doing this, God gifts you with openings and higher spiritual stations, however she points out that you cannot force yourself into these prematurely, rather they are gifts from God given at the appropriate time. Additionally, one has to be mindful of one's ego and the disturbances of the Satan. This is akin to the concept of God as light and Satan as darkness, hence one must feed the former and be aware of the latter.

Imam Suhrawardi (1991) when discussing spiritual advancement, stated that it is moving from one state of consciousness to a higher state of consciousness: "Hence his advance from *maqām* (station) to *maqām* is by God's sway and of His gift—not of his own acquisition." In the light of the above, Ibn Abbad says, "There is no arrival to God but by God, as well as there is no veil between the servant and the Lord but his *nafs* (ego). One does not fight the *nafs* by the *nafs* by God" (Schimmel 1975). Thus, it the ego, the I, me, mine, that is being self-centred and selfish and which acts as an obstacle for getting close to God and it is through His Grace that you arrive.

5.6.2 The Sheikh as an Exemplar

The Sheikh, who is the leader of this Organisation, is the immediate focal point for all spiritual seekers, both the general one's and the residents. He is the exemplar or the living role model that they aspire to as Fig. 5.8 indicates. The Sheikh himself models on the Prophet. The references by the respondents in the survey to the Master-Imam and Tuan Guru (Sheikh) are actually to the same person here, even though it has been presented as two names in the figure, with a score of 32%, while the Prophet himself is rated as 19% (Fig. 5.8). This higher rating of the Sheikh is perhaps due to the seekers themselves being able to directly relate to someone who is in their immediate physical presence, even though there is reference of emulating the Prophet in the interview data extract, especially from the resident Imam. The Sheikh's prime role model is the Prophet himself and thereafter followed by others in the spiritual path.

In terms of role-modelling, parents and the resident's Centre supervisor follow with a score of 6% and 3%. One of the central reasons for the high rating of the Sheikh is his code of conduct or behaviour, where he is able to provide a nurturing environment for the seekers. As Fig. 5.9, the five most important traits of the Sheikh with the highest rated qualities indicated in order of priority are: patience (59%), humbleness (53%), forgiveness (50%), love (47%), wisdom (44%), honesty (41%), and trust (41%).

The attributes of the Sheikh's character are thus seen to be crucial, especially for those who want to reform themselves and have been negligent in the past. He is seen as one who has been bestowed with blessings from God and has a genealogy connecting to the Prophet (Sidek 2014). It is important to note that there are several

5.6 Spiritual Modelling

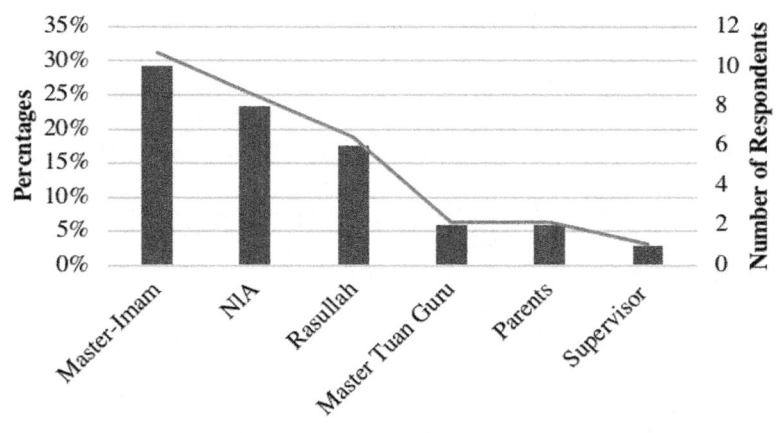

Fig. 5.8 Immediate role model

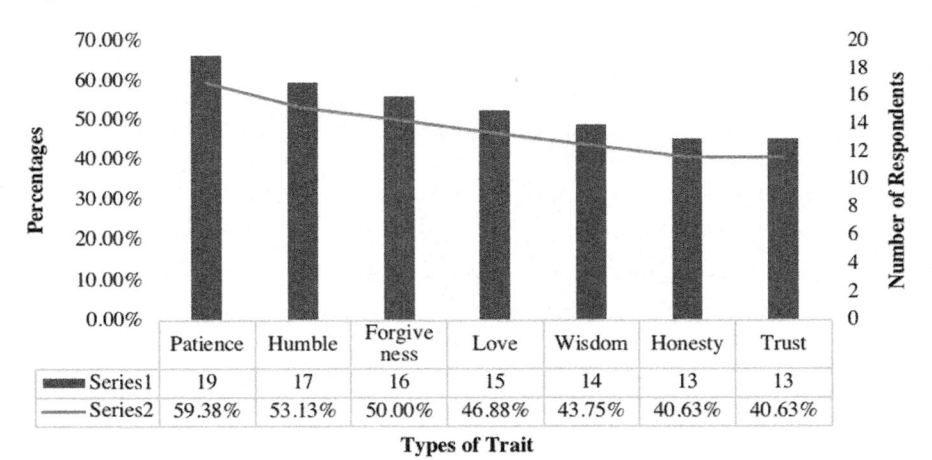

Fig. 5.9 Most important traits of the Sheikh

conditions to becoming a Sheikh, as outlined below, detailing the requirements and characteristics an individual has to have.

1. Needs to be one learned in the science of *Fiqh* and confident about it;
2. Needs to perfect his knowledge about the properties of the heart, have polite manners, be aware about its illnesses and on how to cure and purify it;
3. Must be compassionate to his disciples, have a lot of patience and be forgiving, be able to give guidance to the disciples until they receive guidance from God;
4. Be able to confide in and not shame anyone;
5. Not have any desire and greed for the wealth of his disciples;
6. Should practice what he preaches and thus be an example;

7. Maximise his time when he sits with his disciples offering the required guidance to clean their hearts;
8. Must honour his words and they should be cleansed of any desire or passion;
9. Must always be tolerant and not too lenient or too harsh;
10. When disciples manifest spiritually elevated positions, he should take measure so as not to inflate the seekers ego;
11. When the perceptions of the disciples have been affected regarding the Sheikh, he needs to readdress this matter;
12. Should not be reckless and be able to facilitate his disciples;
13. When disciples share their spiritual experiences, he should be able to guide them accordingly;
14. Must provide facilities for disciples for undertaking their seclusions;
15. He should not expose too many details of his life to his disciples;
16. He should prohibit disciples from overeating and becoming slaves to their habits;
17. Should discourage disciples from meeting very high officials unless there is a specific requirement;
18. Should speak to his disciples with gentleness and not speak harshly about disciples;
19. When invited by someone he should accept the invitation with humility;
20. He should sit quietly and patiently with his disciples and conduct himself in the best manner;
21. He should not avoid his disciples and pray for their goodness;
22. He must feel concern for his disciples and help them if he/she requires help.

The above criteria set the basis to distinguish between who is a reliable Sheikh and who is not, and this is important especially for those who are seeking to find a proper Sheikh to guide them in taking this path. Sidek (2014) also outlines the detailed guidance on the mannerisms of the disciples towards the Sheikh, the mannerisms of the Sheikh towards seekers, as well as mannerisms towards others.

5.6.3 Spiritual Modelling and Mode of Transmission of Practices and Knowledge

The essential learning from the Sheikh that the seekers find most useful are reflected in Fig. 5.10, where the highest rated are 'being silent' (rated by 66% of respondents), and 'saying a prayer' (56%). This is followed by getting advice from others, supplicating to God and being patient.

In terms of the Sheikh imparting codes of behaviour (Fig. 5.11), the most important modes were, firstly, by setting an example (referring to his role models primarily the Prophet, (56%); second, through the Sheikh demonstrably acting as an exemplar through his own behaviour (50%) as well as setting ground rules (50%);

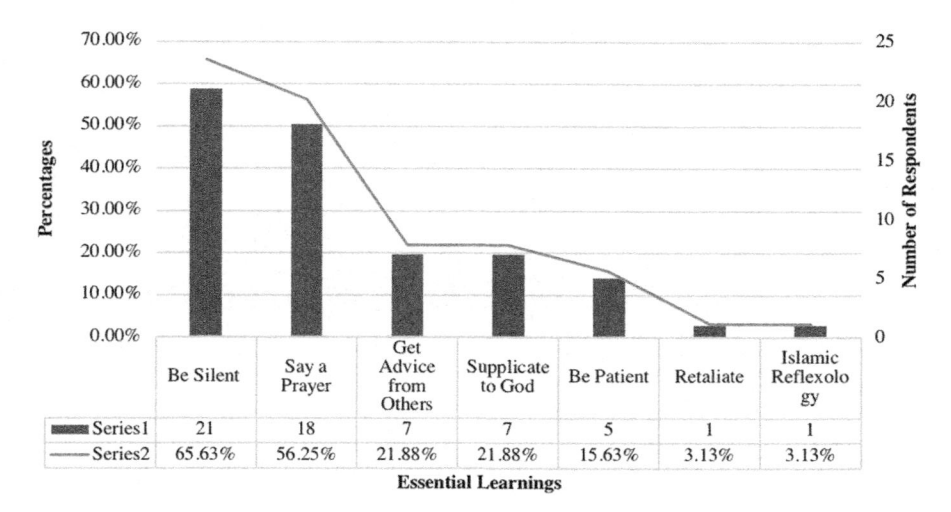

5.6 Spiritual Modelling

Fig. 5.10 Essential learnings from the Sheikh for self-development

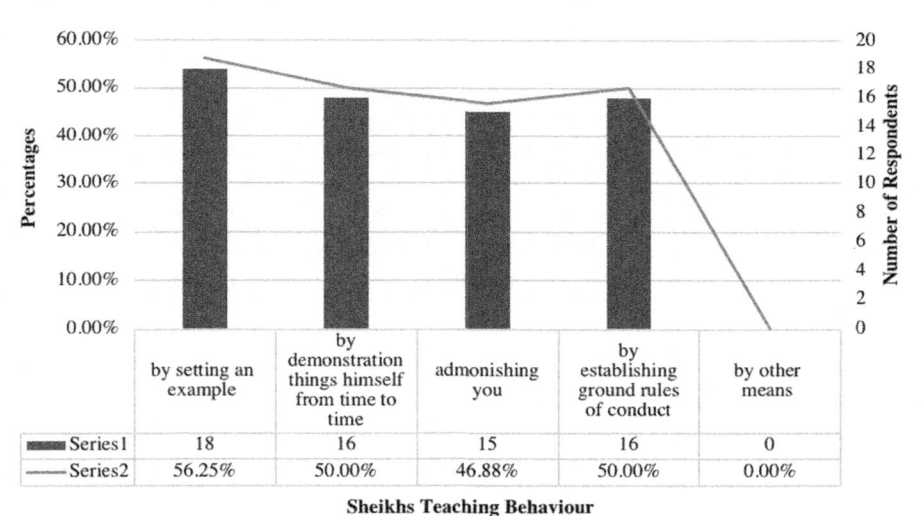

	Be Silent	Say a Prayer	Get Advice from Others	Supplicate to God	Be Patient	Retaliate	Islamic Reflexology
Series1	21	18	7	7	5	1	1
Series2	65.63%	56.25%	21.88%	21.88%	15.63%	3.13%	3.13%

Essential Learnings

Fig. 5.11 Sheikh imparting codes of behaviour to the group

	by setting an example	by demonstration things himself from time to time	admonishing you	by establishing ground rules of conduct	by other means
Series1	18	16	15	16	0
Series2	56.25%	50.00%	46.88%	50.00%	0.00%

Sheikhs Teaching Behaviour

and third, by admonishing seekers (47%) with regards to their speech or actions that are not within the framework of Islam.

The 1st ranked most beneficial acts of worship (Fig. 5.12) include doing individual *dhikr* (22%), collective *dhikr* (15%), *salah* (6%), supplication (3%) and all of the previous (3%). There was a relatively high score where respondents stating not applicable (19%), where the seekers found it difficult to rank acts or worship, or did

	Individual Dhikr Silent	N/A	Zikr	Daily Prayers	Salah	All of the above mentioned	Supplication
Series1	7	6	5	2	2	1	1
Series2	21.88%	18.75%	15.63%	6.25%	6.25%	3.13%	3.13%

Acts of Worship

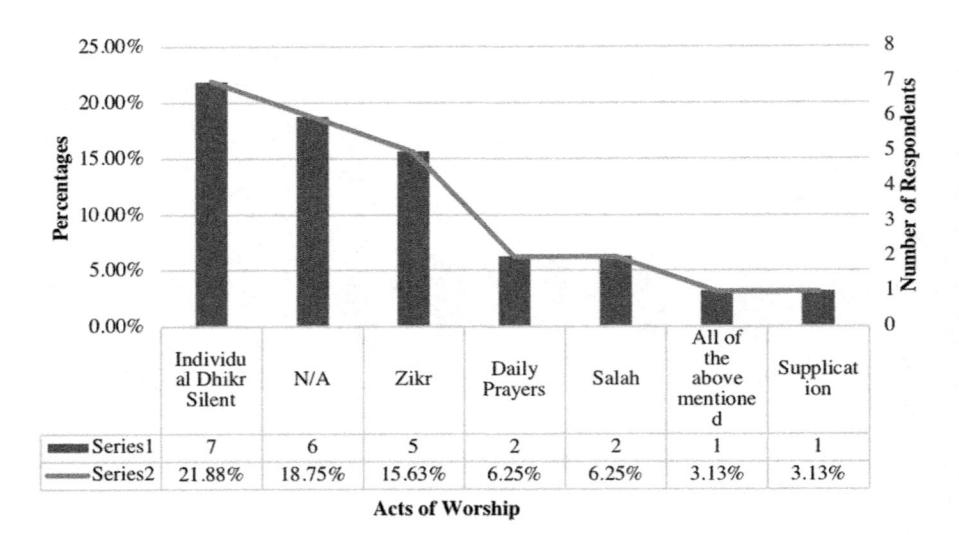

Fig. 5.12 1st ranked beneficial acts of worship

not fully understand the question. The more traditional methods such as by teaching, giving verbal instructions, giving special prayers gained comparatively lower scores.

The two above seeker residents highlight ten virtuous traits that they have learnt from the Sheikh and which they are trying to emulate and is a recurring theme. These form a part of the core traits required for development of the self as outlined below: *baraka* (blessings), *shukr* (gratitude), *tawakal* (trust), *tauba* (repentance), *sabr* (patience); *taqwa* (piety), *zuhd* (poverty), *amal* (hope), *riḍa* (acceptance), *ākhira* (next life).

They go on to give some examples: "*Amal* means hope, you want to get it, you are not confident to get it. Day by day, you use your hand for *du'ā* (supplication), something like you hope for something." In addition: "*riḍa* (contentment) means like something happened to you it is okay. It is from God but you accept it." They add: "*zuhd* (poverty) means being normal and sufficient: to buy something that is normal and not to show off; these things are like all given by Allah." (Appendix 3 Documents 2 and 4).

The above sentences portray the virtues-ruinous framework (see Sect. 3.1.5), which has been articulated by many Islamic scholars, where the virtuous part forms the basis on which sound and ethical characteristics are built. The above two seekers point out that:

"If you have these ten things (set of values) you are (very close) with Him. Thats why when we go to lectures or when our guru is preaching we have to take notes." (They say when they go for *kulliyyah* (lectures) they take notes and they say): "For me with these ten things in Islam you build trust in Allah (and) "So when you can do all this, Allah will accept you or Allah will listen. You are looking for him but you cant see him but He can see you." (Interview Document No: 2 and 4 - Appendix 3).

5.6 Spiritual Modelling

This is the first time that I have seen a demonstrable value framework outlined and evidence of people working towards achieving it day in day out. This seems a useful way to inculcate values and this in turn can have a positive impact on behaviour and transformation. For me, this was something new, which I had not thought about and see that it constitutes a useful way to imbibe and practice to inculcate these values into ones life.

Another essential element that emerges from the data set is the emulation of the Sheikh by the seekers through modelling him by observation (Figs. 5.9 and 5.10) and by taking notes and trying to inculcate the ten values mentioned above. When asked if they had thought like this before, they stated:

> "No...maybe certain of the ten..." (They say): "We have learnt it from the Tuan Guru (Sheikh)...So I still have to catch up and I am not perfect yet...You think about it from down to top, that is, from ākhira (next life) and then work your way up." (Both seekers expand on it): "Because you must...if you dont think ākhira, you never get it. If you think that ākhira is true Allah says, He will stay in the heart and...(and you will) be scared. How are we to face Allah in the ākhira?" (He further expands on it): "It's the way Allah gives, you can discuss which part you want....you are rich but the property you have got is not yours. You want to give it to anyone, you can give, but it is not yours. Yes, the thing is mine but if you want you can have it, that is what our guru said last night in the *kulliyyah* (lecture). This palace is mine, you want to stay, you are welcome you can stay." (Interview Document No: 2 and 4 - Appendix 3).

The influence of the Sheikh seen here is creating awareness of the temporality of this world and based on the realisation that we come to this world alone and leave alone without taking any possessions. The end product of death and the next life becomes a starting point to intensify one's worship, and also to work on one's behaviour setting these ten traits as a value-based framework, where one tries to inculcate it.

Al-Attas (2001) distinguishes between the Islamic and the Western worldview, where he points out that for Muslims, the framework is dunya-ākhira (world-next life). It is a Prophetic tradition to frequently focus on death, so that one does not lose one's orientation and enables one to maintain the required equilibrium. The above seekers, when asked about how they process the information that they learn from the lecure of the Sheikh, provided their insights:

> "I have to learn how to get this done deeply, by going to lectures, by doing *dhikr*, by humbling oneself with people, the way that we talk, the way that we give things, the way that we are scared of Allah...everything that is wrong so that we don't do it again. But it is very hard to get these ten things. Even me at the moment, but one day I will get. *Inshā'Allah* (God willing), if Allah opens my heart and softens my tongue to speak and to read Qur'ān *Inshā'Allah* I will be someone. I would love to go deeply, more deeply." (Interview Document No: 2 and 4 - Appendix 3).

There are many aspects that are underscored above, notably the three main dimensions of building oneself, worship (*'ibādah*) through ritual prayers and *dhikr*, cultivating good character or morals through humility and dealing with people well (*akhlāq*—morality and mu'amalat—dealing with people), and building one's relationship with God (*taqwa*). His desire to 'go deeply, more deeply' is the process of intensifying one's God consciousness, where over time and with mercy, one gets into deeper level of consciousness. When prodded on the reason for this, he says:

> "Getting to know Allah is the key because you always speak about Him, you always talk about Him, and you remember Him, so He remembers you. So wake up, if you want to come to Me then you speak My name, you call My name I will be there anytime you need me by your side, let's say like the song... if you remember Him, you think about Him He will be there for us anytime. He will be there for us and He will listen although we can't see Him, but He can see us and what we are doing. We want to look for Him, but we can't see Him. But He can see what we are doing." (Interview Document No: 2 and 4 - Appendix 3).

Here he is referring to the saying of the Prophet, which comes from ḥadith which states that 'Be mindful of Allah and you will find Him in front of you' (al-Tirmidhi, Hadith No:19, Ibrahim and Johnson-Davies 1977). He elaborates:

> "That is in Islam, nobody can teach you about rukun iḥsān (pillars of sincerity/excellence). If you do worship or *'ibādah* Allah can see you. No, if you do *'ibādah* you see Allah, if you cannot see Allah that He is seeing you. Nobody can give a proper or good information to understand that. You must do it to get it..." (Interview Document No: 2 and 4 - Appendix 3).

When he points out that '*iḥsān*' (excellence) cannot be taught he is referring to a key element which is derived from the *Jibril ḥadīth* (Muslim, Hadith No:2, Ibrahim and Johnson-Davies 1977), when the Prophet was asked what *iḥsan* is he said, 'It is worshiping God as if you see him, while you see Him not He sees you'. This refers to a method of meditation called '*murāqaba*', a state of watchfulness with engrossed attention that God is watchful of you. This kind of meditation, which is called '*wuquf qalbi*' is a primary method used in the Order under study.

The concept of *wuquf qalbi* (act of being present in the heart) is a symbolic form of remembering Allah with a state of alertness to other intruding thoughts other than (Him 'Abd al-Majid in Omarand and Zarrina 2011, p 94). *Wuquf qalbi* refers to two things done by the disciples. First, the disciples call upon the meaning of each name of Allah chanted, that is He is the Ultimate and Incomparable (al-Baghdadi al-Khani in Omarand and Zarrina 2011, p 94). The action's purpose is to eliminate the intrusion of thoughts other than Allah. The second step in *wuquf qalbi* is for the disciple to focus all his senses towards his inner heart which is located under the left breast towards the left side ('Abd al-Majid in Omarand and Zarrina 2011, p 94). The seeker seems to have varying kinds of experiences and sometimes openings, which cannot be taught and frequently cannot be captured in words.

During the interview with the Sheikh (Interview Document No: 5—Appendix 3), he points out that there are three tiers of worship: (1) Islam, with its general body of knowledge and rituals for the public (*awam*). There is tendency toward ghaflah or forgetfulness in this group. The people are hoping and/or expecting rewards for their deeds; (2) Awam—Khawas (elite). There is some degree of awareness in this group. In this group, there is '*al-riḍa*' (being content); (3) *Iḥsan*: Khawas-ul-Khawas (elite among the elite)—this is the group of excellence, also known as Ulul al-Bab (people of the core-wisdom); the *muḥsineen* (a category of people close to God).

5.6 Spiritual Modelling

In this group, worship is only for Allah and there is no expectation of reward. In response to the above three categorisations, it was asked whether this is aligned to the stages of development of the *nafs*, which was articulated in Sect. 2.1, to which the Sheikh responds affirmatively. This will be further elaborated in the Chap. 6 on discussion.

The Sheikh points to the verses below in terms of finding inner peace:

$$\text{الَّذِينَ آمَنُوا وَتَطْمَئِنُّ قُلُوبُهُم بِذِكْرِ اللَّهِ ۗ أَلَا بِذِكْرِ اللَّهِ تَطْمَئِنُّ الْقُلُوبُ}$$

"Those who believed and whose hearts find rest in the remembrance of Allah. Verily, in the remembrance of Allah do hearts find rest." (Qur'ān, al Ra'd 13:28)

$$\text{وَالَّذِينَ اجْتَنَبُوا الطَّاغُوتَ أَن يَعْبُدُوهَا وَأَنَابُوا إِلَى اللَّهِ لَهُمُ الْبُشْرَىٰ ۚ فَبَشِّرْ عِبَادِ}$$

$$\text{الَّذِينَ يَسْتَمِعُونَ الْقَوْلَ فَيَتَّبِعُونَ أَحْسَنَهُ ۚ أُولَٰئِكَ الَّذِينَ هَدَاهُمُ اللَّهُ ۖ وَأُولَٰئِكَ هُمْ أُولُو الْأَلْبَابِ}$$

"Those who shun the worship of false gods and turn to Allah, for them are glad tidings; so announce the good news to My servants. Those who listen to the Word and follow the best thereof, those are (the ones) whom Allah has guided and those are men of understanding." (Qur'ān, al-Zumar 39:17–18)

In the light of the above, there are different levels of worship (*'ibādah*) by the seekers, and each of their levels have varying levels of knowledge, where spiritual progression brings about a greater level of understanding. The Sheikh points out that this is also consistent with the Qur'ān,

$$\text{وَعِبَادُ الرَّحْمَٰنِ الَّذِينَ يَمْشُونَ عَلَى الْأَرْضِ هَوْنًا وَإِذَا خَاطَبَهُمُ الْجَاهِلُونَ قَالُوا سَلَامًا}$$
$$\text{وَالَّذِينَ يَبِيتُونَ لِرَبِّهِمْ سُجَّدًا وَقِيَامًا}$$

"And the servants of the Most Gracious are those who walk on the earth in humility, and when the foolish address them they say; 'Peace'. And those who spend the night in worship of their Lord, prostrate and standing." (al-Furqan 25:63–64)

The Sheikh makes further reference to the Qur'ān:

قَدْ أَفْلَحَ الْمُؤْمِنُونَ

الَّذِينَ هُمْ فِي صَلَاتِهِمْ خَاشِعُونَ

وَالَّذِينَ هُمْ عَنِ اللَّغْوِ مُعْرِضُونَ

وَالَّذِينَ هُمْ لِلزَّكَاةِ فَاعِلُونَ

وَالَّذِينَ هُمْ لِفُرُوجِهِمْ حَافِظُونَ

إِلَّا عَلَىٰ أَزْوَاجِهِمْ أَوْ مَا مَلَكَتْ أَيْمَانُهُمْ فَإِنَّهُمْ غَيْرُ مَلُومِينَ

فَمَنِ ابْتَغَىٰ وَرَاءَ ذَٰلِكَ فَأُولَٰئِكَ هُمُ الْعَادُونَ

وَالَّذِينَ هُمْ لِأَمَانَاتِهِمْ وَعَهْدِهِمْ رَاعُونَ

وَالَّذِينَ هُمْ عَلَىٰ صَلَوَاتِهِمْ يُحَافِظُونَ

أُولَٰئِكَ هُمُ الْوَارِثُونَ

الَّذِينَ يَرِثُونَ الْفِرْدَوْسَ هُمْ فِيهَا خَالِدُونَ

"Successful indeed are the believers. Those who humble themselves in their prayers. And who turn away from all that is frivolous And those who pay the *zakah* (obligatory alms). And those who guard their private parts except with their wives or whom their right hand possess, for then, they are free from blame. But whoever seeks beyond that, then those are the transgressors. Those who are faithfully true to their trusts and covenants. And those who strictly guard their prayers. These are indeed the heirs. Who shall inherit Paradise: and shall dwell therein forever." (al-Mu'minun 23:1–11).

The Sheikh states concerning worship, that one needs to have the consciousness of God or mindfulness and seek the light of Allah. He explains that with regard to the verse 'Light upon Light' cited in the Qur'ān, the first light is the *waḥy*—revelation, and the second light is the Prophet Muhammad (see Appendix 3 Document no:5). In terms of worship, there are two aspects, firstly, referring to the physical aspects of one's life and efforts and, secondly, the events of the heart and its processes: Allah looks at the state of your heart, some hearts are alive and have consciousness of God while others are dead.

The Sheikh in discussing the impact of *'ibādah* (worship) on *akhlāq* (morality), cites the Qur'ānic verses below:

5.6 Spiritual Modelling

$$\text{فَأَصْحَابُ الْمَيْمَنَةِ مَا أَصْحَابُ الْمَيْمَنَةِ}$$

$$\text{وَأَصْحَابُ الْمَشْأَمَةِ مَا أَصْحَابُ الْمَشْأَمَةِ}$$

$$\text{وَالسَّابِقُونَ السَّابِقُونَ}$$

$$\text{أُولَئِكَ الْمُقَرَّبُونَ}$$

"So those on the right – how (fortunate) will be those on the right! And those on the left – how (unfortunate) will be those on the left! And those foremost will be foremost. These will be the nearest (to Allah)." (al-Waqi'ah 56:8–11)

The Sheikh details that the companions of the right hand are those who are drawn nigh (to Allah) and have three spiritual characteristics; *iman* (faith), *'amal* (actions) and remembrance of Allah. The Sheikh then cites the following verse, referring to those who have spiritually developed themselves and their movements towards their Lord:

$$\text{اَا أَيَّتُهَا النَّفْسُ الْمُطْمَئِنَّةُ}$$

$$\text{ارْجِعِي إِلَىٰ رَبِّكِ رَاضِيَةً مَّرْضِيَّةً}$$

$$\text{فَادْخُلِي فِي عِبَادِي}$$

$$\text{وَادْخُلِي جَنَّتِي}$$

"O tranquil soul! Come back to your Lord – well pleased and well-pleasing! Enter then among My servants, and enter My Paradise." (Qur'ān, al-Fajr 89:27–30)

The Sheikh then sums it up in terms of the human characteristics that are required to cultivate it and the impact of both akhlāq (morality) and *'ibādah* (worship), as well as the reward that one gets from their Lord, in reference to this he cites the Qur'ān:

أَفَمَن يَعْلَمُ أَنَّمَا أُنزِلَ إِلَيْكَ مِن رَّبِّكَ الْحَقُّ كَمَنْ هُوَ أَعْمَىٰ إِنَّمَا يَتَذَكَّرُ أُولُو الْأَلْبَابِ
الَّذِينَ يُوفُونَ بِعَهْدِ اللَّهِ وَلَا يَنقُضُونَ الْمِيثَاقَ
وَالَّذِينَ يَصِلُونَ مَا أَمَرَ اللَّهُ بِهِ أَن يُوصَلَ وَيَخْشَوْنَ رَبَّهُمْ وَيَخَافُونَ سُوءَ الْحِسَابِ
وَالَّذِينَ صَبَرُوا ابْتِغَاءَ وَجْهِ رَبِّهِمْ وَأَقَامُوا الصَّلَاةَ وَأَنفَقُوا مِمَّا رَزَقْنَاهُمْ سِرًّا وَعَلَانِيَةً وَيَدْرَءُونَ بِالْحَسَنَةِ السَّيِّئَةَ أُولَٰئِكَ لَهُمْ عُقْبَى الدَّارِ
جَنَّاتُ عَدْنٍ يَدْخُلُونَهَا وَمَن صَلَحَ مِنْ آبَائِهِمْ وَأَزْوَاجِهِمْ وَذُرِّيَّاتِهِمْ وَالْمَلَائِكَةُ يَدْخُلُونَ عَلَيْهِم مِّن كُلِّ بَابٍ
سَلَامٌ عَلَيْكُم بِمَا صَبَرْتُمْ فَنِعْمَ عُقْبَى الدَّارِ

"Shall he then who knows that what has been revealed unto you from your Lord is the truth, be like him who is blind? But it is only the men of understanding that pay heed. Those who fulfil the covenant of Allah and break not the trust. And those who join that which Allah has commanded to be joined and fear their Lord, and dread the terrible reckoning. And those who remain patient, seeking their Lords Face, perform the *salah*, and spend out of that which we have bestowed on them, secretly and openly, and repel evil with good, for such there is a good end. And Gardens, which they shall enter and (also) those who acted righteously from among their fathers, and their wives, and their offspring. And angels shall enter unto them from every gate (saying): Salamun Alaykum (peace be upon you) for our persevered in patience! Excellent indeed is the final home!" (al-Ra'ad 13: 19–24)

The distinguishing point in the above verses are the juxtaposition that is drawn between those who have knowledge and spiritual insight and those who do not, where God says that they are not the same. Knowledge is combined with those who have good qualities or a code of conduct, set apart from hypocrites who break their covenant and are not true to themselves and their Lord. It is only those who sustain their acts of worship and help others in need that will enter the Garden (Ibn Kathir 2003).

5.6.4 The Process of Modelling by the Seeker

Two Centre residents were posed the question, "How are you going to process the information yourself, in relation to the virtuous traits that you learnt from the Sheikh?" They responded, "I have to learn how to get this done deeply. I think I have only one or two virtuous traits." When asked, "What kind of deeply is that deeply?" they stated:

"By going to *kulliyyah* (lecture), by *dhikr*, by humbling with people the way that we talk, the way that we give things, the way that we are scared of Allah… But it is very hard to get these ten virtuous traits… but one day I will get. *Inshā'Allah*, if Allah opens my heart and

5.6 Spiritual Modelling

softens my tongue to speak and to read Qur'ān *Inshā'Allah* (if God wills) I will be someone. I would love to go deeply, more deeply." (Interview Document No: 2 and 4 - Appendix 3).

The reference is how people learn and it touches on social learning theory of understanding, internalising, testing and reproducing behaviour (Bandura 2011). Here there is a process of ongoing self-assessment when he says, "I have only two traits out of ten." The ten traits taught by the Sheikh are viewed as a target towards which the seekers aspire. The Sheikh was posed a question regarding how he motivated the seekers. He responded by saying that the motivation is gained through attaining equilibrium and quotes a verse from the Qur'ān:

$$\text{وَيَرْزُقْهُ مِنْ حَيْثُ لَا يَحْتَسِبُ وَمَن يَتَوَكَّلْ عَلَى اللَّهِ فَهُوَ حَسْبُهُ إِنَّ اللَّهَ بَالِغُ أَمْرِهِ قَدْ جَعَلَ اللَّهُ لِكُلِّ شَيْءٍ قَدْرًا}$$

"And He will provide him from where he never could imagine. And whosoever puts his trust in Allah, then He will suffice him. Verily, Allah will accomplish his purpose. Indeed Allah has set a measure of all things." (al-Talāq 65:3)

The Sheikh adds that "based on one's *taqwa* (piety), Allah will relieve you in many ways, in order to settle all problems" (Appendix 3 Document no:5). The Sheikh says that he motivates the seekers through the exposition of the two dimensions of Allah, that is the Jalāl and the Jamāl and each of these has its attributes (ṣifat). The Jamāli (beautiful) attributes are: Raheem (Merciful), Rahmān (Beneficent), 'Aleem (All Knowing), Wadūd (Most Loving), Haleem (The Clement), Ghaffūr (Forgiving) etc. The Jalāli (Majestic) attributes are: Muqtadir (Powerful), Muntaqim (Avenger.) etc. These two dimensions can be seen as a continuum, with the Jalali or the Uluhiya (God-like) attributes embodying the main aspect of fear, while the Jamāli or the Rubbibiya (Lord-like) attributes embody hope and mercy. He adds that when the Prophet referred to 'ummatan wasatan', the reference was to the attainment of this balance between the Jalāli and the Jamāli attributes. The Sheikh says that, "It is a tight rope to walk on and it is to maintain the balance of fear and hope. This will prevent one from going beyond hope to hopelessness or despair."

The above use of the 'tight rope' metaphor is to navigate the fine balance in life between the Jalāli—Majestic and the Jamāli—Beautiful, which has many manifestations including the fearful and hopeful. The Sheikh motivates his *murid*s through various methods including lectures, circles of *dhikr* and ritual practices. He refers to the story of Prophet Yusuf in the Qur'ān, where his father, Prophet Ya'coub (Jacob), demonstrates the power of his faith through his constant hope in God:

$$\text{يَا بَنِيَّ اذْهَبُوا فَتَحَسَّسُوا مِن يُوسُفَ وَأَخِيهِ وَلَا تَيْأَسُوا مِن رَّوْحِ اللَّهِ إِنَّهُ لَا يَيْأَسُ مِن رَّوْحِ اللَّهِ إِلَّا الْقَوْمُ الْكَافِرُونَ}$$

"O my sons! Go you and inquire about Yusuf and his brother, and never give up hope of Allah's mercy. Certainly no one despairs of Allah's mercy, except the people who disbelieve." (Yusuf 12:87)

This is an example of how the Sheikh draws lessons from the Qur'ān to teach his students, especially with those residents who are recovering drug addicts and HIV patients, as they are in a state of hardship both physically and mentally and thus it is essential that they do not lose hope in God's mercy. In fact, he says that this is the motivation part to know that God will grant you relief and His mercy is ever present

The Manager of Reflexology responds to a query about what he has learnt from Tuan Guru and how he has taken that and made it his own knowledge, by saying:

"I have learnt when I am in front of him there's a flow of light. I feel that when he taught me the words of the Qur'ān, I thought that I got more understanding of that than in the majlis (the gathering) there are so many books that you can read but you don't quite understand it. In this way there is more understanding." (Interview Document No: 3 - Appendix 3).

He was asked what else he had learnt, how he had learnt and translated it into meaning for himself:

"I learn what he taught me - every knowledge of the Qur'ān ... It has very special power, very special knowledge, very special *waḥy* (the revelation). For example, one was a word *fee fight* (yes fight), *fee dalam* (yes inside) you only know the inside but you don't know what is inside the inside, that is, what has woken me up... Okay, what is inside of inside, it is what knowledge Allah given to you." (He adds) "Flow of *limpahan noor* (flow of light). This is really what he gives you when he teaches you..." (Interview Document No: 3 - Appendix 3)

The Manager of Reflexology further expounds:

"You mention about doing more *dhikr*, putting ourselves down so that Allah can see an empty glass. We remember what the words are in the Qur'ān ... We always remember. That's the first thing, how to honour the *tawheed* (unity of God). It's a very interesting question... How to honour the *tawheed*. It is by mentioning Allah name, that is how you honour the *tawheed*... Allah, Allah (remembrance of God)." (Interview Document No: 3 - Appendix 3).

The above rendition by the manager encapsulates many key spiritual or metaphysical aspects, firstly, the he refers to the flow of light (*limpahan noor*), which is from God, alluding to the Qur'ānic verse of 'Light upon light!' (Qur'ān, al-Noor 24:35). Secondly, this light enlightens one's heart, which facilitates learning and the unveiling of divine knowledge (ma'rifa)... of (the) heart (Ghazāli, 1995). This can be called the process of awakening oneself. Thirdly, the reference by this seeker to the 'inside of the inside' is the increasing immersion into this divine knowledge. Imam Qushayri (2002), defined this as "a measure of one's alienation from one's own ego that one attains direct knowledge of one's Lord", while Abu Ali Daqqaq says it "'is the achievement of deep awe and reverence for God... Gnosis requires stillness of the heart, just as learning outward quietness. If someone's gnosis increases, his tranquillity increases." This type of direct knowledge is what he says, 'woke me up', meaning when he became spiritually awake.

5.7 Approaches, Methods and Tools for Self-Development 181

In explaining the inter-link between *tauba* (repentance), *sabr* (patience), *shukr* (gratitude), the manager generates a number of questions:

"...then you realise what kind of person is he, is he patient or not? Can he be grateful (*shukr*) or not? Is he going to complain or not? Is he humble towards the people or not? Then you know, you can change the person. What the Qur'ān says and what we say, what the Qur'ān asks you to do and what you do. The Qur'ān says you *lumbu hati*...(refers to the state of the heart – careful-attentive) not the same then, where we keep on judging the person? But we cannot mention it, we have to keep it and preserve our own knowledge. So what kind of person are you? Sometimes we see this is for Allah. He puts whatever he wanted to put, he puts down everybody and he also puts up, we cannot choose." (Interview Document No: 3 - Appendix 3).

Here the discussion is about the various attitudes of different types of people towards life and their attitude of turning towards God with submissions and patience. The process of questioning is one of self-critique and reflection, which is required to open oneself for introspection. The traits mentioned above form the virtuous elements articulated in Sect. 2.2. The state of the heart of a person who is patient, grateful and humble is closer to God.

5.7 Approaches, Methods and Tools for Self-Development

The methods and tools for the development of the self can be broadly categorised into three key categories, namely: (1) *tarqiyah* or spiritual grooming of the seeker; (2) *tarbiyah*, which essentially means education; and (3) *tazkiyah* signifying the process of purification.

1. *Tarqiyah*—spiritual grooming
2. *Tarbiyah*—education
3. *Tazkiyah*—purification

The above three key categories in combination lay the foundation for the progress of the development of self as indicated by the data set that has been generated.

5.7.1 Tarqiyah (Spiritual Grooming)

This concept of *tarqiyah*, which was outlined by the Manager of the Centre, has the concept of spiritual grooming as a major part of it, where the Sheikh, through his constant interactions with the seekers, molds them so that they acquire a better character (modelling). This is seen by the responses to the questionnaire, notably in Fig. 5.8, the spiritual modelling of the Sheikh by the seekers and in Fig. 5.11 in seeing the Sheikh as 'setting an example'. The Manager of the Centre, who is one of the senior most seekers explain the main methods relating to self-development:

"There is a terminology that we use. We have the three: ta'līm (methods), *tazkiya* (purification) and *tarbiyah* (education). There is this terminology that is called *tarqiyah* (the path or Order)." (He goes on to explain *tarqiyah* as) "...spiritual grooming...the interaction between the word spirit but it is something, the interaction between the *ruḥ* (spirit) and the *nafs*(soul)." (He adds that) "...*tarqiyah* (order) is what you get from reading and listening to lectures and all that...*tarqiyah* that one is again within the knowledge realm...*tarqiyah* is also education, with a little bit more understanding actually." (Interview Document No: 1 - Appendix 3).

The resident imam, who was a former drug addict and HIV patient and now acts as a peer role model for other residents, who look up to him. He often leads the prayers and provides guidance to the other residents. He says about this organisation:

"It is very different because this Naqshabandiyyah (Order) is very tight and has very good discipline, good *adab* (conduct). You are facing seniority. You are facing your Tuan Guru, you must do things properly. And then, in here as well whatever you do, you must know that Allah— everything you do, that Allah sees you really." (Interview Document No: 2 - Appendix 3).

The sense of discipline in the Order comes out in the above statement by the resident imam. This refers back to the concept '*wuquf qalbi*', awareness of God's witnessing over you, which has already been elaborated upon. The resident Imam says in terms of taking a deep dive:

"If you go into learning about Islam, the background opens up your heart. Door by door, deep by deep inside that's why Allah says to Rasulullah (Prophet) to humble himself...He went on *isra* and *mi'raj* (referring to the heavenly journey). For Rasulullah it was a proper humbling, where he repented (*tauba*) seventy times per day." (Interview Document No: 2 - Appendix 3).

The seeker here is outlining the process of unravelling of his experiences and insights that he is gains from the immersion, which is referred to as 'door by door, deep by deep' referring to getting into the depths of consciousness. In this light, he cites the night journey of the Prophet, where after his heart was cleansed by the angels in Makkah, he undertook the night flight on a heavenly creature to Masjid al-Aqsa (Jerusalem) and then vertically to the seven heavens, where there were numerous spiritual experiences. The seeker is appreciating the humbleness of the Prophet in spite of his lofty spiritual status.

Bay'a is an oath of allegiance that the seeker makes with the Sheikh, this involves adhering to the religious obligations and code of conduct of the Order, was a recurring theme in the narrative of the seekers as evident in this section. The professional banker who is one of the seekers outlines that:

"The oath of allegiance (*bay'a*) forms one of the central elements by which the seekers form a spiritual and social bond with the Sheikh." (He says): "You know the most important when you take *bay'a* with any Sheikh, you have to sabr (be patience), meaning you have to follow the Sheikh actually. Not meaning that when you do already have *bay'a* then you just, you do it by yourself. No, you have to have sabr." (Interview Document No: 7 - Appendix 3).

This above-mentioned seeker discussing his own *bay'a*:

5.7 Approaches, Methods and Tools for Self-Development

"In 1990, with Sheikh Imam Issak (the Master of the current Sheikh) himself ... the most important thing is to make people change, it is not only worship, they have to do some *tauba* (repentance); a lot of repentance; a lot of praise on the Prophet; a lot of *tauba*, yes, will help. Then don't think too much about this world, the things that are stopping you from *tauba* (repentance)" (Interview Document No: 7 -Appendix 3).

Here, the first oath was taken from the Master of the Sheikh and then when the Master passed on, he continued with his current Sheikh. What transpires in this narrative is the intensity of the spiritual acts, with repeated reference to seeking forgiveness and having a sense of detachment, as Prophet himself said, "Be in this wordily life as if you are a stranger or a traveller" (An-Nawawi 1977). In response to the question, "What is *bay'a* for you?", the banker answers:

"... when you actually *bay'a* you are in front of the Sheikh, where you promise on our Qur'ān:"

$$\text{لَقَدْ رَضِيَ اللَّهُ عَنِ الْمُؤْمِنِينَ إِذْ يُبَايِعُونَكَ تَحْتَ الشَّجَرَةِ فَعَلِمَ مَا فِي قُلُوبِهِمْ فَأَنْزَلَ السَّكِينَةَ عَلَيْهِمْ وَأَثَابَهُمْ فَتْحًا قَرِيبًا}$$

"Indeed, Allah was pleased with the believers when they gave the pledge to you under the tree. He knew what was in their hearts, and He sent down al-sakinah upon them, and He rewarded them with a near victory." (Fath 48:18)

The reference to the heart is meant to be taken as a reference to their level of truthfulness, trustworthiness, obedience and adherence, while al-sakinah refers to calmness and tranquillity. The seeker says:

"I make *bay'a*, it's a promise; it's not a promise to me, actually, it is a promise to Allah. You know we have this Qur'ān ... very important to life. That is why when you recite the Qur'ān, verse Fath, you promise someone or your *bay'a* in front of somebody, actually you are under promise... If you do good you know Allah will give you good things..." (Interview Document No: 7 - Appendix 3)

This act of the oath of allegiance is sometimes misunderstood by a segment of Muslims as allegiance to the Sheikh, rather than an allegiance to God. When asked the question whether there is a difference between before *bay'a* and after *bay'a*, the banker says:

"The difference is that then only when you know who Allah is, then you will know... who you are actually. So here we cannot know you before you know Allah, you would think that you have the power, you have strength, you have this... you do that. Then when I joined, I knew who makes me earn money, where does the money come from, then you realise that is all Allah... it's not me... I cannot do anything if Allah is not helping me. It is actually Allah. You want to eat it is Allah who is moving your hand." (He is paraphrasing the Qur'ān, al-Hijr(15):25) "It's Allah, if Allah doesn't move your hands you cannot eat. So, then you know this is Allah. When you see, don't just look at the tree. If you look at the tree you will see the tree, God is a creator, and God can create a tree, be it tall or be it small. When we think Allah already knows what we are thinking. We think that we are so intelligent... Allah is moving our brains to think actually, so when you know who is Allah, you know you are down to earth." (Interview Document No: 7 - Appendix 3)

So, seen here is the shift in perception from believing in oneself, to believing that all things proceed from the Universal Force: God, the necessary Causer of all things, a fundamental belief in Islam. This seeker reinforces this stating that:

> "Actually that's why I told you just now, before *bay'a*, I still prayed but I was thinking who Allah is. I don't know who Allah is because that time I didn't have any *tauba* (process of repentance), you know lack of *tauba* and *istighfar* (repentance)..." (Interview Document No: 7 - Appendix 3).

This points to a renewed orientation of the seeker and his deepening understanding of the nature of God through his repentance and meditative practices of remembrance of God. Even though the ritual prayer in Islam is sacrosanct, the Qur'ān says that, "The remembrance (praising) of Allah is greater indeed" (Qur'ān, al-Ankabut, 29: 45), that is, putting the emphasis on *dhikr*.

In this light, Lings (2005) says that one of the meanings of this passage is "that turning towards the inner centre is 'greater' than turning towards the outer centre." The ideal, however, is to do it simultaneously and is best captured in the saying, "Our performance of the rites of worship is considered strong or weak accordingly to the degree of remembrance of God while performing them" (Sheikh al-Alawi in Lings 2005). Responding to the question as to whether the oath is binding, the above seeker says:

> "If you disobey or break your promise you will get kifara (punishment) from Allah. Yes, it is binding. So, there is a lot of difference between before *bay'a* and after *bay'a*. Before *bay'a* you don't know to whom you are praying.... I follow the fasting, I follow all the *fiqh* rules and things but yet there were no changes. The only thing that you do is pray, without knowing to whom you are praying. You don't know. So there is no khushu (concentration) on the *salah*." (Interview Document No: 7 - Appendix 3).

The reference above is to a change in orientation from not being fully aware of the purpose and focus of worship to becoming aware and mindful. A process of trying to integrate one's body and mind, while the focus on the spiritual heart. This is also to come to a state of realisation and as the Prophet said, "Consult your heart. Righteousness is that about which the soul and the heart feel tranquil..." (An-Nawawi 1977). The question was posed to the Manager of the Centre about the nature of *bay'a*, and he responded:

> "*Bay'a* means a promise. There is a verse in the Qur'ān saying that between you and that person, your follower – this is the words in the Qur'ān. It is not between you and the person but with God. So actually, a testimony is between you and God. And there is a Qur'ān verse and I showed you many." (He was requested to outline what occurs in a *bay'a*): "Something to motivate you to *bay'a* otherwise if there is nothing binding you, then you wouldn't want to be part of it. If you do, you get the blessing or you get the reward. So after *bay'a* that person must have the ambition to perform it so it almost becomes compulsory, because the first you have to say the *bay'a*." (Interview Document No: 1 - Appendix 3).

He describes what occurs immediately after *bay'a* and the focus of the *dhikr* or remembrance on the different parts of the body on what is called the subtle spiritual organs (latifa) starting with the heart:

> "So, the first one after *bay'a* you must say at least 5000 times per day, and that one is focused into your qalb (heart) and later on, after some time, to join it with the *rūḥ* (soul),

5.7 Approaches, Methods and Tools for Self-Development

sirr (inner secret), *khafi* (inner most secret), akhfa (inner most inner), *nafs*(self) and *kulli jism* (the whole body from top to bottom), then you will get your promotion to the next lataif." (Interview Document No: 7 Appendix 3 and diagram in Figure 3).

Here the seeker is outlining the process of *dhikr*, where after taking the oath of allegiance, you draw your attention to your spiritual heart (just below the physical heart), and this is followed by shifting the attention to other areas as mentioned above, located in the different parts of the chest and head. This is a whole system unique to the Naqshbandiyyah order, where the seven points in the body are used to focus one's attention, while the explicit overall focus is on God. This particular focus on the different parts of the body starting from the heart on the left side and then working one's way through the different regions of the body is not a known orthodox Islamic practice. The focus areas are the heart (qalb), the spirit (*rūḥ*), the secret (*sirr*), the inner most secret (khafi), and the inner most inner (akhfa), the ego (*nafs*) and the king of the crown (sultan al-adhkār). The terms qalb, *rūḥ*, *sirr*, *nafs*occur in the Qur'ān and are generally not associated with any particular physical locations. These physical locations have perhaps been identified by those who have done deep contemplation and been able to come out with it. The principle of remembering God in every situation remains valid. Figure 5.21 illustrates the points of these spiritual entities by means of physical locations in the body.

The above seeker reinforces this by stating that:

"*Bay'a* it is also a motivation and obligation. The motivation is because you have joined the group. And the obligation is to perform it, there are no excuses. There shouldn't be any excuses. This is the one which must prompt you to go on to do the sunnah (practice of the Prophet), where I was saying although it is sunnah, it is wājib (obligatory)... If you don't do it means you have missed something—just like our prayer, our daily five prayers, if you don't do it you have sinned. And the compulsion it is (an) obligation." (Interview Document No: 7 - Appendix 3).

Here the emphasis is cultivating the prayers and the Prophetic way (sunnah) as a habit, so that is becomes a part of you. Even though there are acts which are termed sunnah, which are not obligatory, for example the *dhikr*, when one becomes constant in these voluntary acts, to miss them causes one to feel discomfort and can be seen as a level of gradation as the seeker moves up the ladder, where one seeks to intensify his/her experiences to further ascend on the spiritual path.

The friend of the resident imam, who had previous difficulties relating to drugs and HIV, articulates his motivation and his experience:

"First of all, before I was becoming a part of the *dhikr* group, every day I see the seeker going (for *dhikr*) and my heart is itching to be with them. So after one month, I told them I want to join and did so. After *bay'a* about two or three weeks, I was really happy that I was doing *dhikr* and learning how to *dhikr*. My idea was how to be in the *dhikr* group and I get close to Allah. As time went on, I had dreams I saw that I am *dhikring* in my dreams, so whether I don't know is it Satan or is it me? Is it me or is it Satan in my dreams that I was *dhikring* with our group?" (Interview Document No: 4 - Appendix 3).

This is a juncture when the role of the Sheikh becomes important to cross-check these types of occurrences based on the framework of his experiences. This signifies a state of internalization of the remembrance of God, as it becomes reflected in dream states. As Jung (n.d.) states, dreams "reveal more than they conceal." What is explicit here is that there is an acute sense of awareness that things that transpire can either be divinely or satanically inspired, and thus the Sheikh's role of guiding the seekers become critical for one's development.

One of the two females in the group relates her experience of the oath:

> "So I follow Tuan Guru... when I started I took the *bay'a*, I had to pray. I prayed *salah tauba* (prayer of repentance) and then asked Allah for guidance with the past. It was a great; you know everybody will be so scared after taking *bay'a* thinking that it is something really wrong. But after taking *bay'a*, I find that more truth is being revealed. The closeness, how we wish to perfection of 'aqīda (creed)." (Interview Document No: 6 - Appendix 3).

The reference here is to the dispelling of her fears and having a renewed experience after she had taken oath and gone through a process of repentance. There seems to be a greater propensity towards God, signifying her statement of more truth being revealed. The reference to the perfection of the 'aqīda is the belief in oneness and gaining close proximity to God.

5.7.2 Tarbiyah (Education)

One of the key themes to emerge was the educational aspects of the faith (*tarbiyah*), including keeping the company of the Sheikh (*sohba*), Qur'ānic recital and lectures (*kulliyyah*). Each of these will now be elaborated.

The Company of the Sheikh (*sohba*): Being present with the Sheikh is one of the most vital elements that enables one comes to grips with oneself and receive the required guidance into the pathway for the development of the self. One of the participants says:

> "Like the sahabas (Prophet's companions) we refer to Abu-Bakr, Omar, Osman and Ali. We have to follow this type of model.... when it is work time you do work, when free time you have to do *du'ā* for your Sheikh. Like me, every weekend I am helping my Sheikh by helping him here, to cook. Actually, I cook for them." (Interview Document No: 7 - Appendix 3).

This aspect of service to others is a key part of the way of the *tarīqa* or the path, where you go beyond your own selfish needs and cater for others. This is one way to debase one's ego and acquire a more selfless character. A counter point is presented, where, if one's intention in serving others is to reinforce the ego, this has a reverse effect. Thus, one is guided that you should act for the sake of God, so as to override your ego state.

Imam Qushayri (2002) says "someone who keeps the company of the Sheikh whose degree is above his own is to give up opposing him, to treat everything that appears from him as beautiful, and to accept his states with faith in him." The motivation to join the organisation and be with the Sheikh is thus flagged as the seeker points out:

> "From (doing) the *dhikr* and also from (understanding) the Qur'ānic verses, you see the mercy of Allah. Yes the (God's attributes) jamālullah (the beautiful), the sifhana sifha

5.7 Approaches, Methods and Tools for Self-Development

jamālullah (the healing and beautiful). The group of attributes of Jalāli (Majestic termed as uluhiya) and Jamāli (Beautiful also termed rubbubiya), such as, Rahmān al Raheem (the most Gracious and Merciful), which is the opposite of the al jalal attribute (the Majestic and Powerful) such as al-Mutakabbir (the Supreme), al-Qahhār (the Ever-Dominating) when we remember...the power (sic) of Allah..." (Interview Document No: 7 - Appendix 3).

The attributes of Jāmal (Beauty) and Jalāl (Majestic), which were referred to earlier by the Sheikh, shows the qualities he should strive to emulate in his own character for emulating and building one's own characteristics. The Sheikh provides the most suitable names to the seekers based on their situation and personality. This emulation of names, especially those attributes of God that are Beautiful such as being compassionate, merciful, forgiving, appreciative etc., is reflected in the Prophetic model, a pathway for 'ennobling one's character', as the Qur'ān states: "And indeed, you are upon a noble conduct, an exemplary manner" (Qur'ān, Nūn 68:4), while there is a reference from the wife of the Prophet "The morals of the Prophet were based on the Qur'ān" (Al-Islam.org n.d.).

The outcome of receiving guidance from the Sheikh and being with him is to try and develop a more holistic way of life as outlined here by the Sheikh himself:

"Yes love, care and fear of Allah and being full of hope of His mercy and to gain a sense of equilibrium, which is the aim. It is not the middle path, which is something else. That's what normally people interpret but the middle path means a state of equilibrium." (Document 5, Appendix 3)

The flux of life the Sheikh mentions highlights the guidance provided by him. He "guides you to the true path ...you walk on the road, walking on tight rope, so you balance, if it isn't balanced you fall off." (Interview Document No: 7—Appendix 3). With 50% of the respondents being drug addicts, HIV patients and a few transgender, the close guidance of the Sheikh is critical, as underscored here by the Sheikh himself:

"That prevents you from going to despair or hopelessness. Both of these are the things used to motivate the *murīds* (seekers); all the attributes, it is the balancing of both the Jamāl and Jalāl. If you can achieve this, then you are okay, you're going in the right path." (Interview Document No: 7 - Appendix 3).

Discussing the methods used by the Sheikh:

"So the *murīds* (seekers) listen to his lecturers and otherwise you don't get anything, you('ve) also got to go for his classes and learn about the actual practice of the *dhikr* and the *ṭarīqa* or the path." (Interview Document No: 7 - Appendix 3).

The Sheikh motivates his seekers through various methods, including lectures and by pointing out that none but people who deny the truth can ever lose hope of God's life-giving mercy, *dhikr* and ritual practices. The Centre Supervisor's says that:

"Ṣohba (companionship) with the Tuan Guru (Sheikh). Everything you get is through companionship. He will teach you how to sort that problem." (Interview Document No: 8 - Appendix 3).

There are some key aspects to discern. First, the Sheikh's reference to 'walking a tight rope' is the reference to the human condition, where one has multiple temptations bombarding them from all sides and thus maintaining one's faith and composure becomes difficult and one must tread carefully. Secondly, the Sheikh's guidance then serves as a pathway to be emulated and be on the track. This helps one to discard one's own pre-conceptions and work towards finding God.

In response to the question regarding what one has learnt from the Sheikh that one can use in one's life, one of the seekers, who has been with the Sheikh for several years, states that:

"One of the things that I have learnt is the practice of *dhikr* (remembrance of God)…(and) "One of the things is the spirit of ṣohba (Sheikh's company), which means that there is a great attachment to him and with that I get attached to my family, friends and folks, especially with those who are within the group of *dhikr* group, there is a bonding." (Interview Document No: 2 - Appendix 3)

The Centre nurse, who is also a seeker, says about modelling the Sheikh:

"What you feel is that he is very patient. We learn…to be like him. You try to copy as much as possible…If you feel a sense of loss then I keep remembering why not, this is how our guru does things and then we absorb that behaviour so you solve the problem." (Interview Document No: 6 - Appendix 3).

The trait of patience is one of the keys to self-development, given its repeated reference both in the interview data set, as well as the survey data as seen in the Figs. 5.9, 5.10, 5.13, and 5.14. Here one observes once again the process of emulating and modelling through, which one learns as outlined in the social learning theory of Bandura (2011), which will be fleshed out in detail in the Chap. 6 discussion.

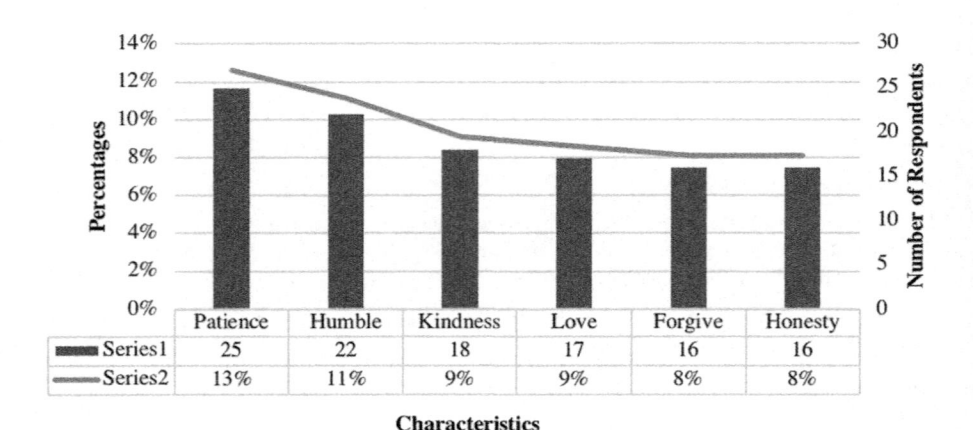

Characteristics	Patience	Humble	Kindness	Love	Forgive	Honesty
Series1	25	22	18	17	16	16
Series2	13%	11%	9%	9%	8%	8%

Fig. 5.13 Most important characteristics for self-development

5.7 Approaches, Methods and Tools for Self-Development

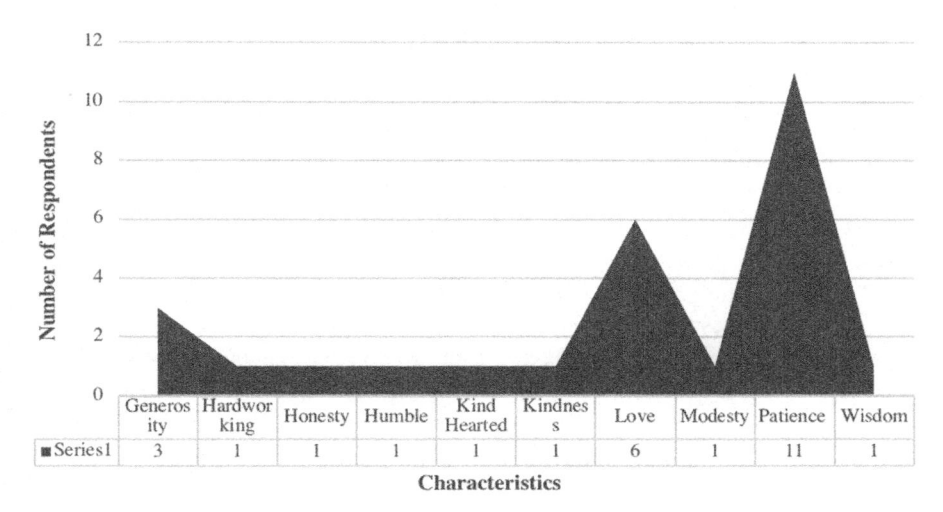

Fig. 5.14 1st ranked virtuous traits

■Series1	Generosity	Hardworking	Honesty	Humble	Kind Hearted	Kindness	Love	Modesty	Patience	Wisdom
	3	1	1	1	1	1	6	1	11	1

The Centre Manager discusses the role of the Sheikh as an educator and in undertaking his spiritual dispensation, as well as how he interacts with the seekers in the various geographical areas:

> "The sheikh appoints the *halaka* (branch) chief. *Halaka* is the group so in each centre we have a chief. He (Sheikh) goes around every month the first week in the month he goes to different sub-centres within Malaysia. They also have some seekers in Brunei and Singapore." (Interview Document No: 1 - Appendix 3).

This denotes a decentralised form of management, with the sub-centre Chief's being empowered, which one assumes makes the functioning of the system more efficient.

Qur'ānic Recital: Turning towards the Qur'ān and its recitation, whether one understands it or not forms a central aspect of Islamic life. It is a reflection of God's guidance and His message, which is a part and parcel of life in this Order. One of the senior seekers says:

> "Yes, actually Allah is not teaching rasulullah (the Prophet) to read, Allah is teaching rasulullah to *dhikr* (remembrance of God) and this translation is real. That time there is no books or something that rasulullah cannot read. This is something that Allah is asking us to do. The meaning here is that you have to *tauba* (repent) and think of Allah. Many people will *tauba* (repent) but they might be somewhere else (in their mind). Believe me, that is why we have a clinic (uzal) for 10 days." (Interview Document No: 2 - Appendix 3).

The seeker implies that what he was essentially transmitted was *dhikr*, that is, remembrance of God or cultivating God consciousness. Secondly, the reference to people being 'somewhere else' denotes a wandering mind and thus pertains to the need to attend the *uzla* or a spiritual retreat, where one can train oneself to be focused in developing one's attention. This represents a process of deepening one's state of meditation through training one's ability to maintain attention.

One of the residents alludes to his schedule of waking up and devotion:

"I wake up for *tahajjud* (night vigil) and do *tauba* (repentance). First, *tauba nasiha* (repentance and good counsel)...yes what sin has come (to me), ...what sin has gone, so Allah please open my heart to follow and soften my tongue to read our Qur'ān because I will still try to learn how to read the Qur'ān, because I don't know how to read the Qur'ān yet." (Appendix 3 Document no: 4).

Repentance or *tauba*, which is seen throughout the data, is seen here as an in-road to getting close to God, with a plea to 'soften my tongue', to be better able to absorb and learn. Psychologically repentance enables one to purge one's toxic thoughts and patterns that one has built up over time and which has caused harm within oneself. You can call it the shedding of toxicity from the ego. This enables the mind to get over the guilt and pain that one is experiencing. This is what essentially Ekhart Tolle (2005) calls the 'pain body' that we carry around with us, which ties us up, with recurring sadness and guilt and a sense of victimhood. Repentance tends to open one's pathway to move towards a more positive state of mind which is conducive to cultivating contentment and bringing about a sense of healing.

This combined with Qur'ānic recital, which is rhythmic chanting and a form of a discursive meditation, where the mind becomes focused on the sound and the meaning of the words, conjuring either a series of images or a state of absorption without a series of images, depending on the person and their state of meditative focus.

In terms of expectations of joining the organisation, the resident Imam says:

"For me, let's say I want Allah to forgive myself for whatever I have done before. The rubbish things relating to my morality (*akhlāq*), where somebody looks at me like I am rubbish. Nobody can say what is wrong with you. But then you still must follow up and then, if you do it truly and... keep at it, then it is like you leave the wrong (behind). If you (become) straight, day-by-day in your heart... Now trusting in Allah is one hundred per cent (but) before you just say that Allah gives your life (but) I don't know how to *salah* (ritual prayer), I don't do fasting, I don't do *salawat* (praise the Prophet). So I ask myself, why are you like that (sic), you know the punishment is very very hard... I learned that I know that I am very scared (now)." (Interview Document No: 2 - Appendix 3).

The above statement details a process in *tasawwuf* known as '*muhasaba*' or self-accounting, which is an essential part of reconciling with oneself and God and coming to terms with one's spiritual position (see Sect. 2.2). Regarding trust, the resident Imam highlights that:

"...my heart is very trusting, so who is Allah and, whatever you think, He is not like that. It is the same, like if I give you honey and you eat that honey, while I saw you eat the honey and then I ask you how was this honey. You say it is very sweet and I say you are also very sweet but how is your sweet?. For me, I say that I don't know what is the difference." (Interview Document No: 2 - Appendix 3).

Here he is discussing the incomprehensibility of God, for as the Qur'ān says, "There is nothing like Him, and He is the all-Hearer, the all-Seer" (Qur'ān, al-Shura 42:11). The concept that *tasawwuf* or the experiential learning of the knowledge of God in effect constitutes only a sense of 'taste' (dhawk) that nobody else but you knows. The reference here is to 'the taste of honey', which is sweet but the actual taste of it differs from one person to another. Lings (2005) highlights that the concept

5.7 Approaches, Methods and Tools for Self-Development

of 'taste' in *tasawwuf* forms one of the central concepts given that knowing God is a personal experience, which varies from one person to another. In responding to the question, "Whereabouts is the trust?", the resident Imam says:

> "That's in your heart. Trust is not being scared and hope Allah will keep you. You know Allah sees you everywhere, whatever you do, whatever is inside your heart Allah. Right or wrong...What Allah gives you and more? What you know about the world the secrets of *dhikr* in the Qur'ān." (...so was there trust before or now?): "Unlike before. Now if something is wrong, my brain is fighting inside with that which is wrong. But I just learned from al-Qur'ān that it said...don't shop lift or take something." (Interview Document No: 2 - Appendix 3).

This ties in with the method of *dhikr* that his Order does, namely, *wuquf qalbi* (Omar and Zarrina 2011), which is a state of witnessing or that God is watchful of you and He is the Knower of the heart, where trust resides. This state of the heart is what is referred to as '*nafs al-lawwama*', where the critical self becomes aware of its wrongs (see Sect. 2.1). The transformation of the resident Imam and why this happened is articulated as thus:

> "It has changed because I hope when Allah...loved me very much whatever I do...He said in the Qur'ān 'if you truly do whatever I say and hope for me to forgive you, you will do it properly and then you will get it.' Now seriously, I follow You, I just get it in my heart. I do not know how to discuss about the heart, you must do what you can to get it, if you do not, then you will not get it." (Interview Document No: 2 - Appendix 3).

Linguistically, apart from Islam deriving from the word peace, its essence also comes from the root word, submission to God. This is exemplified where the seeker says that if you obey what God has commanded, then He will be with you, and this is through the heart. Aside from the literal meaning ascribed to Islam, another interpretation is that by surrendering to God, or to frame it another way, by recognising your own ego identity and overcoming the egoic tendencies, see reality as it truly is and thus, the heart is in a state to become connected to God.

Kulliyyah (Lectures): The lecture sessions conducted by the Sheikh are held periodically in different mosques as well as when the group and the Sheikh gather for *dhikr*. The perceptions of the seekers are outlined below. The resident Imam says:

> "Apart from that we learn that the *ta'lim* (educational method) part, we learn a lot of things from him (Sheikh), especially those pertaining to the *tasawwuf* or Sufism" (Interview Document No: 2 - Appendix 3).

These are the main lecture type sessions rendered by the Sheikh, which provide key guidance pertaining to *tasawwuf*, although this is communicated both verbally and non-verbally. These are either noted down or becomes a part of the memory of the seekers, which is factored in as a part of their learning (Interview Document No: 17—Appendix 3). The female seeker reveals her point of contact with the Sheikh:

> "So every time he (Tuan Guru-Sheikh) came to teach, I was one of the few out of the whole village who made use of it." (She says): "Yes Tuan Guru was looking for me and was asking some students, what happened to me and why I haven't come for so long. At that time, I was looking after my mother who had a stroke, it was the end stage of her life, so she was very dependent. So when they came, I was actually caring for my mother and so they were

surprised. But during that period, I was actually praying to Allah and asking Allah. I did that *tawāṣul*...(an approach to draw close to God)" (She went through a process of questioning herself): "Where is the truth, what am I doing down here and how I missed the lectures. I miss going to the *tawajjuh* (spiritual attention of the Sheikh) but how am I going for it, I feel that basically helpless. So when you *tafakkur* (reflection) and of course the *dhikr* I do it every day..." (Interview Document No: 6 - Appendix 3).

Here she is describing how despite her circumstances that didn't allow her to be a part of the lessons, she was able to undertake the practices that she had learnt from the Sheikh to connect herself to the path. There is a notion within *tasawwuf* that when the student is ready the Sheikh comes along and fulfils this role, and it was from this that she eventually became fully involved with the Order. There are three concepts that she refers to: namely, *tawāṣul*, which is requesting God to fulfil a wish; *tawajjuh* or getting spiritual attention from the Sheikh; and *tafakkur*, a state of reflecting on one's own spiritual states. She reiterated the impact of the lectures:

"Yes *'ibādah* (worship) also has an impact on your *akhlāq* (morality) and the Tuan Guru also impacts on your *akhlāq* because when you also keep getting close to (him), since almost every day as long as there's a lecture and rules. In the mosque, we always follow the programme, so there, in the lessons that he imparts to us, there is also knowledge there for people who remember *akhlāq*... *'ibādah* even when you are treating other people or looking after the sick, it's all *'ibādah* isn't it? So whatever you do, the servitude to the Lord, then it is the *'ibādah*." (Interview Document No: 6 - Appendix 3).

Here one can discern that there is a systematic approach by the Sheikh in terms of having a program and dispensing it to the *murīds* or seekers. She is pointing out that the acts of worship, as well as the Sheikh's guidance, have an impact on morality (*akhlāq*). She is evoking the holistic concept within Islam where the services that you do in order to help others form an act of worship.

5.7.3 Tazkiyah (Purification)

This section on '*tazkiyah*' examines one of the keys to self-development as flagged by the seekers. It deals with some critical approaches and methods that are needed for this purpose including the development of virtuous traits, *uzla* (retreat), repentance (*tauba*), ritual and optional prayers (*salah*), remembrance (*dhikr*), night vigil (*tahajjud*), supplication (du'ā) and serving others (*ukhuwwah* or solidarity).

Morality (*Akhlāq*) and the Heart: Here we begin with some insight into what is good and evil and then move on to discuss core values and vices. The Sheikh points out that:

"Values (human) and their manifestation depends on the stages of the heart of the worshipper. They are influenced by emotions and attributes. Some of the key values are: repentance, thankfulness, patience, asceticism, love, contentment... The heart of a *muḥsin* has humility and is awake." (Interview Document No: 5 - Appendix 3)

The Sheikh is here distinguishing between a Muslim (one who has professed the faith) and a muḥsin (a doer of good), with the latter's devotion being with

5.7 Approaches, Methods and Tools for Self-Development

full orientation towards God. The Sheikh links worship and morality by citing the Qur'ān:

$$\text{فَأَصْحَابُ الْمَيْمَنَةِ مَا أَصْحَابُ الْمَيْمَنَةِ}$$
$$\text{وَأَصْحَابُ الْمَشْأَمَةِ مَا أَصْحَابُ الْمَشْأَمَةِ}$$
$$\text{وَالسَّابِقُونَ السَّابِقُونَ}$$
$$\text{أُولَئِكَ الْمُقَرَّبُونَ}$$

"So those on the right – how (fortunate) will be those on the right, and those on the left – how (unfortunate) will those be on the left! And those foremost will be foremost, these will be nearer (to Allah)." (al-Waqi'ah 56: 8–11)

The Sheikh says that the companions of the right hand are those who are drawn near (to Allah), they have three spiritual characteristics: *iman* (having faith), *'amal* (doing good deeds) and *dhikr* (remembrance of Allah). Al Suddi (Ibn Kathir 2003d), a companion of the Prophet, explains there are three groups of people: those of the right, those of the left (that is those who have gone astray) and the third, that is, the residents of the fire, while Muhammad Asad's (2011) reference to the latter group is those on the left or those 'losing oneself in evil'. The group at the forefront are those who will be with the Prophet in the next life. The Sheikh next cites another verse from the Qur'ān:

$$\text{وَيَقُولُ الَّذِينَ كَفَرُوا لَوْلَا أُنزِلَ عَلَيْهِ آيَةٌ مِّن رَّبِّهِ قُلْ إِنَّ اللَّهَ يُضِلُّ مَن يَشَاءُ وَيَهْدِي إِلَيْهِ مَنْ أَنَابَ}$$
$$\text{الَّذِينَ آمَنُوا وَتَطْمَئِنُّ قُلُوبُهُم بِذِكْرِ اللَّهِ أَلَا بِذِكْرِ اللَّهِ تَطْمَئِنُّ الْقُلُوبُ}$$

"And those who disbelieve say: Why is not a sign sent down upon him by his Lord? Say: Surely Allah makes him who will go astray, and guides to Himself those who turn (to Him). Those who believed and whose hearts are set at rest by the remembrance of Allah; in the remembrance of do hearts finds rest." (al-Ra'ad 13:27–28)

Ibn Kathir comments:

"He guides to Him those who repent, turn to Him, beg Him, seek His help and humbly submit to Him... for their hearts find comfort on the side of Allah, become tranquil when He is remembered and pleased to have Him as Protector and Supporter." Ibn Kathir (2003b).

There are many aspects covered by these verses referred to by the Sheikh, which point out that by aligning with the divine writ and in doing that which has been ordained one strengthens one's acts of worship and focus on the remembrance of God. All of this puts the seeker on track, while changing their behaviour for the

[Chart]

	1st Ranked Anger	Anxiety	Arrogance	Fraud	Forgetfullness	Greedy	Hedlessness & Laziness	Love of the World	Materialistic	Pride	Superiority	N/A
Series1	8	1	2	1	2	1	5	2	1	1	2	6

Types of Vices

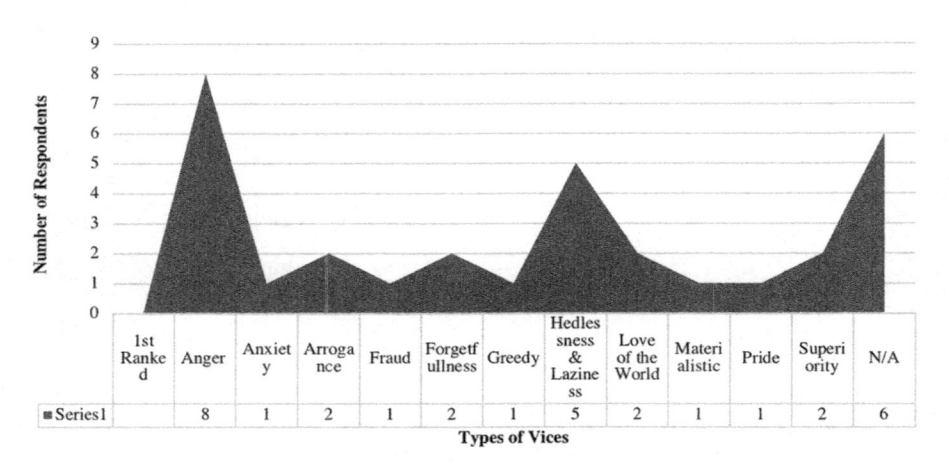

Fig. 5.15 1st ranked vices affecting self-development

better. Thus, there are two aspects as outlined above: one is that of one's own realisation (discussed in Chap. 6) and the other the hope that change will come. This verse is very pertinent for the residents of the Centre where they see impending death with their HIV conditions, while God highlights hope and life-giving qualities.

Core Value System: Virtues and Vices This section deals with the various features that relate to the development of the self, including facets connected with virtuous traits, as well as vices and an essential teaching of the Sheikh. The five most important traits scored by the respondents that were viewed as important for self-development were: patience (13%); humbleness (11%); kindness (9%), love (9%), with forgiveness and honesty both being 8% (see Fig. 5.13). In Fig. 5.14, these virtuous traits were further ranked by the respondents, with highest ranked being patience and love, followed by generosity. The rest followed with the same score including wisdom, modesty, kindness, hard work, humbleness and honesty.

The vices identified by the seekers were further prioritised in order to get the first ranked (Fig. 5.15) and this resulted in anger being the most highly ranked, followed by heedlessness. This was followed by similar scores for superiority, love of the world, forgetfulness and arrogance. There were a comparatively high percentage of respondents who did not give a response to this task.

It is interesting to compare the type and level of vices before and after joining the group as shown in Figs. 5.16 and 5.17 respectively. Before joining the group, there is a high range of vices with decreasing levels including: anger, forgetfulness, heedlessness, anxiety, and laziness. There were other responses, which had much lower scores including the inability to accept one's mistake, sinning, jealousy, lying, sulking, and a lack of confidence in being able to do things. Anger being specified by the seekers as one of the worst vices corroborates with the scholarly views of Imam Ghazāli, where he has flagged anger-hatred as core ruinous traits that give rise to other ruinous traits of envy, ridicule, contempt, back-biting etc. (see Sect. 2.2 and Fig. 2.4).

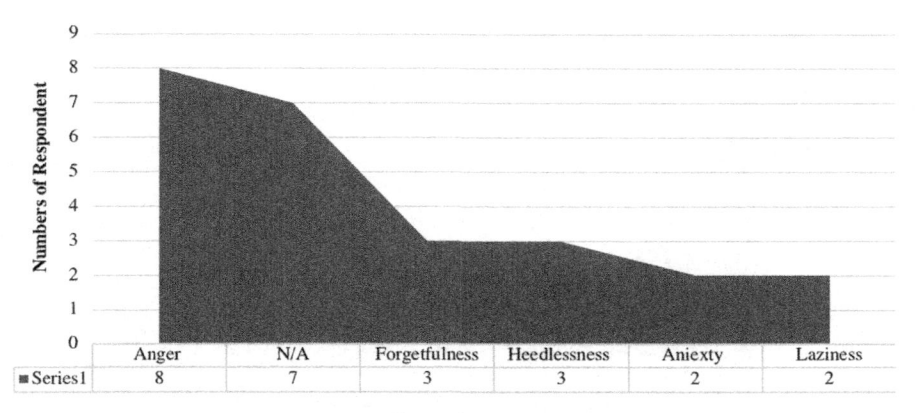

5.7 Approaches, Methods and Tools for Self-Development

Fig. 5.16 1st ranked vices before joining the group

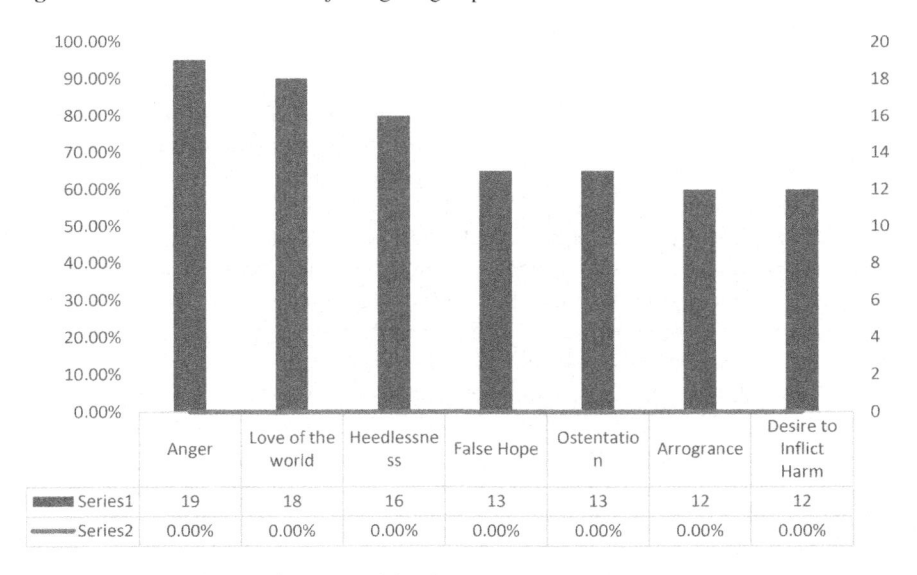

	Anger	N/A	Forgetfulness	Heedlessness	Aniexty	Laziness
Series1	8	7	3	3	2	2

Types of Vices

Fig. 5.17 1st ranked vices affecting self-development

	Anger	Love of the world	Heedlessness	False Hope	Ostentation	Arrogance	Desire to Inflict Harm
Series1	19	18	16	13	13	12	12
Series2	0.00%	0.00%	0.00%	0.00%	0.00%	0.00%	0.00%

There was an observation made of the traits before and after joining the Order. It is found that many other traits remained the same before and after joining the organisation, while some key changes were noted and are highlighted in the proceeding section. In Figs. 5.16 and 5.18, it is to be noted that there was a high level of non-responses. There was also another instance (Fig. 5.15) where there was a high rate of non-responses and both these were associated with ranking traits. In Fig. 5.18, there is an inappropriate indication of calmness as one of the vices, which is followed forgetfulness, heedlessness, laziness. These three traits seem to be recurrent in the data set. Perhaps the reference to calmness as one of the vices

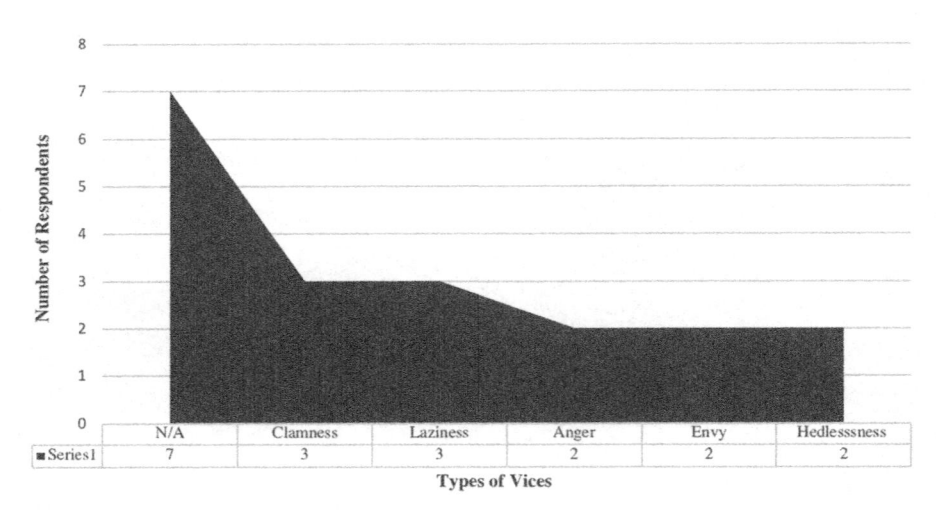

	N/A	Clamness	Laziness	Anger	Envy	Hedlesssness
Series1	7	3	3	2	2	2

Fig. 5.18 Vices after joining the group

could be due to its conflation with laziness and inactivity. The rest of the vices had a much lower score including arrogance, forgetfulness, being materialistic, love for this world, malice, and superiority. There seems to be an indicative reduction in the scores especially relating to anger (from 8 to 2), heedlessness (from 3 to 2) and laziness where the score was slightly higher after joining the organisation.

Figures 5.16 and 5.18 show anger is seen as the most destructive vice, which affects self-development. This is followed by heedlessness plus laziness followed by arrogance, love of the world, forgetfulness and superiority. There was a sizeable percentage that stated non-applicable as either they (Fig. 5.16) did not understand what was to be done or else did not want to respond to it (Figs. 5.15 and 5.18). In Fig. 5.19 changes within yourself after joining the group was explicit (18 per cent), followed by the way the seekers treat themselves and others (16 per cent). This is followed by the way the seekers treat their family, friends and the less privileged as compared to before, What is also underlined is the way the seekers worship and conduct themselves more positively.

When asked about the essential teachings of the Sheikh on anger management (Fig. 5.20), the following were scored: being silent and saying prayer being the highest (66% and 56% respectively), getting advice from others and supplicating to God (26% each) and being patient scoring 16%. The rest of the strategies on anger management had lower scores including: being realistic, Islamic reflexology, *salawāt* (prayers upon the Prophet), *dhikr* and retaliation.

Ulza—The Spiritual Retreat The Sheikh articulates that seclusion (*uzla* or *khalwa*) is outlined as an activity that is essential for gaining the knowledge of God and experiencing the beloved meaning God, which is an essential part of the Prophetic tradition (Sidek 2014). He outlines the twenty conditions that guide the retreat:

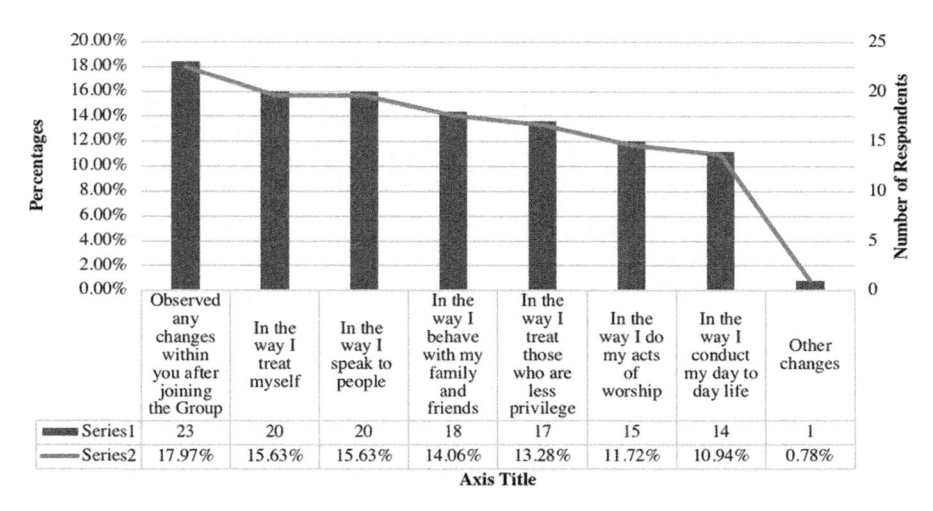

5.7 Approaches, Methods and Tools for Self-Development

Fig. 5.19 Changes within yourself after joining the group

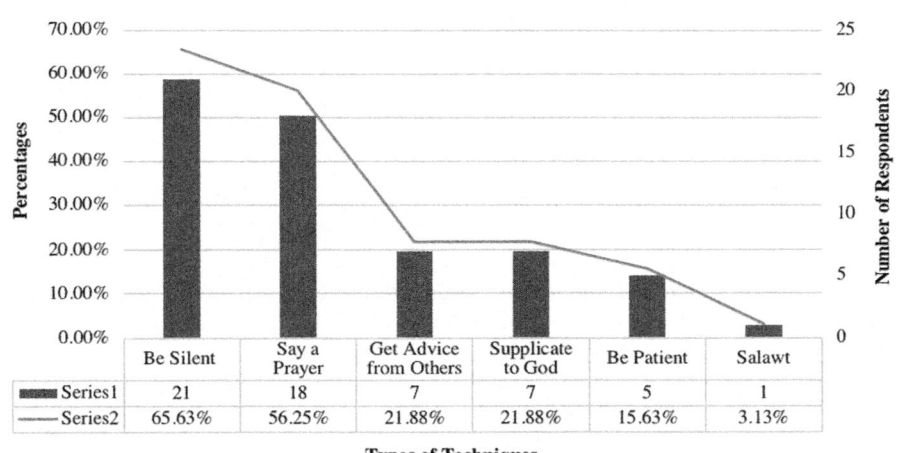

	Observed any changes within you after joining the Group	In the way I treat myself	In the way I speak to people	In the way I behave with my family and friends	In the way I treat those who are less privilege	In the way I do my acts of worship	In the way I conduct my day to day life	Other changes
Series1	23	20	20	18	17	15	14	1
Series2	17.97%	15.63%	15.63%	14.06%	13.28%	11.72%	10.94%	0.78%

Fig. 5.20 Essential teachings on anger management

	Be Silent	Say a Prayer	Get Advice from Others	Supplicate to God	Be Patient	Salawt
Series1	21	18	7	7	5	1
Series2	65.63%	56.25%	21.88%	21.88%	15.63%	3.13%

1. having the sincere intention to cleanse oneself;
2. requesting the Sheikh to pray for the disciple, and also taking the oath of allegiance (*bay'a*);
3. practicing solitude, staying awake and experiencing hunger;
4. stepping into the *khalwa* with the right foot, while seeking help from Allah to keep away Satan and reading the 114th chapter of the Qur'ān (al-Nās);
5. always be in a state of ritual purity (*wuḍū'*);
6. not to focus on the desire to achieve sanctity;
7. the disciple should not lean against the wall or the like;

8. the disciple should always imagine his teacher;
9. the disciple should fast;
10. he should be silent except for the remembrance of God or when it is necessary to speak out;
11. beware of the four enemies: Satan, the world, lust and the self;
12. should be far away from loud noise;
13. be mindful of the Friday prayers and congregational prayers, which is the sunnah of the Prophet;
14. cover the head and up to the knees, and look down only;
15. should not sleep unless very sleepy and must be in a state of cleanliness;
16. must maintain a state of awareness and with a balanced state so as not to overeat;
17. in the midst of the *khalwa* (retreat), should not open the door to others except for the Sheikh;
18. if there are any openings (spiritual), should feel that this came through the Sheikh and Prophet from Allah;
19. should reject any thinking, whether good or bad since this would disrupt the heart, which is focusing on Allah;
20. always maintain remembrance as guided by the Sheikh until he is asked to stop or leaves the *khalwat*.

The Manager states that:

"Beneficial is the Qur'ān, it is very peaceful. When you had *tahajjud* (night vigil)..." (what is it about reading the Qur'ān which makes it like that?) "To me it is peaceful; when I do not understand (the meaning) I ask the imam and he explains to me what this is." (Interview Document No: 1 - Appendix 3).

There are different things that cause people to feel at peace and in this case, it is found that the recitation of the Qur'ān seems to elicit this peaceful state of mind. In the context of the current mindfulness culture, this is termed 'passage meditation' (Shapiro et al. 2008), where one concentrates on scriptural messages. During the retreat, the *dhikr* and the recitation of the Qur'ān become intensified in order to facilitate greater immersion into the depths of one's mind. The professional banker discusses *uzla* (seclusion):

"They went for ten days already. Sometime, most of the time in Ramadan...lot of rules, less talk, you cannot simply talk and then you just don't sit like this and start talking. Your duty is *dhikr* only... Yes five times, we pray five times. We do *jammah* (congregational) you cannot do *salah* (ritual prayer) alone. The rule is doing things together." (he expounds): "And then there are rules you know, we sleep in a mosquito net. It's like a grave and when you sleep in there, it feels like the last time...food, only rice and vegetables. This is for the ten days. After ten days you go and eat meat, it's okay. We cannot give in...we are afraid. We cannot give in for we have *shahawath* (desire)." (Interview Document No: 7 - Appendix 3).

Here the respondent is referring to the environment of their spiritual retreat and the rules governing it, where the main focus is on ritual prayers and *dhikr* (remembrance of God). The key aspect is that it provides a setting conducive to

5.7 Approaches, Methods and Tools for Self-Development

detachment, away from their normal life, with the restriction of food and desires, which prevents lethargy from setting in from consuming too much food. All of these are done to enable the mind to free itself from daily machinations and become freer and more focused. The question here is to establish if this *ṭarīqa* is following the Sharī'a (that is, referring to their five daily prayers, the congregational prayers, which they usually do) or is it going beyond the prescribed to those acts that are deemed optional, that is doing *dhikr* and many sunnah (optional) prayers, as well as maintaining a state of physical purity or *wuḍū'* (ablution). The intention of the retreat is to restrict the connection with the outside world as much as possible, and sustain a minimalistic living in all senses including diet, sleep, sensations etc. The above seeker says in terms of sleep:

> "It's up to you. When you get tired, you take a rest then you start when you wake up. When you get up in the morning it is 4:30am, you have to wake up and start to *dhikr* while waiting for morning prayers. And then you know you cannot sleep after iftār (breaking the fast). That is the rule actually. Every day in your lifetime... You have to be in *wuḍū'* (ablution) 24 hours. What you do in *uzla* (seclusion), you have to bring it to your life (everyday)." (Interview Document No: 7 - Appendix 3).

In the above narration, he is pointing to the intense regime that they follow by waking up early in the morning then involving themselves in *dhikr* (remembrance of God). The importance of the transfer of one's learning from the retreat to the normal life outside, which forms the essence of cultivating it as a way of life, is clearly stated. The above seeker outlines the extent of *dhikr* within the *uzla*:

> "As many times as possible... So, you report to the Sheikh, you increase your *dhikr* to your whole being and also for the *latifa qalbi* (heart) and *latifa rūḥi* (soul). You have two places where you *dhikr*, outside in *uzla* it is double, being for the whole being ten thousand times. Your (remembrance of God aimed at) *latifa qalbi* is 10,000 and *latifa rūḥi* is two thousand. And then a few after that in the night you have got to report. He (Sheikh) could say increase some more until eleven thousand. Eleven thousand but in *uzla* it can be 22 thousand. It's not that you *dhikr* too much. No, it takes about half an hour to forty-five minutes, but when you *dhikr*, always think of Allah always – 'laisa ka mithlihi shay' (there is none comparable to Him), not when you *dhikr* your mind is somewhere... it should be towards Allah. But when you want to *dhikr*, it is very difficult too." (Interview Document No: 7 - Appendix 3).

Here the respondent is discussing performing intensive *dhikr* on the specific locations of the seven *lataifs* or subtle organs within the body. This is combined with the awareness that God is All Witnessing (*wuquf qalbi*)and that there is none comparable to God. This focus and intensity of remembrance of God (*dhikr*) enables the seeker to plunge into a deeper state of meditation, thereby connecting with oneself and gaining a sense of close proximity to God.

The Head of Reflexology was queried about his experience and in reference to a spiritual breakthrough was asked, "When did you say that the... breakthrough came? and did it come through because you were doing the *dhikr*?" He replied:

> "With the mercy of Allah, no Muslim or human being is going for *uzla* (retreat) to undergo that type of experience... you have to leave yourself to the (guidance) Sheikh. Whatever the Sheikh wants to do to you, just let yourself. Then when you go for the classes, whatever the Sheikh says *Inshā'Allah* is the knowledge from our Qur'ān. For example, whatever

happened to Abu-Bakr, when Prophet Mohammed received his revelation, where he said that I have now finished my work, where I already completed.. Islam. What Abu-Bakr heard and saw he understood that the Prophet will not be with us for long ... something like that." (Interview Document No: 3 - Appendix 3).

The articulation of the breakthrough here is through the continuous remembrance of God and the guidance of the Sheikh to reach a spiritual state, that some are able to achieve and others not. These are spiritual states called 'ḥāl' (temporary states) and spiritual stations termed as '*maqām*' (a more permanent state), where one experiences closeness to God. The kind of knowledge that he is pointing out goes beyond mundane knowledge to one that is called *ḥaqīqa* or reality. This will be elucidated further in the discussion chapter. The manager of the Reflexology Unit describes the spiritual retreat (*uzla*) and the *dhikr* (remembrance of God):

"We the group... are under one leader, only one Sheikh ... we *salah* (prayer) time, (then) we go out and we (get) *majlis thawajju* (group spiritual attention) and when we finish, we go to our room, everybody has a room. We have only *dhikr* for night and day, day and night. When you go for *dhikr* there are three parts. First *intiba*, you are starting *dhikr*. The second part *iqbar*. The third part *alhizol*. So, you pass through these three ..." (He was asked what is *intiba*?): "*intiba* is like you just woke up from the bed. Just wake up... *ikbar* is that you are getting more, everything you remember is only Allah... and then *alhizol* is where you will be born second time. Using your soul. Your soul can input what every knowledge that Allah gives." (Interview Document No: 3 - Appendix 3).

Here he is describing the different states of consciousness that the seekers go through, where they wake up to the reality or *intiba*, and then move on to another state where they see God in all the states of their remembrance (*ikbar*), which results in a state of being born again (*alhizol*). He alludes to different forms of consciousness, which seem to somewhat mirror the states of the development of the souls referenced in Sect. 2.1, that is, the *nafs ul ammara* (beastly state); *nafs ul lawwama* (the critical self); and the *nafs ul muttummainna* (the peaceful self). This will be taken up in more detail in Chap. 6.

The professional banker says that:

"So, (for) you to make your heart, your whole being, always do *tauba*. We have a place we called *uzla* – spiritual retreat. We have *uzla* for ten days every year. Sometimes twice a year. Ten days, somewhere in June and then sometime in November... that is what we call a clinic of treatment of the heart. Because actually a lot of people are praying five times, fasting but still yet the behaviour of the people is not changing at all. Some day they do wrong things. People say don't smoke, but (are) still smoking. Because last time I was smoking. I stopped maybe for 5 years or 7 years. In *uzla*, you do *dhikr* for 24 hours, you can rest one, two or three hours. During that time there is no food that contains meat, eggs. No that time, you have to eat right because *Rasulullah uzla* in Hira (the Prophet's meditative retreat in the cave close to Makkah) ..." (Interview Document No: 7 - Appendix 3).

He is referring to some key aspects of *uzla* (retreat), that is, the discipline, speaking only when necessary, maintaining silence with focus on *dhikr*, all of which are prerequisites for making the retreat effective. The concept of *uzla* or retreat derives from the life of the Prophet, where he meditated for 13 years by isolating himself on top of a mountain in a cave called Hira in close proximity to Makkah. Subsequently, this was replaced by what is called '*i'tikāf*', which is retreating to the

5.7 Approaches, Methods and Tools for Self-Development

mosque for a set period of days. The reference to the spiritual clinic, which offers one the possibility to cleanse one's heart as a basis for changing behaviour, does not happen in the normal passage of life in spite of people observing the obligatory ritual activities. The banker further explains certain aspects of the retreat:

> "Yes, as you go up and down but actually people don't know what he (the Prophet) does not eat meat...during that time...you know he only took *zam zam* and dates, that's it. If you eat meat during that time you are.. what we call ...*shahawah*(desires). We have to control the *shahawah*...it will stop you from *tauba* (remembrance of God) and actually we are fighting our *nafs*(self). This is a big fight...we fight with the people, this is not big issue...so, before that there are a lot of things. First, I was hot tempered, I prayed but my hot temper did not reduce. *Alhamdulillah* (Praise the Lord) I would have still been there (that state) before (earlier) I prayed (but) I don't know to whom I pray." (Interview Document No: 7 - Appendix 3).

The above seeker is describing his past life and the anger that he had. The fundamental issue or obstacle in the path to self-development is one's desire, and one of the first steps in self-development is to become aware of one's inherent weaknesses, in this case anger (see Figs. 5.16 and 5.17), and immersing oneself in *dhikr* may enable one to triumph over it. This is not an easy fight and it needs to be sustained over time while continually supplicating to God for His mercy in order for change to happen.

The Supervisor of the residential Centre explains his involvement in the organisation, as well as about the retreat:

> "Then it's only these last five years that I started doing it properly after I went for *Sulook* (the spiritual retreat). Since these past five years I went there five or six times, 60 days already. ('what does that do to you?') "It changed me a lot. Before this I was a very angry person, who got angry very easily (and) out of limits. I just wanted to fight people. But now days, I have my limits. I know, I cannot go through, this is bad for me." (Interview Document No: 8 - Appendix 3).

The term *sulook* refers to a seeker adorning the spiritual path. The seeker is alluding to some of the changes, which came from the multiple methods that are utilised in the retreat or *uzla*, which over time rectifies one's character and in this case it seems that it lessened his angry temperament and he gained more self-control. Similarly, this change was also observed with the banker as outlined above who was able to change this state of mind becoming calmer.

One of the vital aspects that emerged from these interviews is the need for the *uzla* from time to time, and to sustain it over many years in order to trigger the change within oneself. This importance of consistency ties in with a saying of the Prophet narrated by his wife Aisha that even if you do a small act, do it regularly (Malik n.d).

The Centre Manager talks about his experience of the retreat, where he outlines the impact of the retreat:

> "It is to be spiritual. Everybody has a different spiritual taste...you cannot translate this thing to others. I don't know how to explain it to you, because you can look at Allah only from there. You can look at the face of the person and get evidence that these people are going to *akhlāq*. Only I say that, because you can look at Allah and the change of the people.

You cannot describe it by telling other people what you get, because this type of secret is for you and with different people, it is different..." (Interview Document No: 1 - Appendix 3).

What is referred to here is a metaphor that is called '*dhāt*' or taste, which means individualised experiential learning, what the heart feels, which varies from person to person (Lings 1983). The other aspect is the manifestation of light in the face referred to as '*noor*', an indication that one is getting close to God. The Manager elaborates on this:

"Yes, this experience is a big one, once it enters into your life. You do (sic) things that you don't break or you don't get far from *rahma* (mercy) that Allah gives you. The important thing is the first time what it (gets) inside your heart... once in your life. At others times, maybe sometimes Satan can come and disturb you. But that's why we have to get to our Guru... he will guide us whether this is right or this is wrong. ..." (Interview Document No: 1 - Appendix 3).

When experiences start emerging, it is important for one to be able to distinguish between those emerging from God, which are laced with the Divine, and those that are not, which are referred to as was-wās or the Satanic whispering into the breast of mankind, which is referred to in the Qur'ān (al-Nas, 114:5) and thus the Sheikh's guidance is necessary.

Within the Islamic framework whatever 'opening' or spiritual states are only afforded by the Mercy (Rahma) of God. One key aspect relating to worship and morality in the context of mercy is what the Prophet said: "The deeds of anyone of you will not save you (from the Hell) Fire). The companions said: "Even you (will not be saved by your deeds), O Allah's Apostle?" He said: "No, even I (will not be saved) unless and until Allah bestows His Mercy on me" (Sahih Bukhari, Book 76, Hadith 470). This is not to diminish effort since one needs to struggle (jihad) in the way of God and the measure one receives depends on one's intention and the mercy as underlined above.

The Centre Manager further explains the sleeping space in the *uzla* (retreat):

"This is sort of like an enclosed one. tempat (place)... each one has got its own... a cubicle, small size one, just like the Japanese one.. where you lie down and that you can't lie down with your full legs. When you lie down you will only be able to do like the babies in the womb. In fact, that was the terminology used, where you go back to the womb, which means your innocence and pure and unadulterated (self). That's why a baby is pure; it is the parent that turned you into Jews or Muslims or whatever religion... to practice together (*uzla*), for you are alone and it is quite difficult and this is the (nature) of the *tarīqa* (Order) actually." (Interview Document No: 1 - Appendix 3).

The symbolic metaphor referring to a state of infancy is in reference to the Qur'ān (Qur'an, l-Rum, (30):30) and the concept of '*fitra*' or the primordial state, where all human beings are born pure.

The professional banker talks about the blessings of the retreat:

"Because you know the Angels (*malaikat*) they like you when you are there. That's why sometimes I have got people asking me that if I open a restaurant, how do I make my restaurant popular? It is very simple, I tell them don't use all those charms, make sure you are clear from all those things. (negative).. they must always be in a state of ablution (*Inshā'Allah*) 24 hours... Be in good mood when they are attending to the customers. While

5.7 Approaches, Methods and Tools for Self-Development

they are cooking, you the owner, you have to be in *wuḍū'* (ablution), then only... your food receives... blessings (*baraka*) and the food... it is delicious. When a rich person came for *uzla* for 10 days, I thought he wants to complain but he said how come (the) vegetables and rice is so delicious. At home I have got fish and meat but it is not so delicious but SubhanAllah (Glory be to God)... you eat vegetable and rice only..." (Interview Document No: 7 - Appendix 3)

What is pointed to here is a state of purity, both externally, through *wuḍū'*, and internally through pure intentions and good character, the result is that what you do will be wholesome and bring in blessings.

The manager of Islamic reflexology outlines his insights and experiences of the retreat:

"So *uzla* is a very hard and difficult part for the people. Because it's using your heart, you transfer from your head to your heart then you understand more. its more real, example like in the Qur'ān it says *nafs al mutma'inna* (soul at peace), you don't know ... but when you go for *uzla* you know what is *mutma'inna* (soul at peace), (where) you will (change) yourself and be born into another person... you were born (through) your mother and now you will be born (again) (through) your teacher, that's the nice part." (Interview Document No: 3 - Appendix 3)

The reference here is to spiritual re-birth, a symbolic metaphor, when, after going through the intense regime for the 10 days the seekers undergo a paradigm shift in their perspective, that results in them feeling renewed and connected. A vital aspect that is pointed out is the heart-brain interconnection. This enables one to get away from mundane needs and distractions and fully focus on their worship. It enables one to cultivate silence since unnecessary chatter is reduced to a minimum by the ground rules and contemplative practices, thus there is silence of the tongue and this is a first step leading to the silence of the heart, as Ibn Arabi (2008) has articulated. This is directly in line with the Prophetic tradition: "He who believes in Allah and the Last Day must either speak good or keep silent" (Book 18 Hadith 1511). When asked about the meaning of the breakthrough, the above seeker explains:

"Meaning something like you want to get inside you (self), like having to break a bamboo, then you get inside (yourself).. something like that. So not all the people came to this (state), so people have to cross this line... they are only using the head's eyes not the heart's eyes. Only when you close your eyes, the heart eyes open, this is the part that *uzla* teaches you. Relating to Nabi Musa (Moses), Allah says you cannot see Me, you can only see Me by closing your eyes, then you see the Tusina (Mountain), only then the *tajjali* (spiritual light) can come in..." (He then talks about some of the changes): "The change, we struggle, what my friend told me after the *uzla* is that, we throw all that teaching, we only take one, we follow every night.. his (Sheikh's) class. That's is the change... we collect all the knowledge from him (Sheikh). Every word he said we collect that. They are like gold... so something like that... every way I feel I keep it, we have to keep (the) secret and it is hard work." (Interview Document No: 3 - Appendix 3).

This affords insight into the seeker's deepening layers of consciousness, where acquired or learnt knowledge refers to the intellect, which is to be discarded and the mind-free to 'the nearness of God and make efforts to realise Him' as stated by Ghazali (1995), which opens up the heart for divine inspiration. To support this, there is a reference in the Qur'ān, which points out that: 'For indeed, it is not eyes that are blinded, but blinded are the hearts which are within the breasts' (al-ḥajj 22:46). Ibn Arabi (2008) says, "When you close your physical eyes, you negate the physical world and you open to the world inside."

The Manager of the Centre discusses some key aspects of the retreat and the book received on its completion:

> "Silsila (chain of spiritual lineage)... I show you... it has a nice cover..(referring to the book and the silsila)... because as I said sometimes to me it is sacred. But not as sacred as the Qur'ān ... of course, we can grasp it. This is a book received on completion of *uzla*..." (He adds): "*uzla* if you have gone through the ... until you finish *murāqaba* (meditation) complete it, then what do we call this? The people who run the *uzla*? They award you with this small book explaining about the *'ibādah* (worship) that you have to do *dhikr*... This book explains about the *lataifs* (subtle spiritual organs), almost the same as the one in *jiwa sufi* (book written by the Sheikh) and other books..." (Interview Document No: 1 - Appendix 3)

The book that is given to the seekers at the end of their completion of *uzla* contains essential elements that they should know, as well as the description of the seven subtle spiritual organs. In response to the question by the researcher, if there are any Qur'ānic commands relating to *dhikr*, he refers to the verse:

> "And keep yourself (O Muhammad) patiently with those who call on their Lord morning and afternoon, seeking His Face; and let not your eyes overlook them, desiring the pomp and glitter of the life of the world; and obey not him whose heart We have made heedless of Our remembrance, and who follows his own lust, and whose affair has been lost." (Qur'ān, al-Kahf, 18:28)

The *uzla* is further expounded by this seeker:

> "... we continue to read, we *istighfar* (repentance) and with *sirr* (silent *dhikr*). those are the practices that *khatm hoja khan* (reading of the Qur'ān)... probably you will know (a state of realisation). These are the quality of the Sheikh, this is the *adab* (code of conduct) towards the *murid* (seeker) and towards the Sheikh." (Interview Document No: 3 - Appendix 3)

The Qur'ānic verse above commands the Prophet, and by extent humanity in general, to be with those who spend their time seeking closeness to God. This is reflected in those involved in the retreat, where there days are governed by worship (*'ibādah*), seeking repentance (*tauba*), mentioning God's name (*dhikr*), recitation of the Qur'ān and its completion (*khatm*). This is combined with code of conduct/good conduct (*adab*) towards the Sheikh and eliciting his guidance.

Repentance-Forgiveness (*tauba*) From the data set it is clearly evident that *tauba* or repentance plays a key role in clearing the mind of the seeker and getting close to God. This is seen to have a compound effect when combined with the ritual cleansing or *wuḍū'* and ritual prayers. The data extracts below indicate its varying positive aspects. In the survey data, repentance is reflected as the most important traits of the Sheikh (Fig. 5.9) and forgiveness as an essential teaching from the Sheikh for self-development (Appendix 3, Fig. 5.10). When asked about repentance (*tauba*) and what kind of *tauba* it is, the resident imam says:

> "Firstly, you must take a shower..and then.. in your heart you say... (When asked are you referring to intention, he replies): "Yes clean my heart and mind (inner) and *zahir*

5.7 Approaches, Methods and Tools for Self-Development

(outer), that is, (for) my body for the wrongs (done)...for thanking Allah and then you take shower. Before that you must take *wuḍū'* (ablution) first...every time you go to God." (He was queried 'you do this every time?', he answers): "Every time, yes and then if you get time before *farḍ* (obligatory prayer) around 15 minutes you do *salah tauba* (prayer of repentance). Firstly, you must be do *salah tauba* and ask for forgiveness." (Interview Document No: 2 - Appendix 3).

Concerning purification of oneself, one of the residents says:

"We have to do a lot of *istighfar* (act of seeking forgiveness)... yes at least one thousand times. If Rasulullah did *istighfar*..about 75 times, we have to do more than Rasulullah. Because as you know one day I have to do *istighfar* 1000 times and *salawat* (salutations on the Prophet) about 1500 times...this is the one being taught by the Sheikh." (Interview Document No: 2 - Appendix 3).

Both of the above seekers outline the process of seeking forgiveness from God, which is key to achieving salvation. As evident in the above narrations, this involves a process of turning to the Creator and asking Him to cleanse one's heart, releasing the burden that one carries within oneself.

The friend of the resident Imam describes his attempt to change himself by joining an organisation;

"I have been with another organisation but I think that group is wrong...there is one in a particular location (in Malaysia)...but they don't do *ṭarīqa*, they have different ways...and then they force us, while here they don't force you here..." (When prompted further he says): "They don't force you here, but you must pray that's all...*jamaah* (congregation) and you pray by yourself. I think it's better that you pray *jamaah* (together), because (of) the thing that is surrounding (us) is very different...is better than the jamaah, where you really concentrate...now we are expected to wake up early.. and do *tauba* and then *dhikr*" (He discusses about his preparation): "I wake up to... *tauba* (forgiveness) ... yes (he says for) what sin has been done, what sin is forthcoming, what sin has gone; so Allah please open my heart to follow and soften my tongue to read our Qur'ān because I will use methods like ritual repentance..." (Interview Document No: 4 - Appendix 3).

The general approach of the *ṭarīqa* (Order) is discussed here, which is an approach not of coercion but of creating awareness and teaching methods such as ritual repentance and supplication, which are ways to the heart. The above resident was asked if the repentance and remembrance of God is done five times:

"Tuan Guru told us this... yes. Five times ... ruku (bow), *sujjud* (prostration), the same *farḍ* (obligation) and then you get chance then do second *rak'a* (second ritual prayer movement). Then you repeat al-Fātiḥa (opening chapter of the Qur'ān) one time and then in the second (movement recite) Qur'ān, al-Ikhlas (112th chapter) three times and then you will do *sujjud* (prostration), it is always like *salah farḍ* (obligatory ritual prayers) and then give salaams, take your tasby (rosary)...and then...inside your heart you say *astaghfirullah*...that means Allah forgive me" (Interview Document No: 4 - Appendix

When asked how many times, he answers:

"It's up to you...Prophet Yunus said '*la ilaha illa anta inni kuntu minal zalimeen*' (there is no God but You and God you alone are sufficient). God forgive me and then for me I do a hundred... firstly, you must *salawat* (praise the Prophet) and then you give your heart to Allah. Please Allah, please forgive me...Bismillah (in the name of the Lord) before I was very weak, very wrong, very poor in my deeds. I (take) blame for whatever I did, which

I never did properly... and then you do it properly with your heart day by day, then your heart wakes up. ... before we take food and then *salah*. Now things have changed, you are rushing for *salah* and then have your food... your heart says *rizq* (provision) Allah gave to you what he has promised to give you. *Salah*, he didn't promise you but you must do it first, that is *baraka* (blessing) for me." (Interview Document -2 - Appendix 3).

The resident here is outlining his change in behaviour and habits, exemplified by a change in orientation towards God, unlike their previous state. This is brought about by a series of contemplative practices including repentance, supplications of the Prophet (see Contemplative Tree, Sect. 2.3), as well as opening oneself up for self-criticism (muhasaba, see Sect. 2.2). The change in behaviour is indicated here with reference to now doing the ritual prayers first and then eating, whereas before eating was a top priority. The above seeker says:

"Turning because I hope when Allah loved me whatever I do because Allah said in the Qurʾān: If you do whatever I say truly and hope for me to forgive you, you will do properly and then you will get it. Now seriously, I follow you, I just get it in my heart, I do not know how to discuss with you about the heart... you must do (it), you can (then) get it, if you do not ever do (it), you will not get it." (Interview Document No: 2 - Appendix 3).

The focus here is on turning one's attention towards God by adhering to God's commandments and internalising it in one's heart, if this is not done, then the change does not occur as per the above seeker's experience. When asked why *tauba* (repentance) is so very important, the above seeker replies:

"If I fall (sin), you must follow up what Guru said. This is very important for *ʿibādah* (worship) and then you do with your heart and nobody forces you, that means, ikhlas (sincerity). You give your heart and you will see yourself through. We know we are human beings and very small. When you do the *ʿibādah*, so that is much better you ask Allah to clean your heart. It also changes your mind, so it links up with akhlāq (morality)... changes your mind and also how you talk to people." (Interview Document No: 2 - Appendix 3).

What the seeker emphasizes here is the importance of sincerity and humility and seeing things in a wider perspective, where the 'I' becomes small. With this kind of perspective, when one indulges in worship, this seems to be the trigger for some changes to occur in one's conduct. When asked if all of this happens through *tauba* or through *dhikr*, he expounds:

"Through *tauba* (repentence)... somebody said work for your *salah* (ritual prayer)? And you have to say (this is) because of Allah. What if you say no... (and then) fall again... to do dosa (sins)? For me it's very simple to let people know why you *salah*. I *salah* because of Allah. That's why I appreciate my Rasulullah (the Prophet). If Rasulullah cannot give this love nobody could have known Allah the Jalili (Majestic). Then Allah parawalaikan (representative) Rasulullah, so who are you not to do *salah*? You say *salah* to Allah because you must respect..." (Interview Document No: 2 - Appendix 3).

The above focus is on one of the most fundamental aspects of Islam, namely following what has been ordained with consistency and good intentions, as the Prophet said: "Actions are but intention and every man shall have but that which he intended." (An-Nawawi 1977) and in this case, the seeker is emphasizing that his turning to prayers is for God. There is also repeated reference to the Prophet and the need to respect and follow his way to gain the love of God.

5.7 Approaches, Methods and Tools for Self-Development

The Sheikh's rendering of the relationship between worship and morality is outlined as conditional to the state of progression of the heart, where he points out that:

> "Values and their manifestation depend on the stages of the heart of the worshipper. They are influenced by emotions and attributes. Some of the key values are: *tauba* (repentance), *shukr* (thankfulness), sabr (patience), zuhd (state of poverty); muhabat (love)..., ridha (acceptance). The heart of a muhsin (someone who does good) has humility and is awake." (Interview Document No: 5 - Appendix 3).

The cultivation of these values was echoed by the resident imam and his friend, and this as evident above, originates from the Sheikh's teaching itself. Apart from the focus on worship, there is an emphasis on assimilating virtuous values which has a bearing on one's akhlāq. My own position is, how valuable is your worship if you are not able to treat others well?, whom God created irrespective of differences in faith. This is the universality of the message that needs to be shared.

Prayers (Obligatory and Optional) One of the essential aspects of being a Muslim is the ritual prayer. The professional banker outlines the quality of prayers and taking the oath of allegiance:

> "So, my behaviour is still like that, I find I follow the fasting, I follow all the fiqh (legal) rules and things but yet there is no changes. The only thing that you do is pray, without knowing to whom you are praying, and you don't know. So, there is no kushu (absorption) in the *salah*." (When prodded what type of kushu): "Your mind is somewhere but you are reading Bismillah Rahim (In the name of the Lord, the Beneficent) you are reading Allah bin Rab (Allah is the Lord) but your mind is somewhere." (When asked, you mean you can focus, he says): "Yes focus is the most important. This prayer is actually to get to you, when we are praying actually, we are thinking of Allah. So, actually when you think about Allah, you have to focus (on) Allah." (Interview Document No: 7 - Appendix 3).

What is understood is that there is a change, which occurs from blindly following rituals to one where there is a sense of awareness after taking the oath of allegiance. The resident Imam says:

> "So, my soul, that is, I must do it properly outside and inside my heart. So, if I read Qur'ān, al-Fātiha (opening verse), I must know what that means. What is the meaning in English and then, that is, something you do very perfectly. You do it perfect, maybe 80 or 70%. Before, I just do it, no percentage. Now, if I *takbir* (signifying the start of the prayers) you know that Allah sees you, really. I don't know how. Just that my brain, my heart knows that, truly. Then (I) go through rukū' (a bowing position), sujūd (prostration)... and Allah sees... I just changed my life. So, when I wanted to start, I did everything in time. I start it now, step by step. In istana budi (the centre). I do... *tahajjud* (night prayers), dhuha (prayer after sun rise). I wake up in the morning and then I don't miss it." (Interview Document No: 2 - Appendix 3).

When the above seeker was queried about his time of waking in the morning he says:

> "2 o'clock in the morning... It's supposed to be fajr (morning prayers) or whatever, because I learnt in the study of hadīth (narration) of Rasulullah (Prophet) that his ankle swelled up (by praying). I think that is a secret inside. I want to know what the secret is and then my Guru's is also... like that. That's the way for me to be reminded of Allah, to think (about) Allah is the best. (He is) very loving and can forgive all your darkness, your dosa (sins). (The

resident imam above mentioned acts of a role-model for his peers, where he highlights that):
"Somebody looked at me and then that gave me the responsibility to control our friends praying, how to do *salah tauba* (prayer of repentance). My Guru said to me, you must do *salah tauba*, shower and get...clean in the outside and inside of your body." (Interview Document No: 2 - Appendix 3).

This particular seeker who was a former drug addict and HIV patient, has by virtue of this devotion and discipline, been able to lead other residents at the Centre in daily worship. He manifests within himself a strong sense of transformation, which is reflected in his behaviour that seems to influence others who take him as an immediate role-model. He is referring to both the brain and the heart coming into play and the manifesting of 'khushu' or being able to worship with absorption that was outlined above. The resident imam's friend was asked how often he had dreams. He replied:

"Quite often...I get dreams, I get down and I pray...each time I get a dream I wake up and pray my *tahajjud* (night prayers)...how grateful to Allah." (His dreams are about:) "...getting closer to God, to change my ways and to remind me who I am. Allah and Rasulullah...to become like (Prophet) Mohammed." (Interview Document No: 4 - Appendix 3).

He was then asked where he felt the dreams to which he said:

"In my heart and in my mind because I think is this true and true to me. And I say this is the last chance that Allah is giving (me) to use it in the right way." (Interview Document No: 4 - Appendix 3).

In the Prophetic tradition dreams are signs of the process of transformation, and this is said to be authentic for those in the path of God. The resident imam now talks about three inter-linking concepts of trust gained through the knowledge facilitated by the Sheikh, with repentance (*tauba*) being the doorway to the heart and transformation:

"...unlike before, relating to trust, if something is wrong my brain is fighting inside that it is wrong...But I just learned that al Qur'ān said...don't shop lift or take something" (Interview Document No:2 - Appendix 3)

When queried how that trust came to him, he explains:

"It comes to me, because one thing I know I have that...ilm or knowledge.. and then you do amal (action) when you *salah* you clean all your body. What you do is *tauba* (repentance), then the hidayah (inspiration) - can go inside your heart. If you don't do *tauba*, maybe that hidayah is from Satan...and not Allah gives you. ...My heart is very cool doing that amal (action) and then Guru gives you another." (Interview Document No: 2 - Appendix 3).

The former sailor, a resident who has travelled widely, encapsulates his previous state of mind:

"It's when you keep thinking about drugs, you keep thinking about alcohol you know? But now no more. I stopped taking drugs for nearly five years now. So the drugs are no more here, it's gone." (He was asked 'So how did it go away?' to which he replies): "I pray a lot, I *dhikr* (remembrance of God) a lot. Sometimes I used to wake up in the night, sit by myself, it's like repenting you know..." (He adds): "Yes and that helped me to mix around that's why I used to say to myself it's better to be less talkative than more talkative. You

5.7 Approaches, Methods and Tools for Self-Development 209

make less sin." (He was queried if he was saying that he is still not ready to go out, what can make him stronger): "Pray to God. I know the more you pray to God the nearer you are to God..." (When asked 'Do you feel it?'): "Yes at midnight normally it is in my mind...one thing with me I always have difficulty in sleeping since I was young until now. I can lie on the bed, I go to bed at nine o'clock I will sleep maybe at around two o'clock." (Interview Documents No: 10 - Appendix 3).

Here, he acknowledges the struggle of breaking the addiction yet his success in changing the orientation of his mind and behaviour was facilitated by his engagement in prayers and meditation and the feeling that he is close to God. As he points out that the thought relating to drugs is still there and can be indication of a need for a greater immersion in what he is doing, in order to fully break the complex habit.

When he was asked 'Is your mind moving all over?' he says "Yes all over" and when further queried, 'Do you think is there anything you can do to slow it down?' he answers, "don't think about it" and when asked 'Is there anything you can do?' he says "Yes I release my stress by smoking, I smoke about one packet a day that's the only thing" and when asked 'Do you feel like you want to stop?' he highlights that "Yes because I have been smoking for a while more than 30 years maybe now I stopped a lot I try and go like 10 min without... 10 min then after that I start." When queried on the negative effects of smoking, he acknowledges that, "Yes I know it's bad at least it's better than alcohol and all that." (Interview Document No: 10—Appendix 3).

From the former sailor's narrative, one finds that there is progress in his ongoing struggle to achieve a focused mind and control his chaotic mind and thoughts, as compared to a 'scattered mind', and in feeling his closeness to God. Some chronic habits, however, seems to still persist. When asked what he has learnt, he now he points out, "The thing I learnt is you have to go in line, before I was far away from God, very far away." When further queried, 'So why do you think it is that you are nearer to God now than before?' he shares this experience:

"Before maybe I was too occupied with my work and now since I don't work, I got nothing to do. You share in prayers with everybody so you have to pray, also before you force yourself to pray and you fight, then after, it slowly comes and automatically you know? Then you start praying with your heart...before you were praying just to show people. Yes like if someone is there, then you start praying after midnight, then this thing comes slowly." (Interview Document No: 10 - Appendix 3).

The reference to 'go in line' is to participate in the rituals, and the remembrance of God, that is a part of his new (disciplined) environment. His night prayers seem to have yielded some special experiences, while overall 'then things come slowly', meaning his closeness to God. The need for connection with the heart seems to be a recurring theme from those interviewed as a means of connecting to God. When asked if that seems to be a rule, he answers:

"Some people take (things) for granted...pray just to eat, but it is not only that. So one day I was just sitting there alone for 'isha (night ritual prayer)...I feel quiet, I feel lonely...because of my past life. Before I used to be very happy. Now I just have to wake up at midnight and pray. Because this thing will come to you and when you keep on doing it, you come to live it." (He says that this is the advice of the Sheikh, and that he followed it.) "Before when I prayed my mind...used to be scattered...my mind was everywhere. But then I got to know." (So this realisation has come to you after coming here or was it there before?) "After coming here, before...I would stay out womanising, taking alcohol and now, none of that." [So is it the environment or is it the prayers or is it the repentance?] "The repentance on things, prayer, the more you pray, it will come through then you have the people..." (Interview Document No: 10 - Appendix 3).

His reference to 'happiness' here is to his earlier care-free life of indulgence, partying and drugs, which seems to have made him happy but led him to becoming a drug addict and infected with HIV. His reference to loneliness is linked to his calmer life (perhaps alienation from former friends through his choice of path) and non-indulgence in things that he used to do. There is a sense of realisation that is, 'when you keep doing it, you come to live it', which is perhaps an increasing awareness and a degree of internalisation of his change of behaviour. The sailor now talks about his family and his relationship with them:

"Those closest to me is my younger sister... she comes to see me. She will never miss, she comes every weekend..." (Does she see the change in you?) "Yes, she is very happy that I changed at least now and she said you have started to become a human being." (So what is it to be like a human being? What is the difference and which is better?) "Now to start believing in something. You have to start believing in something but now yes, the goodness of Allah is with me. Now I know the meaning of praying. Before I do not know." (Interview Document No: 10 - Appendix 3).

Being a human being refers to having a sense of meaning and direction in life, which in this case, is God. This indicates a process of transformation of the seekers, indicated in his change of behaviour, as noticed by his little sister.

Dhikr: Its Nature and Type The Centre Manager discusses the organisation and some of its methods:

"The Naqshabandiyyah, I think there is a lot of terminologies in Sufism. One is about *sirr* (silent remembrance) and *jihar* (loud remembrance) and these are the differences of the methodology of *dhikr*.... This one I don't know whether its practiced or not *khatm* or *dhikr*, that is, in our practice especially the *uzla* (retreat) before we do the *sirr* (silent) and *jihar* (loud) - then we have this *khatm hoja khan*, which is reading the *fātiha* (opening verse of the Qur'ān) a number of times which is six and twelve times and then the Surah Ikhlas (112th Qur'ānic chapter), then the minimal of a hundred times...the Ikhlas probably like a thousand times I think. This is within *uzla*." (Interview Document No: 1 - Appendix 3).

What are outlined here are the methods of *dhikr* from the loud pronunciation (*jihar*) to the silent (*sirr*), where God is remembered in your heart. This is succeeded by the recitation of the Qur'ān several times. In terms of contemplative practices (Sect. 2.3—contemplative tree), one sees stillness practices like silent *dhikr* as well as cyclic practices of ritual prayers as well as generative practices of loud *dhikr* and Qur'ānic recital. The manager of the Centre says:

"You say one time if it is total or full *ijāza* (permission granted by the Sheikh)... You say one time Allah it is like mentioning it five trillion times Allah said by all the living cells in the body. I think that one (resonates) with some of them." (Here he is referring to the effect on the residents and it was pointed out that one of the resident's mentioned this where he responds:) "I am very happy. You know why? I approached the scientific sort of angle. So

5.7 Approaches, Methods and Tools for Self-Development

when I tell them from the tip of your hairs to the tip of your toes, every cell is also saying the same thing Lā ilāha ill Allāh (no God but God). If you say one thousand you plus another three zero there it becomes... This is very good... that is the reason why the *tasbih* or prayer beads is just a trigger. Just to keep the rhythm on and on, because without the *tasbih* you can still say inside. Sometimes you forget as well." (Interview Document No: 1 -Appendix 3).

The manager is using his scientific training to illustrate the Islamic notion that everything is in a state of remembrance of God (*dhikr*) including all of the cells in the body, this concept seems to have evoked a profound sense of awe in the seekers since some of the seekers have referred to it during the interviews. He makes reference to the use of prayer beads in creating rhythm, the rapid clicking sound of which is said to synchronise with one's heartbeat. This then sets the word of God in motion, which is a specific method in their Order. He acknowledges the human factor of forgetfulness, for which collective gathering and guidance helps remedy. The manager elaborates further on the methods that he uses to teach the seekers:

"I told them, if you look at the sky on a very clear night, you see lots of stars. Millions of stars. In your brain, I said we have also millions of cells, neurones, brain cells, with both the grey matter and the white matter. And these neurones are the units of the brain cells. They are sparkling like those cakerawala (stars). They find this there is very interesting, where some of them (who were) sleeping they woke up... otherwise, they get up and go and they also get very fed up." (Interview Document No: 1 - Appendix 3).

Not all residents join the collective *dhikr* group, which is held on a weekly basis outside the Centre. They join of their own volition, when they feel ready for it, since some are recovering from physical ailments, while others don't feel mentally ready. When asked what else he had learnt from the Sheikh, the manager says:

"By watching and hearing how to *dhikr* and what is the right way to *dhikr*. After that we learnt the right way to, I tried to give it up but no, then I saw that this thing is good for me and good for everybody who really wants to change their ways who really wants to go in Allah's ways and spiritual ways. See when you *dhikr* you get closer to Allah straight away, there's no other way..." (Interview Document No: 1 - Appendix 3).

What is distinctly outlined here are some key elements of the 'social learning theory' (Bandura 2011), where one models by observing the leader and others in the group, that is, peer modelling. This latter type of modelling is significant in the sense that the Sheikh sets an example and the actual practice of it takes place with peers who help the seeker to practice it over time. This is, for example, seen in the resident Imam teaching the former sailor or the friend of the resident imam.

The Centre manager, when queried, 'Where does the *dhikr* and all that fit into this?' replied, "Yes at all the prayer times we have some *dhikr*" and concerning the residents he points out that, "10 out of them goes for *dhikr* with Tuan Guru, they join us." This is out of 30 residents. Some of them have gone for *sulook* (retreat). He adds that for this, "It's in isolation sort of area, in Kuantan in Pahang (two sub-centres). We have a *soora* or prayer place out there" (Interview Document No: 1—Appendix 3).

The practice of *dhikr* is cultivated during the five ritual prayer times, while collective *dhikr* is done both with the general seekers and the residents in the presence of the Sheikh, and held in different sub-centres. This is an example of a third of the residents actually taking part in spiritual activities outside their own centre and together with other general seekers. This is where after prayers *dhikrullah* in a nearby mosque, and following a lecture, the collective *dhikr* takes place, where both the loud (*jihar*) but mainly the silent (*sirr*) *dhikr* is done under the supervision of the Sheikh. During this process some of the selected senior seekers go around facilitating the individuals in their method of doing the *dhikr*. The above seeker also indicates:

> "So you know about the *dhikrullah*, one day you have to sit; you have to find your free time, you don't miss your *dhikr*. You have to *dhikr* every day, you have to *dhikr* at least 5000 times. How to use the *tasbih* or prayer beads... You want more, you want profit, so you make more than that." (Interview Document No: 7 - Appendix 3).

The reference here is to invest in spiritual acts, which will yield results. It is to be noted that regularity is the key to developing practice, its perfection and the reaping of its benefits. Consistency is a part of Prophetic tradition, and when the Prophet was asked what deeds are most loved by Allah, he said, "The most constant deeds even though they may be a few" (Al-Bukhari 1994). Here one observes that by using the beads the *dhikr* is accelerated, a method that allows one to track quantity and progress.

The professional banker expresses his feelings thus:

> "*Dhikrullah* is the basic, where your *'ibādah* (worship) will be so beautiful... you are feeling so scared when you know Allah through *dhikrullah*... The fiqh (law) is important but the most important is the *dhikrullah* because actually when you *dhikrullah* you know wherever you go, what (ever) you are doing... you always *dhikrullah* in your heart. In your whole being you always *dhikrullah*." (When asked what kind of *dhikr*:) "*Dhikrullah* since my late mentor that was Sheikh Imam Bin Mohammed Arif. I sat a lot with him, so he taught me *dhikrullah* by only saying Allah... *sirr* (silent), when (we do) *jihar* (loud) we will Lā ilāha illa Allāh (No God but God). We got two types of *dhikrullah sirr* and *jihar*." (Interview Document No: 7 - Appendix 3).

A distinction is made here between *dhikr* and the Islamic law or fiqh, the seeker emphasises the importance of *dhikr* in bringing about experiential learning, leading for example to spiritual openings and the 'taste' of the Beauty and Majesty of God. A key point that he makes is to take the *dhikr* from its immediate surroundings, the heart and mind of the individual, to the external environment, such that it becomes part of their daily activities, which means that it has to be internalised. This is the essence of developing God consciousness in everyday life. When asked if the *dhikr* is silent, he says:

> "Yes silence... in your whole being. You can do it anywhere, for example, in the toilet, but you cannot do in by *jihar* (loud) its haram (not permissible)." (So if I understand you right you say that basically the normal activities are good, however, we need to do *dhikrullah* to go deeper?) "What I am saying is that basically without *dhikrullah*, first of all you have to do *dhikrullah* and it takes time. Without *dhikrullah* it is difficult to change behaviour. Actually that's why I just told you just now, before *bay'a*, (oath) I still prayed but I was thinking who Allah is. I don't know who Allah is because that time I didn't have any *dhikrullah*, you know lack of *dhikrullah* and istighfar (repentance)." (Interview Document No: 7 - Appendix 3).

5.7 Approaches, Methods and Tools for Self-Development

Fig. 5.21 Lataifs—subtle spiritual organs—focal points for *Dhikr*

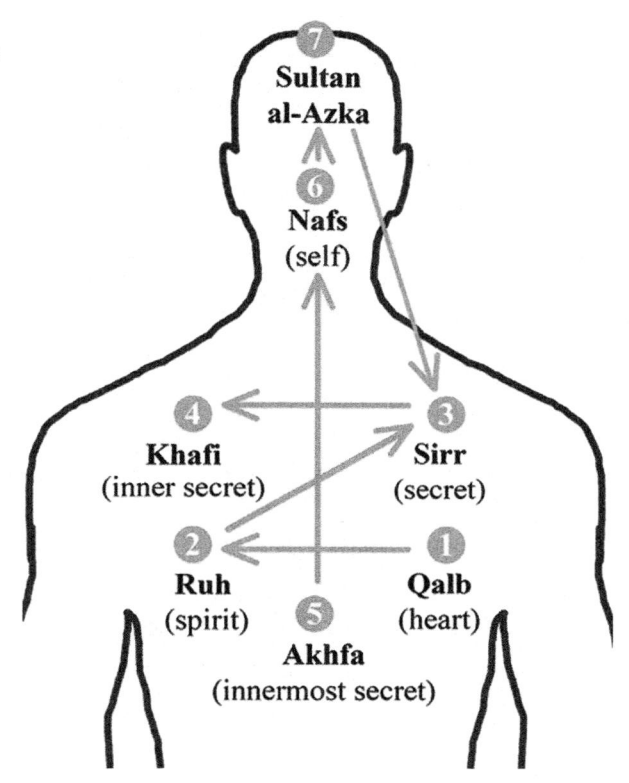

- ⑦ Sultan al-Azka
- ⑥ Nafs (self)
- ④ Khafi (inner secret)
- ③ Sirr (secret)
- ② Ruh (spirit)
- ① Qalb (heart)
- ⑤ Akhfa (innermost secret)

Three essential factors of change are articulated here: firstly, the need to have God consciousness at all times and this is accomplished by doing *dhikr*; secondly, he is alluding to the loud and silent *dhikr*, which are different methods of remembrance, which can vary from order to order; thirdly, seeking forgiveness from God.

Methodology of *Dhikr* (Remembrance of God) In order to justify the use of the latāif, the physical locations in the body which correspond to the subtle spiritual organs, in *dhikr*, the above seeker (Fig. 5.21) cites several Qur'ānic verses. This reference by the manager is to the first subtle spiritual organ (latāif). Figure 5.21 highlights the seven latāif within the frame of the body. This is the heart or 'qalb' located just below the physical heart according to the Naqshabandiyyah system. He then makes reference to a Qur'ānic verse relating to the second lataif, the rūḥ:

$$\text{وَيَسْأَلُونَكَ عَنِ الرُّوحِ قُلِ الرُّوحُ مِنْ أَمْرِ رَبِّي وَمَا أُوتِيتُم مِّنَ الْعِلْمِ إِلَّا قَلِيلًا}$$

"And they ask you concerning the rūḥ (the spirit). Say: The rūḥ (the spirit) is one of the things, the knowledge of which is only with my Lord, And of knowledge, you (mankind) have been given only a little." (Qurʻān, al-Isra,17:85)

Muhammad Asad's (2011) explains that both Imam Zamakhshari and Imam Razi refer to the soul as the seat of divine inspiration. The latāif of the rūḥ is located on the right side and in parallel to the heart according to the Naqshabandiyyah way (Fig. 5.21). Ibn Kathir's (2003d) commentary explains that rūḥ is the origin and essence, while the nafs consists of the rūḥ and is connected to the body. He, then refers to the third subtle spiritual organ called the *sirr* (inner secret) and links the Qurʼānic verse, which says:

$$وَإِن تَجْهَرْ بِالْقَوْلِ فَإِنَّهُ يَعْلَمُ السِّرَّ وَأَخْفَى$$

"Save what God may will (thee to forget), for, verily,He (alone) knows all that is open to (man/women's) perception as well as all that is hidden (from it) and (thus) shall We make easy for thee the path towards (ultimate) ease" (Qurʻān, Taha, 20:7)

This lataif is located on the left side but above the heart in this system (Fig. 5.21). In reference to the above verse Muhammad Asad's (2011) writes that: 'He knows not only man's unspoken, conscious thoughts but also all that goes on within the sub-conscious self.' He then refers to the fourth latāif, termed khafi (Appendix 4L), where he quotes:

$$إِلَّا مَا شَاءَ اللَّهُ إِنَّهُ يَعْلَمُ الْجَهْرَ وَمَا يَخْفَى وَنُيَسِّرُكَ لِلْيُسْرَى$$

"Save what God may will (thee to forget), for, verily,He (alone) knows all that is open to (man/women's) perception as well as all that is hidden (from it) and (thus) shall We make easy for thee the path towards (ultimate) ease." (Qurʻān, al-Aʻla, 87:7–8)

Muhammad Asad explains that all that is intrinsically beyond the reach of human perception (al-ghayb), the implication being that since human knowledge must, forever, remain imperfect, man cannot really find his way through life without the aid of divine revelation. The last sentence is outlined: i.e. towards an ease of mind and peace of the spirit. Khafi is the fourth lataif on the right side parallel to the *sirr*, while the fifth is at the centre of the solar plexus and called the akhfa accordingly to the Naqshabandiyyah system.

The manager says that, "The sixth lataif is now referred to in terms of its link to the lataif nafs", as per the verse:

$$وَاذْكُر رَّبَّكَ فِي نَفْسِكَ تَضَرُّعًا وَخِيفَةً وَدُونَ الْجَهْرِ مِنَ الْقَوْلِ بِالْغُدُوِّ وَالْآصَالِ وَلَا تَكُن مِّنَ الْغَافِلِينَ$$

5.7 Approaches, Methods and Tools for Self-Development

"And remember your Lord within yourself, humbly and with fear and without loudness in words in the morning and in the afternoon, and be not of those who are neglectful." (Qur'ān, al-A'rāf, 7:205)

Ibn Kathir's commentary says that Allah wants that He be remembered more often in the morning and afternoon, in secret and not loudly, with earnestness and fear, thus it is recommended that *dhikr* is not performed in a loud voice.

The seventh lataif referred to is called the sultan al-adhkār, where the whole body is involved, with the Qur'ānic verse says:

اللَّهُ نَزَّلَ أَحْسَنَ الْحَدِيثِ كِتَابًا مُتَشَابِهًا مَثَانِيَ تَقْشَعِرُّ مِنْهُ جُلُودُ الَّذِينَ يَخْشَوْنَ رَبَّهُمْ ثُمَّ تَلِينُ جُلُودُهُمْ وَقُلُوبُهُمْ إِلَىٰ ذِكْرِ اللَّهِ ذَٰلِكَ هُدَى اللَّهِ يَهْدِي بِهِ مَن يَشَاءُ وَمَن يُضْلِلِ اللَّهُ فَمَا لَهُ مِنْ هَادٍ

"Allah has sent down the Best Statements, a Book, its parts resembling each other, (and) oft-repeated. The skins of those who fear their Lord shiver from it. Then their skin and their hearts soften to the remembrance of Allah. That is the guidance of Allah. He guides therewith whom He wills; and whomever Allah sends astray, for him there is no guide." (Surah Zumar, 39:23)

This *dhikr*, which is done from top down and embraces the whole body is the central *dhikr*, where it affects the five trillion cells in the body accordingly to the above seeker's view. He makes reference to nafi isbat—illahulaha illah (No God but Allah). When asked 'What is that?', he say it is "Lā ilāha illa Allah . . . not even *jihar* (loud) it is still *sirr* (silent)" (Interview Document No: 1—Appendix 3). Here, the whole methodology of doing silent *dhikr* at the seven points within the body, is in order for the body to be consumed by it. The focus is to deny or negate everything except God.

With regards to the above verse, Ibn Kathir's commentary (2003c) refers to parts of the Qur'ān resembling one and repeating another, while Muhammad Asad's (2011) uses Razi's explanation and says that it points to statements of polarity of light and darkness, general and specific and to consistency. Ibn Kathir comments on the second part of the verse: while the fear of the Lord makes their skin shine and due to hope for His mercy and kindness their skins and heart soften with His remembrance.

The resident Imam, as well as his resident friend, both discuss their experience of the path (Document 2, Appendix 3): "So certain of the other people are going there (for *dhikr*). Maybe the hidāyah (guidance) is from Allah. Hidāyah is a good gift from Allah to somebody. If your heart is very clear. . . Allah will keep you wherever you are." He was asked, "So if your heart is clear Allah can be with you?", to which they respond:

"Yes. You have dengki. . . means bad feeling for other people. . . and you like to talk about people. . . You see something that you do not want and. . . say no to it, you go.. in your heart and *sirr* (silent *dhikr*)..." (The other resident says:) "And nobody can change you or anything. You shall do it, that is, change yourself... nobody can depend on your life; you yourself have to depend on your own." (Interview Document No: 2 (there were a couple of interviews that both of the resident imam and his friend were present together) - Appendix 3).

What they are expressing here is the emptying of the heart of ill feelings and infusing it with the love of God, so that one's heart clears itself of the debris that it has collected over time. This process of consultation with your heart, a process called 'istigara', where one prays to God with your heart and seeks for a sign. This forms the basis of bringing about change. This closely links with the Qur'ānic verse, "Verily, Allah will not change the (good) condition of a people as long as they do not change their state (of goodness) themselves" (Qur'ān, al-Ra'ad 13:11).

The friend of the resident imam was asked how he intended to process the information that he receives from the Sheikh to which the resident imam replied:

"By going to kulliyyah (lectures), by *dhikring* (remembering God), by humbling with people, the way that we talk, the way that we give things, the way that we are scared of Allah. Normally, everything that is difficult we don't do. But it is very hard to get these ten things (virtuous traits)... even me at the moment, but one day I will get. *Inshā'Allah*, if Allah opens my heart and softens my tongue to speak and to read Qur'ān *Inshā'Allah* I will be someone. I would love to go deeply, more deeply." (Interview Document No: 2 - Appendix 3).

This reference has already been made to the ten virtuous traits that the seekers are trying to inculcate (chapter 2.5). The friend of the resident Imam points out that:

"You never do that alone without Allah... but the best of me is after I got into the *dhikr* almost two months ago. I have been in *dhikr* and I saw changes in me. You see I don't set alarm to get up for morning prayers, now I set up my own mind. I get up before five, I mean 4:45 am... I have a shower and I will be down there for *dhikr* early, after my *tauba* (repentance) I do my *dhikr*. Before I got into *dhikr*, I get up after the azan (call for prayer). I don't need to set on the phone [alarm] I set my own by 4:45am I will be up by myself. No need to even knock on my window." (Interview Document No: 2 - Appendix 3).

What is seen here is the establishing of a routine of practice and habits for worship, which in-effect is a discipline, such that they become internalised and second nature, as seen in his example of waking up at dawn without an alarm. When asked for the reason behind this, the above seeker says:

"Getting to know Allah is the key because you always speak about Him, you always talk about Him and you remember Him so He remembers you. So, wake up, you want to come to Me, you speak My name, you call My name, I will be there anytime you need Me by your side, let's say like the song. ...If you remember Him, you think about Him, He will be there for us anytime. He will be for us and He will listen although we can't see Him but He can see us and what we are doing..." (Interview Document No: 5 - Appendix 3).

Here, what is seen is the rendition of the ḥadīth of the Prophet: "Be mindful of Allah, and you will find Him in front of you", this concept of God's constant companionship, coupled with His mercy has been inculcated in the minds of the seekers and acts as a positive force that both motivates and comforts them. (Ibrahim and Johnson-Davies 1977).

5.7 Approaches, Methods and Tools for Self-Development

The Sheikh provides insight into the nexus between morality and worship:

> "The akhlāq (morality), depends on the state of your heart. There are two aspects, first, the emotions and second the ṣifat or attributes. If the heart is good, the deeds and interactions will also be good. Allah does not count your deeds only, but he accounts for the values in your heart." (Interview Document No: 5 - Appendix 3).

The cleaner your heart, the more pure your intentions and consequently the purer your behaviour will be. When asked what the meaning of changing one's heart was, he replied:

> "It is through adapting the path, with the remembrance of God (*dhikrullah*). When Ali asked the Prophet Muhammad to teach him *'ibādah*, he said 'O Ali you must remember Allah in your heart and in your voice.' "(Interview Document No: 7 - Appendix 3).

The reference to adapting the path is what is called 'tarqiyah' or spiritual grooming, which entails one coming under the guidance of an accomplished Sheikh and adopting a spiritual path.

Night Vigil (*Tahajjud*) This refers to the night prayers, which are done in the very early hours of the morning before the breaking of dawn. The manager of the Centre explains about getting into the depth of worship (Interview Document No: 1—Appendix 3):

> "...and the other thing is that as a Sufi, prayer alone at night when nobody knows that you are praying is just as good, as you're praying not in terms of the rewards. So, we are not bothered. I'm not trying to say that you don't have to go to Mecca and pray, no. The things we perform here is just as good as you go to Mecca. So, you perform well here... what's the terminology— keeping the night alive."

When asked if this refers to a special prayers or night vigil called tahujjud, he says yes and also refers to another optional prayer, which he does:

> "Qiyam al-layl (optional night prayer) - I do it personally. I do a lot of before and after the dawn prayer. So, I get both of the two worlds." (He expounds that:) "Before and after dawn. Before because that's the time when there's no sound, it's very quiet. Nobody knows what I am doing. And before dawn, get up by around 4 or 5 am and ... and then you wait for the prayer call. Sometimes, I go to the mosque, after that, I come back." (Interview Document No: 1 - Appendix 3).

As noted, all the residents who were interviewed seem to pray the night prayer (*tahajjud*), as it is of the most special times to be spiritually active as it is a time of complete stillness, isolation and without the busyness of the day, allowing one to connect with oneself and God. This has a profound effect on the body and mind. The resident Imam then elaborates further on his dawn routine (Interview Document No: 2—Appendix 3), where he says:

> "*Salah tauba* (ritual forgiveness prayer) we do (it) every day around fajr (morning prayer)... I do before *du'ā*(supplication) before *du'ā tauba* (prayer of repentance) and then go *salah dhuha* (an optional prayer after morning prayers) ...yes then follow up *shukr salah* (prayer of gratitude)... and *tahajjud* (night vigil)...." (When queried about the time, he says:) "...yes in the night from 3:00 am early in the morning part of night and then sleep afterwards. You are thinking of what time can I wake up around? If you do like that,

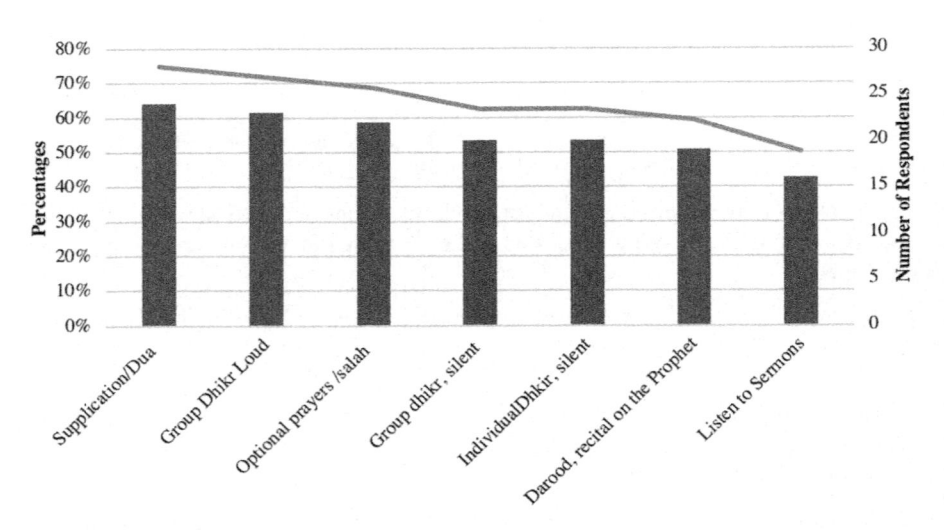

Fig. 5.22 Voluntary acts of worship

a mala'ika (angel) will shake you ... wake up... you must remain with Allah and now this is very nice for me."

Once again there is evidence of a string of acts of worship while giving gratitude to God—a ritual prayer of repentance before the ritual morning prayers, which can lead to an awakened state of mind. This also serves as a process of detoxifying oneself of one's sins and bringing about a sense of reconciliation. What is witnessed in his last sentence is what is called an 'opening' from God in *tasawwuf*, when someone 'will shake you and wake you.' The voluntary activities that the seekers perform is captured in Fig. 5.22.

Supplication (Du'ā) Supplication to God forms an important act of worship, it exemplifies the relationship between man and his Creator, where ones humbles to the Bestower of grace and refuge. This is reflected in the survey data in Figs. 5.10, 5.12, and 5.20. Here the resident Imam highlights his experience of the process:

"Yes now I pray to Allah. *salah tauba* (prayer of repentance) ...I give my face to Your face, give my heart to Your heart. If You do not forgive me, where would (sic) I go...I mention my faults (and say) forgive me. Now I want to say, I want to know Allah...and then I mention my faults..." (Interview Document No: 2 - Appendix 3).

One of the divine ḥadīth that plays a central role in people finding the 'mental space' for forgiving oneself is where God says in a Prophetic tradition that:

"O son of Adam, were your sins to reach the clouds of the sky and you were then to ask forgiveness of Me, I would forgive you..." (An-Nawawi 1977).

This kind of narrative provides a channel for making amends with God and with oneself. This also involves forgiving yourself and being certain that God in His mercy will forgive you. This then becomes a process of personal reconciliation and psychological healing.

One key aspect which is emerging especially amongst the residents is that they see changes within themselves and this is evident in a number of discussions that have been articulated in this case study. It is to be noted that most of them have been in the Centre for a relatively short time, with a few having been there for a much longer time (Fig. 5.4). The real test for the residents will be when they go back into mainstream society and integrate, seeing if their changes still hold and they do not revert to their old habits.

Serving Others and Solidarity (futuwwa and ukhuwwah) The concept of serving others is one of the central aspects in Islam. In this light, one of the residents says:

> "So now there is the one which I'm now encouraging our residents here. All these years you have never prayed. So when you come here the first thing is you must perform the compulsory prayer... and even taking your friend to the toilet, feeding him, helping him to change, dress up, clean his bed... sometimes it is more than the reward, higher than the prayer. Just one sought of counselling that we give, and that also becomes a motivation to them. So there will be a lot ukhuwwah (solidarity) and this feeling of brotherhood amongst these residents. Even reading the Qur'ān for the person—reminding of death—and of course saying remembrance of so they are encouraged to sit with the Qur'ān and help a lot. Even giving salams and greetings... so those are the things, small things but it makes a lot of difference." (Interview Document No: 4 - Appendix 3).

Several of the seekers volunteer at the Centre, doing gardening, cooking, cleaning and other acts of service. Serving others forms one of the cornerstones in '*tasawwuf*' (inward science) for developing the self since it enables one to go beyond oneself and one's ego, from being selfish to moving towards selflessness. This is the epitome of a self-actualized or spiritual being no matter what faith you belong to. In this light, Imam Qushayri (2002) outlines three fundamental aspects of true companionship: (1) keeping the companionship of those above you is essentially service; (2) those below you need sympathy and compassion in the one who is followed, and harmony and respect in the follower; (3) those who are peers, preferring others to oneself, while sustaining the standard of chivalry (futuwwa).

5.8 Wellbeing and the Worshipper

5.8.1 Impact on the Seeker

This section looks at the impact of worship and morality on the seeker, which subsumes their spiritual experiences. Here the holistic concept of worship is underlined, where it is not only confined to the recitation of the Qur'ān and the ritual prayers but also includes servitude to God and caring for others. Responding to the query, "What have you learnt from Tuan Guru? And how do you take that knowledge and make it your own?", the manager of Islamic Reflexology says:

"I have learnt when I am in front of him (Sheikh) there's a limpahan noor (flow of light). I feel that when he taught me the words of the Qur'ān...that there is more understanding, that is, what I learnt in that majlis (congregation), because so many..books you can read but you don't quite understand and here there is more understanding." (Interview Document No: 3 - Appendix 3).

The living connection between the seeker and the Sheikh is characterized in the flow of light (noor), that the manager describes. Light is traditionally symbolic of piety and divine knowledge, and its penetration into the heart is perhaps caused by the insight and explanations of the Sheikh himself. The above seeker further expresses his feelings:

"Other times, yes, that I feel that I am nobody. You feel *tawajjuh* ...although there is Prophet Mohammed the highest level but he is as a slave to Allah ' ubudiyya (slave). Then in person, there are a few on this level, for example, those with patience or sabr. First, we start with *tauba* (repentance), then the sabr (patience) and *shukr* (gratitude)...so at this level we will feel serious what people do to you...You go for kulliyyah (lectures) and then you come back late everyday...You have to be patient. A lot of patience. So when you are lucky enough to flourish for all this things you have to be patience and this sabr (patience) has very high potential." (Interview Document No: 3 - Appendix 3).

The concept of '*tawajjuh*' referred to here is "a process of spiritual inducement brought about by the special attention of an accomplished...master unto a seeker" (Khan 1976). He is touching upon the virtuous traits like repentance, patience, and gratitude that are required to flourish within oneself as per his own articulation. These three traits (repentance, patience, gratitude) were also flagged by respondents from both the Centre residents as well as the general seekers in the survey data (Figs. 5.9, 5.10, 5.13, and 5.14). Thus, these form key traits which are required to be inculcated in order to further the development of the self. Imam Junayd, Imam Ghāzali (both in Ghazali 1995 and Ibn Hazm al-Andalusi 1998) point to patience as one of the most fundamental virtues (see Sect. 2.5—table on virtues). The opposite of the spectrum of patience is anger, which has been indicated as the one of the worst traits both by the seekers themselves and this corroborates with their portrayal of it. The essential teaching by the Sheikh against anger is to be silent, say prayers, get advice from others, supplicate to God, be patient and say praise on the Prophet (salawāt).

Concerning ritual prayer, the feeling of wellbeing felt by the seekers as demonstrated in the interview quotes mentioned below, as well as indicated in the Figs. 5.23, 5.24, 5.25, and 5.26 corroborates the physiological effect of lowering of the heart rates during resting, sitting and especially during prostration (Table 5.1) and the state of relaxation by the lowering of brain waves activities, which falls with the alpha frequency range of 8–13 Hz (Table 5.2) during Muslim prayers (*salah*) and increases to the alpha rhythm coherence (Alwasiti, Aris and Jantan 2010). Another study (Doufesh, Ibrahim, Ismail and Ahmad 2014) found that during *salah*, there is a decrease in the sympathetic activities of the brain, while the parasympathetic one's increase (increase in the alpha wave activities in the occipital and the parietal regions of the brain), which seems to promote relaxation, minimize anxiety, and reduce cardiovascular risk. This is in concordance with another study (Doufesh, Faisal Lim et al. 2012), where an increase in the alpha waves was found particularly in the prostration position in *salah*.

5.8 Wellbeing and the Worshipper

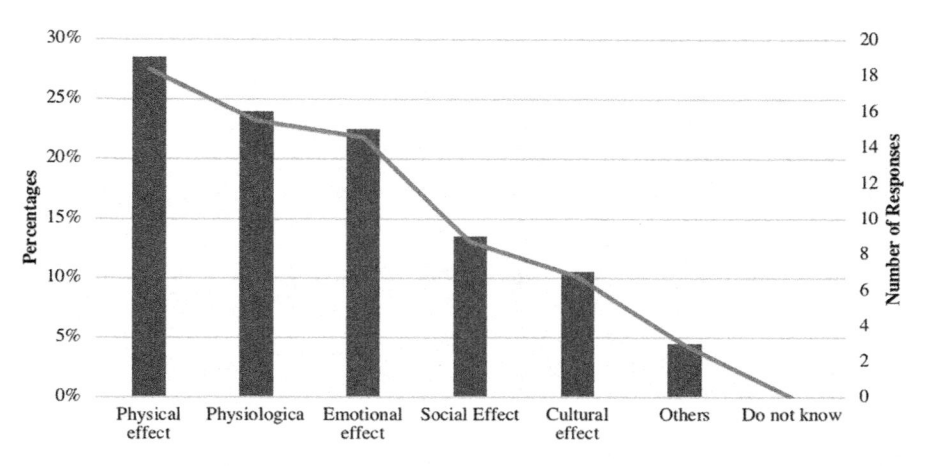

Fig. 5.23 Effects of worship on self

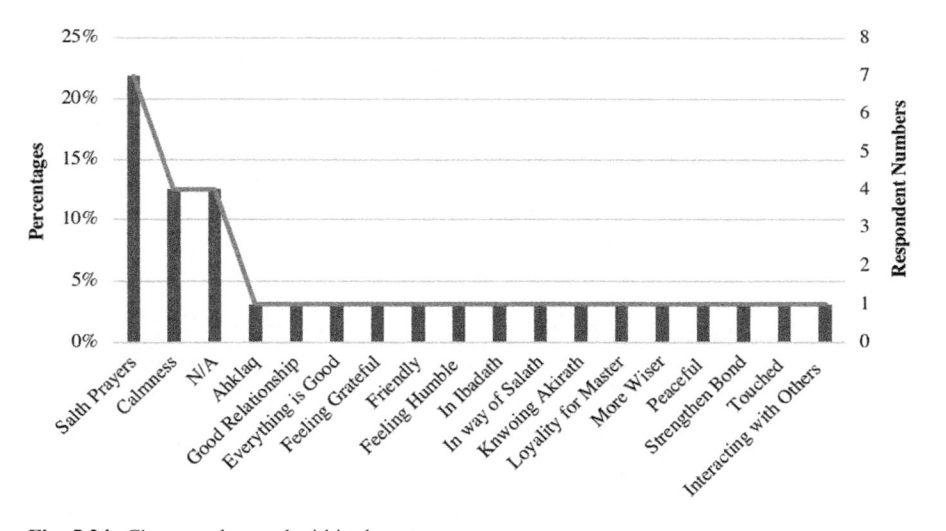

Fig. 5.24 Changes observed within the group

Two of the residents, including the resident Imam, who are transforming their lives, outline their learnings from the Tuan Guru through the kulliyyah or lecture exercise:

> "So like Tuan Guru said last night, there are ten traits: *baraka* (blessings), *shukr* (gratitude), *tawakkal* (trust), *tauba* (repentance), sabr (patience), zuhd (spiritual poverty), amal (hope), riḍa (acceptance) and takut (fear)." (They outline that): "So the brain and the heart are different. So Allah says, if you never use your brain and heart properly to *dhikr*, they must be (done) together. It must be in our brains and in our heart...that we do well, we get good from it and we stay good okay." (They say that): "You want to get it and you are not confident of getting it, day by day, you use your hand to make *du'ā*(supplication). *Du'ā*is something like you hope for..." (Interview Document No: 2 - Appendix 3).

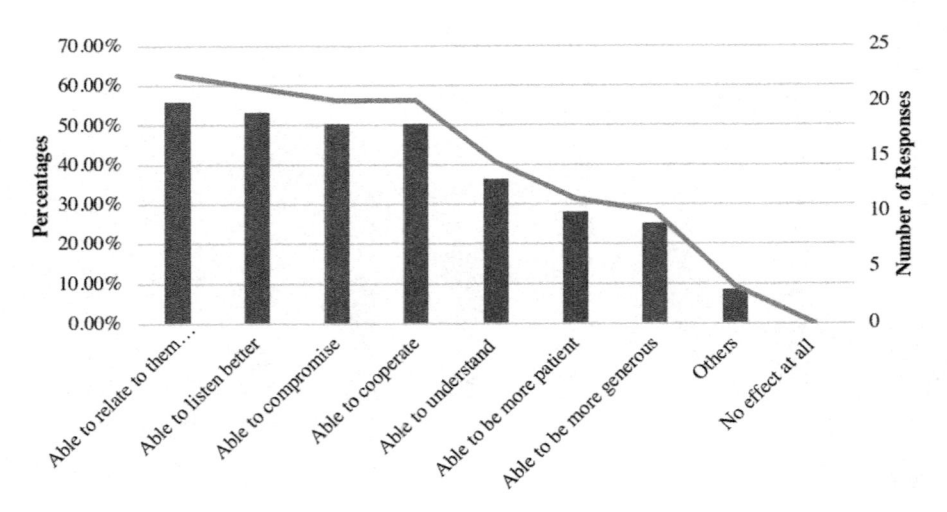

Fig. 5.25 Effects of worship on family and friends

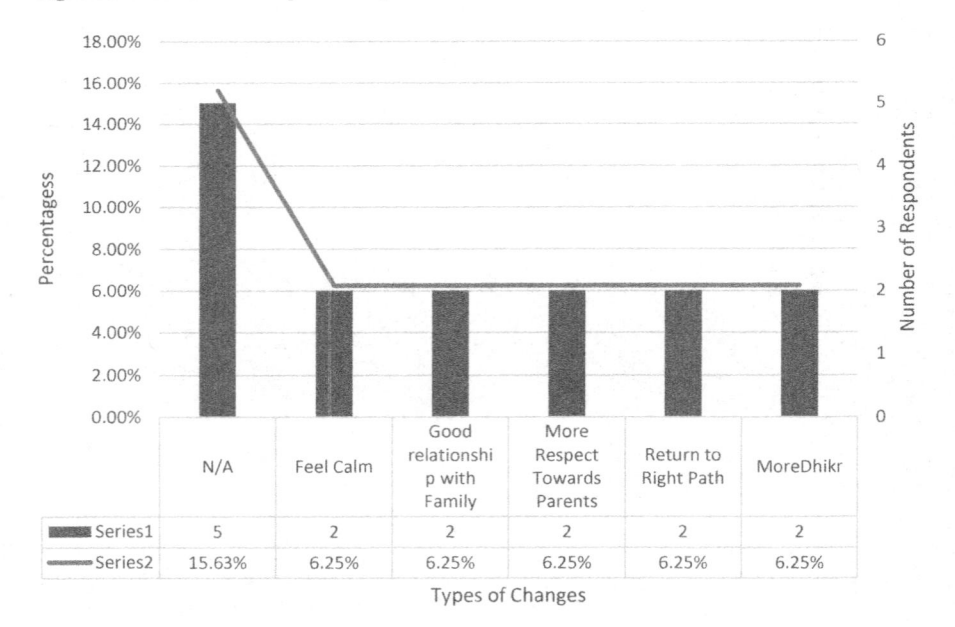

Fig. 5.26 Worship and behaviour

The above seekers reiterate that *riḍa* (acceptance):

"This is in God's will and not mine... you accept it. One needs to think about the ākhira (the next life), so that they have *baraka* (blessings) in this world and that they need to have *shukr* (grateful), *tawakkal* (trust) in Allah, *taubat* (repentance), *sabr* (patience), *takut* (fear) of Allah." (They continue): "If you get these 10 things then you are very close to Allah"

5.8 Wellbeing and the Worshipper

Table 5.1 Heart rate during ritual prayer (salah)

Average heart rate (beats per minute)		
Positions	Correct sequence	Reverse sequence
Resting	75	75
Standing	87	90
Bowing	79	81
Prostration	72	73
Sitting	78	78

Table 5.2 Type of Brain Waves during different states of consciousness

Type of Brain Wave	Frequency	Characteristic
Gamma	>30 Hz	Processing activity
Beta	13–30 Hz	Awake
Alpha	8–13 Hz	Relaxed state
Theta	4–8 Hz	Sleepy, half-awake
Delta	0.5–4 Hz	Deep sleep

(and): "That's why when we go to kulliyyah or our Guru is preaching we have to take notes. So when you can do all this, Allah will accept you or Allah will listen. You are looking for Him but you can't see Him but He can see you" (Interview Document No: 2 - Appendix 3).

The importance of the key traits highlighted by the seekers are shown in Fig. 5.13 as the most important for self-development being patience, humbleness, kindness, love, forgiveness and being honest.

There are two central aspects that they are discussing. Firstly, the ten virtuous traits that form the road on which one has to walk on the spiritual path. These core values are the drivers for change in one's behaviour and there is a concerted effort by the seekers to assimilate them. Secondly, the orientation of the next world within the framework of dunya-ākhira (this world-the next world), which gives the right perspective for immersion in these types of activities. This is a Prophetic perspective of living a truthful life in this world and preparing the next life, while being frequently reminded of impending death (see Sect. 2.6 on the spiritual life of the Prophet).

5.8.2 The Heart—Brain Connection

One of the most recurring themes that is very significant to this research is the frequent citation of the heart and brain connection, as it is captured in the various narratives of both the centre residents and seekers. The resident imam and his resident friend, when asked about the heart brain connection and whether it is something that they have heard from someone:

> "Our own and not... heard from someone." (asked about the type of heart-brain connection:) "For me, brain receives whatever we can think of... and the heart is very special..." (The friend adds:) "To me when I set my brain, all right, in my heart I say I cannot lie to myself.

I did that before, now I have changed a bit, so if I lie to people that means I have lied to myself. So, the brain connects to that. The brain and mind and the heart must come together as one, so when your brain sees something your heart must commit to it. We try hard..." (Interview Document No: 2 - Appendix 3).

An interesting convergence is made here in relation to intention, emotion, the process of thinking and realisation, where there is the brain—mind and heart coming together. Here he is referring to the mind, that is, a cognitive frame of reference, where the intention comes from, while with emotion he is referring to the heart—about 'not being able to lie now as before'. This indicates a form of interaction between the brain and the heart. Thus, it is not only the thought process, but the commitment of the heart and emotion that connects actions together. The resident imam responds to the question "Is there a difference between the brain and the heart?" by saying:

"Yes a difference, now, for example, you close your eyes...you look where your kitchen is in your house is, where is your book in your library you know...who sent the picture to your brain? Is it your brain? Only just, look at whatever, the heart can sense...the heart can go everywhere. The heart can move..." (Interview Document No: 2 - Appendix 3).

In reference to what he is saying, there could be a mix up between memory, imagination and the spiritual heart at one level, as from a metaphysical perspective, the memory is contained within the faculty of the spiritual heart as articulated by Ghazali (1995). This is a divergent view from a modern psychology, where memory resides in part of the brain.

The question was posed "So when you close your eyes and then you are going to the library, what is it, is it the heart or the brain?":

"Heart leads first then the brain. When you close your eyes, seems like you talk to your heart, like you talk to your brain. When you talk to my heart, I know where the book is. I have to tell you where the book is. You just go there and you pick the book. You know the book is there every day, you set the brain (and) you are moving your hand to take the book or to pick it...seems like what I said, the memory is in your heart...The memory is (your) heart and then the speed is in your brain...basically, the information that you collect by talking, hearing, tasting, touching all the senses that you are getting goes into the brain, and the brain will tell out what to do. But the heart is different...The heart is (open)when you close your eyes." (Interview Document No: 2 - Appendix 3).

Here there is an attempt to delineate the functions of the brain and the sensory perceptions, with that of the heart, which functions beyond the sense perception level, where reference is made to the heart becoming activated 'when you close your eyes'. The resident imam clarifies this concept further:

"I will make it simple, I give to you example, somebody is blind, he can go everywhere, why is this? Even as he sees, he can walk, he knows his way where there is a tree and that is the heart. Very simple, example that I will give you is that if from when you are born today you are blind. Logically if you are blind, you cannot see. Most things you know is by the hearing it because you cannot see." (Interview Document No: 2 - Appendix 3).

The friend of the resident imam says:

5.8 Wellbeing and the Worshipper

"Light...better than light. This proceeds inside your heart to your whole body. But sometimes we can connect with people by using our hearts and our minds." (Interview Document No: 4 - Appendix 3).

Here the respondent is relating this to telepathy and how the heart scans and detects persons, whom you happened to be thinking about. The description ties with the nature of the soul, which Ghazali (1995) uses synonymously with the heart having the power to know through the process of intuition. In referring to the Qur'ān, the above resident poses a series of questions and then responds to it himself:

"In the Qur'ān, Allah said We say *salawat* (praise on the Prophet). So why do you never do that? For me, why are you never following Rasulullah (Prophet) like my Guru, do all the practices - sunnah. I mentioned to myself that I must do that." (Who taught you to recite and that you do many things?) "It comes from Allah...Tuan Guru does amal (good deeds). To do something you must do it properly, while struggling smartly and then get it with your brain and your heart. Your brain and your heart are the same, you learn al-Fātiḥa (opening Qur'ānic chapter) your brain and your mouth say Alhamdulillah about al-Fātiḥa your heart will read al-Fātiḥa." (Interview Document No: 2 - Appendix 3).

The resident imam is pointing out the heart-brain connection, where there is synchronism of intention and worship. One has to learn to practice and this is where one needs cognition, where memory is involved, while any act that you are doing only becomes meaningful when the heart feels it and thus it becomes internalised.

The resident imam and another resident point to an interesting aspect of worship (Interview Document No: 2—Appendix 3):

"That's why in the Qur'ān Allah said...you (are) listening, are you hearing....Allah teaches you how good your eyes, ears and your mouth are, where there is rhythm....That process is faster better than light. This proceed inside your heart and your whole body."

He demonstrates this by using an example:

"You have seen like that you go to around the supermarket, you see somebody crossing you. Your heart says is this Dr. Ahmed. Suddenly he faces you, says hi to you...your heart is very powerful. He does not hear you, he doesn't know whether you are around, then he is facing you...it is a heart connection." (Interview Document No: 2 - Appendix 3).

Here the seeker is outlining a process of telepathy, some may call it a coincidence, where a person's thought (in the heart) is perceived by another without the cognitive faculties being involved. He relates this ability to the heart, which is able to feel and connect with the thoughts and emotions of another. One could attribute this to coincidence but if this occurs more than once, the tendency is to think otherwise. Your existing hypothesis is reinforced, which George Kelly (1963) terms the human constructs of the evolving reality around us, where what you experience becomes internalised and your working hypotheses are reinforced by live and repeated examples.

The manager of reflexology (Interview Document No: 3—Appendix 3) outlines some aspects of the inner transformation, and when asked about this switch from head to heart says:

"That switch we have to mention (is) Allah's name, he only gives you that nice *iman* (faith), he can only give you the life (sic). So you have to mention his name everyday morning and night, day and night until it breaks through... sometime people get sometime people don't get."

He then quotes a Qur'ānic verse:

$$\text{اَلَّذِينَ يَذْكُرُونَ اللَّهَ قِيَامًا وَقُعُودًا وَعَلَىٰ جُنُوبِهِمْ وَيَتَفَكَّرُونَ فِي خَلْقِ السَّمَاوَاتِ وَالْأَرْضِ رَبَّنَا مَا خَلَقْتَ هَذَا بَاطِلًا سُبْحَانَكَ فَقِنَا عَذَابَ النَّارِ}$$

"Those who remember Allah standing, sitting, and lying down on their sides, and think deeply about the creation of the heavens and the earth, (saying): Our Lord! You have not created this without purpose, glory to You! Give us salvation from the torment of the Fire." (Qur'ān, al Imran, 3:191)

The first part of the Qur'anic statement refers to mindful remembrance of God in all stages of one's action and movement. The second part of the statement points to a deep state of reflection on the earth that we inhabit with all its fauna and flora and the human existence and its intricate relationship with the ecosystem, as well as the universe with its constellations and rhythmic orbit and functions. Here the term 'breakthrough' is mentioned by the above seeker to describe getting into the realm of God consciousness, where the mundane mind set is broken through by an 'opening' from God into another realm. This is one aspect that has emerged in some interviews of nearness to God, and having a type of spiritual experience, which is elaborated on in the next section.

5.8.3 Impact of Worship on Self and Others

The state of mind before prayers forms a base line to understand varying levels of consciousness (see Fig. 5.27). For most, when they approach ritual prayer, they state that they are calm (69%), while others have a range of emotions including agitation and anxiousness (both 22%), with frustration (9%) and anger (6%) following.

Apart from the obligatory acts of worship, which constitute the ritual five times daily prayers, there were several acts of voluntary worship cited (see Fig. 5.22), which signify different types of worship, with the highest scores being: supplication to God (75%), loud group *dhikr* (72%) and optional prayers (69%). The silent group *dhikr* as well as silent individual *dhikr* scored 62% followed by darood or recital on the Prophet (59%) and listening to sermons (50%).

The various acts of worship were listed and the respondents ranked them in their order of priority, with the scores being as follows: silent individual *dhikr* ranked first (22%), while 19% did not provide a score. This was followed by *dhikr* in general (16%), followed by ritual prayers both obligatory and voluntary having a score of 6% (Fig. 5.12).

As seen in Fig. 5.23, the respondents were asked to score the effects of worship on their general wellbeing, with the highest being the physical effects (28%), followed

5.8 Wellbeing and the Worshipper

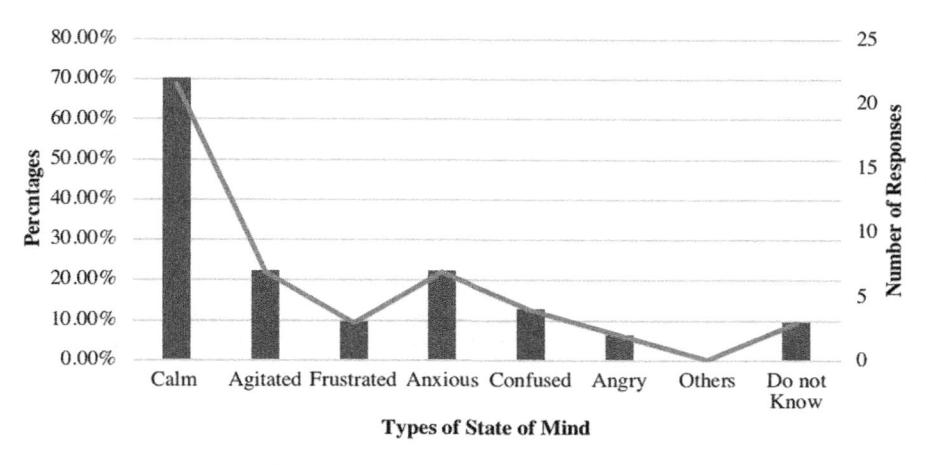

Fig. 5.27 State of mind before prayers

by physiological (23%), emotional (28%), social (13%) and cultural (10%), with a small response for other non-defined options (4%). All of these responses indicate a sense of wellbeing by being involved in the various acts of worship. This can be linked to the emerging evidence within neuroscience of the wellbeing of people involved in acts of worship and meditation and this is elaborated on in Chap. 6 (see Munsoor and Munsoor 2017).

In Fig. 5.19, 18% of the respondents observed 'changes within oneself after joining the group', while highlighting the types of changes ranging from: in 'the way I treat myself' and 'the way I talk to people' both scoring 16% each. This is followed by 'the way I behave with my friends and family' (14%), 'the way I treat those who are less privileged' (13%), 'the way I do my acts of worship' (12%), and 'the way I conduct my day to day life' (11%). It is to be noted that these groups of seekers had changed their lifestyle and intensified both their obligatory and optional acts of worship. This sense is expressed as feelings of wellbeing as some of the discussions that follows indicates.

As shown in Fig. 5.24, two marked changes were observed by the seekers within their respective groups, that is people observing their *salah* prayers on a regular basis (22%), accompanied by 'a sense of calmness' (13%). There were several other changes indicated, with much lower scores including 'better morality' (akhlāq), 'having good relationships', 'feeling good', 'feeling grateful' etc., each having a standard score of 3%. Figure 5.24 represents the effects of worship on family and friends, with the highest scores being, 'the ability to better relate to them' (63%), 'ability to better listen' (59%), and 'ability to compromise' as well 'as cooperate', being both 5%. Also mentioned were 'to better understand' (41%), 'be more patient' (31%) and 'be generous towards others' (28%).

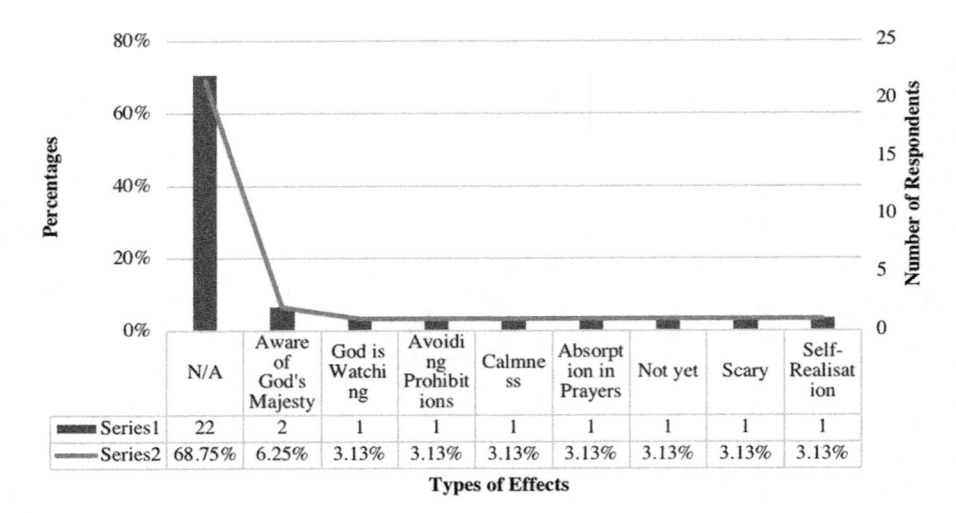

Fig. 5.28 Spiritual experiences

Types of Effects	N/A	Aware of God's Majesty	God is Watching	Avoiding Prohibitions	Calmness	Absorption in Prayers	Not yet	Scary	Self-Realisation
Series1	22	2	1	1	1	1	1	1	1
Series2	68.75%	6.25%	3.13%	3.13%	3.13%	3.13%	3.13%	3.13%	3.13%

5.8.4 Spiritual Experiences

When it comes to sharing information about spiritual experiences, there is a natural reluctance and this is evident from the survey data or it could be that they did not have any spiritual experiences or find it difficult to describe it (Fig. 5.28). Only a few responded, while a large number did not respond at all. For the few who responded, some of the experiential aspects were being aware of the Majesty of God, a state where God is watching you, having the courage to avoid prohibitive things, having a sense of calmness and absorption in prayers, while one reported having a sense of fear as well as self-realisation. All of these reasons can be considered as anchors that are necessary to bring about the needed focus in contemplation or meditation.

From the interview data, there were a number of items including dreams that comes true, kinds of telepathy, premonitions and some states of mind that were not possible to capture in words but some examples have been already cited in the cases of the resident imam, as well as the head of reflexology. In terms of the most profound learning (Fig. 5.29) achieved from joining the organisation, this ranged from calmness (16%), learning silence (6%) and group remembrance (9%), increased understanding (3%), being mindful of others (3%) and greater peacefulness, while there were respondents who did not state anything (44%).

The evidence of the impact of worship and morality on the seekers mentioned in this chapter and derived from the data-set (interviews and survey) from both from the Sheikh and the seekers will be discussed in the light of the emerging humanistic and neuroscientific evidence in Chap. 6.

These points of significance of worship are corroborated by the survey data as seen in the figures and what was the most profound spiritual experience was

5.8 Wellbeing and the Worshipper

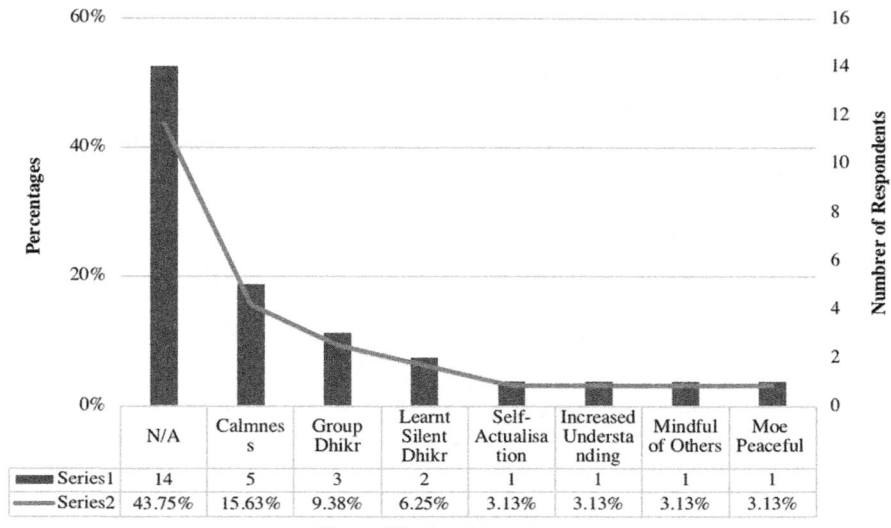

	N/A	Calmness	Group Dhikr	Learnt Silent Dhikr	Self-Actualisation	Increased Understanding	Mindful of Others	Moe Peaceful
Series1	14	5	3	2	1	1	1	1
Series2	43.75%	15.63%	9.38%	6.25%	3.13%	3.13%	3.13%	3.13%

Types of Profound Learnings

Fig. 5.29 Most profound learning

awareness of the Majesty of God (Fig. 5.28) and the first ranked beneficial act being 'individual silent *dhikr*' (Fig. 5.12).

A seeker further explains the essence of *dhikr*:

> "In 1994 or 1995, I was with Sheikh J. Sidiq [current Sheikh] after that I gained something that is through *dhikrullah*. Allah teaches us. When Allah is not happy you can see the things that are from Satan... our focus now is *dhikrullah* and just asking about Allah and seeing that when you *dhikrullah* there is something coming into your ear, something or someone is whispering to you... when you close your eyes you can see something inside there. That is stopping you from *dhikrullah*, actually this is the obstacle that stops you from thinking of *dhikrullah*." (Interview Document No: 7 - Appendix 3).

This *waswās*, the inner whisperings that prompt to evil, is explicated in the Qur'ān, al-Nās, verse 114, which as the seeker explains, diverts one from the path of God. This can be linked to the concept of darkness, which if indulged in can take you down, while the concept of light, which is being God conscious, is that which takes you to God.

The Sheikh underlines that *dhikr* means "mindfulness in consciousness, meaning you don't think of anything else apart from Allah." The translator of the Sheikh explains:

> "What the Guru says is you have to do something about it and one of the main methods we use is *dhikr*. When Ali (companion of the Prophet) asked Rasulullah (Prophet) to teach him *'ibādah*, the best *'ibādah*, he said, you must *dhikrullah* to strengthen your *iman*.... you don't learn very much, you also have to go for his (the Sheikh's) classes and learn about the actual practice of the *dhikr* and the *ṭarīqa* (the Order)." (Interview Document No: 5 - Appendix 3).

The concept of mindfulness which is currently a growing trend globally (Esch 2014), essentially means to become aware of oneself and one's thoughts without evaluating it. The context of the Sheikh's usage of it refers to a heightened sense of awareness of yourself and of God watching you (murāqaba). A seeker expounds on distinguishing experiences and the need for a Master:

> "After all, only sometimes one does (experience) and it is a gift from God actually. But there is another thing that it could also be the devil, but you must be able to distinguish and that is the main reason why we have the Guru. You have to tell your experience to the Guru. During the *dhikr* I feel like some sort of vision, visualize, but the most important part, is the part that you feel within your heart. So that is the reason why we have to be close to the Guru, and there is this terminology ṣoḥba, the closeness with the Prophet. So sometimes, if there is any problem you approach the Guru and tell him this is my problem and especially with regard to somethings..." (Interview Document No: 1 - Appendix 3).

In this tradition of *tasawwuf* (inward science), the need for the Sheikh is paramount since everyone needs to be guided, especially in relation to religion and developing one's character.

The Centre manager says, "All the *dhikr* that we do is *jihar*...No sound or anything, all from the soul." He was queried if '*jihar*' was the loud *dhikr* to which he responds:

> "In fact, if you may interpret it, you're actually letting your soul do, this is the concept of wuquf qalbi. So, that is wuquf qalbi, there's no work, there's no sound. It's nothing actually. But we sort of trigger the heart by pushing the beads... it's all in the soul. It's all in the soul." (Interview Document No: 1 - Appendix 3).

He describes using the prayer beads in a way that creates a clicking sound and he was asked, is that why you do the pushing of the bead, he answers:

> "That's a trigger, because as long as it moves, they install ... then the inside is removed." (You mean it synchronizes?) and "Yes synchronizes. Not necessarily because even if you touch ..one... it is triggered." (The researcher observed that during the *dhikr* sessions there was no noise except for a clicking sound. This seekers was thus asked the question, "How can you count 5,000 times?") "The *jihar* (loud) part, if possible and time permits we need to do at least 1,000. There we spend about half an hour— twenty minutes to half an hour to get to 1,000 times *jihar*. But in the 1,000s is so quick actually... a few seconds." (Do you repeat Allah, Allah, and Allah?) "Yes, so quickly... It's just like electronics-mechanical... We have the mechanical clock— tick, tick, tick, tick, but the initiation is via your batteries and also you are (basically) electronic within. We also have the digital cloak which is electronic, fully electronic and that has no moving parts. The same thing is with *jihar* and *sirr*. *Jihar* is a moving part because you have to move your lips and your vocal chords." (Interview Document No: 1 - Appendix 3).

The symbolic metaphor here is to the internal landscape within oneself having a clock work mechanism, which is activated by a physical trigger process, in this case the prayer beads, which in turn infuse the name of God within one's heart. When asked about the nature of silent *dhikr* (*sirr*), the resident Imam says it is, "Depth of heart. The waswās (whispering), where you fight back—you get whatever you want to do." In terms of it having an effect on him and what kind of an effect, he says, "Yes! Contended or happy, not anger only love." He reflected that the most

5.8 Wellbeing and the Worshipper

important thing he had learnt was, "*Dhikr* first...it changed my life. Before I do *salah* but no *dhikr* or 'top up'. It has the power shine or 'top up.' "When asked about its effect, he outlines:

> "Self-healing from inside...need for guidance from the Sheikh. Need to change and not be a hypocrite. Thinking of how to change. When I came here 360 degree change – the environment, stories, study, *dhikr* ...The *dhikr, sirr* and *jihar* changed my mind and habit and after feel peace." (Interview Document No: 2 - - Appendix 3).

It is underlined here that the link of *dhikr* with the heart produces a state of nearness to God that facilitates the transformation that takes place as a result of it. The survey data corroborates this sense of peace or calmness by the seekers (Figs. 5.7, 5.23, 5.24, 5.25, 5.26, 5.27, and 5.28), and this can be validated by the neuroscience data (Ibrahim et al. 2008), which indicates the changing pattern of alpha brain waves and a creation of a sense of relaxation and peace due to certain neurological processes that occur (elaborated in the next chapter). The most profound learning of the seekers is reflected in Fig. 5.29. What emerges is the integrated nature of the approach to transformation, which subsumes spirituality, methods, tools and the various aspects of the organisation including the leadership of the Sheikh.

The question was posed to the manager of the Centre, who has been with the Sheik for 17 years, about what he has learnt and how he has translated this into his life. He outlines that:

> "To begin with, it goes back to the principles of the practice of the *dhikr*. The symbols of the practice of *dhikr*, where there will probably will be the changes from one maqām (spiritual station) to the other. Everybody has to experience the first one, probably even me." (Interview Document No: 1 - Appendix 3).

The reference here is to the changing states of consciousness, which comes through practice, where seekers move from one spiritual station to the other. This is described as a journey that the seeker goes through and this is well articulated in some scholarly works (Suhrawardi 1991, Muhasibi 1950). Ghazali (1995) states:

Qualification (*wasf*) is called "station" (*maqam*) if it is stable and endures and it is called "state of soul" (*hāl*) if it passes away and disappears without delay...What is not stable is called "state of soul" because it disappears to give its place to another state rapidly. This is true of all the qualifications of the heart.

The above seeker adds:

> "I was saying about the changes, because to me – this is my whole sort of impression – if you're practicing *dhikr* then probably if you're totally involved then you would achieve faster...to the seven stages or something like that. But because I am engaged with a lot of worldly things and roles, it is not that easy to come to destiny, because you need total devotion, it is important in terms...of course I have sort of neglected my duty and my ability to do *dhikr* and join the congregation, listen to the talks by the Guru or the guidance. And in cases they have to make decisions in everything. I normally refer to him for advice." (Interview Document No: 2 - Appendix 3).

What is pointed to here is the difficulties of progressing through the seven stages of consciousness[8] due to diversion caused by worldly distractions. These seven states of consciousness are articulated in Sect. 2.1 (Figure 2.2). This aspect of learning is further expounded by him:

> "Yes, if you follow up the Naqshabandiyyah discipline, every day you must *dhikr* and you hope Allah can help you... You are trying to be a *khalīfah* (vicegerent on earth)... if you *dhikr* for 15 years then Allah will give you something you've never thought about before... Your brain will think a lot faster... You must take the time. One day you must make time for Allah, maybe two hours out of 24 hours. For me that is not enough. Every day, the entire day you must *khusus* (special) ... someone says that is time due to Allah only. Nobody should disturb you, give your heart..." (He questions himself) "Why did you not do *salah* today? Why did you not *dhikr* last night? and then you give a bad reason, no way." (Interview Document No: 2 - Appendix 3).

Here he points to the need to allocate time for worship, for the remembrance of God. Evident in his above statement is the employment of the concept of *muhasaba*, taking oneself to account, (see Sect. 2.3) and an increased level of awareness that one brings upon oneself, called *nafs-al-lawwama* or the critical self (see Sect. 2.1 and Fig. 2.1). The resident imam continues:

> "Every day at a certain time you must just say, Allah. Allah, help me. Allah gives me *rizq* ..give me to eat... So, how do we say thank you to Allah – it is by doing or praying and take two hours out of 24 hours. Leave your work and sit... and in early morning it is you and Allah... I want to know, where the willpower comes from? Who gives it to you? I learnt that— the thing for me is (the) very very depths of my heart... now, if you do this, if you wake up at 2 o'clock in the morning and go up to *subhu* (morning prayers) and again sleep for a while and like somebody shakes you... and then you take a bath prepare you and say Allah. So, in here, I get it... so, before you want to stick to your thinking. When your eyes are closed, you sleep. Now, I don't think like that. If your heart sleeps, you sleep. If your heart does something like Allah, Allah, Allah, you'll never sleep. Its only your eyes that are closed. Your heart is still carrying on – Allah, Allah. That is a good for your *nafs* (self). I do fasting. My people get lunch while I fast. I come sit around and they see that I'm fasting." (Interview Document No: 2 - Appendix 3).

There are some vital aspects that are underlined in the above narrative. Firstly, the sense of gratitude by offering prayers, Secondly, making 'space' for oneself by allocating time to contemplate. Thirdly, his reflection and willpower, where it translates into what he says, 'the very very depths of my heart'. Fourthly, the need for consistency in one's actions. Fifthly, the change of habit patterns to wake up early. Finally, the internalisation of the *dhikr*, which, if done properly and regularly, manifests itself even at a subconscious level.

The professional banker outlines his experience with *dhikr*:

> "When you *dhikrullah* (the act of doing *dhikr*) you are happy. You know before, I was hot tempered and it is very difficult to *dhikr*. Before treatment early morning after *subuh* we

---

[8]It is to be pointed out that, apart from the seven stages of consciousness outlined in figure 2.2, there are also the seven stations or maqamats that a salik or spiritual traveller goes through, that is, repentance (tawba), wara (repentance), zuhd (renunciation), faqr (poverty(, sabr (patience), tawakkul (trust) and satisfaction (rida).

5.8 Wellbeing and the Worshipper

have to *dhikr* first and that is 22,000 times and then *salah* (ritual prayer)...because you know if the patient tends to be good or bad, it's from Allah. It's not us. We only just do our job. We are from Allah. It is Him that we ask to cure this human." (Interview Document No: 7 - Appendix 3).

The reference to treatment here is to Islamic reflexology, which is done to get rid of physical ailments, as well as mental impurities. This is preceded by intense *dhikr* and a self-realisation that the origin of one's whole being is from God and that He is the Healer, while Satan on the other hand afflicts you. The above seeker continues:

"Allah says we argue, we get sick because of Satan...So that I can always remember and *dhikrullah* to you...But it is just for Allah my life, my tongue and my whole being. I want to *dhikr* and then here, so in verse 41–42...Allah said..."

He cites the Qur'ān in relation to this:

$$\text{وَاذْكُرْ عَبْدَنَا أَيُّوبَ إِذْ نَادَىٰ رَبَّهُ أَنِّي مَسَّنِيَ الشَّيْطَانُ بِنُصْبٍ وَعَذَابٍ}$$
$$\text{ارْكُضْ بِرِجْلِكَ هَٰذَا مُغْتَسَلٌ بَارِدٌ وَشَرَابٌ}$$

"And remember Our servant Ayyub (Job), when he invoked his Lord (saying): Verily, Satan has afflicted me with distress and torment. (Allah said to him) Strike the ground with your foot. This is (a spring of) water to wash in, cool and a drink." (Sad 38:41–42)

The banker further explains:

"Allah said are you keeper of the earth and there will be very cool water coming out. So you take your bath there and drink it. So that is the problem of drinking water with ice. So the Western people they say, it is not good for your health, they say it is not good but in Islam but it is very good...." (Interview Document No: 7 - Appendix 3).

The concept of the cool being good for you and the hot being not is not a mainstream Islamic view but a certain interpretation or perspective of this verse. As a part of the Islamic reflexology treatment, an ice water bath is given as a means to purification to try and cleanse oneself.

In response to the question, "What else have you learnt from the Sheikh and other peers?", the friend of the resident imam says:

Through friends by watching and hearing how to *dhikr* and how to do it in the right way to *dhikr*, like Fātiḥa (prayers) to Tuan Guru, and through our eyes we can really concentrate after *dhikr* and we see that we are dying and will be buried. (Interview Document No: 4 - Appendix 3).

This reference to 'watching and hearing' and doing are key aspects of Modelling the Sheikh and the peers, apart from the remembrance of God. It is a Prophetic tradition to remember death every day, so that it sobers one's mind and gives it the right perspective. However, a point to note is that 'one should not long for death' (Al Bukhari 1994) as the Prophetic tradition states, since life is precious and one needs to maximise one's time on earth. The friend of the resident imam, when asked how he thought the personality of people changes, answered, "Because I saw the changes. You see myself, I am actually a soft person I like to help people, I like to do things right, so the thing then come to me so it's more better and better each day." (Document no:4 Appendix 3). He was then asked, "What things come to you?", to which he says:

> "To help people here like on their last few months. I met my roommate and then he passed away, so if I don't change myself I will be like him... but he cannot do anything, cannot get up by himself, cannot eat by himself, you must feed him and so I don't want to be like him. I want to die peacefully on my bed, without any sickness that I won't trouble people, I don't like to trouble people. My late father said you are so soft hearted, even when you don't have money you like to help people. When I have money, I will spend on my friends. When I have, I will give, when I don't have I don't mind, I will help people but I know Allah will give me..." (Interview Document No: 4 - Appendix 3).

This reflects a heightened sentience (the capacity to feel, perceive or experience subjectively) and a greater receptiveness to his surroundings, that allow him to draw lessons from it and improve his life. The above resident here outlines some of the obstacles of the path:

> "But yes, like Allah says, I will send Satan to disturb you. To see how well you can fight yourself. I hope one day I will be someone to help to cure people and I will bring more friends here to change their lives like what I have been through... I tried to bring someone but it's difficult, he cannot set his mind and soul here, so he stayed for round one week and went away, he is on drugs too. But I like to bring friends who really want to change their lives, to anyone who wants to get involved with *dhikr*. I would like to do that I still got a lot to learn from Guru and the *dhikr* group." (Interview Document No: 4 - Appendix 3).

Here is someone who seems to be changing for the better, with an aspiration to heal others, as well as to bring about changes to others who have an issue of addiction. When he says that he brought a friend who was a drug addict, who later left, he points to the fact that there needs to be a degree of self-realisation on the part of the seeker and a will in order to change. In terms of learning from the group itself, the above seeker points out:

> "How to really give, how to really pronounce the word *dhikr* and listen how they *dhikr* in the right way... Yes this is from the seniors and one day I would like to *belajar* (learn) to *dhikr* in one place for several hours then we can get into the real *dhikr*..." (Interview Document No: 4 - Appendix 3).

This indicates an example of how the seekers try to model their peers, not only the Sheikh, in this case for learning the method of *dhikr*. This supportive learning is found to be a key facilitative element amongst the seekers.

The resident nurse discusses her lack of encounter with the Sheikh:

> "Where is the truth, what am I doing down there and how I missed the lectures? I miss going to the *tawajjuh* (spiritual attention from the Sheikh) but how am I going? I feel that basically helpless. So when you tafakkur (reflect) and of course the *dhikr*, I do it every day." (Interview Document No: 6 - Appendix 3).

When asked if the Sheikh taught her *dhikr*, she says:

> "We ladies, we do the loud one when we go to Tuan Guru's house. And we only do the *dhikr* (silent); that one is a daily practice, we have to do it. Before the food, once a day but it is better to do... just once a day, even that (when) you miss, you really feel so sad like really

5.8 Wellbeing and the Worshipper

you have lost something and then so just let Allah open the passage." (Interview Document No: 6 - Appendix 3).

Here she is pointing to being with the Sheikh and receiving his spiritual attention (*tawajjuh*), the reflection (tafakkur) here is on 'soḥba' or being with the Sheikh, while interacting with him and listening to what he has to say and trying to emulate him. It is noted that the women are not excluded from the activities as the researcher observed their participation in the Sheikh's house. Here, men and women sit separately from each other but do the same *dhikr* and listen to the same lectures. When asked about how the *dhikr* has affected her, she says:

> "*Dhikr* has of course affected me a lot, it's the basis of our existence, the more you practice *dhikr* and the more you are closer (to God). The Guru always tells us that everything, the whole universe... all are in *dihkrullah* (remembrance of God), so how come we are not in *dihkrullah*?. So that is a lot to do with *tafakkur* (reflecting). We have to do that a lot and that will affect... on your *akhlāq* (morality). You have to let Allah nourish you with that." (Interview Document No: 6 Appendix 3I).

The above seeker adds that:

> "It is a gift (*dhikr* and its manifestations) because when you find difficulty you have to let Allah help you with that... If Allah feels like you're ready to be gifted then Allah gifts you at that time. So, you cannot be impatient knowing that you put yourself in that station, which is not meant for you, yet so that is wrong and that's when all the nafs and the Satan will all come in. So, you always have to be aware about the practice of *dhikr* (that) is so important. You always have to be aware that Satan is always trying to destroy the relationship with the Khāliq (Creator). Realise the position of 'abd (servant) the more you feel that you are 'abd, keep polishing as the Tuan Guru says until you die..."(Interview Document No: 6 - Appendix 3).

There are three fundamental aspects that she is outlining, firstly, of doing *dhikr* through a cognitive process of reflection (tafakkur) using the mind. Secondly, the *dhikr* that you do through your heart, where you separate the mundane thought process by focus on the name or attributes of God. Thirdly, she is alluding to the 'whispering' or 'waswās' that one's experiences in the process, where one needs persevere until God gives one spiritual openings. Fourthly, the concept of 'abd-Khāliq (slave-Creator), which defines the position of humans in relation to God, enabling him/her to humble themselves to the Lord, while gaining the aptitude to serve others and could enable the casting of the ego aside. She clarifies further the relationship between worship and morality:

> "'*Ibādah* (worship) also has an impact on your *akhlāq* (morality)... Guru also impact on your *akhlāq* because when you also keep getting close to (God) because almost every day, as long as there's a lecture (and) rules... in the mosque... We always follow, so therein (is) the lessons that he imparts to us, also knowledge... for people who remember *akhlāq* (morality) it's not just that we stay at home. Our *'ibādah* at home is not only on the *'ibādah* even when you are treating other people or looking after the sick, it's all *'ibādah* isn't it? So whatever you do, the servitude to the Lord, then it is the *'ibādah*..." (Interview Document No: 6 - Appendix 3).

She outlines several factors that impact morality including worship, the teaching of the Sheikh, and the rules of fiqh (Islamic law). In her articulation of the holistic concept of worship, she points out that servitude to God's creation is servitude to God.

The resident Imam was asked about his expectation when he joined the organisation:

"Let's say I want Allah to forgive me whatever I have done before. The rubbish things of my *akhlāq* (morality)...nobody can say what is wrong with you...but then you still must follow up and then...when you do, like you leave the wrong parts...if you do it day by day, you start to feel how small you are. If Allah doesn't hurt you, nobody can do anything, Allah will not let it happen. Now that trusting of Allah is 100%." (Interview Document No: 2 - Appendix 3).

Now the above seeker questions himself:

"Before you just say that Allah gives your life, so I go anywhere, I don't know how to *salah*, I don't do fasting, I don't do *salawat* (praise on the Prophet). So why are you (sic) like that? And you know the punishment is very very hard.... say whatever, it is Allah who gives punishment? It is the longing, not forgetting everything. I learned (and) know that I am very scared." (Interview Document No: 2 - Appendix 3).

The seeker here identifies his past life of sins as being the cause that led him to seek the path to forgiveness and God's pleasure. The path is undertaken through consistent steps, "day by day" focusing on the heart, and by realising humility before God, "a small being". He outlines the need to fully trust God, which is the concept of tawakkul (exert effort and then put your trust in God), who is the Source of everything. When asked "How do these experiences happen to you?", he points out that:

"There is *sulook* for 10 days (retreat), I go to it one time,.... la ilaha ilallah (no God but God)...One whole day you must *dhikr*, and then sleep for only like two hours and then wake up and take a shower and then *dhikr*...you can do the *salah* and all this...All of this maybe around 100,000 (times of remembrance) or over in around ten days and then when your heart be changed, you also see as Guru says how it's easy, my heart is very relaxed, cool..." (Interview Document No: 2 - Appendix 3).

This is getting into the depths of remembrance of God, with the Sheikh guiding, where you, yourself, are pushing beyond normal boundaries. The concept of '*uzla*' (retreat) leads the heart or oneself to become more composed and relaxed, which is backed by the emerging evidence of neuro-science (Fatima et al. 2008), where vital signs like the basal metabolism slows down. It is beneficial to the mind-body (see Sect. 2.4) and corroborated by the seekers in the survey in terms of achieving wellbeing or state of calmness (Figs. 5.7, 5.23, 5.24, 5.25. 5.26, 5.28, and 5.29). When queried about the Sheikh's role and the experience, the above seeker says:

"How are you different during the 10 days in *sulook* . You do *dhikr*...Allah, Allah, Allah. Rukun *iḥsan* (pillars of excellence/virtue/sincerity), you know *iḥsan*, if you do *'ibādah* Allah sees you, even though you never get to see Allah. There is a word with a secret meaning...only just Allah and you (know)...that is secret (between) you and Allah alone." (Interview Document No: 2 - Appendix 3).

5.8 Wellbeing and the Worshipper

The actual experience of indulging in *dhikr* is cited here, where the personal connection one feels with God is clear in his words "secret between you and Allah alone.". A reference is made to the concept of '*iḥsan*', which has a range of meanings from virtue to excellence and sincerity, this is a door to gain proximity to God. There has been much emphasis on repentance or *tauba*, and he describes its process and its ensuing merits:

> ...(When asked is that intention and how often he does it, he says:) "Yes to clean my heart, mind, my arms, zahir (outer) and my body for the wrong before...it is for thanking Allah and then you take shower. Before that you must take *wuḍū'* (ritual ablution)...every time you go to God." (Interview Document No: 2 - Appendix 3).

The process here is gaining outer cleanliness and then through repentance gaining the way to inner cleanliness from the wrong that one has done to one's body and mind. The *wuḍū'* or ritual purification is a preparation for prayers and constitute both the physical and the mental washing away of any sins that one has done through the five senses. When asked whether the Sheikh had told him this, the seeker says:

> "Yes. Five times and then do another...ruku (bowing), *sujjud* (prostrating) same *fard* (obligation) and then you get chance then do second *rak'a* (one complete ritual prayer cycle). Then you repeat al-Fātiḥa (opening verse of the Qur'ān) one time and then second in the Qur'ān, al-Ikhlas (Qur'ān, 112)...three times. And then you will do *sujjud* it is always like *salah fard* (obligatory prayers) and then salaams of the prayer (taslīm) ...take your *tasbih* (prayer beads)...and then has been inside your heart *astaghfirullah*...that means Allah forgive me." (Interview Document No: 2 - Appendix 3).

The process of seeking repentance which has been taught by the Sheikh in this case involves a kind of ritual prayer, while using the *tasbih* refers to a louder form of *dhikr* and then seeking forgiveness within yourself.

The professional artist discusses his expectations from joining this organisation:

> "One thing is that when I came here, I only wanted to know the right way of how to do the *dhikrullah* because I always got the wrong impression. I mean the wrong people, they have a different idea of these *ṭarīqa* (spiritual order), *sulook* (the path) and *tasawwuf* (inward science) and I was not happy with the attitude towards it. So, when I came here, when I told [Centre manager]...I just want to know the right way...because I think that when I look at Tuan Guru for me he is like so cool, so relaxed so that is the right way. Not like, you have to be angry, scold people that is so wrong. So, I am looking forward for the *dhikrullah* and I hope I can do on my own." (Interview Document No: 9 - Appendix 3).

He makes reference to a common misperception of *ṭarīqa*s or orders that results in them being labelled as not following 'proper' Islam. Most critique comes from people who have not actually been a part of spiritual orders, labelling their practices outright as innovation (bid'ah) without having knowledge of or trying to understand how Islam is translated into their practice. They may see one aspect, which may not necessarily be a part of mainstream Islam, and then they label it as innovation (bid'ah). Thus, the good aspects are thrown out together with those termed as bad. This is where one loses an overall sense of the objectivity or benefits one can gain from being a part of a community of practice. However, the seeker himself has come to a realisation that the Sheikh and the Order have something to offer him and which he can benefit from. In this case, the desire for change came through the exemplary model of the Sheikh being calm, relaxed and non-threating.

In order to overcome this apathy, the Manager says:

> "Bored yes. That is why I encourage them to read or talk in any language. And encourage them to you know? We are starting a new sort of trend about the *nasheed* (Islamic oriented songs). *Nasheed* are the holy songs... the holy places, the praise of God, the attributes of God, Allah. Allah Qayyum (Eternal) and all those things. At least if you sing or lie down, you sing about the nighty nine attributes of God. That is better than just dreaming about nothing or at least you want to *salawat* (praise on the Prophet). That is even better as I said because God says, 'I and the angels say I am good tidings to Mohammed.' Yes so, I say God has commanded you to say it and you just do not care a damn." (Interview Document No: 1 - Appendix 3).

His approach to combatting it is to encourage interaction, reading, Islamic songs, praise of God and the prophet. Occupying their time and importantly, their minds and hearts, with beneficial activities, such that they remain focused on God consciousness.

References

Alwasiti, H., Aris, I., & Jantan, A. (2010, September 01). EEG activity in Muslim prayer: A pilot study. *Maejo International Journal of Science and Technology, 4*(3), 496–511

Abu al-Zahra', 'Uways bin 'Abd Allah. (2002). *al-Isharat al-Saniyyah li Saliki al-Tariqah al Naqshabandiyyah*. Qahira: Dar al-Mustafa.

Al-Islam.org (n.d.), *Dimension of Manner and Morals of the Holy Prophet, Ahlul Bayt Library Project. (1995–2016)* (pp. 288). Al-Islam.org. https://www.al-islam.org/prophethood-and-prophet-islam-ayatullah-ibrahim-amini/dimensions-manner-and-morals-holy-prophet.

An-Nawawi. (1977). An-Nawwai's Forty Hadiths. In Ibrahim, E. & Davies, D. J. (Eds.) Damascus: Holy Qur'ān Publication

Asad, M. (2011). *The Message of the Quran*, Trans. and explained by Muhammad Asad, new edition. Kuala Lumpur: Islamic Book Trust.

Attas, S. M. N. (2001). *Prolegomena: To the Metaphysics of Islam: An Exposition Of The Fundamental Elements of the Worldview of Islam* (pp. 1–358). Kuala Lumpur: International Institute of Islamic Thought and Civilisation (ISTAC).

Bandura, A. (2011). *Most Human Behaviour Is Learned Through Modeling in the Psychology Book* (p. 288). London: DK.

Bukhari, Al. (1994). Chapter 32, 100:103 in Al-Imam Zia-ud-Din Ahmad bin Ahmad in Abdul-Lateef Az-Zuaidi Summarized Sahih Al-Bukhari: Book of Knowledge (Khan, M.K., Trans.). (Original work published in ninth Century-810-870 CE). Riyad: Maktaba Dar-us-Salam.

Doufesh, H., Faisal, T., Lim, K. S., & Ibrahim, F. (2012). EEG spectral analysis on Muslim prayers. *Applied Psychophysiology and Biofeedback, 37*(1), 11–18.

Doufesh, H., Ibrahim, F., Ismail, N. A., & Ahmad, W. A. W. (2014). Effect of Muslim prayer (Salat) on α electroencephalography and its relationship with autonomic nervous system activity. *The Journal of Alternative and Complementary Medicine, 20*(7), 558–562. https://doi.org/10.1089/acm.2013.0426.

Esch, T. (2014). *The Neurobiology of Meditation and Mindfulness, Meditation—Neuroscientific Approaches and Philosophical Implications* (Vol. 156). New York: Springer.

G. hazali, A. H. (1995). *Book of religious learning III, Ihiya Ulum-din: Revival of the religious sciences (pp. 4–10)*. New Delhi: Islamic Book Services.

References

Ibn Hazm al-Andalusi. (1998). *Al-Akhlāq wa'lsiyar, In Pursuit of Virtue: The Moral Theology and Psychology of Ibn Hazm al-Andalusi* (Laylah, M.A., Trans.). London: Ta Ha Publishers Ltd.

Ibn Kathir, I. (2003a). *Abridged by Shaukh Safiur-Rahman Al-Mubarakpuri* (Vol. 2, 2nd edn.). Riyad: Darussalam, July 2003; 347.

Ibn Kathir (2003b). *Tafsir Ibn Kathir* (Vol. 5). Trans. and abridged by Al-Mubarakpuri, S.R and group of scholars, Riyadh: Darussalam.

Ibn Kathir (2003c). *Tafsir Ibn Kathir* (Vol. 8). Trans. and abridged by Al-Mubarakpuri, S.R and group of scholars, Riyadh: Darussalam.

Ibn Kathir (2003d). *Tafsir Ibn Kathir* (Vol. 9). Trans. and abridged by Al-Mubarakpuri, S.R and group of scholars, Riyadh: Darussalam.

Ibn Kathir (2003f). *Tafsir Ibn Kathir* (Vol. 6). Trans. and abridged by Al-Mubarakpuri, S.R and group of scholars, Riyadh: Darussalam.

Ibn Arabi, M. (2008). In Hirtenstein, S. (Eds.) *The Four Pillars of Spiritual Transformation: The Adornment of the Spiritually Transformed (Hilyat al-abdal) (Mystical Treatises of Muhyiddin Ibn 'Arabi). Bilingual Ed.* Oxford: Anqa Publishing.

Ibrahim, F., Abas, A. B. W., & Ng, S. C. (2008). *Salat: Benefit from the Science Perspective.* Malaysia: Department of Biomedical Science, University of Malaya.

Ibrahim, E., & Johnson-Davis, D. (1977). *An-Nawawi's Forty Hadith*, Trans. Ezzedin Ibrahim and Denys Johnson-Davies (p. 68). Damascus: Holy Qur'an Publishing House.

Jung, C. (n.d.). *The Dream Theories of Carl Jung*. http://dreamstudies.org/2009/11/25/carl-jung-dream-interpretation/.

Kabbani, M. H. (1995). *The Naqshbandi Sufi Way History and Guidebook of the Saints of the Golden Chain*. Chicago: Kazi Publication Inc.

Kelly, G. (1963). *The Psychology of Personal Construct*. New York: W.W. Norton & Company, Inc.

Khan, M. A. Y. (1976). *Dalail-Us-Sulook: An Objective Appraisal of the Sublime Sufi Path. (Abu Talha Idarah-E-Naqshbandiah Trans.)*. Owaisiah: Pakistan.

Lings, M. (1983). *What is Sufism?*. Lahore: Suhail Academy.

Lings, M. (2005). *What is Sufism*. Lahore: Sohail Academy.

Malik, I. (n.d.). *Muwatta Chapter No: 16, Burials, Hadith no: 53*. http://ahadith.co.uk/searchresults.php?q=born+in+a+state+of+fitra

Munsoor, M. S., & Munsoor, H. S. (2017). Well-being and the worshiper: A scientific perspective of selected contemplative practices in Islam. *Humanomics, 33*(2), 163–188.

Omar, S. H. & Zarrina, C. S. (2011). The Practice of Wuquf Qalbi in the Naqshbandiyyah Khalidiyyah Order and it's Practice in Malaysia. *International Journal of Business and Social Science, 2*(4), 93. http://ijbssnet.com/journals/Vol._2_No._4;_March_2011/11.pdf

Picken, G. (2011). *Spiritual Purification in Islam: The Life and Works of al-Muhasibi*. UK: Routledge.

Qushayri, Abu-al Qasim Abd-al-Karim bin Hawazin (2002). On the Hearts Direct Knowledge of God (Marifahbillah). In *The Risolat: Principles of Sufism in Bakthiar, L.. Great Books of the Islamic World* (Harris, R., Trans.). Chicago: Kazi Publications Inc.

Schimmel, A. M. (1975). *Mystical Dimensions of Islam*. USA: The University of North Carolina Press.

Shapiro, S. L. et al. (2008). Cultivating Mindfulness. *Journal of Clinical Psychology, 64*(7), 840–862.

Sheikh Shahab-ud-Din Umar B. Muhammad Suhrawardi. (1991). *The Awarif-ul-Ma'arif (Lieut-Col. H. Wilberforce Clarke)*. Lahore: Sh. Muhammad Ashraf Publishers.

Sidek, J. (2014). *Membentuk Sufi Jiwa*. Selangor, Malaysia: Falah Publication. Smith, Margaret*

Smith, Margaret (1980), Al-Muhasibi: An Early Mystic of Baghdad, Islamic Book Foundation, Publication No: 52, Lahore, Pakistan

Yucel, S. (2010). *Prayer and healing in Islam, with addendum of 25 remedies for the sick by said Nuris*. New Jersey: Turga Books

Chapter 6
Spiritual Leadership and Self-Development Model

In light of this research, it's primary objective (chapter 1.1),[1] the outlined knowledge gap (chapter 1.4) and in order to put things into a holistic perspective, a thematic map has been developed as outlined below in Fig. 6.1. These main themes are outlined, namely, the organizational features, spiritual leadership, the workings of the Order, transformation of its seekers, the performance and outcomes with it's related sub-themes. In this chapter, these themes and sub-themes derived from chapter 5 are integrated into a holistic narrative, while synthesizing it with various theories as well as concepts based on the conceptual frameworks, which was outlined in chapters 2 (worship) and 3 (morality).

As is evident in the review of literature (Chaps. 2 and 3), there is a plethora of text and commentaries on Islamic spirituality or *tasawwuf*, known in modern parlance as 'Sufism', which deals with morality as well as worship. The immersion

---

[1] Primary objectives: i) Based on an in-depth assessment of the spiritual Order, to develop a model exploring the associations between spiritual leadership and self-development of its seekers. ii) To understand the nature of the spiritual Order, its leadership, and the impact has on its seekers. Specific objectives: i) To identify, through a non-intrusive process of inquiry, the spiritual landscape of the Order including its concepts, metaphors, and the guiding principles that enhance and contribute to self-development. ii) To identify the essential features and traits of the relevant spiritual role models or exemplar-Sheikh. iii) To develop a model of the state of excellence of the role model, namely, the Sheikh and the workings of his Order. iv) To identify spiritual practices that go towards positively contributing to the spiritual and emotional wellbeing of practitioners. Knowledge gaps:

- To develop a model of spiritual leadership and self-development after mapping out the metaphoric, symbolic, and conceptual landscape of a spiritual leader within the order;
- To develops the nexus between worship and morality, as well as the rational (brain) versus the non-rational (heart), which needs to be better articulated within English-language Islamic literature;
- To provide empirical data and first-hand insight into contemplative practices within Islam, including a framework relating to meditation-contemplation and neuro-science.

in these spiritual practices for purifying and developing the inner self is advocated for by Muslims but especially by spiritual orders (*ṭarīqas*), which have their own Sheikhs. Criticism has been levelled against Sufism and *ṭarīqas*, especially by those belonging to emerging 'Salafi' types of movements[2], the focus of which has been on perceived deviations, unorthodox ritual practices and the reverence of its Sheikhs. While acknowledging that there are Sufi type of orders whose practices are not within the Islamic tradition and this has been criticised by eminent Sufi oriented scholars themselves including Al-Ghazali (1995) amongst others, there are acts of certain Salafi type of orders themselves, which do not follow the practice of the Prophet, especially relating to tolerance and understanding of others. The important thing is not to lay blame on one another but to maximise one's worship and actions towards oneself and others, so that one lives an exemplary life being mindful that one does not know of their own final exit or state. As the Prophet himself mentioned that it is only by the Grace of God that we shall all enter the garden.

A study on the nature of the '*ṭarīqa* Islam' (Marzouqi 2013), which attempted to 'deconstruct' it from within points out that:

> Having noted the existence of the same harmonising form of reason in both *ṭarīqa* and orthodox Islam, one can once again see that this discourse could never have continued within the Islamic space unless it had based itself on the solid core of Islamic epistemology and its structure of ideas. Islam would not have ensured the conditions for its epistemological survival in the Arab Islamic space without having imitated the structure of jurisprudential reason, which is based on analogical reason as a collective principle of knowledge that holds sway over the discourse of orthodox Islam.

Essentially, what this study highlights is that the concept of modelling that the *ṭarīqa* employs is largely within Islamic orthodoxy, even though one discerns variations in the methodologies of rituals and *dhikr* that the different *ṭarīqas* utilise. Thus, it cannot be simply dismissed, as is done by some quarters, as not being within the boundaries of Islam. In this context, it is appropriate to decipher the thoughts of one of the most influential scholars in the Malay world, Haji Abdul bin Abdul Amrullah (Hamka), who was known through the multiple titles of rational Sufi, moderate Sufi, a Sufi without a *ṭarīqa*, and someone who says on authentic Sufism (*tasawwuf sejati*):

---

[2]The Amman Message (https://ammanmessage.com) is a statement calling for tolerance and unity in the Muslim world issued on 9th November 2004, by 500 Islamic Scholars from over 50 countries. This is related to such matters as defining who is a Muslim, excommunication from Islam (takfir) and principles related to delivering religious opinion (fatwa). According to this message Muslims include Sufiá's, Salafiá's, Shiá's, Sunniá's and several other Muslims groups with different orientation and theological perspectives. The scholars who supported the Amman message included Grand Imam Shaykh Al-Azhar, the Grand Ayatollah Al-Sayyid Ali Al-Sistani, the Mufti of Egypt, the leading Shi'a clerics (both Ja'fari and Zaydi), the Grand Mufti of the Sultanate of Oman, the Islamic Fiqh Academy in the Kingdom of Saudi Arabia, the Grand Council for Religious Affairs of Turkey, the Grand Mufti of the Hashemite Kingdom of Jordan and the Respectable Members of its National Fatwa Committee, and the Shaykh Dr. Yusuf Al-Qaradawi.

6 Spiritual Leadership and Self-Development Model

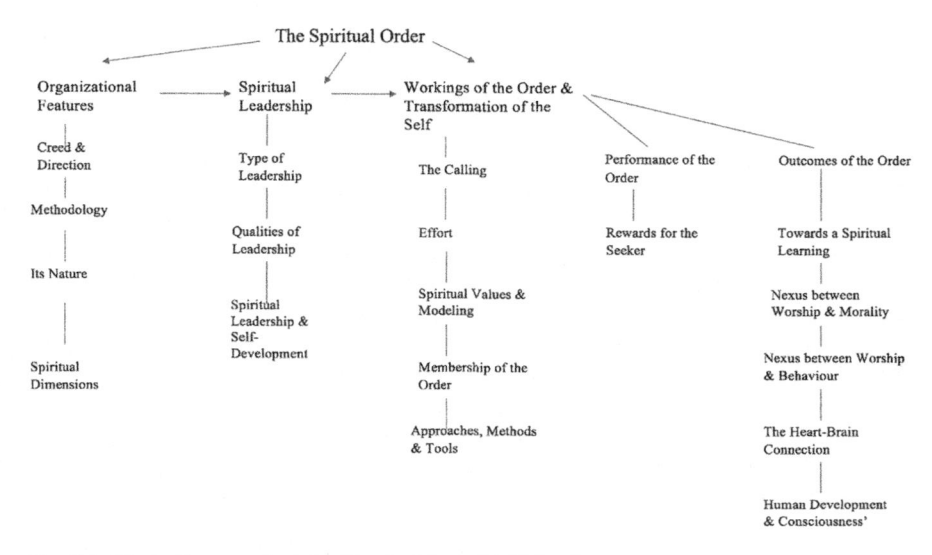

Fig. 6.1 Thematic map of spiritual leadership and self-development

[Thematic map diagram with the following structure:

The Spiritual Order branches into three main areas:

- **Organizational Features**: Creed & Direction → Methodology → Its Nature → Spiritual Dimensions
- **Spiritual Leadership**: Type of Leadership → Qualities of Leadership → Spiritual Leadership & Self-Development
- **Workings of the Order & Transformation of the Self**: The Calling → Effort → Spiritual Values & Modeling → Membership of the Order → Approaches, Methods & Tools
- **Performance of the Order**: Rewards for the Seeker
- **Outcomes of the Order**: Towards a Spiritual Learning → Nexus between Worship & Morality → Nexus between Worship & Behaviour → The Heart-Brain Connection → Human Development & Consciousness']

True Sufism does not enjoin the fleeing of man from the realities of life, true Sufism serves as a guide for one to confront the challenges of life. True Sufism does not encourage the flight to forest other than to immerse in the heart of society. Because the society needs spiritual guidance. (Aljunied 2016).

He adds:

...cleanse the soul, educate and refine the emotions, enliven the heart to be in constant prayer, and enable the character (while) suppressing greed and gluttony, battling excessive lust that goes beyond what is needed to achieve calmness. (Aljunied 2016).

...modified *tasawwuf* as a remedy for modern materialism...judged scripturalist Islam (i.e. the narrowly dogmatic and legalistic Islam of his fellow Muslim modernist) insufficient sustenance in the modern world...rule-focused Islam calls upon only 'the brain' (*otak*) and 'logic'; (*logika*), neglecting the esoteric faculty of spiritual feeling (*rasa zauq*). Without cultivating the inner spiritual faculty, people find it difficult to resist the materialism of the modern world, and also the vices of the body that have always been with us ... Spiritual exercises not only offer intellectual assent to his faith, 'clean the heart (*hati*) and enable the believer not only to offer intellectual assent to his faith, but feel close to God.' (Aljunied 2016)

What is best exemplified in the discourse of contemporary scholars and thinkers, such as Hamka, has already been dealt with in great detail in the seminal works of Imam Al-Ghazāli (2005), where he was able to build a bridge between Islamic orthodoxy and the mystics. The quintessential point here is the unification of the sense-perceptions and cognitive faculties with that of spirituality and the heart. This aspect is discussed as a part of the research in a later section that deals with the heart-brain connection[3].

Part of the issue within the modern-day context is that, on a general note, most '*ulamās*' (religious scholars) do not seem to take pains to expound on both on the internal and external dimensions of Islam and its inter-linkages, while Muslims themselves do not find time to read traditional scholarly works. If this was done, then it would lay a sound foundation for a wholesome life based on the Qur'ān and sunnah, while dispelling some of the more problematic issues emanating from theologians (*mutakallimūn*), the esoteric interpretation of the scriptural sources (*bāṭiniyyah*), the philosophers (*falāsifa*) and the mystics (Sufis).

There have been multiple research studies on various *ṭarīqas* (e.g. Fujii 2010, Hill 2014, Pasilov and Ashirov 2007, De Jong 1983, Gammer 1994, Bousfield 1993 and Van Bruinessen 1998) covering the spatio-temporal landscape in terms of their objectives, their historical role in resistance, impact on local communities, nature of the *dhikr*, gender dimensions, rituals and practices, genesis of the movements and the misrepresentations of *ṭarīqas*. It is rare, however, to see one that attempts to establish a model pertaining to its organisational functioning, its leadership and the impact on its seekers in the light of the related sciences as this research demonstrates.

At the core of the spiritual order is what can be called spiritual modelling (Oman and Thoresen 2003) as this study demonstrates, which is a neglected field within the light of traditional religions as well as contemporary spirituality. This is despite the very valuable skills and knowledge that spirituality offers, as seen in its adaption within mindfulness-based therapies, including MBSR (mindfulness

---

[3] What is referred to here as the brain-mind comprises sense perceptions, where information is received through the 5 senses are processed by the brain with its related cognitive faculties, while the spiritual heart refers to revelation, intuition, illumination, virtuous emotions (compassion, love, empathy, wisdom...). There are those who only vouch for the existence of the brain- mind with consciousness residing in the brain, a materialist point of view, what is now called the 'hard problem'. In a spiritual sense, both the brain-cognitive and the spiritual heart is required to achieve a sense of equilibrium, where the latter is required for going beyond the mind into the metaphysical realm, where meditation and prayers are instruments for developing the spiritual heart. In this case, consciousness is theorized to be outside the material brain with emerging evidence supporting this phenomenon, which challenges the current and mainstream scientific paradigm. From an Islamic perspective the heart is used synonymously with the soul by Imam Al-Ghazali (1995), which can be termed as consciousness within it's current usage of this term. Chapter 2.1 details this out where the soul and its attributes are outlined with special reference to western psychology. For current insights into scientific research on consciousness please see the materials outlined below: See Professor Stanislav Grof, Implication of Consciousness Research for Psychiatry, Psychology and Psychotheraphy: Observations from half a century of consciousness research, https://www.youtube.com/watch?v=o0YDzLAI5X8, 27th April 2017; Chalmers, David (2014) is a scientific materialist. How do you explain consciousness, David Chalmers, 14th July 2014, https://www.youtube.com/watch?v=uhRhtFFhNzQ&t=931s; Hoffman. D, Donald (2019), Reality is not as it seems, a dialogue with neurologist Dr. Suzanne O'Sullivan hosted by Steve Paulson, Nour Foundation, 14th Feb 2019; https://www.youtube.com/watch?v=3MvGGjcTEpQ

based stress reduction) and MBCT (mindfulness based cognitive therapy).[4] This study develops a model of spiritual leadership and self-development.[5] This model is built around the patterns of variables that have been identified from emerging data, generated from both the survey data, as well as the interview data set. The survey response forms a more precise response from the seekers, while the interview data captures their authentic flowing narratives. The flow of these two primary data streams are integrated with the secondary data from the literature reviews, as well as with relevant theories and concepts. Apart from traditional Islamic sources, relevant evidence from neuroscience and humanistic theories are woven into the fabric of the discussion to augment the ensuing synthesis of the discussion. This makes it relevant to the contemporary context and thus produces a powerful narrative of the inward aspects of Islam, which are generally lesser well known as compared to the Hindu, Buddhist or the Christian monastic meditative traditions.

The structure of this chapter is as outlined below, with the sections/sub-section cited within brackets: First, the organisational features of the Order (Sect. 6.1); Second, presentation of a model of spiritual leadership and self-development (Sect. 6.2); Third, the calling of the seekers (Sect. 6.3); Fourth, the efforts of the seekers (Sect. 6.4); Fifth, the spiritual Order—The Sheikh as an exemplar (Sect. 6.5); Sixth, the membership of the Order (Sect. 6.6); Seventh, the performance of the Order (Sect. 6.7); Eight, the rewards of the seekers (Sect. 6.9); Ninth, the outcomes of the Order (Sect. 6.10).

6.1 Organisational Features of the Order

6.1.1 Creed and Direction of the Order

Given the criticism from some sections of the Islamic faith with regard to Sufi types of movements, attention was given to understanding the creed and the direction of the Order. This will to a large extent determined if this Order is within the Islamic orthodoxy. As was evident in both the interview and survey data, this can be categorised as a mainstream order, with the belief in the Oneness of God and testifying that Prophet Muhammad is the final Prophet. It is observed that all of the

---

[4] Mindfulness based stress reduction (MBRS) therapy and Mindfulness based Cognitive therapy (MBCT). Both of these therapies have been developed based on the Buddhist mindfulness based meditation.

[5] The concept and model that has been developed for this study outlined in figure 6.1 below is generally used in quantitative research within the framework of cause and effect aimed at developing causal models. Given that this is primarily a qualitative research, I have used it to develop a conceptual framework to identify the key variables and then label them according to their inherent nature and explain how they correlate and work in relation to each other (model). This should enable the reader to understand the workings of the order in a more systematic manner.

obligatory rituals prescribed by the Sharī'a are being performed in addition to the optional acts relating to prayers, fasting and remembrance of God (*dhikr*).

According to the seekers the objective of the Order is to inculcate the Oneness of God and exert efforts to achieve *ma'rifa* (divine knowledge of God). There is special focus on the *dhikr* both the silent (*sirr*) and the loud (*jahir*), following the methodology of a particular Sufi order, the Naqshabandiyyah (see Sect. 5.2). The principle of remembering God is replete in the Qur'ān and sunnah and the Order strives in this direction. What is not evident in the sunnah may be the particular methodology used for *dhikr* of this Order specifically, which is derived from the Naqshabandiyyah way. This can be a basis for critique, where one can, however, argue that this is adopted based on the general principles of remembrance in Islam, with the particular methodology being developed later on. Therefore, the methods are well grounded in the principles enshrined within the Qur'ān and its replete references to *dhikr* (see Sects. 2.1, 2.2, and 2.3).

6.1.2 The Order and Its Methodology

The Naqshabandiyyah Khālidiyyah model is based on the transmission of its '*silsila*' or lineage[6], which carries with it the related methodological approaches. It traces its organisational roots from Malaysia through Indonesia to different parts of the world, based on the origins of its Sheikh or leadership (Appendix 2). As seen in the case study (Chap. 5) one of the central drivers of the spiritual change is by the Sheikh himself and in this sense the 'Order is good as its Sheikh' as Knysh has outlined in his detailed study (Knysh 2007). The methodology of the Order is not seen to have changed significantly over generations as indicated by previous researchers (Hadzrullathfi and Sa'ari 2011) who investigated the Order. This is well articulated by a key information in one of the few ethnographic studies (Pasilov and Ashirov 2007) in Central Asia, that says:

> if in the *khufi* (silent) *dhikr* a Sufi makes the *dhikr* only by soul (*qalb*), in the *jahri dhikr*, the Soul (*qalb*), the body (*badan*) and the tongue (*til*) of a person participates.

Interestingly when one compares other Orders, namely Naqshbandiyyah Haqqani (Kabbani 1995) or Naqshbandi Awaisiya (Khan 1976), both of which have significantly different '*silsilas*' or lineages, the essential methods of the silent *dhikr* and the focus on the subtle spiritual organs, known as 'lataif' are essentially similar. This refers to some congruence in the methodology pertaining to *dhikr*

---

[6]Silsila or lineage generally refers to the line of Sheikhá's or exemplars of any spiritual order, representing a master-student relationship, where one of the studentá's eventually becomes the master after being given permission (ijaza) as well the knowledge and the spiritual beneficence to carry forward the spiritual teachings. It is a physical one-to-one transmission, however, there are a few spiritual orders, where there in a break in the physical link and there is a transmission from an exemplar who has passed on. This is called the awaisiya or distant spiritual transmission.

6.1 Organisational Features of the Order

or remembrance of God particularly in the Naqshabandiyyah *ṭarīqa* in spite of its variance in certain aspects. There is, however, some opposition to the method of *dhikr* as outlined here:

> Yet to many an outsider the Naqshbandiyyah system of *dhikr lataif* (system according to which the *dhikr* is circulated progressively through the seven subtleties of the body each of which has a spiritual location and proximity to the truth or *ḥaqīqa*) appears most 'unorthodox' and would not meet with the approval from wahabi (the movement seeking to root out all 'innovations' in Islam) or modernists alike. (Bousfield 1993)

Even though the Prophet and his companions have not undertaken this method of *dhikr* specifically, the above opposition is counteracted by the citation of a *ḥadīth qudsi* (divine inspiration from God) cited by one of the foremost narrators, al-Bukhari:

> Allah (God) has angels who wander in the paths searching for those who remember Allah... then they surround them with their wings up to the nearest heaven... thereupon Allah says 'therefore, I call you to witness that I have forgiven them'... the angels then say 'among them there is so and so who is not one of them, as he has come for some (other) purpose'. Allah says, 'They are such person that whomever sits with them is not to be miserable' (An-Nawawi 2004). There are other famous narrations as outlined below:
>
> I am as My servants thinks I am, and I am with him when he remembers Me. If he remembers Me to himself, I remember him to Myself; and if he remembers Me in a gathering, I remember him in a gathering better than it. If he draws near to Me a hand's span, I draw near to him an arm's length; I draw near to him a fathom's length; and if he comes to Me walking, I do to him with haste. (An-Nawawi 2004)
>
> Abu Ma'bad, the freed slave of Ibn Abbas said 'In the lifetime of the Prophet, it was the custom to remember Allah (*dhikr*) by glorifying, praising and magnifying Allah aloud after compulsory congregational *salah* (prayers).' Ibn Abbas further said 'When I heard the *dhikr*, I would learn that the compulsory congregational *salah* (prayer) had ended.' (Al Bukhari 1994)

The first two authentic narrations clearly outline the importance of *dhikr*, as well as people gathering for this purpose. The methodologies of how the *dhikr* is done have not been articulated in the above *ḥadīth* except that it is the remembrance of God, which is done individually and/or in groups. The third above mentioned reference cited in Burkhari points out to loud *dhikr* (*jihar*) being done at the Prophet's mosque after ritual prayers. This is in spite of some opposition against loud *dhikr*, which was said not to have been performed during the time of the Prophet, although somehow this specific practice has been lost in the passage of time especially in the context of the Middle East.

6.1.3 Nature of the Order

Some of the distinct features of the Order are:

i. Both men and women participate in the *dhikr* and the lectures, even though the participation of men is greater;

ii. The ruling of the Sharī'a is followed where men and women are segregated but have access to what is going on;
iii. In terms of socio-economic strata, it has people from the various social classes and therefore does not appear to be an elitist order;
iv. In terms of education, the subjects' qualifications varied from degree holders to those who have completed their secondary education;
v. The age range of the subjects also varied from the younger group, with a large slice being in the middle age range, with a few older subjects;
vi. The most predominant reasons for joining the Order was to prepare for the next life;
vii. The expectation from joining the Order was to develop themselves spiritually and do service to others

This Order from an Islamic point of view and in terms of following the Prophetic model (see Sect. 3.2.2, Table 3.2.1) of social justice and inclusion, includes the poorer classes and females and therefore is both class and gender sensitive.

6.2 Towards a Model of Spiritual Leadership and Self-Development

6.2.1 An Overview—Spiritual Dimension

This work was informed by Louis Fry's (2003) research on 'spirituality and workplace' but it is essentially different in terms of its subject matter, content and methodology. Fry's articulation was adapted and contextualised within the framework of the Prophet, where the essential qualities of spiritual leadership was articulated in terms of vision, altruistic live and hope, as well as faith in Sect. 3.2.2 on the spiritual leadership of the Prophet (see Sect. 3.2.2 and Table 3.2.6).

Even though spiritual leadership encompasses both transformation as well as situational leadership elements, it differs from them and is distinct from for example Fry's model. As Fry states, given that the spiritual leadership model is an 'intrinsic' one, motivated mainly by internal factors, it distinguishes itself from the transactional model of leadership. The latter model is largely dependent on extrinsic factors, and performance is dependent on external rewards and governed by maintaining organisational stability but not necessarily promoting change or enhancing growth.

The style and model of leadership of the spiritual order seems twofold:

i. On one hand it is a transformational type of leadership as exemplified by the Prophetic model in light of his set of values and behaviour. This was congruent to what he set out to his community of followers, which now forms a basis for emulation as outlined in Sect. 3.2. It is a transformation from two points of view: first, overall it is not a centralised one where the Sheikh controls and

6.2 Towards a Model of Spiritual Leadership and Self-Development

manages all the various branches of the order. It is left to those deputised for this purpose, where in the various geographical areas, the khalīfas (deputies) run their own branch operations. In order to guide them, there are certain protocols and rules that are unwritten yet seem to be followed. Thus, the khalīfas are able to function and develop themselves independently. Second, the seekers are not forced to perform spiritual acts or join the *dhikr* group as evident in the interviews (Chap. 5). They join out of their own volition and both the survey and the interview data clearly indicated change within themselves, as well with regard to their relationship with peers and family.

ii. It has been observed that there are many aspects of situational leadership, where the Sheikh has one-to-one counselling with each seeker and each is assessed with regards to their spiritual growth or the lack of it and are given appropriate guidance. Seekers feel that there is considerable flexibility and that they are able to discuss their situations with the Sheikh or else in the case of residents with the Centre manager or supervisor.

There is a concept that the Project Management Institute (PMI) uses for this combination of leadership, which is called interactional leadership (PMI 2018). This type of leadership offers a wide spectrum of leverage for those who are followers to operate, as well as providing the leaders themselves with the space to guide and facilitate decision making.

The data generated from this study, which has been encapsulated in the model that is presented below (Fig. 6.1), provides a spiritual leadership model where there is a meeting point for the values and goals of the individuals with those of the leader and the organisational values and culture. Contrary to Fry's above postulation, it contains both the intrinsic and extrinsic intervening factors.

Spiritual leadership within the Islamic ethos is based on the development of virtuous traits and aligned with the Islamic value system (see Sects. 3.1 and 3.2), as well as that of other faiths be it Hinduism, Buddhism, Judaism, Christianity and others. Therefore, it is seen as having universal traits that cut across numerous cultures including the indigenous ones. Thus, kindness, forgiveness, compassion, honesty, patience, calmness, courage, trust, wisdom, and loyalty, good relationships are those which facilitate the development of the self and the soul, as evident from the survey data extracted from this research (see Chap. 5).

The comparison in Table 6.1 shows the commonality of Louis Fry's conceptualisation of the qualities of leadership, where as seen in Table 6.1 there are close similarities with both sets, while the current research data is much more elaborate. The virtuous and the vices tree (Fig. 6.1) derived from this research is framed within the continuum of both ends of the spectrum of these traits. As seen in Fig. 6.1, there are traits conducive to self-development, while the other are vices or ruinous traits (Fig. 6.2).

The virtuous traits identified are also those who have self-actualised from Maslow's perspective (Maslow 2011) or become a full human being as articulated by Rogers (1991) from a psychological viewpoint. Within a spiritual framework, it represents not only a manifestation of values but also changes in the state of consciousness of those who are being spiritually transformed. This was the original

Table 6.1 A comparison of Louis Fry's conceptualisation of Qualities of Spiritual Leadership with the data extracts from this research

Vision—derived from Louis Fry (2003)	Vision—interview data from this research	Altruistic love—derived from Louis Fry (2003)	Altruistic love—survey data from this research	Reference of the research survey data
Broad appeal to key stakeholders	Appeal to the seekers and ex-addicts of different socio-economic groups	Forgiveness	Forgiveness	Chapter 5—Figs. 5.9, 5.13
Defines the destination and journey	This world (*dunya*) and the next world (*ākhira*)	Kindness	Love	Section 2.1 and Chap. 5—Figs. 5.9, 5.13, 5.14.
Reflects high ideals	High ideals set against the Qur'ān and the sunnah	Integrity	Integrity	The Prophetic Model—Sect. 2.5
Encourages hope-faith	Hope (*amal*) and Faith (*taqwa*) are fundamentals of Islam	Empathy/compassion	Empathy/Benevolence	Sheikh's reference to Qur'ānic verse in Chap. 5... and Fig. 5.25
Establishes a standard of excellence	Virtuous—excellence and sincerity (*iḥsan*)	Honesty	Honesty	Jibreel ḥadīth referred to by the Sheikh (Chap. 5—Figs. 5.9, 5.13, 5.14.)
		Patience	Patience	Figures 5.9, 5.13, 5.14, 5.20.
		Courage	Courage	Figure 5.19—The concept of Futuwwa (Chaps. 5 and Sect. 6.2.2.1)
		Trust / loyalty	Trust / loyalty	Figure 5.9
		Humility	Modesty/humbleness	Figures 5.9, 5.13, 5.14, 5.25.
			Wisdom	Figures 5.9, 5.14.

thesis of trying to find a link between worship (*'ibādah*) and morality (*akhlāq*) and how one influences the other. This then changed to trying to establish a model for

6.2 Towards a Model of Spiritual Leadership and Self-Development

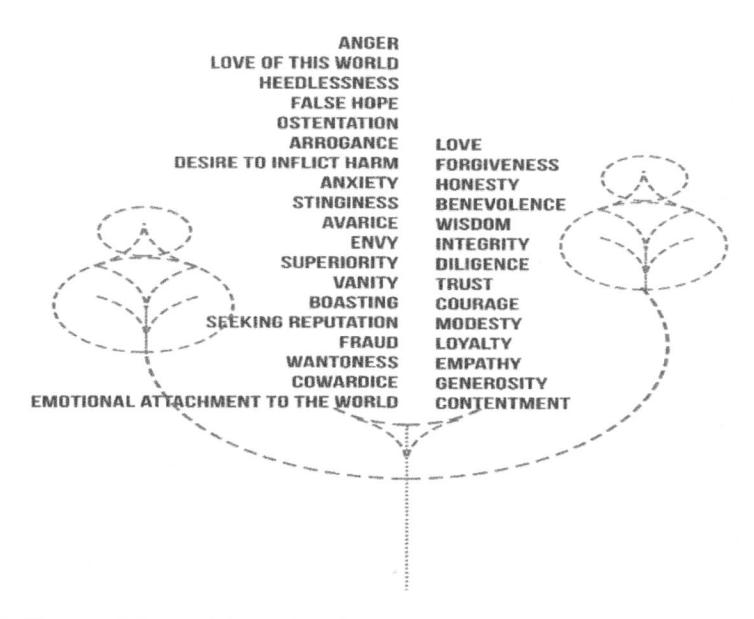

```
                    ANGER
         LOVE OF THIS WORLD
              HEEDLESSNESS
                FALSE HOPE
                OSTENTATION
                  ARROGANCE      LOVE
        DESIRE TO INFLICT HARM   FORGIVENESS
                    ANXIETY      HONESTY
                  STINGINESS     BENEVOLENCE
                    AVARICE      WISDOM
                      ENVY       INTEGRITY
                 SUPERIORITY     DILIGENCE
                    VANITY       TRUST
                   BOASTING      COURAGE
           SEEKING REPUTATION    MODESTY
                     FRAUD       LOYALTY
                  WANTONESS      EMPATHY
                  COWARDICE      GENEROSITY
 EMOTIONAL ATTACHMENT TO THE WORLD  CONTENTMENT
```

Fig. 6.2 The tree of vices and virtues from the seekers perspective

spiritual leadership and self-development, which essentially subsumed the former and gave credence to establishing this link.

The reference to this above link of worship and morality in the research data set is in reference to the seekers experiencing change within themselves. This led them to critically examining themselves, while experiencing a change in their levels of consciousness from being dependent on external things such as drugs to a naturally induced state of contentment, calmness and patience-silence. They state that not only has their promiscuous behaviour changed but they experience and feel different. We can say that there has been an altered or more appropriately a non-ordinary state of consciousness, where the states (*ḥāl*) are moving towards stations (*maqām*), which indicates a more stable position.

From an Islamic view point this can best be represented as moving from the *nafs al-ammāra bi-su* (animal self), where one is prone to worldly dependencies and vices to the *nafs al-lawwāma* (the critical self) of becoming aware of one's faults and working on improving oneself. This then creates the grounds for moving towards a state of contentment or *nafs al-mutma'inna* (the self at peace). These stages are seen as progressive stations of the evolving consciousness, where the individual moves from a lower to a higher stage of self-development. Section 2.1 deals with this aforementioned graduation process in some detail. In Islamic metaphysical literature there are seven stages outlined (discussed in the latter section), whereas only the three-dimensional stages are outlined here.

This experiential insight can be argued to have some bearing on the understanding and experience of the conception of God that is often gained through prayers and meditative practices. In Islam God is 'formless, shapeless and beyond one normal comprehension', a reason why worshipping statues is forbidden. Furthermore, God is both immanent, or accessible within the physical realm, as He states that 'he is closer to you than your jugular vein'(Qur'ān, Qaf 50:16) while also being transcendent, traversing all boundaries beyond the normal physical experience and laws. This is a paradox within our logical perception and which can only be understood within a metaphysical frame of reference.

The next section attempts to develop a model for spiritual leadership and self-development based on both the interview and the survey data that has been generated from this study.

6.2.2 The Spiritual Leadership and Self-Development Model

From this study, it will be difficult to single out one act alone that is the most positively impactful on the seekers and their behaviour. It is more a systemic approach and a combination of methods that is seen to bring forth a sense of discipline, giving people a sense of core values, meaning and direction, as well as some measure of peace. Even though spiritual modelling (Hall and Bodenhamer 2006) is largely an intrinsically motivated model as per Fry's postulation, it is argued that the extrinsic factors are vital to bring about this spiritual fusion. In this sense, it significantly differs from Fry's model and brings in a new perspective.

The above inferences derive from the full data set of multiple factors that clearly testify to the evidence from the literature review from the conceptual frameworks on worship ('ibādah) and morality (akhlāq) in Chaps. 2 and 3. This conceptualises multiple methods and tools relating to worship as seen in the tree of contemplative practices (Fig. 2.8), as well as the diseases of the heart and their treatments in Table 2.2, to the value system and characteristics and acts of worship of the Prophet outlined in Chap. 3.

Figure 6.3 utilises Fry's causal model of spiritual leadership as a frame of reference. It, however, goes well beyond it with two additional dimensions, namely, it is modelled on primary data set generated from the research within the spiritual order Naqshbandiyyah Khālidiyyah and it is framed within the Islamic spiritual tradition. It underlines both intrinsic and extrinsic factors, which are required for the effective functioning of this model. The model is developed and presented in Fig. 6.3, where each of the essential components are elaborated.

There are three control variables, namely, the calling, leadership-values and membership, these are key where if they were taken out the model would collapse. This is also called the constant variable. The independent variable is the 'effort', which is also called the change variable, where if it were to change, it would affect all the other variables especially the dependent variable. It is also called the cause variable. The dependent variables are the reward and performance, i.e. that which can be measured or observed and can change. It is also called the effect variable.

6.2 Towards a Model of Spiritual Leadership and Self-Development

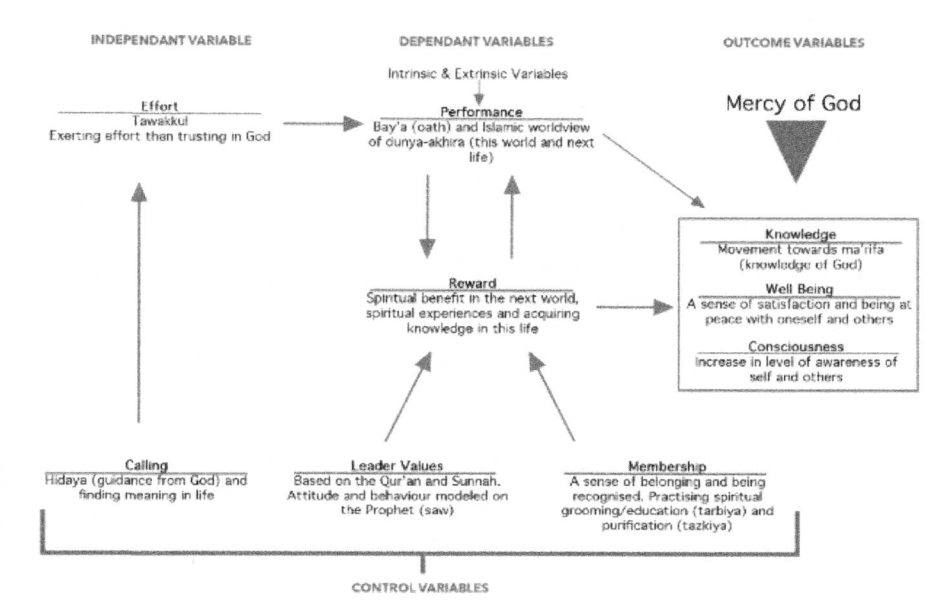

Fig. 6.3 The model of spiritual leadership and self-development

The outcome variable is in this case knowledge and state of contentment, which form the outcomes of the whole process.

Concept of Futuwwa (Chivalry) One of the threads which comes through the case study is the concept of futuwwa (Abdullah n.d.), derived from the Arabic lexicon 'fata', which generally refers to 'any young man/woman of virtue'. This has an array of meanings derived from its place in history and the context within which it was used. It quintessentially represents a 'code of conduct' adhered to, which arises from societal norms or results from spiritual initiation. It predates Islam and has become one of the central concepts within Islam. There are several conceptions of futuwwa (Qushayri 2002), which include: always paying attention to the care of others, over-looking the faults of others and not counting oneself superior to others. This is encapsulated in the Prophetic model as outlined in identifying the key traits of the Prophet, as well as his profile ranging from generosity to equity and consideration. This research presents a positive interventionist model of the theory and practice of Islam contrary to the general negative perceptions as portrayed by the media and some quarters of society.

The Prophet Muhammad says, "God Most High attends to the needs of a servant as long as the servant attends to the needs of his Muslim brother/sister." Imam Qushayri's defines his conception thus, "The fata is the one who destroys the idol", substantiated by his comments that "the idol of all men/women is their ego." (Qushayri 2002)

This concept of moving beyond one's ego was captured both in the interviews and the survey data. Out of the examples a few are cited here: where the professional banker was seen devoting his time at the residential centre to work in the garden and cooking for the residents; while the residential imam helped others with improvements in their practices; to his friend caring for those dying. The Sheikh and his wife were described by the seekers as being loving and caring, this formed a foundational aspect of the success of the Centre as seen from the viewpoints of the seekers including the residents of the Centre.

It was found that the seekers' immediate environment was conducive to fostering their growth but it should not be perceived that there was no discipline enforced. As a matter of fact, a sound routine and a sense of discipline was instilled by the Centre manager and the resident seekers followed suit, and while the Sheikh was found to be kind and approachable, one observes that the ground rules are followed by the seekers. This is one of the factors that makes the system work effectively.

6.3 The Calling—Self-Realisation and Seekers' Need for Spiritual Survival

6.3.1 Calling

One of the most fundamental themes expressed by seekers is the calling, which would be called *hidāya* (inspiration from God) that is bestowed on the seekers. At a human level it is rooted in the process of self-realisation of the seekers, which was found to be a key trigger to seeking an Order where they can find direction and meaning in life. This is also described as spiritual awakening (*yaqzah*) in the spiritual traditions. Thus, there are two facets of the calling, one from God, and the other from one's own volition. It is the calling that sets the seekers on their spiritual journey and they are rewarded depending on their efforts which influence their performance. As seen from the survey data, they are motivated to prepare for the next life, learn better behaviour, do good to others, have the company of the like-minded and learn spiritual practices (Fig. 5.6). Seekers profess an expectation that they have changed themselves for the better, become calmer, gained blessings, learned more spiritual practices and learned more about faith (Fig. 5.7).

The calling is a control variable, where if removed from the model would make it falter. It is thus one of the most fundamental triggers and the most important variable, and is especially meaningful for those seekers who were drug addicts and HIV patients (50 per cent of participants), as it has provided them with a basis for changing their lives.

6.4 Efforts

Effort effectively forms the independent variable, which influences the dependent variables of the model, namely, performance and rewards, which are dealt with in the proceeding sections. Effort is linked with the concept of '*tawakkul*' or exerting effort and then putting trust in God. The context of *tawakkul* is the belief that whatever the eventual outcome, there is 'khair' or goodness in it and God knows best. The concept of '*Jihad*' or struggle is closely associated with effort, and this worldly life is typified by struggle throughout man's time on earth. This is where prime importance is given to the virtue of patience as evident in the survey data (Figs. 5.9, 5.13, 5.14, 5.20.). This is buttressed by supplication to God (*du'ā*) (Figs. 5.10, 5.12, 5.20, 5.22) and reconciling oneself with one's sins and past life through seeking forgiveness and repentance (*tauba*) (Figs. 5.9, 5.13). This evolving state of consciousness is akin to the critical stage of awareness (*nafs al-lawwāma*) as outlined in Sect. 2.1.

This key variable, effort, can be linked with rituals and practices that are important to transform seekers' lives since it is through this that they have been able to adhere to their contemplative-meditative practices, as well as advocate their code of conduct. Effort in this case was triggered by their motivation, which comes from their calling or self-realisation to seek and change themselves for the better.

6.5 The Spiritual Order—The Sheikh as Exemplar

6.5.1 Spiritual Leadership and Values

One central concept that defines '*tasawwuf*' or the inward science of Islam is *akhlāq* or morality, and this is exemplified by the Qur'ānic statement, 'And indeed, you are upon a noble conduct, an exemplary manner' (Qur'ān, 68:4) and that 'he is an example of good conduct'. These statements are in reference to the Prophet being sent down to help people to perfect their character and who is seen as a model of excellence. The Sheikh himself models the Prophet, and his ways including speech, conduct and habits that have been codified in the sunnah.

The Sheikh or the exemplar is one of the most critical control variables after the calling, where if his part was absent then it will make the whole model collapse. It is generally conceived within the inward sciences that it is a rare exception to be able to develop oneself without a Sheikh since there are things that one may not necessarily observe about oneself. Drawing on the concept of the Johari Window from psychology, this can be called our blind side that others can point out to us. This is one of the reasons that the Sheikh comes into play apart from his role to guide the seekers in terms of the Sharī'a (body of knowledge) and law (*fiqh*) associated aspects of the faith.

One's behaviour in all circumstance becomes very crucial and the data from the seekers indicates that the nexus between worship (*'ibādah*) and morality (*akhlāq*) unfolds as being one inexplicable entity, which cannot be separated from one another. Thus it can be seen from the whole data set, including in both surveys and interviews, that worship is paramount for wellbeing manifested as calmness (Figs. 5.23, 5.24, 5.26, 5.27, 5.28, 5.29) and so is behaviour with others (Figs. 5.19, 5.23, 5.24, 5.25, 5.26). The changes brought about by worship and behaviour precipitate the transformation of the seekers over time (Figs. 5.19, 5.23, 5.24, 5.25, 5.26, 5.28) where, concurrently, the seekers are trying their utmost to model the Sheikh especially in terms of his behaviour (Figs. 5.8, 5.9, 5.10, 5.11, 5.20, 5.29).

The section under membership of the Order elaborates on the leadership as well as core value system within the dimension of a concept termed as spiritual grooming (*tarqiya*), which is associated with the seekers developing within this Order. This is corroborated by the scholarly writings on values and its importance in overcoming the vices or ruinous traits articulated in Chap. 2 (Figs. 2.4 and 2.6 and Table 2.1, Table 2.3) and in inculcating virtuous praiseworthy traits as outlined in Chap. 3 (Tables 3.2, 3.3 and 3.4).

6.5.2 The Sheikh as the Exemplar

Concerning role modelling, the Sheikh plays the central role in the whole process of providing the space, which enables to re-model the *murids* or seekers. Based on the data set (interviews—Appendix 3), the Venn diagram in Fig. 6.4 was developed, which indicates the perspective of the seeker, where the Sheikh is seen as the person who is the closest to them, thus occupying the position of an immediate role model (Fig. 5.8). The Sheikh is perceived by the seekers as being loving, wise, forgiving, honest and someone who can be trusted (Figs. 5.8, 5.9). This affinity is reinforced further when the seekers, after having inherently accepted the Sheikh, adopt the multiple methods of worship (*'ibādah*), follow the rules of conduct (*adab*) and swears allegiance through a process of oath taking (*bay'a*).

This taking of the oath or *bay'a* was seen as one of the most crucial and recurring themes in all of the interviews. This is a ritual modelled on the Prophetic incident, where the companions took an oath (*bay'a*) with him, and this practice is followed by this Order as well as by other Sufi orders. This is an act of allegiance to the Sheikh and the Order, as well as a type of social control that gives a sense of discipline since

Fig. 6.4 Venn diagram of the affinity of the seeker

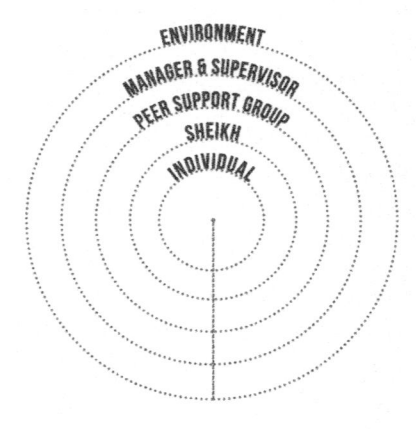

it sets social and psychological boundaries for the seekers. It has been observed in interaction with the seekers that this forms a structured basis for interaction with the Sheikh especially for the former drug addicts and HIV patients, who need a structured path due to their earlier promiscuous life. It acts as a tangible, potentially lifelong, connection between them and the Sheikh.

This affinity to the Sheikh enables the seekers to turn their attention and energy to the path that is being set for them by way of a combination of spiritual acts, both those that are obligatory and the optional or voluntary acts. The combination of the Sheikh's lead is seen in the *kulliyyah*, that is, lectures, and the group *dhikr*, which brings all seekers together in his presence. During this time the *dhikr* is conducted both in a loud manner, and then followed by the silent one, which reinforces solidarity and togetherness with the Sheikh, as well as with the other seekers. Kynsh (2007) points out that what is relevant to the seeker is the Sheikh himself, and not necessarily the *ṭarīqa* or the '*silsila*' (lineage). Even though this is an important point, it is worth stating that based on the emerging data from this research apart from the role of the Sheikh, the intrinsic and extrinsic factors outlined in this study are of utmost importance, which hold it all together. Thus, Kynsh's point is partially correct and but should be qualified since without other variables falling into place the transformation will be slow to catalyse. It is seen that after the Sheikh, the closest to them are the other seekers who are resident with them, that is, their peer group. From the data it is evident that especially the resident imam, as well as the other seekers, teach and guide each other. This peer-to-peer learning and support is a crucial factor in their growth and can often be over looked.

Given that the residents who live with each other day-in-and-day-out have an intricate routine starting from the very early hours of the morning and ending at night, whatever the Sheikh teaches the group or individual is discussed, refined and internalised by the seekers. Thus this provides a powerful platform for unlearning, relearning and reinforcing the intricacies of the learnings within the Order. Imam Ghazāli (1995) in his most famous work—the revival of religious sciences—discusses this process as the heart unravels itself when the seeker plunges inward and God casts knowledge into their hearts through a form of intuition (badīha), and as the seeker advances they are illuminated with the grace of God.

Given that the mind is consistently engaged in scripting, there is a tendency for it to get involved in 'rumination', where one's mundane scripts are repeated over and over again which can lead one into a state of anxiety and eventually depression (Esch 2014). Thus a guide or Sheikh is required in order to distinguish between what appears not to be right or wrong, thus a Sheikh can guide the seeker in overcoming negative thoughts and creating a mental space of tranquillity, God consciousness and positivity. The intensive contemplative practices include meditation through which the seekers point out they gain psychological benefits (Sears 2014, Ibrahim and Ng 2008), have less negative thoughts, feel calmer, as well as having improvements in executive functions of attentions and working memory, have greater clarity of thought, all of which corroborates with the emerging neuro-scientific data as outlined by several studies (Kaltwasser et al. 2014, Chisea 2010, Doufesh et al. 2012, Esch 2014), which have used both tracking of the brain wave patterns using neuro-imaging, as well as through physiological markers. Thus, the psychological as well as the physiological benefits of meditation cuts across the various faith traditions.

The next layer of beneficial interaction is the manager of the Centre and his supervisor, both of them not only manage the administration and the logistics of the Centre but are themselves seekers. This provides both of them with the platform to share their own thought processes to the residents. This is best illustrated by the manager of the Centre by virtue of his scientific training, who discusses the millions of cells in the body that gets activated during the prayers or *dhikr* where all of them are in a state of remembrance of God, and was echoed by the residents during their interviews. While the crucial role of the Sheikh has been emphasised, the roles of facilitators and the guidance of the peers within spiritual orders has not been given adequate emphasis though this may form a key factor in the growth of the seekers.

It has to be said that the immediate environment where love, cooperation and spiritual practices are performed provides the seekers some sense of meaning and healing. This is especially so for the residents of the Centre since they are living without their families. The care given by the Sheikh and his wife, highlighted by the residents, provides them with a sense of familial care and orientation. This provides the seekers with a psychological anchor and a spiritual point of reference.

The ground rules and discipline set by the Centre manager and his supervisor for the residents forms a boundary within which the residents operate, and this is important given the history of the residents who were ex-drug addicts and formerly lived a much more liberal lifestyle. This active cooperation and sharing with each other and keeping their residence clean and tidy, all goes towards ordering their lives. This creation of space for the general seekers and residents, combined with the purpose and direction, forms a basis for developing a contented form of life as expressed by the seekers themselves. This supports Seligman's (2012) findings, where purpose and direction was one of the three factors most important for a happy life.

6.5.3 The Sheikh's Impact on the Seeker

In terms of role-modelling, it is important to see how the Sheikh imparts his behaviour to the seekers. The Venn diagram above derived from the survey indicates that most of the respondents indicate that they learn the most by the Sheikh 'setting an example', which was followed by 'demonstration', then 'admonishment' and then 'the establishment of ground rules' (Fig. 5.11).

This shows that the seeker's observational skills, which is primarily non-verbal, plays an important role, combined with demonstrations by the Sheikh, which shows both an active form as well as the passive or silent one. The essential teaching of the Sheikh is on anger management (Fig. 5.20) that imparts the seekers to be silent, say a prayer, get advice from others, supplicate to God, be patient and says *salawat* (praise on the Prophet). This is a manifestation of the example of the Prophet and his behaviour, which has been elaborated on in Sect. 2.5 based on several early sources. Thus, we see here the Sheikh himself emulating and modelling the Prophet.

The next section now deals with the process and content of modelling of the Sheikh utilising an unorthodox methodology called Neuro-Semantic and Neuro-Linguistic Programming (NS-NLP).

6.5.4 Neuro-Semantic (NS) and Neuro-Linguistic Programming (NLP) Modeling of the Sheikh

Here, a technique and format from NS-NLP has been utilised, to capture the essential features of the Sheikh, aimed at gaining a better understanding of why and how he functions. Within NS-NLP there are meta-states, which is a sense of awareness of what is going on: while meta-programmes are a process used for formalising or structuring one's thinking, emotions and perceptions (see Chap. 4.6 on methodology, also Hall and Bodenhamer 2006), in this sense it is a filter through which one see the world. Here, an attempt is made to capture some aspects of the Sheikh's meta-states and meta-programmes.

The NLP modelling format presented below was populated by the author based on the survey and the interview data, which was validated by explaining and sharing it with the Centre manager. Each of the main components are clarified here:

Skills The Sheikh has several skills in that, apart from being a spiritual guide, he is an academic and writer, able to skilfully mentor seekers, both residents and general. He is able to speak in public as well as offers one-to-one counselling.

Strategies An integrated approach to spirituality including treating the mind-body-soul. The Sheikh evokes the role of the Prophet and references the past sheikhs as well as sharing narratives, demonstrating virtuous behaviour and writing and reading stories.

The element with most impact which can be discerned about this Order is that it advocates a holistic approach to spirituality and in dealing with its seekers. By this it is meant that those residents who are taking medication continue to do so, while they are taught to develop their spiritual activities, which is a combination of lectures, *dhikr* (remembrance of God), chanting liturgy (*wird*), one-to-one counselling, repentance, supplication, learning patience, Islamic reflexology, and various types of prayers including the obligatory and optional. The approach of the Sheikh is one which is very composed, as one seeker put it 'staying cool' and is an iterative approach to teaching and learning, which provides the seekers time to reflect, test things out, and internalise them. The combination of techniques mentioned above are used by the Sheikh for the general seekers, and he rotates his visits to different locations utilising mosques and the Orders sub-centres as well as have sessions in his own home.

Screen Play on the Mind The Sheikh uses a combination of techniques to imprint on the minds and hearts of the seekers, including sharing narratives of the Prophet, his companions (*sahabas*) and other role-models, by writing about the field of '*tasawwuf*' (inward sciences), public speaking, interactive methods including group gatherings, and one-one-counselling.

States and Intensity This is difficult to capture given that there is an array of activities undertaken by the seekers to which the researcher was not privy. However, the varying states of energy, with high intensity was observed during the group loud and silent *dhikrs*, which is done using voice (auditory) and breathing (kinaesthetic). This combined with the therapeutic approach including Islamic reflexology gives it both the extensiveness, as well as the intensiveness of these activities as observed by me.

Primary States (Movie Mind) States consists of mind-body-emotions, the sum total of all neurological and physical processes within an individual at any moment in time and a holistic phenomenon of mind-body-emotions-moods. VAK is used for the sensory representation systems of Visual, Auditory and Kinaesthetic. The 'visual' refers to seeing and imaging, the representation systems of sight (Hall and Bodenhamer 2006). The 'auditory' is used for the sense of hearing; a basic sensory representation system. The last one (K) includes smells (olfactory) and tastes (gustatory). 'Kinaesthetic' are sensations, feelings, tactile sensations on surface of skin, proprioceptive sensations inside the body, including the vestibular system. These states are elaborated below in the section of primary states. These includes Visual-auditory plus Visual and kinaesthetic plus Auditory-visual and Auditory kinaesthetic, and Kinaesthetic-visual and Kinasesthetic-auditory (the capitalisation signifying which is dominant at one point in time). Figure 6.5 captures the main sensory processes and sub-processes.

Meta-States: Significance, connected, excused, feel the self
Gestalt State: Growth (self) and contributions to the life of other
Frames: In oneness of God
Belief: In the hereafter (next life)
Values: Serve others, forgiving, tolerant, charitable, gratitude, humble, polite
Decisions: To lead others towards God
Identification: Main Sunni stream of Islam with focus on the inward sciences (*tasawwuf*), understanding/background knowledge: Qur'ān, sunnah and *tasawwuf*.
Attractors: Service to God.

Meta-Programmes:

Primary States There is a combination of many aspects on how the mind and body receive information and how it is processed and disseminated. The Sheikh

Fig. 6.5 The different types of primary-states combination

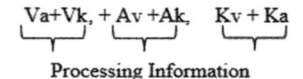

$Va+Vk, + Av +Ak, Kv + Ka$

Processing Information

6.5 The Spiritual Order—The Sheikh as Exemplar 261

uses the visual (V) and auditory (A) modes, that is, through his lectures (A) and in discussions he evokes imagery (V) to explain things of importance. For example, he cites verses from the Qur'ān and narrates the Prophetic *ḥadīth*. In reality, there are combinations of the VAK (visual-auditory-kinaesthetic) that are used in different variations since in many instances movement of the body is involved on the part of the Sheikh, as well as the seekers, especially during *dhikr* (see Figs. 5.12, 5.22, 5.29). He then explains these verses and sayings, which lends itself to the auditory aspects and some visualisation (Av). The kinaesthetic visualisation (Kv) element is pronounced in the group *dhikr* where there is intense sensation and interaction between the Sheikh as well as those facilitating the *dhikr*. Pronunciation of the word of God and the breathing movement with focus on God are kinaesthetic, while selected seekers go around and offer guidance to the seekers who tend to visualise - 'worship God as they see Him and if they do not see Him, He sees them' (An Nawawi 2004). During the sessions, one finds a 'flow of energy' (Ka—Kinaesthetic auditory) given that the whole group is performing the *dhikr* simultaneously, with a very intense feeling brought about by vibrations like the buzzing of bees. The psycho-physiological changes and effects on the seekers through intense meditation (*dhikr*) are well corroborated by neuro-scientific work (see Sect. 2.4).

Skills: Mentoring, writing, counselling, coaching and public speaking.

Meta-states and Meta-programmes (See Table 6.2) These states are of a higher-level order and differ from the primary states of information processing by the seekers. The meta states or programmes refer to what makes people 'tick' and motivates them and in the case of the Sheikh, it can be stated as being that of making significance, feeling connected, the development of the self and being meritorious. For example, within the core-values framework (see Fig. 6.2) it can be stated that a movement away from the ruinous (evil) to the virtuous traits provides the trajectory for the seekers to develop themselves. To this effect, the Sheikh uses a variety of means to teach and share (VAK) with the seekers including the philosophical approach of raising key questions about the meaning and purpose of life (cognitive), to exercising patience and being compassionate (emotional-feeling—emotive states).

The conative (meaning) aspects are seen in the Sheikh striving to set goals for the seekers, while trying to do things to perfection. His style of management is very much decentralised as evident in his delegation to his khalifas or deputies to lead and conduct their own sub-centres, while he attempts to work in a collaborative manner so that the deputies and seekers feel empowered. One of the key aspects of the Order is the mind-body integration, where the focus is on 'eating to live' (rather than living to eat), and an intense form of worship, which are aimed at unravelling experiential learning from within, which is the essence of the meditative process. In this sense, there is the aspect of de-learning and re-learning and developing the ten core values that were articulated by the resident imam and his friend which were outlined in the case study chapter.

Gestalt State This is the highest order state, which forms the core-construct or key values of the Sheikh, or to put it another way, why the Sheikh is doing what he

Table 6.2 Modelling template for Leader-Sheikh behaviour

Focus	(Thinking) Cognitive	(Feeling) Emotional	(Choosing) Conative	(Meta-Meaning) Semantic
Meta-programs:	Representation	Persistence	Goal striving	Self-experience
	VAK/Language	(Patience)	Perfectionist	Mind, body, emotions will
	Epistemological Intuitor-sensor		Optimalist Management	Self-integrity Harmonious, integration
	Conceptualizing-Experiencing		Delegate Collaborative	Responsibility Healthy responsibility
	Philosophical Why/origins		Flexible	Time zones Past-present-future
	How/solutions Understanding-Getting results Information kind			Values List of values: Needs-wants Important-urgent
	Quantity-Quantitative			

is doing. The response based on the survey and interview data can be outlined as promoting the growth of himself spiritually as well as to the development of others, in this case the seekers' spiritual growth.

Frame of Reference and Belief The main frame of reference is the belief in One God, and the belief in not only this life (*dunya*) but the hereafter (*ākhira*). In this sense, the core values of the Sheikh as seen both in the interview and survey data includes serving others, forgiving, exercising tolerance, being charitable, gratitude to God, courteousness to the seekers etc. (Figs. 5.9, 5.10).

Values and Decision One of the key findings is that the Sheikh and the Order have developed a core value system that is wide ranging and includes serving others, being patient, loving, generous, forgiving, tolerant, charitable, gratitude, humble, polite etc. (see Figs. 5.9, 5.10, 5.13, 5.14). What I found most relevant is that this value framework is presented and utilised actively by the seekers to better themselves. They are seen to consciously practice and reflect on these values by mirroring and checking between themselves their progress or lack of it, which was a revelation for me.

Identification and Attractors Given the criticism of these types of spiritual Orders, it was important to identify their source of guidance, which in this case was the divine writ (Qur'ān) and the Prophetic actions and saying (*ḥadīth*) as well as following the inward tradition of '*tasawwuf*'. The fundamental attractor is service towards God, with the aim of gaining knowledge possibly leading towards *ma'rifa* (divine knowledge) and experiential learning.

6.6 The Membership of the Order

Similar to the 'calling' and the 'leadership of the Sheikh', 'membership' forms an important control variable, without which the stated outcomes variables cannot be accomplished as a general rule: that is, it is key to transformation. There is a sense of belonging to the Order, which is apparent in the various dialogues manifested in the interviews and that this Order is different to others that they had experienced. This is solidified by three main aspects that form the approach, methods and tools of the Order, known as *tarqiyah* (spiritual grooming), *tarbiyah* (education), and *tazkiyah* (purification) and these aspects are highlighted below. Goleman best captures this when he points out the need for overcoming negative emotions by retraining one's attention (education), change of perceptual habits (process of purification) and sitting in the company of those who have transformed (being with the Sheikh and peers).

6.6.1 Approaches, Methods and Tools—Tarqiyah (Spiritual Grooming), Tarbiyah (Education), Tazkiyah (Purification)

Tarqiyah (Spiritual Grooming) The role of the exemplar or the Sheikh as already seen in previous sections is most fundamental in guiding the seeker along the path, having successfully traversed it himself. It is from him that the seekers observe the characteristics they seek to emulate, and receive the knowledge they seek to implement as well as the guidance they need to overcome the obstacles in their way.

One of the most significant findings of this study, apart from the role of the exemplar, is the methods of worship that are a part of the core value system, which is the driver and the motivator both from the point of view of the Sheikh as well as the seekers. From the perspective of the Sheikh, he uses the framework of the attributes of God as a core value system for the seekers to model. These attributes can be broadly classified into two categories; the majestic and powerful (Jalāli) and the beautiful and merciful (Jamāli).

Some of these, especially the ten core values, some of which are derived from the attributes of God and the others to spiritual states of being that seekers experience in their journey, and this is explicitly evident in the dialogue that is pursued with the resident Imam and his friend, where they outline these ten which they try to emulate during their course of life, namely: *baraqa* (blessings), *shukr* (gratitude), *tawakkul* (trust), *tauba* (repentance), *sabr* (patience), *zuhd* (spiritual poverty), *amal* (hope), *riḍa* (acceptance) and *takut* (fear). There is a narrative that these are spiritual stations (makamas) that the seeker has to traverse in his/her journey to reach the goal.

The survey data extracts refer to the most important traits for the development of the self, as well as the worst vices from the perspective of the seekers, these can be developed into a tree of virtues and vices as illustrated above (Fig. 6.2). Vices in order of the seekers priority includes: anger (1), love of this world (2), heedlessness (3), false hope (4), ostentation (5), arrogance, a desire to inflict harm, anxiety, stinginess, avarice, envy, superiority, vanity, boasting, seeking reputation, fraud, wantonness, inequality, cowardice, and emotional attachment to the world.

It is interesting to note that the most important traits that the seekers identified in the Sheikh (Fig. 5.9) were: patience (59 percent), humbleness (53 per cent), forgiveness (50 per cent), love (47 per cent), wisdom (44 per cent), honesty (41 per cent) and trust (41 per cent). The traits that they selected mirror what the seekers feel is important to their own lives and is based on their own choosing and understanding these above mentioned values.

Concerning the vices that the seekers felt were most detrimental, based on their experiences are listed as the follows in order of rank: anger, heedlessness and laziness, superiority, arrogance, love of the world, forgetfulness, anxiety, fraud, greedy, materialism and pride (Figs. 5.15, 5.16, 5.17, 5.18). This closely corroborates with the ruinous traits outlined by five eminent scholars, Sheikh Abul Hasan al-Kharaqāni, Imam Mawlud al-Ya'qūbi, Imam Abu Hāmid al-Ghazāli, Imam Ibn Jawziya, and Imam Ibn Hazm al-Andalūs (see Sect. 3.5).

While striving towards perfection is the ideal in this Order, there is no claim by the Sheikh of being so and no excessive veneration of him has been seen, which is often the criticism levelled against Sufi type of movements. However, there could be some similar movements where the extreme adulation of the Sheikh is questionable and may border on the impermissible from an strict orthodox viewpoint.

Tarbiyah (Education) There were a number of methods of education that were used within the Order and these include attending lectures (*kulliyyah*), one to one counselling by the Sheikh, recital and understanding of the Qur'ān and reading of the *ḥadīth*. This is very much a cognitive strategy and involves memory, attention, comprehension, and application of what one has learnt. It can be observed that although on one hand there is a cognitive process of learning, there is much emphasis on experiential learning and getting to know God by the unravelling of the conditioned self.

Teacher-Educator: The concept of teacher-educator is one of the most important aspects of spiritual education in its real sense[7] and this is seen broadly as the

---

[7]Even though there are contrary views on the philosopher and teacher Jiddu Krishnamurti the way he perceived religion and God, his rendition of education is very useful in terms of understanding what it is all about. His conversation with Dr. Allan.W.Anderson, San Diego, February 16th, 1972 is very insightful (what is the point of education?—https://www.youtube.com/watch?v=-

method of teaching of the Sheikh. This is demonstrated in the case study narrative of Chap. 5, where in the classical sense, the loving relationship of the teacher-Sheikh with the seekers was evident, where he was seen as loving, humble, caring, unassuming and 'cool' who provided the space to enthuse people to learn and grow. He brings in a quality of intelligence more than mere information by his story telling, one-to-one counselling, demonstration of practice etc. As some of the graphs indicated, the seekers learnt from him by watching him, his humbleness, his silence, his integrity and practising what he preached. There is seen a profound respect for him, which is not to be confused with veneration of the Sheikh, which is a critique from some quarters about the leaders of the spiritual orders (tariqas).

***Tazkiyah* (Purification)** Essentially this refers to a process of cleansing one's inner self, especially from vices, and learning to cultivate virtuous traits. Through their interactions with the Exemplar or Sheikh and through his teachings, the seekers are able to implement a daily regime of spiritual acts, which are wide ranging, starting well before dawn with the physical purification of oneself (*wuḍū'*), night vigil and prayers (*tahajjud*), accompanied by the ritual prayers (*salah*), fasting (*saum*), seeking repentance (*tauba*), supplication to God for change (*du'ā*), methods of remembrance of God (*dhikr*), and Qura'nic recital and the reading of the acts and words of the Prophet (*ḥadīth*). As is evident in the interviews and the surveys, seeking forgiveness, supplicating to God and the ritual and obligatory prayers form a sustained method in this process of mind-body cleansing. All of these acts follow the Prophetic practices as seen in Sect. 3.2.4, Tables 3.3 and 3.4, which sets the foundational standards for the Sheikh to follow, which was then transmitted to the seekers.

***Dhikr* (Remembrance of God)** Apart from the ritual prayers, one of the integral aspects of Islam is the remembrance of God or *dhikr*. On a general note, the focus on *dhikr* has somehow been lost in the process of time and almost weeded out as a focused form of worship. There are only certain groups with Sufi orientation who consciously perform *dhikr* as a focused methodology, while Salafi oriented groups do not do it as a methodological process. It has been embroiled within the politics of the differences between Sufi and Salafi groups. It needs to be pointed out that *dhikr* can take many forms, including ritual prayer, which can be called movement meditation, the recitation of the Qur'ān also called scriptural meditation, supplication to God (*du'ā*), repentance (*tauba*) and recital of praise upon the Prophet (*salawat*) etc.

5o2hJTllqc&t=1070s). His views closely align with the traditional concept of teacher-educator and the way that they taught students (*murids*) and the close relationship that they had with them, where there were loving relationships and at the same time open to them being critical about various subject and attaining diverse views. This follows the Prophetic model on the way he interacted and conducted this teaching, which caused the transformation of his disciples. As time moved on, the emergence and the variations in the four major schools of thought and law (the four Mazhabs) even though all of them had a teacher-student relationship with each other, they differed in their views and this is a solid example on this matter.

While agreeing to all of the above as some form or type of meditation, the focus here is on *dhikr* as a focused form of worship and as a methodological process. This, if properly done, has a profound effect on the mind-body, as indicated by emerging neuroscientific data. From my own experience, my ritual prayers were enhanced in terms of focus and absorption following my deep immersion into silent *dhikr*. Both the quality of my prayers and my life seem to have been enriched by it, while concurrently enabling me to let go of addictions that I used to have. This, to me, has been transformative in shaping how I receive and respond to information and stimuli, characterised by greater patience and understanding, which was clearly not the case before.

In terms of *dhikr* itself, there are several citations from the Qur'ān as well as the Prophetic narrations as follows:

> Recite what has been revealed to you of the Book, and perform the *salah* (prayer). Verily, the *salah* prevents from al-faḥsh (immoral sins) and al-munkar (evil deeds) and the remembering (praising) of Allah is greater indeed (Surah al-Ankabut 29:45).

There are two interpretations of this, in Ibn Kathir's version (2003a) the remembrance of God is included within the ritual prayer, while in the literal translation, as is stated above, there is a separation of recital of the Qur'ān, the ritual prayers and the remembering of God (*dhikr*), this is supported by an authentic Prophetic narration, which is seen to put *dhikr* into a category of its own with the emphasis of it being greater. A striking Prophetic *ḥadīth*[8] in this regard is outlined below:

> 'Shall I tell you about the best of deeds, the most pure in the sight of your Lord, about the one that is of the highest order and is far better for you than spending gold and silver, even better for you than meeting your enemies in the battlefield where you strike at their necks and they at yours?' The Companions replied, 'Yes, O Messenger of Allah!' The Prophet, peace be upon him, said, 'Remembrance of Allah.'

Another Qur'ānic verse (al-Baqara 2:151–152) extols the remembrance of God, supported by a Prophetic narration of Divine speech (*ḥadīth qudsi*) (An-Nawawi 2004) that follows it:

> We have sent among you a Messenger of your own, reciting to you Our verses and purifying you, and teaching you the book, and the wisdom and teaching you that which you did not know. Therefore, remember Me. I will remember you, and be grateful to Me, and never be ungrateful to Me.
>
> I am as My servant thinks I am, and I am with him when he remembers Me. If he remembers Me to himself, I remember him to Myself; and if he remembers Me in a gathering, I remember him in a gathering better than it. If he draws near to Me a hand's span, I draw near to him an arm's length; if he draws near to him an arm's length, I draw near to him a fathom's length; and if he comes to Me walking, I go to him with haste.

These above proclamations reinforce the need for silent contemplation (*dhikr khafi* or *dhikr qalb*) and consistently remembering God, without referring to a

---

[8]It is narrated by the Prophet's companion Abu Darda, and is cited in many sources including Imam Malik's Muwatta, the Musnad of Imam Ahmed, the Sunan of Tirmidhi, Ibn Majah and the Mustadrak of Hakim and categorised as authentic (sunnah.org n.d.).

specific act of worship. There is a subtle difference in translation of the above Qur'ānic verse, Mubarakpuri chose 'purifying you' while Muhammad Asad (2011), interpreted it as, 'to cause you to grow in purity', signifying the concept of 'tazkiatun nafs' or the purification of the self.

As already stated there is evidence from authentic *ḥadīth* that there was a form of loud *dhikr* during the time of the Prophet, when the ritual prayer (*salah*) was completed as stated by the companions Amr Ibn al-Asr and Ibn Ma'bad. The evidence for the silent *dhikr* comes from one of the authentic *ḥadīth*, where the Prophet and his companions were seated absolutely still as if a bird was perched on their heads, indicating some form of contemplation. There is no exact methodology stated in *ḥadīth* literature or in the Qur'ān about the silent *dhikr* except a verse calling on mankind to remember God within ourselves, in silence, with humility and reverence (7:205). Aside from this, there are many verses in the Qur'ān that refer to doing *dhikr* outside the ritual prayers, while a Prophetic saying testifies to its effects as the polishing of the heart.

In the in the absence of an explicit methodology of *dhikr* being outlined in the *ḥadīth* or the Qur'ān, people have either completely eliminated it from their practices or have developed their own methodology. For the Naqshbandiyyah Khālidiyyah both its loud and silent *dhikr* take its methodology from the founder of the Naqshabandiyyah *ṭarīqa* Bahā' al-Dīn Naqshabandiyyah. After learning from his sheikhs, he developed a system which outlines seven points in the physical body (see Chap. 5, Fig. 5.21). These points, called '*latāifs*' or subtle spiritual organs, which are also called faculties of supra sensory, are effectively energy points that are enlightened through a process of remembering God. This leads one to gain closer access to the path of God and opens up new vistas of knowledge. This is said to lead one to '*ma'rifa*' or knowledge of the divine or higher reality, which as we have noted was one of the key objectives of this spiritual Order.

It is necessary to point out that *tasawwuf*, which includes '*tazkiyatun nafs*', means the purification of one's self and this is an essential aspect of Islam. Even though there are proponents within Islam who deem this aspect as an innovation, the strongest point of reference is the Qur'ān, which states,"Consider the human self, and how it is formed in accordance with what it is meant to be, and how it is imbued with moral failings as well as with the consciousness of God. To a happy state shall indeed attain he who causes this (self) to grow in purity, and truly lost is he who buries it (in darkness)" (Qur'ān, al-Shams 91: 7–10). Thus, Islamic scholars (Yusuf 2015a,b; Winters 2015) recognise that '*tasawwuf*' is a Qur'ānic based science, even though there are variations on its methodology and what is acceptable within the framework of orthodox Islam.

There has been an increasing number of resources including written as well as audio-visual materials, which discusses in some detail about Islamic meditation and the *latāifs* (subtle spiritual organs in the body) (Mendes 2014, Shah 2012, Mirhamadi 2016a,b, Alexander 2015). Some say that this system is similar to 'chakras in the yogic system and the Chinese 'Tao' system. However, there are references to these points in the Qur'ān—heart (*qalb*), spirit (*rūḥ*), inner secret (*sirr*), although there is no specific scriptural (Qur'ān and *ḥadīth*) indication relating to its methodology. The system of *latāifs* may have been developed through experiential learning and contemplation and not necessarily be modelled on the yogic or the Chinese system. There is ample evidence for systems and values to be developed independently. For example, one finds great variation in geographic locations yet there are similarities in aspects of their practices, such as, the universal value system, which has roots in all religions, the practice of prostration seen in both monotheistic and polytheistic religions and spiritual experiences including near death states of consciousness are examples of these.

As already evidenced in some neuroscientific studies, this type of meditation has a profound impact on the neurophysiology apart from the impact that we have already outlined by performing ritual prayer (*salah*). The combination of both prayers and dhikr (remembrance), which is seen to be similar to mindfulness, is enhanced by meditation, where in this case the researcher monitored the transcendental meditation process (TM) (Aldahadha 2013). Within the Islamic Sufi tradition there are both loud and silent *dhikrs*, the latter being similar to TM, with a whole system of metaphysics to support it, which has unfortunately not been scientifically or rigorously researched, and is well worth the exploration for those interested in this science. Figure 6.6 (Ibrahim 2008)[9] shows the varying heart rate in the Muslim ritual prayer positions, where the prostration records the lowest heart rate, while Fig. 6.7 (Cheok 2008)[10] indicates dominant alpha signals during prostration, which shows mental calmness.

This is further supported by an increasing number of studies (Ibrahim et al. 2008; Doufesh et al. 2012; Hisham 2008), where beneficial effects were found from EEG and physiological measurements, especially relating to ritual and voluntary prayers, fasting and *dhikr*, which range from emission of alpha waves, increase in the capacity of cellular fluids, decrease in Heart Rate Variability (HRV) and lowering of the metabolic rate. Further research in this field is required, in terms of having a larger sample size, as well as more longitudinal studies to robustly corroborate these initial findings.

Regarding the development of the self, Imam Ghazāli (1995) provides a comprehensive framework, which encapsulates many of its aspects including *mushārata* (taking account of passion), *murāqaba* (deep meditation), *muḥāsaba* (taking account of oneself), *mu'āqaba* (punishment of oneself), *mujāhada* (exerting efforts) and *mu'ātaba* (self-rebuke). This has been elaborated on in Sect. 2.4 on contemplative practices. These key aspects of contemplative practices have ceased to be part of main-stream narrative and need to be revived in the contemporary

---

[9]This picture is courtesy of Professor Fatimah Ibrahim, from "Heart Rate" (2008) by Fatimah Ibrahim in "Salat: Benefit From the Science Perspective" by Fatimah Ibrahim, Wan Abu Bakar Wan Abas and NG Siew Cheok. Faculty of Engineering, University of Bio-Engineering, University of Malaya, Malaysia. (pp. 46).

[10]This picture is courtesy of Professor Fatimah Ibrahim, from "The Brain" (2008) by NG Siew Cheok in "Salat: Benefit From the Science Perspective" by Fatimah Ibrahim, Wan Abu Bakar Wan Abas and NG Siew Cheok. Faculty of Engineering, University of Bio-Engineering, University of Malaya, Malaysia. (pp. 74).

6.6 The Membership of the Order

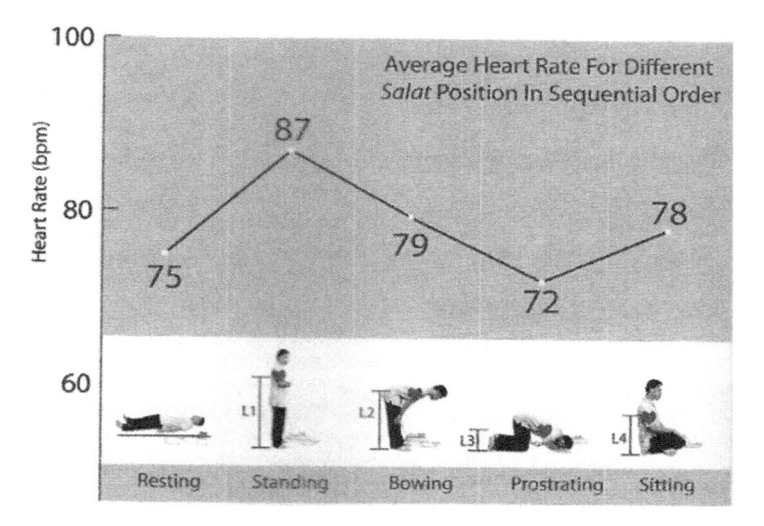

Fig. 6.6 Average heart rate for different *Salah* (ritual prayer) positions in sequential order

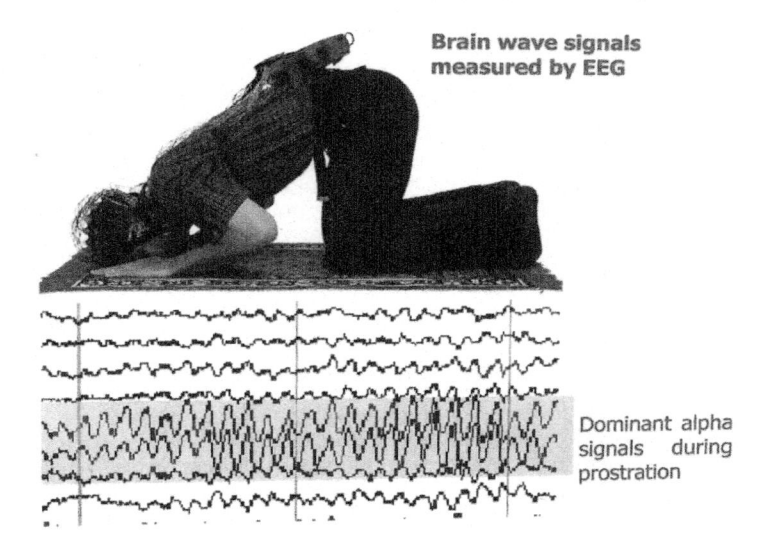

Fig. 6.7 Brain wave signals measure by EEG

context, where it is most needed due to the hectic lifestyle and stresses one experiences. We seem to be so preoccupied with the outer aspects of the faith that the spirit of the inner is either overlooked or lost in the process.

Ibn 'Arabi (2008) in his pillars of spiritual transformation refers to four fundamental aspects for this purpose, which includes keeping vigilance (*sahar*), being in a state of hunger (*ju*), maintaining silence (*samt*) and seclusion (*'uzlah*), these corroborate with the data generated from this research, which subsumes all of these contemplative practices by the seekers of the Order. Ibn 'Arabi puts these salient aspects into a holistic context when he points out, "We empty our hears of reflective thinking, and we sit together with the al-Ḥaqq (The Real) on the carpet of *adab* (pious conduct) and *murāqaba* (spiritual attentiveness) and presence and readiness to receive whatever comes to us from Him—so that it is God who takes care of teaching us by means of unveiling and spiritual realisation" (Morris 2005). In this light, the seekers focus is on"perfect collectedness in contemplation (*murāqaba*) and if God's grace persists then he may attain vision (*mushāhada*)" (Schimmel 1975).

6.7 The Performance of the Order

This can be categorized as a 'dependent variable', which is influenced by the 'efforts' exerted by the seekers. One of the key aspects within the metaphysical perspective is that, the blessings of God are channelled through the Sheikh to the seeker called *tawajjuh* (spiritual attention), which is also termed the spiritual beneficence. In this sense the seekers are supported in their spiritual journey by the facilitation of their Sheikh, as well as exerting their own effort or struggle (*jihad*). This concept of *tawajjuh* is challenged by some within the Islamic community, who argue that blessings are only from God. The counter argument to this is that being in the company of those who are spiritually elevated and connected to the Divine brings about benefits by virtue of their station and nearness to God and His messenger, while blessings and guidance originate solely from God, whatever the circumstances.

My own thoughts on the subject are that most of us need a mentor to facilitate our spiritual journey since the mind is complex and often we cannot see our own faults—the blind spot (see Sect. 3.1, Figure 3.1—the Johari window) and machinations of the mind. A guide or a mentor is someone whom you are able to openly converse about your life and spiritual journey, and who is able to use his/her wisdom to facilitate, while providing you with related prayers and supplication to enhance this process. Moreover, it was the tradition amongst the companions of the Prophet to ask each other about their individual state of affairs and blemishes, with the aim of rectifying themselves (see Chap. 3). This is representative of peer to peer reflections, which was found to be of important especially with the Centre's resident seekers.

One of the fundamental factors for those aspiring to improve performance is experiential learning, both in terms of *dhikr* as well as ritual prayers (*salah*). This type of experience can sometimes be shared, while at other times it cannot due to its richness of it, and the limitations of words to express it. This, combined with the aim of trying to perfect the outward practices, reinforces performance according to the seekers. There are many factors that influence performance, and these can be categorised into intrinsic and extrinsic factors as outlined below.

6.8 Intrinsic and Extrinsic Factors Impacting Self-Development

There are several factors that were indicated by the seekers, both the centre residents and the general seekers, that can lead to the development of the self. These can be divided into internal and external factors. Each of these categories is briefly explained below. Both external and internal factors were found to be important for the seekers but as the survey data indicates the internal factors superseded the external.

Intrinsic Factors There were a number of intrinsic factors that were highlighted as being the key:

i. Self-realisation was seen as a vital aspect; the seekers found it to be a motivational factor in initiating the desire for change;
ii. The heart–brain connection was the most interesting finding, which catalyses the change. This is further expounded in the next section;
iii. Learning lessons, testing and refining were found to be aspects which facilitated internalisation and habit formation;
iv. Observation of the Sheikh and self-modelling over time formed one of the platform that made change possible;
v. Testing new ideas, practices and concepts helped to re-define what they had learnt in the past, a trigger to change habits;
vi. Self-reflection on their past led to repentance, which formed the basis for setting in motion a process in self-purification and adhering to good habits;
vii. Adaptation to the new environment and to the other seekers and changing circumstances as they observed the change, reinforced the change in behaviour;
viii. Dreams formed a vehicle for receiving messages of change and reinforcing their faith.

Extrinsic Factors There were a number of extrinsic factors, a combination of which facilitated the interaction of the residents in the Centre, as well as helping the seekers with their personal growth:

i. One to one counselling by the Sheikh with the seekers, helping them to become centred, helped to give them the confidence to sustain their change;
ii. Kulliyah—intermittent lectures by the Sheikh to groups in various locations, which the seekers attend depending on their proximity. The topic of the lectures varies, from sharing the ten most virtuous traits, to methods of worship and stories of the Prophets and the Sages;
iii. Setting of ground rules and their reinforcement by the manager and supervisor of the Centre helped the seekers structure their prayers, ritual acts and lifestyles, aiding their transformation;
iv. Peer group facilitation was found to be very vital for the seekers to learn, adapt and internalise their change and transformation;

v. The immediate environment plays an important part in facilitating the growth of the residents, as well as for the general seekers. This includes learning the rituals and rules of conduct as well as social interaction, which is seen to foster caring and is directed towards the worship of one God;
vi. Needs based therapy, whereby residents get their required medical treatment combined with the spiritual practices. This includes meditative and contemplative practices, and is reinforced with what is called Islamic reflexology, which seems to have positive mental effects.
vii. The love and care of the Sheikh and his wife to the seekers both general and more importantly those Centre residents who see them as anchors providing them with spiritual nourishments and guiding them when needed.

One observes that there are internal changes and states of these seekers, where some of these methods and devotional acts leads them to a state of deep meditation and hence a state of relaxation and a sense of peace, as reported in the interviews and survey data. This state benefits both body and mind is corroborated by neuroscientific findings as articulated in Sect. 2.4 by the research of Ibrahim et al. (2008), Doufesh et al. (2012) and Aldahadha (2013). These practices have been upheld for more than a thousand year, and those seekers who have experienced the power of its transformations did not need scientific explanations for pursuing it.

This change which occurs when practicing contemplative practices can be stated as changing levels of consciousness or altered consciousness as some would call it, which comes through a process of a combination of factors both intrinsic and extrinsic as outlined above. It is worthy of noting that within the Islamic framework there are seven major branches, which can be condensed into three dimensions as shown in the contemplative tree in Sect. 2.3: (1) the practices where the mind and more specifically the heart predominate, namely, stillness (prayers, meditation) and creative practices (poetry, prose, art); (2) practices where collective behaviour predominates including generative (loud prayer, congregational prayer, loud *dhikr*) and relational practices (dialogue, mentoring, spiritual guidance); (3) practices where the body predominates including activist ('Umrah, voluntary services), movement (mindfulness while sitting, walking, journeying) and ritualistic (obligatory prayers, Hajj, Ramadan).

Self-restraint was found to be one of the more difficult concepts that seekers had to learn and implement, given their earlier state of promiscuity. Dreams were reported as a way of indicating change and reinforcement of their progress. While the inner state was seen as crucial, the external environment facilitated and reinforced the change process: these include peer support which we have seen as being paramount to learning, motivating and refining.

Relating to the Centre's residents, the setting of ground rules and an infusion of a sense of discipline by the manager and supervisor are key to establishing order and functionality and keeping residents on track. The majority of the residents had been abandoned by their families due to their earlier unsociable and harmful behaviour, however after joining the Centre it has been demonstrated that they are better able to reconnect with them and be accepted back into the fold. It is worthy of noting that the Centre encourages this process of family reconciliation.

6.9 The Reward for the Seekers

The reward for the seekers, like the variable 'performance', can be categorised as a 'dependent variable' and is influenced by 'efforts' of the seeker and the Grace of God, where the latter is part of the core belief. Rewards are intimately connected with 'performance' and reinforce each other. On a general note, the better the performance, the greater the reward, and this is dependent on the guidance of the spiritual leader, as well as the approach, methods and tools embedded within the 'membership' of the Order. The drive and motivation of the seekers comes from the spiritual reward or merits (*baraqa*) that they will get by performing these spiritual acts. It is to be noted that for some seekers the reward is slower in being generated and this is where patience as well as the guidance of the Sheikh comes in and where the sustainment of these practices over time pays off.

There are two kinds of rewards from an Islamic perspective, that is, first, the spiritual merits (*baraqa*) that one gets from participating in religious or virtuous activities and, second, what one is to receive in the next life.

As seen by the response of the seekers, they feel a sense of peace and serenity that comes from the acts of worship including meditation (*murāqaba*), which is now evidentially backed by neuroscience data on wellbeing, as well as from observing the effects of virtuous traits including patience, gratitude, humbleness, honesty, trust, forgiveness, tolerance etc. on the individual. Here one finds that inter-link between worship and morality, where apart from worship, behaviour by itself has an effect on the mind-body, for example, by observing patience in testing situations one remains composed with no major change in one's psychology or physiology, which would otherwise negatively affect the concerned individual. When one meets a truly spiritual person, one generally finds that person to be calm, well behaved and helpful, which represents a sense of deep spirituality and connectedness.

Performance and rewards are intertwined, whereby one reinforces the other by way of motivation, and these two aspects serve as an engine for driving forth the spiritual quest of the seekers, which is outlined below.

6.10 The Outcomes of the Order—Wellbeing and the Worshipper

6.10.1 Outcomes of the Order

The product of the whole process is the positive transformation that seekers experience, especially in the case of the residents overcoming addictions, including a sense of peace and togetherness with their peers and families, as evident in the survey data results (Figs. 5.19, 5.23, 5.25). The seekers experience benefits that are spiritual, physical, physiological, emotional, social and cultural among others. This essentially forms the key dimensions of human wellbeing within the Islamic tradition, as outlined in Figure 3.2.3 (Sect. 3.2) and elaborated in this section.

The improvements in wellbeing highlighted above by the seekers in this research are well corroborated by an increasing number of scientific studies that have been recently carried out on Muslim ritual prayers and *dhikr* (Doufesh et al. 2012, Ibrahim et al. 2008, Afifi 1997, Roky et al. 2003). There are beneficial effects derived from the spiritual practice of fasting, including reduced oxidative stress and inflammation in overweight women at risk with breast cancer (Harvie et al. n.d.; Teng et al. 2011), and a reduction of body weight and fat, as well as elevation of mood for ageing men. Section 2.4 deals with these in greater detail and adds credence to the findings of this research. An ethnographic study in Central Asia (Pasilov and Ashirov 2007) points out:

> the ceremony of the *jahri dhikr* was quite often held for healing (curing) people from various diseases. In our field research, we also were witnesses of the still existing practice of treating people with the help of the important factors attesting this *dhikr*.....in our opinion....an atmosphere of strict regimen and regular participation of patients in the sessions of the jahri represents very important factors attesting this.

This study is supported by an interesting series of experimentations done with a Buddhist type of meditation called vippasana on prisoners in India, where the transformation was evident in inmates who were drug addicts, thieves, murderers and other types of criminals. This has been recorded through a series of documentaries (Karuna Films 2013). Vippasana is a non-discursive type of meditation; one does not focus on any object only observing one's self. This is similar to the silent *dhikr*, where the focus within this Order is on one's spiritual heart, no object is associated with it since God in Islam is formless, shapeless and beyond human comprehension. Thus, some similarities are observable although there are clear metaphysical differences between Buddhist and Islamic ideology and thoughts on the final destination.

As already detailed in Sect. 2.4, wellbeing refers to the 'absence of negative conditions or feelings, the result of adjustment and adaptation to a hazardous world' (Corey and Keyes 1998). Thus, the aggregated impact of the communities of practices like the spiritual Order under study can go beyond the physiological and psychological realm and be transmitted from an individual to a community and societal level, culminating in producing a global perspective. This in-effect represents the Therapeutic Life Change (TLC) that Walsh (2011) refers to in his study on mental health that can start from an individual level and evolve into a community of practices, which has implications on wider society. This is discussed in Sect. 2.4, Table 2.4.2, which sums up the impact and implications at individual, community, societal and global levels.

With regards to the transformation of the seekers, Walsh's (2011) articulation well captures the situation of the resident seekers of this study: Differences in just four lifestyle factors—smoking, physical activity, alcohol intake, and diet—exert a major impact on mortality, and even small differences in lifestyle can make a major difference in health status (Khaw et al. 2008). He further states that there has been an underestimation by health care professionals of the role of lifestyle changes on reducing multiple diseases, bringing about related psychopathologies, and on psychological and social wellbeing, while preserving and optimising cognitive capacities and neural functions.

6.10.2 Spirituality and SDGs

One finds spirituality completely excluded from the discussion on SDGs. Indeed, one seldom finds reference to it in any development or humanitarian literature. What is presented here from the data collected, is that, there is a direct correlation between spirituality and the SDGs, especially in terms of well-being and good health (SDG 3), quality education (SDG 4) and in terms of gender inclusion (SDG 5). Even though there does not seem to be a direct link with SDG goal number 16 relating to peace and justice since the framing of it is in the context of external peace, data is presented from this study, which is framed within an internal socio-psychological and spiritual dimension towards contributing to peace.

For SDG goal 3 (ensure healthy lives and promote well-being for all ages), from the data-set one can discern improvements in well-being due to their spiritual practices as expressed by the seekers, where they point out that they felt better physically, physiologically, emotionally, socially and culturally (Chap. 5, see Fig. 5.23). This is supported by, for instance, the reduction in heart rate during the prostration, sitting and resting phases of the prayer (Chap. 5, Table 5.1 and Fig. 6.6), as well as the emission of alpha waves (Chap. 6, Table 5.2 and Fig. 6.7), with all of these changes tending to contribute to their well-being. As the seekers have expressed in their narratives in Chap. 5, these neurophysiological changes make them calmer and more relaxed making them feel emotionally better, which then positively impacts their health status both physically and mentally. During this period, all of those who were interviewed had not taken drugs and stated that they had no desire to do so. Apart from this direct correlation on their well-being, the seekers also pointed out the improvement in their socio-cultural relationships with family, friends and enabled them to partake in various activities (Chap. 5, Figs. 5.24, 5.25, 5.26). This in a way contributes to two indicators within SDG goal 3, to promote mental health and well-being (3.4) and to strengthen the prevention and treatment of substance abuse, including narcotic drug abuse and harmful use of alcohol (3.5). This is significant given that half of the seekers whom I interviewed were ex-substance users, who had overcome their addiction through their interaction with the Order, and were given psychological support whilst dealing with HIV.

Education, in this case spiritual education, includes learning and practicing morality, ethics, learning of rituals, methods of contemplation and the study of hadith and Qur'an. This is augmented importantly with experiential learning, peer to peer engagement and modelling the Sheikh or guide. Thus, this involves both cognitive and non-cognitive or heart-based learning, which have different approaches and method as compared to formal education. The way that the seekers foster education is by improving their literacy through the books available especially for the resident seekers, as well as from the oral tradition of storytelling by the Sheikh, which is seen to form a basis on which they are able to discuss and reflect amongst themselves. This forms a peer-to-peer mirroring platform, where they can monitor their own progress and emulate the virtuous framework that they use which includes such virtues as *tauba* (repentance), *shukr* (thankfulness), *sabr* (patience), *zuhd* (state of poverty); *muhabat* (love), *ridha* (acceptance) etc. This virtuous framework is set as a goal towards which they, where this has been discussed in detail in Chap. 5.

Some aspects of SDG goal 4 is seen to be achieved within the Order, that is, to ensure that all learners acquire the knowledge and skills needed to promote sustainable lifestyles, promotion of peace and non-violence (4.7). This is seen in their tolerance with each other, the way they treat others, their re-engagement with their once estranged families and respect for outsiders, especially relating to the resident seekers. Some reflections can be made with regards to SDG 4.a, to build and upgrade education facilities that are child, disability and gender sensitive and provide safe, non-violent, inclusive and effective learning environments for all. The Order itself, as well as the treatment centre which is linked to it, has provided a space for interactive learning and transformation through the methodology of spiritual grooming (*tarqiyah*), education (*tarbiyah*) and purification (tazkiyah), which has been outlined in detail in Sects. 5.7.1, 5.7.2 and 5.7.3 respectively. As evidence to the above claims, there are several essential aspects of learning from modelling others to essential learning on anger management, type of learning and teaching methods and behaviours are captured in the Chap. 5, Tables 5.8, 5.9, 5.10, 5.11, 5.17, 5.20 and 5.29.

In terms of women's involvement in the Order (SDG goal 5), there is a sizeable proportion of women and this is evident in the attendance of the Sheikh's sessions. However, following the Islamic Shari'a code, men and women are segregated but sit together in the same space. Women are introduced to all of the spiritual methods and techniques as their male counterparts but are encouraged to perform it as and when they find time, amidst their multiple other duties. This study was only able to interview a couple of women, and this forms one of the limitations of this study from a gender perspective.

Given the inclusion of women in the spiritual Order, this goes towards fulfilling part of the indicators, that is, SDG goal 5.5 to ensure women's full and effective

6.10 The Outcomes of the Order—Wellbeing and the Worshipper

participation and equal opportunities for leadership at all levels of decision-making. In the latter point, women are fully participating members of the Order, but due to the innate nature of the structure of the Order women are not in leadership or key decision making positions as far as I observed. These types of orders are generally accessible to people from all walks of life, in this particular order there were ex-drug addicts, HIV patients and transgender individuals, as well as both men, women and children contributing to its working albeit in different capacities. Thus, they are inclusive in many aspects.

An important SDG goal is number 16, Peace, Justice and Inclusive Societies, which is largely developed around external variables of strengthening relevant institutions, policies and legislatures, while combating terrorism and trafficking etc. Perhaps only part of the two indicators 16.1, to reduce all forms of violence, and 16.2, to end abuse and exploitation, in a limited way, could be relevant to spirituality. The way this SDG is framed, its relevance is largely from an external point of view of making peace and not as much making peace with yourself, while having a pluralistic values and mind-set. This resonates on a global scale with what Dalai Lama[11] says "1. Universal humanitarianism is essential to solve global problems; 2. Compassion is the pillar of world peace; 3. All world religions are already for world peace in this way, as are all humanitarians of whatever ideology; 4. Each individual has a universal responsibility to shape institutions to serve human needs". The initiatives for achieving outside peace are necessary and negotiations and treaties are crucial, however, this could well be short lived if there is no peace within oneself underlined by a universal set of values that all religions both theistic and non-theistic faiths possess.

From the data-set what is evident is that the seekers of this Order have achieved a sense of inner peace as explicitly stated in Figs. 5.7 and 5.9. They consciously cultivate characteristics of patience, humbleness, forgiveness, love, kindness and trust (Figs. 5.12 and 5.13). The imbibing of this calm mind-set and these values comes about through a combination of tools, such as, being silent, mindful prayers, getting advice, being patient, supplicating to God, invoking praise upon the Prophet (Figs. 5.20, 5.24, 5.26) and modelling the Sheikh (see Figs. 5.8, 5.9, 5.10 and 5.11). The changes are manifested in the ways the seekers treat themselves, treat their once estranged families and others (see Figs. 5.19 and 5.24).

6.10.3 Towards a Spiritual Learning Theory

The research data is used here to try and work towards a spiritual learning theory based on Albert Bandura's social learning theory, which postulates that people learn

---

[11]This is a message from his Holiness the 14th Dalai Lama of Tibet in his writing A Human Approach To World Peace, https://www.dalailama.com/messages/world-peace/a-human-approach-to-world-peace.

not through reward and punishment but through observing others, where he argued that 'most human behaviours are learnt through modelling' (Bandura 2012). Some key elements of constructing a spiritual learning theory that are derived from the research data can be summarised as:

i. **Observing-Attention:** The seekers emulating the Sheikh-Exemplar by observing his verbal and non-verbal behaviour.
ii. **Reflection:** The seekers reflect on what they have observed from the Sheikh, as well as test out the ten virtues that they have learnt from him.
iii. **Self-Accounting:** The seekers take account of themselves vis-a-vis their past behaviours, which is a type of self-accounting.
iv. **Supplication:** The seekers elicit change through intense daily prayers, supplicating God to change their situation while asking others to pray for them.
v. **Mirroring:** Based on the self-modelling that the seeker is going through, they cross check or mirror their behaviour with their peers with an intent of improving it.
vi. **Testing and Retention:** They retain these behaviours and test them over time.
vii. **Reproduction:** The seekers physically reproduce these behaviours.
viii. **Internalisation and Motivation:** The seekers then internalise these behaviours reinforced by their cohort, which provide the motivation for them to share.

What is different about Bandura's social learning theory is that there are some spiritual features taken from the Islamic tradition:

i. **Reflection (*tafakkur*):** After their initial and sequential observations the seekers are seen to reflect (*tafakkur*) on it.
ii. **Self-accounting and Rebuke (*muḥāsaba* & *muataba*):** They take account of themselves (*muḥāsaba*) and self-rebuke (*muataba*) their past behaviour and take account of the changes that are occurring in them.
iii. **Supplication (du'ā):** They supplicate to God (du'ā) to change their situation, as well as asking others to pray for them.
iv. **Mirroring, internalisation and Motivation:** Thereafter, they cross-check with their peers or mirror those who have been able to internalise it, which provides the needed motivation.

There are some narratives that are reflected, especially in the dialogue of the resident imam and his friend, where for example he says, "I wake up to.....*tauba* (repentance) ....yes what sin has been done, what sin is forthcoming, what sin has gone (sic), so Allah please open my heart to follow and soften my tongue to read our Qur'ān because I will use methods like ritual repentance...", and in the changes outlined by the professional banker, who says, "During the *dhikr* I feel like some sort of vision, visualise, but the most important part, is that you feel within your heart. So that is the reason why we have to be close to the Sheikh, and there is this terminology *ṣoḥba* (sitting with the group and the Sheikh), the closeness with the Prophet." The female seekers highlighted that she went through a process of questioning herself:

where is the truth, what am I doing down here and how I missed the lectures. I miss going to the *tawajjuh* (spiritual attention from the Sheikh and the gathering) but how am I going for it (sic), I feel that basically helpless. So when you *tafakkur* (reflection) and of course the *dhikr* I do it every day...

There is a need for more elaborate observations with other spiritual orders to cross-check the emerging patterns. The key mechanism that Bandura outlines is the cognitive nature of the process, which mediates between the observing and imitating. However, in the elements that will go towards the future formation of a spiritual theory that is being postulated, there are non-cognitive factors related to the heart within the realm of contemplative practices that come into play. This is illustrated by the resident imam when he says,

> The brain and mind and the heart must come together in one, so when your brain sees something your heart must commit to it. We try hard.

This, then, defines and distinguishes the spiritual theory of learning from the social theory of learning, where some of the concepts are different in the latter as outlined above and that it is based on experiential learning from this Order. What has been proposed here is termed as towards a spiritual learning theory is really a framework since for it to become a spiritual theory, there is a need to do more extensive research, which replicates similar findings and builds on this to develop a comprehensive explanation, which then becomes a spiritual theory.

6.10.4 *The Nexus Between Worship ('Ibādah) and Morality (Akhlāq)*

Types of Worship and its Impact: Given the difficulty of having a working definition of prayer due to its complexities as well as its subtleties, Andresen (2000) divides it into two main categories, namely, the discursive and the non-discursive, which has already been outlined in Sect. 2.4 (Wellbeing and the Worshipper). The Islamic practices falls largely with the domain of non-discursive as defined by Andresen, which generally refers to "mental states that entertain a single thought/object serially, where the focus is on one God. This is characterised by the mind being focused upon a single object without voluntary discussion or involuntary distraction towards the objects." While discursive practices, are "mental states that entertain thoughts/objects serially. The mind focuses on a series of thoughts and images".

Ascertaining the practices within the Order under study, the obligatory and optional ritual prayers, the supplications, the repentance and especially the methods used during *dhikr* (remembrance of God) can all be categorised as a non-discursive method of practice (some parts of Table 6.2). This is so since within all of these practices the focus is on a single object, namely God. Andresen points out that the non-discursive methods are found to be more effective from a neurological point of view. This also corroborates with from my own as well as feedback from others that the non-discursive and silent type of meditation is more effective. For these practices to be effective, however, from a spiritual viewpoint the intention needs to be right, and it has to be done with 'khushu' or absorption as the Prophetic practice deems it to be. This spiritual position concurs with the physiological and neurological effectiveness when worship is done properly as the studies of Ibrahim et al. (2008, 2013) indicate, which support the states the seekers felt (Fig. 5.23). Thus, there appears to be a correlation between observing proper worship and the emerging neurological changes as indicated in neurological studies, where this seems to cut across all faiths as highlighted in numerous studies cited in Sect. 2.4, Chaps. 5 and 6.

Table 6.2 encapsulates the various and divergent methods of worship that the seekers undertake including both discursive and non-discursive types of worship. This table also highlights some examples of how the seekers model the Sheikh, that is, spiritual modelling as well as being facilitated by others in the Order.

Nexus Between Worship and Behaviour: One of the fundamental areas explored in this thesis is the nexus between worship and behaviour, or to frame it another way, does worship have an effect on one's behaviour denoting changes in morality or adapting a core value system? It was found that there appears to be an interconnection between the depth of worship and the behaviour of the seekers, and this is achieved through a process of adapting a combination of contemplative practices, modelling or emulating the Sheikh, as well as the peers and others around them. Thus, there seems to be a correlation between worship and its impact on behaviour, as both the survey and the interview data as outlined below.

One can discern from the survey as well as the interview data, that the seekers experienced various mental states as a result of sustained worship, including calmness, good behaviour towards their family and others, respect towards their parents, returning to the right path and reduced anxiety. It will be noted that these changes resulted from the sustained acts of worship by the seeker. This impact on the mental states of the individual worshipper and their behaviour does have a scientific basis.

There are a number of factors that are said to change one's behaviour including repentance, remembering God (*dhikr*), which needs to be internalised, as well as taking the oath of allegiance (*ba'ya*). The deepening of *dhikr*, which is done within their retreat, accelerated the transformation process through intensity and this is confirmed by neuroscientific evidence (Newberg and D'Aquili 2000) within the context of mindfulness meditation. This type of silent meditation is very similar to the method that is used in this Order (*ṭarīqa*) but goes much deeper since it is a regular activity combined with night vigil, individual as well as collective *dhikr* and retreats.

The Heart–Brain Connection: One of the most powerful messages to be articulated by the seekers is the connectivity of the heart and brain. Table 6.3 and its illustration in Fig. 6.8, where an attempt have been made to qualitatively cross tabulate, worship and morality with the brain and the heart as perceived by the seekers. The results demonstrate the reference to the brain and the heart in the context of spiritual development: the reference to the heart is much more in terms of impact on worship and morality than that of the brain. In this case, 10 references were made by the seekers to the heart and its effect on morality, while 26 references

6.10 The Outcomes of the Order—Wellbeing and the Worshipper

Table 6.3 Examples of methods and spiritual modelling

Method	Medium	Description
Sheikh's guidance	Group Dhikr—heart focused	The Centre Manager cites that the group *dhikr* enhances the depth of meditation. He himself spurs the other seekers on by stating that the millions of cells also perform the dhikr.
Individual Dhikr	Silent (*sirr*) and Loud (*jihar*) *dhikr*—heart focused	The professional banker who used to be hot-tempered before says that *dhikr* is the answer, which made him calmer.
Divine names of God	Repetition and Internalisation of divine names—Brain–heart focused	The resident imam and his friend have learnt 10 Divine names from the Sheikh, of which they try to emulate the values-attributes contained within them.
Repentance and Supplication	Repentance via voluntary *salah* and seeking forgiveness for past actions—heart focused	The majority of the seekers cited the practices of both repentance and supplication as exerting a profound impact on the heart and mind.
Obligatory prayers	Movement meditation—brain–heart focused	All 5 ritual prayers performed with the resident Imam in the lead. This is followed by loud *dhikr* and praise of the Prophet.
Optional prayers (silent)	Movement meditation—mainly heart focused	The seekers in general including the residents perform the night prayers plus all other optional prayers with particular focus on gratitude and repentance.
Obligatory and optional fasting	Regulation of physiology and psychology via restriction on food-drinks and curtailing of 5 senses—heart focused	The obligatory fast by those who are able, while the optional fasts done by selective groups. A time of intense devotion.
Sheikh's/exemplar's lectures	Listening and reflection—brain-heart focused	Many seekers cite the impactfulness of the lectures and emulation of the Sheikh.
Recital of the Divine scripture—Qur'ān	Passage meditation—recital and reflection. Brain-heart focused.	The ex-sailor who speaks about his earlier scattered mind has now become more focused says the recitation of the Qur'ān gives him a sense of peace.
Modelling the Sheikh	Non-verbal observations of the Sheikh and emulating him.	The Sheikhs traits of humbleness, patience, wisdom and his forgiving and calm nature make him a role model worthy of emulating in the eyes of the seekers.
One-to-One Counselling by the Sheikh	Structured guidance.	The professional artist who earlier had a misconception about ṭarīqas and Sheikhs found an inspiration in the Sheikh, seen to be 'cool and composed and not angry'.
One-to-One Counselling by the Peers	Informal conversation and fellowship.	Both the ex-sailor and the friend of the resident Imam say that they have derived great benefits from the resident Imam through interaction with him.

Heart-Brain - Results Preview

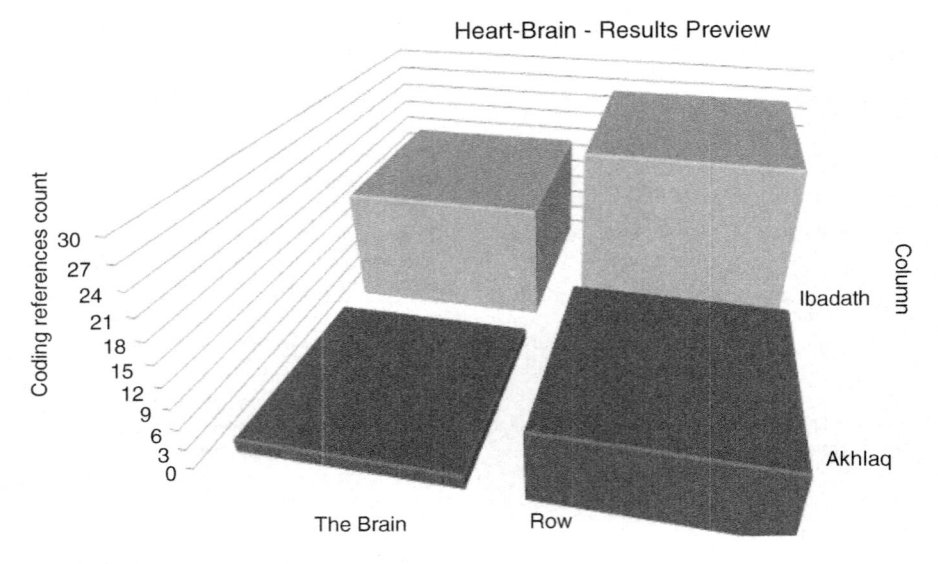

Fig. 6.8 The heart–brain connection

were made to its impact on worship. In the case of the brain, 2 references to its effect on morality and 17 citing its impact on worship. While one may call these subjective perceptions, it demonstrates the well-grounded feelings of the seekers themselves, which cannot be disregarded. Thus, from a seekers' point of view, the emphasis on the heart is greater than on the brain even though both aspects, that is, worship ('Ibādah) and morality (*akhlāq*) are important. This is illustrated as a diagram in Fig. 6.8, where the scores were higher with the heart (in the back end) than with the brain (in the front side—shaded as darker blue).

This is best illustrated in the saying of the resident imam, who highlights that "Before we prayed but only with our brain, and now we use our hearts" and "The brain and the heart must come together as one". What is meant by this is that previously prayer was going through the motions guided cognitively, but now both the brain and the heart are merged to create presence in and connection to the prayers, to oneself and to the Divine. This can be conceptualised as represented in Fig. 6.9, which shows the alienation of the brain and the heart especially for those who do worship out of obligation or whose minds and hearts wander and thus lack presence in their worship. When the connectivity of the heart and the brain come together as articulated by the seekers mentioned above, then this is seen to positively impact on both the quality of their worship, as well as on their morality, or values and behaviour.

Neuroscience validates that in contemplative states, when one is able to access different states of consciousness, one neurobiologically reduces the activity of the default-mode network and mind wandering (Walach 2014). It has been found that during meditation, there are neurobiological auto-regulations, with the secretions

6.10 The Outcomes of the Order—Wellbeing and the Worshipper

Fig. 6.9 The heart–brain connection relating to worship and morality

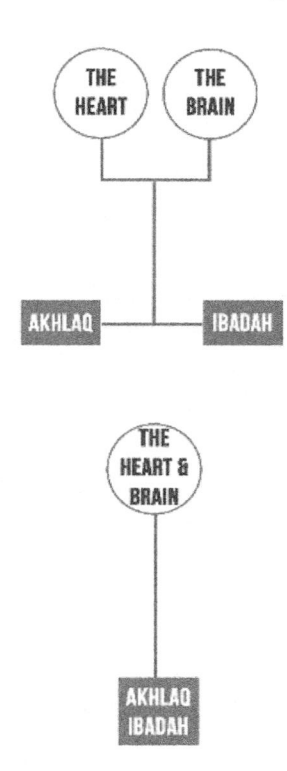

of dopamine and melatonin and the reduction of the stress hormones cortisol and norepinephrine (Esch 2014). These findings, as Esch (2014) points out, have implications especially for the health care and therapeutic systems linked to behaviour and lifestyle changes including for the treatment of addictions.

The Zen Buddhist school encourages getting beyond the chattering mind, through contemplative practices, to a state which has the following attributes: openness, receptivity, clarity, wordlessness, no thought, instantaneity and discernment. This state is needed to see reality as it is and to get away from the usual field of the mind being too preoccupied with its self-centred subjective thought streams (Austin 2014). Should this not be our state of mind when we indulge in Islamic ritual prayers and other forms of worship rather than the wandering mind that people seem to often experience? As demonstrated by the seekers especially the Centre residents, this movement towards this open state of mind is possible, which is backed by what Goleman (1991) points out of the ability of attention to be trained or retrained. This is supported by my own experience of practising the silent meditation (*dhikr*) for two decades, which has opened the door from the usual disruptive mind to one of a much calmer state. By performing meditation and as a result of retraining our consciousness, we modulate our own brain structures (Walach 2014). This seems to me a way in which we are able to alter our states of mind, transcending old behavioural patterns, which ties in with the concept of the neuroplasticity of the brain.

This is reflected in seeing the transformation of those who are ex-drug addicts and HIV patients, and have been able to change their behaviour, as well as feel a sense of peace. This state of mind has been highlighted by many of the residents. Taking another perspective, there are those who pray but their behaviour manifests negative emotions of envy, hatred, jealousy and/or other vices, indicating the disconnection of the brain and the heart. Figure 6.9 shows the state of the mind and its divergence before the seekers joining the path and after their transformation, where the mind and the heart have come together to shape their morality and their character.

It is interesting to look at the seekers' narrative within the context of the developing scientific perspective of the connection between the heart and brain, which effects the physiology as well as psychology of individuals. In line with the neuro-visceral integration model (Thayer and Lane 2009), there are direct and indirect neural pathways linking the brain and the heart, which are involved in cognitive, autonomic and affective responses. The key factor in the regulation of this neural pathway is the heart rate variability (HRV), which is the difference in time between heart beats, which serves as a marker for detecting diseases, where for example, reduced HRV is associated with conditions like congestive heart failure, diabetic neuropathy, increased levels of anxiety and post-traumatic stress disorder (PTSD). Thus, it serves as an indicator of the heart-brain health.

6.11 Spirituality Wellbeing and Emotional Intelligence

Table 6.4 presents a summary of the various acts of worship and their neurophysiological effects. This is presented within the context of Islamic worship and practices. The primary evidence from this study, which obtained responses from seekers through both interviews and surveys, corroborates their subjective sense of wellbeing with their own sense of wellbeing as the ensuing discussion indicates.

Apart from the spiritual dimension of proximity to God and the development of oneself, emerging evidence points to the physical and mental wellbeing of seekers as evident in the survey data in Figs. 5.19, 5.24, 5.23, 5.25, 5.26, 5.28, 5.29. From the seekers' perspectives, there is a clear correlation between worship and wellbeing given that they feel content and have meaning and direction in life, while also being able to relate to themselves and others better. This can be validated by the findings generated from neurophysiological studies outlined in Table 6.4.

The related evidence carried out on a more quantitative research approach has been flagged in Sect. 2.4 on neuroscience and Islam, where results of numerous studies indicate the wellbeing of the worshipper outlined in research carried out by Ibrahim et al. (2008, 2013) on ritual prayers, Doufesh et al. (2012) on brain wave patterns, and Yucel (2010) on healing and prayers.

In a meta-analysis of 100 studies examining the relationship between religiousness and mental health conducted by Koenig and Larson (2001), religious beliefs and practices were related to greater life satisfaction, happiness, positive affect and higher morale in 79 (nearly 80%) of the studies. Of 12 prospective cohort studies

Table 6.4 The Seekers view of impact of the brain and the heart on morality and worship

Dimension	The brain	The heart
Akhlāq (morality)	2	10
'Ibādah (worship)	17	26

identified in their meta-analysis, 10 reported a significant relationship between greater religiousness and greater well-being. Similar levels of positive association were found between religiousness and hope, optimism, purpose and meaning; of 14 studies examining these relationships, 12 reported significant positive associations among these variables and two found no association with religion.

In the context of Islam, Hisham's (2008) research points out that:

> Overall, the results were noteworthy in several respects. First, the PMIR (Psychological Measure of Islamic Religiousness) was relevant to Muslim participants and suggested that Muslims adhere to different Islamic beliefs, adopt various Islamic religious attitudes, and observe a diverse array of Islamic religious practices. Second, Islam is multidimensional; factor analysis of the PMIR resulted in 6 factors (Islamic beliefs, Islamic ethical principles and universality, Islamic religious struggle, Islamic religious duty, obligation and exclusivism, Islamic positive religious coping and identification, and punishing Allah reappraisal) that possessed good to high internal consistency. These findings highlight the fact that Islam plays a central role in the well-being of Muslims and stress the need for paying more attention to the Islamic religion when dealing with Muslim populations.

As indicated above, the results from both the survey and the interviews of this research indicate a sense of wellbeing from the seekers' point of view even though this research did not use a robust quantitative methodology as, for example, the PMIR as utilised above. The data already highlighted in the case studies in Chap. 5, lays down some evidence indicating the psychological, spiritual and physiological wellbeing of the seekers.

Apart from the above mentioned study, there is some burgeoning research that corroborates the findings of this study with that of neuroscience data (Esch 2014), which points out that methods such as mindfulness meditation, which is similar to the silent *dhikr* (*sirr*) method practiced by the Order, leads "to an increase in the degrees of freedom, i.e. internal flexibility, since adaptation to reality, perceived control, self-efficacy and self-management skills are strengthened."

As already highlighted, it has also been observed that the meditative types of practices impact "therapeutic behaviour, lifestyle modification, and addiction treatment" (Esch 2014). This is what has been observed and documented, especially in relation to those seekers who were drug addicts and the HIV patients who were able to transform themselves as encapsulated in the case study (Chap. 5).

One study (Haider et al. 2010) on EEG activity in Muslim prayer indicates that while some of the findings validate previous meditation studies—alpha rhythm slowing, increased alpha rhythm coherence—it does not show an increase in alpha and/or theta power as indicated in most meditative studies. This seems to counter the findings generated both by Cheok (2008) and Doufesh et al. (2012), which showed an increase in the alpha amplitude with a relaxed state of mind during prayer especially during prostration, which they say correlates with other studies done on spiritual practices (Arambula et al. 2001).

Given the small sample size in the study (9 subjects), Doufesh et al. (2012) proposes further studies with a larger sample size. The authors of the EEG pilot study on Muslim prayers (only 1 subject) propose that 'a systematic and standardised roadmap for future Muslim prayer EEG research' is needed, as is further studies in the field of Islamic methods of worship. This widening of scope forms a deeper part of mindfulness research, that Islam has a lot to contribute to. The factors that need to be taken into account while doing such kinds of experimentation can range from level of concentration, level of anxiety, type of spiritual practices to the experience of the worshipper, age, gender, types of environments etc. which then calls for a cross-sectional and preferably longitudinal types of studies to come to any meaningful conclusions.

What transpires from the data set in terms of the process of transformation of the seekers, especially those in the resident centre, is the cultivation and development of emotional intelligence. Emotional intelligence is defined as 'the ability to recognize and regulate emotions in self and others' (Goleman in Revees, 2005, p. 173). There are four major components of emotional intelligence: awareness of self and others and management of self and others (Goleman et al. in Revees, 2005, p. 173). This can be seen from the research data set are the following:

(i) Their increasing awareness about themselves. This can be seen in the data relating to Fig. 5.27—State of mind before prayers, that is, being calm or agitated or frustrated; Fig. 5.19—Changes within yourself after joining the group, that is, in the way I treat myself, in the way I speak to people, in the way I behave with my family and friends, the way I treat those who are less privileged.
(ii) Their relationship with others and helping their peers: Fig. 5.26—Worship and behavior, feeling calmer, having a good relationship with family and friends, having more respect towards others and being patient. Figure 5.25—Effects on family and friends, the ability to relate to them, ability to listen, ability to compromise, ability to cooperative, having greater understanding, being more patient and being generous.
(iii) The ability to manage themselves: Fig. 5.20—Essentials of anger management, learning to be silent, learning to say a prayer, learning to supplicate to God, leaning to be patient. Fig. 5.24—Changes observed within the group, that is, being able to pray, being able to be calm, having good morality, maintaining good relationships, having a good attitude (everything is good), feeling grateful and feeling humble.

In this sense, it is to be recognized that spiritual development is closely linked to the emotional development of the seeker population within this Order, if not to seekers generally.

6.11.1 Consciousness and Spirituality

The concept of consciousness has been used in our literature review (Chap. 2), and the seekers have cited this in their narratives in Chap. 5, where it has been referred to as a level of awareness, which varies and transforms itself. Consciousness is one of the most intriguing and contested concepts that has been and is being discussed in various fields including religion-spirituality, psychology, neuroscience, evolutionary biology and philosophy; where there is no clear agreement on what it is, while generally agreeing that there is such a conception. There are two fundamental views relating to consciousness, namely the physicalist and the non-physicalist theory. In the former, experiences are reduced to the physical stratum, the brain, known as the reductionist perspective, while in the latter, these experiences occur outside our physical entity and is independent of it, known as phenomenal experiences (Kriegel (2006) in Ali and Sulam 2018).

While a precise definition and understanding of consciousness seems to elude us, a working definition is, 'the subjective experience of the mind and the world... fundamental facts of human existence... the inner movie' (David Chalmers 2014[12]). The term 'qualia' is important in capturing the essence of consciousness, which could be understood in the context of the 'sense-datum' theory, as intrinsic non-representational properties.... sensory experiences are ultimately analysed—whether, for example, they are taken to involve relations to sensory objects or they are identified with neural events or they are held to be physically irreducible events... they have intrinsic, consciously accessible features that are non-representational and that are solely responsible for their phenomenal character' (Stanford 2017).

There is an argument that there cannot be a science of consciousness since science is objective and consciousness is subjective, however there has been work done in terms of trying to correlate the activities of the brain with different activities and states of consciousness. This, however, is the science of correlation of what the brain areas do and not one that explains why it is that all of the physical activities of the brain are accompanied by consciousness, which David Chalmers (2014) points out as the hard problem of consciousness. He offers two radical theories moving beyond the accepted fundamentals of space, time, mass and charge; which are not able to explain consciousness. First, that consciousness is the fundamental building block of nature, that is, it is the basis of everything. This, he says, opens up for its study and how it connects with space, time, mass, charge and processes. Second, that it may be universal, meaning that everything has some degree of consciousness, a panpsychist view (pan—all and psychic—mind) not that all things are intelligent but that they have a raw subjective feeling, a precursor to consciousness' (2014). In

---

[12]Philosopher Professor David Chalmers is a scientific materialist. How do you explain consciousness, David Chalmers, 14th July 2014, https://www.youtube.com/watch?v=uhRhtFFhNzQ&t=931s.

terms of understanding he links this up to the level of information processing, which can be simple or complex, and where consciousness varies in its degree accordingly.

The above postulation by Chalmers (2014) of the fundamentality of consciousness is supported by Donald Hoffman[13] (2019) although he disagrees with the panpsychist view, which seems to be dualistic, instead proposing a monistic theory. Hoffman ventures further to suggest that consciousness exists outside ourselves and that we are a part of a complex network of consciousness, with different levels of consciousness agents. These levels constitute different levels of complexity, which can go up to infinite consciousness says Hoffman (2019), this resonates with spiritual theory, where space, time and reality as we perceive it are interfaces, and that there is a deeper reality. Infinite consciousness could be construed as a higher power or higher order Being, which is akin to God.

From an Islamic perspective there are some beliefs which resonate with the above mentioned particular scientific view but goes beyond it in its scriptural and narrative explanations. What can be discerned from the various scholarly rendition and its interpretation is as follows:

(i) Consciousness is embedded within the fluid immaterial structure composed of the soul-self-heart, with the intellect being a part of it together with the spirit (*rūḥ*), being separated by something resembling a ray of light (Ibn Juryi in Picken 2011). This immaterial structure is the life-giving entity with its states of consciousness. Even though these above-mentioned facets can be differentiated they are intrinsically interlinked, as Imam Muhasibi highlights (Smith 1980).

(ii) The human soul is an indivisible, identical entity, a spiritual substance, which is the reality or very essence of man (Al-Attas 2001b). The differences are in the way of its attributes and not in terms of entity (Ibn Qayyim in Khan 1976).

(iii) It is a spiritual entity, which is not confined by space and time (Ghazali in Sa'ari 2007). Therefore, even though the spiritual entity animates the body, it has an independent existence.

(iv) What gives humans unique sense of knowledge is the connection to the Divine, which is evident in the Qur'ān (Al-Hijr, verse 28-29) "Behold! Thy Lord said to the angels, I am about to create man, from sounding clay form mud moulded into shape; When I fashioned him (in due proportion) and breathed into him of My spirit....".

(v) This spiritual entity is in existence prior to human life, in the domain of the Divine, and is infused into the fetus to give it life, which lives until physical life ceases and then moves on to its after-life phase (Al-Haddad 1990). This is supported by the scriptural verses: Before birth all souls are with God and they all bear witness that Allah is their Lord (Qur'ān, Surah al-A'raf, 7:172),

---

[13]Cognitive scientist Professor Donald. D. Hoffman in the video—Reality is not as it seems, a dialogue with neurologist Dr. Suzanne O'Sullivan hosted by Steve Paulson, Nour Foundation, 14th Feb 2019; https://www.youtube.com/watch?v=3MvGGjcTEpQ.

(ii) Life on earth, where our purpose is to worship Allah (Qur'ān, Surah al-Dhariyat, 51:56), (iii) The Hereafter, where we will be held accountable for all our actions and be either rewarded or punished (Qur'ān, Surah al-Qari'ah 101:5–8).

(vi) Whatever has transpired in the human life, the network of information, is carried within the soul and spirit, which is imbibed with consciousness, with information of what one does in this life, which one has to account for in the next realm.

(vii) A typology of the state of self is categorised into consciousness and death (*wafat*). Consciousness is sketched out as awareness and arousal, and *wafat* as sleep and death, where the former has the normal physiological, that is, sleep and the abnormal—pathological e.g. coma (Ismail 2008).

(viii) The Qur'ānic verse (39:42) refers to the above "It is Allah Who takes the souls at death and those who die not (He takes) during their sleep. Those on whom He has passed the decree of death, He keeps back (from returning to life). But the rest He sends (to their bodies) for a term appointed. Verily in this are signs for those who reflect".

(ix) Religious consciousness is the awareness of oneself, of God and the act of surrendering to the Creator and from an Islamic context relates to *iman* (faith) and *taqwa* or God consciousness (Ali and Sulam 2018).

(x) Consciousness embedded within the soul-heart has the ability to transform itself into higher levels or else descend into the depths of darkness as explicitly outlined in the Qur'ān (Sura Shams 91: 8–10) "And by the soul and He Who perfected it, Then inspired it to understand what is wrong and (what is) right for it, Indeed he succeeds who purifies it, And indeed he fails who corrupts it".

(xi) There are different types of conscious agents that the Divine has created, these include plants, animals, humans, angels, spirits (jinns), satan (iblis) and others that we have no knowledge of, they all serve their functions and originate from the Infinite or Divine Consciousness.

(xii) There are numerous instances recorded of the Prophet's communication with inanimate objects which are authenticated narrations . An example of this is when the Prophet spoke to and consoled the palm tree that was weeping.[14]

(xiii) The Qur'ān supports this state of consciousness of inanimate objects, where God says "We did offer indeed the Trust to the Heavens and the Earth and the Mountains: but they refused to undertake it, being afraid thereof: but man undertook it.....' (Al-Ahzab, 33:72). This refers to humans being

---

[14] This particular hadith as well as other hadiths are reported in several sources including Bukhari (Manaqib 25, Jum'a 26), Ibn Majah (Iqamat al-Salat 199), Nasa'I (Jumu'a 10), Tirmidi (Jum'a 10, Manaqib 6), Darimi (Muqaddima 6, Salat 202), Musnad (i: 249); Miracles Concerning Trees, Questions on Islam, 2003–2020, https://questionsonislam.com/article/miracles-concerning-trees.

given knowledge[15] and consciousness and made vicegerents on earth, which they are to use judicially and protect life and earth and what it is contained within it.

6.11.2 Consciousness, Spirituality and Human Development

One of the fundamental aspects of spiritual orders is to identify the obstacles seekers face during the process of gaining knowledge, both outwardly as well as inwardly. This is part of the '*jihad*' or struggle in the way of God that the seekers must undergo. In this light, the Sheikh, during the course of the interview had defined three stages of the development of the seekers, which coincides with the Qur'ānic references to the stages of the evolving soul (Table 6.5), alluding to the different levels of gaining knowledge or advancing one's state of consciousness. The term conscious and consciousness has been interchangeably used to represent a wide spectrum of mental phenomena. This is seen to be consistent with cross-cultural and cross-spatial observations within the anthropological and religious sphere pointing out to differentiation of religion experiences, which are called 'religious consciousness' (Andresen 2000). This is found to be distinct from other types of conscious experiences.

One can discern that these stages of consciousness have to correlate with the changing states and development of one's self from being self-centred to one that reaches out to others and is engrossed in a state of worship of God (see Sect. 2.1, Figures 2.1.1 and 2.1.2). This is inter-linked with knowledge and in Islam, one needs to understand the nature of knowledge, which has some fundamental differences compared to the Western realm of scientific knowledge, which does not have the metaphysical dimension. A comparison from different perspectives are made below, together with a greater exposure into the changing consciousness within the Islamic framework.

Perspectives from Psychology In order to put things into a contemporary perspective and drawing on humanistic sciences, the above underlined progression or evolution of consciousness (Table 6.5) has some parallels in psychology, where it can be viewed firstly through the lens of; (i) Concept of Self-Actualisation (Table 6.6), and (ii) Concept of 'On Becoming' or 'Full Humanness' that of a state of evolved consciousness (Table 6.7). The Sheikh of the spiritual Order modelled the Prophet, and therefore it would be relevant to draw out some parallels from the above two mentioned perspectives (see Tables 6.4, 6.6, and 6.7).

---

[15] A detailed exposure of knowledge is presented in the journal article - Mohamed Safiullah Munsoor and Che Zarrina Saari, Knowledge and Islam on the Non-Rational and Rational-Heart-Brain Inter-Connection, Journal Afkar, Vol. 19 Issue (2017): 129–162.

6.11 Spirituality Wellbeing and Emotional Intelligence

Table 6.5 Types of Islamic worship and its effects on the mind-body

Type of worship	Its effect	Observations/comments
Ritual prayer (*salah*):	On Body Composition: (i) High Phase angle (PA): from less than 7 degrees to >7.4 degrees. (ii) High Body Capacitance (BC) from less than 800 pF to 808 pF. (iii) Lower body resistance value: from above 513 to <513... (iv) Improved lower back muscles: high activation of muscles including biceps femoris, rectus femori, gastrocnemius and lumbar region. On Neurophysiological: The Brain: (i) Lowering of Gamma (>30 Hz) and Beta (13–30 Hz) waves and increase in Alpha frequency brain waves (8–13 Hz). The Heart: (i) Lowering of heartrate in certain postures (standing 87 rpm, bowing: 79 bpm, prostration: 72 bpm and sitting: 78 bpm).	On Body Composition: (i) Higher phase angle indicates large quantities of intact cell membranes and body cell mass. This is one of the indicators of the efficient functioning of the internal organs and the immune system... (ii) BC is the ability of cells to store energy and high BC indicates the efficient storage of energy in the cells. This means the individual will be more energetic and fit. (iii) A decrease in the body resistance values means that there is an increase in the elasticity of the blood vessels. This enables a better blood flow to the whole body. (iv) Due to the stretching of the various muscles, the whole sequence of the prayer (*salah*) is considered as a moderate form of exercise if done properly. On Neurophysiological: (i) Brain waves are affected by physical, emotional and spiritual states. During prayer (*salah*), there is a lowering of the gamma and beta waves, while there is an increase in alpha waves. This brings about a state of relaxation. (ii) Lowering the head, as in the bowing and prostration positions, reduces the distance between the heart and base level/gravity. This is seen to reduce the heart-beat rate while increasing blood flow to the brain. These effects are said to be good for the overall health.

(continued)

Table 6.5 (continued)

Type of worship	Its effect	Observations/comments
Fasting combined with voluntary prayers (*taraweeh*)	(i) Increase in the phase angle by 4% within 20 days, with increase in the cell membrane integrity in the body. This increase reflects that the cells are in a healthy condition. (ii) A reduction of glucose level in the blood from 4.35 mmol/L to 4.29 in a 140 minutes prayer session (*taraweeh*). (iii) The physical movements in the prayer (*taraweeh*) increase the muscle activity, with increased the basal metabolic rate (bmr). This has an effect on the fat mass (fm) as much as 21%. (iv) A decrease in the resistance value was found, which indicates an increase in the elasticity in the diameter of the blood vessels due to the shrinking of fat mass.	The increase in the phase angle, with increases in bmr (basal metabolic rate) and a reduction in the glucose levels and resistance indicates an overall improvement in the health status. This combination is equated to doing a regime of exercise with a balanced diet.
Fasting (*Saum*)	(i) In elderly men it was found to reduce body weight and fat, while elevating mood. (ii) Reduction in oxidative stress and inflammation in overweight women at risk of breast cancer. (iii) Shown to have a conservatory effect against aging and the prevention of related diseases. (iv) Shown improvements in cognitive functions in overweight women and elderly men.	The evidence from animal and human data suggests that fasting can play a beneficial role in optimising health and reducing the risk of disease.

(continued)

6.11 Spirituality Wellbeing and Emotional Intelligence 293

Table 6.5 (continued)

Type of worship	Its effect	Observations/comments
	v) Those with mild chronic impairments demonstrated improved visual memory, cerebrospinal fluids biomarkers and brain bioenergetics.	
Remembrance of God (*Dhikr*)	A study was done combining Muslim prayer with transcendental meditation. The effect of this was found to be beneficial.	The questionnaire of MPM (Muslim Praying Meditation) and the Kentucky Inventory of Mindfulness Skills (KIMS) were applied before training to answer the first question, while KIMS was only applied again as post testing after 3 months of training of TM. The results revealed an effect for TM in enhancing the level of KIMS after 3 months of training

The Development and Representation of Self (Egoistic versus Spiritual self): In the light of the above mentioned discussion and before we move on to the discussion relating to self-actualisation and spiritual actualisation, it is important to unravel the notion of 'self' within the Islamic tradition and in comparison to secular notions. There are different notions of the definition of self emerging within varying fields of study including phenomenology, developmental psychology, neuroscience and spirituality, where the latter is the focus on the study. In order to accomplish this, the empirical model generated (see Fig. 6.11) from this research draws upon the classical understanding of the concept of self from an Islamic tradition and discusses it in the light of humanistic psychology and neuroscience.

There are two fundamental approaches in this regard, firstly, self as a knower, which is akin to most spiritual traditions including Islam. Secondly, self as an object of what is known. The first proposition was totally rejected in the secular tradition, while the second was referred to from an individual viewpoint as belonging to himself including the material self (own body, his family and possessions), the social self (views others hold of the individual), and spiritual self (emotions and desires). Self is viewed as having unity and differentiation and being intimately associated with emotions as mediated through self-esteem.

A conceptual framework (Fig. 6.10), which is informed by psychology and neuroscience is utilised to explain the concept of self and its representation (Trautwein et al. 2014, p 182).

In the diagram above, two levels are outlined, one at the bodily- affective level and the other at the cognitive-conceptual level, which is inter-linked by the states of self-centredness and self-other-connectedness. Based on the self's intention and course of interaction, it moves either from being rooted in self-centredness or shifting to a state of self-other inclusion or coupling, the latter producing empathy and compassion.

Table 6.6 The type of personality and the development of the self-soul

Stage of man (*Awam*)	The development of the Soul	Scriptural reference	Levels of consciousness
Awam	Nafs al-ammāra bi-su	"And yet, I am not trying to absolve myself: for, verily, man's inner self does incite (him) to evil, and saved are only they upon whom my Sustainer bestows His grace!" (Qur'ān, Yusuf, 12:53)	Primitive level of human consciousness—1st level—biological ground of human reality—domineering self: aggressiveness and territoriality. Violent urge for survival.
Awam Khawas	Nafs al-lawwāma	The Lord says, "But nay I call to witness the accusing voice of man's conscience!" (Qur'ān, al-Qiyamah, 75:2) To this Asad (2011) clarifies that the man's reproaching soul is the sub-conscious awareness of his own short comings and failings.	A greater sense of awareness and consciousness—2nd level: Search for human values and for fruitful and disciplined life. Critique of self-impulses and critique of dominant ego.
Awam Khawas al-Khawas	Nafs al-mutma'inna	The Lord says "(But unto the righteous God will say,) O thou human being that has attained to inner peace! Return thou unto thy Sustainer, well-pleased (and) pleasing (Him): enter, then, together with My (other true) servants—yea, enter thou My paradise!" (Qur'ān, al-Fajr, 89:27–30)	A heightened level of consciousness and self-actualisation—3rd level: awakening to our true nature. Fulfilled or satisfied self. Human potential unfolding harmoniously, while ethical and religious ideas are in full flower (Sharī'a).

Scientific investigations have focused on contemplative practices of meditation largely associated with Buddhism, as well as the Yoga,[16] where one can say provide relevant approaches and methods to enable one to move from a point of self-centredness along the continuum of self-other-connectedness. Most of the research on meditative practices have dealt with the processes associated with attention and emotional regulation, while the change in the nature of self is informed by Buddhist theory (Trautwein et al. 2014). Some evidence resulting from neuroscientific studies indicates that during meditation there is reduction in the activities in the default

---

[16] Much of the research relating to meditation and its neurophysiological impact on the mind-body has been done on practices associated with Buddhism (Theravada, Zen) and Hinduism (Yoga, TM). There is a need for researches to do more in terms of meditative-contemplative practices within Islam (*muraqaba*), Christianity (heart based contemplation) and Judaism's kabbalistic tradition, which has a rich treasure of meditative methods-tools within its tradition. This can prompt a cross-religious study, which is important in the current context since many traditions have lost their silence-stillness and relational practices over time and is in need of such practices in order to deal with the stresses and strains of modern life to ride over anxiety, depression, suicidal tendencies etc.

6.11 Spirituality Wellbeing and Emotional Intelligence

Table 6.7 Values of being (B values) and examples of those in peak experiences

Being values	Qualities and examples	Key prophetic examples
Integrated	Less split or dissociated; less fighting against himself; more at peace with himself; less split between experiencing self and observing self; more one-pointed, more harmoniously organised; more synergistic, with less internal friction.	Never argumentative, he would leave if there was an argument and saw anger as a kind of insanity. When asked about the Prophet, his wife Aisha stated, "Verily, the character of the Messenger of Allah was the Qur'ān" and what the Qur'ān, Nun, 68; (4) says "Indeed you are of a great moral character", meaning that he practiced what he preached.
Aligned	As he gets to be more purely and singly himself, able to fuse with the world (refers to becoming one, without differentiation); For example, a mother being one with her child (he feels one with his community). This is going beyond oneself, where the person can then become egoless or selfless.	Aligned with himself and with his community (*ummah*), which he saw as one body.
Fully Functional	At the peak of his powers utilising his capacities and to its fullest. Feels more intellectual, more perspective, stronger and more graceful than at other times.	Always seen to be full of vigour either in a state of worship or when interacting with family and community. Always presented a balanced position and stated that his faith was of the middle way—*ummatan wasatan*.
Effortlessness	Ease of functioning. What took effort, straining and struggling at other times, comes effortlessly without much effort, that is comes of itself. One sees sure calmness and rightness, while things are being done wholeheartedly, without doubt or hesitation.	Many a time, when his community had difficulty and were struggling, he performed it effortlessly, for example, in the battle of the trench, where he broke the rock when others could not; his calm state amidst his prosecution in Makkah etc.
Prime Mover	More self-determined, fully responsible, fully volitional and for an observer becomes more trustworthy, more reliable, more dependable.	Was the prime mover of faith and consolidating the conflicting tribes of Arabia. He was known as the trustworthy—al-Amin, and was seen to be always dependable.
More Spontaneous	More spontaneous, more expressive, behaving more innocently, more naturally, more free-flowing. Authentic identity.	The Prophet's speech, actions and behaviour were in unison. This was seen especially the way that he dealt with children that he loved. He preached as well as practiced. In this sense, he was an authentic person.

(continued)

Table 6.7 (continued)

Being values	Qualities and examples	Key prophetic examples
More creative	More creative in a particular sense, with his cognition and behaviour coming out of a greater self-confidence.	The Prophet used to mend his own shoes and stitch his own cloths, as well as doing all work that needed to be done in the house?.
Uniqueness	The uniqueness is manifested, where they are different from others during spiritual experiences and when receiving revelations (*wahi*).	His personality was unlike others, unique in every sense, and people tried to emulate him in every aspect—a role model. Had many spiritual experiences through the process of intuition and revelation.
Here and now	Fully present, while being free of the past and the future. He is beyond desire and does not react based on fear, hate or whim.	Be in this world as a traveller, said the Prophet. This implies not being attached, living for the moment and not too pre-occupied with the past or future.
Completion-of-the acts	This person has a sense of closure of things, that is, a complete discharge, climax, culmination, emptying or finishing. The outer and inner world in some way related.	The Prophet said, "Even if you do a little worship, do it well and be consistent with it."
Pure psyche and less a thing-of-the-world	More determined by intra-psychic laws rather than non-psychic reality insofar as they are different. Respecting-loving myself and respecting-loving the other, each permitting, supporting and strengthening each other.	"Love for others what you love for yourself, to have complete iman (faith)" said the Prophet.
Non-striving and Non-needing	Everything now comes of its own accord, pouring out, without will, effortless, purposelessly. His behaviour and experience become per se, and self-validating, end-behaviour and end-experience, rather than means-behaviour and means-experience.	Within the Prophet life, the divine revelations (Qur'ān) were revealed to him, which he dictated to his companions to record. In a similar vein, he was inspired out of which came forth the *ḥadīth qudsi* or the inspired narrations.
Playfulness of a certain kind.	It is simultaneously mature and child-like. A feeling of gratitude, in religious people to their God, in other to fate, to nature, to people, to the past, to parents to the world, to everything and anything that helped this wonder possible. This spills into worship, giving thanks, adoration, giving praise; which fits into a religious framework.	The Prophet was playful with his wife and this is seen in the example of him racing Aisha on more than one occasion. He was very fond of children and it is recorded that he used to carry his grandchildren and pray with them. His worship and gratitude went beyond normal human endeavour.

(continued)

6.11 Spirituality Wellbeing and Emotional Intelligence

Table 6.7 (continued)

Being values	Qualities and examples	Key prophetic examples
Communication poetic, mythical and rhapsodic	A natural flow of a natural kind of language to express such states of being. This kind of authentic persons are like Prophets.	When the Qur'ān was revealed, and he used to chat to the Makkans eloquently, some called him a poet but divine scriptures re-asserted than he was not a poet or a soothsayer but a Prophet.

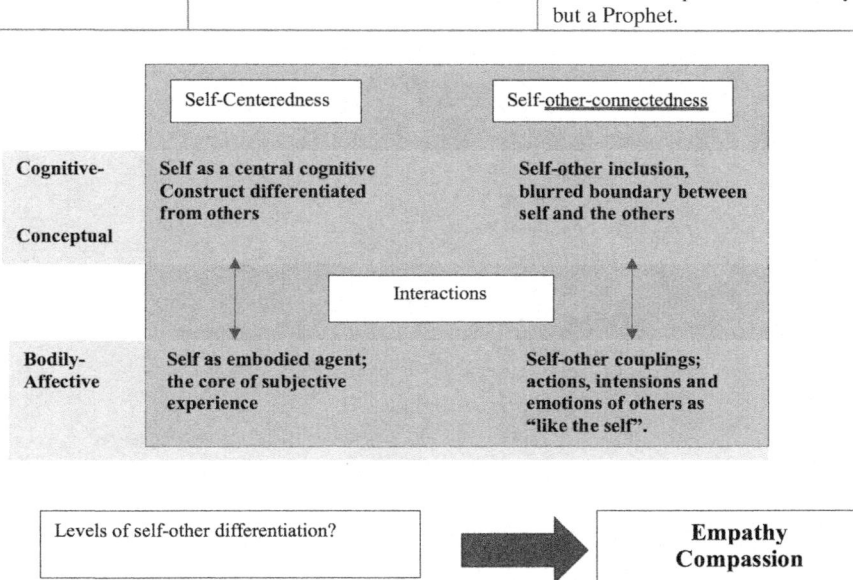

	Self-Centeredness	Self-other-connectedness
Cognitive-Conceptual	Self as a central cognitive Construct differentiated from others	Self-other inclusion, blurred boundary between self and the others
	↕ Interactions ↕	
Bodily-Affective	Self as embodied agent; the core of subjective experience	Self-other couplings; actions, intensions and emotions of others as "like the self".

Levels of self-other differentiation? ➡ **Empathy Compassion**

Fig. 6.10 A framework of mental functioning of a cognitive-conceptual and bodily-affective level of self-representation

mode network during intensive mindfulness meditation, suggesting a corresponding '...decrease in self-centredness arising from the dis-identification from the mental contents on the conceptual level' (Trautwein et al. 2014, p 184). Another meditation technique called loving kindness meditation (metta) was seen to '..increase self-other connectedness on the bodily-affective level' (Trautwein et al. 2014, p 192), where it is able to identify or empathize with the other enabling a shift in cognition.[17]

The Islamic conception of the self, its nature and evolution, can be expounded by the conceptual framework for spiritual development (Fig. 6.11) that has been developed from the data and the literature of this study.

---

[17] The authors highlight that these studies while being cross-sectional, has been done on a small sample and therefore is seen as preliminary, where more research is called for in the light of the impact that it can have on reducing conflicts and enhancing human flourishing vis-à-vis the others.

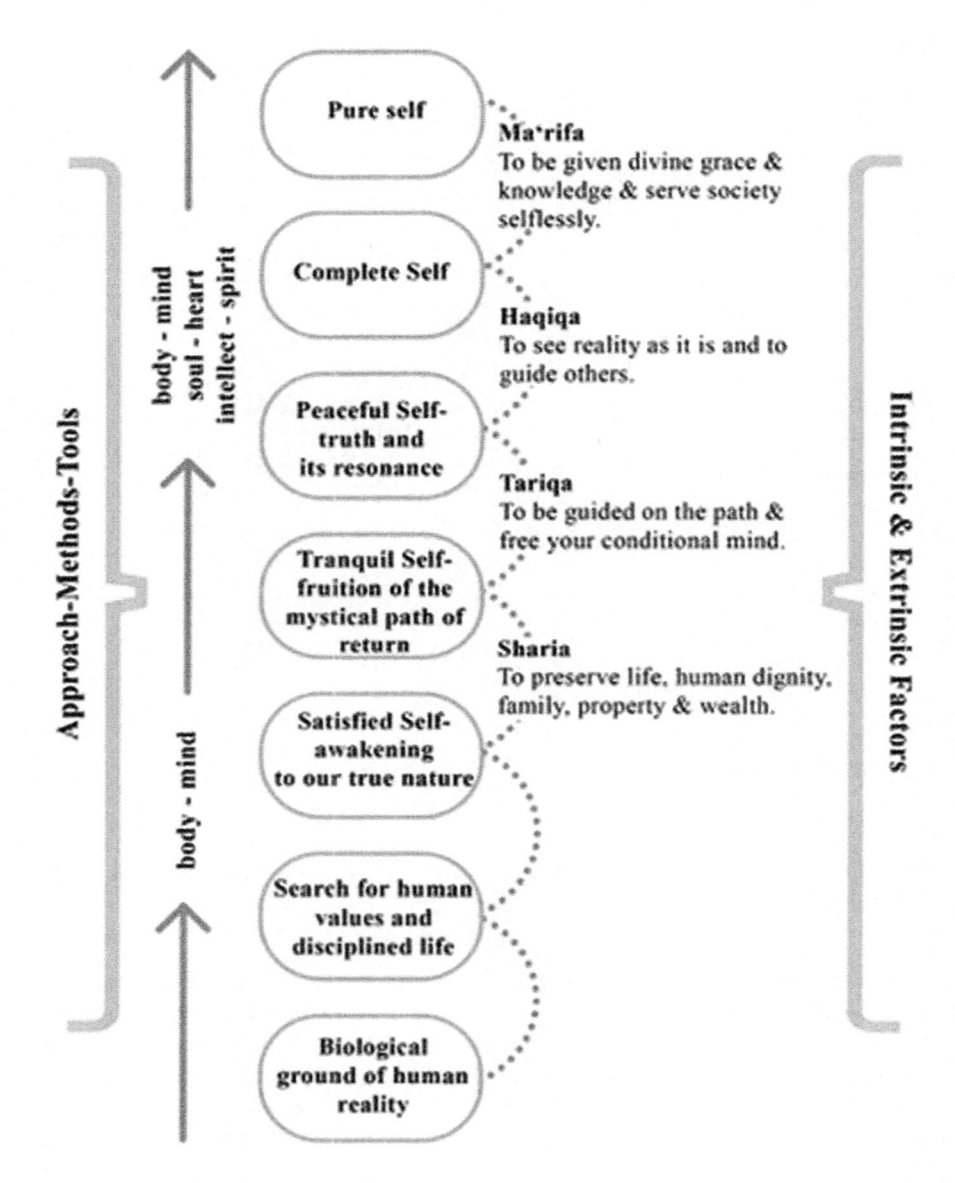

Fig. 6.11 An integrated framework for spiritual development

The self is not simplistic but a complex entity,[18] where the Qur'ān refers to it as '*nafs*' interchangeably used to mean self or soul, whereas there is also reference to

---

[18]Section 2.1 has gone into great details to explain these essential spiritual entities, while citing various references to elucidate it (Imam Ghazāli, Imam Al-Jawziya).

6.11 Spirituality Wellbeing and Emotional Intelligence

the heart (*qalb*) and the intellect (*aql*) and the spirit (*rūḥ*). What we can discern from the various Islamic scholarly deliberations (elaborated in Sect. 2.1) is that the self-soul in any child is primordially of a pure nature (*fitra*), it is only as the child grows that it gathers the various aspects of the world and then known by different names depending on its nature—beastly self, self-critical self, peaceful self and spiritual self. What can be ascertained from the literature in Sect. 2.1 is that there is a close link between the self-soul and the heart. The intellect (*aql*) aids the process of the development of the self-soul by serving to distinguish between right and wrong and guide the life process. The spirit (*rūḥ*) according to Al-Ghazali (1995) is the electric element which animates the body and gives life to it. The greater the transformation of the person towards good and Divine the greater is the integration of the spirit (*rūḥ*) with the self-soul (*nafs*), the feeling of integration where 'we are one with the Universe' and close to God.

What can be discerned from traditional scholarship (Sect. 2.1) is that self-soul forms the platform on which all else is embedded, that is, the heart, the intellect with the spirit (*rūḥ*) being an independent entity from the command of the Lord, which aligns with the above platform as one develops spiritually with closeness to the Divine. The Islamic conception is that consciousness which is animated by the spirit (*rūḥ*) and constitutes the soul-heart is not a material entity and therefore while it is connected with the body, it is independent of the body. This concurs with the emerging views of both Chalmers (2014) and Hoffman (2019) that consciousness is not a part of the physical substratum of the brain (called the hard problem) and is therefore not localised. It is the body that materialise and withers away, while the spirit has been there before, it animates us while we are here and moves on after bodily life ceases.[19]

What takes place during contemplative practices and how the self is transformed in its spiritual journey is captured in Fig. 6.11 above, which attempts to provide a comprehensive conceptual outline of the process by using data from this research, as well as integration Islamic scholarly views, which is based on their understanding of the Qur'ān and the traditions (sunnah) of the Prophet.

In Chap. 2, Figs. 2.1 and 2.2 it was outlined that from an Islamic perspective, the human self goes through a process of transformation from the beastly self to a critical self and then to a peaceful self, traversing through these states before reaching the '*ma'rifa*' (Divine knowledge). These states are outlined in greater detail

---

[19]One of the appropriate ways of finding out if consciousness is monitoring of those who have had cardiac arrests where the blood flow to the brain has ceased and ascertaining if these persons have been able to see, hear or feel the presence of people around or near them. Studies have been done in this direction and it appears that there have been cases, where people have been able to report on what was exactly going on, where the inference being made is that consciousness in not depend on brain function and leads to it being independent. This has also been report in what is called near death experience and out of body experiences. Further studies are needed to build a robust case for this observation. This discuss is reported in the video—reality is not as it Seems, Nouf Foundation, 14th February 2019, with a groups of Scientists as panelist, https://www.youtube.com/watch?v=3MvGGjcTEpQ.

by the Chishti (2007) spiritual order within the context of meditative progression and consciousness is independent of the body as: (i) the biological ground of human reality (Qur'ān, 12:53[20] (filled with impulses which is in conflict with what is defined as moral good"), (ii) search for human values and disciplined life (Qur'ān, 75:2[21]), (iii) awakening to our true nature or satisfied self-sha'ria, (91:7[22] (refers to the human personality with it complex nature of body, mind—intellect, emotions, and the grandeur of the universe and compelling evidence of God's creative force)." (iv) fruition of the mystical path of return—the tranquil self—*tariqa*, (Qur'ān, 89:27[23]."), (v) truth and its resonance—the peaceful self—haqiqa (Qur'ān, 89:28[24]."), (vi). The complete self—*ma'rifa* (89:22[25]), (vii) the pure self, *ma'rifa* (Qur'ān). Here it is evident that there is a process of evolution and gradations, which is not conceptualised in the works of Maslow or Rogers.

Each of these above stations (*maqamas*)—*shar'ia, tariqa, haqiqa* and *ma'rifa*—has its own objectives, which are encapsulated in Fig. 6.11 From an Islamic perspective the shar'ia is required to ground oneself at a conceptual level and begin the journey taking the path towards tariqa, haqiqa and finally *ma'rifa*, where, as one proceeds one's conceptual identity unravels leading to other-self connectedness (see Fig. 6.10), as well as transcending one's one conditional self towards knowing one's primordial self, which is beyond the mental and cognitive framework. Thus, the declaration of one's faith (shahada), which was in the first instance verbal and cognitive, now moves on to become one that is grounded experientially in the realities that one experiences, which are blessings (*baraqa*) or openings (*fath*) from the Divine. This is not to be mistaken that all is good since there will be highs and lows, however, the response to the struggle (*jihad*) is not egoistic but patience and gratitude. This factor shapes one's depth of faith, where one moves on from being a Muslim (declared the faith and practices) to a *mu'min* (declared the faith, practices and develops both the outer and inner aspects) and then a *muhsin* (includes all aspects of both the aforementioned categories and has reached a level of excellence and mastery—*ihsan*).[26] The Sheikh of the Order has outlined the three types mentioned here but the formulation is more comprehensive as seen in

---

[20]Qur'ān, 12:53 (sura Yusuf)—"And yet, I am not trying to absolve myself: for, verily, man's inner self does incite to evil, and saved are only they upon whom my Sustainer bestow His grace.

[21]Qur'an, 75:2 (sura Al-Qiyamah)—"But nay! I call to witness the accusing voice of man's own conscience" (sub-conscious awareness of one's one short-comings and failings).

[22]Qur'ān, 91:7 (sura Shams)—"Consider the human self and how it is formed in accordance with what it is meant to be

[23]Qur'ān, 89:27 (sura Al-Fajr)—"O thou human being that hast attained to inner peace!

[24]Qur'ān, 89:28 (sura Al-Fajr)—"Return thy onto thy Sustainer, well-pleased (and) pleasing (Him)

[25]Qur'ān, 89:22 (sura Al-Fajr)—"...and (the Majesty of) thy Sustainer stands revealed" (God's revelation of His transcendental Majesty and the manifestation of His judgement). All of the above mentioned brief commentaries of the Qur'ān within the brackets are from The Message of The Qur'ān, trans. and explained by Muhammad Asad, Islamic Book Trust, Kuala Lumpur, Malaysia.

[26]The difference between a muslim and a *mu'min* and why, Qura'nic connection.tv, https://www.quranicconnection.tv/the-difference-between-a-muslim-and-a-mumin-and-why/.

6.11 Spirituality Wellbeing and Emotional Intelligence

Table 6.6, where the stages are linked with its related brief description. This is the process and states of human flourishing and where God Himself points out "Say, is the one who knows equal to the one who does not know" (Qur'ān, 39: 9).

It is important to note that it is not meditation-contemplation alone which facilitates and enhances the inward and outward human transformation but an array of factors, which includes the following as outlined in Fig. 6.11 :

(i) The Approach, Methods and Tools:

Approach and Ethical Foundation: An integrated approach, where the mind-body-soul-heart-intellect-spirit are involved in varying degrees, which is premised on a strong ethical foundation and where worship (*ibadah*) and morality (*akhlāq*) combines.

Ethical Dimension: In conjunction with all other practices outlined below, the ethical dimension is demonstrated by the seekers cultivating and modelling values including some attributes of God and others, such as, compassion, empathy, forgiveness, gratitude, helping others in need, repentance, humbleness, honesty etc. (see Chap. 5). The ethical dimension is crucial since ruinous traits or vices, such as anger, jealousy, greed, miserliness, envy, dishonesty etc. (see Sects. 2.2 and 2.3) clouds the mind-heart and impedes spiritual progress. This is the case with all the major spiritual and faith traditions—theistic and non-theistic—towards achieving their respective metaphysical goals.

As conceptualised in Figures 2.4 and 2.6, Tables 2.2 and 2.3, there are numerous vices identified and their possible treatments outlined as per the Islamic tradition. What we have seen from experiences of the seekers (Chap. 5) is that it has been a struggle (*jihad*) for them, fighting their inner self (*nafs*) through various means including meditation (*dhikr*), ritual and voluntary prayers, turning to God in repentance (*tauba*) and supplication (*dua*), lectures and discussions, one-to-one counselling, peer-to-peer support, love and acceptance from the Sheikh and family, Islamic reflexology etc. It has not be an easy journey for the seekers but what is expressed by them in terms of their positivity and resilience is a testimony to their transformation especially for those who have been able to get over their addictions. This resonates with the Prophetic *ḥadīth*[27] (narration) where after returning from a

---

[27] This particular narration seems to be debated with some scholars citing it as authentic, while others rejecting it as a weak narration. From an overall perspective *jihad* (struggle) refers to the daily struggle against oppression and in maintaining a life of spiritual freedom. This is demonstrated in the Makkan period of Prophet's life, where there was 'patient forbearance', where the Prophet and Muslims were prosecuted and some of the Muslims had to migrate first to Ethiopia and then the Prophet and others to Medina. During the Medina period the Muslims had to wage defensive wars against those who saw them as a threat, where the *jihad* in this sense was known as qital (fighting in self-defence) as opposed to *sabr* during the Makkan period. In this light, Asma Afsaruddin (2020) says "two main dimensions of *jihad*, ṣabr and qitāl, were renamed *jihād al-nafs* (the internal, spiritual struggle against the lower self) and jihād al-sayf (the physical combat with the sword), respectively. They were also respectively called al-jihād al-akbar (the greater *jihad*) and al-jihād al-aṣghar (the lesser *jihad*)." In these kinds of extra-Qur'ānic literature, the different ways of promoting what is good and preventing what is wrong are included under the broad

battle he said that this is a smaller *jihad* (struggle) as compared with the greater *jihad* (struggle), which is the battle against one's own *nafs* (self).

Contemplative practices: ritual and supererogatory prayers, Qur'ānic recital, fasting, charity, reflection (*tafakkur*), recollection (*tazkar*), self-accounting (*muḥāsaba*), self-rebuke (muaqaba), focus on God's attributes (taddabur), observation (*mushahada*) and state of witness-mindfulness (*muraqaba*).

Psycho-Spiritual practices: repentances, supplication, making peace with others, one-to-one counselling, peer-to-peer support and consultation.

Organisation: Interactional Leadership style (transformation and situational leadership) and decentralised management.

(ii) Internal and the external factors:

Intrinsic factors: Self-realisation: the main trigger for opening the heart to receive guidance (the Zen mind) or learning methods-techniques to unravel one's mind. Learning lessons, testing, refining and internalising. Modelling: Observing the Sheikh and role-modelling both through non-verbal and verbal cues. Adapting: This is done within one's self, which comes about through reflection of oneself and in relation to others. Dreams: this is used as a vehicle for discussing and interpreting with the help of the Sheikh.

Extrinsic factors: Setting of ground rule: This is set by the Sheikh, which the seekers are encouraged to follow. Needs based therapy: Islamic reflexology for treating a number of psycho-somatic aliments. Love and Care: Both the Sheikh and his wife are adored by the seekers for the love their demonstrate to the seekers.

It is thus an adornment of a whole way of a holistic life and not focusing only on one or two facets of an integrated approach that aids this process. This above mentioned holistic approach responds to the query that mindfulness meditation leads to be decrease in self-centred functioning but does not lead to a radical transformation of one's self (Trautwein et al. 2014, p 184). In this case the reference is to the goal of Buddhist practices but this is true of any spiritual tradition, which carried with it, contemplative practices, an ethical-virtuous foundation and the community of practice. This is one of the issues with the secularisation of these meditative practices in the contemporary context not fully comprehending what is required for the preparation and undertaking of this journey. In the spiritual journey, openings or peak experiences as Maslow (1970) calls it occurs unexpectedly, while its growth and flourishing into plateau experiences comes from a consistent process of practice and full spiritual experiences are rare occurrences only afforded to select individuals in the course of history (further expounded below).

One point that needs to be flagged is that, while there is a defined goal that the seekers are to work towards as outlined in Fig. 6.11, there is no promise of reaching

---

rubric of al-jihād fī sabīl Allāh, "striving in the path of God…A well-known *ḥadīth* (narration) therefore refers to four primary ways in which *jihad* can be carried out: by the heart, the tongue, the hand (physical action short of armed combat), and the sword". https://www.britannica.com/topic/Egyptian-Islamic-Jihad, Encyclopaedia Britannica, 2020.

the goal. It is only by Divine grace that people get openings as in peak experiences or states (*hal*) that arises unexpectedly, and where people strive (*jihad*) to reach stations (*maqam*) or plateau experiences.

In the Islamic tradition, there is a general discouragement of discussion of one's spiritual experiences with others due to the ego getting in the way, and also rousing negative feelings within oneself and in others. If there is an experience that the seeker had, where he/she has the urge to discuss it then they can do so with the Sheikh. For those seeker who think that they have arrived spiritually, it is said that they have lost it. As Al-Ghazali (1995) says it is not learning new knowledge but unravelling the heart and removing the veils that covers us from reaching the light and knowledge in the heart. It is the inward journey that takes one to his/her spiritual home, which has many rooms and floor or levels as outlined in Fig. 6.11.

An interesting parallel of the above mentioned Islamic mystical map of spiritual progression (Fig. 6.11) is the evolution or change in states of consciousness can be drawn from the mind map developed within the yogic and the Vedanta and the other orthodox Indian systems—darsana (Sears 2014), where all of the below outlined six levels can be experienced:

i. Senses (experiencing through the five senses);
ii. Discursive thinking (thinking in word as in internal discourse);
iii. Discriminative intellect (discriminative mental functioning with coherent use of words);
iv. Pure individuality or ego (no phenomenological objects such as sensation, thoughts and images of the above mentioned levels i–iii but with the presence of (I);
v. Pure bliss (pure positive affect—contains no phenomenological content and subject-objects are absent);
vi. Pure consciousness (pure emptiness—non-being or absence of every conceivable thing).

The first two levels are experienced by ordinary persons, while discriminative thinking comes from the development of the individual, with levels four, five and six occurring in those persons who have trodden the spiritual and meditative path and generally outside the remit of ordinary range of experiences (Sears 2014).

There have been some studies on the different levels of consciousness and its neurobiological correlates, which largely refers to the above mentioned level vi, that is, pure consciousness. Sears (2014, p 68) outlines that this has come out of the traditions of Yoga, Transcendental Meditation (TM) and Zen and some neurophysiological markers of this state are: (i) experience and suspension of perceptible respiration, with no changes of CO_2 and O_2 levels in the blood or compensatory breathing afterwards[28], (ii) High level of frontal EEG alpha coherence. (iii) Robust

---

[28] Austin, J.H. (1998) Zen and the brain, Cambridge, MA: MIT Press. Badawi, K.K et al. (1984). Electrophysiologic characteristics of respiratory suspension periods occurring during the practice of the TM programme, Psychosomatic Medicine 46 (3): 267–276. Farrow, J.T., and Herbert,

gamma band oscillation and long-distance phase-synchrony[29] in Advanced Tibetan Buddhist Monk meditators (Lutz et al. 2004).

The type of silent meditation with the breath done by the Order under study and the one footnoted in Chap. 5 (footnote no: 15) has similar parallels with the yogic including transcendental meditation and Buddhist meditation (anapana sati and vipassana) and thus offers an Islamic version of meditative for neuroscientific studies. This system has been in place for over a millennia in the Islamic world generally on a low profile basis, where many people may not have heard of it. Douglas-Klotz (2002, p 9) support this claim by pointing out that various Sunni and Shi'ite circles have developed methods that harnesses "interpenetrating attention", utilising breathing, body awareness and chanting. This is based on the doctrine of unity (*tawhid*), which is posited in the divinely inspired narration (*ḥadīth qudsi*), which states that:

> My servant draws near to me through nothing I love more than the religious duty I require of him. And my servant continues to draw near to me by supererogatory worship until I love him. When I love him, I become the ear by which he hears, the eye by which he sees, the hand by which grasps, and the foot by which he walks. If he asks me for something, I give it to him, if he seeks protection, I provide it to him (Ibn Daqiq al-'Id 2014, p 155).

The testing of the hypothesis of the 'human witnessing' model is very interesting, where it is postulated that those who are not directly participating in transcendental meditation may radiate the harmony and psychological benefits, that is, increase in 5-HIAA-to-decreased cortisol ratio,[30] to those who outside the group but observing it (Van Wijk et al. 2014, p 372–373). This increase was found to be correlated to a reduction in anger, anxiety, aggression, as well as other negative emotions (Walton and Pugh in Van Wijk et al. 2014, p 368). This seems to have resonance to the Prophetic divinely inspired narration[31] that highlights that those who sit and meditate (*dhikr*) in circles, their state is projected as light as seen by the angels

---

J.R (1982) Breath suspension during the Transcendental Meditation technique, Psychosomatic Medicine 44 (2): 133: 143.

[29] The gamma brain waves are high frequency (25–42 Hz) and it was found that is seen to increase in the EEG of high-amplitude gamma oscillations rhythm to slow oscillatory rhythms for long-term meditators during mediation (non-referential compassion meditation—objectless meditation. Benevolence and compassion pervade the mind as a way of being, thus termed pure compassion or non-referential compassion) that was not present in the base-line and the control group. The gamma brain waves patterns are linked to high-order cognitive and affective processes that affects our attention, working memory, learning or conscious perception. The results from this study indicates that this type of meditative training involves the temporal integrative mechanisms in the brain and may induce short-term and long-term neural changes (Lutz et al. 2004).

[30] 5-HIAA—Hydroxyindoleacetic acid, which is a main metabolite of serotonin, which is seen to have a calming effect on the mind, while cortisol is the stress hormone, where higher levels are found in those experiencing stress and that which decreases with meditation.

[31] This is the narration by Abu Hurayah, which is very detailed and has been summarized here, with variations in what is meant by *dhikr*—remembrance of God. This is cited in many sources including Muslim, al-Bukhari, at-Tirmidhi, and an-Nasa'i; 40 *ḥadīth qudsi*; https://sunnah.com/qudsi40.

and that tranquillity descends upon them. Even a passer byer who sits with them also benefits from his sitting with those who are doing their remembering of God (*dhikr*). They have been granted sanctuary and forgiveness by God and such people shall not suffer says the Lord.

Irrespective of the religious traditions and the metaphysical differences, these higher stages are known as 'non-being or emptiness' in Buddhism, 'pure consciousness' and 'pure being' in Yoga and Vedanta, whereas Taoism captures it as 'non-being or nothingness', while Islam refers to it as '*ma'rifa*' or the 'divine knowledge of God'. Sears, supported by Samdong Rinpoche, states that 'all major traditions share the same phenomenological-defined experience despite the traditions often strenuous metaphysical difference' (Sears 2014, p. 61). Rinpoche points out that the discerning levels of experiences outlined above of the Vedantic tradition are 'readily recognisable within his Tibetan Buddhist tradition'.

Self-Actualisation The Maslow hierarchy of needs (Maslow 2011; Learning Theories.com 2014) is represented as a pyramid, with the physiological or lower needs forming the base, followed by security and safety, belongingness, esteem, and with self-actualisation being at the top of the pyramid or the highest stage. This latter stage has some resonance to the evolving states of consciousness where seekers are said to move from the *nafs al-ammāra* (beastly or lower state) to the *nafs al-lawwāma* (a self-reproaching or self-critical self) and progressing on to the *nafs al-mutma'inna* (a peaceful self) and beyond (see Fig. 6.11). These are called D-Needs or deficiency needs given that humans are driven because of their need to fulfil it or the lower state, and that which evolves into higher states of self-actualisation or the peaceful self (B values). Table 6.7 outlines the beta values and provides Prophetic examples of each characteristic.

1. Physiological: air; food, water, sex, and other factors related to homeostasis etc.;
2. Safety: Security of environment; resources, health, property etc.;
3. Belongingness: love, friendship, intimacy, family etc.;
4. Self-Esteem: confidence; self-esteem; achievement, respect etc.;
5. Self-actualisation: morality, creativity, problem solving etc.;

Table 6.6 outlines the B Values articulated by Maslow and then provides Prophetic examples for each:

Even though there are critiques of the Maslow's hierarchy of needs, who argue that needs are not sequential and can vary according to personalities and circumstances, it still remains a useful framework to understand the various human needs and its categories. In contrast to the above, D-needs, B-Values or Values of Being as Maslow calls them, are driven by personal desire to reach the highest in human potential. This is not triggered by any deficiency as with D values. These B-Values, Maslow postulates, are to be found in those who have self-actualised and have peak experiences as outlined below. For each of the B-Values that he has identified and explained, the Prophetic life examples are given to best fit it, as Sect. 3.2 expounds behaviour related to this value set.

It can be seen from Table 6.7 that there is an emergence of a person who has had peak and plateau experiences and self-actualised, which is based on life experiences that have been largely drawn from the earliest biographies of the Prophet. This can be validated against the work of Carl Rogers, the founder of Humanistic Psychology based on his extensive experience with the method that he developed, called the client-centred approach (Rogers 1991). The Prophet was able to have a great one-to-one relationship with his community, treating every individual as special, while building a strong sense of community (ummah), that still prevails to this date. This is what is seen in the Sheikh of the Order, where he offered one-to-one counselling to the seekers especially to those who were drug addicts and the HIV patients (see Chap. 5).

Table 6.7 captures some of the generalisations from his years of work that can be articulated, which are grounded in his experience on 'becoming a person' or 'full-humanness'. From the well-grounded generalisation that has emerged from Carl Roger's clinical work (Table 6.8), the Prophet fits into all four categories, being open to experience; trusting one's organism (self); a locus of evaluation; and willingness to be a process. Thus, from the perspective of the work of both Maslow as well as Rogers, the Prophet is seen as a self-actualised being, as well as reaching the full human potential. Both from Maslow's and Roger's perspective, the Sheikh of the Order himself demonstrates some of these traits as outlined in the analysis of the NS-NLP in Fig. 6.2 and as seen from the seekers' view as indicated in Chap. 3 (Figs. 5.8, 5.9, 5.10, 5.11).

Spiritual Actualisation

Self-actualisation from the above mentioned rendition represents the development of traits and concurrently varying levels of consciousness, where both Maslow and Rogers have articulated experiences based on their interviewees who had undergone these types of experiences within the sphere of humanistic psychology. It is a process whereby humans are able to achieve their highest potential following peak experiences[32] (Maslow, 1970, p xiv)", accompanied by a sense of wholeness and meaning in life. Maslow (1970) argues that these types of peak-experiences, ecstasies or transcendental experiences can be achieved by ordinary people. His perception is that this is something that is innate in humans and can be experienced by all irrespective of philosophy, ethnicity, language, culture etc.; which when stripped back can be called 'core religious experiences' or 'transcendent experience' (Maslow 1970, pp 19–20). As conceptualised by Maslow there seems to be no involvement of the Divine.

Self-actualisation outlined within the light of the Prophetic model and his characteristics sits well within spirituality given its inherent nature of 'becoming fully human' or Being values (B values) and Being cognition (B cognition). However, spiritual actualisation, I argue, is much more in the sense that even though it operates in the mind-body realm, it goes beyond it through the agency of the

---

[32] An experience characterised by "a poignantly emotional, climatic, autonomic response to the miraculous, the awesome, the sacralized, the Unitive, the B-Values.

6.11 Spirituality Wellbeing and Emotional Intelligence

Table 6.8 On becoming a person (Rogers 1991)

Generalisations	Prophetic examples
Openness to Experience: This is the opposite of being defensive. Openly aware of his feelings and attitude as they exist in him at the organic level. Thus, more aware of reality as it exists outside of himself, instead of pre-conceptions. He is able to take in the evidence in a new situation as it is, rather than distorting it to fit a pattern which he already holds. An openness of awareness to what exists in this moment in oneself and the situation.	The classical example is of the Prophet when his delegation was prevented by the Quraish (Makkans) from proceeding to Makkah to perform their pilgrimage. Firstly, the Prophet agreed to this and an agreement was drawn out between the parties to this effect and that they would proceed the following year. Secondly, since the delegation felt dejected and frustrated, he took the advice of his wife Umm Salama to do the rites then and there, and this led to all of his companions doing the same. Even though most of his companions were against this pact, this changed the situation. Thirdly, his profound life and society changing experience at Mount Hira, Makkah where he received the first revelation, which he was not expecting, represents his openness to both innate experiences and how it translated outside of himself to society.
Trust in one's Organism: It seems that the person increasingly discovers that his own organism is trustworthy, that it is a suitable instrument for discovering the most satisfying behaviour in each immediate situation. He has a relatively accurate perception of this external situation in all of its complexity. He is better able to permit his total organism, his conscious thought participating, to consider, weigh and balance each stimulus, need, and demand, and its relative weight and intensity.	From an Islamic perspective, guided by the Divine, there are many situational decisions of the Prophet that made him an example and turned the minds of others to accepting him. For example, listening to others and discussing things through appealing to reason and doing this confidently as well as kindly, changed the minds of the harshest persons. This was testified by the Qur'ān when it was said, "If you had spoken to them harshly, you would have dispersed them." Another example is of the water carriers, who complained to the Prophet of waking up very early for prayers given that their work was arduous, and he told them, pray when you wake up and he shortened the prayers when he heard the children who were with the women crying.
A Locus of Evaluation: The individual increasingly comes to feel that this locus of evaluation lies within himself. Less and less does he look to others for approval or disapproval; for standards to live by; for decisions and choices. The key question of the creative individual is: Am I living in a way which is deeply satisfying to me and which truly expresses who I am?	Despite being a leader and the complexity surrounding him, he was seen to be with a smile most of the time, and prayed for people, was tolerant to people from all walks of life, and prayed long hours, and when asked by Aisha, why do you have to pray so much since your sins are forgiven, he responded by saying, "Should I not be grateful to my Lord?" Whatever wealth he received, he gave it all away and would not return home until all his money was distributed. He lived an austere life and was content with it.

(continued)

Table 6.8 (continued)

Generalisations	Prophetic Examples
Willingness to be a Process: It is that the individual seems to become more content to be a process than the product. One can see here both the expression of trust in the organism, and also the realisation of self as a process. It means that a person is a fluid process, not a fixed and static entity; a flowing river of change, not a block of solid material, a continually changing constellation of potentialities, not a fixed of traits.	"Live in this world as a stranger" said the Prophet, indicating detachment from this world and focus on living with the moment, as life with all its vagaries is uncertain and tomorrow is promised to no one. The Prophet said, "Be satisfied if you have a roof over your head, enough to eat and that you wake up in the morning for this is a blessing."

heart (*qalb*) and the spirit (*rūḥ*), transcending the physical and mental realms to the spiritual realm from an Islamic perspective. This type of people are seen to have a high degree of piety (*taqwa*) that leads them to a righteous (*birr*) life, where one becomes selfless, caring for others as themselves, and connected with the Divine. Spiritual actualisation can be defined as gaining knowledge of the Divine (*ma'rifa*), which is the highest state of consciousness in the Islamic tradition.

The extent of the peak, plateau and spiritual experiences can vary with individuals and within the Islamic framework of consciousness as outlined below. The experiences of the Prophets can be said to be of a highest nature, whereby, they are recipients of divine scriptural messages, which were then shared with the wider populace through oral or written means and then has been shared with people orally or written down. This has prompted the formation of religions, which has influenced humanity and brought about social reformation and changes to their respective lives and society. Nonetheless, it is acknowledged that religion or rather its misunderstanding and misinterpretation has caused problems to society. In terms of spiritual experiences, however, not everyone has been bestowed with this kind of mega-core religious experience that has changed the course of history. In this context, the peak experiences that Maslow is referring to above is not the same as authentic Prophetic experiences since his worldview resides only in the realm of the mind-body and not in the spirit realm, which is in the domain of the Divine what ever be ones conception of God.

In order to understand the process of self-actualisation and spiritual actualisation, one needs to examine the world view of Islam in comparison to scientific perspectives or the western secular model. There are several realms that one can discern (see Fig. 6.12), the physical/somatic/bodily realm, the psychological realm and the spiritual realm. One of the distinct features of psycho-somatic experiences, which operates in the body-mind realm as articulated by modern Psychology. This is as compared to spiritual experiences in which case, the body-mind and importantly the soul-heart and spirit (*rūḥ*) is involved in the process. Spiritual

6.11 Spirituality Wellbeing and Emotional Intelligence

Spiritual sphere

Psychological Sphere

Human Being

Physical/Somatic /Bodily

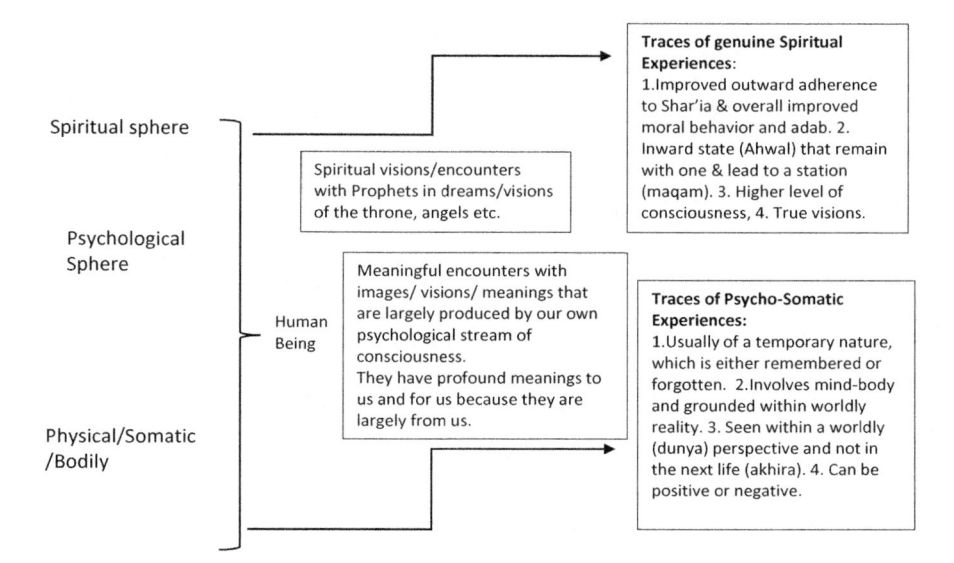

Spiritual visions/encounters with Prophets in dreams/visions of the throne, angels etc.

Traces of genuine Spiritual Experiences:
1. Improved outward adherence to Shar'ia & overall improved moral behavior and adab. 2. Inward state (Ahwal) that remain with one & lead to a station (maqam). 3. Higher level of consciousness, 4. True visions.

Meaningful encounters with images/ visions/ meanings that are largely produced by our own psychological stream of consciousness. They have profound meanings to us and for us because they are largely from us.

Traces of Psycho-Somatic Experiences:
1. Usually of a temporary nature, which is either remembered or forgotten. 2. Involves mind-body and grounded within worldly reality. 3. Seen within a worldly (dunya) perspective and not in the next life (akhira). 4. Can be positive or negative.

Fig. 6.12 Varying spheres and nature of experiences

experiences within the Islamic tradition are generally explained within the context of the metaphysical realm, where human beings have the body-mind-soul-heart and spirit being involved within the context of this world and the next life (*dunya-akhira*) (Imam Ghazāli 1995, Al-Attas 2001b). Some of the experiences of the seekers outlined in Chap. 5, particularly of the resident imam, his friend and the manager of reflexology, demonstrate that the type of experiences that they were having are related to the spiritual realm, call it peak or plateau experiences.

A diagram outlined in Fig. 6.12 below by Samir Mahmoud (2020) has been used to present different realms, with relevant insertions by myself specifically relating to the traces of psycho-somatic experiences. I argue that 'self-actualisation' (Maslow 2011) and 'becoming human' (Rogers 1991), when seen within the context of peak and plateau experiences, is part of spiritual experience albeit it is a step in the ladder of the ascending levels of consciousness. This is a theistic perspective, which views the spirit (*rūḥ*) being from God, with a potential to connect to Him. The peak and plateau experiences, however, are different to the full-fledged spiritual experiences and the process of spiritual actualisation that the Prophets and Sages have manifested, which are at a much higher level of consciousness. Their experiences lead from spiritual states (*hal*) to spiritual stations (*maqams*) scaling the hierarchies of consciousness with the grace of God, which represent close proximity to the Divine. To use Hoffman's (2019) theory of consciousness there are different conscious agents-networks, which increases in its level of complexity reaching to an infinite consciousness. To represent this, two core-religious experiences are presented below, which are a different level from Maslow's conception of the above mentioned type of experiences.

One of the most enduring examples, which operates in the spiritual realm within the Islamic ethos of spiritual actualisation is the what is known as '*al Isra wal mi'raj*'[33] This is the night journey of the Prophet first from Makkah to Jerusalem (horizontal journey), where he was in communion with all other Prophets leading them in ritual prayers. This was followed by the Prophet taking flight to the seven heavens (vertical journey). In order to confirm his horizontal journey, he was able to provide signs along the way including the trail of caravans, which was confirmed since they arrived later in Makkah. The signs and symbols that he witnessed in his vertical journey are outlined in some detail in selected Islamic scholarly works. Another process of spiritual actualisation are the revelations (*wahi*)[34] that the Prophet experienced over a period of 23 years during which the whole of the divine Qur'ān was transmitted in a sustained stream, embodying the process of spiritual actualisation. The process of revelation itself took many forms including visions, primordial sounds, dreams, direct contact through Angel Jibreel, etc.

While, the above mentioned is the process of spiritual actualisation of the Prophet Mohammed, there are other examples from other Prophets and Sages, where there were varying experiences in their attainment of this process of enlightenment. From time to time some ordinary people are offered some spiritual openings of much lesser depths, with the grace of God, which seems to transform them thereafter. This process of spiritual actualisation, where the spirit is involved traverses beyond the physical and psychological realm into a spiritual realm, which is beyond the normal time-space continuum. In this light, one of the things that has been left behind for us after the Prophet are good dreams,[35] which takes place in the spiritual realm, and according to the Prophet are 1/46 part of prophethood (Muslim 2007).[36] People are seen to have spiritual experiences from time to time, which are from God as opposed to ones prompted by the ego or Satan (see Fig. 6.12).

---

[33] There are three renditions selected of this spiritual journey '*al-isra-wal-miraj*', which provides are useful account of this and puts into context. One is by Sheikh Al-Yaqoubi, The miracles isra and miraj, of 21st May 2016, https://www.youtube.com/watch?v=zLwsd-4DiTk. The second one is by Sheik Hamza Yusuf, The Night Journey, 15th December 2018, https://www.youtube.com/watch?v=qos482OGXII. The third version The Night Journey – Story of Muhammad by Sheikh Dr. Yasir Qadhi, 24th November 2019, https://www.youtube.com/watch?v=59I-t50ZEhs.

[34] The context of the revelation is presented in these selected videos: (i) The remarkable story of Qur'ān's revelations, Dr. Shabir Ally, 17th July 2014, https://www.youtube.com/watch?v=u-4GJ5KyXbg. (ii) How the Qur'ān was reveled and compiled, Sheikh Hamza Yusuf, Foundations of Islam Series: Session 1, 24th February 2011, https://www.youtube.com/watch?v=ICu3ITHnBoM. (iii) Dr. Garry Will and the Qur'ān, What the Qur'ān Meant, Chicago Humanities Festival, 7th November 2017, https://www.youtube.com/watch?v=h6NWfVWxqSM.

[35] Some selected videos on dreams: (i) Dreams (Islamic Interpretation), Imam Karim AbuZaid, 16th June 2012, https://www.youtube.com/watch?v=6p3YBoWoL-I. (ii) Interpreting Dreams, Sheikh Husain Abdul Sattar, 21 December 2012, https://www.youtube.com/watch?v=3A9ypzvs1ZA. (iii) Dream Interpretation: Understanding different types of Dreams, Abdul Rahim Harun Sheikh Abu Suhaib Bassaam Ali Abul Haaj, 29th April 2015, https://www.youtube.com/watch?v=09wzi8i5fdE.

[36] There are multiple narrations on this as narrated by the companions of the Prophet including Abu Qatada, Abu Huraira, Anas bin Malik and Ibn Umar as reported in Sahih Muslim.

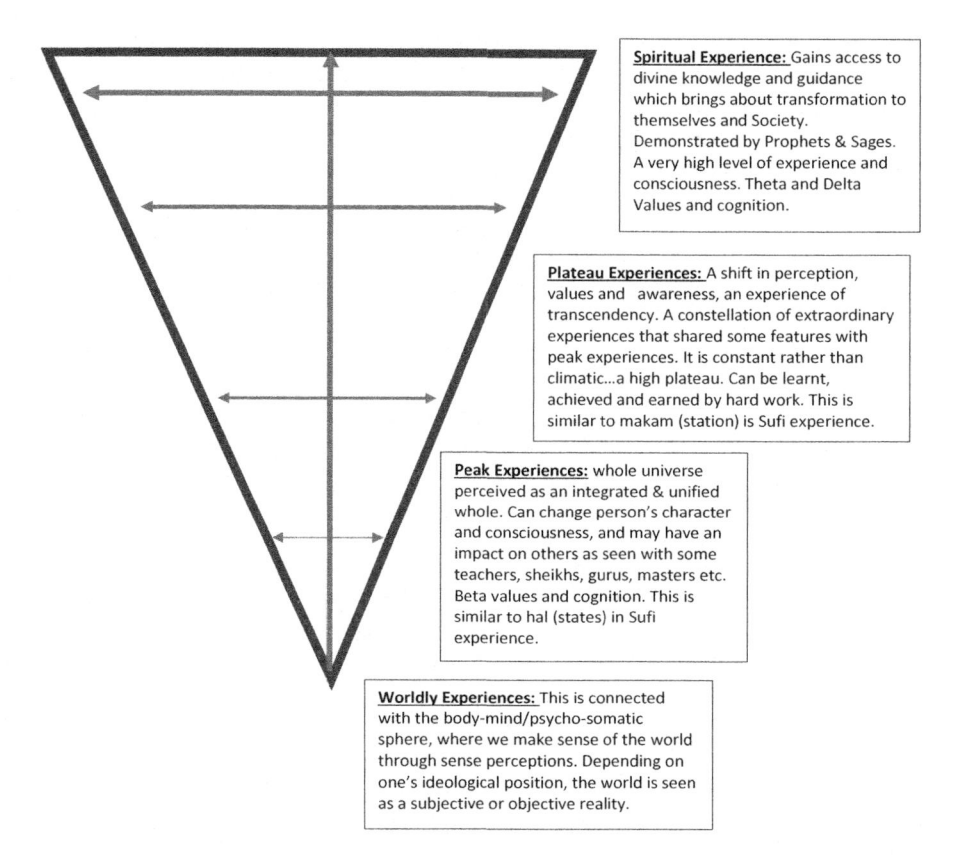

6.11 Spirituality Wellbeing and Emotional Intelligence

Spiritual Experience: Gains access to divine knowledge and guidance which brings about transformation to themselves and Society. Demonstrated by Prophets & Sages. A very high level of experience and consciousness. Theta and Delta Values and cognition.

Plateau Experiences: A shift in perception, values and awareness, an experience of transcendency. A constellation of extraordinary experiences that shared some features with peak experiences. It is constant rather than climatic...a high plateau. Can be learnt, achieved and earned by hard work. This is similar to makam (station) is Sufi experience.

Peak Experiences: whole universe perceived as an integrated & unified whole. Can change person's character and consciousness, and may have an impact on others as seen with some teachers, sheikhs, gurus, masters etc. Beta values and cognition. This is similar to hal (states) in Sufi experience.

Worldly Experiences: This is connected with the body-mind/psycho-somatic sphere, where we make sense of the world through sense perceptions. Depending on one's ideological position, the world is seen as a subjective or objective reality.

Fig. 6.13 Inverted pyramid hierarchy of types and levels of experiences

Types and Levels of Experiences In order to further elucidate and put the types and levels of experiences into perspective, the diagram conceptualised below represents an ascending hierarchy of the types of experiences (Fig. 6.13). The worldly experiences relates to the body-mind and its related psycho-somatic patterns is grounded within each individuals conditioning. On the other hand, the peak experiences occurs unexpectedly and this from a Islamic perspective are openings bestowed with the grace of God. As Maslow (1970) points out from his interviews with those who have had this type of experiences, where they feel unified with themselves and their environment. These experiences are explosive in their nature and do not last but they have an impact on the concerned persons, where their perspectives and attitude are transformed. Maslow (2011, p 104) says expression and communication in peak experience '...tend to become poetic, mythical and rhapsodic, as if this were the natural language to express such states of being'. This peak experience is similar to what is termed in the Sufi tradition as states (*hal*), which are intermittent in its nature, where there is difficulty in expressing their experiences in words. Some of the seekers experiences based on the case study narrative in Chap. 5, seems to belong to this category with their insight into their experiences and dreams.

The plateau experiences, which Maslow (Gruel 1995) himself is said to have experienced is a more stable experience, where there is a shift in perception and values and is transcendent in nature. Maslow (1970, xiv) points out that this type of experience '…always has a noetic and cognitive elements, which is not always true for peak experience, which can be purely and exclusively emotional. It is far more voluntary than peak -experiences are'. Even though it shares some elements with peak experiences, it is not climatic and more enduring. This is similar to stations (*maqam*) in the Sufi tradition.

According to Maslow (1970), the plateau experience can be achieved by learning and hard work. It can be asserted that the Sheikh who has been in the spiritual path could be said to be within this category, where stability is demonstrated in terms of how he deals with himself and others and the way he is able to facilitate the transformation of the seekers. This is to an extent supported by the modelling and the meta-programme completed in chapter 5, which puts into context the experiences of the Sheikh. Cleary and Shapiro cite Maslow (Gruel 1995, p. 45) that "individuals capable of having transcendent experiences lived potentially fuller and healthier lives than the majority of humanity because (they) were able to transcend everyday frustrations and conflicts and were less driven by neurotic tendencies" (Cleary and Shapiro 1995, p. 6). This seems to resonate with some selected seekers of the Order who have undergone this type of experiences who are seen to be at peace with themselves, despite the difficulties that they had undergone in the past. For those who are having peak and plateau experiences, Maslow (1970) called them transcending self-actualisers, the Theory Z people, while contrasting them to non-transcending self-actualisers, or Theory Y people. According to Gruel (1995) not much research has been since done on further exploring these type of experiences as well as with the theory Z.

What is appropriate for discussion within Maslow's above mentioned conception is the Islamic Sufi tradition of advances experiences of '*fana*' and '*baqa*'.[37] Murata (2018) elucidates these two concepts, where the former is a process and state by which human selfhood is annihilated in the 'sheer presence of God', while in the latter, the 'human self-returns and subsists', where people can operate normally in

---

[37]The concepts of *fana* and *baqa* is said to have been originally conceived by 'Abu'l-Fayż Du'l-Nūn (d. 245/860), developed by Sahl b. Abd-Allāh Tostarī (d. 283/896), spread in Sufi circles by Abu'l-Qāsem Jonayd (d. 298/910), publicly proclaimed by Ḥosayn b. Manṣūr Ḥallāj (d. 309/922), and enigmatically articulated by Abū Bakr Šeblī (d. 334/945)'. This refers to the original standing of man (waqfa) before God at the primordial covenant (before becoming human and when we were souls), when 'man received his own intellect in and through his profession of God's oneness, is reactualized by the Sufi in his dying to worldly existence and his returning to his original, primal state in the presence of God' (Böwering, pp. 153–57, 185–207), *fana* and *baqa*, Encyclopaedia Iranica Foundation Inc, 2020, http://www.iranicaonline.org/articles/baqa-wa-fana-sufi-term-signifying-subsistence-and-passing-away.

society. There are other pairs of opposites that are used for this purpose such as spiritual 'intoxication' (*sukr*) and 'sobriety' (*sahw*), 'expansion' (*bast*) contraction (*qabd*), as well as 'gathering' (*jam*) and 'separation' (*tafriqa*). This is seen by the Sufi's to be the state of the Prophet (Murata 2018), where he had deep spiritual experiences and lived amongst his family and community. This is said to be supported by the Qur'ānic verse (55:26–27), where God says "Everything upon the earth is undergoing annihilation, but there subsists the face of your Lord, Possessor of Majesty and Generous giving".

My own perspective is that spiritual experiences particularly those that the Prophets and the Sages transcends all of the other types of experiences, given the high and more evolved state of consciousness as in the above mentioned experiences of '*fana*' and '*baqa*'. Maslow (2011, p 198) alludes to this where he differentiates "low Nirvana (enlightenment) from a high Nirvana (enlightenment), union downwards from union upwards" Not everyone has this type of experience even though it has covered traversed diverse geographic areas as witnessed in the various divine scriptures throughout history. The persons who have experienced this type of consciousness from an Islamic perspective is one who is nearest to God, and his spirit (*rūḥ*) is able to transcend time and space in terms of receiving scriptural revelations, known as messengers (*rasuls*) or transmitting the previous divine messages (*nabi*) that has been received.

The distinctive difference between self-actualisation and spiritual actualisation is that, in the former the potential is actualised within oneself, whereas in the latter the self is not actualised within oneself but in the knowledge of God (*ma'rifa*), where there is no place for the ego, there is no I, me and mine. There could well be intermediary levels of experiences involving the spirit (*rūḥ*), where God graces people with and these can be alluded to as peak and plateau experiences that Maslow discusses. As the famous mystic Suhrawardi (1991) points out, which can be seen within the seven levels of the spiritual hierarchy (Chishti 2007) is that very few people go beyond the first few levels of consciousness (see Fig. 6.11). The people who truly have spirit (*rūḥ*) based experiences are totally transformed and have had the potential and light to bring about transformation to other as did the Prophets and selected Sages across time and space.

Brain Wave Patterns It is useful to examine the brain wave patterns which are likely to be present in the various types of experiences that has been described above. While studies have to be done in order to capture the type of brain wave patterns during peak, plateau and spiritual experiences, there is some available data that suggests that theta and delta brain waves are seen to be present in meditative states (Sanchetee 2020). There is emerging evidence that in meditation and prayer, there is a change in the type of brain waves that are emitted. Generally when there is a high level of activity, one is in the gamma range (38–42 Hz), which the fastest brain waves being of high frequency, while being subtle, where the mind has to be quiet to access these waves. It is found to be highly active when one is in a state of universal love, altruism, as well as in expanded consciousness and spiritual emergencies (Sanchetee 2020).

On the opposite end of the range of gamma are delta (0.5–3 Hz) and theta waves (4–8 Hz), which are of much lower frequencies, where they are detected in deepest meditation and dreamless sleep. They are said to suspend external awareness and become a source of empathy where healing and regeneration are triggered. The latter theta waves are emitted in sleep and in deep meditation. Similar to delta, the focus is shifted from the external world to ones within oneself, this is the state in which dreams occur, generation of vivid imagery, intuition and information which is normally beyond normal consciousness (Sanchetee 2020). It is most likely that gamma, delta and theta states of consciousness occurs in the peak, plateau and spiritual states but to what extent, there seems to be no data for this purpose.

Where there is clear data is in ritual prayer (*salah*), especially in prostration, there is emission of a high level of alpha waves (8–12 Hz) as seen in Fig. 6.7 (Cheok 2008). This demonstrates a relaxed state of the brain and that which aids overall mental coordination, calmness alertness, mind/body integration and learning. This was clearly seen in the feedback from the seekers and this has been presented in Chap. 5 (Figs. 5.19, 5.23, 5.24, 5.25, 5.26 and 5.28), whereby seekers were able to reconcile with themselves, better related to friends and family and experience a sense of calmness and spirituality, which they did not have before they undertook the spiritual practices.

6.11.3 Spiritual Order (Ṭarīqa), Islamic Psychotherapy and Therapeutic Communities (TCs)

Islamic spiritual orders have been in existence for over a 1000 years as outlined in Chap. 5, where they have taken myriad forms, with their distinct approaches and methodologies. They have become embedded in the various communities around the world serving not only a spiritual function but providing a space for social, cultural and therapeutic interventions. The spiritual Order that is the focus of this study served the function of rehabilitating of drug addicts and HIV patients (they consisted of half the sample of seekers), who by and large were rejected by their families. As demonstrated in Chaps. 5 and 6, the Order itself has had a positive impact on transforming their attitudes and behaviours and providing them with a set of values for their personal growth. One of the types of Islamic meditation called *muraqaba*[38] (a state of witnessing), which has been referred to in Sect. 2.3 and

---

[38] *Muraqaba* is a silent meditation carried out with the breath within the Order that I cultivated my meditative practice, the Naqshabandiyyah Awasiya, for nearly two decades. It has two phases, one is vigorous movement with the breath on the seven lathaifs in the body (subtle spiritual organs), where the focus on the names of God and the heart is used as an anchor. The second phase, is of complete silence, where one in a state of witnessing of the heart, where there is no sound or movement but the awareness of the presence of God. Within this phase, one moves up to different stations (*maqams*) depending on the maturity of the seekers being monitored by the Sheikh. There are no active thoughts, no judgement or no mental involvement and as in mindfulness meditation, if a thought arises you take note and come back to the state of witnessing. This deep type of meditation has had a transformative impact on my being and enabled me to shed

6.11 Spirituality Wellbeing and Emotional Intelligence

Table 6.9 Types of meditation and therapeutic/clinical implications

Meditation-based therapy	
Techniques of Muraqaba	Therapeutic/clinical implications
Mushahada (observation)	Presence
Tasawwur (imagination)	Focused attention and open monitoring
Tafakkur (contemplation of creation)	Creativity
Tadabbur (contemplation of God's names/attributes)	Connecting with self, nature, and higher power
Muhasaba (self-assessment)	ClaritySerenity

Chap. 5 is being practiced by the Order being researched. This is being integrated into mainstream psychotherapy as *Muraqaba* Mindfulness-based therapy in Islamic Psychotherapy (Isagandarova 2019). Imam Ghazāli (1995) discussion six types of meditation (Sect. 2.3), most of which is reflected in Table 6.9 (Isagandarova 2019 2019, p. 1150), which deals with the methods as well as their therapeutic/clinical implications:

While *muraqaba* can be used as meditative-based therapy within the domain of Islamic Psychotherapy; psychotherapist, counsellors, spiritual caregivers are beginning to use *muraqaba* as a psychotherapeutic method and integrating it with mainstream therapies[39] such as MBSR, MBCT, DTC, ACT and MBRP. More research is needed to further develop and integrate the various methods contained within the Islamic tradition into psychotherapy. Given the results which has be generated from this spiritual Order, it will auger well to verify these claims and study what is beneficial especially for the drug addicts, as well as those with other types of addictions.

A very useful resource that brings much of the information and analysis together in terms of developing the self from an Islamic Psychotherapy perspective is

---

negative thoughts and external addictions. I see that this transformational aspects are mirrored in others whom I have met from different parts of the world. An important point to labour is that, it is not only the meditation itself but the adherence to the ritual prayers, observing fasts, charity, the value system, the guidance of the Sheikh, the spiritual attention, the peer learning etc., as highlighted in the model that was developed in this study Fig. 6.2—The Model of Spiritual Leadership and Self-development, in combination contributes to transformation with the grace of God. The book Dalael-ul-Sulook (the objective appraisal of the Sufi path) gives an overview of the methods/techniques as well as its states and stations, written by the Sheikh of this Order Maulana Allahyar Khan (1976 cited and referenced in Sect. 2.1), who had both a (conservative Islamic orientation) Deobandi and Sufi orientation (an unusual combination), having mastered Islamic traditional studies and *fiqh* (law). The Order adhered to the Shar'ia and concurrently focusing on the inward development (*tasawwuf*) as was the case with the Order that was researched in this study.

[39] Mindfulness Based Stress Reduction (MBSR), Mindfulness Based Cognitive Therapy (MBCT), Dialectic Cognitive Therapy (DCT), Acceptance and Commitment therapy (ACT) and Mindfulness Based Relapse Prevention (MBRP).

Abdallah Rothman's (2020)[40] series of videos, which maps out the literature that it captured in Chaps. 2 and 3, and the theoretical framework discussed in detail in Chap. 5. Most of the contemplative methods that Rothman outlines has been put into practice within the spiritual Order that was studied, within a community of practitioners under the guidance of the Sheikh. It will be well worth a study in terms of understanding of these methods/tools and the approach of the Order, can enhance Islamic psychotherapy.

This Order is seen to have resonance with what is called 'therapeutic community' (TC), which started in 1960s in US and Europe and hinges on people coming together to initiate and sustain social and psychology change (Vanderplasschen et al. 2014). They have been associated with a range of treatment traditions and approaches based on a specifically designed social environment aimed at offering a drug free space in which people live together. TCs has the characteristics of utilising the community itself as an agent of change. Residents participate, where they model the peers and emulate the philosophy and values of the TC system. Several assessments conducted to ascertain its effects points out that compared to other interventions there "..are lower substance use and recidivism rates in more than half of the selected studies", which is demonstratively positive (Vanderplasschen et al. 2014, p 55).

From an Islamic perspective, spiritual orders (*ṭarīqas*) can serve as TCs, so long as they can model on existing *ṭarīqas* as in this case of the Naqshabandiyyah Khāliddiyyah order. This *ṭarīqa* has been able to develop a rehabilitation model within its spiritual domain and offer a safe space and nurture personal transformation and growth of its seekers. They can extend beyond the boundaries of the TCs given their wide horizon of spiritual growth and communities, which have been seen to organically sustain themselves.

References

Abdullah, T., Al-Hajj, A. (n.d.). *The origins and meaning of al-futuwwa*. Institute of Islamic – African International, SANKORE. https://siiasi.org

Afifi, Z. E. M. (1997). Daily practices, study performance and health during the Ramadan fast. *The Journal of the Royal Society for the Promotion of Health, 117*(4), 231–235.

Al-Attas, S. M. N. (2001a). *Prolegomena: To the metaphysics of Islam: An exposition of the fundamental elements of the worldview of Islam* (pp. 1–358). Kuala Lumpur: International Institute of Islamic Thought and Civilisation (ISTAC).

---

[40] This is one of the few series on the development of the self-articulated by Dr. Abdallah Rothman, which covers a wide range of topics within the inward aspects of Islam (*tasawwuf*), providing theoretical and practical tips drawn from traditional Islamic sources. The video has 20 sessions which covers various areas within the above mentioned field in a systematic manner. What is referenced in only Session 20, which provides an overall summary of this but all other videos can be accessed on-line.

References

Al-Attas, S. M. N. (2001b). *Prolegomena to the metaphysics: An exposition of the fundamental element of the Worldview of Islam* (2nd ed.), Kuala Lumpur, Malaysia: International Institute of Islamic Thought & Civilisation (ISTAC).

Al-Ghazali. (1995). *Ihya Ulum Id-Din* (Vol. 3) (M.F. Karim, Trans.). New Delhi: Islamic Book Services.

Al-Ghazāli. (2005). *Deliverance from error and the beginning guidance.* (W. Montgomery Watt, Trans.). Kuala Lumpur: Islamic Book Trust.

Al-Haddad, I. A. A. (1990). *The lives of man* (M. Badawi, Trans.) Aligarh, India: Premier Publishing Company.

Al-Mubarakpuri, S. R. (2003a). *Tafsir Ibn Kathir* (Vol. 2). Riyadh: Darussalam.

Aldahadha, B. (2013). The effects of Muslim Praying Meditation and Transcendental Meditation Programs on mindfulness among the University of Nizwa Students. *College Student Journal, 47*(4), 668–676.

Alexander, I. (2015). *Meditation in Islam.* https://www.youtube.com/watch?v=WmgAkaHFZY8

Ali, K. K., & Sulam, M. B. (2018). *The Paradigms of Consciousness, Department of Management and Humanities.* Universiti Teknology, PETRONAS, 32610, Seri Iskandar, Perak, Malaysia, SHS Web Conferences 53, 04003, ICHSS. https://www.shs-conferences.org/articles/shsconf/pdf/2018/14/shsconf_ichss2018_04003.pdf

Aljunied, K. (2016). *Reorienting Sufism: Hamka and Islamic mysticism in the Malay World, Indonesia,* No. 101 (April 2016) (pp. 69–84). Cornell University: Southeast Asia Program Publications. http://www.jstor.org/stable/10.5728/indonesia.101.0067

An-Nawawi (2004). In A. Adbul-Fattah & R. Youssif Shakei (Eds.), *A selection of authentic (sacred) Hadiths with An-Nawawi's forty Hadiths.* Compiled by Muhammad. Egypt: Dar Al-anarah.

Afsaruddin, A. (2020). *Jihad,* Encyclopaedia Britannica, Inc. 28 February 2020. https://www.britannica.com/topic/jihad.

Andresen, J. J. (2000). Meditation meets behavioral science: The story of experimental research on meditation. cognitive models and spiritual maps: The interdisciplinary explorations of religious experience. *Special Issue of the Journal of Consciousness Studies, 7,* 11–12, 20.

Arambula, P., Peper, E., Kawakami, M., & Gibney, K. H. (2001). The physiological correlates of Kundalini Yoga meditation: a study of a yoga master. *Association for Applied Psychophysiology and Biofeedback, 26*(2), 147–153.

Asad, M. (2011). *The Message of the Qur'ān.* Kuala Lumpur: International Book Trust.

Austin, H. J. (2014). In S. Schmidt & H. Walach (eds.), *The meditative approach to awaken selfless insight-wisdom, meditation – Neuroscientific approaches and philosophical implications. Studies in neuroscience, consciousness and spirituality* (Vol. 2, pp. 23–55). Cham, Switzerland: Springer International.

Bandura, A. (2012). *Social learning theory in the psychology book.* London: DK.

Bousfield, J. (1993). Adventures and misadventures of the new Sufis: Islamic spiritual groups in contemporary Malaysia, Sojourn. *Journal of Social Issues in Southeast Asia, 8*(2), 328–344. http://www.jstor.org/stable/41056867

Bruinessen, M. V. (1998). *Studies of Sufism and the Sufi orders in Indonesia. Die Welt des Islams, New Series* (Vol. 38, Issue 2, pp. 192–219). http://www.jstor.org/stable/1570744

Bukhari, M. (1994). *The translation of the meanings of summarized Sahih Al-Bukhari, Compilation by Al-Imam Zain-ud-Din bin A.L. Az-Zubaidi, Translated by Muhammad Mushin Khan* (pp. 1–1096). Riyadh: Dar-us-Salam.

Chalmers, D. (2014). Is a scientific materialist. *How do you explain consciousness, David Chalmers,* 14th July 2014. https://www.youtube.com/watch?v=uhRhtFFhNzQ&t=931s

Cheok, N. S. (2008). The brain. In F. Ibrahim, A. B. W. Abbas, & S. Ng (Eds.), *Salat: Benefits from Science Perspective.* Kuala Lumpur: Department of Biomedical Engineering/Malaysia: University of Malaya.

Chisea, A. (2010). Vippassana meditation: Systematic review of current evidence. *Journal of Alternative and Complementary Medicine, 16*(1), 37–46.

Chisea, A. V. (2010). Meditation: Systematic review of current evidence. *Journal of Alternative and Complementary Medicine, 16*, 1.
Chishti (2007). The stages of the development of the soul, last modified 2nd October 2007. 1945 Retrieved from: https://www.chisthi.ru/soul_development.html.
Cleary, T., & Shapiro, S. (1995). The plateau experience and the post-mortem life: Abraham. H. Maslow's unfinished theory. *The Journal of Transpersonal Psychology, 27*(1), 1–23.
Corey, L., & Keyes, M. (1998). Social well-being. *Social Psychology Quarterly, 61*(2), 121.
De Jong, F. (1983). The Sufi orders in nineteenth and twentieth-century Palestine: A preliminary survey concerning their identity, organisational characteristics and continuity. *Studia Islamica, 58*, 149–181. http://www.jstor.org/stable/1595345
Doufesh, H., Faisel, T., Lim, K.-S., & Ibrahim, F. (2012). EEG spectral analysis on Muslim prayers. *Applied Psychophysiology and Biofeedback, 37*, 11–18.
Douglas-Klotz, N. (2002). *Re-hearing Qur'ān in Open Translation: Ta'wil, Postmodern Inquiry and a Hermeneutics of Indeterminacy, Edinburgh Institute of Advance Learning*. A juried paper presented in the Arts, Literature and Religion Section of the American Academy of Religion Annual Meeting, Toronto, Ontario, Canada, November 23rd, on the theme of Hermeneutics.
Esch, T. (2014). The neurobiology of meditation and mindfulness. In S. Schmidt & H. Walach (Eds.), *Neuroscientific approaches and philosophical implications, studies in neuroscience, consciousness and spirituality* (Vol. 2, pp. 155–173). Cham, Switzerland: Springer International Publication.
Fry, L. (2003). Towards a theory of spiritual leadership. *The Leadership Quarterly, 14*, 693–727.
Fujii, C. (2010). Ritual activities of Ṭarīqas in Zanzibar. *African Study Monographs*, Supplementary Issue 2010, 4. https://doi.org/10.14989/108281
Gammer, M. (1994). The beginnings of the Naqshbandiyyah in Dāghestān and the Russian conquest of the Caucasus. *Die Welt des Islams, 34*(2), 204–217. http://www.jstor.org/stable/1570930
Goleman, D. (1991). Tibetan and Western models of mental health. In D. Goleman & R. Thurman (Eds.), *Mindscience: An East-West dialogue* (pp. 89–102). Massachusetts, Boston: Wisdom Publications.
Haider, H., Alwasiti, I. A., & Adznan, J. (2010). EEG activity in Muslim prayer: A pilot study. *Maejo International Journal of Science and Technology, 4*(03), 496–511. www.mijst.mju.ac.th
Harvie, N. M., Pegington, M., Mattson, M. P., Frystyk, J., Dillion, B., Evans, G., et al. (n.d.). The effects of intermittent or continuous energy restriction on weight loss and metabolic disease risk markers: A randomised trial in young overweight women. *International Journal of Obesity, 35*(5), 714–722.
Hill, J. (2014). Picturing Islamic authority: Gender metaphors and Sufi leadership in senegal. *Islamic Africa, 5*(2), 275–315. http://www.jstor.org/stable/islamicafrica.5.2.275
Hisham, A. R. (2008). *A Psychological Measure of Islamic Religiousness: Evidence for Relevance, Reliability and Validity* (Doctoral Dissertation). Graduate College of Bowling Green State University.
Hoffman, D. (2019). *Video—Reality is not as it seems, a dialogue with neurologist Dr. Suzanne O'Sullivan hosted by Steve Paulson*, Nour Foundation, 14th Feb 2019; https://www.youtube.com/watch?v=3MvGGjcTEpQ
Ibn Daqiq al-'Id (2014). *A Treasury of Hadith, A Commentary on Nawawi's Selection of Forty Prophetic Traditions* (M. Guezzou, Trans.). Leicester, UK: Kube Publisher.
Ibrahim, F., Abu Bakar, W. A., & Cheok, N. S. (2008). *Salat: Benefit from science perspective*. Kuala Lumpur: Department of Biomedical Engineering, Faculty of Engineering, University of Malaya.
Ibn 'Arabi, M. (2008). *The four pillars of spiritual transformation* (trans.: Hirtenstein, S.). Oxford: Anqa Publication in Association with Ibn Arabi Society.
Isagandarova, N. (2019). Muraqaba as a mindfulness-based therapy in Islamic psychotherapy. *Journal of Religion and Health, 58*, 1146–1160
Kabbani, M. H. (1995). *The Naqshabandi Sufi way: History and guidebook of the saints of the golden chain*. Chicago: Kazi Publications, Inc.

References

Kaltwasser, V., Sauer, S., & Kohls, N. (2014). Mindfulness in German Schools (MISCHO): A specifically tailored training program: Concept, implementation and empirical results. In S. Schimdt, H. Walach (Eds.), *Meditation - neuroscientific approaches and philosophical implications*. Studies in neuroscience, consciousness and spirituality (pp. 381–404). Cham: Springer.

Karuna Films LTD. (2013). *Doing Time Doing Vippasana*. https://www.youtube.com/watch?v=WkxSyv5R1sg

Khan, A. Y. (1976). *An objective appraisal of the sublime Sufi path* (A. Talha, Trans.). Pakistan: Idarah-E-Naqshbandiah Owlish.

Khaw, K.T., Wareham, N., Bingham, S., Welch, A., Luben, R. et al. (2008). Correction: Combined impact of health behaviours and mortality in men and women: The EPIC-Norfolk prospective population study. *PLOS Medicine 5*(3), e70. https://doi.org/10.1371/journal.pmed.005007.

Knysh, A. (2007). Contextualizing the Salafi-Sufi conflict (from Northern Caucasus to Hadaramawth). *Journal of Middle Eastern Studies, 43*(4), 527.

Koenig, H. G, & Larson, D. B (2001). Religion and mental health: Evidence for an association. *International Review of Psychiatry, 13*(2), 67–78.

Learning Theories.com (2014). *Maslow's Hierarchy of Needs*.http://www.learning-theories.com/maslows-hierarchy-of-needs.html

Lutz, A., Lawrence, L. L., Greischar, N., Rawlings, B., Ricard, M., & Davidson, R. J. (2004). Long-term meditators self-induce high-amplitude gamma synchrony during mental practice. *Proceedings of the National Academy of Science, 101*(46), 16369–16373. https://www.pnas.org/content/101/46/16369

Mahmoud, S. (2020). *Lessons from the Cave – Session 3, Companion of the Caves*. Cambridge, UK: Cambridge Muslim College. Last retrieved 18th May 2020. https://www.youtube.com/watch?v=V6yKIffG8Lg&t=522s

Marzouqi, H. (2013). *Ṭarīqa Islam: Layers of Authentication*. 20–21, 44. Doha, Qatar: Arab Center for Research and Policy Studies.

Maslow, A. (1970). *Religions, values, and peak-experiences*. New York: Penguin Compass.

Maslow, A. H. (2011). *Towards a psychology of being*. Eastford, USA: Martino Publishing.

Mendes, A. M. (2014). *Theory and practice of Islamic Meditation*. Al Maqasid: Part 1 https://www.youtube.com/watch?v=_eFZbRuWFlg&t=19s. Part 2 https://www.youtube.com/watch?v=ti5oApIMIjg&t=18s. Part 3 https://www.youtube.com/watch?v=vLT9OyNYJIk&t=3s. Part 4 https://www.youtube.com/watch?v=EDpO44QpXxQ&t=2s. Part 5 https://www.youtube.com/watch?v=9tWoOiNu8b0

Mirhamadi, N. J. (2016a). *Islam and your spiritual energies chakras/lataifs*. https://www.youtube.com/watch?v=HSS9gYfeXEQ

Mirhamadi, N. J. (2016b). *Islamic Meditation and the Opening of the Heart Murāqaba/Muhabat (Love)/Huddur (presence), Fana/ annihilation*. https://www.youtube.com/watch?v=DOiGKgQ7s_g

Morris, J. W. (2005). *The reflective heart: discovering spiritual intelligence in Ibn Arabi's Meccan illumination*. Louisville: Fons Vitae.

Murata, K. (2018). *Fana and Baqa, Introduction, Oxford Bibliographies, 2020*. Oxford, UK: Oxford University Press. Last retrieved 9th June 2020. https://www.oxfordbibliographies.com/view/document/obo-9780195390155/obo-9780195390155-0256.xml

Muslim. (2007). English Translation, 1st Edition, Sahih Muslim, Volume 6, pp 121–123, compiled by Imam Abul Hussain Muslim al-Hajjaj, Ed. Hafiz Abu Tahir Zubair ' Ali Za'I, Trans., Nasiruddin al-Khattab, Darussalam, Riyadh, Saudi Arabia.

Nicole Gruel, M.A. (1995) The plateau experience: An exploration of its origins, characteristics, and potential. *The Journal of Transpersonal Psychology, 47*(1), 44–63. Newport, NSW Australia

Newberg, A., & D'Aquili, E. (2000). Neuropsychology of religious & spiritual experience. In J. J. Andersen & R. K. C. Foreman (Eds.). *Cognitive models and spiritual maps* (Vol. 255). Exeter, UK: Imprint Academic.

Oman, D., & Thoresen, C. E. (2003). Spiritual modeling: A key to spiritual and religious growth? *The International Journal for the Psychology of Religion, 13*(3), 149–165.

Pasilov, B., & Ashirov, A. (2007). Revival of Sufi Traditions in Modern Central Asia: 'Jahri Zikr' and its ethnological features. *Oriente Moderno, Nuova serie*, Anno 87, Nr. 1 (pp. 163–175). http://www.jstor.org/stable/25818119

Picken, G. (2011). *Spiritual purification in Islam: The life and works of al-Muhasibi*. UK: Routledge.

Programme Management Institute – PMI (2018). *Project Management Body of Knowledge (PMBOK)*, PMI, USA.

Qushayri, A. Q. A. K. (2002). *The Risalah - Principles of Sufism*, Translated by Harris, R, Edited by Bakhtiar, L with series Editor Nasr, S.H. (pp. 1–513). Chicago: Great Books of The Islamic World.

Revees, A. (2005, April). Emotional intelligence recognizing and regulating emotions. *AAOHN Journal, 53*(4), pp 172–178.

Roky, R., Chapotot, F., Benchekroun, M. T., Benaji, B., Hakkou, F., Elkhalifi, H., & Buguet, A. (2003). Daytime sleepiness during Ramadan intermittent fasting: Polysomnographic and quantitative waking EEG study. *Journal of Sleep Research, 12*(2), 95–101.

Rogers, C. (1991). *On becoming a person: A therapist view of psychotherapy*. New York: Houghton Mifflin Company.

Rothman, A. (2020). *Midnight moments, session 20, continuing the journey*. Cambridge, UK: Cambridge Muslim College. https://www.youtube.com/watch?v=I3DE5MpfiPk&list=PLBUQOvJ_NYrAawK3603c13NXfHhxPia0f

Sa'ari, C. Z. (2007). *Al-Ghazali and intuition: An analysis*. (al-Risalah al-Ladunniyyah, Trans.). Kuala Lumpur: University of Malaya.

Sanchetee, P., & Sanchetee, P. (2020). Meditation and brain: An overview. In S. C. Prajna, B. Narendra, N. L. Kachhar (Eds.), *Jain philosophy: A scientific approach to reality*. (pp. 284–301). Ladnun: BMIRC, JVBI, 2018.

Sears, J. (2014). Meditation as a first-person methodology: Real promise – and problems in meditation. In S. Schmidt & H. Walach. In *Neuroscientific approaches and philosophical implications*. Cham, Switzerland: International Springer Publication.

Seligman, M. (2012). Happy people are extremely social. *The psychology book*. London: DK Publishers

Shah, I. (2012). *The Latifas*. https://www.youtube.com/watch?v=VnfKjVYE9vo Sunnah.org (n.d.) Dhikr is the Greatest Obligation and a Perpetual Divine Order. http://sunnah.org/ibadaat/dhikr.htm

Smith, M. (1980). *Al-Muhasibi: An early Mystic of Baghdad, Islamic book foundation, publication no: 52*. Pakistan: Lahore.

Stanford. (2017). *Qualia*, Encyclopedia of Philosophy, Centre for the Study of Language and Information, Stanford University, USA.

Suhrawardi, Shahab–ud–Din 'Umar b. Muhammad. (1991). *The Awarif-ul-Maarif* (trans.:Wilber-2072 force Clarke, H.). Lahore: Sh. Muhammad Ashraf.

Teng, N. I. M. F., Shahar, S., Manaf, A. A., Das, S. K, Taha, C. S. C., & Ngah, W. Z. W. (2011). Efficacy of fasting calorie restriction on quality of life among aging men. *Journal of Physiology and Behaviour, 104*(5), 1059–1064.

The 14th Dalai Lama. (2016, November 22). A Human Approach to World Peace. https://www.dalailama.com/messages/world-peace/a-human-approach-to-world-peace.

Trautwein, F.-M., Naranjo, J. R., & Schmidt, S. (2014). Meditation effects in the social domain: Self-other connectedness as a general mechanism? In *Meditation - neuroscientific approaches and philosophical implications*, Studies in neuroscience, consciousness and spirituality (pp. 175–198). Cham: Springer International.

Thayer, J. F., & Lane, R. D. (2009). Claude Bernard and the Heart-Brain connection: Further elaboration of the of a model of neuro-visceral integration. *Neuroscience and Behavioral Reviews, 33*, 81–88.

References

Van Wijk, E., Ackermen, J., & van Wijk, R. (2014). Meditation: A link to spirituality and health. a novel approach to a human consciousness field experiment. In S. Schmidt & H. Walach (Eds.). *Meditation – Neuroscientific Approaches and Philosophical Implications* (pp. 365–380). Cham, Switzerland: Springer.

Vanderplasschen, W., Vandevelde, S., & Broekaert, E. (2014). *Therapeutic communities for treating addictions in Europe: Evidence, current practices and future challenges*. Lisbon, Portugal: European Monitoring Centre for Drugs and Drug Addiction.

Walach, H. (2014). Towards an epistemology of inner experience, neuroscientific approaches and philosophical implications. In S. Schmidt & H. Walach (Eds.). *Studies in neuroscience, consciousness and spirituality* (Vol. 2, pp. 7–22). Switzerland: Springer International.

Walsh, R. (2011). Life Style and mental health. *American Psychologist, 66*(7), 579–592. www.apa.org/pubs/journals/release/amp-66-7-579.pdf

Winters, T. (2015). *Is orthodox Islam possible without Sufism by Sheikh Abdul Hakim Murad*. https://www.youtube.com/watch?v=uQWNeGyRu0k

Yucel, S. (2010). *Prayer and Healing in Islam, with addendum of 25 Remedies for the Sick by Said Nuris*. New Jersey: Turga Books.

Yusuf, H. (2015a). Sufism: A brief talk. https://www.youtube.com/watch?v=vSoj80fmVb0

Yusuf, H. (2015b). *Sufism, Dhikr, spiritual states and Islam: A brief talk*. https://www.youtube.com/watch?v=0Y6N2e4ED10

Chapter 7
Summary and Conclusion

7.1 Methodological Uniqueness

This research is unique since it attempts to landscape and build a model of spiritual leadership and the development of the self, which is presented in light of the Islamic tradition, contemporary humanistic sciences, psychology, organisational development and neuroscience. There are other studies of Islamic spiritual orders, but they have focused on other dimensions as outlined in Chap. 1. This study is augmented by the use of a combination of methodology within Interpretative Phenomenological Analysis (IPA),[1] as well as utilising a survey questionnaire (see Appendix 2).

This study is enriched by the insights and understanding of the researcher's own grounding and experience with spiritual orders, with first hand experiences of contemplative practices within the Hindu tradition (*yoga* and *yogic meditation*), Buddhist meditation (*vippasana* and *anapanasathi*) and the Islamic contemplative practices (*dhikr*—loud—focused concentration and silence—mindfulness-witnessing). Given the various facets outlined above, it is a trail blazing empirical research in the context of understanding spiritual orders from the point of view of the role of its Sheikh, how it functions, and the impact that it has on the seekers from a multi-disciplinary perspective.

---

[1] This consisted of the 'clean language approach' of developing an non-intrusive interviews based on which authentic narratives were developed; the use of Neuro Linguistic Programming—Neuro-Semantics (NLP-NS) to build a leadership model of the Sheikh, as well as thematic analysis of the set of data.

© The Author(s), under exclusive license to Springer Nature Switzerland AG 2021
M. S. Munsoor, *Wellbeing and the Worshipper*, Studies in Neuroscience,
Consciousness and Spirituality 7, https://doi.org/10.1007/978-3-030-66131-1_7

7.2 Conceptual Frameworks

The comprehensive literature review that was carried out in Chaps. 2 and 3 essentially established that there is a spiritual architecture relating to spiritual leadership and the development of self within Islam. The conceptual framework relating to worship (Chap. 2) covers the nature of the soul, its diseases and treatments, a multi-dimensional contemplative framework, which offers the methods and tools for wellbeing for the worshipper, that includes neuroscientific evidence to support it. The conceptual framework of morality (Chap. 3) provided an exposure of a multiple based value system and the spiritual journey of the Prophet aimed at understanding the Prophetic spiritual journey and his model of existence.

It was found that even though worship and morality are conceptually separate, both are intertwined with one another and forms the basis to transform consciousness, modelled on an exemplar (Sheikh), who becomes the role model. This theoretical understanding was tested empirically with the spiritual Order (Chap. 5) that was researched and the results are what was presented and integrated with evidence from contemporary sciences (Chaps. 6 and 7).

The Order that was researched was of the Sunni tradition (*tasawwuf*-Sufism), while reference was made in the text to the Shia mystical tradition (*irfan*) where necessary. It was found that both spiritual traditions were closely intertwined in the early stages of history but parted ways due to histro-political reasons. Even though the terms were different in the Sunni and Shi'a traditions, their concepts and the approach to developing oneself is very similar. The distinct difference is that in the Shia traditions the spiritual lineage on a general note follows through from the Shia Imam's, who are decedents of the Prophet's family, while in the Sunni tradition, the Sheikh can be from other lineages, so long he is a pious person and the virtuous character, which has been outlined in Chap. 5.

7.3 Spirituality & SDGs

Given the importance of the UN global SDG framework, it is timely to make this connection between spirituality and the SDGs, where positive changes are observed in terms of health and well-being, education, participation of women and peace as well as tolerance, as seen from the data-set of the Order. Otherwise, one will be leaving out a vital component of well-being. The SDGs while very comprehensive and more expansive than the previous MDGs[2], lacks the dimension of inward spiritual development. This poses a real issue since it overlooks the gains accumulated from the spiritual dimension, where faith in God and its accompanying prayers, meditation, fasting and other spiritual practices as outlined in chapter 2.4

---

[2]We can end poverty: United Nations Millennium Development Goals https://www.un.org/millenniumgoals/.

still play a vital role in the lives of majority of the world's population[3]. In this context, Sulmasy's (2002) biopsychospiritual model, which includes spirituality is more comprehensive and is in line with grounded reality.

In light of the above, what is proposed to the global community is a twofold intervention: First, these types of spiritual orders oriented towards inward development or transformation is seen to generate positive results, representative all faiths, should be recognized and factored into the development and humanitarian narrative. The question that needs to be posed and debated is whether there can be development from without when there is no development within, and whether there can be peace without when there is no peace within? While pursuing these very important SDG goals, there needs to be an attempt to incorporate the inner dimensions of spiritual practices given that there is increasing evidence from a psychological and neuroscientific point of view on its impact on the mind-body and behaviour as outlined in this study. Secondly, there is a need to build inter-religious and intra-religious platforms and networks, forged especially based on their universal or common values, which forms a basis on actively including the SDGs in terms of understanding the contents, methods, processes and results generated. This has been a neglected area in the past but it is currently an emerging field, which is beginning to have global recognition as seen in the resolution (GA/12226) of the United Nations fostering peace and interreligious dialogue[4], which has been put into practice by organisations such the UNAoC[5] (United Nations Alliance of Civilisation) and KAICIID (King Abdul Aziz International Dialogue Centre)[6], as well as several other organisations representing all faiths.

7.4 Spiritual Leadership

It is evident in relation to the seekers, the central anchor points include the Sheikh as a role-model, as well as the institutional framework of the spiritual order (*tarīqa*) which lays down the path with its underpinning philosophy, rules and regulations, methods-tools and its peer group support.

---

[3] Is Belief in God Necessary For Good Values? Global Survey on Religion and Morality, Christine Tamir-Aidan Connaughton-Ariana Salazar - https://www.pewresearch.org/global/2020/07/20/the-global-god-divide/.

[4] General Assembly Adopts Three Resolutions on Culture of Peace, Highlighting Need to Foster Interreligious Dialogue, Moderate Social Media," 2019, https://www.un.org/press/en/2019/ga12226.doc.htm.

[5] "UNAoC High Representative's Remark at the High Level Meeting on Interreligious Dialogue for Peace: Promoting Peaceful Co-Existence and Common Citizenship," UNAoC, May 4, 2018, https://www.unaoc.org/2018/02/hlm-interreligious-dialogue-for-peace-vienna/.

[6] What We Do, KAICIID and the UN, KAICIID, 4th May 2020, https://www.kaiciid.org/what-we-do/kaiciid-and-un.

The spiritual leadership style of the Sheikh is categorised as 'interactional', which includes on one hand 'transformational' aspects empowering the seekers through providing a motivation, methods/tools and a value system, while on the other, it is 'situational', where there is customisation of guidance depending on the seekers personalities. Thus, it involves the body, mind, soul, heart, intellect and the spirit, as well factoring in contextual dimensions, characterising the specific nature of the spiritual Order—namely the Naqshabandiyyah Khālidiyyah leadership.

Teacher-Educator: This is one of the most important findings, that the Sheikh is a teacher-educator, which is a traditional spiritual concept, whereby, seekers (*murids*) finds a designated teacher-educator, who then becomes his/her spiritual parent so to speak. A loving and caring spiritual relationship is seen to be established, where the seekers become eager to learn and they are imparted knowledge and how to think and approach life apart from memorising scriptural verses and liturgies. The earlier epoch of Islamic history had a wide horizon in terms of learning and knowledge, which covered numerous subjects and the end-products was a learned person (A'lim) who is really knowledgeable and can guide others. Unfortunately, the current Islamic School (*madarassa*) system, in general, does not mirror this approach to learning, and has become very narrow in its approach, methodology and content. Some spiritual orders (*ṭarīqas*) still have this traditional approach and the Order that was researched tries to adopt this kind of learning style even though it is confined largely to religious and spiritual education.

The role of the Sheikh is seen to be paramount with the seekers trying to model him and, as pointed by Kynsh, it is more the Sheikh than the Order itself that is the key. In the case of the Order under study, even though the methods were highlighted to be of utmost importance in helping them to be connected with God, the very essence is the Sheikh, his functionality and characteristics, helps the seekers to steer the course towards self-development. While acknowledging that the Sheikh's role is key, there are both intrinsic and extrinsic factors that contribute and shape the growth and development of the seekers including peer-to-peer learning. Thus, it is a combination of factors that causes the transformation of the seekers including grace of God and not the Sheikh alone.

7.5 Ethical Dimension: Core-Values

The core-value system is the central feature of the Order and there is a conscious effort to emulate the Sheikh and his characteristics. The ten values set by the Sheikh serve as a good base for the seekers to work towards within the framework of the *Jamāli* (Beauty)—*Jalāli* (Majestic) attributes of God. This value system forms the enabler for the development of the self and therefore seems to mould the behaviour of the seekers. The concept of *futuwwa* (chivalry), which includes *ukhuwwah* or brotherhood/sisterhood, was flagged as being an important way of serving others, as well as overcoming one's own ego, which otherwise is an obstacle for self-development.

Practically, the seekers are seen utilising the value framework and adapting it to their need, which is something that I have not seen being overtly practiced. This is seen to establish core values within the seekers, where they aspires to achieve it through the struggle (*jihad*) that they undergo on a daily basis. This is a method of testing specific values for example, patience, compassion, love, humbleness, helping others, forgiveness, gratitude, cultivating hope etc. that are espoused as goals and tried out by the seekers, as one journeys through life in order to improve oneself. Some of seekers were seen to cross check their progress with each other, as did some of the companions of the Prophet—the concept of mirroring.

7.6 Wellbeing and the Worshipper

The multiple tools and methods of worship including ritual and optional prayers (*salah*), as well as remembrance of God (*dhikr*), repentance (*tauba*), supplication (*du'ā*), night vigil (*tahajjud*), and charity (*sadaqa*); all form channels through which the seekers detoxify themselves and try to resolve their sins and difficulties. Thus, it becomes a process of self-healing. This is seen to lead the seekers to a sense of calmness and happiness, which is supported by the neurophysiological evidence relating to the benefits of contemplative practices. The seekers are then able to reconcile both with themselves and with others, as outlined by them in Chap. 5.

7.7 The Heart-Brain Link

The emerging evidence from the data set is that there is an inextricable link between consistent worship (*'ibādah*) and the developing of good manners (adab) leading to improving one's morality (*akhlāq*). This is best exemplified by the seekers often referencing the heart-brain connection, where they now seem to be using both of these faculties, whereas before it was only their brain functioning (cognitive) as cited by some seekers. The heart here refers to feelings, emotions, being mindful and connected to the Divine—a meditative process, which has a different neural pathway—lower default mode network and reduced mind wandering shifting from purely a cognitive process of activation (Mrazek et al. 2014, p 228–234). This combination of working on worship and morality is the quintessential aspect aimed at the development of a holistic self from an Islamic point of view. This is a process towards spiritual actualisation, where the spirit (*rūḥ*), is essential different to the way self-actualisation, is conceptualised from a Western secular perspectives relating to humanistic psychology of Abraham Maslow (1970, 2011) and Carl Rogers (1991), grounded within worldly realities and operates within the mind-body realm. I argue that for such experiences to occur the soul-heart and spirit is engaged since according to the Islamic perspective is from the domain of God and therefore could transcend time and space. The levels of spiritual actualisation, with its different states of consciousness is captured in the section below.

7.8 States of Consciousness and the Development of the Self

Consciousness, Self-Actualisation and Spiritual Actualisation Some of the contemporary theories of consciousness points to consciousness as being fundamental (Chalmers 2014 and Hoffman 2019) that all things have varying degrees of it (Chalmers 2014). Consciousness from an Islamic perspective is referred to in the Qur'an and Prophetic traditions can be discerned from the scholarly reading as being embedded within the fluid structure of the soul-heart, intellect and the spirit. Hoffman's (2019) theory of conscious agents having different degrees of complexity and resulting in an infinite consciousness seems to have resonance well within the Islamic framework (see Chap. 6).

The transformation of the seekers from an Islamic perspective is linked to the changing state of consciousness from a beastly state (*nafs al-ammāra bi su*) to a self-critical self (*nafs al-lawwāma*) to a state of peacefulness (*nafs al-mutma'inna*). A more elaborate levels of consciousness is given the Chisti order's rendition, where there are seven levels of ascension including *sharī'a* (body of knowledge), *ṭa'rīqa* (the path), *ha'qiqa* (the reality) and *ma'rifa* (gnosis), which is in the realm of the divine knowledge of God. Figure 6.11 encapsulates these ascending levels of consciousness, where the mind-body, soul, heart, intellect and spirit is involved in varying degrees depending on the states and stations of the seekers. As noted in this figure, there are several factors that facilitates and enhances this upward process, including the approach-methods and tools on one hand and the intervention of both intrinsic and extrinsic factors. Thus, it is not meditation alone that causes this transformation.

In this state of *ma'rifa* (divine knowledge), higher levels of consciousness are experienced such as **fana** (annihilation of the human selfhood in the sheer presence of God) and *baqa* (where the human selfhood returns and subsists). These are rare stations (*maqāms*) of the Prophets and perhaps of some selected Sages. This is not to be misunderstood as becoming one with God but tasting some droplets from the divine realm, which is afforded by the grace of the Divine. Islam encourages mysticism or spirituality in everyday life, where, whatever is the state or station of one, he/she has to be a part of society and actively contribute to it, and this was exemplified by the life of the Prophet himself. While there is a role definite role for seclusion and retreat in Islam, it is situating oneself within these human and societal boundaries to lead a spiritual life, which can affect others positively.

A comparison of these states can be made to Maslow's self-actualisation and Roger's becoming fully human is rooted within the material world, with the difference being the absence of an explicit metaphysical dimension (dunya-world and arkhira-next world) and role modelling vis-à-vis the Sheikh. I argue that in

Maslow's peak and plateau experience, which is akin to states (*hal*) and stations (*maqāms*) respectively in the Islamic tradition, there is an opening that God provides, and this is related to the soul-heart and spirit (*rūḥ*) being involved, where one feels a sense of harmony, being at peace, united with others and the environment etc (peak experiences). There are other sort of experiences, which are attributed to which is either from the ego (mind-body realm) or from the satan or forces that are not of God. The inverted pyramid of the nature of types of experiences that has been constructed (Fig. 6.11) offers a useful framework for this purpose. In light of the varying levels of levels and consciousness, Maslow (2011) himself points to the low and high Nirvana (enlightenment), where differences exists between these types of experiences.

One of the essential differences that is made in our discussion is that self-actualisation as Maslow conceptualised is related to the mind-body, with openings from time to time, where the spiritual experiences (epiphany) are involved which through hard work can build up to plateau experiences. I suggest that this is not only confined to body-mind but where the soul-heart and the spirit is involved, which affords these experiences. However, the full spiritual experiences has had by the Prophet are different in its scope and depth especially relating to Isra wal Mi'rage, as well as the revelations of the Qur'an over the 23 years, which descended in various forms are different both in nature and the level of consciousness. This would have been similar, with its own unique variations, to the spiritual experiences of other Prophets like Noah, Abraham, Moses, David and Jesus (Archprophets- *Ulu'Azm* who received the book-messages). It is important to note that there are countless other Prophets some of whom are mentioned in the Qur'ān and others not, where every nation in the world had been sent one. From an Islamic perspective, one is to believe in all of the Prophets and all of the Scriptures revealed, which essentially makes it a universal religion. Unfortunately, the preaching or transmission of the message of Islam sometimes takes a localised form, which does not do justice to its core universal message.

7.9 The Model for Spiritual Leadership and Self-Development

The evidence from this research indicates that apart from the Sheikh, who is seen as an exemplar, there are other factors that contribute to self-development including: the multiple methods of worship, the core value system practiced within the Order; and the immediate environment, that is, the surroundings, with the peer group support system, the general group dynamics, the decentralised nature of the operations, where the deputies or the *khalifas* are empowered to play a key role in energising the Order and keeping its momentum intact.

With particular regard to the residents of the Centre, who formed about 50% of the research sample (drug addicts, HIV patients and trans-gender), it was found that joining the Order has benefitted them spiritually, psychologically, as well as physiologically (Chap. 5). This is manifested in the way they felt about themselves, their relationship with others and in their escape from their earlier dependency on drugs and wayward lifestyle, testifying to their spiritual transformation.

The real test, however, of their change can only be objectively ascertained once they return to mainstream society, where they will confront their earlier environment and dependencies. For the general seekers, the changes that they have described seem to have benefited them and seem more permanent in nature since they are already living within mainstream society. The Order seems to provide the seekers with a direction and meaning, as per their stated expectations of joining the Order.

This spiritual Order with its rehabilitation centre seems to resonate the 'Therapeutic Community' model (Vanderplasschen et al. 2014), where transformation is seen of the drug addicts by way of them becoming drug free and reduced recidivism. However, the Order goes beyond the TCs by virtue of the *tarīqa*'s (Order) wider spiritual horizons and its sustainability over generations, which was one of the criteria of selection for the study.

The spiritual model of the Order outlined in this research goes beyond Fry's causal model of spirituality in the workplace (Fry 2003; OmanandThoresen 2003) through the inclusion of the metaphysical and mystical dimensions that are embedded within this Order. Within the Islamic framework it is through spiritual transmission and the mercy of God that enables both the Sheikh and the seekers transcend their current reality. As seen in the models (Figs. 6.2 and 6.11), it is through a holistic and integrated approach that the seekers are provided with the space (both externally and internally) to develop themselves spiritually, which has numerous benefits, including neurologically. This essentially constitutes a process of expanding their mental space and initiating the process of healing for them.

All of the above key findings have been conceptualised into a model of spiritual leadership and self-development (Fig. 6.2), whereby the most important variables (control) are the 'calling' of the seeker, the 'leadership of the Sheikh', and the 'Membership' of the 'Spiritual Order'. These lay the foundation, and the 'effort' (independent variable) influences the 'performance' and the rewards (dependent variables), the latter two closely reinforcing each other. All of these result in the 'wellbeing' and the acquisition of the knowledge of the seeker (outcome variable). In the context of the above, contrary to general and often skewed perception, Islam does provide an underlying philosophy, a comprehensive spiritual architecture for the development of the self and carries the required approaches, methods, tools and role-models for this purpose.

Integrated Approach with a Combination of Methods The picture that emerges from all of the data, both survey and interviews, is that, an integrated approach that was advocated by the Order, with the use of a combination of the approach and methods-tools. The Order itself as seen to use a diverse methods within an integrated approach to engage with the seekers including—individual and group contemplative practices (ritual and voluntary prayers and *dhikr*), recitation of the Qur'ān (scriptural meditation), the act of repentance and supplication, the teacher-educator sessions, one-to-one counselling, setting the ground rules, peer to peer counselling etc. These practices are best comprehended through the contemplative tree of Islamic practices constructed in Sect. 2.3.1 (Chap. 2). Its effectiveness is seen when the ritual and voluntary prayers are combined with *dhikr*-meditation (remembrance of God) both on an individual as well as a collective basis. These acts when done properly with mindfulness and absorption (*khushu*) is seen to yield better results in terms of both seekers views as seen in a number of their response but also from a neurophysiological stand point as indicated from the results from studies done within the light of Islamic practise as outlined by Aldahadha (2013), Ibrahim et al. (2008), Doufesh et al. (2012), Haider et al. (2010), and Hisham (2008). The model of spiritual leadership and self-development, that has been generated through this study encapsulates the total workings of this spiritual Order including the outcomes of this journey and processes (Figs. 6.2 and 6.11).

7.10 Islamic Spiritual Architecture

What clearly comes through both from a comprehensive review of literature (Chaps. 2 and 3), and more importantly from the practice of these approaches, concepts, methods and tools by the seekers and the Sheikh (Chaps. 5 and 6) is that there is an Islamic spiritual architecture with its accompanying philosophies deeply embedded with the Qur'ān and the Prophetic narrations. Several Qur'ānic citations and Prophetic narrations in this study backs this up. Apart from the occurrences of peak type of experiences, which is from the grace of the Divine, there is a plethora of contemplative practices including: stillness, generative, relational, creative, activist, all of which can be used mindfully to enhance ones spiritual journey. Figure 6.11 provides a comprehensive framework for understanding spiritual growth and development, however, it is only by experiential learning and practice that one can move towards the Divine, with what Maslow would call Being values, Being cognition and what Roger's calls being fully human. The Prophetic model including both the outer and inner states of being and characteristics, which aligns with what has been outline by Maslow and Roger's, if followed to the human extent possible can carve out a path for human flourishing.

In conclusion, it can be said that there are eight significant findings generate by this research:

Firstly, the spiritual modelling of the Sheikh as well as following of the path of the Order are seen to have multiple benefits for the seekers. The claims of their changes and how they feel about themselves are supported on a general level both by neuroscientific data as well as humanistic physiological evidence. This is especially notable in terms of the rehabilitation of the seekers who have dependencies, including drug addiction and promiscuity, which previously led them to socially deviant behaviour. Secondly, there is a need for development and humanitarian practitioners to closely look at the work of the spiritual orders and to make referrals especially of those who have been traumatised in conflict and post-conflict countries apart from main-stream society itself, which has an increasing level of psychological and mental health related issues.

Thirdly, the heart-brain connection is seen to be a significant finding from both the point of view of wellbeing and the worshipper, as evident in neuroscientific research, as well as its importance from the state of mindfulness of the worshipper.

Fourthly, this study attempts to formulate a model of spiritual leadership and self-development. This needs to be tested to validate it with further empirical research, which is beyond the scope of the current research on spirituality and development of self. As outlined in the discussion from a more secular viewpoint, leading psychologists also point in the direction of self-actualisation and on becoming a person with full potential, which seems to mirror the initial state of spiritual development. The spiritual model goes well beyond the therapeutic or the psychological model since it affords a broader framework for the participants who are part of a community of practice, as well as the Order that has been sustained over several generations.

These types of research within the Islamic framework, incorporating evidence in neuroscience as well as humanistic science, are required in the contemporary context, to abate maladies linked to external dependencies such as substance abuse, anxiety and depression. The spiritual Order under study presents a platform for transformation, providing its tools and methods, as well as bringing a sense of meaning and direction.

One of the key elements that is generated from the data set is cultivation and development of emotional intelligence (Chap. 6.11), that is, the seekers becoming more aware about themselves and the other, and being able to effectively manage themselves. More research is required in the area of emotional intelligence and how it relates to spirituality.

Fifthly, building on Bandura's social learning theory, this thesis postulates working towards a spiritual learning theory, which includes factors beyond his theory and includes: observation-attention, reflection, self-accounting, supplication, mirroring, testing and retention, reproduction, internalisation, and motivation.

Sixthly, the inner experiences of the seekers, which are feeding into their transformation, cannot be fully expounded and can only be understood by the metaphors that they use such as 'inner of the inner', 'step by step', 'deep by deep' etc.; all of which refer to the various depths of consciousness that they have been able to experience.

There is a suggested correlation between deep contemplation-meditation and neurophysiological effects, but this has to be tested in conjunction with various Islamic practices. This then, is entering a dimension beyond neuroscience, which is the mystical or the metaphysical realm of experiencing God through His various manifestations or openings that God provides to the seekers. The most contemporary scientific research into consciousness where it is seen as fundamental (Chalmers 2014 and Hoffman 2019), and where consciousness is seen as a network of conscious agents, where there is an infinite Consciousness resonates well with the Islamic perspective and world view.

7.10 Islamic Spiritual Architecture

Seventhly, the picture that emerges is the veracity of the integrated nature of the approach, with a combination of methods, which is utilised in this Order to engage and motivate the seekers both residents of the Centre, as well as the general seekers, which is seen to produce overall positive benefits.

Finally, the Islamic spiritual framework (Fig. 6.11) can be selectively integrated into the Islamic formal educational curriculum, informal and formal training and the *madarassa* curriculum to introduce its wide scope and the benefits that it can avail the seekers from all walks of life.

Future research in this area can benefit from the following directions:

1. Need for further exploratory research with other Islamic Spiritual orders (*tarīqa*s) in order to test if the model developed in this research in terms of its applicability and replicability (see Fig. 6.2).
2. The results of this research need to be tested on a larger sample size, while having a control group to enable the generalisability of these findings. Future studies can use both the treatment and the control group to track the changes.
3. Studies can be carried out utilising IPA, including the combination methodology of this research, to re-test the model and the claims made in order to validate it or repudiate it. I found the use of the 'clean language' approach to interviewing a non-intrusive and excellent way of building the internal spiritual landscape and authentic narratives of the seekers of the Order (see Chap. 4 on methodology and Appendix 1B).
4. This type of research can be conducted with groups or orders, which have both a 'Sufi' as well as a 'Salafi'[7] orientation, to explore the processes and outcomes.
5. There is a need for researchers to identify meditative approaches and methods-tools within Islam, Christianity, Judaism, Jainism and other faiths, given that much of the research so far has been on Buddhist and Hindu related practices. The findings from these type of multi-religious research will enhance psychotherapy in general since most people feel comfortable within their own faith traditions and would like to be treated within this context. Given their faith predisposition and the related core personal constructs[8] (George Kelly 1963)

---

[7]Given that divisiveness of the Sufi and Salafi, as well as the Sunni and Shia orientation and the rhetoric that accompanies it; understanding is required that if the core belief system is the same (the shahada, the five pillars, the six articles of faith the effort to excel in virtue), then it is important to accept the differences that natural occur, be it is the area of theological understanding or laws which has diverse viewpoints or in the matter of interpretations of the scripture etc (see the Amman message—https://ammanmessage.com of who constitute as Muslims). It is human nature to be different as the Qur'ān, 49:13 states—"O mankind! We created you from a single (pair) of a male and a female, and made you into nations and tribes, that ye may know each other (not that ye may despise (each other)). Verily the most honoured of you in the sight of Allah is (he who is) the most righteous of you. And Allah has full knowledge and is well acquainted (with all things)". A detailed treatment of the Universal message of Islam is presented in Dr. Kazemi, Reza Shah, m (2006) book, The Other in the Light of the One: The Universality of the Qur'ān and Interfaith Dialogue, The Islamic Texts Society, UK.

[8]The personal construct theory of George Kelly (former Professor of Psychology and President, Clinical and Consulting Division, American Psychological Association) is based on his extensive

based on which they tend to operate their lives, their recovery and healing from various maladies can be accelerated.

6. There is a need to conduct further neuroscientific studies on Islamic worship, which has seven types of contemplative practices (Sect. 2.3 and Figure 2.8), in order to ascertain the changes that occur during this process and its impact on the seekers. The silent meditative practices type (stillness practices and heart based contemplation) which uses the breath (focused attention) and objectless meditation (*muraqaba*) is a very good candidate for this type of neuroscientific studies and it has a basis of comparison to other faith traditions including the Yogic, Buddhist (see Sect. 2.4) and the heart-centred Christian Meditation.

7. One area of explorative research that is required is the linking up of Maslow's (1970) peak[9] and plateau experiences, as well as spiritual experiences with neuroscientific experimentations to find out if there can be relevant neurobiological correlates for different types of experiences.

8. In the light of the above, there is a need to select the more advanced meditators-contemplators[10] for the purposes of the research. Given the difficulties of meditative research including stabilisation of neural activities, the tracking of the plateau and spiritual experiences can be done with the more seasoned meditative participants along the lines of Lutz et al. (2004) cited in Chap. 6.

9. Concurrently, the above research can catalog the characteristic and values of the subjects in the study who have underdone the above type of experiences to come out with a framework for spirituality in the light of contemporary sciences. This can follow the lines of the research studies that have been carried out in neuroscience like Sect. 2.4 and Chap. 6, that has already demonstrated the neural changes with occurs during prayers and meditation.

---

work with many of his patients, where he postulated that people develop personal constructs about how the world works. He said that people's processes are psychologically channelled by the way they anticipate events rather than the ways the react to them. The patterns of our make-up, which he termed as constructs are the key to changing old patterns and habits. A construct includes such things as intelligence, motivation, anxiety, fear; it can be a skill, attribute or ability that is based on established theory or philosophy. People utilise these personal constructs to make sense of their observation and experiences. While the world in which we live in the same, the way people experience, interpret and relate to each other is very different. In this sense, each religion offers a particular worldview, while there are some essential universals, which are common to all. It is important to operate from this perspective, while engaging with each other as well as mentoring, guiding or treating others on equal terms.

[9]Peak experiences are very difficult to measure since it occurs at unexpected times and is a state, which can come and go without warning. However, the plateau and spiritual experience, which are stabilised over times known within Islamic traditions as states (*maqams*). Based on my own interaction with a number of seekers (*murids*) who have been meditating for several years using the Islamic mindfulness type of meditation and have gained a high level of awareness; they are good candidates for this type of neurophysiological experimentation.

[10]This can be measured with those seekers who have been with these types of spiritual orders over decades and are advance meditators. General getting access to some of these spiritual orders could be difficult since they are not commercially oriented entities themselves but this can be negotiated through known seekers, who are trusted by the concerned spiritual orders.

10. There is a defined therapeutic role of Islamic Spiritual orders based on their approach, methods, tools and role-models, which can be a basis for integrating it into Islamic Psychotheraphy as is in the case of some of the *muraqaba* meditative-contemplative practices, which are now being used in the above mentioned field. This needs to be further studied, with a view of its therapeutic role and its efficacy.
11. What would be most appropriate would be to carry out longitudinal studies in terms of Islamic contemplative practices, which will enable the tracking of groups and individuals over time in order come to firmer conclusions.

Notwithstanding the limitation in its scope, this research offers a rich tapestry of primary data integrating different perspectives through methodological triangulation and development of a model to understand the intricate mechanisms and workings of a spiritual order. This forms one of the few studies to use an integrated approach to understanding and mapping out the spiritual process, its leadership and the impact on the seekers. This, therefore, has brought together the fields of spirituality, humanistic psychology, organisational development and neuroscience in understanding a spiritual order to sketch out its multi-dimensional nature.

References

Aldahadha, B. (2013). The Effects of Muslim Praying Meditation and Transcendental Meditation Programs on mindfulness among the University of Nizwa Students. *College Student Journal, 47*(4), 668–676.

Chalmers, D. (2014) is a scientic materialist. *How do you Explain Consciousness, David Chalmers* (2014). https://www.youtube.com/watch?v=uhRhtFFhNzQ&t=931s.

Doufesh, H., Faisel, T., Lim. K-S., & Ibrahim, F. (2012). EEG Spectral Analysis on Muslim Prayers. *Appl Psychophysical Biofeedback, 37*, 11–18.

Fry, L. (2003). Towards a Theory of Spiritual Leadership. *The Leadership Quarterly 14*, 693–727.

Haider, H. Alwasiti, I. A., & Adznan, J. (2010). EEG activity in Muslim Prayer: A Pilot Study. *Maejo International Journal of Science and Technology, 4*(03), 496–511. www.mijst.mju.ac.th.

Hisham Abu Raya. (2008). *A Psychological Measure of Islamic Religiousness: Evidence for Relevance, Reliability and Validity* (Doctoral Dissertation). New York: Graduate College of Bowling Green State University.

Hoffman, D. D. (2019). *Video—Reality is not as it Seems, a Dialogue with Neurologist Dr. Suzanne O'Sullivan Hosted by Steve Paulson* (Nour Foundation, 14th Feb 2019). https://www.youtube.com/watch?v=3MvGGjcTEpQ.

Ibrahim, F, W., Abu Bakar, W.A. & Cheok, N. S. (2008). *Salat: Benefit from Science Perspective.* Kuala Lumpur: Department of Biomedical Engineering, Faculty of Engineering, University of Malaya.

Is Belief in God Necessary for Good Values. (2020). Pew Research Center. https://www.pewresearch.org/global/2020/07/20/the-global-god-divide/

KAICIID. (2020) What We Do. Retrieved from https://www.kaiciid.org/what-we-do

Kazemi, Reza Shah, m. (2006). The Other in the Light of the One: The Universality of the Qur'an and Interfaith Dialogue, UK: The Islamic Texts Society.

Kelly, G. (1963). *A Theory of Personality: The Psychology of Personal Constructs, Norton Publishers, USA* Knysh, A. (2007). Contextualizing the Salafi-Sufi Conflict (From Northern Caucasus to Hadaramawth). *Journal of Middle Eastern Studies, 43*(4), 527.

Lutz, A, Lawrence, L. G., Nancy, B. R., Matthieu, R., & Richard, J. D. (2004). Long-term meditators self-induce high-amplitude gamma synchrony during mental practice. *Proceedings pf the National Academy of Science, 101*(46), 16369–16373. https://www.pnas.org/content/101/46/16369.

Maslow, A. (1970). *Religions, Values, and Peak-Experiences*. New York: Penguin Compass.

Maslow, A. H. (2011). *Towards A Psychology of Being*. USA: Martino Publishing.

Mrazek, D. M., Mooneyham, W. B., & Schooler, W. J. (2014). *Insight from Quiet Minds: The Converging Fields of Mindfulness and Mind-Wandering; Meditation—Neuroscientific approaches and Philosophical Implications, Studies in Neuroscience, Consciousness and Spirituality* (Vol. 2, pp. 228–234). Switzerland: Stefan Schmidt and Harald Walach, Springer International Publishing.

Oman, D. & Thoresen, C. E. (2003). Spiritual modeling: A Key to Spiritual and Religious Growth? *The International Journal for the Psychology of Religion, 13*(3), 149–165.

Rogers, C. (1991). *On Becoming a Person: A Therapist View of Psychotherapy*. New York: Houghton Miin Company.

Sulmasy, D. P. (2002). A biopsychosocial-spiritual model for the care of patients at the end of life. *Gerontologist, 42*, Spec No 3, 24–33. https://doi.org/10.1093/geront/42.suppl_3.24

UN MDGs. (2014). We Can End Poverty. https://www.un.org/millenniumgoals/

UNAoC High Representative's Remark at the High Level Meeting on Interreligious Dialogue for Peace: Promoting Peaceful Co-Existence and Common Citizenship. (2018). UNAoC High Representative's Remark at the High Level Meeting on Interreligious Dialogue for Peace: Promoting Peaceful Co-Existence and Common Citizenship. https://www.unaoc.org/2018/02/hlm-interreligious-dialogue-for-peace-vienna

Vanderplasschen, W., Vandevelde, S., & Broekaert, E. (2014). Therapeutic communities for treating addictions in Europe: Evidence, current practices and future challenges, Lisbon, Portugal. In *European Monitoring Centre for Drugs and Drug Addiction*.

Appendices

Appendix 1

Appendix 1A

Clean Language Model Questionnaire

Identify/Developing Questions
- And what would (you/X) like to happen?
- And that's ( ) like what?
- Is there anything else about that?
- Whar kind of....is..that...?
- Where is ....?
- Whereabout is...?
- That's ....like what?
- Does....have a size or a shape?
- How many....are there?
- Is....on the inside or outside?
- In which direction is/does...?

Relation Across Time (within and Between Events)
- And then what happens?
- And what happens next?
- And what happened just before (events)?
- Where does/could....come from?

Relation Across Time (within and Between Events)
- And when/as (X), what happens to (Y)?
- And is there a relationship between (X) and (Y)?
- Is...the same or different to...?

- Other Questions: How do your know....? What's happening now? What just happened? (.....) = A client's exact word or phrase.

Appendix 1B

Appendix 1B1

Key Questions and Pointers for the Leader-Sheikh using Clean Language format

Developing Questions
1. I am exploring the relationship between worship and morality as a vehicle for the development of one Self, what is your view on it?
2. Why are you doing, what you are doing?
3. What kind of concepts, tools, methods and principles are available for this purpose?
4. Is there anything else about it?
5. Is... on/from the inside or outside?
6. What happens when one puts into practice these concept, methods, tools and principles?
7. Is there any evidence to it...?

Relationship Over Time
8. Does it have an effect over time?
9. And if it does what kind of effect does it have?
10. Where does/could... come from?

Relationship Over Space
11. Is there any relationship between any of them? If so what is the nature and type of relationship?
12. Is... the same or different to...?
13. What is your role in this process?

Desired Outcome
14. Why are you doing what you are doing and have you got any expectations?
15. What would you like to have happen?

Appendix 1B2

Key Questions and Pointers for the Seekers-Followers Using Clean Language Format

Developing Questions
1. I am exploring the relationship between worship and morality as a vehicle for the development of one Self, what is your view on it?
2. What kind of concept, methods, tools and principles are there?
3. Can you give examples of it?

Relationship Over Space
4. And are there any relationship between them? If so that is the nature of it?
5. Are there any similarities or differences in it?

Relationship Over Time
6. And what does it do to you?
7. What happens before it?
8. What happens after it?
9. Where does/could... come from?

Relationship Over Time
10. What would you like to happen to you?
11. What needs to happen for...?
12. How will you know if there are any changes?

Appendix 1C

Template of Meta-Programmes

Appendix 1C - Meta Modeling Framework: NS-NLP

Cognitive–thinking	Emotional–feeling	Conative–choosing	Semantic–meaning
1. Representative—Visual, auditory, kinaesthetic, language. A preferred learning system of information processing through sensory or language	19. Convincer representative (VAL and language): refers to the state of feeling convinced. What convinces you. Looks right, sounds right as compared to makes sense and feels right	34. Convincer representation—Number of times—length of time: some are never convinced, while others are automatically giving the benefit of doubt. Most people are convinced by repetition, which drives values, beliefs, knowledge. Some need a specific period of time to do so	48. Self-experience—mind; body; emotions; will; roles; dis-identified: refers to beliefs and understanding that we use and operate from in defining ourselves, as well as how we experience ourselves. One's self-experience is based on thoughts, emotions, choice, body, status, roles, experiences
2. Epistemological: sensors—see, hear, feel mode, with preference for empirical data. Intuitions—preference for meaning—values, beliefs, experience. Gut-feeling	20. Movie position: stepping-in-stepping out (emotional state); association-dissociated; feeling-thinking: refers to viewing and feeling things from a first person position having somatic and kinaesthetic sensations as compared to being a second or third person and thus not really into the experience	35. Motivational direction: away from—towards; avoidance—approach; aversion—attractions. Refers to our orientation in the world in terms of who we take action, and make choices. Makes first choice based on safety, avoidance of problems, as compared to moving towards what a person wants, goals, dreams, outcomes etc.	49. Self-instruction—compliant—strong willed: refers to our relationship with choice, instruction, command, authority, power, control etc.; those who are able to take orders well and comply with it either in a fearful way or recognising authority. Others define themselves has being strong willed and freedom of choice
3. Scale-scope Global—Specific: From the bigger picture or generality (deductive) as compared to very small details to very large general understanding (inductive)	21. Exuberance—desurgency—surgency; shy-outgoing; timid-bold (emotional intensity): refers to how much emotional exuberance or lack of it especially in relation to others. Experiences emotions very strongly felt through out the body as compared to low level of emotional intensity, where values certainty, predictability and stability	36. Organisational style—procedures—options; sequential—alternatives: refers to the adaptation style in terms of seeking for specific procedures, processes, structures, organisations, as compared to seeing things in terms of options or choices, or exploring new ways of doing things	50. Self-confidence—low—high: refers to one's feeling of confidence, trust, or faith in their skills and abilities. Low refers to those who lack it do accomplish a particular thing and distrust their ability. As compared to, those having confidence and trust that they can learn and develop

(continued)

Appendix 1C -Meta Modeling Framework: NS-NLP

Cognitive–thinking	Emotional–feeling	Conative–choosing	Semantic–meaning
4. Relationship comparison: sameness (matching)— seeking to understand how somethings fit in with what already knows. Differences (mismatching)— seeking to understand somethings in terms of there differences	22. Stress coping— passive-aggressive; assertive: refers to moving away from danger, stressors, threats (use type B stress response), as compared to moving towards and going at threats etc.; (type A stress response). While assertive or mindful response (type C) results from training in thinking and managing stresses	37. Adaption— judging—perceiving; controlling— releasing: refers to how we adapt ourselves as we move through the world. Views the world, as well as makes choices by seeking control or management over the world characterised by taking charge, acting, innovating etc.; In contrast, views the world more holistically, where it is to observe, experience etc.; This is fitting in with the natural rhythms of the world being passive, enjoy, observe etc.	51. Self-esteem: low—high; conditional— unconditional: refer to a higher level belief frame that we operate from in relation to our conceptual understanding of the value and dignity of the self. Feeling self-esteem based upon conditions belief systems; culture, social norms and trends—ego always on the line. The other feeling self-esteem as not subjected to conditions—feeling full, complete—little ego concerns given that they are centred
5. Information Staging— counting— discounting	23. Authoritative source (referencing style)—internal— external: refers to locus of control, those who seek for outside views, opinions and authorities. While self or internal reference points to depending on one's own thoughts, values choices mostly	38. Modus operandi— impossibility; necessity; desire, possibility; choice: style of operating with regards to events, tasks, people, information. The world of should, must's signified by rules, compulsions, laws, as compared to the world of wants, desires, hopes etc.; the other being cant's, impossibilities— limitations inhibitions, as compared to the can's, possibilities—hopes and dreams	52. Self-integrity— conflicted— harmonious; incongruity— integration; refers to how well one lives upto their values, belief, rules etc.; degree of self-integrity. Feeling and actualizing your ideal self and being integrated, congruous and living upto one's ideals. Those that feel torn, conflicted, un-integrated, incongruous etc.

(continued)

Appendix 1C -Meta Modeling Framework: NS-NLP

Cognitive–thinking	Emotional–feeling	Conative–choosing	Semantic–meaning
6. Scenario type (attribution sort) pessimistic—optimistic: seeking for problems or solutions: refers to one who looks for problems, dangers, difficulties (worst case scenario) or for solutions, opportunities etc. (best case scenario). Helpless vs. empowered	24. Attention—self-other	39. Preference—people, place; things; activity; information; time; systems: refers to what we prefer as most important or significant. People and related issues and emotions, as compared to things, objects, technology etc. Focus on activities, events, tasks, projects, while some value places, locations, environments. There are those who value, information, data, as compared to importance of time and when we do things	53. Responsibility—under-responsible; healthy responsibility; over-responsible
7. Classification scale: either—or—continuum—multidimensional (emotional direction sort): experiences emotions as staying contextualized to referent object and frames as compared to experiencing emotions as spreading all over and contaminating others facets of life	25. Emotional containment—unit-dimensional—multidimensional (emotional direction): refers to emotion being as staying contextualized in relation to object and frames as compared to emotions spreading all over the contaminating other facets of life	40. Goal striving—skeptic—perfectionist; Optimalist: refers to how we adapt as well as respond to expectations, goals, outcomes etc.; negatively anchored to concept, while refusing to set goals or compete. Flawless perfection, with focus on end-product—never good enough as compared to those enjoying process and achieve aim mindful of constraints	54. Ego strength—weak—strong; unstable—stable: refers to how well we face the world, facts, degree of adjustment. Ego points to our cognitive and perceptual mind in facing what exist. The state of mind-and-emotions when facing a problem

(continued)

Appendix 1C - Meta Modeling Framework: NS-NLP

Cognitive–thinking	Emotional–feeling	Conative–choosing	Semantic–meaning
8. Nature (reality structure sort): (thinking about external reality) static—systemic Aristotelian—non-aristotelian: sorts in terms of things being static, permanent and solid as micro level as compared to sorts in terms of process, movement, change and non-linear	26. Rejuvenation—introvert—extrovert; ambivert: refers to how we interact with and need or avoid people when we are feeling low or discouraged. There are those who perception turns outward to others, desires companionship, encouragement and support (E). The perception turns inward to self, wants privacy, time by self etc.; (I). The other uses both in a more balanced way with a sense of choice (A)	41. Buying—cost—time—quality: refers to how we think, perceive, pay attention and sort for when it comes to purchasing and deciding to purchase	55. Morality—weak super-ego; strong super-ego; overly strong super-ego: refers to conscience, following moral and ethical principles. Those with weak one's tend not to recogsnise or sort for true guilt-the violation of a true moral standard, thus disregarding obligatins, rules, ethics, morals—live self-indulgently. Those with strong, seek for rightness and wrongness of events. Their internal moral consciousness makes them responsible, personally disciplines, with a strong sense of duty
9. Focus: screening—non-screening: more focused and easier time concentrating as compared to being highly distracted and less selective	27. Somatic responses—inactive—reflective; active—reactive: refers to how we act out our thoughts, emotions and choices. It refers to a response style that generates little action—procrastinating resulting in inactivity, as compared to acting quickly on our thoughts, feeling, emotions an doing something about it. Reactive refers to unthinking acting	42. Social convincer—distrusting—trusting; suspicious—naïve: refers to how we feel convinced, and how we sort for and respond to others. Immediately think the worse of others, distrust, jealousy, envy, defensiveness, shallow relationship etc.; this is as compared to those immediately responding to others, assuming trust, connections, leads to openness—can lead to being duped easily	56. Self-monitoring—low—high; external—internal

(continued)

Appendix 1C - Meta Modeling Framework: NS-NLP

Cognitive–thinking	Emotional–feeling	Conative–choosing	Semantic–meaning
10. Philosophical: why (origins)—how (solutions): seeking for the past, source, origins as compared to its use, purpose, practical concerns	28. Social presentation—artless—genuine; shrewdly—artful: refers to how we relate to and interacting with others in a social context. Filters for the social impression that we make, our presentation to others, carefully manages impression, fearful of negative impressions and judgment (S&A). Filters for being real, not a fake, being one's own person, saying and thinking that one truly does, disvalue judgments of other (G&A)	43. Interactive—competitive—cooperative; win/lose; win/win	57. Time zones—past—present—future: refers to which time zone one prefers to seek for, pay attention to, and utilize in the calculation of things. Some use past events, past learnings, while others use the present, the now, and to value current experiences and feelings. There are those who prefer future possibilities as a point of reference—lead to visionary thinking, dreaming or else fearful worrying about dangers
11. Communication: verbal—non-verbal Digital-analogue: seeking for words, language, terms and content of messages as compared to body expressions, breathing, posture, muscle tone, eye scanning, tone and volume	29. Dominance—power; achievement; affiliation (achievements). Refers to sorts for accomplishing things, getting things done, end-products: evaluating motives in terms of interacting with others in terms of one's motivational preferences between power (dominance, competition, politics); affiliation (relationship, courtesy, cooperation) and achievement (results, goals, objectives). Use 100 point scale to distribute it amongst the above	44. Directness—direct—inferential; low context—high context	58. Time—experience—in time—through time; random—sequential. Refers to how we code and process our time-lines. Living in-time, where the primary state of living in time, with little awareness of time itself—makes us spontaneous, systematic and random in orientation and behavior. Those that are being out of time, where the time-line is outside of us—gives us more perception and awareness of time leading to being more sequential, linear and on time

(continued)

Appendix 1C -Meta Modeling Framework: NS-NLP

Cognitive–thinking	Emotional–feeling	Conative–choosing	Semantic–meaning
12. Durability (perceptual durability sort): permeability—impermeable (what is the quality of our internal construction): difficulty of keeping an idea front and centre in the mind as compared to the concepts being strong and stable	30. Work style—independent; dependent; team player, manager; bureaucrat—leader: refers to how we sort work situation with other people. Preferring to work alone and assuming sole responsibility for a task in one's own hand (I). Works with others and keeps responsibility for a task in one's own hand (D). Works and shares responsibility for an assignment with others and believes in the synergism of people working together (TP). Those people who find it easy to manage others (M). Those who see and create new visions and setting new frames (L)	45. Management—control; delegate; collaborative; flexibility	59. Quality of life—be—do—have [t]
13. Causation: causeless, linear, complex, personal, external, magical, correlational: refers to how we sort for causes. What makes things happen? No causes, all is by chance, random as compared to simplistic, stimulant response world (L). There are many contributing influences, systemic (MCE). I cause whatever happens (PCE), as compared to I cause nothing, it comes from without (ECE). Superstitious beliefs about entities and forces in the universe causing things (MCE). Recognising things can happen simultaneous without a causational relationship	31. Change adaptor—closed; halfway; open; late; medium; early	46. Risk taking—aversive-embracer; fearful-excite	60. Values—list of values; needs—wants; important urgent: this occurs from and takes form, from our thoughts, ideas, and understanding about what we deem as important (significant and meaningful). Makes it a perceptual sorts for who we pay attention to things and perceive things. Values arise from our drive meta-programme

(continued)

Appendix 1C - Meta Modeling Framework: NS-NLP

Cognitive–thinking	Emotional–feeling	Conative–choosing	Semantic–meaning
14. Completion: closure—non-closure: refers to sorting for the fullness or lack thereof of information. Sorts for completeness, fullness of information, closure, story finished, loop ended ©. Does make this sort, nice but not necessary. Rests easily with ambiguity, confusion open-ended processes (NC)	32. Attitude— serious-playful	47. Decision making— cautious—bold	
15. Information kind (comparison sort): quantitative— qualitative: refers to how we filter as we compare things. Perceive things via quanta—numbers, ranks, orders, measurement, standards (Q). Perceive things via quality—of an experience, person, or event (Q)	33. Persistence— patient—impatient		
16. Stream of consciousness: focused—diffused			
17. Conventional: conformist—non-conformist			
18. Speed: deliberate and slow Witty and quick			

Meta-Modelling Template for Leader-Sheikh Attachment 1C

Behaviour
- Skills
- Strategies
- Screen Play on the Mind

States—What—Intensity
- Primary States (movie mind)
- Meta-States
- Gestalt State

Focus
- Meta-Programmes

Frames
- Belief
- Values
- Decisions
- Identification
- Understanding/Background Knowledge
- Attractors

Appendix 1D

INOVA Dashboard with Some Key Features

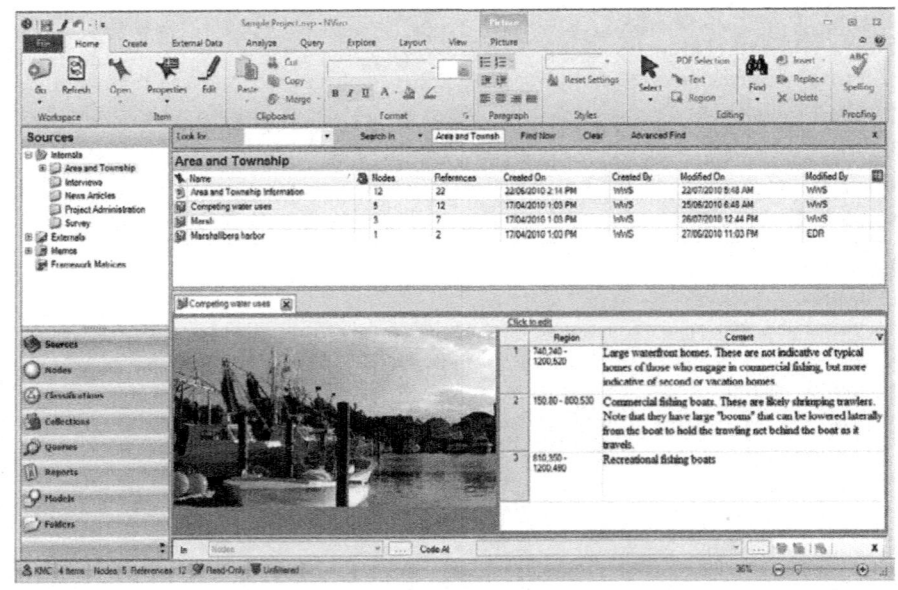

Munsoor-Annex1D

Appendix 2: Personal Interviews Document Numbers and 97

Names of Those Interviewed in the Naqshadandiyyah 98 Khalidiyyah Spiritual Order 99 Interview Details (Detailed Transcripts available on request-Interviews were carried out during the months on March-April 2015) 101

- Interview Document No: 1—Interview with GF and G at Kuang, Malaysia
- Interview Document No: 2—Interview with P, Kuang Malaysia
- Interview Document No: 3—2nd Interview with P and D at Kuang, Malaysia
- Interview Document No: 4—Interview with FX, Kuang, Malaysia
- Interview Document No: 5—Second Interview with GF at Kuang, Malaysia
- Interview Document No: 6—Interview with GZF, Kuang, Malaysia
- Interview Document No: 7—Interview with HQ (with translation by GF) at Kuang, Malaysia
- Interview Document No: 8—Third Interview with GF, Kuang, Malaysia

Appendices

- Interview Document No: 9—Third Interview with P, Kuang, Malaysia
- Interview Document No: 10—Interview with L, Kuang, Malaysia
- Interview Document No: 11—Second Interview with D, Kuang, Malaysia
- Interview Document No: 12—Interview with I, Kuang, Malaysia
- Interview Document No: 13—Fourth Interview with P, Kuang, Malaysia
- Interview Document No: 14—Interview with DQ, Kuang, Malaysia
- Interview Document No: 15—Second Interview with the FX, Kuang, Malaysia
- Interview Document No: 16—Interview with NZG, Kuang, Malaysia
- Interview Document No: 17—Fifth Interview with GF, Kuang, Malaysia
- Interview Document No: 18—Sixth Interview with P and 3rd interview with D, Kuang, Malaysia
- Interview Document No: 19—Fifth Interview with GF, Kuang, Malaysia
- Interview Document No: 20—Written notes sent to me by the HQ after the above interview with him titled: Impact of Ibadah (worship) towards Akhlaq (morality).
- Interview Document No: 21—Second Interview with GZF, Kuang, Malaysia
- Interview Document No: 22—Sixth Interview with GF, Kuang, Malaysia
- Interview Document No: 23—Seventh Interview with GF, Kuang, Malaysia
- Interview Document No: 24—Eighth Interview with R and 4th interview with D, Kuang, Malaysia
- Interview Document No: 25—Second Interview with HQ with translation by GF, Kuang, Malaysia
- Interview Document No: 26—Eighth Interview with GF, Kuang, Malaysia.

Appendix 2A

Soal Selidik

untuk program EXCEL Analisis berbasis Web

Jawablah soal selidik ini dengan benar dan jujur. Jawapan dalam soal selidik ini merupakan jawapan Anda berdasarkan pengalaman Anda sendiri – dan bukan pengalaman orang lain.

Bagian I – Karakteristik Responden

1. Usia : (Age)	2. Pendidikan Terakhir: (Education)
3. Jantina : (lGender)	4. Pekerjaan: (Employment)

5. Sudah berapa lama Anda menjadi anggota kumpulan tarikat ini?

(How long have you been the member of this Group?)

Bahagian II – Konteks dan Hasil
(Questionnaire Part I – Context & Outcome)

Sila pilih jawapan Anda. Pilihan jawapan boleh lebih dari satu:
(Please tick one or more as relevant)

6. Hal apakah yang mendorong Anda bergabung dengan kelompok tarikat ini? Pilihlah jawapan yang paling relevan? Pilihan jawapan boleh lebih dari satu.

(What motivated you to join this group (most relevant one or more)?

Berkumpul dengan orang-orang berpikiran sama (To have company of the like-minded)	Memperluas jaringan (To access a wider network)
Agar dapat berbuat baik untuk orang lain (To do good to others)	Melatih berperilaku lebih baik (To learn better behaviors)
Belajar melakukan kegiatan spiritual (To learn spiritual practices)	Persiapan menghadapi kehidupan selanjutnya (Akhirat) (To prepare for the next life)
Lain-lain, jelaskan:......... (Others – Explain)	

7. Apa yang Anda harapkan terjadi pada diri Anda setelah bergabung dengan kumpulan tarikat ini?

(What would you like to have happened to you by joining the Group?)

Perubahan diri yang lebih baik. (To have changed myself for the better)	Memperoleh lebih banyak ketenangan (To have become calmer)
Mendapatkan berkat (To have gained blessings)	Belajar lebih jauh tentang iman (To have learned more about the Faith)
Belajar lebih jauh tentang kegiatan spiritual (To have learned more spiritual practices)	Lain-lain, jelaskan (Others – Explain)

Bahagian III – Akhlak dan Tata-Perilaku (Adab)
(Questionnaire II – Akhlaq (Morality) & Code of Behavior)

Pilih jawapan yang paling relevan. Jawapan boleh lebih dari satu.
(Please tick one or more, most relevant)

8. Pilih lima (5) sifat positif yang paling penting bagi pengembangan diri seseorang?

(What are the five (5) most important positive characteristics for one's self-development?)

Kasih-sayang (Love)	Sabar (Patience)	Empati (Empathy/ Compassion)	Rendah hati (Humble)	Lain-lain (Others...)
Murah-hati/ Darmawan (Benevolence /Generosity)	Boleh dipercaya (Trust)	Baik hati (Kindness)	Berani (Courage)	
Bijak (Wisdom)	Bersahaja (Modesty)	Integritas (Berhimma) (Integrity)	Rajin dan kerja keras (Diligent and hardworking)	
Adil (Justice)	(Pemaaf) (Forgiveness)	Setia (Loyalty)	Jujur (Honesty)	

Susunlah kelima pilihan Anda di atas menurut skala prioritas. Mulai dari nombor 1 yang paling penting hingga nombor 5 yang kurang penting.

(Among the characteristics you selected, rank five (5) characteristics in your order of priority (from most important to least important)?)

> 1.
> 2.
> 3.
> 4.
> 5.

9. Menurut Anda, sifat buruk apakah yang paling berpengaruh buruk terhadap pengembangan diri seseorang.

(What are Vices, which you feel, are harmful for one's self-development? Pick five (5) at the most)

Berbagai bentuk sifat buruk Types of Vices				
Pemarah (Anger, al-Ghalab) – a feeling of displeasure or wrath)	Gelisah/ Cemas (Anxiety/ al-Hamm – distress or uneasiness caused by fear, danger or misfortune.)	Cinta Duniawi Love of the World (Hubb d'Dunya)	Dengki/Hasad (Malice (al-Hiqd) - desire to inflict harm or injury on another.)	
Kikir / Bakhil (Miserliness (Bukhl) – stingy or does not want to share things)	Tinggi hati/ Ujub (Vanity, al-Ujb) – excessive pride in ones looks, behavior, capabilities)	Menceroboh (Wantonness; batar) – lawless or unrestrained behavior)	Takbur(Boasting; fakhr – to speak bout oneself with excessive pride)	
Tamak Avarice (al-Tama) - insatiable greed for riches & desire to hoard.)	Tidak adil (Iniquity; baghl) – gross injustice or wickedness)	Penakut (Cowardice (al-Jubn) – lack of courage to face danger, pain, difficulty or pain)	Iri-hati (Envy; hasad – a feeling of discontent with the success of another)	Lalai lagi Malas (Heedlessness and Laziness (al Ghabawah wa 'l Kasalah). Careless, thoughtless)
Menunjuk-nunjuk (Seeking Reputation (sum'ah) – seeking fame and status)	Angkuh Arrogance (al-kibr) – offensive display of superiority or self-importance)	Ingkar janji False Hope (tatwil al-'amal) – giving people false hopes)	Riya Ostentation (al-Riya) – showing off to attract others)	Menipu (Fraud (Ghish) – trickery, deception, gaining something unfairly)
Materialistik Attachment - (al-Hirs); an enduring emotional bond to person or things.	Lengah/ Ghaflah (Headlessness (Ghaflah) – unmindful, and disinterested, slow)	Meninggi Diri (Superiority, al-Azamah)		

10. Sebutkan lima (5) sifat buruk yang sangat mempengaruhi pengembangan-diri Anda.

(Rank the worst five (5) vices in your opinion affecting your self-development?)

Appendices 353

1. 2. 3. 4. 5.

11. Sebutkan sifat buruk yang Anda miliki **sebelum** mengikuti kumpulan tarikat ini?

(What characteristics - vices did you have before you joined the Group?)

12. Apakah sifat buruk yang Anda miliki **sesudah** mengikuti kumpulan tarikat ini?

(What characteristics – vices did you have after joining the Group?)

13. Sesuai yang diajarkan Tuan Guru agama Anda, apa yang harus Anda lakukan ketika dalam keadaan marah, frustasi, cemas, dsb.? Pilih maksimum tiga (3) dari pilihan berikut atau sebutkan hal lainnya)

(What have you been taught to do by your Sheikh, when you are angry, frustrated, anxious etc; ? (pick maximum three (3) of the following or suggest on your own)

1. Menenangkan diri (Be silient)
2. Berdoa / Solat Sunat (Say a prayer)
3. Mencari nasihat/pandangan orang lain (Get advice from others)
4. Memohon pada Tuhan (Doa) (Supplicate to God)
5. Bersikap Sabar (Be patient)
6. Beladiri (Retaliate/offensive)
7. Lain-lain, sebutkan (Others, please explain)

14. Siapakah orang yang menjadi ikutan (Role Model) Anda

(Who are your role-models?)

1. 2. 3.

15. Sebutkan lima (5) sifat yang ada pada ikutan (Role Model) Anda tersebut

(Give only five (5) key characteristics that your role-model is most like?)

Peribadi Pengasih Love – warm personal attachment.	Bersikap adil Justice – being fair and equitable.	Pemaaf Forgiveness – willingness to let go on things or forgive.	Berani (menghadapi kesulitan dan bahaya) Courage – quality of the mind and spirit to face danger or difficulties without fear.
Bersikap dermawan Benevolence (Generosity) – desire to do good to others and be charitable.	Penyabar Patience – ability or willingness to wait in the light of difficulties being faced.	Bersikap ramah Kindness – friendly feeling, likeness.	Jujur Honesty – uprightness and fairness
Bijak Wisdom – ability to think and action with understanding, common sense and insight.	Boleh dipercayai Trust – someone who is reliable and can have confidence.	Berhemah Integrity – has moral and ethical standards and is dependable.	Setia pada komitmen dan kewajiban) Loyalty – faithfulness to commitments and obligations.
Rendah diri Humble – courteous, respectful and now arrogant.	Bersahaja Modesty – decency of behavior, speech and dress.	Empati Empathy/Compassion – identifying with the feeling, thoughts and attitude of another person.	

16. Prilaku manakah yang ada pada ikutan (Role Model) Anda tersebut yang sangat penting sebagai rujukan dan untuk pengembangan diri Anda?

(What behavior (key actions & key words) of the role-model have been most crucial for the guidance and self-development of you? (Please mention, not more than five (5))

1. 2. 3. 4. 5.

17. Bagaimanakah Tuan Guru agama Anda menyampaikan **pengetahuannya** pada kelompok tarikat ini

(How does your Sheikh transmit knowledge to the Group?)

Memperlihatkan ajarannya melalui perilakunya (by demonstrating it through his own behavior)	Dengan kerap kali merujuk pada perilakunya yang dapat menjadi ikutan (Role Model) (by mentioning his own role models frequently)
Dengan melakukan hal-hal baik bersama Anda secara berkala (by periodic engagement/ do good deeds together)	Dengan merujuk pada Al Quran & Hadith (by spiritual recital)
Dengan pengajaran (by teaching)	Dengan memberi doa atau bacaan khusus (by giving special prayers or recitation)
Dengan instruksi lisan (by verbal instructions)	Dengan duduk bersama Anda (by sitting with you)
Dengan instruksi/cara bukan-lisan – (by non-verbal means)	Dengan mengamati Anda dan memberi maklum balas (by observing you and giving feedback)
Lain-lain, sebutkan… (Other methods – Please state it)	

18. Bagaimanakah Tuan Guru agama Anda mengajarkan **tata-perilaku** pada kumpulan tarikat ini? (How does your Sheikh transmit/impart codes of behavior to the group?)

Dengan memberi contoh (by setting an example)	Beliau sendiri menunjukkan berbagai hal dalam beberapa kali (by demonstration things himself from time to time).
Menasehati Anda (admonishing you)	Dengan mendirikan aturan dasar perilaku (Hukum-hukum Adab) (by establishing ground rules of conduct)
Lain-lain, mohon sebutkan (by other means – Please state it)	

19. Apakah Anda merasakan perubahan pada diri Anda setelah bergabung dengan kumpulan tarikat ini? (Have you observed any changes within you after joining the Group?)

- Ya
  (Yes)
- Tidak
  (No)

Bila Ya, sebutkan dalam hal apa Anda merasakan perubahan:
(If Yes, please mention in what way you observed changes)

Dalam cara saya melayani diri saya   (In the way I treat myself)
Dalam cara berbicara dengan orang lain   (In the way I speak to people)
Dalam cara kelakuan saya di tengah keluarga dan kawan-kawan –   (In the way I behave with my family and friends)
Dalam cara kelakuan saya ke atas mereka yang kurang beruntung   (In the way I treat those who are less privileged)
Dalam cara saya beribadah   (In the way I do my acts of worship)
Dalam cara kelakuaan saya sehari-hari   (In the way I conduct my day to day life)
Lain-lain, sebutkan   (Other changes – Please state it)

20. Apakah Anda menemui (melihat) perubahan yang lebih baik pada anggota kumpulan tarikat ini.

(Have you observed any better changes within the Group Members?)

- Ya
  (Yes)
- Tidak
  (No).

Bila Ya, sebutkan dalam hal apa Anda merasakan perubahan:
(If Yes, please mention in what way you observed changes)

1.   2.   3.   4.   5.

Bahagian IV – Ibadah
(Questionnaire III – Ibadath (Worship))

Silahkan pilih jawaban yang relevan untuk Anda
(Please tick the most relevant to you)

21. Selain ibadah wajib, perbuatan ibadah apalagi yang Anda lakukan secara berkala?

(What are the acts of worship that you perform on a regular basis (apart from the obligatory ones?)

Solat selain di luar solat wajib (Optional prayers /salah)	Membaca Qur'an (Recital of Qur'an)	Berdoa (Supplication/Dua)	Zikir berjama'ah dengan suara terdengar (Jihar) (Group Zikr, loud)
Zikir berjama'ah, tanpa suara (Sirr) (Group dhikr, silent)	Zikir sendiri, dengan suara terdengar (Individual Dhkir – loud)	Zikir sendiri tanpa mengeluarkan suara (Individual Dhkir, silent)	Shalawat Nabi (Darood, recital on the Prophet)
Mendengar khotbah (Listen to Sermons)	Berpuasa (Fasting)	Melakukan amal (Charity)	Lain-lain, sebutkan (Others. Please state it)

22. Dari lima jenis perbuatan ibadah yang Anda pilih tersebut di atas, mohon susun kelima ibadah tersebut menurut prioritas dari nombor 1 yang paling penting hingga no 5 yang kurang penting.

(How would you order the acts of worship (maximum five (5) in the rank of your priority? (Except obligatory acts of worship)

1.
2.
3.
4.
5

23. Di antara semua ibadah tersebut di atas, manakah yang paling bermanfaat untuk peribadi Anda?

(Personally, which acts of worship is/are most beneficial to you?)

24. Apakah pengaruh perbuatan ibadah tersebut pada diri Anda?

(What sort of effects does these acts of worship have on you?)

Fizikal (Physical)	Fisiologis (Physiological)
Emosi (Emotional)	Sosial (Social)
Budaya) (Cultural)	Lain-lain... (Others)
Tidak tahu (Do not know)	

25. Bagaimana Anda mengetahui bahwa ibadah tersebut telah mempengaruhi Anda?

(How do you know it has an effect on you)?

Perubahan fisikal (changes physically)	Perubahan emosi (changes emotionally)
Perubahan secara fisiologi (changes physiologically)	Perubahan kepribadian (changes my personality)
Tidak dapat menjelaskan (Cannot Explain it)	Tidak tahu (Do not know)
Alasan-alasan lain (Other reasons)	

26. Bagaimanakah keadaan pikiran Anda sebelum melakukan suatu perbuatan ibadah? Sila pilih jawapan berikut ini. Pilihan boleh lebih dari satu.

(What sort of state of mind are you in before an act of worship (state which ones)? This could be one or more)

Tenang (Calm)	Gelisah (Agitated)
(Frustasi) (Frustrated)	Cemas (Anxious)
Bingung (Confused)	Marah (Angry)
Lain-lain (Others)	Tidak tahu (Do not Know)

27. Bagaimanakah keadaan pikiran tersebut mempengaruhi hubungan Anda dengan keluarga dan kawan-kawan setelah Anda melakukan ibadah?

(How does this state of mind after the relevant acts of worship effect your relationship with your family and friends?)

mampu berhubungan lebih baik dengan mereka (able to relate to them better)	mampu menjadi pendengar yang lebih baik (able to listen better)
mampu bertolak ansur (able to compromise)	boleh bekerja sama (able to cooperate)
mampu lebih memahami mereka (able to understand)	menjadi lebih sabar (able to be more patient)
bisa lebih bersikap murah-hati (able to be more generous)	Lain-lain (Others)
tidak berpengaruh sama sekali (No effect at all)	

28. Apakah Anda merasakan adanya perhubungan antara perbuatan ibadah Anda dan perilaku Anda? Kalau ya, mohon jelaskan keterkaitan tersebut?

(Have you observed any relationship between your act of worship and your behavior?

- Ya
  (Yes)
- Tidak
  (No)

   Bila Ya, sebutkan dalam hal apa Anda merasakan perubahan:
   (If Yes, please mention in what way you noticed the changes)

29. Apakah Anda memiliki pengalaman spiritual yang membawa Anda ke tingkat kesedaran yang lebih lanjut.

(Have you had any spiritual experiences that lead to a greater level of awareness/spirituality?)

   Mohon jelaskan jenis pengalaman tersebut
   (Please explain the types of experiences)

30. Apakah hal yang paling mendalam yang Anda sudah pelajari dari Tarikat ini dan ingin Anda berkongsi dengan orang lain?

(What is the most profound thing that you would like to share with others that you have learnt from being in the Group?)

| Mohon jelaskan |
| (Please explain) |

Appendix 3: Personal Interviews Document Numbers and Names of Those Interviewed in the Naqshadandiyyah Khalidiyyah Spiritual Order

Several interview documents have been combined, where for example, the interviews were held with the same person twice, or else, there are some interviews which were held with more than one person. Therefore, this has been consolidated to 10 documents. Transcripts of all documents are available with the author.

Consolidated Appendix 3A

- Document no: 1 (Manager AAA): Transcripts nos: 1 + 4 + +8 + 12 + 15 + 17 + 18 + 19 + 22 + 23 + 25 + 26
- Document no: 2 (Resident Imam BBB): Transcript nos: 2 + 5 + 10 + 13 + 17 + 18 + 20 + 24
- Document no: 3 (Head Reflexology CCC): Transcript nos: 11 + 12
- Document no: 4 (Friend DDD): Transcript nos: 3 + 5 + 8 + 23
- Document no: 5 (Sheikh EEE): Transcript nos: 6 + 7 + 24
- Document no: 6 (Resident Nurse FFF): Transcript nos: 9
- Document no: 7 (Banker GGG): Transcript nos: 14 + 21
- Document no: 8 (Supervisor HHH): Transcript nos: 16
- Document no: 9: (Artist): Transcript nos: 21
- Document no: 10 (Sailor): Transcript nos: 22 + 25
- Total number of Participants/Documents 10 & 26 interview transcripts

Appendix 3B: Interview Details (Detailed Transcripts available on request—Interviews were carried out during the months on March–April 2015)

- Interview Document No: 1—Interview with GF and G at Kuang, Malaysia
- Interview Document No: 2—Interview with P, Kuang Malaysia
- Interview Document No: 3—2nd Interview with P and D at Kuang, Malaysia
- Interview Document No: 4—Interview with FX, Kuang, Malaysia
- Interview Document No: 5—Second Interview with GF at Kuang, Malaysia
- Interview Document No: 6—Interview with GZF, Kuang, Malaysia
- Interview Document No: 7—Interview with HQ (with translation by GF) at Kuang, Malaysia
- Interview Document No: 8—Third Interview with GF, Kuang, Malaysia
- Interview Document No: 9—Third Interview with P, Kuang, Malaysia
- Interview Document No: 10—Interview with L, Kuang, Malaysia
- Interview Document No: 11—Second Interview with D, Kuang, Malaysia
- Interview Document No: 12—Interview with I, Kuang, Malaysia
- Interview Document No: 13—Fourth Interview with P, Kuang, Malaysia
- Interview Document No: 14—Interview with DQ, Kuang, Malaysia
- Interview Document No: 15—Second Interview with the FX, Kuang, Malaysia
- Interview Document No: 16—Interview with NZG, Kuang, Malaysia
- Interview Document No: 17—Fifth Interview with GF, Kuang, Malaysia
- Interview Document No: 18—Sixth Interview with P and 3rd interview with D, Kuang, Malaysia
- Interview Document No: 19—Fifth Interview with GF, Kuang, Malaysia
- Interview Document No: 20—Written notes sent to me by the HQ after the above interview with him titled: Impact of Ibadah (worship) towards Akhlaq (morality).
- Interview Document No: 21—Second Interview with GZF, Kuang, Malaysia
- Interview Document No: 22—Sixth Interview with GF, Kuang, Malaysia
- Interview Document No: 23—Seventh Interview with GF, Kuang, Malaysia
- Interview Document No: 24—Eighth Interview with R and 4th interview with D, Kuang, Malaysia
- Interview Document No: 25—Second Interview with HQ with translation by GF, Kuang, Malaysia
- Interview Document No: 26—Eighth Interview with GF, Kuang, Malaysia Appendix 3B.

Printed in Great Britain
by Amazon